Keen's
Latin American
Civilization

NINTH EDITION

Keen's Latin American Civilization

History and Society, 1492 to the Present

Edited by

Robert Buffington
University of Colorado at Boulder

Lila Caimari
CONICET

Westview
PRESS

A Member of the Perseus Books Group

Westview Press books are available at special discounts for bulk
purchases in the United States by corporations, institutions, and
other organizations. For more information, please contact the
Special Markets Department at the Perseus Books Group, 2300
Chestnut Street, Suite 200, Philadelphia, PA 19103, or call (800)
810-4145, ext. 5000, or e-mail special.markets@perseusbooks.com.

Library of Congress Cataloging-in-Publication Data
    Keen's Latin American civilization : history and society, 1492 to
the present / edited by Robert Buffington and Lila Caimari. —
9th ed.
        p. cm.
    Includes bibliographical references.
ISBN 978-0-8133-4408-9 (pbk. : alk. paper) 1. Latin America—
Civilization. 2. Spain—Colonies—America—History. 3. Latin
America—History. I. Keen, Benjamin, 1913– II. Buffington,
Robert, 1952– III. Caimari, Lila M., 1962– IV. Title: Latin
American civilization.
F1408.3.L274 2009
980—dc22
                                                        2008042452

10 9 8 7 6 5 4 3 2

Contents

PART SIX: INDEPENDENCE AND ITS AFTERMATH

PART SEVEN: CONSTRUCTING THE NATION-STATE

PART EIGHT: CONSOLIDATING THE NATION-STATE

Preface

AS CONSCIENTIOUS TEACHERS concerned about the ever-increasing cost of education, we debated putting out a new edition of *Latin American Civilization* just five short years after the eighth edition of Benjamin Keen's classic text appeared. There were things we wanted to change about the eighth edition (almost as soon as it appeared), but nothing that couldn't wait another year or two, and certainly nothing that could justify the added financial cost to students or the time commitment on our part.

Then, a couple of years ago, Latin America became a much different place as regional politics took a sharp left turn. There had been warning rumbles of a political seismic shift with the earlier election of Hugo Chávez in Venezuela (1998) and Luiz Inácio Lula da Silva in Brazil (2002), but despite their political leanings both men looked familiar enough to political observers. No one, however, would have predicted that by 2008, Latin Americans would have elected as president two leftist women (Michelle Bachelet in Chile and Cristina Fernández de Kirchner in Argentina), an indigenous coca grower/union organizer (Evo Morales in Bolivia), and a radical priest (Fernando Lugo in Paraguay). Moreover, hand in glove with its political shift, a region at the forefront of 1990s globalization efforts had begun to reconsider its enthusiastic commitment to neoliberal economic restructuring programs.

Given the magnitude of this political/economic shift, we decided the time had come for a ninth edition of *Latin American Civilization*. It features several new excerpts dedicated to current events: an influential essay by former Mexican foreign minister Jorge Castañeda on Latin America's left turn and interviews with Michelle Bachelet and Evo Morales. To round out this heavy dose of presidential politics, we added excerpts that address the public safety concerns of Brazilian city dwellers, the changing sexual politics of the Cuban revolution, and a provocative declaration by indigenous rights groups seeking the establishment of "plurinational" states.

These selections appear in a new Chapter 17, "Globalization and Its Discontents," which replaces "Contesting Power, Fighting Inequality" in the previous edition. At the request of our loyal readers and following the dictates of our own better judgment, the excerpts from the "Contesting Power" chapter have been inserted into appropriate chronological chapters. This should make it easier on students and teachers alike.

We took the opportunity to add new selections to earlier chapters as well. Chapter 8 now includes Sor Juana's brilliant poem/exposé of male "foolishness." Chapter 14 features a revised and expanded version of José Guadalupe Posada's popular perspective on modernity with clearer images and a sharper interpretive focus. Chapter 15 adds an important manifesto from Victor Raúl Haya de la Torre, the founder of Peru's APRA party (back in power in 2006). Chapter 16 includes a short excerpt from Brazilian Marxist Carlos Marighella's *Minimanual for Urban Guerrillas* and replaces Leo Masliah's brilliant but confusing essay on "Turning the Nation into a Prison" with Rodolfo Walsh's impassioned and more accessible "Open Letter to the Military Junta."

We also added—by popular demand—three new selections to the thematic chapter on U.S.-Latin American relations (Chapter 18). "The White Man's Burden" is a series of five turn-of-the-century political cartoons from the United States depicting its new Caribbean charges (acquired in the 1898 Spanish-American War) as young women and native children. "Dissent Within the Ranks" excerpts a 1965 speech by Senator J. William Fulbright condemning the Johnson administration for doctoring intelligence to justify intervention in the Dominican Republic. "Covert Operations" includes selections from a controversial CIA manual used to train Nicaraguan Contras in a U.S.-sponsored guerrilla war against the Sandinista government.

A complex project like *Latin American Civilization* requires teamwork. We couldn't have managed without the enthusiasm, patience, good advice, and gentle prodding of the editorial staff at Westview Press, especially Karl Yambert, Brooke Kush, Kelsey Mitchell, Annie Lenth, and Chrisona Schmidt. Richard Shindell gave invaluable editorial advice. Pedro Porben provided crucial background on Cuban comics and the Virgilio cartoon from *Mella*. This is a much better book thanks to their help. For its inevitable defects, we accept full responsibility.

Robert Buffington
University of Colorado at Boulder

Lila Caimari
CONICET

PART ONE

INDIAN

AND

HISPANIC

ORIGINS

1

ↄﾟ

ANCIENT AMERICA ON

THE EVE OF CONQUEST

Latin American colonial society, and especially Spanish American colonial society, was shaped largely by the interaction of Hispanic (Spanish and Portuguese) invaders with the Indian peoples who had inhabited the Americas for thousands of years. The Indians usually responded to the arrival of European invaders with armed resistance. After the European conquest, the Indians continued to resist with a variety of strategies, including revolts, flight, riots, and sabotage. Sometimes they turned their masters' legal codes to their own advantage. Thanks to this unyielding spirit and despite immense loss of life and inestimable suffering, the Indian communities in key areas of Latin America survived the storm of conquest and colonial oppression with their cultural identity largely intact. However, the Indians did undergo some acculturation in the form of a more or less nominal acceptance of Christianity and a more willing acceptance of European tools, work animals, crafts, foods, and other material elements. Resistance to Hispanic rule, however, characterized Indian-Hispanic relations in general and was a major source of tension in colonial life.

Indian culture and the Indians' response to the Hispanic invaders were shaped by a long history on the American continents. The Indians arrived from Asia by way of the Bering Strait no fewer than forty thousand years ago and in the course of time spread through North and South America and eventually developed a wide range of cultural types, ranging from nomadic groups of hunters and food gatherers to the elaborate empires of the Aztecs and the Inca and the culturally advanced Mayan states. These three civilizations had certain features in common. All were based on intensive farming that supported the development of a large sedentary population and considerable division of labor. These civilizations, however, also evolved along distinctive lines. Mayan culture was distinguished by impressive achievements in writing, calendrical science, mathematics, and architecture. The Aztecs were mighty warriors, and a distinctive feature of their religion was large-scale human sacrifice. The Inca were the greatest empire builders of ancient America, and they made a serious and largely successful effort to unify the institutions and language of their extensive empire.

Modern scholars recognize that despite the decapitation and degradation of these states by the conquest, many of their institutions and much of their culture survived into the nineteenth century and even down to the present. Thus the history and culture of colonial Latin America (and even modern Latin America) cannot be understood without a knowledge of the high civilizations of ancient America.

1. AZTEC WARFARE

Warfare was the basis of Aztec existence, and warriors shared with priests the place of greatest honor and influence in Aztec society. An important object of warfare was procuring captives to be sacrificed on the altars of the gods whose goodwill brought victory to the Aztec banners. Thus, in the words of George C. Vaillant, "War led to sacrifice and sacrifice led back to war, in ever-widening cycles." Our principal source of information concerning Aztec life and customs is the monumental work of the Spanish friar Bernardino de Sahagún (1499–1590), who carefully recorded a vast store of material obtained from native informants. His great General History of the Things of New Spain *contains the following native account of an Aztec military campaign.*

The ruler was known as the lord of men. His charge was war. Hence he determined, disposed, and arranged how the war would be made. First he commanded masters of the youths and seasoned warriors to scan the [enemy] city and to study all the roads—where [they were] difficult, where entry could be made through them. This done, the ruler first determined, by means of a painted [plan], how was placed the city which they were to destroy. Then the chief noted all the roads—where [they were] difficult, and in what places entry could be made.

Then he summoned the general and the commanding general, and the brave warriors, and he commanded them how they were to take the road,

---

Fray Bernardino de Sahagún, *The Florentine Codex: General History of the Things of New Spain*, bk. 8, *Kings and Lords*, trans. Arthur J. O. Andersen and Charles E. Dibble (Santa Fe, N.M.: School of American Research, 1954). Reprinted by permission.

what places the warriors were to enter, for how many days they would march, and how they would arrange the battle. And he commanded that these would announce war and send forth all the men dexterous in war to be arrayed, and to be supplied with provisions for war and insignia.

The ruler then consulted with all the majordomos. . . . He ordered them to take out all their [goods held in] storage, the tributes, costly articles—insignia of gold, and with quetzal feathers, and all the shields of great price.

And when the majordomos had delivered all the costly devices, the ruler then adorned and presented with insignia all the princes who were already able in war, and all the brave warriors, the men [at arms], the seasoned warriors, the fearless warriors, the Otomí, and the noblemen who dwelt in the young men's houses.

And when it had come to pass that the ruler adorned them, when he had done this to the brave warriors, then the ruler ordered all the majordomos to bear their goods, all the costly devices, and all the valuable capes there to battle, that the ruler might offer and endow with favors all the [other] rulers, and the noblemen, and the brave warriors, the men [at arms] who were about to go to war, who were to be extended as if made into a wall of men dexterous with arms. And the ruler forthwith called upon the rulers of Texcoco and Tlacopan and the rulers in all the swamp lands, and notified them to proclaim war in order to destroy a [certain] city. He presented them all with costly capes, and he gave them all insignia of great price. Then he also ordered the common folk to rise to go forth to war. Before them would go marching, the brave warriors, the men [at arms], the lord general, and the commanding general.

The lords of the sun, it was said, took charge and directed in war. All the priests, the keepers of the gods, took the lead; they bore their gods upon their backs, and, by the space of one day, marched ahead of all the brave warriors and the seasoned warriors. These also marched one day ahead of all the men of Acolhuacan, who likewise marched one day ahead of all the Tepaneca, who similarly marched one day ahead of the men of Xilotepec; and these also marched one day ahead of all the so-called Quaquata. In like manner the [men of] other cities were disposed. They followed the road slowly and carefully.

And when the warlike lands were reached, the brave warrior generals and commanding generals then showed the others the way and arranged them in order. No one might break ranks or crowd in among the others; they would then and there slay or beat whoever would bring confusion or crowd in among the others. All the warriors were extended there, until the moment that Yacauitztli, [god of] the night, would descend—that darkness would fall. And when they already were to rise against the city to destroy it, first was awaited tensely the moment when fire flared up—when the priests brought [new] fire—and for the blowing of shell trumpets, when the priests blew them.

And when the fire flared up, then as one arose all the warriors. War cries were raised; there was fighting. They shot fiery arrows into the temples.

And when they first took a captive, one fated to die, forthwith they slew him there before the gods; they slashed his breast open with a flint knife.

And when the city had been overcome, thereupon were counted as many captives as there were, and as many Mexicans and Tlatilulcans as had died. Then they apprised the ruler that they had been orphaned for the sake of Uitzilopochtli; that men had been taken captive and been slain. And the ruler then commanded the high judges to go to tell and inform all in the homes of those who had gone to die in war, that there might be weeping in the homes of those who had gone to war to die. And they informed those in the homes of as many as had gone to take captives in war that they received honors there because of their valor. And they were rewarded according to their merits; the ruler accorded favors to all—costly capes, breech clouts, chocolate, food, and devices, and lip rods and ear plugs. Even more did the ruler accord favors to the princes if they had taken captives. He gave them the offices of stewards, and all wealth without price—honor, fame, renown.

And if some had done wrong in battle, they then and there slew them on the battlefield; they beat them, they stoned them.

And if several claimed one captive, and one man said, "He is my captive," and another man also said, "He is my captive": if no man verified it, and also if no one saw how they had taken the captive, the lord of the sun decided between them. If neither had an advantage of the two who claimed the captive, then those who had taken four captives, the masters of the captives, decided that to neither one would the captive belong. He was dedicated to the Uitzcalco [or] they left him to the tribal temple, the house of the devil.

And when the city which they had destroyed was attained, at once was set the tribute, the impost. [To the ruler who had conquered them] they gave that which was there made. And likewise, forthwith a steward was placed in office who would watch over and levy the tribute.

2. THE HALLS OF MOCTEZUMA

The political organization of the Aztec state on the eve of the Spanish conquest represented a mixture of theocracy and royal absolutism. The barbaric splendor and elaborate ceremony that marked the household of the great war chief Moctezuma are vividly described by an eyewitness, the conquistador and historian Bernal Díaz del Castillo (1492–1581?).

Bernal Díaz del Castillo, *Historia verdadera de la conquista de Nueva España*, 4 vols. (Buenos Aires, 1914), 2:31–33. Excerpt translated by the editors.

The great Moctezuma was close to forty years old, of good height and well proportioned, slender and lean. His skin was not particularly dark but the proper color and shade for an Indian. He wore his hair not too long, just so it covered his ears; his few whiskers were dark, well trimmed, and sparse. His face was rather long and cheerful with pleasant eyes, and he showed in his expression and in his gaze, at times affection and when necessary sternness. He was very neat and clean, bathing daily in the afternoons. He had many concubines, the daughters of lords, but he also had two legitimate wives who were chiefs in their own right. When he slept with them it was done so secretly that only a few of the servants knew about it. He was quite free of sodomies ["unnatural" sex acts]. The robes or clothes that he wore one day were not worn again for three or four days. He had a guard of over 200 chieftains in rooms adjacent to his and only a select few were permitted to speak to him. When they went to talk with him, they had to take off their fancy cloaks and put on others of less value (although clean) and they had to enter barefoot and with their eyes downcast. They made three bows and with each bow they had to say, "Lord, my Lord, my great Lord." When they had delivered their message, he dispatched them with just a few words. They didn't turn their backs on him as they took their leave but faced him with their eyes on the ground, and they didn't turn their backs as they were leaving.

And another thing I noticed: that when the great lords who came from faraway lands on legal matters or business arrived at Moctezuma's dwelling, they had to go barefoot and with modest robes, and they couldn't enter straight into the palace but had to wait awhile beside the door, because to enter in a hurry was considered disrespectful.

As regards eating, his cooks prepared over thirty different types of dishes which they kept warm by placing them over small clay braziers. From the dishes offered to the great Moctezuma, they produced over 300 meals and sometimes as many as 1,000 for his guard. On these festival occasions Moctezuma would sometimes come with his retinue and the cooks would point out the best dish and explain which fowl and other things were included, and whatever they suggested he was obliged to try. But he came only once in a while and just to pass the time. I've heard tell that they used to cook the flesh of young boys, and, since there were so many different dishes and things, no one could tell that it was human flesh because every day they cooked chickens, turkeys, pheasants, partridges, quail, tame and wild ducks, venison, wild boar, waterfowl, pigeons, hares, rabbits, and all manner of birds and things from that country of which there are so many that I'll never finish naming them—so I'll stop here. I do know for certain that once our captain [Cortés] reprehended them for sacrificing and eating human flesh they stopped the practice.

But we'll leave off talking about this and return to the way Moctezuma was served at mealtimes. This is the way it was: if it was cold they made a big fire from the embers of a smokeless tree bark. The embers from that bark gave off a fragrant smell and, so that it gave off no more heat than he wanted, they placed in front of it a screen worked with gold and other figures of idols. He was seated on a low stool, luxurious and soft, with a table also low and made in the same style as the stools. On this they put white table clothes and some rather long napkins of the same material. Four women, very beautiful and clean, brought him water for his hands in a kind of deep bowl called a *xical* below which they held a kind of plate to catch the water, and they handed him towels [to dry his hands]. Two other women brought him tortillas. When he had begun to eat they put in front of him a gilded wooden screen so that no one could see him eat and the four women were dismissed. Then he was joined by four elderly lords who Moctezuma chatted with from time to time and questioned about things. To show his favor he gave each man a plate of food taken from his personal dishes. They said that those old men were his closest kinsmen and counselors and magistrates. The food Moctezuma gave them they ate standing up and with great respect, and all without looking at his face. He was served on earthenware from Cholula, some of it red and some black.

While he ate, the guards in the adjoining rooms didn't dare make a ruckus or speak loudly. The servers brought him all kinds of fruit from the region but he ate very little and only from time to time. They brought him a special cocoa drink in a sort of cup made of pure gold and they say that it was to ensure success with women so we'll look no further into it. But what I did see was that they brought him over fifty big mugs full of good frothy cocoa, and that he drank from them, and that the women served him with great deference. Occasionally at dinnertime there were hunchbacked Indians—very ugly because their small bodies were bent in half. Among them were jesters and buffoons who praised him, and others who sang or danced for him because Moctezuma was fond of entertainment and singing. To these entertainers he gave leftover food and mugs of cocoa. Meanwhile, the same four women cleared the tablecloths and gave him fresh water for his hands, always with great deference. And Moctezuma talked to those old men about issues that concerned him, and they took leave of him with great reverence, and he stayed behind to rest.

3. AZTEC INDUSTRY AND COMMERCE

The division of labor and the development of craftsmanship among the Aztecs attained perhaps the highest level compatible with what was essentially an Upper Stone Age technology. The vast scale on which goods and services were exchanged is shown by the activity at the great market at Tenochtitlán, as described below by Cortés in a letter to Emperor Charles V. Trade was not confined to Aztec territory.

The city has many squares where markets are held, and trading is carried on. There is one square, twice as large as that of Salamanca, all surrounded by arcades, where there are daily more than sixty thousand souls, buying and selling, and where are found all the kinds of merchandise produced in these countries, including food products, jewels of gold and silver, lead, brass, copper, zinc, stone, bones, shells, and feathers. Stones are sold, hewn and unhewn, adobe bricks, wood, both in the rough and manufactured in various ways. There is a street for game, where they sell every sort of bird, such as chickens, partridges, quails, wild ducks, flycatchers, widgeons, turtle-doves, pigeons, reed-birds, parrots, owls, eaglets, owlets, falcons, sparrow-hawks and kestrels, and they sell the skin of some of these birds of prey with their feathers, heads, beaks, and claws. They sell rabbits, hares, and small dogs which they castrate and raise for the purpose of eating.

There is a street set apart for the sale of herbs, where can be found every sort of root and medical herb which grows in the country. There are houses like apothecary shops, where prepared medicines are sold, as well as liquids, ointments, and plasters. There are places like our barber shops, where they wash and shave their heads. There are houses where they supply food and drink for payment. There are men, such as in Castile are called porters, who carry burdens. There is much wood, charcoal, braziers, made of earthenware, and mats of diverse kinds for beds, and others, very thin, used as cushions, and for carpeting halls, and bedrooms. There are all sorts of vegetables, and especially onions, leeks, garlic, borage, nasturtion, watercresses, sorrel, thistles, and artichokes. There are many kinds of fruits, amongst others cherries, and prunes, like the Spanish ones. They sell bees-honey and wax, and honey made of corn stalks, which is as sweet and syrup-like as that of sugar, also honey of a plant called maguey, which is better than most; from these same plants they make sugar and wine, which they also sell.

They also sell skeins of different kinds of spun cotton, in all colors, so that it seems quite like one of the silk markets of Granada, although it is on a greater scale; also as many different colors for painters as can be found in Spain and of as excellent hues. They sell deer skins with all the hair turned on them, and of different colors; much earthenware, exceedingly good, many sorts of pots, large and small, pitchers, large tiles, an infinite variety of vases, all of very singular clay, and most of them glazed and painted. They sell maize, both in the grain and made into bread, which is very superior in its quality to that of the other islands and mainland; pies of birds, and fish, also much fish, fresh, salted, cooked and raw, eggs of hens, and geese, and other birds in great quantity, and cakes made of eggs.

Hernán Cortés, *Fernando Cortés: His Five Letters of Relation to the Emperor Charles V*, 2 vols., ed. and trans. Francis A. McNutt (New York: Arthur H. Clark, 1908), 1:257–259. Reprinted by permission of the publisher.

Finally, besides those things I have mentioned, they sell in the city markets everything else which is found in the whole country and which on account of the profusion and number, do not occur to my memory, and which also I do not tell of, because I do not know their names.

Each kind of merchandise is sold in its respective street; and they do not mix their kinds of merchandise of any species; thus they preserve perfect order. Everything is sold by a kind of measure, and, until now, we have not seen anything sold by weight.

There is in this square a very large building, like a court of justice, where there are always ten or twelve persons, sitting as judges, and delivering their decisions upon all cases which arise in the markets. There are other persons in the same square who go about continually among the people, observing what is sold, and the measures used in selling, and they have been seen to break some which were false.

4. THE CONDITION OF THE AZTEC PEASANTRY

Among the Aztecs, as among many other peoples of ancient Mexico, the basic social unit was a group called the calpulli *(pl.* calpultin*), which was a territorial as well as a kinship organization. The* calpulli *offered its members a certain collective security and other advantages, but the life of the Aztec free commoners was probably a fairly hard one. Even harder was the lot of serfs (*mayeque*) attached to the private estates of Aztec nobles. The royal chronicler of the Indies, Gonzalo Fernández de Oviedo y Valdés (1478–1557), describes the condition of these people and other aspects of the Aztec social order.*

The Indians of New Spain, I have been told by reliable persons who gained their information from Spaniards who fought with Hernando Cortés in the conquest of that land, are the poorest of the many nations that live in the Indies at the present time. In their homes they have no furnishings or clothing other than the poor garments which they wear on their persons, one or two stones for grinding maize, some pots in which to cook the maize, and a sleeping mat. Their meals consist chiefly of vegetables cooked with chili, and bread. They eat little—not that they would not eat more if they could get it, for the soil is very fertile and yields bountiful harvests, but the common people and plebeians suffer under the tyranny of their Indian lords, who tax away the greater part of their produce in a manner that I shall describe. Only

Gonzalo Fernández de Oviedo y Valdés, *Historia general y natural de las Indias,* 14 vols. (Asunción, Paraguay, 1944–1945), 10:110–114. Excerpt translated by Benjamin Keen.

the lords and their relatives, and some principal men and merchants, have estates and lands of their own; they sell and gamble with their lands as they please, and they sow and harvest them but pay no tribute. Nor is any tribute paid by artisans, such as masons, carpenters, feather workers, or silversmiths, or by singers and kettle drummers (for every Indian lord has musicians in his household, each according to his station). But such persons render personal service when it is required, and none of them is paid for his labor.

Each Indian lord assigns to the common folk who come from other parts of the country to settle on his land (and to those who are already settled there) specific fields, that each may know the land that he is to sow. And the majority of them have their homes on their land; and between twenty and thirty, or forty and fifty houses have over them an Indian head who is called *tiquitlato*, which in the Castilian tongue means "the finder (or seeker) of tribute." At harvest time this *tiquitlato* inspects the cornfield and observes what each one reaps, and when the reaping is done they show him the harvest, and he counts the ears of corn that each has reaped, and the number of wives and children that each of the vassals in his charge possesses. And with the harvest before him he calculates how many ears of corn each person in that household will require till the next harvest, and these he gives to the Indian head of that house; and he does the same with the other produce, namely kidney beans, which are a kind of small beans, and chili, which is their pepper; and *chia*, which is as fine as mustard seed, and which in warm weather they drink, ground and made into a solution in water and used for medicine, roasted and ground; and cocoa, which is a kind of almond that they use as money, and which they grind, make into a solution, and drink; and cotton, in those places where it is raised, which is in the hot lands and not the cold; and *pulque*, which is their wine; and all the various products obtained from the maguey plant, from which they obtain food and drink and footwear and clothing. This plant grows in the cold regions, and the leaves resemble those of the cinnamon tree, but are much longer. Of all these and other products they leave the vassal only enough to sustain him for a year. And in addition the vassal must earn enough to pay the tribute of mantles, gold, silver, honey, wax, lime, wood, or whatever products it is customary to pay as tribute in that country. They pay this tribute every forty, sixty, seventy, or ninety days, according to the terms of the agreement. This tribute also the *tiquitlato* receives and carries to his Indian lord.

Ten days before the close of the sixty or hundred days, or whatever is the period appointed for the payment of tribute, they take to the house of the Indian lord the produce brought by the *tiquitlatos*; and if some poor Indian should prove unable to pay his share of tribute, whether for reasons of health or poverty, or lack of work, the *tiquitlato* tells the lord that such-and-such will not pay the proportion of the tribute that had been assigned to him; then the lord tells the *tiquitlato* to take the recalcitrant vassal to a *tianguez* or market, which they hold every five days in all the towns of the land, and there sell him into slavery, applying the proceeds of the sale to the payment of his tribute. . . .

All the towns have their own lands, long ago assigned for the provision of the *orchilobos* or *ques* or temples where they kept their idols; and these lands were and are the best of all. And they have this custom: At seeding time all would go forth at the summons of the town council to sow these fields, and to weed them at the proper time, and to cultivate the grain and harvest it and carry it to a house in which lived the pope and the *teupisques, pioches, exputhles* and *piltoutles* (or, as we would say, the bishops, archbishops, and canons and prebendaries, and even choristers, for each major temple had these five classes of officials). And they supported themselves from this harvest, and the Indians also raised chickens for them to eat.

In all the towns Montezuma had his designated lands, which they sowed for him in the same way as the temple lands; and if no garrison was stationed in their towns, they would carry the crops on their backs to the great city of Temestitan [Tenochtitlán]; but in the garrison towns the grain was eaten by Montezuma's soldiers, and if the town did not sow the land, it had to supply the garrison with food, and also give them chickens and all other needful provisions.

5. AN AZTEC MOTHER ADVISES HER DAUGHTER

On the eve of the Spanish conquest the simpler Indian societies (tribes and bands) were typically characterized by gender equality and male–female complementarity, which recognized the equal importance of the special tasks performed by men and women. The situation with respect to the more complex societies like the Aztec, Inca, and Maya is another matter. In these societies the rise of militarism and a warrior class to which women had no access had eroded women's status to a significant degree. Some historians argue that Aztec male–female complementarity was maintained by symbolic means that equated giving birth with capturing a prisoner, dying in childbirth with being captured or killed in battle. A man's success in battle corresponded to the care that a woman took of his household. Aztec women were active in a wide variety of professions ranging from priest and doctor to sorcerer and prostitute. But Aztec sources and Spanish accounts based on them make clear that patriarchal family relations existed in Aztec society. This is evident from the "speeches of the ancients," passed on by memory from generation to generation, in which Aztec elders counseled the young. The following excerpt reveals some tampering by pious hands that substituted the Christian God for the Aztec supreme divinity, but it provides a sense of the coloring of Aztec speech and offers insight into Aztec social and family relations. It also points up an apparent contradiction in Aztec civilization: the "Assyrians of America," whose plunder empire rested on the foundations of war and human sacrifice, advised their children in speeches that are full of tender affection and precepts of charity and fair dealing.

My daughter: I bore you and have taught you good breeding and good order, and your father has honored you. If you are not what you should be, you may not live with good and virtuous women; nor will any man take you for wife.

Hardship and suffering are our lot in this world, and our powers daily waste away. We must serve God that He may aid us and give us health; we must live with diligence and care to obtain our needs.

See to it, then, beloved daughter, that you are not careless or lazy. Be cleanly and diligent, and look after the house and keep all in order as it should be, each thing in its place. Thus will you learn what you must do in your house when you marry.

Wherever you go, go with great modesty. Do not hurry or laugh as you walk, and do not glance about, either at those coming toward you or at any other, but go your way; and thus will you gain honor and good name.

See that you are well behaved and speak soberly; reply civilly to any who question you.

Perform your household duties, weave and embroider; and so you will be well beloved and will merit the food and clothing you receive. In this labor you will find comfort and will thank God that he fitted you for it.

Give yourself not to sleeping, to the bed, to laziness. Do not be used to sitting in the fresh cool shade; for this teaches sloth and vice, and with such a habit one does not live well or decorously. Women who give themselves over to it are not loved.

Whether seated or standing, walking or working, my daughter, always think good thoughts and work well; and do what you must do to serve God and your parents.

If you are called, do not wait to be called a second time, but go promptly to do what you are ordered to do, to avoid giving offense or making it necessary to punish you for your sloth and disobedience. Listen well to what you are ordered to do, and do not give a rude reply. If you cannot do what is asked of you, make your excuses civilly, but do not lie or deceive anyone; for God sees you.

If another is called and she does not promptly respond, do you go diligently and hear and do what that one had to do; and thus will you be loved.

Alonso de Zorita, *Life and Labor in Ancient Mexico*, ed. and trans. Benjamin Keen (New Brunswick, N.J.: Rutgers University Press, 1963), pp. 148–151.

If someone offers you good counsel, take it; do not reject it, lest that person grow angry with you and hold you in scorn.

Walk modestly and quietly, not in such a way that men will think you giddy.

Be charitable; do not scorn or hate others; and be not avaricious.

Do not assign a bad sense to the words of others; do not envy the good that God was pleased to do to others.

Do not cause others hardship or suffering; for thereby you will bring the same on yourself.

Do not do evil; and do not follow the promptings of your heart; for thereby you will make yourself evil and will ensnare yourself to your own hurt.

Do not keep company with women who lie, or are lazy, or gad about, not with low women, lest you harm yourself. Attend to your housework, and do not frivolously leave your house. Do not frequent the market place, or the public squares or baths; for this is very bad and leads to perdition and harm. And one who follows evil courses finds it difficult to give them up; for evil inspires evil desires.

If a man speaks to you, do not believe him and do not look at him; be quiet and pay no attention to him. If he follows you, do not reply to him, lest your speech trouble his heart; and if you take no heed of him, he will stop following you.

Do not enter a stranger's house without cause, lest he bring some charge against you.

If you enter the house of relatives, show respect to them and be not lazy; do what you see is fitting for you to do, and do not simply look at the women who are working.

When your parents give you a husband, do not be disrespectful to him; listen to him and obey him, and do cheerfully what you are told. Do not turn your face from him; and if he did you some hurt, do not keep recalling it. And if he supports himself by your industry, do not on that account scorn him, or be peevish or ungracious; for you will offend God, and your husband will be angry with you. Tell him meekly what you think should be done. Do not insult him or say offensive words to him in front of strangers or even to him alone; for you will harm yourself thereby, and yours will be the fault.

If someone visits your husband, thank him for coming, and do him some service. If your husband is disabled, you must show him how he is to live; and you must take care of the household, and secure persons to work your fields and store the harvest; and you must not be negligent in anything.

Do not waste your estate, but aid your husband; and you will obtain what you need for yourselves and your children.

My daughter, if you do what I have told you, all will love and esteem you. I have complied with my duty as a mother. If you take my advice, you will live happily; if you do not, the fault will be yours, and the future will show you the results of not heeding this advice. It shall never be said that I failed to advise you as a mother.

6. Mayan Industry, Commerce, and Agriculture

The Spanish bishop Diego de Landa's (1524–1579) Relation of the Things of Yucatán *is our principal source of information on the native way of life in northern Yucatán before and after the conquest. In the following extract Landa mentions the use of foreign trade, money, and credit, pointing to the existence among the ancient Maya of a complex economy in which exchange played a significant part. Landa's references to cooperative effort in agriculture, hunting, and fishing suggest the importance of the communal element in Mayan life.*

The trades of the Indians were making pottery and carpentering. They earned a great deal by making idols out of clay and wood, with many fasts and observances. There were also surgeons, or, to be more accurate, sorcerers, who cured with herbs and many superstitious rites. And so it was with all the other professions. The occupation to which they had the greatest inclination was trade, carrying salt and cloth and slaves to the lands of Ulua and Tabasco, exchanging all they had for cacao and stone beads, which were their money; and with this they were accustomed to buy slaves, or other beads, because they were fine and good, which their chiefs wore as jewels in their feasts; and they had others made of certain red shells for money, and as jewels to adorn their persons; and they carried it in purses of net, which they had, and at their markets they traded in everything which there was in that country. They gave credit, lent and paid courteously and without usury. And the greatest number were the cultivators and men who apply themselves to harvesting the maize and other grains, which they keep in fine underground places and granaries, so as to be able to sell (their crops) at the proper time. Their mules and oxen are the people themselves. For each married man with his wife, they are accustomed to sow a space of four hundred feet, which they call a "hun uinic," measured with a rod of twenty feet, twenty feet wide and twenty feet long.

The Indians have the good habit of helping each other in all their labors. At the time of sowing those who do not have their own people to do their work, join together in groups of twenty, or more or less, and all together they do the work of all of them (each doing) his assigned share, and they do

---

Diego de Landa, *Relación de las cosas de Yucatán* in "Landa's *Relación de las cosas de Yucatán*," ed. and trans. Alfred M. Tozzer (Cambridge: Peabody Museum of Archaeology and Ethnology, 1941), 18:94–97. Reprinted by permission of the author and the Peabody Museum of Archaeology and Ethnology, Harvard University.

not leave it until everyone's is done. The lands today are common property, and so he who first occupies them becomes the possessor of them. They sow in a great number of places, so that if one part fails, another may supply its place. In cultivating the land they do nothing except collect together the refuse and burn it in order to sow it afterwards. They cultivate the land from the middle of January and up to April, and they sow in the rainy season. They do this by carrying a little bag on their shoulders, and with a pointed stick they made a hole in the ground, and they drop there five or six grains, which they cover over with the same stick. It is a wonder how things grow when it rains. They also joined together for hunting in companies of fifty, more or less, and they roast the flesh of the deer on gridirons, so that it shall not be wasted, and when they reach the town, they make their presents to their lord and distribute the rest as among friends. And they do the same in their fishing.

7. THE MAYAN SOCIAL ORDER

Ancient Mayan society was highly stratified and divided into four "classes": nobility, priesthood, commoners, and slaves. A hereditary ruler with civil, religious, and military functions headed the government. The hierarchical order of society was reflected in the pattern of settlement in the Mayan towns. The homes of the nobles, the priests, and the wealthy were clustered around the ceremonial center, and the huts of the peasantry lay on the outskirts. For this, as for other aspects of Mayan life, Bishop Landa's Relation *is our chief source.*

After the departure of Kukulcan, the nobles agreed, in order that the government should endure, that the house of the Cocoms should have the chief power; because it was the most ancient or the richest family, or because at this time he who was at the head of it was a man of the greatest worth. This being done, since within the enclosure there were only temples and houses for the lords and the high priest, they ordered that other houses should be constructed outside, where each one of them could keep some servants, and to which the people from their towns could repair, when they came to the city on business. Each one then established in these houses his majordomo, who bore for his badge of office a short and thick stick, and they called him *caluac*. He kept account with the towns and with those who ruled them; and to them was sent notice of what was needed in the house of

Landa, *Relación*, pp. 26, 62, 85–87.

their lord, such as birds, maize, honey, salt, fish, game, cloth and other things, and the *caluac* always went to the house of his lord, in order to see what was wanted and provided it immediately, since his house was, as it were, the office of his lord.

It was the custom to seek in the towns for the maimed and blind, and they supplied their needs.

The lords appointed the governors, and if they were acceptable confirmed their sons in the offices, and they charged them with the kind treatment of the poor people, the peace of the town and to occupy themselves in their work of supporting themselves and the lords.

All the lords were careful to respect, visit and to entertain the Cocom, accompanying him, making feasts in his honor and repairing to him with important business, and they lived in peace with each other amusing themselves with their accustomed pastimes of dancing, feasts and hunting. . . .

Before the Spaniards had conquered that country, the natives lived together in towns in a very civilized fashion. They kept the land well cleared and free from weeds, and planted very good trees. Their dwelling place was as follows: in the middle of the town were their temples with beautiful plazas, and all around the temples stood the houses of the lords and the priests, and then (those of) the most important people. Then came the houses of the richest and of those who were held in the highest estimation nearest to these, and at the outskirts of the town were the houses of the lower class. And the Wells, if there were but few of them, were near the houses of the lords; and they had their improved lands planted with wine trees and they sowed cotton, pepper and maize, and they lived thus close together for fear of their enemies, who took them captive, and it was owing to the wars of the Spaniards that they scattered in the woods. . . .

Beyond the house, all the town did their sowing for the nobles; they also cultivated them (the fields) and harvested what was necessary for him and his household. And when there was hunting or fishing, or when it was time to get their salt, they always gave the lord his share, since these things they always did as a community. If the lord died, although it was the oldest son who succeeded him, the other children were very much respected and assisted and regarded as lords themselves. And they aided the other *principales* inferior to the lord in all these ways, according to whom he was and the favor which he enjoyed with his lord. The priests got their living from their offices and from offerings. The lords governed the town, settling disputes, ordering and settling the affairs of their republics, all of which they did by the hands of leading men, who were very well obeyed and highly esteemed, especially the rich, whom they visited, and they held court in their houses, where they settled their affairs and business usually at night. And if the lords went out of their town, they took with them a great many people, and it was the same way when they went out of their homes.

8. MAYAN RELIGIOUS LIFE

The great object of Mayan religion and worship was, as Landa concisely puts it, "that they [the gods] should give them health, life, and sustenance." The priesthood owed its influence to its assumed intimacy and power of intercession with the divine beings. Human sacrifice, vividly described below, was practiced from a very early period, but it did not assume mass proportions among the Maya until the tenth century and was a result of growing Mexican influence.

The natives of Yucatan were as attentive to the matters of religion as to those of government, and they had a high priest whom they called Ah Kin Mai and by another name Ahau Can Mai, which means the Priest Mai, or the High-Priest Mai. He was very much respected by the lords and had no *repartimiento* [allocation] of Indians, but besides the offerings, the lords made him presents and all the priests of the towns brought contributions to him, and his sons or his nearest relatives succeeded him in his office. In him was the key of their learning and it was to these matters that they dedicated themselves mostly; and they gave advice to the lords and replies to their questions. He seldom dealt with matters pertaining to the sacrifices except at the time of the principal feasts or in very important matters of business. They provided priests for the towns when they were needed, examining them in the sciences and ceremonies, and committed to them the duties of their office, and the good example to people and provided them with books and sent them forth. And they employed themselves in the duties of the temples and in teaching their sciences as well as in writing books about them.

They taught the sons of the other priests and the second sons of the lords who brought them for this purpose from their infancy, if they saw that they had an inclination for this profession.

The sciences which they taught were the computation of the years, months and days, the festivals and ceremonies, the administration of the sacraments, the fateful days and seasons, their methods of divination and their prophecies, events and the cures for diseases, and their antiquities and how to read and write with the letters and characters, with which they wrote, and drawings which illustrate the meaning of the writings.

Their books were written on a large sheet doubled in folds, which was enclosed entirely between two boards which they decorated, and they wrote on both sides in columns following the order of the folds. And they made this paper of the roots of a tree and gave it a white gloss upon which it was easy to write. And some of the principal lords learned about these sciences from cu-

---

Landa, *Relación*, pp. 27–28, 108–113, 115–120.

riosity and were very highly thought of on this account although they never made use of them publicly. . . .

They had a very great number of idols and of temples, which were magnificent in their own fashion. And besides the community temples, the lords, priests and the leading men had also oratories and idols in their houses, where they made their prayers and offerings in private. And they held Cozumel and the well of Chichen Itza in the same veneration as we have for pilgrimages to Jerusalem and Rome, and so they used to go to visit these places and to offer presents there, especially to Cozumel, as we do to holy places; and if they did not go themselves, they always sent their offerings, and those who went there were in the habit of entering the abandoned temples also, as they passed by them, to offer prayers there and to burn copal. They had such a great quantity of idols that even those of their gods were not enough; for there was not an animal or insect of which they did not make a statue, and they made all these in the image of their gods and goddesses. They had some idols of stone, but very few, and others of wood, and carved but of small size but not as many as those of clay. The wooden idols were so much esteemed that they were considered as heirlooms and were (considered) as the most important part of the inherited property. They possessed no idols of metal, since there was no metal there. They knew well that the idols were the works of their hands, dead and without a divine nature; but they held them in reverence on account of what they represented, and because they had made them with so many ceremonies, especially the wooden ones. The greatest idolaters were the priests, *Chilans*, the sorcerers and physicians, *Chacs*, and *Nacoms*. The office of the priest was to discuss and to teach their sciences, to make known their needs and the remedies for them, to preach and to publish the festival days, and to offer sacrifices and to administer their sacraments. The duty of the *Chilans* was to give the replies of the gods to the people, and so much respect was shown to them that they carried them on their shoulders. The sorcerers and physicians performed their cures by bleedings of the parts which gave pain to the sick man; and they cast lots so as to know the future in their own duties and in other things. The *Chacs* were four old men who were always chosen anew for each occasion, to aid the priest in carrying on the festivals well and thoroughly. The *Nacoms* were two officers; the first was perpetual and did not bring much honor with it, since it was he that opened the breasts of the human victims whom they sacrificed. The second was a choice made of a captain for war and for other feasts. His duties lasted three years, and he was held in high honor. . . .

Besides the festivals in which they sacrificed persons in accordance with their solemnity, the priest or *Chilan*, on account of some misfortune or necessity, ordered them to sacrifice human beings, and everyone contributed to this, that slaves should be bought, or some in their devotion gave their little children, who were made much of, and feasted up to the day (of the festival), and they were well guarded, so that they should not run away or pollute themselves with any carnal sin. And in the meanwhile they led them from town to town with dancing, while the priests, *Chilans* and other officers fasted. And when the day arrived, they all came together in the court of the temple, and if the victim was to be sacrificed with arrows, they stripped him naked, and anointed his body with a blue color, and put a *coroza* on his head. When they had reached the victim, all, armed with bows and arrows, danced a solemn dance with him around the stake, and while dancing they put him up on it and bound him to it, all of them keeping on dancing and gazing at him. The foul priest in vestments went up and wounded the victim with an arrow in the parts of shame, whether it was a man or woman, and drew blood and came down and anointed the faces of the idols with it. And making a certain sign to the dancers, they began one after another to shoot, as they passed rapidly before him, still dancing, at his heart, which had been marked beforehand with a white mark. And in this way they made his whole chest one point like a hedgehog of arrows. If the heart of the victim was to be taken out, they led him with a great show and company of people of the temple, and having smeared him with blue and put on a *coroza*, they brought him up to the round altar, which was the place of sacrifice, and after the priest and his officials had anointed the stone with a blue color, and by purifying the temple drove out the evil spirit, the *Chacs* seized the poor victim, and placed him very quickly on his back upon that stone, and all four held him by the legs and arms, so that they divided him in the middle. At this came the executioner, the *Nacom*, with a knife of stone, and struck him with great skill and cruelty a blow between the ribs of his left side under the nipple, and he at once plunged his hand in there and seized the heart like a raging tiger and snatched it out alive and, having placed it upon a plate, he gave it to the priest, who went very quickly and anointed the faces of the idols with that fresh blood. Sometimes they made this sacrifice on the stone and high altar of the temple, and then they threw the body, now dead, rolling down the steps. The officials below took it and flayed it whole, taking off all the skin with the exception of the feet and hands, and the priest, all bare, covered himself, stripped naked as he was, with that skin, and the others danced with him. And this was considered as a thing of great solemnity amongst them. The custom was usually to bury in the court of the temple those whom they had sacrificed, or else they ate them, dividing him among those who had arrived (first) and the lords, and the hands, feet and head were reserved for the priest and his officials, and they considered those who were sacrificed as holy. If the victims were slaves captured in war, their master took their bones, to use them as a trophy in their dances as token of victory. Sometimes they threw living victims into the well of Chichen Itza, believing that they would come out on the third day, although they never appeared again.

9. MAYAN ORIGIN MYTH

Spanish efforts to eradicate Mayan religious practices resulted in the destruction of all but a few scattered hieroglyphic texts probably used by the Maya in divination. At the same time, European alphabetic writing—an integral part of the education of elite Native American children—provided new, if generally covert ways to preserve traditional religious beliefs. Written down sometime during the mid-sixteenth century in Quiché (one of the principal Mayan languages) and intended to inform the councils of Quiché leaders, the Popol Vuh *is a splendid example of the subversive appropriation of one of the principal weapons of conquest—written language—and it also provides a unique glimpse into Mayan religion. Unlike pre-Conquest hieroglyphic texts, which required extensive expertise to interpret, the* Popol Vuh *integrated the divinatory aspects of Mayan religion into a compelling narrative that included mythical figures like the hero twins, Hunahpu and Xbalanque, whose adventures culminate in a heavenly ascent as part of a detailed account of the four stages of human creation. "Discovered" and preserved by a Spanish friar, Francisco Ximénez, the* Popol Vuh *continues to play a role in Quiché religious life. This selection tells the story of the successful fourth creation that followed three failed attempts to create humans from animals, mud, and wood. Munro Edmonson's translation highlights the mixture of ritual invocation and storytelling that characterize this hybrid creation myth.*

And this is the beginning when man was invented, / And when that which would go
into man's body was sought.
Then spoke the Bearer, / And Engenderer,
Who were Former / And Shaper, / Majesty /And Quetzal Serpent by name,
"The dawn has already appeared; / The creation has already been made,
And there is clearly a nourisher appearing, / A supporter,
Born of light, / Engendered of light.
Man has already appeared, / The population of the surface of the earth," they
said.
It was all assembled and came / And went, their wisdom,
In the darkness, / In the night time,
As they originated things, / And dissolved things.
They thought; / And they meditated there
And thus came their wisdom directly, bright / And clear.
They found / And they maintained / What came to be / Man's body.

The Book of Counsel: The Popol Vuh of the Quiche Maya of Guatemala, ed. and trans. Munro S. Edmonson (New Orleans: Middle American Research Institute, Tulane University, 1971), pp. 145–155. Reprinted by permission of the Edmonson family.

That was just a little later / There not having appeared
The sun, / Moon / And stars / Over the heads
Of Former / And Shaper.

In Cleft, / In Bitter Water by name,
There came then yellow corn ears / And white corn ears.

And there are the names of the animals; / These were the bringers of the food:
Wildcat, / Coyote, / Parakeet / And Crow.
They are the four animals / Who told the news
Of the yellow corn ears / And white corn ears to them.
There they went then to Cleft / To point out the Cleft road,
And there they found the food / Whence came the flesh
Of the formed people, / The shaped people.
And water was their blood; / It became man's blood.
There came to Bearer / And Engenderer the corn ears.
And they rejoiced then / Over the discovery
Of the marvelous mountain, / Filled / With quantities / And quantities
Of yellow corn ears, / And white corn ears,
And also loads of cacao / And chocolate,
Numberless mameys, / Custard apples, / Anonas, / Nances, / Soursops / And
*   honey.*
It was full of the sweetest foods, / In the town
At Cleft, / And at Bitter Water by name.
There was food there / From the fruit of everything:
Small vegetables, / Big vegetables, / Small plants / And big plants.
The road was pointed out / By the animals.
And the yellow corn was ground / And the white corn,
And nine bushels / Were made by Xmucane.
The food came / With water to create strength,
And it became man's grease / And turned into his fat
When acted upon by Bearer / And Engenderer,
Majesty / And Quetzal Serpent, as they are called.
And so then they put into words the creation, / The shaping
Of our first mother / And father.
Only yellow corn / And white corn were their bodies.
Only food were the legs / And arms of man.
Those who were our first fathers / Were the four original men.
Only food at the outset / Were their bodies.

These are the names of the first men who were made, / Who were shaped:
The first was Jaguar Quiche, / And the second in turn was Jaguar Night,
And the third in turn was Nought, / And the fourth was Wind Jaguar,

And these are the names of our first mothers / And fathers.
Only formed, / Only shaped they were said to be.
They had no mother; / They had no father.
Just heroes by themselves / We have said.
No woman bore them; / Nor were they engendered
By the Former / And Shaper, / The Bearer / And Engenderer.
Just power, / Just magic
Was their forming, / Their shaping
By the Former / And Shaper,
Bearer / And Engenderer, / Majesty / And Quetzal Serpent.
And when they looked like men / They became men.
They spoke / And they talked; / They saw / And they heard;
They walked; / They grasped;
They were fine men. / They were handsome. / Manly faces / Were
*   their features.*
They had breath / And existed.
And they could see too; / Immediately their sight began.
They came to see; / They came to know
Everything under heaven / If they could see it.
Suddenly they could look around / And see around
In the sky, / In the earth.
It was scarcely an instant / Before everything could be seen.
They didn't have to walk at first / So as to gaze at what was under heaven:
They were just there and looked. / Their understanding became great.
Their gaze passed over trees, / Rocks, / Lakes, / Seas, / Mountains /
*   And valleys.*
Truly then / They were the most beloved of men,
Jaguar Quiche, / Jaguar Night, / Nought / And Wind Jaguar.

And then they were asked by the Former / And Shaper:
"How pleasant is your existence? / Do you know? / Can't you see? /
*   Can't you hear?*
Isn't your language good / And your walking?
And look now / At what you see under heaven!
Aren't the mountains clear? / Do you see the valleys?
Then try it now!" / They were told.
And so then they came to see everything under heaven, / And so then they
*   gave thanks*
To Former, / And Shaper,
"Truly then twice thanks, / Thrice thanks that we are created already,
And that we are mouthed / And faced.
We can speak; / We can hear; / We ponder; / We move;
We think very well; / We understand

Far / And near,
And we can see large / And small,
What is in heaven, / What is on earth.
Thanks then to you / That we are created, / We are formed, / We are shaped,
We exist, oh our grandmother, / Oh our grandfather,"
They said / As they gave thanks
For their forming, / Their shaping.
They came to understand everything; / They saw it:
The four creations, / The four destructions
The womb of heaven, / The womb of earth.
And not very happily / Did they listen to this,
The Former / And Shaper.
"It is not good / What they said,
Our forming, / Our shaping:
We know everything great / And small," they said.

And so they took back again / Their knowledge,
Did Bearer / And Engenderer.
"How shall we make them again / So that their sight reaches only nearby?
So that it will just be a little space / Of the surface of the earth that they see?
It is not good / What they say.
Aren't their names just formed / And shaped?
But quite like gods / Will they become then
Unless they begin to multiply / And begin to grow numerous
When it whitens, / When it brightens:
Unless it increases. / Then so be it!
Let's just undo them a little more. / That's what is still needed.
It isn't good what we have found out. / Won't they just equate their deeds
     with ours
If their understanding reaches too far / And they see everything?" they were told
By the Heart of Heaven, / 1 Leg, / Dwarf Lightning, / Green Lightning,
Majesty, / Quetzal Serpent, / Bearer, / And Engenderer, / Xpiacoc, / Xmucane,
Former/ And Shaper, as they are called.
And then they made / Their life over
For their forming, / Their shaping.

And their eyes were chipped / By the Heart of Heaven.
They were blinded like the clouding of the surface of a mirror; / Their eyes were
     all blinded.
They could only see nearby then, / However clear things might be,
And thus they lost their understanding, / And all the wisdom of the four men
At the start, / At the beginning.
And thus was the forming, / The shaping

Of our grandfathers, / Our first fathers
By the Heart of Heaven, / The Heart of Earth.
And then there were their mates; / And their wives came to exist.
Only the gods / Invented them too.
Thus it was just in their sleep/ That they brought them then.
Truly they were beautiful / And they were women
For Jaguar Quiche / Jaguar Night, / Nought / And Wind Jaguar.
When their wives were there they were properly brought to life / At once their
hearts rejoiced again over their mates.
And these are their names; / Their wives were these:
Red Sea House was the name / Of the wife of Jaguar Quiche;
Beauty House was the name / Of the wife of Jaguar Night;
Hummingbird House was the name / Of the wife of Nought;
Parrot House was the name / Of the wife of Wind Jaguar.
And these were the names of their wives, / Who became queens.
They were the bearers of the little tribes, / The great tribes,
And this was the root of us / Who are Quiche people.
And the worshippers became many, / And the sacrificers.
They came to be no longer four, / Though four were the mothers of us Quiche
people.
Different were their names / For each of them.
Then they multiplied there / At the sunrise.
Many were their names. / They became the peoples:
Majesties, / Ballplayers, / Maskers, / Children of Lords,
As they continued to be called, / The names of the people.
And there / At the sunrise they multiplied. . . .

10. How the Inca Formed a Nation

The Inca made a systematic attempt to unify the institutions and even the language of
their extensive empire; they were so successful that today five-sixths of the Indians of
the Andean area still speak Quechua, the official language of the empire. The Inca ob-
tained their results with the aid of an elaborate bureaucracy that brought every inhab-
itant of the empire under the direct and continuous control of an official appointed by
the emperor. An important factor in the success of the Inca plan of unification was the
policy of resettlement or colonization, described below by Father Cobo.

———————

Bernabé Cobo, *Historia del Nuevo Mundo*, 4 vols. (Sevilla, 1890–1893), 3:222–225. Excerpt translated by Benjamin Keen.

The entire empire of the Inca, though so extensive and composed of so many diverse nations, was a single commonwealth, ruled by the same laws, statutes, and customs and observing the same religion, rites, and ceremonies. . . .

The first thing that these kings did after conquering a province was to re- move six or seven thousand families, more or less, as seemed best to them, taking into account the capacity and temper of the population, and to trans- fer these families to the quiet, peaceful provinces, assigning them to different towns. In their stead they introduced the same number of people, taken from the places to which the former families had been sent or from such other places as seemed convenient; among these people were many nobles of royal blood. Those who were thus domiciled in new lands were called *mitimaes*— that is, newcomers or strangers, as distinct from the natives. This term ap- plied to the new vassals as well as to the old ones who were sent in their places, since both went from their own to foreign lands; even today we use the word in this sense, calling *mitimaes* all those newcomers who have settled in the provinces of this kingdom. In these transfers of population they saw to it that the migrants, both the newly conquered persons and the others, were moved to lands whose climate and conditions were the same as, or similar to, those which they had left behind and in which they had been reared. . . .

The Incas introduced these changes of domicile in order to maintain their rule with greater ease, quiet, and security; for since the city of Cuzco, their capital, where they had their court and residence, was so distant from the provinces most lately acquired, in which there were many barbarous and war- like nations, they considered that there was no other way to keep them in peaceful submission. And since this was the principal purpose of the transfer, they ordered the majority of the *mitimaes* whom they sent to the recently conquered towns to make their homes in the provincial capitals, where they served as garrisons, not for wages or for a limited time but in perpetuity, both they and their descendants. As soldiers they received certain privileges to make them appear of nobler rank, and they were ordered always to obey the slightest commands of their captains and governors. Under this plan, if the natives revolted, the *mitimaes*, being devoted to the governors, soon reduced them to obedience to the Inca; and if the *mitimaes* rioted they were repressed and punished by the natives; thus, through this scheme of domiciling the ma- jority of the people of some province in other parts, the king was made secure against revolts in his dominions, and the social and commercial intercourse among the different provinces was more frequent and the entire land was better supplied with all its needs.

The Inca profited further by this transfer of their vassals from one part to another in that throughout the length and breadth of the Empire similarity and conformity prevailed in religion and government. All the nations learned and spoke the language of Cuzco, which thus came to be general throughout Peru; for through this change of domicile the newly conquered peoples, re- moved into the interior of the kingdom, learned all this quickly and without difficulty or coercion, and the old vassals who were resettled in place of the new subjects who were being pacified taught it to the natives. The Inca required everyone to absorb their language, laws, and religion, with all the beliefs about these matters that were established at Cuzco; they either partly or wholly abolished their former usages and rites and made them receive their own. In order to introduce and establish these things more effectively, in addition to transferring people they would remove the principal idol from a conquered province and set it up in Cuzco with the same attendance and worship that it had formerly had; all this was seen to by persons who had come from that province, just as they had done when they had had the idol in their own country. For this reason Indians from every province of the kingdom were at all times in residence in the capital and court, occupied in guarding and ministering to their own idols. Thus they learned the usages and customs of the court; and when they were replaced by others according to their system of *mitas*, or turns, on their return to their own country they taught their people what they had seen and learned in the court.

11. THE VILLAGE BASIS OF INCAN SOCIETY

The basic unit of Incan social organization was the ayllu, *a kinship group whose members claimed descent from a common ancestor. An Inca village typically consisted of several* ayllu. *The chronicler Garcilaso de la Vega (1539–1616), son of a Spanish noble and an Incan princess, drew an idyllic picture of Indian village life and of the relations between the Inca and their subjects. His account of a happy peasantry going forth singing and rejoicing to labor in the service of their king is at serious variance with what is known of the chronic unrest and frequent revolts of conquered tribes against their Incan rulers.*

In the matter of working and cultivating the fields they also established good order and harmony. First they worked the fields of the sun, then those of the widows and orphans and of those disabled by old age or illness: all such were regarded as poor people, and therefore the Inca ordered that their lands should be cultivated for them. In each town, or in each ward if the town was large, there were men assigned exclusively to look after the cultivation of the fields of the persons that we would call poor. These deputies were called *llactamayu*, or town councilors. It was their task, at the time of plowing, sowing, and harvesting the fields, to ascend at night towers that were made for this purpose, to blow on a trumpet or shell to attract attention,

Garcilaso de la Vega, *Comentarios reales de los Incas*, 2 vols. (Buenos Aires, 1943), 1:227–229. Excerpt translated by Benjamin Keen.

and loudly announce: "On such-and-such a day the fields of the disabled persons will be cultivated; let each betake himself to his assigned place." The people in each precinct already knew, by means of a list that had been made, to which fields they must go; these were the fields of their relatives or closest neighbors. Each one had to bring his own food, whatever he had in the house, so that the disabled persons would not have to provide for them. For they said that the aged, the sick, and the widows and orphans had trouble enough of their own, without being burdened with the troubles of others. If the disabled persons had no seeds they were provided from the storehouses, of which we shall have more to say hereafter. The fields of the soldiers who were away at war were also worked in common, for when their husbands were absent on army duty the wives were counted as widows. And so they performed this favor for them as for needy people. They took great care in the rearing of the children of those who were killed in the wars, until such time as they were married.

After the fields of the poor had been cultivated, each one tilled his own, and they helped each other in groups, cultivating their fields in turn. Then they tilled the fields of the *curaca*, the chief, and these were the last to be worked in each town or province. In the time of Huaina Capac, in a town of the Chacapuyas, one Indian town councilor gave precedence to the fields of the *curaca*, a relative of his, before those of a widow. He was hanged for breaking the rule that the Inca had established for the cultivation of the fields, and the gallows was set upon the land of the *curaca*. The Inca decreed that the fields of their vassals should have precedence before their own, for they said that the prosperity of his subjects was the source of good service to the king; that if they were poor and needy they could not serve well in war or in peace.

The last fields to be cultivated were those of the king. They worked them in common; all the Indians went to the fields of the king and the sun, generally with great good cheer and rejoicing, dressed in the vestments and finery that they kept for their principal festivals, adorned with gold and silver ornaments and wearing large feathered headdresses. When they plowed the land (and this was the labor that gave them the greatest pleasure), they sang many songs that they composed in praise of their Inca; thus they converted their work into merrymaking and rejoicing, because it was in the service of their God and of their kings.

12. TWO VIEWS OF THE INCAN EMPIRE

The debate on the nature of the Incan state that began soon after its downfall continues into our own times. Successive generations of historians, consciously or unconsciously influenced by political, social, or sentimental biases, have found in the Incan empire whatever type of governmental system or social order they perhaps wanted to find. Some of the pros and cons of this debate are presented in the following selections, written by men who do not clearly belong to either of the two major schools and who are highly regarded for their honesty and objectivity. The first reading is from the Chronicle of Peru, *written in 1551 by Pedro de Cieza de León (1518–1560), a soldier who had traveled throughout the Andean region studying Indian customs and institutions. The second is from the previously cited work of Father Cobo.*

Part 1

Since these kings ruled over a land of such great length and vast provinces, and in part so rugged and full of snow-capped mountains and sandy, treeless, arid plains, they had to be very prudent in governing so many nations that differed so greatly in language, law, and religion, in order to maintain them in tranquility and keep peace and friendship with them. Therefore, although the city of Cuzco was the head of their empire, . . . they stationed deputies and governors at various points; these men were the wisest, ablest, and most courageous that could be found, and none was so young but that he was in the last third of his age. And since the natives were loyal to such a governor and none dared to rebel, and he had the mitimaes on his side, no one, no matter how powerful, dared to rise against him; and if such a rebellion did take place, the village in which the uprising occurred was punished and the instigators were sent to Cuzco. Hence the kings were so greatly feared that if they traveled through the kingdom and merely permitted one of the hangings on their litters to be lifted so that their vassals might see them, the people raised such a great cry as to cause the birds flying on high to fall and be captured by hand; and so great was their fear that they dared not speak ill of even the shadow that the Inca cast. And this was not all; . . . if any of his captains or servants went out to visit some part of the kingdom, the people came out to receive him on the road with many presents, never failing, even if he were alone, to comply in detail with his every order.

So greatly did they fear their princes, in this extensive land, that every village was as well organized and governed as if their lord were present in it to punish those who disobeyed him. This fear arose from the power that these lords enjoyed, and from their justice, for all knew that if they did wrong they would certainly be punished and that neither pleas nor bribes would help them. And the Incas always did good works for their subjects, not permitting them to be wronged or burdened with excessive tribute or outraged in any way. They helped those who lived in barren provinces, where their forefathers

Pedro de Cieza de León, *Del señorio de los Incas* (Buenos Aires, 1943), pp. 34–35; Bernabé Cobo, *Historia del Nuevo Mundo*, 3:279–281. Excerpts translated by Benjamin Keen.

had lived in great need, to make them fertile and abundant, providing them with the things they required; and to other provinces where they had insufficient clothing, for lack of sheep, they sent flocks of sheep with great liberality. In fine, it was understood that these lords knew not only how to be served by their subjects and to obtain tribute from them but also how to keep up their lands and how to raise them from their first rude condition to a civilized state and from destitution to comfort. And through these good works and through constantly presenting their principal men with wives and jewels, they gained the extreme good will of all, and were so greatly loved that I recall with my own eyes having seen aged Indians, visiting Cuzco, gaze upon the city with tearful lamentations, as they contemplated the present time and recalled the past, when that city so long housed their natural lords, who knew how to gain their service and friendship in other ways than those used by the Spaniards.

Part 2

The yoke that weighed down the necks of these miserable Indians was so heavy that I doubt if all the men in the world, joining together to invent a species of subjection and tyranny as oppressive as that in which they lived, could improve on what the Incas achieved to keep these Indians in a state of submission.

And anyone who carefully considers the system they maintained in administering and conserving their empire will find that all was directed solely toward this end. I could easily prove this by describing in detail the actions they ordered for oppressing their subjects, but it will suffice to say that these poor people were not allowed to own anything privately without the permission of the Inca or his governors, not even to slaughter a sheep or to have two suits of clothes; nor could they eat what they chose, but they had to observe the wishes of the Inca or his governors; nor could they marry whomever they pleased, and still less could they marry off their daughters at their pleasure; nor (what is worse) were they masters of their own wives and children, for the lords took away the wives of some to give them to others, and they took their children to slay them in the sacrifices.

The *caciques* made the round of their districts several times a year, to make sure that the Indians had no more than was allowed them, for they were not permitted to possess gold or silver or to wear fine clothes. They could not own a flock of more than ten animals without special permission; this privilege the Inca would grant to the *caciques*, but in a specified number, which never exceeded fifty or a hundred heads; and the *caciques* themselves could not wear fine clothes unless they received them from the Inca as a reward for some distinguished service. Daughters ordinarily were in the power of their parents until the age of ten, and thereafter they were at the disposition of the Inca.

All persons, no matter how noble their rank, when entering the presence of the king took off their sandals and placed light burdens on their shoulders as a sign of homage and reverence. In speaking to the Inca they kept their eyes lowered and did not look him in the face, while he maintained a visage of notable gravity and replied with few words, spoken in such a low voice that they could scarcely be heard. Only the great lords, by special privilege, seated themselves before him.

And since the Incas had no other aim in their method of government than to place their vassals daily in a state of greater subjection and servitude, to please them each of their governors and *caciques*, both high and low, applied himself to the attainment of their objective, which was to exhaust the strength of the Indians until they were unable to raise their heads. And since the Incas were very capable men, they were not found wanting in the craft and skill required for the difficult task of taming nations so barbarous and indomitable. The principal method that they used for this purpose was to keep their subjects poor and continually occupied with excessive labors, so that being oppressed and abased they might lack the fire and spirit to aspire to revolt. To this end they built great fortresses, opened roads, constructed terraces on the hillsides, and compelled them to bring tribute to Cuzco from distances of three and four hundred leagues. With the same aim they introduced many cults and burdened them with many rites and sacrifices, so that when they were free from other labors and services this work alone sufficed to leave them without time to take breath or rest. . . .

Moreover, the Incas were much aided in their designs by the great esteem and respect that the Indians felt for them, through which these simple people came to believe that the Incas not only were different from other men in valor and strength but had close kinship, familiarity, and intercourse with the sun and with the *huacas*, basing this erroneous opinion on the testimony of the Incas themselves, who boasted of this relationship, and on the religious claims which the Incas always advanced in making their conquests. And by reason of these things, and because of the diligence with which the Incas propagated the worship of their religion, consuming in its honor so much wealth and so many people that it became the principal occupation of the whole land, the Indians concluded that the gods must be under a great sense of obligation and duty toward the Incas, never failing to favor their designs. They were daily confirmed in this view by the many victories that the Incas won over all kinds of nations, and by the fact that although at the outset they had been so few in number they had placed this whole great empire under their sway. And the esteem that the Indians felt for the Incas was not a little enhanced by the admirable order and harmony that they established in all matters, both in what concerned the good of the commonwealth and in the aggrandizement of the cult of their gods. To this also contributed the nonsense the Incas daily fed their subjects, as a result of which these simple people conceived the Incas to be very close to the gods and endowed with super-human wisdom, particularly when they saw the beauty and majesty with which the Incas had adorned their court, for which the Indians felt great reverence. . . .

Nevertheless, I believe that these measures would not have sufficed to establish so firmly the power of the Incas and the subjection of these peoples if the Incas had not also resorted to severe measures, inflicting deaths and exemplary punishments upon those who attempted to overthrow the existing order. Actually, there were numerous revolts on the part of their subjects, who tried to regain their liberty by this means. . . . Many of these terrible chastisements are still fresh in the memories of living men, since their stories have been handed down from father to son. I will cite here two or three of these cases. In a place near Payta an Inca slew five thousand men at one time, and to strike greater fear into his subjects he ordered the hearts of the slain men to be plucked out and placed around the fortress in a circle. In the towns of Otavalo and Caranque, Guaynacapac put to death all the males (except the boys), and for this reason the inhabitants of those towns were long called Guambracuna, which means "lads." . . . From which I conclude that it was through strictness and cruelty, more than by any other means, that the Incas succeeded in breaking the spirit of their subjects, in placing them in the strict servitude in which they kept them, and in developing in them the abject submissiveness with which they were obeyed and revered. For theirs was a slavery so rigorous that it is difficult to imagine a worse one, even if we reviewed all the governments of the world of which we have any knowledge.

13. WAR AND CANNIBALISM
AMONG THE BRAZILIAN INDIANS

The complex, stratified Aztec, Maya, and Inca societies represent the peaks of Indian cultural development before the coming of the Europeans. A far greater number of Indian groups were organized simply as bands or tribes; some lived by hunting and gathering, and others practiced a shifting slash-and-burn agriculture and supplemented their diet by hunting and fishing. Typical of this tribal level were the Tupi Indians, a linguistic family of tribes inhabiting the eastern seaboard of Brazil. These Indians lived in villages composed of long huts, each sheltering many interrelated families; they cultivated manioc and other food plants, and also hunted and fished. Each hut had its chief, and a council of elders and a paramount chief met regularly to discuss the entire tribe's affairs; chiefs had little power in the egalitarian Tupi societies. A characteristic of the Tupi way of life was constant intertribal warfare waged to capture prisoners; these captives were later ritually executed and their flesh was cooked and eaten to gain their spiritual strength and perpetuate the tribal feud. André Thevet (1504–

1592), a French cosmographer who briefly lived among the Tupinamba of coastal Brazil, describes their mode of warfare and ritual cannibalism.

These savages are much given to warring with their neighbors. . . . Having no other way of settling their disputes, they valiantly fight each other. They assemble in groups of six, ten, or even twelve thousand men, with villages pitted against each other. They also fight whenever they meet by chance. . . . Before carrying out any great enterprise of peace or war, these savages, especially the older men, assemble to discuss the matter; women and children do not take part in these meetings. In these assemblies they display much gravity and decorum, taking turns speaking and carefully listening to each speaker. A few, because of their distinguished lineage or for some other reason, are permitted to sit on their hammocks.

These Indians, like people in other parts of the world, use stratagems to surprise their enemies. . . . They stage surprise attacks at night more often than during the day; for this reason they are especially watchful at night, assembling in great numbers to guard against their enemies. As soon as they suspect that their enemies are approaching, they plant innumerable pieces of wood with sharp points (like the traps we use in France) in the earth for a distance of a bowshot around their huts. The points of these sticks protrude from the earth and are very hard to see in the dark. The enemies impale their feet, which are bare like the rest of their bodies, on these sticks; this makes it easy to kill some of the wounded and take the rest prisoners.

These savages consider it a very honorable thing to leave their homes and invade enemy territory, and he who returns home with a number of enemy prisoners is honored like a great king or lord. When the people of one village want to ambush the people of another village they hide like foxes in the nearby woods for a certain period of time, emerging only when they see an opportunity to take their enemies by surprise. Entering the enemy village, they set the huts on fire to force the people to come out with their wives, children, and all their possessions. When these people come out, the two sides attack each other with clubs and wooden swords, and shoot arrows at each other at random; they also bite every part of their enemies' bodies that they can reach, including their perforated lips. Sometimes, in order to intimidate their enemies, they hold up the bones of the men they have killed in war and eaten. In short, they do everything possible to anger their enemies. The prisoners are led away, tied up and trussed like thieves. You cannot imagine the howls and endearments with which warriors are greeted when they return home victorious.

André Thevet, *Les singularités de la France antarctique*, ed. Paul Gaffarel (Paris, 1878), pp. 184–204. Excerpt translated by Benjamin Keen.

Wives accompany their husbands to war—not to fight, like Amazons— but to carry food and munitions, for warriors sometimes travel as long as five or six months without returning to their villages. When they leave for war they set fire to all their huts and bury their most prized possessions in the earth until they return. The number of wives a man has to serve him varies with his importance. . . .

One may wonder why these savages make war against each other since they have more than enough land for their needs, and no rulers or great riches. All I can say is that their wars have little foundation, and that they fight only from a desire for vengeance, like wild animals. They are incapable of reaching any settlement, and justify their continual warfare with the simple statement that the people they fight have been their enemies from time immemorial. As I said above, they assemble in great numbers to march against their enemies, especially if they have recently suffered some injury from them. When they meet they first shoot flights of arrows at each other, then join in hand-to-hand combat, seizing each other by the arms and ears, and dealing each other blows with their fists. . . .

So great is their mutual hatred that they sometimes spend an entire day standing the distance of an arquebus shot from each other, hurling threats at their enemies, with such deafening howls and cries that they drown out the sound of thunder, raising their wooden swords and clubs on high, and saying, "We have eaten your relations and we will eat you," and making fearsome faces and other silly threats at each other.

The greatest, cruelest vengeance that these savages can take is to eat their enemies. If they have taken some war prisoners and are not strong enough to carry them away before an attempt is made to rescue them, they will cut off a prisoner's arms and legs and eat them before leaving him, or perhaps each will carry away a piece of his flesh, large or small. But if they can bring their prisoners to their own country, they will eat them just the same. . . .

It remains for me to describe how the savages treat these captives. For four or five days they are well treated, after which each captive is given a wife, who may be the captor's daughter, to sleep with him and satisfy his other needs. The captive is given the best food available, and they try to fatten him up like a capon until he is killed. After the prisoner has been well fattened, they kill him, thinking they do him a great honor.

In order that the prisoner may be more easily recognized, they put around his neck a necklace of cotton thread strung with some round fruit or the bones of some fish or animal, resembling rosary beads. If they want to keep him for a space of four or five moons, they attach that number of beads, and remove them one at a time as each moon wanes, killing him when the beads are all gone.

Sometimes, instead of these beads, the savages tie as many little necklaces around the prisoner's neck as he has moons to live. (Note that these savages count only up to five, and mark time only by moons, instead of days, months, or years.) . . .

If a child is born of the union between the prisoner and the wife given to him, the savages fatten the child for some time and then eat him or her because the child is the offspring of their enemy.

For the solemn occasion of the execution the savages invite all their friends to come from afar and partake of the prisoner's flesh. On the appointed day the captive, made fast with chains (whose use they have learned from the Christians), lies in his hammock, singing day and night songs like the following, "Our friends the Marakajas are honest men, strong and powerful warriors; they have taken and eaten many of our enemies, and they will eat me the day it pleases them, but I have killed and eaten the relatives and friends of the man who took me prisoner," and much more of the same. One can see from this how little fear they have of death. Once, out of curiosity, I asked some prisoners, strong and handsome men, if they were not anxious about being killed from one day to the next. Laughing and joking, with great coolness and assurance, they replied, "Our friends will avenge us." If someone even suggested the possibility of their being ransomed and freed from the hands of their enemies, they treated it as a great joke.

They treat women and girls taken in war like the men, but give them no husbands. They are not held captive as closely as the men, however, being free to go here and there. But they are made to work in the gardens and to fish for oysters.

I return to the execution. As I noted above, the owner of a prisoner invites all his friends to partake of pieces of the prisoner's flesh, which is served up with great quantities of *cahouin*, a beverage made of coarse millet and certain roots. All who attend this solemn occasion are adorned with beautiful plumes of different colors, or paint themselves all over. The man who is to deal the fatal blow puts on his best finery and carries a wooden sword richly adorned with various plumes.

As the preparations for his death advance, the prisoner displays ever greater signs of joy. At last he is led, firmly tied with cotton cords, to the public place of execution. He is accompanied by ten or twelve thousand of his enemies. There, after various ceremonies, he is clubbed over the head, as if he were a pig. When he is dead, the wife he has been given makes some slight show of mourning. After his body has been cut into pieces, the savages wash their male children in his blood to teach them to be brave, explaining that when they come of age they must do the same to their enemies. By watching this ceremony the children also learn that the same fate awaits them when they are taken captive. After the body has been dismembered and cooked, it is distributed to all those present, each receiving a piece. The women commonly eat the entrails, while the head is hung up on the end of a pole among the huts as a trophy or symbol of victory. . . .

As soon as the execution is over the executioner takes to his bed and remains in his hut without eating or drinking for a space of three days. If he must go somewhere he must be carried, for they foolishly believe that if he walks he will suffer some misfortune or even die. Soon afterwards, using a lancet made from the teeth of an animal called the Cutia, he makes various incisions on his chest and other parts of his body, so that he looks like a mass of slashes.

In response to my questions, several savages informed me that the executioner does this as a token of the honor he derives from having killed his enemy. When I remonstrated with them, pointing out the cruelty of these killings, they rebuffed me, saying that it was shameful for us to pardon our enemies after we had made them prisoners, that it was better to kill them so they would not make war on us a second time. This is the mode of reasoning of these brutish people.

2

HISPANIC SOCIETY ON THE

EVE OF THE CONQUEST

THE INSTITUTIONS, TRADITIONS, and values brought to the Americas by Hispanic invaders shaped the future of Latin America more decisively than did the culture of the vanquished Indians. Five centuries of struggle against the Muslims had made warfare almost a way of life and created a large class of titled fighting men who regarded manual labor and most forms of commerce with contempt. The Reconquest (*Reconquista*), as that struggle is called, was also accompanied by a growing concentration of land in the hands of the Christian nobility and the Church. Although serfdom in Castile had virtually ceased to exist by the end of the fifteenth century, in contrast to the situation in Aragón, the great majority of the peasants were heavily burdened by rents, seigneurial dues, taxes, and tithes. With some regional exceptions, there was little industry. The most lucrative economic activity in Castile—the export of wool to Flanders and Italy—enriched the great nobility who owned vast herds of sheep and extensive pasturages. The Portuguese economy displayed similar disparities. The claim of some scholars that a thriving "capitalism" existed in late medieval Spain and Portugal does not bear scrutiny. On the eve of the conquest of the Americas, the economies and societies of both countries presented a predominantly feudal aspect.

A turning point in Iberian peninsular history occurred in 1469, when the heirs apparent to the thrones of Aragón and Castile—Ferdinand and Isabella—married. The Catholic Sovereigns—the title given to them by the pope in recognition of their crusading zeal—broke the power of the great nobility but allowed it to retain and even expand its social and economic privileges. The crowning domestic achievement of Ferdinand and Isabella's reign was the surrender of the Muslim city and kingdom of Granada in 1492, after a ten-year siege. More unified politically and religiously than ever before, and avid for the gold and silver that symbolized power and wealth in the age of the commercial revolution, Spain stood ready to launch the great enterprise of the Indies.

1. THE CATHOLIC SOVEREIGNS

The joint reign of Ferdinand of Aragón and Isabella of Castile was rich in dramatic and important events. They worked to unify Spain, subdue feudal lawlessness, and activate Spanish industry, but they nevertheless contributed to Spain's ultimate decay through their policies of religious intolerance and systematic weakening of the autonomy and political influence of the Spanish towns. This negative aspect of their world was not apparent to the patriotic Jesuit Father Juan de Mariana (1535–1625), whose history of Spain contains a glowing tribute to the Catholic Sovereigns.

Truly it was they who restored justice, previously corrupted and fallen into decay, to its proper place. They made very good laws for governing the towns and settling lawsuits. They defended religion and faith and established public peace, putting an end to discords and tumults, at home as well as abroad. They extended their dominions, not only in Spain but to the farthest parts of the earth. Most laudably, they distributed rich rewards and dignities not on the basis of noble birth or as private favors but according to individual merit, and thus encouraged their subjects to devote their intellects to good work and literature. There is no need to describe the benefits of all this; the results speak for themselves. Truly, where in the world are to be found more learned and saintly priests and bishops, or judges of greater wisdom and rectitude? Before their day one could list very few Spaniards distinguished in science; since their time who can count the Spaniards who have gained fame as scholars?

The king and queen were of average stature and well built; they carried themselves majestically, and their facial expressions were gravely pleasant. The king's naturally fair skin had been tanned in military campaigns; he wore his chestnut hair long and shaved his beard more often than necessary. He had wide eyebrows, a smooth face, a small crimson mouth, narrow teeth, wide shoulders, a straight neck, and a sharp voice; he spoke quickly and thought clearly; his manner was smooth, courteous, and kindly. He was skilled in the art of war, unexcelled in the business of government, and so conscientious that labor seemed to relax him. He was not self-indulgent; he ate simply and dressed soberly. He was a skillful horseman; as a youth he enjoyed playing cards and dice; as he grew older he practiced hawking, and took much pleasure in the flights of herons.

Juan de Mariana, *Historia de España*, 2 vols. (Madrid, 1909), 2:239. Excerpt translated by Benjamin Keen.

The queen had a pleasant face, blonde hair, and light blue eyes; she used no cosmetics and was exceedingly dignified and modest in appearance. She was devoted to religion and fond of literature; she loved her husband, but her love was mixed with jealousy and suspicion. She knew Latin, an accomplishment that King Ferdinand lacked because he had not received a liberal education; he liked to read histories, however, and to talk with scholars. On the day of his birth, it is said, a certain saintly Carmelite friar of Naples said to King Alfonso, his uncle: "Today in the Kingdom of Aragon is born a child of thy lineage; heaven promises him new empires; great riches, and good fortune; he will be very devout, a lover of the good, and an excellent defender of Christianity."

Considering human frailty, it was almost inevitable that among so many virtues there should be certain defects. The avarice that is charged against him can be excused by his lack of money and by the fact that the royal revenues were diverted from their proper use. The severe punishments that also are charged to him were occasioned by the disorder and depravity of the time. Foreign writers have implied that he was a crafty man and one who sometimes broke his word if it was to his advantage. I do not propose to discuss whether this be truth or fiction concocted out of hatred for our nation; I would only point out that malicious men often assign the name of vices to true virtues and, conversely, praise the deceitful vices that resemble virtues; for the rest, the king merely adapted himself to the times and to the language, methods, and strategies that were then in use.

2. THE SPANISH INQUISITION

All of Spain's troubles since the time of Ferdinand and Isabella should not be laid at the door of the Spanish Inquisition, but the operations of the Holy Office unquestionably contributed to the picture of economic decay that Spain presented by the close of the sixteenth century. The blows struck by the Spanish Inquisition at the conversos (Jewish converts and their descendants, who were frequently charged with heresy) fell on an important segment of Spain's merchant and banking class, the social group that in England and Holland was transforming economic life and preparing the way for the Industrial Revolution. The Santangel mentioned was condemned by the civil court to burn at the stake, as the findings of the inquisitors required. Ironically, he was a kinsman of Luis de Santangel, Ferdinand's treasurer, who at the last moment persuaded Isabella to support Columbus's project and who obtained at least half the money needed for the enterprise.

Cited in Manuel Serrano y Sanz, *Orígenes de la dominación española en América* (Madrid, 1918), pp. 114–116. Excerpt translated by Benjamin Keen.

It appears that the accused, the said Luis de Santangel, has openly and very clearly practiced heresy and apostasy from our holy Catholic Faith, performing and maintaining rites and ceremonies of the old law of Moses, as a true and consummate Jew, especially observing the Sabbath with entire faith and devotion, abstaining on that day from engaging in business, travel, or other lowly tasks, as much and as well as he could, keeping it a holiday with all zeal and devotion, as the Jews do, eating on that day meat and amin and many other Jewish foods, both those prepared in his house on Friday for use on Saturday and those brought and sent from the ghetto, getting and lighting clean candles on Friday evening in honor of the Sabbath, as the Jews do, donning a clean shirt and performing other ceremonies such as the Jews on that day are wont to perform. And likewise he zealously observed the holiday of the thin bread, eating ceremonially of the said thin bread, and of no other, this bread being sent to him by Jews, and on such days he would eat from new plates and bowls, keeping and observing the said holiday as best he could. Moreover, he observed the fasts that the Jews call the Great Kippur and Haman, abstaining from food until nightfall and then breaking fast with meat, as the Jews do. Moreover, he did not observe the Christian holidays, or attend mass, or observe the fasts of the Holy Mother Church, but on the contrary he ate meat at Lent; in particular we find that he ate meat stewed in a pan on Good Friday. And that he continually prayed in the Judaic manner, his face turned to the wall, looking toward heaven through a window, bowing and reciting the psalms of David in Spanish, in the Judaic manner; and at the end of each psalm he said not gloria patri but instead Adonai, Adonai, and he had a psalter in the Spanish language that did not have gloria patri or the litany of the saints. And that he had faith and true hope in the said law of Moses, rather than in the evangelical law of our Lord Jesus Christ, defending the said law of Moses as superior to that of Jesus Christ; and that he gave oil for the lamps of the synagogue, and other alms to Jews; and that he had no oratory or other Christian practice. Nor did he kneel at the sounding of the orisons or at the elevation of the Corpus Christi, or cross himself, or say "Jesus." And when riding horseback, if the beast should stumble, in place of saying "Jesus" he used to say Sadday, and Adonai, as the Jews do; and he abstained from eating the foods forbidden by the law of Moses as much as he could, eating instead the meat of animals slaughtered by Jewish hands, cleansing away the tallow, salting it to draw out the blood before cooking, and removing a certain small round body from the leg. Nor did he eat the flesh of game or birds that had been strangled, but instead he had his chickens and other fowls slaughtered by Jews; and the other game that he purchased he would kill or have killed with a well-sharpened knife, in the Judaic manner.

And as we already had information of the aforementioned matters, the said Luis de Santangel, suspecting this and suspecting that orders had been issued for his seizure, came before us with lying and deceitful words, saying that he, as a good Christian, wished to submit to our justice and confess completely certain errors that he had committed against the faith, and of his own will he bound himself to the punishment of a relapsed heretic if he should not tell the whole truth, and he gave in writing a certain confession in his handwriting, in which he confessed that he had observed certain Judaic ceremonies and fasts, by which it immediately became evident that he had committed perjury and relapsed into heresy, to which charge he had exposed himself of his own will; and after the above-cited confession, with the hope of being released from prison and even of having his goods returned, as we lawfully know, he made other confessions, more extensive than the first, although in none of these did he confess all the heresies that he had committed.

In fine, it appears that the said Luis de Santangel has been and is a negative, obdurate heretic, and that he came to seek reconciliation to the Holy Mother Church with a lying tale, and not in a sincere or contrite spirit, as the case required, and that he is unworthy of forgiveness or of admission to the Holy Mother Church; concerning all of which we have resolved and deliberated with learned men of good conscience, who have seen and examined the said process and the said confessions. And desiring to extirpate and eradicate completely, as by our office we are most strictly bound and held to do, in the name of the Church, all such vile, grave, and wicked errors, so that the name of Jesus Christ may be truly believed, exalted, adored, praised, and served, without any pretence, hypocrisy, or sham, and so that no one may bear the name of a Christian and the air of a lamb who is truly a Jew and has the heart of a wolf; and having before our eyes Our Lord, from whom proceed all just and righteous judgments, we find that we must pronounce and declare, as by these presents we do pronounce and declare, that the said Luis de Santangel has been and is a true heretic and apostate from the faith, negative and obdurate. . . . We moreover declare all his goods confiscated for the Treasury and exchequer of the King our lord. . . . And since the Holy Mother Church cannot and should not do anything more against the said heretic and apostate, except to withdraw from him its protection and remit him to the secular justice and arm that he may be punished and chastised according to his demerits, therefore, with the customary protestations established in canon law, we remit the said Luis de Santangel, heretic and apostate, to the excellent and virtuous Juan Garcez de Marcella, chief justice of the King our lord in this city, and to its judge and justices, that they may dispose of him as in law and justice they may decree.

3. THE SPANISH CHARACTER

The great movement of the Reconquista—*the reconquest of Spain from the Muslims— left an enduring stamp on the Spanish character. The soldier of the* Reconquista *was reborn in the conquistador of America. Italian historian and diplomat Francesco*

Guicciardini (1483–1540), who represented Florence in the court of King Ferdinand, left an acid—yet often perceptive—account of the Spanish character at the opening of the sixteenth century.

The Spaniards are of melancholy and choleric disposition, dark skinned, small in stature, and haughty by nature. They believe no other nation can compare with them; in speech they brag and puff themselves up all they can. They have little love for foreigners and are very rude to them. They are more inclined to arms, perhaps, than any other Christian nation, and that because they are extremely agile, skillful, and light in movement. In war they have a high regard for honor, and would rather suffer death than dishonor. . . .

In their wars they have begun to adopt the Swiss formation, but I question whether this conforms to their nature, for when they form a compact front or wall, in the Swiss manner, they cannot make use of their nimbleness, the quality in which they surpass all others. All Spaniards carry arms, and in the old days they took part not only in foreign wars but in domestic broils, each man siding with one faction or another. For this reason Spain formerly had more cavalrymen, and more skillful ones, than now. In the reign of Queen Isabella peace and order were restored to the kingdom, and that, in my opinion, is why Spain is less of a military power today than at any time in the past.

Spaniards are generally regarded as ingenious and astute people, but they have little taste for the mechanical or liberal arts. Almost all the artisans in the royal court are from France or some other foreign country. Nor do Spaniards devote themselves to commerce, for they think it shameful, and all give themselves the airs of a hidalgo. They would rather eat the meager fare of a soldier, or serve some grandee, suffering a thousand privations and inconveniences, or—before the time of the present king—even take to the roads as a highwayman, than devote themselves to commerce or some other work. True, in certain places they have begun to pay attention to industry, and in some regions they are now producing textiles, clothing, crimson damasks, and gold embroideries. They do this in Valencia, Toledo, and Seville. In general, however, the Spaniards have no liking for industry. Thus the artisans work only when driven by necessity, and then they rest until they have used up their earnings. This is the reason why manual labor is so expensive. It is the same in the countryside, for the peasants will not work hard unless compelled by extreme need. Each one works much less land than he could, and the little land that is farmed is badly cultivated.

There is great poverty in Spain, and I believe this arises less from the quality of the country than from the nature of its people, who lack the incli-

Francesco Guicciardini, "Relazione di Spagna," in *Opere*, ed. Vittorio de Caprariis (Milano, 1961), pp. 29–31. Excerpt translated by Benjamin Keen.

nation to devote themselves to industry and trade. The problem is not that Spaniards leave their country, but that they prefer to export the raw materials that the kingdom yields and buy them back in the form of finished goods; this is the case with wool and silk, which they sell to other nations and then purchase back in the form of woolen and silk cloth. From the resulting poverty arises the misery of the people. Aside from a few grandees of the realm, who live sumptuously, the Spaniards live in very straitened circumstances, and if they have some money to spend, they spend it on clothing and a mule, making a greater show in the street than at home, where they live so meanly and eat so sparingly that it is a marvel to see. Although they can manage with very little, they are not free from greed for gain. Indeed, they are very avaricious, and, since they know no trade, they are given to robbery. Formerly, when there was less rule of law in this kingdom, the whole land swarmed with assassins, a thing favored by the nature of the country, which is very mountainous and sparsely settled. Their astuteness makes them good thieves. There is a popular saying that the Frenchman makes a better lord than a Spaniard, for, although both extort from their subjects, the Frenchman immediately spends what he takes, whereas the Spaniard hoards it. For the rest, the Spaniard, being more clever, surely robs better.

They are not given to letters. One finds little knowledge of Latin among the nobility or among the rest of the population, and that among very few persons. In demonstrations and outward show they are very religious, but not in fact. They are very ceremonious, with many deep bows, great verbal humility, and much use of titles and hand kisses. They assure everyone that he is their *señor*, that they are at his orders; but it is best to keep one's distance with them and give little credit to their words.

Dissimulation is natural to this nation, and one finds masters of this art among all classes. This is the basis of their reputation for astuteness and ingenuity; for the rest, they are not especially faithless or treacherous. In this matter of dissimulation the Andalusians surpass all others, particularly those of the ancient and famous city of Córdoba, home of the Great Captain [Gonzalo Fernández de Cordoba (1453–1515), a Spanish general celebrated for brilliant victories in the Italian wars]. From this dissimulation arise their ceremoniousness and their great hypocrisy.

4. THE MAN COLUMBUS

Christopher Columbus was a transitional figure. His thought and aspirations reflected both the waning of the Middle Ages and the rising sun of rationalism and capitalism. A major source of information about the Columbian epic is the monumental History of the Indies *of Bartolomé de las Casas (1484–1566), who was with Columbus on Hispaniola in 1500 and whose father and uncle accompanied Columbus on his second voyage. Las Casas describes the appearance and character of the Discoverer. This excerpt and the one that follows offer interesting insights into Spanish notions of manhood at the time of the conquest.*

As concerns his appearance, he was fairly tall, his face long and giving an impression of authority, his nose aquiline, his eyes blue, his complexion light and tending to bright red; his beard and hair were fair in his youth but very soon turned gray from his labors. He was witty and gay in speech and, as the aforementioned Portuguese history relates, eloquent and boastful in his negotiations. His manner was serious, but not grave; he was affable with strangers and mild and pleasant with members of his household, whom he treated with dignity, and so he easily won the love of those who saw him. In short, he had the appearance of a man of great consequence. He was sober and moderate in eating and drinking, in dress and footwear; he would often say, whether jokingly or angrily: "God take you, don't you agree to that?" or "Why did you do that?" In the matter of Christian doctrine he was a devout Catholic; nearly everything he did or said he began with: "In the name of the Holy Trinity I shall do this" or "this will come to pass," or "may this come to pass." And at the head of everything he wrote he put: "Jesus and Mary, attend us on our way." I have many of these writings in my possession. Sometimes his oath was: "I swear by San Fernando"; when he wanted to affirm the truth of something very important, especially when writing to the King and Queen, he said: "I swear that this is true." He kept the fasts of the Church most faithfully, confessed and took communion very often, said the canonical offices like any churchman or monk, abhorred blasphemy and vain oaths, and was most devoted to Our Lady and the Seraphic Father Saint Francis. He appeared very grateful for benefits received at the divine hand; and it was almost a proverb with him, which he repeated frequently, that God had been especially good to him, as to David. When gold or precious objects were brought to him he would enter his chapel and kneel, asking the bystanders to do the same, saying: "Let us give thanks to the Lord, who made us worthy of discovering such great wealth." He was most zealous in the service of God; he was eager to convert the Indians and to spread the faith of Jesus Christ everywhere, and was especially devoted to the hope that God would make him worthy of helping to win back the Holy Sepulcher. . . . He was a man of great spirit and lofty thoughts, naturally inclined—as appears from his life, deeds, writings, and speech—to undertake great and memorable enterprises; patient and long-suffering . . . quick to forgive injuries and wishing

---

Bartolemé de las Casas, *Historia de las Indias*, 3 vols. (México, 1951), 1:29–30. Excerpt translated by Benjamin Keen.

nothing more than that those who offended him should come to know their error and be reconciled with him. He was most constant and forbearing amid the endless incredible hardships and misfortunes that he had to endure, and always had great faith in the Divine Providence. And as I learned from him, from my own father, who was with him when he returned to settle the island of Hispaniola in 1493, and from other persons who accompanied and served him, he was always most loyal and devoted to the King and Queen.

5. COLUMBUS SETS THE STAGE

The log of Columbus's first voyage to the New World is obviously an important historical document. The first recorded encounter between the Old World and the New, it provides a revealing look at European attitudes at a crucial juncture in world history. It also offers considerable insight into the subsequent history of Latin America. Columbus begins the log with a message to his sponsors, Queen Isabella and King Ferdinand of Spain, in which he places his voyage in historical context and outlines his understanding of their contract.

In the Name of Our Lord Jesus Christ. Most Christian, exalted, excellent, and powerful princes, King and Queen of the Spains and of the islands of the sea, our Sovereigns: It was in this year of 1492 that Your Highnesses concluded the war with the Moors who reigned in Europe. On the second day of January, in the great city of Granada, I saw the royal banners of Your Highnesses placed by force of arms on the towers of the Alhambra, which is the fortress of the city. And I saw the Moorish king come to the city gates and kiss the royal hands of Your Highnesses, and those of the Prince, my Lord. Afterwards, in that same month, based on the information that I had given Your Highnesses about the land of India and about a Prince who is called the Great Khan, which in our language means "King of Kings," Your Highnesses decided to send me, Christopher Columbus, to the regions of India, to see the Princes there and the peoples and the lands, and to learn of their disposition, and of everything, and the measures which could be taken for their conversion to our Holy Faith.

I informed Your Highnesses how this Great Khan and his predecessors had sent to Rome many times to beg for men learned in our Holy Faith so

---

Christopher Columbus, *The Log of Christopher Columbus*, ed. and trans. Robert H. Fulton (Camden, Me.: International Marine, 1987), pp. 51–53. Reprinted by permission of the editor and translator.

that his people might be instructed therein, and that the Holy Father had never furnished them, and therefore, many peoples believing in idolatries and receiving among themselves sects of perdition were lost.

Your Highnesses, as Catholic Christians and Princes devoted to the Holy Christian faith and to the spreading of it, and as enemies of the Muslim sect and of all idolatries and heresies, ordered that I should go to the east, but not by land as is customary. I was to go by way of the west, whence until today we do not know with certainty that anyone has gone.

Therefore, after having banished all the Jews from all your Kingdoms and realms, during this same month of January, Your Highnesses ordered me to go with a sufficient fleet to the said regions of India. For that purpose I was granted great favors and ennobled; from then henceforward, I might entitle myself Don and be High Admiral of the Ocean Sea and Viceroy and perpetual Governor of all the islands and continental land that I might discover and acquire, as well as any other future discoveries in the Ocean Sea. Further, my eldest son shall succeed to the same position, and so on from generation to generation for ever after.

I left Granada on Saturday, the 12th day of the month of May in the same year of 1492 and went to the town of Palos, which is a seaport. There I fitted out three vessels, very suited to such an undertaking. I left the said port well supplied with a large quantity of provisions and with many seamen on the third day of the month of August in the said year, on a Friday, half an hour before sunrise. I set my course for the Canary Islands of Your Highnesses, which are in the Ocean Sea, from there to embark on a voyage that will last until I arrive in the Indies and deliver the letter of Your Highnesses to those Princes, and do all that Your Highnesses have commanded me to do.

To this end I decided to write down everything I might do and see and experience on this voyage, from day to day, and very carefully. Also, Sovereign Princes, besides describing each night what takes place during the day, and during the day the sailings of the night, I propose to make a new chart for navigation, on which I will set down all the sea and lands of the Ocean Sea, in their correct locations and with their correct bearings. Further, I shall compile a book and shall map everything by latitude and longitude. And above all, it is fitting that I forget about sleeping and devote much attention to navigation in order to accomplish this. And these things will be a great task.

6. THE PORTRAIT OF THE CONQUEROR

Historians and biographers do not agree in their estimate of the character and actions of Hernando Cortés. The chronicler Francisco López de Gómara (1511?–1562?), who lived in Cortés's household as his private chaplain for some years, had no doubts con-

cerning the righteousness of either Cortés's actions or the civilizing mission of the Spanish conquest. His history of the conquest of Mexico, which is actually a biography of Cortés, contains an intimate and not altogether flattering description of his former patron.

Ferdinand Cortés was of good size, broad in shoulders and chest, and of sallow complexion; his beard was light colored, and he wore his hair long. He was very strong, high spirited, and skilled in the use of arms. As a youth he was given to adventurous pranks, but in later years he acquired a mature dignity and thus became a leader in both war and peace. He was mayor of the town of Santiago de Barucoa [in Cuba], which fact the townspeople still regard as their chief title to fame. There he acquired a reputation for the qualities that he later displayed. He was passionately attracted to women, and indulged this proclivity without regard to time or place. It was the same with games of chance; he played dice exceedingly well and with great enjoyment. Although he drank moderately he was a very hearty eater and kept an abundant table. He bore hunger with great fortitude, as he showed on the march of Higueras and on the sea to which he gave his name. He was very contentious and so was involved in more lawsuits than suited his condition. He spent freely on warfare, on women, on his friends, and to satisfy his whims, but showed himself niggardly in some things; hence some people called him a "wet-weather stream," one that ran high one day and dry the next. He dressed neatly rather than richly, and kept himself scrupulously clean. He took pleasure in keeping a large house and family, with a great display of plate, both for use and for show. He bore himself like a lord, and with such gravity and discretion that it neither caused disgust nor appeared presumptuous. A story has it that as a boy he was told that he was fated to conquer many lands and become a very great lord. He was jealous of the honor of his own house but forward in the homes of others—a common trait of lustful men. He was devout and prayerful, and knew many prayers and psalms by heart; he was very charitable, and on his deathbed especially charged his son with the giving of alms. He usually gave the Church a thousand ducats a year, and sometimes he borrowed money for giving alms, saying that he redeemed his sins with the interest on the money. On his shields and coats of arms he put the motto: *Judicium Domini apprehendit eos, et fortitudo ejus corroboravit brachium meum* [The judgment of the Lord overtook them, and his strength supported my arm]—a text very appropriate to the conquest.

Francisco López de Gómara, "Conquista de Méjico," in *Historiadores primitivos de las Indias*, 2 vols., ed. Enrique de Vedia (Madrid, 1852–1853), 1:454–455. Excerpt translated by Benjamin Keen.

PART TWO

CONQUEST AND
COLONIZATION

3

CONQUEST

THE DISCOVERY OF AMERICA is linked to a number of great European movements: the decline of feudalism and the rise of the nation-state; the rapid growth of the merchant class and international trade; a series of advances in navigational science and shipbuilding that facilitated European overseas expansion; and a new intellectual climate (the Renaissance) that helped dispel old geographical dogmas and fired men's curiosity to penetrate the unknown.

More immediately, the discovery of America by Christopher Columbus resulted from the search for an all-water route to the East. That search was promoted by the monarchs of Portugal and Spain in an effort to break the Italian-Arab monopoly of European trade with the East.

From its primary base on Hispaniola, the Spanish conquest of the Americas branched out to the other great Antilles (Puerto Rico, Cuba, Jamaica) and simultaneously sent out weak offshoots to the coasts of South and Central America. Slave-hunting and exploring expeditions gradually mapped the coasts of Central America and Mexico and revealed Indian societies far wealthier and more advanced than those found in the West Indies.

The discovery of these societies led to the invasion of Mexico by Hernán Cortés in 1519. According to some scholars, the superstitious fears of the Aztec emperor Moctezuma led him to identify Cortés as the god and priest king Quetzalcoatl, who was believed to have left Mexico centuries before. These fears enabled Cortés to enter the Indian capital without opposition, but unprovoked aggression by his lieutenant Pedro de Alvarado precipitated a mortal struggle. Cuauhtémoc, the last Aztec ruler, surrendered to Cortés in 1521 only after Tenochtitlán lay in ruins and its native defenders were dead or starving. From Mexico the stream of conquest flowed south into Guatemala and Honduras; in Nicaragua it joined another current formed by Spaniards coming north from Darién.

The town of Panama, founded in 1519 across the isthmus from Darién, became a base for expeditions seeking kingdoms of gold that were rumored to lie southward. After repeated failures, Francisco Pizarro and his companions achieved their aim of reaching and conquering the Incan empire (1532). Before Incan resistance was entirely overcome, however, the conquerors fell out among themselves, and by the time peace was restored in Peru all the leading conquerors of Peru had come to a violent end.

Contrary to romantic tradition, only a small minority of the *conquistadores* were *hidalgos* (nobles), although many claimed to be such. The majority were plebeians—peasants, artisans, sailors, and soldiers, some with dubious pasts. As the conquest advanced and consolidated its gains, however, the *conquistadores* were joined by a growing number of clergy, lawyers, royal officials, merchants, and other middle-class types. The number of women immigrants was extremely small in the first stages of the conquest but increased as the sixteenth century wore on.

1. OCTOBER 12, 1492

In this excerpt from his log, Columbus writes about the events of October 12, 1492, the first recorded encounter of Europeans and Native Americans in the New World (although Columbus persisted in believing he was off the coast of Asia). The elaborate ceremony of possession and Columbus's paternalistic attitude portended things to come. The admiral's biographer, the great "Protector of Indians" Bartolomé de las Casas, made much of his comment that the Indians "are a people who can be made free and converted to our Holy Faith more by love than by force." Columbus's attitude, however, shifted quickly in the first days after this initial encounter from sympathy and condescension to suspicion and coercion. His subsequent treatment of conquered Native American peoples as the governor of Hispaniola was appalling even by the standards of the time.

At dawn we saw naked people, and I went ashore in the ship's boat, armed, followed by Martín Alonso Pinzón, captain of the *Pinta*, and his brother, Vincente Yáñez Pinzón, captain of the *Niña*. I unfurled the royal banner and the captains brought the flags which displayed a large green cross with the letters F and Y at the left and right side of the cross [for Ferdinand and Ysabella]. Over each letter was the appropriate crown of that Sovereign. These flags were carried as a standard on all of the ships. After a prayer of thanksgiving I

Christopher Columbus, *The Log of Christopher Columbus*, ed. and trans. Robert H. Fulton (Camden, Me.: International Marine, 1987), pp. 75–77. Reprinted by permission of the editor and translator.

ordered the captains of the *Pinta* and *Niña*, together with Rodrigo de Es-
cobedo (secretary of the fleet) and Rodrigo Sánchez of Segovia (comptroller
of the fleet) to bear faith and witness that I was taking possession of this island for the King and Queen. I made all the necessary declarations and had
these testimonies carefully written down by the secretary. In addition to
those named above, the entire company of the fleet bore witness to this act.
To this island I gave the name *San Salvador*, in honor of our Blessed Lord.

No sooner had we concluded the formalities of taking possession of the
island than people began to come to the beach, all as naked as their mother
bore them, and the women also, although I did not see more than one very
young girl. All those that I saw were young people, none of whom was over
30 years old. They are very well-built people, with handsome bodies and very
fine faces, though their appearance is marred somewhat by very broad heads
and foreheads, more so than I have ever seen in any other race. Their eyes
are large and very pretty, and their skin is the color of Canary Islanders or of
sunburned peasants, not at all black, as would be expected because we are on
an east-west line with Hierro in the Canaries. These are tall people and their
legs, with no exceptions, are quite straight, and none of them has a paunch.
They are, in fact, well proportioned. Their hair is not kinky, but straight, and
coarse like horsehair. They wear it short over the eyebrows, but they have a
long hank in the back that they never cut. Many of the natives paint their
faces; others paint their whole bodies; some, only the eyes or nose. Some are
painted black, some white, some red; others are of different colors.

The people here called this island *Guanabaní* in their language, and their
speech is very fluent, although I do not understand any of it. They are
friendly and well-dispositioned people who bear no arms except for small
spears, and they have no iron. I showed one my sword, and through ignorance he grabbed it by the blade and cut himself. Their spears are made of
wood, to which they attach a fish tooth at one end, or some other sharp
thing.

I want the natives to develop a friendly attitude toward us because I know
that they are a people who can be made free and converted to our Holy Faith
more by love than by force. I therefore gave red caps to some and glass beads
to others. They hung the beads around their necks, along with some other
things of slight value that I gave them. And they took great pleasure in this
and became so friendly that it was a marvel. They traded and gave everything
they had with good will, but it seems to me that they have very little and are
poor in everything. I warned my men to take nothing from the people without giving something in exchange.

This afternoon the people of San Salvador came swimming to our ships
and in boats made from one log. They brought us parrots, balls of cotton
thread, spears, and many other things, including a kind of dry leaf that they
hold in great esteem. For these items we swapped them little glass beads and
hawks' bells.

Many of the men I have seen have scars on their bodies, and when I made signs to them to find out how this happened, they indicated that people from other nearby islands come to San Salvador to capture them; they defend themselves the best they can. I believe that people from the mainland come here to take them as slaves. They ought to make good and skilled servants, for they repeat very quickly whatever we say to them. I think they can easily be made Christians, for they seem to have no religion. If it pleases Our Lord, I will take six of them to Your Highnesses when I depart, in order that they may learn our language.

2. THE DISCOVERY OF THE PACIFIC

Amerigo Vespucci's theory that the land mass said by Columbus to be part of Asia was really a new continent gained wide though not universal approval in the decade after 1502. If Vespucci was right, then there was another ocean to cross between the New World and Asia. Confirmation of this view was forthcoming in 1513 when Vasco Núñez de Balboa, standing "silent, upon a peak in Darien," looked out upon the waters of the Pacific. The Spanish chronicler Gonzalo Fernández de Oviedo y Valdés, who came to Darién in 1514 in an official capacity, tells the story of Balboa's feat, with some mention of the exploits of his remarkable dog, Leoncico.

For four years the Christians had been in Tierra-Firme; they fought under Captain Vasco Núñez de Balboa, and had made peace with certain *caciques*, in particular with the chieftains of Careta, which lies on the west coast, twenty leagues west of Darien, and of Comogre, and both of them had been baptized. The *cacique* of Careta was called Chima, and they named him Don Fernando, and he had as many as two thousand Indian warriors; the *cacique* of Comogre was a greater lord, and his proper name was Ponquiaco, but they gave him the baptismal name of Don Carlos; he had more than three thousand warriors and ruled over more than ten thousand persons. These *caciques* had grown so peaceful that they sent messengers and canoes; they came and went to and from Darien to see the Christians and communicated with them as with friends. Vasco Núñez, filled with hope by the information that he had secretly obtained from these *caciques*, resolved to set out on Friday, the first day of September, 1513; and he departed from the town of Santa María de la Antigua with eight hundred men in a galleon and nine canoes to search out the secrets of the land, on the pretext of going to seek for mines. On the following Sunday, the fourth day of September, half of this

Gonzalo Fernández de Oviedo y Valdés, *Historia general y natural de las Indias*, 14 vols. (Asunción, Paraguay, 1944–1945), 7:92–95. Excerpt translated by Benjamin Keen.

company arrived at Careta in the canoes, and the galleon came later with the rest; there Vasco Núñez disembarked. The *cacique* Don Fernando received him and all his people very well, both those who came in the canoes and those in the galleon. After they had arrived and assembled, Captain Vasco Núñez selected those whom he wished to take with him and left there those who were to guard the galleon and the canoes, and set out for the interior on the sixth day of the month. After a two-day march over a rough, difficult, and mountainous route he approached the vicinity of the *cacique* of Ponca, only to find that he and his people had fled to the hills.

Before proceeding further, I should state that the town that the Christians now call Acla was founded in the abovementioned port of Careta. I also want to tell of a dog that belonged to Vasco Núñez, called Leoncico, a son of the dog Becerrico of the isle San Juan [Puerto Rico] and no less famous than his father. This dog gained for Vasco Núñez in this and other conquests more than a thousand gold pesos, for he received as large a share in the gold and slaves as a member of the company when the division was made. So, whenever Vasco Núñez went along, the dog was assigned wages and a share like the other captains; and he was so active that he earned his reward better than many sleepy comrades who like to gain at their ease what others reap by their toil and diligence. He was truly a marvelous dog, and could distinguish a peaceable from a wild Indian as well as I or any other who went to these wars. When Indians had been taken and rounded up, if any should escape by day or by night the dog had only to be told: "He's gone, go get him," and he would do it; and he was so keen a pointer that only by a miracle could a runaway Indian escape him. After overtaking him, if the Indian remained still the dog would seize him by the wrist or hand and would bring him back as carefully, without biting or molesting him, as a man could; but if the Indian offered resistance he would tear him to pieces. He was so much feared by the Indians that if ten Christians went with the dog they went in greater safety and accomplished more than twenty without him. I saw this dog, for when Pedrarias arrived in the following year, 1514, he was still alive, and Vasco Núñez lent him for some Indian wars that were made afterwards and gained his shares as was told above. He was a dog of middle size, reddish in color, with a black muzzle, and not elegant in appearance; but he was strong and robust, and had many wounds and scars of wounds that he had received fighting with the Indians. Later on, out of envy, someone gave the dog some poisoned food, and he died. . . .

On September 13 came the *cacique* of Ponca, reassured by Captain Vasco Núñez, who did him much honor, gave him shirts and hatchets, and made him as comfortable as he could. Since this *cacique* found himself so well treated, he told Vasco Núñez in secret a great deal about the secrets and treasures of the land, which gratified the captain; among other things, he said that a certain number of days' journey from there was another *pechry*, which in their language means "sea"; and he presented Vasco Núñez with some very finely worked pieces of gold. . . .

On the twentieth of that month, Vasco Núñez set out from the land of this *cacique* with certain guides that Ponca assigned to go with him till they reached the land of the *cacique* Torecha, with whom Ponca was at war; and on the twenty-fourth day of that month they came by night upon the *cacique* Torecha and his people. This was ten leagues beyond the land of Ponca, and was reached by a most difficult route and by crossing rivers in rafts, at great peril to themselves. And there they took some people and some gold and pearls, and Vasco Núñez obtained more extensive information concerning the interior and the other sea, to the South. In Torecha he left some of his people, and set out with about seventy men; on the twenty-fifth of the month, the same day that he had left, he arrived at the village and seat of the *cacique* called Porque, who had absented himself; however, this did not matter to Vasco Núñez, and he went ahead, continuing his search for the other sea. And on Tuesday, the twenty-fifth of September of the year one thousand five hundred and thirteen, at ten o'clock in the morning, Captain Vasco Núñez, leading all the rest in the ascent of a certain bare mountain, saw from its peak the South Sea, before any other of his Christian companions. He joyfully turned to his men, raising his hands and eyes to the skies, praising Jesus Christ and his glorious mother the Virgin, Our Lady; then he sank on his knees and gave thanks to God for the favor that had been granted to him in allowing him to discover that sea and thereby to render such a great service to God and to the Catholic and Most Serene King of Castile, our lord. . . . And he ordered them all to kneel and give the same thanks to God for this grace, and to implore Him to let them discover and see the hoped-for great secrets and riches of that sea and coast, for the exaltation and increase of the Christian faith, for the conversion of the Indians of those southern regions, and for the greater glory and prosperity of the royal throne of Castile and its princes, both present and to come.

3. THE MEETING OF CORTÉS AND MOCTEZUMA

Few incidents in history have the romantic quality of the meeting between Cortés and Moctezuma at the entrance of Tenochtitlán. Two cultures met in the persons of the Indian chieftain and the Spanish conquistador. The remarkable speech of welcome made by Moctezuma, as reported by Cortés, supports the view that Moctezuma regarded the conqueror as an emissary of the departed Quetzalcoatl, if not Quetzalcoatl himself, about to return to his Mexican realm.

Hernán Cortés, *The Letters of Cortés to Charles V*, 2 vols., ed. and trans. Francis A. McNutt (New York, 1908), 1:232–236.

I followed the said causeway for about half a league before I came to the city proper of Temixtitan. I found at the junction of another causeway, which joins this one from the mainland, another strong fortification, with two towers, surrounded by walls, twelve feet high with castellated tops. This commands the two roads, and has only two gates, by one of which they enter, and from the other they come out. About one thousand of the principal citizens came out to meet me, and speak to me, all richly dressed alike according to their fashion; and when they had come, each one in approaching me, and before speaking, would use a ceremony which is very common amongst them, putting his hand on the ground, and afterward kissing it, so that I was kept waiting almost an hour, until each had performed his ceremony. There is a wooden bridge, ten paces broad, in the very outskirts of the city, across an opening in the causeway, where the water may flow in and out as it rises and falls. This bridge is also for defense, for they remove and replace the long broad wooden beams, of which the bridge is made, whenever they wish; and there are many of these bridges in the city, as Your Highness will see in the account which I shall make of its affairs.

Having passed this bridge, we were received by that lord, Montezuma, with about two hundred chiefs, all barefooted and dressed in a kind of livery, very rich, according to their custom, and some more so than others. They approached in two processions near the walls of the street, which is very broad, and straight, and beautiful, and very uniform from one end to the other, being about two thirds of a league long, and having, on both sides, very large houses, both dwelling places, and mosques. Montezuma came in the middle of the street, with two lords, one on the right side, and the other on the left, one of whom was the same great lord, who, as I said, came in that litter to speak with me, and the other was the brother of Montezuma, lord of that city Iztapalapan, whence I had come that day. All were dressed in the same manner, except that Montezuma was shod, and the other lords were barefooted. Each supported him below his arms, and as we approached each other, I descended from my horse, and was about to embrace him, but the two lords in attendance prevented me, with their hands, that I might not touch him, and they, and he also, made the ceremony of kissing the ground. This done, he ordered his brother who came with him, to remain with me, and take me by the arm, and the other attendant walked a little head of us. After he had spoken to me, all the other lords, who formed the two processions, also saluted me, one after the other, then returned to the procession. When I approached to speak to Montezuma, I took off a collar of pearls and glass diamonds that I wore, and put it on his neck, and, after we had gone through some of the streets, one of his servants came with two collars, wrapped in a cloth, which were made of colored shells. These they esteem very much; and from each of the collars hung eight golden shrimps executed with great perfection and a span long. When he received them, he turned towards me, and put them on my neck, and again went on through the streets, as I have already indicated, until we came to a large and handsome house, which he had prepared for our reception. There he took me by the hand, and led me into a spacious room, in front of the court where we had entered, where he made me sit on a very rich platform, which had been ordered to be made for him, and told me to wait there; and then he went away.

After a little while, when all the people of my company were distributed to their quarter, he returned with many valuables of gold and silver work, and five or six thousand pieces of rich cotton stuffs, woven, and embroidered in divers ways. After he had given them to me, he sat down on another platform, which they immediately prepared near the one where I was seated, and being seated he spoke in the following manner:

We have known for a long time, from the chronicles of our forefathers, that neither I, nor those who inhabit this country, are descendants from the aborigines of it, but from strangers who came to it from very distant parts; and we also hold, that our race was brought to these parts by a lord, whose vassals they all were, and who returned to his native country, and had many descendants, and had built towns where they were living; when, therefore, he wished to take them away with him they would not go, nor still less receive him as their ruler, so he departed. And we have always held that those who descended from him would come to subjugate this country and us, as his vassals; and according to the direction from which you say you come, which is where the sun rises, and from what you tell us of your great lord, or king, who has sent you here, we believe, and hold for certain, that he is our rightful sovereign, especially as you tell us that since many days he has had news of us. Hence you may be sure, that we shall obey you, and hold you as the representative of this great lord of whom you speak, and that in this there will be no lack or deception; and throughout the whole country you may command at your will (I speak of what I possess in my dominions), because you will be obeyed, and recognized, and all we possess is at your disposal.

Since you are in your rightful place, and in your own homes, rejoice and rest, free from all the trouble of the journey, and wars which you have had, for I am well aware of all that has happened to you, between Puntunchan and here, and I know very well, that the people of Cempoal, and Tascaltecal, have told you many evil things respecting me. Do not believe more than you see with your own eyes, especially from those who are my enemies, and were my vassals, yet rebelled against me on your coming (as they say), in order to help you. I know they have told you also that I have houses, with walls of gold, and that the furniture of my halls, and other things of my service, were also of gold, and that I am, or make myself, a god, and many other things. The houses you have seen are of lime and stone and earth. And then he held up his robes, and showing me his body he said to me, "Look at me, and see that I am flesh and bones, the same as you, and everybody, and that I am mortal, and tangible." And touching his arms and body with his hands, "Look how they have lied to you! It is true indeed that I have some things of gold, which have been left to me by my forefathers. All that I possess, you may have whenever you wish."

"I shall now go to other houses where I live; but you will be provided here with everything necessary for you and your people, and you shall suffer no annoyance, for you are in your own house and country."

I answered to all he said, certifying that which seemed to be suitable, especially in confirming his belief that it was Your Majesty whom they were expecting. After this, he took his leave, and, when he had gone, we were well provided with chickens, and bread, and fruits, and other necessities, especially such as were required for the service of our quarters. Thus I passed six days well provided with everything necessary, and visited by many of the lords.

4. TWILIGHT OVER TENOCHTITLÁN

For three months the Aztec nation fought for its independence with incredible valor and fortitude. Not until a great part of the city was in ruins, the streets and canals choked with corpses, did the gallant Cuauhtémoc, the last Aztec war chief, surrender in the name of his people. An Aztec account of the fall of Tenochtitlán conveys with simple eloquence the pathos of the surrender and the terrible aftermath of the conquest.

And when night had fallen, then it rained and sprinkled at intervals. Late at night the flame became visible; just so was it seen, just so it emerged as if it came from the heavens. Like a whirlwind it went spinning around and revolving; it was as if embers burst out of it—some very large, some very small, some like sparks. Like a coppery wind it arose, crackling, snapping, and exploding loudly. Then it circled the dike and traveled toward Coyonacazco; then it went into the middle of the lake there to be lost.

None shouted; none spoke aloud.

And on the next day, nothing more happened. All remained quiet, and also our foes [so] remained.

But the Captain [Cortés] was watching from a roof-top at Amaxac—from the roof-top of [the house of] Aztauatzin—under a canopy. It was a many-colored canopy. He looked toward [us] common folk; the Spaniards crowded about him and took counsel among themselves.

Bernardino de Sahagún, *The Florentine Codex: General History of the Things of New Spain*, bk. 12, *The Conquest*, chaps. 39–40, trans. Arthur J. O. Andersen and Charles E. Dibble (Santa Fe, N.M.: School of American Research, 1953). Reprinted by permission.

And [on our side] were Quauhtemoc and the other noblemen—the vice ruler Tlacotzin, the lords' judge Petlauhtzin, the captain of the armies Motelchiuhtzin; the constable of Mexico; and the lord priest; and also the noblemen of Tlatilulco—the general Coyoueuetzin; the commanding general Temilotzin; the army commander Topantemoctzin; the chief justice Aueli-toctzin; the captain of the armies Uitziliuitzin; and the courier Uitzitzin. All of these noblemen were assembled at Tolmayecan; they appeared to consult among themselves how to do that which we were to undertake and how we should yield to [the Spaniards].

Thereafter only two [men] took Quauhtemoc in a boat. The two who took him and went with him were the seasoned warrior Teputzitoloc, and Yaztachimal, Quauhtemoc's page. And the one who poled [the boat] was named Cenyaotl.

And when they carried Quauhtemoc off, then there was weeping among all the common folk. They said: "Now goeth the young lord Quauhtemoc; now he goeth to deliver himself to the gods, the Spaniards!"

And when they had betaken themselves to bring and disembark him thereupon all the Spaniards came to see. They drew him along; the Spaniards took him by the hand. After that they took him up to the roof-top, where they went to stand him before the Captain, the war leader. And when they had proceeded to stand him before [Cortés], they looked at Quauhtemoc, made much of him, and stroked his hair. Then they seated him with [Cortés] and fired the guns. They hit no one with them, but only made them go off above, [so that] they passed over the heads of the common folk. Then [some Mexicans] only fled. With this the war reached its end.

Then there was shouting; they said: "Enough! Let it end! Eat greens!" When they heard this, the common folk thereupon issued forth. On this, they went, even into the lagoon.

And as they departed, leaving by the great road, once more they there slew some, wherefore the Spaniards were wroth that still some again had taken up their obsidian-bladed swords and their shields. Those who dwelt in house clusters went straightway to Amaxac; they went direct to where the ways divide. There the common folk separated. So many went toward Tepey-acac, so many toward Xoxouiltitlan, so many toward Nonoalco. But toward Xolloco and toward Macatzintamal no one went.

And all who lived in boats and [in houses] on poles, and those at Tol-mayecan, went into the water. On some, the water reached to the stomach; some, to the chest; and on some it reached to the neck. And some were all submerged, there in the deeps. Little children were carried on the backs [of their elders]; cries of weeping arose. Some went on happy and rejoicing as they traveled crowding on the road. And those who owned boats, all the boatmen, left by night, and even [continued to] leave all day. It was as if they pushed and crowded one another as they set out.

And everywhere the Spaniards were seizing and robbing the people. They sought gold; as nothing did they value the green stone, quetzal feathers and turquoise [which] was everywhere in the bosoms or in the skirts of the women. And as for us men, it was everywhere in [our] breech clouts and in [our] mouths.

And [the Spaniards] seized and set apart the pretty women—those of light bodies, the fair [-skinned] ones. And some women, when they were robbed, covered their face with mud and put on old, mended shirts and rags for their shifts. They put all rags on themselves.

And also some of us men were singled out—those who were strong, grown to manhood, and next the young boys, of whom they would make messengers, who would be their runners, and who were known as their servers. And on some they burned [brand marks] on their cheeks; on some they put paint on their cheeks; on some they put paint on their lips.

And when the shield was laid down, when we gave way, it was the year count Three House and the day count was One Serpent.

5. Rendezvous at Cajamarca

As the conquest of Peru unfolded, it repeated in a number of ways the sequence of events in Mexico. In one important respect, however, the story of Peru differs from that of Mexico. If Montezuma was undone by his passive acceptance of the invaders' divinity and their inevitable triumph, Atahualpa erred disastrously in his underestimation of the massed striking power of the small Spanish forces. Francisco de Xérez (1504–?), secretary to Francisco Pizarro and an active participant in the conquest, describes the fateful meeting between Spaniards and Inca at Cajamarca.

When the Governor saw that it was near sunset, and that Atabalia [Atahualpa] did not move from the place to which he had repaired, although troops still kept issuing out of his camp, he sent a Spaniard to ask him to come into the square to see him before it was dark. As soon as the messenger came before Atabaliba, he made an obeisance to him, and made signs that he should come to where the Governor waited. Presently he and his troops began to move, and the Spaniard returned and reported that they were coming, and that the men in front carried arms concealed under their clothes, which were strong tunics of cotton, beneath which were stones and bags and slings; all of which made it appear that they had a treacherous design. Soon the van

Reports on the Discovery of Peru, ed. and trans. C. R. Markham (London: Cambridge University Press, 1872), pp. 52–56.

of the enemy began to enter the open space. First came a squadron of Indians dressed in a livery of different colors, like a chess board. They advanced, removing the straws from the ground, and sweeping the road. Next came three squadrons in different dresses, dancing and singing. Then came a number of men with armor, large metal plates, and crowns of gold and silver.

Among them was Atabaliba in a litter lined with plumes of macaws' feathers, of many colors and adorned with plates of gold and silver. Many Indians carried it on their shoulders on high. Next came two other litters and two hammocks, in which were some principal chiefs; and lastly, several squadrons of Indians with crowns of gold and silver.

As soon as the first entered the open space they moved aside and gave space to the others. On reaching the centre of the open space, Atabaliba remained in his litter on high, and the others with him, while his troops did not cease to enter. A captain then came to the front and, ascending the fortress near the open space, where the artillery was posted, raised his lance twice, as for a signal. Seeing this, the Governor asked the Father Friar Vicente if he wished to go and speak to Atabaliba, with an interpreter? He replied that he did wish it, and he advanced, with a cross in one hand and the Bible in the other, and going amongst them: "I am a Priest of God, and I teach Christians the things of God, and in like manner I come to teach you. What I teach is that which God says to us in this Book. Therefore, on the part of God and of the Christians, I beseech you to be their friend, for such is God's will, and it will be for your good. Go and speak to the Governor, who waits for you."

Atabaliba asked for the Book, that he might look at it, and the Priest gave it to him closed. Atabaliba did not know how to open it, and the Priest was extending his arm to do so, when Atabaliba, in great anger, gave him a blow on the arm, not wishing that it should be opened. Then he opened it himself, and, without any astonishment at the letters and paper, as had been shown by other Indians, he threw it away from him five or six paces, and, to the words which the monk had spoken to him through the interpreter, he answered with much scorn, saying: "I know well how you have behaved on the road, how you have treated my Chiefs, and taken the cloth from my storehouses." The monk replied: "The Christians have not done this, but some Indians took the cloth without the knowledge of the Governor, and he ordered it to be restored." Atabaliba said: "I will not leave this place until they bring it all to me." The monk returned with this reply to the Governor. Atabaliba stood up on the top of the litter, addressing his troops and ordering them to be prepared. The monk told the Governor what had passed between him and Atabaliba, and that he had thrown the Scriptures to the ground. Then the Governor put on a jacket of cotton, took his sword and dagger, and, with the Spaniards who were with him, entered amongst the Indians most valiantly; and, with only four men who were able to follow him, he came to the litter where Atabaliba was, and fearlessly seized him by the arm, crying out Santiago. Then the guns were fired off, the trumpets were sounded, and the troops, both horse and foot, sallied forth.

On seeing the horses charge, many of the Indians who were in the open space fled, and such was the force with which they ran that they broke down part of the wall surrounding it, and many fell over each other. The horsemen rode them down, killing and wounding, and following in pursuit. The infantry made so good an assault upon those that remained that in a short time most of them were put to the sword. The Governor still held Atabaliba by the arm, not being able to pull him out of the litter because he was raised so high. Then the Spaniards made such a slaughter amongst those who carried the litter they fell to the ground, and, if the Governor had not protected Atabaliba, that proud man would there have paid for all the cruelties he had committed.

The Governor, in protecting Atabaliba, received a slight wound in the hand. During the whole time no Indian raised his arms against a Spaniard. So great was the terror of the Indians at seeing the Governor force his way through them, at hearing the fire of the artillery, and beholding the charging of the horses, a thing never before heard of, that they thought more of flying to save their lives than of fighting. All those who bore the litter of Atabaliba appeared to be principal chiefs. They were all killed, as well as those who were carried in the other litters and hammocks. One of them was the page of Atabaliba, and a great lord, and the others were lords of many vassals, and his Councillors. The chief of Caxamalca was also killed, and others; but, the number being very great, no account was taken of them, for all who came in attendance on Atabaliba were great lords. The Governor went to his lodging, with his prisoner Atabaliba, despoiled of his robes, which the Spaniards had torn off in pulling him out of the litter. It was a very wonderful thing to see so great a lord, who came in such power, taken prisoner in so short a time.

6. How the New Laws Were Received in Peru

A heavy atmosphere of intrigue, broken by recurrent cycles of murderous violence, hung over Peru in the time of the great civil wars. Early in 1544 a new viceroy, Blasco Núñez Vela, arrived in Lima to proclaim the edicts known as the New Laws of the Indies. These laws, the fruit of years of devoted labor on the part of Fr. Bartolomé de las Casas to save the Indians from destruction, evoked outraged cries and appeals for their suspension from the Spanish landowners in Peru. When these pleas failed, the desperate conquistadores rose in revolt and found a leader in Gonzalo Pizarro, brother of the murdered Francisco Pizarro. The chronicler Gómara describes the reception accorded the New Laws in Peru.

Blasco Núñez entered Trujillo amid great gloom on the part of the Spaniards; he publicly proclaimed the New Laws, regulating the Indian tributes, freeing the Indians, and forbidding their use as carriers against their will and without pay. He took away as many vassals as these laws permitted, and vested them in the crown. The people and the town council petitioned for repeal of these ordinances, except for those which regulated Indian tribute and prohibited the use of Indians as carriers; of these provisions they approved. He did not grant their appeal, but instead set very heavy penalties for those judges who should fail to execute the laws, saying that he brought an express order of the emperor for their enforcement, without hearing or granting any appeal. He told them, however, that they had reason to complain of the ordinances; that they should take their case to the emperor; and that he would write to the king that he had been badly informed to order those laws.

When the citizens perceived the severity behind his soft words, they began to curse. Some said that they would leave their wives. Actually, some were ready to leave them for any reason, good or bad, since many had married their lady-loves or camp-followers only on account of an order that stripped them of their estates if they did not do so. Others said that it would be much better not to have a wife and children to maintain, if they were to lose the slaves who supported them by their labors in mines, fields, and other pursuits; others demanded payment for the slaves that were being taken from them, since they had bought them from the crown fifth and they bore the royal brand and mark. Still others said that they were ill requited for their labors and services, if in their declining years they were to have no one to serve them; these showed their teeth, decayed from eating toasted corn in the conquest of Peru; others displayed many wounds, bruises, and great lizard bites; the conquerors complained that after wasting their estates and shedding their blood in gaining Peru for the emperor, he was depriving them of the few vassals that he had given them. The soldiers said that they would not go to conquer other lands, since they were denied the hope of holding vassals, but instead would rob right and left all they could; the royal lieutenants and officials complained bitterly of the loss of their allotments of Indians, though they had not maltreated them, and held them not by virtue of their officers but in return for their labors and their services.

The priests and friars also declared that they could not support themselves nor serve their churches if they were deprived of their Indian towns; the one who spoke most shamelessly against the viceroy and even against the king was Fray Pedro Múñoz, of the Mercedarian Order, saying how badly the king rewarded those who had served him so well, and that the New Laws

Francisco López de Gómara, "Historia de las Indias," in *Historiadores primitivos de las Indias*, 1:251. Excerpt translated by Benjamin Keen.

smelled of calculation rather than of saintliness, for the king was taking away the slaves that he had sold without returning the money received for them, and that he was taking away Indian towns from monasteries, churches, hospitals, and the conquistadores who had gained them; and, what was worse, they were laying a double tribute and tax on the Indians whom they took away in this fashion and vested in the crown, and that the Indians themselves were weeping over this. There was bad blood between this friar and the viceroy because the latter had stabbed the friar one evening in Málaga, when the viceroy was *corregidor* there.

7. THE MAN WHO WOULD BE KING

After Gonzalo Pizarro prevailed over the viceroy Vela, Pizarro's advisers urged him to proclaim himself king of Peru. But Pizarro hesitated to avow the revolutionary meaning of his actions. An envoy of the crown, Pedro de la Gasca, arrived and announced the suspension of the New Laws and offered pardons and rewards to all repentant rebels, leading to a trickle of desertions from Pizarro's ranks that in time became a flood. In the end the rebellion collapsed almost without a struggle, and its leaders ended on the gallows or the block. Garcilaso de la Vega describes the execution of Gonzalo Pizarro.

It remains only for me to tell of the pitiful death of Gonzalo Pizarro. He spent all of his last day in confession. . . . The ministers of justice, coming and going, sought to hasten the execution of his sentence. One of the gravest of them, angered by the delay, said loudly: "Well! Are they not done with the fellow yet?" All the soldiers who heard him took offense at his disrespect and hurled a thousand oaths and insults at him, but though I remember many of them and knew the man, I will not set them down here nor give his name. He went without saying a word, before it came to blows, something he had reason to fear in view of the indignation and annoyance that the soldiers displayed at his rudeness. A little later Gonzalo Pizarro came out and mounted a saddled mule that was held ready for him. He was covered with a cape; although one author says that his hands were tied, it was not so. They threw one end of a halter over the neck of the mule, in compliance with the law. In his hands he bore an image of Our Lady, to whom he was most devoted. He continually implored her to intercede for his soul. Halfway along he asked for a crucifix. A priest, one of the twelve that accompanied him, gave him

---

Garcilaso de la Vega, *Historia general del Perú*, 3 vols. (Buenos Aires, 1944), 2:276–277. Excerpt translated by Benjamin Keen.

one. Gonzalo Pizarro took it and gave the priest the image of Our Lady, kissing with great affection the hem of the dress of the image. With the crucifix in his hands, never taking his eyes from it, he came up to the platform that had been made for his execution. This he ascended, and, standing at one side, he spoke to the people who were watching him. Among them were all the men of Peru, soldiers and citizens, excepting only the grandees who had turned against him—and even some of them were there, disguised and muffled up. He said in a loud voice:

> Gentlemen, your worships know well that my brothers and I gained this empire. Many of your worships hold *repartimientos* of Indians that the Marquis, my brother, gave you; many others hold them from me. Moreover, many of your worships owe me money that you borrowed from me; many others have received money from me as free gift. I die so poor that even the clothes I wear belong to the executioner who will cut off my head. I have nothing with which to ensure the good of my soul. Therefore I appeal to those of your worships who owe me money, as well as those who do not, to grant me the alms and charity of having as many masses as possible said for my soul, for I place hopes in God that by the blood and passion of Our Lord Jesus Christ, His Son, and through the alms that your worships grant me, He will have pity of me and will pardon my sins. And may your worships remain with God.

Before he had finished his plea for alms, there arose a general lament, with great moans and sobs and tears, from those who heard his pitiful words. Gonzalo Pizarro kneeled before the crucifix that he bore, and which was placed on a table on the platform. The executioner, who was named Juan Enríquez, came up to place a bandage over his eyes. Gonzalo Pizarro said to him: "I do not need it." And when he saw that Enriquez was raising the sword to cut off his head, he said: "Do your task well, brother Juan." He meant that he should do the job cleanly, and not prolong the agony, as frequently happens. The executioner replied: "I promise it to your Lordship." Saying this, with his left hand he raised his beard, which was long, about eight inches, and round, for it was not the fashion in those days to clip beards. And with one back stroke he cut off his head as easily as if it were a lettuce leaf and held it in his hand, and the body fell slowly to the ground. Such was the end of this good gentleman. The executioner, true to his trade, wanted to despoil him of his clothing, but Diego Centeno, who had come to inter the body safely, forbade him to approach it and promised him a good sum of money for the clothing. And so they bore the body to Cuzco; they buried Pizarro in his clothes, for there was no one to offer him a burial shroud. They buried him in the Convent of Nuestra Señora de las Mercedes, in the same chapel where were buried the two Don Diegos de Almagro, father and son, in order that they might be equal and comrades in all things—

in their common conquest of the land, in the common death of all three on the executioner's block, and in the pauper's burial of all three in a common grave, as if they even lacked earth enough to cover each one separately. Fortune made them equal in all things, as if to prevent any one of them from lording it over the others and as if to prevent all three from setting themselves above the Marquis Francisco Pizarro, who was brother of the one and comrade of the other and who was likewise slain and buried in a pauper's grave, as was told above. Thus all four were brothers and comrades in all and for all. Such is the way of the world (as those remarked who viewed these matters dispassionately) with those who serve it most and best, for such was the end of those who won that empire called Peru.

8. ADVICE TO A WOULD-BE CONQUEROR

The conquest of the Americas, like similar enterprises before and after, attracted a wide variety of people. A common figure was the adventurer, who frequently had a military background and not infrequently a past that he preferred to forget. Such, assuredly, were the "fine-feathered birds and great talkers" that Oviedo warns against below. But there were also many young and high-spirited hidalgos, "men of good family who were not reared behind the plow," who sailed in the ships bound for the Indies. It is probably safe to assume that of the trinity of motives usually assigned to the Spanish conquistador (God, gold, and glory), the second was uppermost in the minds of most.

Sir captain: Understand me and understand yourself. When you make up a company to go to the Indies, and especially in Seville (for it is there, on the steps of the cathedral, that the soldiers are wont to gather), you should first examine the face of each; having scrutinized the face, you will see part of the evil beneath. But because the outward aspect may deceive you in the choice of a soldier, you should make secret inquiry concerning his habits, his mode of life, his skills, and his nationality; for even in that sacred there are some who will lie about their countries and even their own names for the sake of going to the Indies. And do not attach much importance to his height and his well-combed beard, but rather try to find out whether he is of good character and family, and a frank and modest man. And if he tells you that he was in the battle of Ravenna, dismiss him, if he is a Spaniard, since he remained alive or was not taken prisoner; and do the same if he speaks of the battle of Pavia;

Oviedo y Valdés, *Historia general*, 5:213–218. Excerpt translated by Benjamin Keen.

and dismiss him if he tells you that he was in the sack of Genoa or Rome, since he did not get rich; and if he was there, and gambled his wealth away or lost it, do not trust him. Those slashed hose and shoes will not do at all for such lands as the Indies, full of ambushes and thick with trees and hawthorns, where there are so many rivers to swim and so many swamps and bogs to cross.

The dress and the person should conform to your needs; above all do not take a man whose faith is suspect, or one less than twenty-five or more than fifty years old. And do not take such fine-feathered birds and great talkers as those I mentioned above, for in the many years that I have seen them in the Indies, and before that in Europe, I have found that few turn out well. As long as there is gold, or they suspect that they will get it through your hands, they will serve you diligently; but be careful, for the minute that things do not go their way they will either slay you or sell you or forsake you, when they find that you promised them more in Spain than you can produce. . . .

And before you begin this examination, examine yourself, and make sure that your aim is to serve God and your king by converting the Indians and treating them well, and by finding a way to lead them to the Republic of Christ. Do not enslave them without cause, or stain your hands with blood without cause or justice, or rob them or remove them from the lands where God created them; he gave them life and humanity not to help you carry out any evil design but in order to save them. . . . And do not say that you are going to the Indies to serve the king and to employ your time as a brave man and an hidalgo should; for you know that the truth is just the opposite; you are going solely because you want to have a larger fortune than your father and your neighbors. However, you can do everything you want to do without hurting others or jeopardizing your soul. And do not seek any estate or treasure that might cost you such a price, if in so doing you lose that invaluable treasure by which you were redeemed and God freed you from Hell. . . .

Comrade and friend: If you decide to go to the Indies, when you are in Seville ascertain first of all whether the captain with whom you are going is a man who will fulfill what he promises, and learn on the basis of what word or guaranty you are entrusting your life and person to his will—because many of these captains promise what they do not have, know, or understand; and they pay for your person with words that are worth less than feathers; because feathers, though the wind bear them away, at least have some substance and you know their purpose, which is to float in the air aimlessly; but the words of a liar are without substance and, having been said, are invisible and vanish like air. . . . Do you not see that he speaks of what is yet to come, and promises what he neither has nor understands? And once you are free of the perils of the sea and the land, which are innumerable, and come to the Indies, if he should succeed, he neither knows nor rewards you; and if you fall ill, he does not heal you; and if you should die, he will not bury you. . . . And if he gives you an allotment of Indians, he does not care to ascertain whether you are competent to teach them or whether you yourself have more need of a teacher than of governing others, in order that both your consciences may be at rest. And since these estates are acquired unjustly, God permits them to be lost, and you with them. . . .

I observe that for every man who has made his fortune in these parts and has returned to Castile with or without it, an incomparably larger number have lost both their fortunes and their lives. You will say: What should I do? Shall I hold back from going to the Indies, where so many go and return rich—men who were formerly poor and do not measure up to me in ability, merit, or capacity for work? Is it fitting that for lack of courage I should fail to do what so many have done who are older than I and not of such good health and presence? I do not counsel you not to go to the Indies, nor to go there; but I do counsel you, whether you come or not, first to justify yourself with God and to commend yourself to Him. I am aware that it is proper and necessary to seek one's fortune, especially for men of good family who were not reared behind the plow; but let the undertaking be well thought out, and once you have determined upon it, never let greed turn you aside from the loyalty that you owe, and never let necessity give occasion for you to be considered an ingrate or to tarnish your good name; for if you only set your mind to it, in the Indies as elsewhere you can live without offense to your fellowmen.

9. LOPE DE AGUIRRE: DISILLUSIONED WARRIOR

The principal instrument of Spain's conquest of the New World was the compaña *(warrior band), whose members shared in the profits of an expedition or campaign according to their rank and services. Despite the ostensibly democratic aspect of the campaigns, the captains, large investors, and royal officials dominated the enterprise of conquest and took the lion's share of spoils, land, and Indians for themselves, often leaving the rank-and-file conquistadors seething with discontent. Typical in some respects of the disinherited of the conquest was the famous Lope de Aguirre, who called himself el Peregrino, the Wanderer. In 1581, a mutiny headed by Aguirre resulted in the death of the leader of an expedition sent from Peru in search of a fabled golden kingdom in the Amazonian wilderness. Aguirre then launched an audacious plan to descend from the Amazon to the Atlantic, capture Panama, and then cross the Andes for the conquest of Peru and the creation of an independent Peruvian state that would properly reward old conquistadors like himself. Aguirre's wildly improbable plan was doomed to fail, but before his death at the hands of his own men he sent King Philip II a letter that offers a vision of the society created by the conquest as seen by its underdogs, bitter over their betrayal by the great captains, the viceroys, cunning* letrados *or judges, and their king. Despite its rambling tone, the letter is marked by originality and a powerful style.*

To King Philip, native of Spain and son of Charles the Invincible. From Lope de Aguirre, the least of your vassals, an Old Christian, of middling parents but an hidalgo, native of the Basque country of the kingdom of Spain and citizen of the town of Oñate.

In my youth I crossed the sea to better my fortunes, lance in hand, and to fulfill the obligation of all good men. In twenty-four years I have done you great service in Peru, in the conquest of Indians, in founding towns, and especially in battles and skirmishes waged in your name, always to the best of my ability, without requesting of your officials pay or assistance, as will appear from your royal records.

I firmly believe, most excellent King and Lord, that to me and my comrades you have been cruel and ungrateful; I also believe that you are deceived by those who write you from these distant lands.

I demand, King, that you deal justly with the good vassals that you have in this land, though I and my comrades, . . . unable to bear further the cruelties of your judges, viceroys, and governors, have resolved to obey you no longer. Renouncing allegiance to Spain, our native land, we make the cruelest war against you that our forces permit. Believe me, King and Lord, that we do this because we can no longer suffer the great oppression and unjust punishments of your ministers, who in order to benefit their sons and hangers-on have robbed us of our good name, honor, and life. Truly, King, it is a pity, the bad treatment we have received.

I am lame in the right leg from two arquebus wounds I received in the battle of Chuquinga, fighting with Marshal Alonso de Alvarado in response to your call against Francisco Hernández Girón, a rebel against your rule as I and my comrades presently are and will remain until death, for we know now how cruel and faithless you are and give less credit to your promises than to the books of Martin Luther. For we remember how your viceroy the Marquis de Cañete hanged Martín de Robles, a man distinguished in your service; and the brave Tomás Vazquez, conquistador of Peru; and the unhappy Alonso Díaz, who labored more in the discoveries of this kingdom than the scouts of Moses in the desert; and Piedrahita, a good captain who fought many battles in your service. In the battle of Pucara these men brought you victory, and had they not, Francisco Hernández would now be king of Peru. And do not believe what your judges tell you about the great services they have rendered

Casto Fulgencio López, *Lope de Aguirre el Peregrino, Primer Caudillo de América* (Barcelona, 1977), pp. 234–240. I am grateful to Professor Thomas Holloway of University of California–Davis for calling my attention to the peculiar interest of the Aguirre episode and allowing me to use his translation of Aguirre's letter.—B.K.

you, for it is all a myth, unless it is a service to have spent 800,000 pesos from your royal treasury on their vices and misdeeds. Punish them as the wicked men they are.

Look here, King of Spain! Do not be so cruel and ungrateful to your vassals, for while your father and you stayed in Spain, free from care, your vassals have won for you all the kingdoms and lordships that you possess in these parts at the cost of their blood and fortune. Consider, King, that you cannot justly take any wealth from these lands where you risked nothing until you have properly rewarded those who gained them for you with their toil and sweat.

I am certain that very few kings go to hell, because there are so few of you, but even if there were many, none would go to heaven. Even in hell, you would be worse than Lucifer, because you all thirst after human blood. . . . For certain, I and my 200 arquebus-bearing . . . conquistadors and hidalgos solemnly swear to God that we will not leave a minister of yours alive, for we know what your clemency amounts to. We who live in these parts of the Indies consider ourselves the luckiest men alive, for we observe the Christian faith and commandments of God in full and uncorrupted, maintaining all that is preached by the holy mother church of Rome, and though sinners in life we are ready to suffer martyrdom in defense of God's commandments. . . .

So great is the dissolution of the friars in these parts that it would be well for you to make them feel your wrath and punishment, for each acts as high and mighty as if he were a governor. And do not believe what they tell you in Spain, for the tears they shed in your royal presence are in the hope of coming here in order to lord over all. If you want to know what sort of life they lead here, it is to buy and sell, acquire worldly goods, and sell the sacraments of the church for a price. They are enemies of the poor, without charity, ambitious, gluttonous, and arrogant, so that even the humblest friar seeks to command and govern all these lands. Correct these things, King and Lord, for by their bad example they weaken the faith of the natives, and if the dissolution of these friars is not checked, it will be a never-ending source of scandal.

If I and my comrades, for the reasons given above and on account of other things that have happened in the past, have determined to die, you, King, have been the cause thereof because you felt no pity for the toil of your vassals and gave no thought to what you owe them. If you do not look after your vassals and close your eyes to the actions of your judges, your government will surely fail. I do not need to present witnesses; consider only what I tell you. Each of your judges receives an annual salary of 4,000 pesos, and an expense allowance of 8,000 pesos, yet at the end of three years in office each has saved up 60,000 pesos, not to speak of their estates and other possessions. Withal, if they were content to be served as ordinary mortals, we would be willing to serve them as we do, but for our sins they want us to drop to our knees whenever we meet them and worship them like Nebuchadnezzar. This is intolerable. As one who has suffered and was made lame in your service (and my comrades have grown old and weary in the same), I must warn you not to entrust your royal conscience to those lawyers. It is in your royal interest to keep a sharp eye on them, for they spend all their time planning the marriages of their children, and think of nothing else. The common refrain among them is, "To the left and the right, I claim all in my sight."

The friars here will not bury the poor Indians, and they have the best estates in Peru. The life they lead is truly hard and burdensome, for by way of penance each keeps a dozen young women in his kitchen and as many boys busy with fishing, hunting partridges, and gathering fruit. They must have a share of everything. As a good Christian, I swear, King and Lord, that if you do not correct the evils of this land, you must suffer the divine wrath. I say these things that you may know the truth, though I and my comrades neither expect nor want mercy from you. . . .

Ah, what a pity it is that the Emperor, your father, should have conquered proud Germany with the power of Spain and spent so much money from the Indies discovered by us, and that you do not care enough about our old age and weariness to satisfy our hunger for a single day! . . .

The captains and other officers whom I lead at present and who promise to die in this enterprise, being men who have suffered great injury, . . . pray to God our Lord that you be victorious in your struggle against the French and the Turks and all others who wish to wage war against you in those parts. In these parts, may God grant that we obtain by force of arms the reward that is by right due us, but that you have denied.

A son of your loyal Basque vassals and rebel until death against you for your ingratitude.

Lope de Aguirre, the Wanderer

10. JOURNEY'S END

Of the many bold captains who rode under the banner of Castile to the conquest of the Americas, few lived to enjoy in peace and security the fruits of their valor, their suffering, and their cruelty. "He that killeth with the sword must be killed with the sword," recalled the old conquistador Oviedo. Certainly there was a kind of poetic justice about the ends met by such notorious and hardened Indian slave catchers and tormentors as Balboa, Ponce de León, and Pedro de Alvarado. Oviedo presents a partial roll call of

Oviedo y Valdés, *Historia general*, 5:150–152. Excerpt translated by Benjamin Keen.

the great adelantados, *or leaders of conquering expeditions, and relates the ends to which they came.*

I do not like the title of *adelantado*, for actually that honor and title is an evil omen in the Indies, and many who bore it have come to a pitiable end. So it was with Don Bartholomew Columbus, the first *adelantado* in the Indies, brother of the first admiral, who left behind him neither heirs nor any other enduring thing. Look at Ponce de León, *adelantado* of Florida, slain by the Indians; the *adelantado* Rodrigo de Bastidas, treacherously slain by the dagger blows of his own soldiers; the *adelantado* Diego Velásquez, who spent infinite sums on the discovery of New Spain, only to see another enjoy it and himself disappointed. Consider Vasco Núñez de Balboa, *adelantado* of the South Sea, and its first discoverer, who was beheaded as a traitor, and others with him, although they were all innocent of treason; the *adelantado* Lucas Vasquez de Ayllón, his Majesty's judge on the Royal Audience that sits here in Santo Domingo, who spent his estate and died in the discovery of a certain province that was given him in the northern regions, and whose body was flung in the sea; Francisco de Garay, *adelantado* of Panuco, who wasted his substance in arming and going to settle a land he knew nothing of, and who lost everything and finally died, although some say he was poisoned.

Antonio Sedeño spent much money on the conquest of Trinidad and Meta, and in the end was ruined and died disastrously; Diego de Ordaz, somewhat madder than the others, left and lost all he had and sought to settle the River Marañón, and in the end, departing for Spain, died and was cast in the sea; the *adelantado* Hernando de Soto, governor of the isle of Cuba, after returning to Spain loaded with gold, went to settle the mainland [of North America] and died there, leaving no trace or memory of himself. The *adelantado* Simón de Alcazaba was treacherously slain by his soldiers; the *adelantado* Diego de Almagro died a good and Catholic death; and, finally, his comrade Francisco Pizarro and his brothers, especially Hernando Pizarro, were slain against all reason and justice by those who were not their judges—but there is another world after this.

The *adelantado* Francisco Pizarro, later a marquis, was wickedly slain by his enemies and soldiers; the *adelantado* Pedro de Heredia, governor of Cartagena, is still alive, and no one can tell how he will end; a worse fate than others befell the *adelantado* Francisco de Orellana, who went to the River Marañón in search of the tribe of the Amazons—or, to put it better, in search of death, although he did not know it—and so met his end at the mouth of the river. . . . The *adelantado* Pedro de Mendoza went to the River Plate and wasted and lost all he had, and sailing for Spain, died and was cast into the sea; the *adelantado* Pánfilo de Narváez and his followers suffered an even worse fate, for some were eaten by their fellows, and of six hundred men only three escaped, while Narváez drowned in the sea; the *adelantado* Pedro de Al-varado lived and died violently, for his horse rolled down a steep hill, with him helplessly entangled underneath, and dragged him from cliff to cliff, leaving him in such a state that he died soon after, but not before receiving the Sacraments like a good Catholic. . . .

And thus, prudent reader, you may see what sort of title is that of *adelan-tado*, that leaves in such conditions those who have held it in the Indies; and it seems to me that after what I have said of the *adelantados* named above, no man of sound sense will seek to obtain this title in that part of the world.

4

❧

COLONIZATION

DEVISING A WORKABLE labor system for the American colonies was the central problem for Spain and Portugal in formulating their settlement policies. The situation that Columbus's second expedition created on the island of Hispaniola has been aptly summed up as "hell on Hispaniola." Columbus, anxious to prove to the crown the value of his discoveries, compelled the natives to bring in a daily tribute of gold dust. Indians who revolted were hunted down, and hundreds were sent to Spain as slaves. Later, yielding to the demand of rebellious settlers for Indian slaves, Columbus distributed the Indians among them in *repartimientos*, or shares, with the grantee enjoying the right to use the forced labor of his Indians. This system, formalized under the administration of Governor Nicolás de Ovando and sanctioned by the crown, became the *encomienda*.

In operation, the *encomienda* in the West Indies became a hideous form of slavery. The first voices raised against it came from a company of Dominican friars who arrived on Hispaniola in 1510. Their spokesman was Fr. Antonio Montesinos, who on Advent Sunday 1511 ascended the church pulpit to threaten the Spaniards with damnation for their offenses against the Indians.

The Dominicans' agitation raised the larger question of the legality of Spain's claim to the Indies. To satisfy the royal conscience, the jurist doctor Palacios Rubios drew up a document, the *requerimiento*, which all conquistadores were supposed to read to the Indians before making war on them. This document called on the Indians to acknowledge the supremacy of the Church and the pope and the sovereignty of the Spanish monarchs over their lands by virtue of the papal donation of the Indies to Spain in 1493. The Indians were threatened with war and enslavement if they refused to acknowledge Spain's hegemony over them.

The famous Bartolomé de las Casas now joined the struggle against the *encomienda* and the doctrines of Palacios Rubios. He won a brilliant but

largely illusive victory in the promulgation of the New Laws of 1542. Faced
with revolt in Peru and the threat of revolt elsewhere, the Spanish crown offered the colonists a compromise. The laws forbidding enslavement and
forced personal service by *encomienda* Indians were reaffirmed, but the right
of *encomenderos* to continue collecting fixed amounts of tribute from the natives was confirmed. The crown, however, rejected the demand that the *encomienda* be made hereditary, and the gradual reversion of the *encomiendas* to
the crown paved the way for the institution's extinction. But in some regions,
such as Paraguay and Chile, the *encomienda* survived almost to the end of the
colonial period.

Indian forced labor, once it was legally separated from the *encomienda*,
soon appeared in another form. The colonists' demand for cheap labor was
satisfied by legal conscription of Indians, who worked in shifts or relays. But
the system was inefficient and could not satisfy the growing need of Spanish
employers for Indian labor. From an early date, therefore, Spanish landowners and other employers resorted to the use of so-called free or contractual
labor; however, they often bound the Indians with advances of money and
goods, thereby turning them into virtual serfs. In certain industries and areas,
however, such as the silver mining area of northern New Spain and the silver
mines of Potosí (Peru), more or less free labor came into fairly wide use.

For Portugal, the labor problem took a different turn. Pedro Alvares
Cabral, a Portuguese captain sent to follow up Vasco da Gama's great voyage
to India, accidentally discovered Brazil in 1500 and claimed it for his country.
Trade and conquest in the Far East claimed Portugal's chief attention at this
time, but Portugal did not completely neglect its new possession. Brazil-
wood, source of a valued red dye, was the first staple of the colony, but sugar
soon established its economic leadership. Sugar cultivation required a considerable labor force and Portuguese settlers, like their Spanish counterparts,
sought to coerce Indians into providing it. The lack of relatively centralized
Indian "empires" and fierce resistance made this more difficult than in Mexico and Peru. Although slave raids on Indian villages continued, after 1550
black slaves imported from Africa provided the bulk of the labor for the plantations and sugar mills.

1. THE STRANGE SERMON OF FR. MONTESINOS

*The struggle for justice for the American Indians was begun by a small group of Do-
minican friars, who were horrified by the sights they witnessed daily on the island of
Hispaniola. They delegated Fr. Antonio Montesinos to preach a sermon that would
drive home to the Spanish settlers the wickedness of their deeds. Montesinos's denunciation infuriated the townspeople, who called on the Dominicans to retract their senti-*

ments in next Sunday's sermon. Otherwise, the townspeople declared, the friars should pack up and sail for home. In reply, Montesinos mounted the pulpit the following Sunday and let loose a second and even more terrible blast against Spanish mistreatment of the Indians. Bartolomé de las Casas describes the opening round in the great controversy over Spain's Indian policy.

Sunday having arrived, and the time for preaching, Father Antonio Montesinos rose in the pulpit, and took for the text of his sermon, which was written down and signed by the other friars, "I am the voice of one crying in the wilderness." Having made his introduction and said something about the Advent season, he began to speak of the sterile desert of the consciences of the Spaniards on this isle, and of the blindness in which they lived, going about in great danger of damnation and utterly heedless of the grave sins in which they lived and died.

Then he returned to his theme, saying, "In order to make your sins known to you I have mounted this pulpit, I who am the voice of Christ crying in the wilderness of this island; and therefore it behooves you to listen to me, not with indifference but with all your heart and senses; for this voice will be the strangest, the harshest and hardest, the most terrifying that you ever heard or expected to hear."

He went on in this vein for a good while, using cutting words that made his hearers' flesh creep and made them feel that they were already experiencing the divine judgment. . . . He went on to state the contents of his message.

"This voice," said he, "declares that you are in mortal sin, and live and die therein by reason of the cruelty and tyranny that you practice on these innocent people. Tell me, by what right or justice do you hold these Indians in such cruel and horrible slavery? By what right do you wage such detestable wars on these people who lived mildly and peacefully in their own lands, where you have consumed infinite numbers of them with unheard-of murders and desolations? Why do you so greatly oppress and fatigue them, not giving them enough to eat or caring for them when they fall ill from excessive labors, so that they die or rather are slain by you, so that you may extract and acquire gold every day? And what care do you take that they receive religious instruction and come to know their God and creator, or that they be baptized, hear mass, or observe holidays and Sundays?

"Are they not men? Do they not have rational souls? Are you not bound to love them as you love yourselves? How can you lie in such profound and lethargic slumber? Be sure that in your present state you can no more be saved than the Moors or Turks who do not have and do not want the faith of Jesus Christ."

Bartolomé de las Casas, *Historia de las Indias*, 3 vols. (México, 1951), 2:441–442. Excerpt translated by Benjamin Keen.

Thus he delivered the message he had promised, leaving his hearers astounded. Many were stunned, others appeared more callous than before, and a few were somewhat moved; but not one, from what I could later learn, was converted.

When he had concluded his sermon he descended from the pulpit, his head held high, for he was not a man to show fear, of which indeed he was totally free; nor did he care about the displeasure of his listeners, and instead did and said what seemed best according to God. With his companion he went to their straw-thatched house, where, very likely, their entire dinner was cabbage soup, unflavored with olive oil. . . . After he had left, the church was so full of murmurs that . . . they could hardly complete the celebration of the mass.

2. THE LAUGHTER OF DR. PALACIOS RUBIOS

The dispute about Indian policy that had begun on the island of Hispaniola and was carried to Spain by the contending parties stimulated discussion of a fundamental question: By what right did Spain claim to rule over the Americas and wage war on the native peoples? The strong tradition of legalism in Spanish life and history as well as the pious professions of the Catholic Sovereigns required that a satisfactory reply be devised to this query. King Ferdinand, who is not particularly remembered by historians for scrupulosity in dealing with his fellow European monarchs, summoned a committee of theologians to deliberate on the matter. The fruit of their discussions was the famous requerimiento *or requirement, drawn up by Dr. Palacios Rubios. This document called on the Indians to acknowledge the supremacy of the Church, the pope, and the Spanish kings and to permit the faith to be preached to them. Not until they had rejected these demands, made known to them by interpreters, could war be legally waged on them. The chronicler Gonzalo Fernández de Oviedo y Valdés, who accompanied the expedition of Pedrarias Dávila to the South American mainland in 1514, records in his great history the first use made of the Requirement, and the ironic laughter of Palacios Rubios as he listened to Oviedo's account of his experience with this curious manifesto.*

After crossing this river we entered a village of some twenty huts; we found it deserted, and the general entered one of the houses, accompanied by all the captains who were there, by the licentiate Espinosa, who was the royal comptroller, factor, and governor, and by his lieutenant Juan de Ayora, and in the presence of all I said to him: "Sir, it seems to me that these Indians do not care to hear the theology of this requirement, nor do you have anyone who

---

Gonzalo Fernández de Oviedo y Valdés, *Historia general y natural de las Indias*, 14 vols. (Asunción, Paraguay, 1944–1945), 7:131–132. Excerpt translated by Benjamin Keen.

can make them understand it. Your worship had better put this paper away until we have caught an Indian and put him in a cage, where he can gradually master its meaning, and the bishop can help to make it clear to him."

And I gave the general the requirement, and he took it, amid the hearty laughter of all who were there. While we were all resting in those huts, waiting for the sun to go down, our sentinels gave the alarm at about two o'clock in the afternoon. And down a very wide and handsome road, bordered with many trees that had been planted for adornment, came more than a thousand Indian bowmen, with much noise and blowing on certain large shells which are called cobos and are heard at a great distance. . . .

The general quickly left the village to meet the Indians on the road and arrayed his men in battle formation, each line separated from the other by a distance of two hundred paces. He also ordered a bronze cannon of about two hundred pounds to be loaded. Two greyhounds, highly praised by their masters, were to be placed on our wings; we were to fire when he gave the signal; and at that instant the dogs should be loosed and we were all to fall upon the enemy and conduct ourselves like valiant men.

I should have preferred to have that requirement explained to the Indians first, but no effort was made to do so, apparently because it was considered superfluous or inappropriate. And just as our general on this expedition failed to carry out this pious proceeding with the Indians, as he was supposed to do before attacking them, the captains of many later expeditions also neglected the procedure and did even worse things, as will be seen. Later, in 1516, I asked Doctor Palacios Rubios (who had written that proclamation) if the consciences of the Christians were satisfied with that requirement, and he said yes, if it were done as the proclamation required. But I recall that he often laughed when I told him of that campaign and of others that various captains later made. I could laugh much harder at him and his learning (for he was reputed to be a great man, and as such had a seat on the Royal Council of Castile), if he thought that the Indians were going to understand the meaning of that requirement until many years had passed.

3. BARTOLOMÉ DE LAS CASAS: GOD'S ANGRY MAN

Among the many personalities who intervened in the great controversy about Spain's Indian policy, the figure of Bartolomé de las Casas (1484–1566) has grown most in stature with the passing of the centuries. The world knows him best for his flaming tract against Spanish cruelty to the Indians, the Brief Account of the Destruction of the Indies *(1552), a work soon translated into most of the languages of Europe and joyously used by Spain's imperialist rivals to discredit its colonial enterprise. Recent studies in the social history of colonial Latin America tend to confirm Las Casas's claims of large pre-Conquest Indian populations and his thesis that a catastrophic population decline occurred as a result of the Conquest. Typical of the tone and contents of the* Brief Account *is its description of the Spanish subjugation of Cuba.*

In the year 1511 the Spaniards passed over to the island of Cuba, which as I said, is as long as from Valladolid to Rome, and where there were great and populous provinces. They began and ended in the above manner, only with incomparably greater cruelty. Here many notable things occurred.

A very high prince and lord, named Hatuey, who had fled with many of his people from Hispaniola to Cuba, to escape the calamity and inhuman operations of the Christians, having received news from some Indians that the Christians were crossing over, assembled many or all of his people, and addressed them thus.

"You already know that it is said the Christians are coming here; and you have experience of how they have treated the lords so and so and those people of Hayti (which is Hispaniola); they come to do the same here. Do you know perhaps why they do it?" The people answered no; except that they were by nature cruel and wicked. "They do it," said he, "not alone for this, but because they have a God whom they greatly adore and love; and to make us adore Him they strive to subjugate us and take our lives." He had near him a basket full of gold and jewels and he said: "Behold here is the God of the Christians, let us perform *Areytos* before Him, if you will (these are dances in concert and singly); and perhaps we shall please Him, and He will command that they do us no harm."

All exclaimed: it is well! it is well! They danced before it, till they were all tired, after which the lord Hatuey said: "Note well that in any event if we preserve the gold, they will finally have to kill us to take it from us: let us throw it into this river." They all agreed to this proposal, and they threw the gold into a great river in that place.

This prince and lord continued retreating before the Christians when they arrived at the island of Cuba, because he knew them, but when he encountered them he defended himself; and at last they took him. And merely because he fled from such iniquitous and cruel people, and defended himself against those who wished to kill and oppress him, with all his people and offspring until death, they burnt him alive.

When he was tied to the stake, a Franciscan monk, a holy man, who was there, spoke as much as he could to him, in the little time that the executioner granted them, about God and some of the teachings of our faith, of which he had never before heard; he told him that if he would believe what was told him, he would go to heaven where there was glory and eternal rest;

Bartolomé de las Casas, "The Brevissima Relación," in Francis A. McNutt, *Bartholomew de las Casas* (New York: Putnam's, 1909), Appendix 1, pp. 328–332. Reprinted by permission of the publishers.

and if not, that he would go to hell, to suffer perpetual torments and punishment. After thinking a little, Hatuey asked the monk whether the Christians went to heaven; the monk answered that those who were good went there. The prince at once said, without any more thought, that he did not wish to go there, but rather to hell so as not to be where Spaniards were, nor to see such cruel people. This is the renown and honour that God and our faith have acquired by means of the Christians who have gone to the Indies.

On one occasion they came out ten leagues from a great settlement to meet us, bringing provisions and gifts, and when we met them, they gave us a great quantity of fish and bread and other victuals, with everything they could supply. All of a sudden the devil entered into the bodies of the Christians, and in my presence they put to the sword, without any motive or cause whatsoever, more than three thousand persons, men, women, and children, who were seated before us. Here I beheld such great cruelty as living man has never seen nor thought to see.

Once I sent messengers to all the lords of the province of Havana, assuring them that if they would not absent themselves but come to receive us, no harm should be done them; all the country was terrorized because of the past slaughter, and I did this by the captain's advice. When we arrived in the province, twenty-one princes and lords came to receive us; and at once the captain violated the safe conduct I had given them and took them prisoners. The following day he wished to burn them alive, saying it was better so because those lords would some time or other do us harm. I had the greatest difficulty to deliver them from the flames but finally I saved them.

After all the Indians of this island were reduced to servitude and misfortune like those of Hispaniola, and when they saw they were perishing inevitably, some began to flee to the mountains; others to hang themselves, together with their children, and through the cruelty of one very tyrannical Spaniard whom I knew, more than two hundred Indians hanged themselves. In this way numberless people perished.

There was an officer of the King in this island, to whose share three hundred Indians fell, and by the end of the three months he had, through labor in the mines, caused the death of two hundred and seventy; so that he had only thirty left, which was the tenth part. The authorities afterwards gave him as many again, and again he killed them: and they continued to give, and he to kill, until he came to die, and the devil carried away his soul.

In three or four months, I being present, more than seven thousand children died of hunger, their fathers and mothers having been taken to the mines. Other dreadful things did I see.

Afterwards the Spaniards resolved to go and hunt the Indians who were in the mountains, where they perpetrated marvelous massacres. Thus they ruined and depopulated all this island which we beheld not long ago; and it excites pity, and great anguish to see it deserted, and reduced to a solitude.

4. ALL HUMANKIND IS ONE

In 1550, in perhaps his finest hour, Las Casas rose to answer the eminent humanist Juan Ginés de Sepúlveda (1490?–1572?), author of a treatise which sought to prove that wars against the Indians were just. The background of the great debate, held before a junta of theologians summoned by Charles V to decide the matter, was a general reaction in the Spanish court against Las Casas's liberal views, as signaled by the partial repeal of the New Laws of 1542. Las Casas founded his argument on his eloquent affirmation of the equality of all races, the essential oneness of humankind. The first of the following extracts is from Sepúlveda's treatise on the subject of Indian wars; the second is taken from Las Casas's Apological History of the Indies.

Part 1

Now compare these [Spanish] traits of prudence, intelligence, magnanimity, moderation, humanity, and religion with the qualities of these little men in whom you will scarcely find even vestiges of humanity; who not only are devoid of learning but do not even have a written language; who preserve no monuments of their history, aside from some vague and obscure reminiscence of past events, represented by means of certain paintings; and who have no written laws but only barbaric customs and institutions. And if we are to speak of virtues, what moderation or mildness can you expect of men who are given to all kinds of intemperance and wicked lusts, and who eat human flesh?

And do not believe that before the coming of the Christians they lived in that peaceful reign of Saturn that the poets describe; on the contrary, they waged continuous and ferocious war against each other, with such fury that they considered a victory hardly worth while if they did not glut their monstrous hunger with the flesh of their enemies, a ferocity all the more repellent since it was not joined to the invincible valor of the Scythians, who also ate human flesh. For the rest, these Indians are so cowardly that they almost run at the sight of our soldiers, and frequently thousands of them have fled like women before a very few Spaniards, numbering less than a hundred. . . .

Could one give more convincing proof of the superiority of some men to others in intelligence, spirit, and valor, and of the fact that such people are slaves by nature? For although some of them display a certain talent for craftsmanship this is not proof of human intelligence, for we know that animals, birds, and spiders do certain work that no human industry can completely imitate. And as regards the mode of life of the inhabitants of New

---

Juan Ginés de Sepúlveda, *Tratado sobre las justas causas de la guerra contra los indios* (México, 1941), pp. 105–113; and Bartolomé de las Casas, *Apologética historia de las Indias* (Madrid, 1909), pp. 128–129. Excerpts translated by Benjamin Keen.

Spain and the province of Mexico, I have already said that they are considered the most civilized of all. They themselves boast of their public institutions, for they have cities constructed in an orderly fashion, and kings, not hereditary but elected by popular vote; and they carry on commerce among themselves in the manner of civilized people.

But see how they deceive themselves, and how much I disagree with their opinion, for in these same institutions I see proof on the contrary of the rudeness, the barbarism, and the inherently slavish nature of these people. For the possession of habitations, of a fairly rational mode of life, and of a kind of commerce is something that natural necessity itself induces, and only serves to prove that they are not bears or monkeys and are not completely devoid of reason. But on the other hand, they have no private property in their state, and they cannot dispose of or bequeath to their heirs their houses or fields, since they are all in the power of their lords, whom they improperly call kings, at whose pleasure, rather than at their own, they live, attentive to their will and caprice rather than to their own freedom. And the fact that they do all this in a voluntary and spontaneous manner and are not constrained by force of arms is certain proof of the servile and abased spirit of these barbarians. . . .

Such, in sum, are the disposition and customs of these little men—barbarous, uncivilized, and inhumane; and we know that they were like this before the coming of the Spaniards. We have not yet spoken of their impious religion and of the wicked sacrifices in which they worshiped the devil as their God, believing that they could offer no better tribute than human hearts. . . . How can we doubt that these peoples, so uncivilized, so barbarous, contaminated with so many infidelities and vices, have been justly conquered by such an excellent, pious, and just king as the late Ferdinand the Catholic, and the present Emperor Charles, and by a nation that is most humane and excels in every kind of virtue?

Part 2

From these examples, both ancient and modern, it is clear that no nation exists, no matter how rude and uncivilized, barbarous, gross, savage or almost brutal it may be, that cannot be persuaded into a good way of life and made domestic, mild, and tractable—provided that diligence and skill are employed, and provided that the method that is proper and natural to men is used: namely, love and gentleness and kindness. . . .

For all the peoples of the world are men, and the definition of all men, collectively and severally, is one: that they are rational beings. All possess understanding and volition, being formed in the image and likeness of God; all have the five exterior senses and the four interior senses, and are moved by the objects of these; all have the natural capacity or faculties to understand and master the knowledge that they do not have; and this is true not only of those that are inclined toward good but of those that by reason of their depraved customs are bad; all take pleasure in goodness and in happy and pleasant things; and all abhor evil and reject what offends or grieves them. . . .

Thus all mankind is one, and all men are alike in what concerns their creation and all natural things, and no one is born enlightened. From this it follows that all of us must be guided and aided at first by those who were born before us. And the savage peoples of the earth may be compared to uncultivated soil that readily brings forth weeds and useless thorns, but has within itself such natural virtue that by labor and cultivation it may be made to yield sound and beneficial fruits.

5. THE PORTUGUESE COLONIZER

Unlike the Spanish conquistadores, who roamed through jungles and mountains searching for kingdoms of gold, their Portuguese counterparts were content to remain on the fertile coast of northeast Brazil, where they established a plantation economy producing sugar for the world market. Yet the Portuguese colonizer could deal hard blows when necessity required, as shown by the story of Duarte Coelho, who undertook to settle the captaincy of Pernambuco. Gabriel Soares de Souza, a planter of Baía who wrote one of the earliest and most valuable accounts of colonial Brazil, tells of Duarte's exploits.

The town of Olinda is the capital of the captaincy of Pernambuco, which was settled by Duarte Coelho, a gentleman of whose courage and chivalry I shall not speak here in detail, for the books that deal with India are full of his deeds. After Duarte Coelho returned from India to Portugal to seek a reward for his services, he sought and obtained from His Highness the grant of a captaincy on this coast; this grant began at the mouth of the São Francisco River in the northwest and ran fifty leagues up the coast toward the captaincy of Tamaracá, ending at the Igaruçu River. . . . Since this brave captain was always disposed to perform great feats, he determined to come in person to settle and conquer this, his captaincy. He arrived there with a fleet of ships that he had armed at his own cost, in which he brought his wife and children and many of their kinsmen, and other settlers. With this fleet he made port at the place called Pernambuco, which in the native language means "hidden sea," because of a rock nearby that is hidden in the sea. Arriving at this port, Duarte Coelho disembarked and fortified himself as well as he could on a high point free of any dominating peaks, where the town is today. There he

Gabriel Soares de Souza, *Tratado descriptivo do Brazil em 1587* (São Paulo, 1938), pp. 27–29. Excerpt translated by Benjamin Keen.

built a strong tower, which still stands in the town square, and for many years he waged war against the natives and the French who fought at their side. Frequently he was besieged and badly wounded, with the loss of many of his people, but he courageously persisted in his aim, and not only defended himself bravely but attacked his enemies so effectively that they abandoned the neighboring lands. Later his son, of the same name, continued to wage war on them, harassing and capturing these people, called Cayté, until they had abandoned the whole coast and more than fifty leagues in the interior. In these labors Duarte spent many thousands of *cruzados* that he had acquired in India, and this money was really well spent, for today his son Jorge de Albuquerque Coelho enjoys an income of ten thousand cruzados, which he obtains from the retithe, from his tithe of the fishing catch, and from the quit rent paid him by the sugarmills (fifty of these have been established in Pernambuco, and they produce so much sugar that the tithes on it yield nineteen thousand *cruzados* a year).

This town of Olinda must have about seven hundred householders, but there are many more within the limits of the town, since from twenty to thirty people live on each of these plantations, aside from the many who live on farms. Hence if it were necessary to assemble these people with arms, they could place in the field more than three thousand fighting men, together with the inhabitants of the town of Cosmos, which must have four hundred mounted men. These people could bring from their estates four or five thousand Negro slaves and many Italians. This captaincy is so prosperous that there are more than a hundred men in it who have an income of from one to five thousand *cruzados*, and some have incomes of eight to ten thousand *cruzados*. From this land many men have returned rich to Portugal who came here poor, and every year this captaincy sends forty to fifty ships loaded with sugar and brazilwood; this wood is so profitable to His Majesty that he has lately farmed out the concession for a period of ten years at twenty thousand *cruzados* a year. It seems to me that such a powerful captaincy, which yields this kingdom such a great store of provisions, should be better fortified, and should not be exposed for a corsair to sack and destroy—which could be prevented with little expense and less labor.

6. THE SLAVE HUNTERS

The expanding plantation economy of the Brazilian northeast required a steady supply of cheap labor. The Portuguese met the problem with raids on Indian villages, returning with trains of captives who were sold to plantation owners. The men of São Paulo, lacking the sugar and brazilwood on which the prosperity of the northeast was based, turned to slave hunting as a lucrative occupation. The prospect of finding gold in the interior made their expeditions doubly attractive. As the coastal Indians were

exterminated or fled before the invaders, the bandeirantes, *the "men of the banner,"*
pushed ever deeper south and west, expanding the frontiers of Brazil in the process. Je-
suit missionaries, almost alone, raised their voices against their predatory activities.
One of them, believed to be the famous Fr. Joseph de Anchieta (1534–1597), describes
the devastation wrought by the slave hunters.

The number of Indians that have been destroyed in this captaincy of Baía
in the past twenty years passes belief; who would think that so many people
could be destroyed in so short a time? In the fourteen churches maintained
by the Fathers they had brought together 40,000 souls, by count, and even
more, counting those who came after—yet today it is doubtful whether the
three churches that remain have 3,500 souls together. Six years ago an honored citizen of this city, a man of good conscience and a city official at the
time, said that in the two preceding years 20,000 souls, by count, had been
brought from the back country of Arabó and that all of them went to the Portuguese plantations. These 20,000, added to the 40,000 of the churches,
come to 60,000. Now for the past six years the Portuguese have been bringing Indians for their plantations, one bringing 2,000, another 3,000, some
more, others less; in six years this must come to 80,000 souls or more. Now
look at the sugar-mills and plantations of Baía, and you will find them full of
Guinea Negroes but very few natives; if you ask what happened to all those
people, they will tell you that they died.

In this way God has severely punished the Portuguese for the many offenses that they committed and still commit against these Indians, for they go
into the interior and deceive these people, inviting them to go to the coast,
where, they say, they would live in their villages as they did in their lands, and
the Portuguese would be their neighbors. The Indians, believing this, go
with them, and for fear they will change their minds the Portuguese destroy
their gardens. On arrival at the coast they divide the Indians among themselves, some taking the women, others their husbands, and still others the
children, and they sell them. Other Portuguese go into the interior and entice the Indians by saying that they will take them to the churches of the Fathers; and by this means they seduce them from their lands, for it is common
knowledge in the backlands that only the Indians in the churches where the
Fathers reside enjoy liberty and all the rest are captives. Matters reached such
a point that a certain Portuguese, going into the back country in search of Indians, shaved his head like a priest, saying that he was a Father seeking Indians for the churches. This happened at a time when Father Gaspar Lourenço
was bound for the interior, and he found these people on the road. When

---

Joseph de Anchieta, *Cartas, informaçoes, fragmentos históricos e sermões do Padre Joseph de Anchi-*
eta, S. J. (1554–1594) (Rio de Janeiro, 1933), pp. 377–378. Excerpt translated by Benjamin Keen.

they heard that the Father was going into the backlands they said: "How can that be, when he who brings us says that he is a Father, and that is why we go with him?" And the Portuguese with the shaven head hid himself, not wanting the priest to see him.

The Portuguese travel 250 and 300 leagues to find the Indians, for the nearest ones are by now a great distance away, and since the land is now depopulated most of them die on the road from hunger. There have been Portuguese who seized on the road certain Indians who were enemies of the ones they were bringing, killed them, and gave their flesh to the captives to eat. And when all these people arrive at the coast, seeing that the Portuguese do not keep the promises they made in the interior but separate them from each other, some flee into the forests, never to emerge again, and others die from grief and chagrin that they, who had been free men, should be made slaves.

7. AIMORÉ: WORD OF TERROR

Brazilian Indians did not accept the loss of land and liberty without a struggle. Indian resistance to white aggression was handicapped by the fatal propensity of the tribes to war against each other, a situation that the Portuguese turned to their advantage. Forced to retreat into the interior by the superior arms and organization of the whites, the natives often returned to make destructive forays on isolated Portuguese communities. As late as the first part of the nineteenth century stretches of the Brazilian shore were made uninhabitable by the raids of Indians who lurked in the forests and mountains behind the coast. One tribe that never sought or granted a truce to the whites was the Aimorés. The chronicler Soares de Souza describes their mode of life and warfare.

It seems proper at this point to state what kind of people are those called Aimorés, who have done so much damage to this captaincy of Ilheos, as I have said. The coast of this captaincy used to be inhabited by the Tupiniquins, who abandoned it from fear of these brutes and went to live in the back country; at the present time there are only two very small Tupiniquin villages, situated near the sugar mills of Henrique Luiz.

These Aimorés are descended from other people that they call Tapuias, from whom departed in olden times certain families that went to live in very rugged mountains, fleeing from a defeat inflicted on them by their enemies; and there they lived many years without seeing any other people; and their descendants gradually lost their language, and developed a new one that is not understood by any other nation in the whole country of Brazil. These

Soares de Souza, *Tratado descriptivo do Brazil*, pp. 56–60. Excerpt translated by Benjamin Keen.

Aimorés are so savage that the other barbarians consider them worse than barbarians. Some of these were taken alive in Porto Seguro and in Ilheos, and they would not eat, preferring to die like savages.

This people first came to the sea at the River Caravellas, hard by Porto Seguro, and roamed this countryside and the beaches as far as the River Camamú; from there they began to launch attacks near Tinharé, descending to the shore only when they came to make an attack. This people is of the same color as the others, but they are larger and of more robust build. They have no beards or any other hair except on their heads, because they pluck out the hairs on the other parts of their bodies. They fight with very large bows and arrows, and are such excellent bowmen that they never miss a shot; they are marvelously light on their feet, and great runners.

These barbarians do not live in villages or houses like other people, and so far no one has come across their dwellings in the woods; they go from one place to another through the woods and fields; they sleep on the ground on leaves; and if it rains they go up to the foot of a tree and squat there, covering themselves with leaves; no other furnishings have ever been found among them. These savages do not have gardens or raise any food; they live on wild fruit and the game they kill, which they eat raw or poorly roasted, when they have a fire. Both men and women cut their hair short, shearing it with certain canes of which they gather a great number; their speech is rough, projected from their throats with much force; like Basque, it is impossible to write down.

These barbarians live by robbing everyone they encounter, and one never sees more than twenty or thirty bowmen at one time. They never fight anyone face to face, but always employ treachery, for they attack in the fields and roads which they travel, waiting in ambush for other Indians and all other sorts of persons, each hidden behind a tree and never missing a shot. They use up all their arrows, and if the people turn on them they all flee in different directions, but if they see that their pursuers have dropped their guard they stop and find a place to hide until their pursuers have passed, when they shoot them in the back with their arrows at will. They do not know how to swim, and any river that cannot be forded presents an adequate defense against them; but in order to find a crossing they will go many miles along the river in search of one.

These savages eat human flesh for sustenance—unlike the other Indians, who only eat it for the sake of revenge and in memory of their ancient hatreds. The captaincies of Porto Seguro and Ilheos have been destroyed and almost depopulated by fear of these barbarians, and the sugar mills have stopped working because all the slaves and the other people have been killed by them. The people on most of the plantations and those who have escaped from them have become so afraid of them that if they merely hear the word "Aimorés" they leave their plantations in search of refuge, the white men among them. In the twenty-five years that this plague has afflicted these two captaincies, they have killed more than 300 Portuguese and 3,000 slaves.

The inhabitants of Baía used to send letters to the people of Ilheos, and men traveled this road along the shore without danger. But when the Aimorés realized this they decided to come to these beaches to wait for the people who passed there, and there they killed many Portuguese and many more slaves. These bandits are such fleet runners that no one could escape them on foot, except those who take refuge in the sea; they dare not enter the ocean, but wait for them to come on shore until nightfall, when they retire. For this reason the road is forbidden, and no one travels it except at great risk of his life. If some means is not found to destroy these savages they will destroy the plantations of Baía, through which they roam at will. Since they are such intractable enemies of all mankind, it was not possible to learn more about their mode of life and customs.

8. Indian Forced Labor in Guatemala

Las Casas died in 1566, at the age of eighty-two, in a convent outside Madrid. Three Spanish kings had listened respectfully to his advice on Indian affairs, had sometimes acted on that advice, and in their Indian legislation gave pious lip service to the principles he advocated. But the realities of colonial existence overruled the voice of morality and religion. Legal slavery and personal service under the encomienda *system had largely disappeared by 1600 in New Spain and Peru, effectively replaced by a system of labor conscription requiring all adult male Indians to give a certain amount of their time to work in mines, factories, and on farms, ranches, and public works, receiving a small wage for their labor. In New Spain this institution was known as the* repartimiento. *Its operation in this area is described by Thomas Gage (1600?–1656), an observant though highly biased Englishman who spent twelve years as a priest in Guatemala before turning apostate and coming home to write an anti-Spanish book about his experiences.*

The miserable condition of the Indians of that country is such that though the Kings of Spain have never yielded to what some would have, that they should be slaves, yet their lives are as full of bitterness as is the life of a slave. For which I have known myself some of them that have come home from toiling and moiling with Spaniards, after many blows, some wounds, and little or no wages, who have sullenly and stubbornly lain down upon their

Thomas Gage, *The English-American: A New Survey of the West Indies*, ed. A. P. Newton (London, 1946), pp. 230–233.

beds, resolving to die rather than to live any longer a life so slavish, and have refused to take either meat or drink or anything else comfortable and nourishing, which their wives have offered unto them, that so by pining and starving they might consume themselves. Some I have by good persuasions encouraged to life rather than to a voluntary and willful death; others there have been that would not be persuaded, but in that willful way have died.

The Spaniards that live about that country (especially the farmers of the Valley of Mixco, Pinola, Petapa, Amatitlan, and those of the Sacatepequez) allege that all their trading and farming is for the good of the commonwealth, and therefore whereas there are not Spaniards enough for so ample and large a country to do all their work, and all are not able to buy slaves and blackamoors, they stand in need of the Indians' help to serve them for their pay and hire; whereupon it hath been considered that a partition of Indian laborers be made every Monday, or Sunday in the afternoon to the Spaniards, according to the farms they occupy, or according to their several employments, calling, and trading with mules, or any other way. So that for such and such a district there is named an officer, who is called *juez repartidor*, who according to a list made of every farm, house, and person, is to give so many Indians by the week. And here is a door opened to the President of Guatemala, and to the judges, to provide well for their menial servants, whom they commonly appoint for this office, which is thus performed by them. They name the town and place of their meeting upon Sunday or Monday, to which themselves and the Spaniards of that district do resort. The Indians of the several towns are to have in a readiness so many laborers as the Court of Guatemala hath appointed to be weekly taken out of such a town, who are conducted by an Indian officer to the town of general meeting; and when they come thither with their tools, their spades, shovels, bills, or axes, with their provision of victuals for a week (which are commonly some dry cakes of maize, puddings of *frijoles*, or French beans, and a little chili or biting long pepper, or a bit of cold meat for the first day or two) and with beds on their backs (which is only a coarse woolen mantle to wrap about them when they lie on the bare ground) then are they shut up in the townhouse, some with blows, some with spurnings, some with boxes on the ear, if presently they go not in.

Now all being gathered together, and the house filled with them, the *juez repartidor*, or officer, calls by the order of the list such and such a Spaniard, and also calls out of the house so many Indians as by the Court are commanded to be given him (some are allowed three, some four, some ten, some fifteen, some twenty, according to their employments) and delivereth unto the Spaniard his Indians, and so to all the rest, till they be all served; who when they receive their Indians, take from them a tool, or their mantles, to secure them that they run not away; and for every Indian delivered unto them, they give unto the *juez repartidor*, or officer, half a real, which is three-pence an Indian for his fees, which mounteth yearly to him to a great deal of money; for some officers make a partition or distribution of four hundred, some of two hundred, some of three hundred Indians every week, and carrieth home with him so many half hundred reals for one, or half a day's work. If complaint be made by any Spaniard that such and such an Indian did run away from him, and served him not the week part, the Indian must be brought, and surely tied to a post by his hands in the marketplace, and there be whipped upon his bare back. But if the poor Indian complain that the Spaniards cozened and cheated him of his shovel, axe, bill, mantle, or wages no justice shall be executed against the cheating Spaniard, neither shall the Indian be righted, though it is true the order runs equally in favor of both Indian and Spaniard. Thus are the poor Indians sold for threepence apiece for a whole week's slavery, not permitted to go home at nights unto their wives, though their work lie not above a mile from the town where they live; nay some are carried ten or twelve miles from their home, who must not return till Saturday night late, and must that week do whatsoever their master pleaseth to command them. The wages appointed them will scarce find them meat and drink, for they are not allowed a real a day, which is but sixpence, and with that they are to find themselves, but for six days' work and diet they are to have five reals, which is half a crown. This same order is observed in the city of Guatemala, and towns of Spaniards, where to every family that wants the service of an Indian or Indians, though it be but to fetch water and wood on their backs, or to go of errands, is allowed the like from the nearest Indian towns.

9. Debt Peonage in Peru

The repartimiento, *known in Peru as the* mita, *could not provide Spanish employers with a dependable and continuing supply of labor. As a result, they turned increasingly to the use of free or contractual wage labor. From the first, however, this so-called free labor was associated with debt servitude. An advance of money or goods required an Indian to work for his employer until his debt was paid, often reducing him and his descendants to the condition of virtual slaves or serfs. Debt peonage became widespread in the seventeenth and eighteenth centuries. The Spanish royal officials Jorge Juan and Antonio de Ulloa offer a precise description of how debt peonage, superimposed on* mita *obligations, operated in the Peruvian province of Quito in the first half of the eighteenth century.*

Jorge Juan and Antonio de Ulloa, *Noticias secretas de América*, 2 vols. (Madrid, 1918), 1:290–292. Excerpt translated by Benjamin Keen.

On farming haciendas, an Indian subject to the *mita* earns from fourteen to eighteen pesos a year, the wage varying with the locality or *corregimiento*. In addition, the *hacendado* assigns him a piece of land, about twenty to thirty rods square in size, to grow his food. In return the Indian must work three hundred days in the year, leaving him sixty-five days of rest for Sundays, other church holidays, illness, or some accident that may prevent him from working. The *mayordomo* of the hacienda keeps careful record of the days worked by the Indian in order to settle accounts with him at the end of the year.

From his wage the master deducts the eight pesos of royal tribute that the Indian must pay; assuming that the Indian earns eighteen pesos, the most he can earn, he is left with ten pesos. From this amount the master deducts two pesos, two *reales* to pay for three rods of coarse cloth, costing six *reales* a rod, from which the Indian makes a cloak to cover his nakedness. He now has seven pesos, six *reales* with which to feed and dress his wife and children, if he has a family, and to pay the church fees demanded by the parish priest. But this is not all; since he cannot raise on his little plot all the food he needs for his family, he must get from the *hacendado* each month a half *fanega* of maize, costing six *reales*, more than double the price if he could buy elsewhere. Six *reales*, times twelve, come to nine pesos, which is one peso, six *reales* more than the Indian has left. Thus the unhappy Indian, after working three hundred days of the year for his master and cultivating his little plot in his free time, and receiving only a coarse cloak and six *fanegas* of maize, is in debt one peso and six *reales*, and must continue to work for his master the following year. . . .

If, to crown his misfortunes, his wife or a child should die, he must somehow find the burial fee demanded by the priest, and so turns to the *hacendado* for another advance. If he is spared the pain of losing a member of his family, the priest demands that he show his gratitude by paying for another church ceremony in honor of the Virgin or some saint, which requires another loan. Thus, at year's end, without money or anything else of value having passed through his hands, the Indian owes his master more than he has earned. The *hacendado* then claims legal control over the Indian and compels him to work for him until the debt is paid. Since it is impossible for the poor Indian to do so, he remains a slave all his life and, contrary to natural law and the law of nations, after his death his sons must continue to work to pay the debt of their father.

10. Dialogue in Yucatán

Some of the early friars in the Indies were saintly and courageous men who preached not only the gospel of Christ but the message of justice to the Indians. Their point of view is well expressed in a dialogue overheard in a Yucatán village by Fr. Tomás de la Torre, one of the Dominican friars who accompanied Las Casas when the great fighter for Indian rights came to southern Mexico as bishop of Chiapas in 1544.

The sun had already set when we came to a clean looking little church, decorated with branches. We were much pleased and greatly heartened, believing that where the signs appeared we were certain to find charity. After saying a prayer we continued on our way as if spellbound, for we knew nothing of these people and did not know how to talk to them. This was our first encounter with the Indians, who certainly could do as they pleased with us without fear of resistance; it was we who were afraid of them.

So we came to a village where many Indians were sitting about. When they saw us they rose and gave us seats, which were small stools, no larger than the distance between the extended thumb and forefinger of one hand. . . . The father vicar said, "Let us stay here this night, for God has prepared this lodging for us." The Indians, seeing how miserable we were, owing to the cold of the lagoon, made a great bonfire, the first that we had needed since leaving Spain. Then the chief came with half a pumpkin shell filled with water; he washed our feet, and they gave us each two tortillas and a piece of fresh fish and another of sweet potato. We ate and felt much better, and were filled with devotion and wonder to see the charity of these Indians, who the Spaniards claimed were so bestial.

At night came Ximénes, who knew their language, and through him we asked them why they had treated us so kindly. They replied that on the road an Indian had seen us and realized that we were thirsty and had told them so, and for that reason they had sent that pumpkin shell of water and accorded us that hospitality, because they knew that we came from Castile for their good. We took great pleasure in the reply of these barbarians.

That night there arrived a peasant who came with the bishop [Las Casas], Zamora by name, and after we had all lain down to sleep, some on boards and others on small mats that the Indians make of rushes . . . Zamora, the recently-arrived peasant from Castile, and Ximénes, an oldtimer in the country and a conqueror of Yucatan, began to talk, and because their conversation was very diverting I shall set down here what I remember of it.

Said Ximénes to Zamora: "You chose a poor place to stable that beast of yours for the night; the Indians will surely take it and eat it."

Said Zamora: "Let them eat it, by God; we Christians owe them a good deal more than that."

Fray Tomás de la Torre, *Desde Salamanca, España hasta Ciudad Real, Chiapas, Diario del viaje, 1544–1545*, ed. Frans Blom (México, 1945), pp. 150–152. Excerpt translated by Benjamin Keen.

Ximénes: "What the devil do you mean by that?"

Zamora: "I mean that you've robbed them of their property and taken their sons from them and made them slaves in their own land."

Ximénes: "They owe us more than that, for we are Christians."

Zamora: "Christians? A Christian is known by his works."

Ximénes: "We are Christians, and we came to this land to make Christians of them."

Zamora: "I'll bet you came over here because your deviltries made Spain too hot a place for you, or else you would not have left your own country. I swear to God that no one comes to the Indies for any other reason, and myself first of all."

Ximénes: "God alone knows why each man came over; but the main thing is that we conquered this country."

Zamora: "And that is why you expect the Indians to give you their food and property—because you murdered them in their own houses! Good friends you proved to be, indeed!"

Ximénes: "You would not say that if you had shed your blood in the war."

Zamora: "I dare say that even if they had killed you they would not go to Hell, because you made war on them."

Ximénes: "They are dogs, and will not believe in God."

Zamora: "And very good preachers they had in you, for certain."

Ximénes: "Surely, Zamora, you will not go back to Castile."

Zamora: "The devil take me if I carry away a cent that I did not earn with my spade; the Indians owe me nothing."

While this dialogue went on the rest of us kept quiet, lying in the dark, but we could hardly keep from laughing at the humor of Zamora's remarks. On the other hand, we were confounded by the clarity and simplicity of the judgments of this illiterate peasant, who said only what his reason dictated. . . .

11. GUAMAN POMA ASSESSES THE CONQUEST

Spanish priests like Las Casas and de la Torre weren't the only ones upset at the cruelty and rapaciousness of the Spanish conquest. In 1615 a Spanish-educated Peruvian Indian named Felipe Guaman Poma de Ayala, who claimed Andean nobility and had some experience as a colonial administrator, addressed an exhaustive and damning 1615 indictment of Spanish excesses to King Philip III. He hoped the king would intervene on behalf of his new Indian subjects, perhaps through the Society of Jesus (Jesuits)—an organization that Guaman Poma considered one of the few redeeming elements of the Spanish conquest. The New Chronicle and Good Government *is an especially important historical source because Guaman Poma had mastered not just the Spanish language (and colonial law) but European iconographic conventions as well. To reinforce his point, Guaman Poma provided copious illustrations for his text, much like a modern photojournalist. To ensure that the king (and his advisers) understood the illustrations, he provided each with a caption. The combination of written denunciation and captioned illustrations make for an impressive and eloquent statement (although there's no evidence that Philip ever saw the* New Chronicle*). The four illustrations that follow depict scenes from before and after the conquest, drawing a sharp contrast between Native American and European societies and styles of governance.*

———————

Felipe Guaman Poma de Ayala, *El primer nueva crónica y buen gobierno*, pp. 252, 308, 503, 507. Reprinted by permission of the Royal Danish Library, Copenhagen. The original manuscript is available at www.kb.dk/elib/mss/poma.

96

Tilling in August

*August / month for breaking land / time of cultivation /
the Inca dance the haylli [dance of tilling].*

Punishment of Adulterers

*Punishment of adulterers / [the bound man is labeled] adulterer, violent /
[the rock-thrower says] "Die, enemy!" / [the bound man replies] "It's my fault, my inca" /
[the judge is named] Quillis Cachi, inca.*

98

CORREGIMIENTO
COREG.º AFRENTA AL
alcalde hordenario por dos guebos que no le da mi tayo.

probincias   como

The Corregidor Insults the Mayor

*Corregidor's district / the corregidor insults the mayor
for two eggs that weren't given him in tribute.*

CORREGIMIENTO
EL COREG, I P, TINIE
manda uelando y mirando la querguen za delas mugeres

Abuses of Women

*Corregidor's district / The Corregidor, priest, and lieutenant
making their rounds and gazing at the shame of the women.*

PART THREE

THE
COLONIAL
POLITICAL
ECONOMY

5

❧

THE COLONIAL ECONOMY

THE ECONOMIC LIFE of the Spanish and Portuguese colonies reflected both New and Old World influences. Side by side with the subsistence and tribute economy of the Indians arose a Hispanic commercial agriculture producing foodstuffs or raw materials for sale in local or distant markets. To some extent this agriculture served internal markets, as in the mining areas of Mexico and Peru, or intercolonial trade, as in the case of the wine industry of Peru. But its dominant trait, which became more pronounced with the passage of time, was production for export to European markets. Spain and Portugal imposed certain restrictions on colonial agriculture in the mercantilist spirit of the age, but this legislation was largely ineffective.

Stock raising was another important economic activity in the colonies. The introduction of domestic animals represented a major Hispanic contribution to American economic life, since in the ancient Americas, aside from a limited region of the Andes, animals were not domesticated for use as food or in transportation. By 1600, the export of hides from Hispaniola to Spain had assumed large proportions, and meat had become so abundant on the island that the flesh of wild cattle was generally left to rot. The export of hides also became important during the seventeenth century in the Plate area (modern Argentina and Uruguay).

Mining, as the principal source of royal revenue, received the special attention and protection of the crown. Silver, rather than gold, was the principal product of the American mines. The great mine of Potosí in Upper Peru was discovered in 1545; the rich mines of Zacatecas and Guanajuato in New Spain were opened in 1548 and 1558 respectively. Silver mining was greatly stimulated in 1556, when the patio process for separating silver from the ore with quicksilver was introduced. As in other times and places, the mining industry brought prosperity to a few, and either failure or small success to the great majority.

The Spanish found a flourishing handicrafts industry in the advanced culture in Mexico, Central America, and Peru. Throughout the colonial period the majority of the natives continued to supply their own needs for pottery, clothing, and other household requirements. With the coming of the Spanish, new manufacturing industries arose in the towns, stimulated by the high prices of imported goods. The artisans were organized in guilds (although Indians were not allowed to be guild masters), which included silversmiths, goldbeaters, and weavers.

The period up to 1700 also witnessed a remarkable growth of factory-type establishments (*obrajes*) that produced cheap cotton and woolen goods for popular consumption. A number of towns in New Spain (Puebla, Guadalajara, Cholula, and others) were centers of the textile industry. Other factory-type establishments produced soap, chinaware, leather, and other products. Internal and intercolonial trade, based on regional specialization and particularly on the rise of mining centers that consumed large quantities of agricultural produce and manufacturers, steadily increased in the sixteenth and seventeenth centuries.

Sugar production, mostly for European markets, dominated the Brazilian colonial economy for over a century. The second half of the seventeenth century, however, saw a crisis in the Brazilian sugar industry, which faced severe competition from Dutch, English, and French sugar colonies in the West Indies. As the first economic cycle of colonial Brazil drew to a close, a second opened with the discovery of gold and diamonds in the regions of Minas Gerais, Goiás, and Mato Grosso, lying west and south of Baía and Pernambuco. But the quantities of gold and diamonds were limited, and production declined sharply after 1760.

As the interior provinces of Minas Gerais and Goiás sank into decay, the northeast enjoyed a revival based on the increasing European demand for sugar, cotton, and other semitropical products. Between 1750 and 1800 Brazilian cotton production made large strides but declined in the face of competition from the more efficient cotton growers of the United States. The beginnings of the coffee industry, the future giant of the Brazilian economy, also date from the late colonial period.

Until the decree of January 28, 1808, which opened the ports of Brazil to the trade of all nations, the commerce of the colony was restricted to Portuguese nationals and ships. A significant exception was made in the case of Great Britain, Portugal's protector and ally. By the Treaty of 1654, British merchants were permitted to trade between Portuguese and Brazilian ports. English ships frequently neglected the formality of touching at Lisbon and plied a direct contraband commerce with the colony. The 1808 decree of free trade confirmed Great Britain's actual domination of Brazilian commerce.

1. THE INDIAN AGRICULTURAL HERITAGE

Indians made important contributions to colonial and world agriculture, including maize, the white potato and sweet potato, pineapple, peanut, cultivated strawberry, lima and kidney beans, squash and pumpkin, cacao, rubber, and tobacco. To Europeans, some of the new American plants appeared to have strange and possibly supernatural qualities. The learned Jesuit José de Acosta (1539?–1600) sought to satisfy Spanish curiosity about the natural products of the New World in his scientific and historical work, the Natural and Moral History of the Indies *(1590). Among the plants Fr. Acosta described are maize, the Indian staff of life; cacao, source of the refreshing chocolate drink first used by the Maya; coca, the magic plant that imparted endurance to the weary frame of the Peruvian Indian; and* maguey, *the Mexican tree of wonders.*

Turning to plants, I shall speak first of those which are more peculiar to the Indies and afterwards of those which are common both to those lands and to Europe. And because plants were created principally for the maintenance of man, and man sustains himself above all by bread, I should speak first of their bread. . . . The Indians have their own words to signify bread, which in Peru is called *tanta* and in other parts is given other names. But the quality and substance of the bread the Indians use is very different from ours, for they have no kind of wheat, barley, millet, panic grass, or any grain such as is used in Europe to make bread. Instead they have other kinds of grains and roots, among which maize, called Indian wheat in Castile and Turkey grain in Italy, holds the first place.

And just as wheat is the grain most commonly used by man in the regions of the Old World, which are Europe, Asia, and Africa, so in the New World the most widely used grain is maize, which is found in almost all the kingdoms of the West Indies; in Peru, New Spain, the New Kingdom of Granada, Guatemala, Chile, and in all the Tierra Firme. In the Windward Isles, which are Cuba, Hispaniola, Jamaica, Puerto Rico, it does not seem to have been used in earlier times; to this day they prefer to use yucca and cassava, of which more later. I do not think that maize is at all inferior to our wheat in strength and nourishment; but it is stouter and hotter and engenders more blood, so that if people who are not accustomed to it eat it in excess they swell up and get the itch.

Maize grows on canes or reeds; each one bears one or two ears, to which the grains are fastened, and though the grains are big they hold a large number of them, and some contain seven hundred grains. The seeds are planted

José de Acosta, *Historia natural y moral de las Indias* (México, 1940), pp. 265–266, 285–289. Excerpt translated by Benjamin Keen.

one by one. Maize likes a hot and humid soil. It grows in many parts of the Indies in great abundance; a yield of three hundred *fanegas* from a sowing is not uncommon. There are various kinds of maize, as of wheat; one is large and nourishing; another, called *moroche*, is small and dry. The leaves of the maize and the green cane are a choice fodder for their beasts of burden, and when dry are also used as straw. The grain gives more nourishment to horses than barley, and therefore it is customary in those countries to water their horses before giving them maize to eat, for if they drank after feeding they would swell up and have gripes, as they do when they eat wheat.

Maize is the Indian bread, and they commonly eat it boiled in the grain, hot, when it is called *mote* . . . sometimes they eat it toasted. There is a large and round maize, like that of the Lucanas, which the Spaniards eat as a delicacy; it has better flavor than toasted chickpeas. There is another and more pleasing way of preparing it, which consists in grinding the maize and making the flour into pancakes, which are put on the fire and later placed on the table and eaten piping hot; in some places they call them *arepas.* . . .

Maize is used by the Indians to make not only their bread but also their wine; from it they make beverages which produce drunkenness more quickly than wine made of grapes. They make this maize wine in various ways, calling it *azua* in Peru and more generally throughout the Indies *chicha*. The strongest sort is made like beer, steeping the grains of maize until they begin to break, after which they boil the juice in a certain way, which makes it so strong that a few drinks will produce intoxication. In Peru, where it is called *sora*, its use is forbidden by law because of the terrific drinking it occasions. But the law is little observed, for they use it anyway, and stay up whole days and nights, dancing and drinking. . . .

The cacao tree is most esteemed in Mexico and coca is favored in Peru; both trees are surrounded with considerable superstition. Cacao is a bean smaller and fattier than the almond, and when roasted has not a bad flavor. It is so much esteemed by the Indians, and even by the Spaniards, that it is the object of one of the richest and largest lines of trade of New Spain; since it is a dry fruit, and one that keeps a long time without spoiling, they send whole ships loaded with it from the province of Guatemala. Last year an English corsair burned in the port of Guatulco, in New Spain, more than one hundred thousand *cargas* of cacao. They also use it as money, for five cacao beans will buy one thing, thirty another, and one hundred still another, and no objections are made to its use. They also use it as alms to give to the poor.

The chief use of this cacao is to make a drink that they call chocolate, which they greatly cherish in that country. But those who have not formed a taste for it dislike it, for it has a froth at the top and an effervescence like that formed in wine by dregs, so that one must really have great faith in it to tolerate it. In fine, it is the favorite drink of Indians and Spaniards alike, and they regale visitors to their country with it; the Spanish women of that land are particularly fond of the dark chocolate. They prepare it in various ways: hot, cold, and lukewarm. They usually put spices and much chili in it; they also make a paste of it, and they say that it is good for the chest and the stomach, and also for colds. Be that as it may, those who have not formed a taste for it do not like it.

The tree on which this fruit grows is of middling size and well-made, with a beautiful top; it is so delicate that to protect it from the burning rays of the sun they plant near it another large tree, which serves only to shade it; this is called the mother of the cacao. There are cacao plantations where it is raised as are the vine and the olive in Spain. The province of Guatemala is where they carry on the greatest commerce in this fruit.

The cacao does not grow in Peru; instead they have the coca, which is surrounded with even greater superstition and really seems fabulous. In Potosí alone the commerce in coca amounts to more than 5,000,000 pesos, with a consumption of from 90 to 100,000 hampers, and in the year 1583 it was 100,000. . . . This coca that they so greatly cherish is a little green leaf which grows upon shrubs about one *estado* high; it grows in very warm and humid lands and produces this leaf, which they call *trasmitas*, every four months. Being a very delicate plant, it requires a great deal of attention during cultivation and even more after it has been picked. They pack it with great care in long, narrow hampers and load it on the sheep of that country, which carry this merchandise in droves, bearing one, two, and three thousand hampers. It is commonly brought from the Andes, from valleys of insufferable heat, where it rains the greater part of the year, and it costs the Indians much labor and takes many lives, for they must leave their highlands and cold climates in order to cultivate it and carry it away. Hence there have been great disputes among lawyers and wise men about whether the coca plantations should be done away with or no—but there they still are.

The Indians prize it beyond measure, and in the time of the Inca kings plebeians were forbidden to use coca without the permission of the Inca or his governor. Their custom is to hold it in their mouths, chewing and sucking it; they do not swallow it; they say that it gives them great strength and is a great comfort to them. Many serious men say that this is pure superstition and imagination. To tell the truth, I do not think so; I believe that it really does lend strength and endurance to the Indians, for one sees effects that cannot be attributed to imagination, such as their ability to journey two whole days on a handful of coca, eating nothing else, and similar feats. . . . All would be well, except that its cultivation and commerce endanger and occupy so many people. . . .

The *maguey* is the tree of wonders, to which the newly-come Spaniards, or *chapetones* (as they call them in the Indies), attribute miracles, saying that it yields water and wine, oil and vinegar, honey, syrup, thread, needles, and a thousand other things. The Indians of New Spain value it greatly, and they commonly have one or several of these trees near their homes to supply their needs. It grows in the fields, and there they cultivate it. Its leaves are wide and thick, with strong, sharp points which they use as fastening pins or sewing needles; they also draw a certain fiber or thread from the leaves.

They cut through the thick trunk when it is tender; there is a large cavity inside, where the sap rises from the roots; it is a liquor which they drink like water, since it is fresh and sweet. When this liquor is boiled it turns into a kind of wine, and if it is left to sour it becomes vinegar. But when boiled for a longer time it becomes like honey, and cooked half as long it turns into a healthful syrup of good flavor, superior in my judgment to syrup made of grapes. Thus they boil different substances from this sap, which they obtain in great quantity, for at a certain season they extract several *azumbres* a day.

2. Spain's Contributions to New World Agriculture

The colonial era saw a notable exchange of agricultural gifts between Old and New Worlds. The Spanish crown displayed much solicitude for the agricultural development of the Indies and paid particular attention to the shipping of trees, plants, seeds, and agricultural implements of all kinds. Fr. Acosta gives an account of the transit of Spanish plants to America and of the rapid rise there of a commercial agriculture producing wine, wheat, sugar, and other products.

The Indies have been better repaid in the matter of plants than in any other kind of merchandise; for those few that have been carried from the Indies into Spain do badly there, whereas the many that have come over from Spain prosper in their new homes. I do not know whether to attribute this to the excellence of the plants that go from here or to the bounty of the soil over there. Nearly every good thing grown in Spain is found there; in some regions they do better than in others. They include wheat, barley, garden produce and greens and vegetables of all kinds, such as lettuce, cabbage, radishes, onions, garlic, parsley, turnips, carrots, eggplants, endive, salt-wort, spinach, chickpeas, beans, and lentils—in short, whatever grows well here, for those who have gone to the Indies have been careful to take with them seeds of every description. . . .

The trees that have fared best there are the orange, lemon, citron, and others of that sort. In some parts there are already whole forests and groves of orange trees. Marveling at this, I asked on a certain island who had planted

Acosta, *Historia natural y moral de las Indias*, pp. 311–315. Excerpt translated by Benjamin Keen.

so many orange trees in the fields. To which they replied that it might have happened that some oranges fell to the ground and rotted, whereupon the seeds germinated, and, some being borne by the waters to different parts, gave rise to these dense groves. This seemed a likely reason. I said before that orange trees have generally done well in the Indies, for nowhere have I found a place where oranges were not to be found; this is because everywhere in the Indies the soil is hot and humid, which is what this tree most needs. It does not grow in the highlands; oranges are transported there from the valleys or the coast. The orange preserve which is made in the islands is the best I have ever seen, here or there.

Peaches and apricots also have done well, although the latter have fared better in New Spain. . . . Apples and pears are grown, but in moderate yields; plums give sparingly; figs are abundant, chiefly in Peru. Quinces are found everywhere, and in New Spain they are so plentiful that we received fifty choice ones for half a real. Pomegranates are found in abundance, but they are all sweet, for the people do not like the sharp variety. The melons are very good in some regions, as in Tierra Firme and Peru. Cherries, both wild and cultivated, have not so far prospered in the Indies. . . . In conclusion, I find that hardly any of the finer fruits is lacking in those parts. As for nuts, they have no acorns or chestnuts, nor, as far as I know, have any been grown over there until now. Almonds grow there, but sparingly. Almonds, walnuts, and filberts are shipped there from Spain for the tables of epicures. I have not seen any medlars or services, but those do not matter. . . .

By profitable plants I mean those plants which not only yield fruit but bring money to their owners. The most important of these is the vine, which gives wine, vinegar, grapes, raisins, verjuice, and syrup—but the wine is the chief concern. Wine and grapes are not products of the islands or of Tierra Firme; in New Spain there are vines which bear grapes but do not yield wine. The reason must be that the grapes do not ripen completely because of the rains which come in July and August and hinder their ripening; they are good only for eating. Wine is shipped from Spain and the Canary Islands to all parts of the Indies, except Peru and Chile, where they have vineyards and make very good wine. This industry is expanding continually, not only because of the goodness of the soil, but because they have a better knowledge of winemaking.

The vineyards of Peru are commonly found in warm valleys where they have water channels; they are watered by hand, because rain never falls in the coastal plains, and the rains in the mountains do not come at the proper time. . . . The vineyards have increased so far that because of them the tithes of the churches are now five and six times what they were twenty years ago. The valleys most fertile in vines are Victor, near Arequipa; Yca, hard by Lima; and Caracaro, close to Chuquiavo. The wine that is made there is shipped to Potosí and Cuzco and various other parts, and it is sold in great quantities, because since it is produced so abundantly it sells at five or six ducats the jug, or arroba, whereas Spanish wine (which always arrives with the fleets) sells for ten and twelve. . . . The wine trade is no small affair, but does not exceed the limits of the province.

The silk which is made in New Spain goes to other provinces—to Peru, for example. There was no silk industry before the Spaniards came; the mulberry trees were brought from Spain, and they grow well, especially in the province called Misteca, where they raise silkworms and make good taffetas; they do not yet make damasks, satins, or velvets, however.

The sugar industry is even wider in scope, for the sugar not only is consumed in the Indies but is shipped in quantity to Spain. Sugar cane grows remarkably well in various parts of the Indies. In the islands, in Mexico, in Peru, and elsewhere they have built sugar mills that do a large business. I was told that the Nasca [Peru] sugar mill earned more than thirty thousand pesos a year. The mill at Chicama, near Trujillo [Peru], was also a big enterprise, and those of New Spain are no smaller, for the consumption of sugar and preserves in the Indies is simply fantastic. From the island of Santo Domingo, in the fleet in which I came, they brought eight hundred and ninety-eight chests and boxes of sugar. I happened to see the sugar loaded at the port of Puerto Rico, and it seemed to me that each box must contain eight arrobas. The sugar industry is the principal business of those islands—such a taste have men developed for sweets!

Olives and olive trees are also found in the Indies, in Mexico, and in Peru, but up to now they have not set up any mills to make olive oil. Actually, it is not made at all, for they prefer to eat the olives, seasoning them well. They find it unprofitable to make olive oil, and so all their oil comes from Spain.

3. THE POTOSÍ MINE

Spain's proudest possession in the New World was the great silver mine of Potosí in Upper Peru (present-day Bolivia), whose flow of treasure attained gigantic proportions between 1579 and 1635. More than any other colonial resource, the fantastic wealth of Potosí captivated the Spanish imagination. The following selection gives some account of this wealth and of mining practices in the late sixteenth century.

It appears from the royal accounts of the House of Trade of Potosí, and it is affirmed by venerable and trustworthy men, that during the time of the government of the licentiate Polo, which was many years after the discovery of the hill, silver was registered every Saturday to the value of 150 to 200,000 pesos, of which the King's fifth (*quinto*) came to 30 to 40,000 pesos, making a

Acosta, *Historia natural y moral de las Indias*, pp. 238–243. Excerpt translated by Benjamin Keen.

yearly total of about 1,500,000 pesos. According to this calculation, the value of the daily output of the mine was 30,000 pesos, of which the King's share amounted to 6,000 pesos. One more thing should be noted in estimating the wealth of Potosí; namely, that accounts have been kept of only the silver that was marked and taxed. But it is well known in Peru that for a long time the people of that country used the silver called "current," which was neither marked nor taxed. And those who know the mines well conclude that at that time the bulk of the silver mined at Potosí paid no tax, and that this included all the silver in circulation among the Indians, and much of that in use among the Spaniards, as I could observe during my stay in that country. This leads me to believe that a third—if not one half—of the silver production of Potosí was neither registered nor taxed. . . . [It should also be noted that] although the mines of Potosí have been dug to a depth of two hundred *estados*, the miners have never encountered water, which is the greatest possible obstacle to profitable operations, whereas the mines of Porco, so rich in silver ore, have been abandoned because of the great quantity of water. For there are two intolerable burdens connected with the search for silver: the labor of digging and breaking the rock, and that of getting out the water—and the first of these is more than enough. In fine, at the present time His Catholic Majesty receives on the average a million pesos a year from his fifth of the silver of Potosí, not counting the considerable revenue he derives from quicksilver and other royal perquisites. . . .

The hill of Potosí contains four principal veins: the Rich vein, that of Centeno, the vein called "of Tin," and that of Mendieta. All these veins are in the eastern part of the hill, as if facing the sunrise; there is no vein to the west. These veins run from north to south, or from pole to pole. They measure six feet at their greatest width, and a *palmo* at the narrowest point. From these veins issue others, as smaller branches grow out of the arms of trees. Each vein has different mines that have been claimed and divided among different owners, whose names they usually bear. The largest mine is eighty yards in size, the legal maximum; the smallest is four yards. By now all these mines are very deep. In the Rich vein there are seventy-eight mines; they are as deep as one hundred and eighty and even two hundred *estados* in some places. In the Centeno vein there are twenty-four mines. Such are as much as sixty and even eighty *estados* deep, and the same is true of the other veins and mines of that hill. In order to work the mines at such great depths, tunnels (*socavones*) were devised; these are caves, made at the foot of the mountain, that cross it until they meet the veins. Although the veins run north to south, they descend from the top to the foot of the mountain—a distance calculated at more than 1200 *estados*. And by this calculation, although the mines run so deep it is six times as far again to their root and bottom, which some believe must be extremely rich, being the trunk and source of all the veins. But so far experience has proven the contrary, for the higher the vein the richer it is, and the deeper it runs the poorer the yield. Be that as it may, in order to work the mines with less cost, labor, and risk, they invented the tunnels, by means of which they can easily enter and leave the mines. They are eight feet wide and one *estado* high, and are closed off with doors. With the aid of these tunnels they get out the silver ore without difficulty, paying the owner of the tunnel a fifth of all the metal that is obtained. Nine tunnels have already been made, and others are being dug. A tunnel called "of the Poison" (*del Veneno*), which enters the Rich vein, was twenty-nine years in the making, for it was begun in 1556 (eleven years after the discovery of those mines) and was completed on April 11, 1585. This tunnel crossed the vein at a point thirty-five *estados* from its root or source, and from there to the mouth of the mine was 135 *estados*; such was the depth of that they had to descend to work those mines. This tunnel (called the *Crucero*) is 250 yards in length, and its construction took twenty-nine years; this shows how much effort men will make to get silver from the bowels of the earth. They labor there in perpetual darkness, not knowing day from night; and since the sun never penetrates these places, they are not only always dark but very cold, and the air is very thick and alien to the nature of men. And that is why those who enter there for the first time get seasick, as it were, being seized with nausea and stomach cramps, as I was. The miners always carry candles, and they divide their labor so that some work by day and rest by night and others work at night and rest during the day. The silver ore is generally of a flinty hardness, and they break it up with bars. Then they carry the ore on their backs up ladders made of three cords of twisted cowhide, joined by pieces of wood that serve as rungs, so that one man can climb up and another come down at the same time. These ladders are ten *estados* long, and at the top and bottom of each there is a wooden platform where the men may rest, because there are so many ladders to climb. Each man usually carries on his back a load of two arrobas of silver ore tied in a cloth, knapsack fashion; thus they ascend, three at a time. The one who goes first carries a candle tied to his thumb, because, as I mentioned, they receive no light from above; thus, holding with both hands, they climb that great distance, often more than 150 *estados*—a fearful thing, the mere thought of which inspires dread. So great is the love of silver, which men suffer such great pains to obtain.

4. THE COLONIAL FACTORY

The Mexican city of Puebla was a leading industrial center in the colonial period, with numerous workshops (obrajes) *producing cotton, woolen, and silk cloth, hats, chinaware, and glass. The Englishman Thomas Gage, who visited Puebla not many*

Antonio Vásquez de Espinosa, *Compendio y descripción de las Indias Occidentales*, 2 vols. (1636), 1:218–220. Excerpt translated by the editors.

years after the visit described below, observed that "the cloth which is made in it . . . is
sent far and near, and [is] judged now to be as good as the cloth of Segovia, which is the
best that is made in Spain."

This city [Puebla] has great workshops in which they weave a quantity of
fine cotton cloth, wool frieze, and ribbed silk from which they make a handsome profit because this business is common in these parts. And although the
workshop owners are compassionate Christians, in order to supply their
workshops with people to make the cloth and ribbed silk, they have persons
hired and paid to deceive poor innocents. When they see some Indian from
out of town, they lure him to the workshop with tricks or on some pretext
like hiring him as a porter and paying him to carry something. When he enters inside the workshop they spring the trap, and the poor soul never again
leaves that jail until he dies and is taken away to be buried. In this way they
have seized and deceived many an Indian, married with children, forgotten
for twenty years or more and for all his life, without his wife or his children
knowing where he is, because even though he might want to leave, he cannot,
since the city gates are well guarded by watchmen. These Indians are kept
busy with carding, spinning, weaving and the other tasks associated with the
making of cloth and ribbed silk. And the owners make their profits by these
unjust and illicit means.

The Royal Council of the Indies, with holy zeal in the service of Our Lord
God, His Majesty, and for the good of the Indians, has tried to remedy the situation through the warrants and ordinances that were sent and continue to be
sent for the proper administration of the Indians and for their relief from this
great burden and enslavement. And the Viceroy of New Spain [Mexico] has
appointed inspectors to visit the workshops and remedy such things. But since
most of those charged with these duties are concerned more with their own
betterment than with helping the Indians—although it might weigh on their
consciences—and since the workshop owners pay them well, the miserable Indians are left in the same slavery. And if some inspectors are carried away by a
holy zeal to remedy these abuses when they go to inspect the workshops, the
owners hold the workers in some previously designated area, where they hide
the Indians against their will so that they are not seen, or found, or able to
voice their complaints. This is so common in all the workshops of this city and
jurisdiction, and that of Mexico City, and those that build and run the workshops do so without scruples—as if it were not a grave mortal sin.

5. ON THE SEA-ROAD TO THE INDIES

Throughout the sixteenth century, men and goods were carried to the colonies in tiny
vessels similar to those in which Columbus made his memorable discovery. Danger and

hardship attended the long voyage to the Indies from the time a ship left Seville to thread its way down the shoal-ridden Guadalquivir to the Mediterranean. Fr. Tomás de la Torre, one of a number of Dominican friars who accompanied Bishop Bartolomé de las Casas when the Protector of the Indians came to Mexico in 1544, describes the trials of an Atlantic crossing in the days of the galleons.

After boarding our ship we passed the day there, exposed to a burning sun. On the following day (July 10) we hoisted sails with a very feeble wind, because the sailors said that once on the high seas we could navigate with any kind of wind. That day all the other ships got off that difficult and dangerous sandbar at San Lucar. Only ours remained in the middle of the bar and its dangers. They put the blame on the land pilot; but it was really the fault of our sailors, who had ballasted the ship badly, loading all the cargo above deck. That day the fleet moved three leagues out, while we remained on the bar in front of the town, enduring miseries that made a good beginning to our labors and perils.

When the townspeople saw that the ship remained there they thought that something had happened, and the Duke [of Alba] sent a boat to express the regrets of himself and his lady, and to say that if boats were needed to get the ship off the bar he would send them. But the crazy sailors, very haughty about all that concerned their business, wanted no help. The captain of the fleet sent a small vessel to let us know that he would wait for us only a day or two. . . . The pilot and master of the ship, named Pedro de Ibarra, went to give an account of himself and to complain of the land pilot, who, in accordance with prevailing custom, is supposed to take the ships off the bar. . . .

The following day, which was Friday, July 11, we raised sails and with perfectly dry eyes lost sight of our Spain. The wind was good but weak. The sea quickly gave us to understand that it was not meant to be the habitation of men, and we all became so deathly sick that nothing in the world could move us from where we lay. Only the Father Vicar and three others managed to keep their feet, but these three were so ill that they could do nothing for us; the Father Vicar alone served us all, placing basins and bowls before us so that we could bring up our scanty meals, which did us no good at all. There were four or five neophytes in our company, on their way to serve God in the Indies, who usually took care of us, but they also became sick and had to be nursed themselves. We could not swallow a mouthful of food, although we were quite faint, but our thirst was intense.

One could not imagine a dirtier hospital, or one that resounded with more lamentations, than ours. Some men went below deck, where they were cooked

Fray Tomás de la Torre, *Desde Salamanca, España, hasta Ciudad Real, Chiapas, Diario del viaje, 1544–1545*, ed. Frans Blom (México, 1945), pp. 70–73. Excerpt translated by Benjamin Keen.

alive; others roasted in the sun on deck, where they lay about, trampled upon, humiliated, and indescribably filthy; and although after several days some of them had recovered, they were not well enough to serve those who were still sick. His Lordship the Bishop donated his own hens to the sick, for we had not brought any, and a priest who was going as a schoolteacher to Chiapa helped the Father Vicar. . . . We were a pitiful sight indeed, and there was no one to console us, since nearly everyone was in the same condition.

When we left Spain the war with France was at its height, so we departed in great fear of the enemy. On the afternoon of that day those who could raise their heads saw sixteen sails. They feared that they were Frenchmen, and all that night the fleet was much alarmed, although the enemy had greater reason to fear us, because of our superior numbers. But in the morning nothing could be seen, so we decided it was a fleet coming from the Indies. . . . In the evening our stomachs quieted down and we did not vomit, but the heat, especially below deck, was intolerable.

Saturday morning we saw a large boat, and, thinking that it was a French spy, a ship went after it. The bark began to escape, when the ship fired a shot, whereupon the bark lowered its sails, was recognized as Spanish, and was permitted to go in peace. The crews of the vessels that heard the shot thought that we had run into Frenchmen and that the ships were firing at each other. When we below deck heard the noise of arms being got ready, we were alarmed and suddenly recovered enough to say a litany; some even confessed themselves. Others made a joke of the whole affair. When we learned it was nothing at all, we returned to our former supine misery. After this there was no more disturbance.

So that those who do not know the sea may understand the suffering one endures there, especially at the beginning of a voyage, I shall describe some things that are well known to anyone who has sailed on it. First, a ship is a secure prison, from which no one may escape, even though he wears neither shackles nor irons; so cruel is this prison that it makes no distinctions among its inmates but makes them all suffer alike. The heat, the stuffiness, and the sense of confinement are sometimes overpowering. The bed is ordinarily the floor. Some bring a few small mattresses; ours were very poor, small, and hard, stuffed with dog hairs; to cover us we had some extremely poor blankets of goat's wool. Add to this the general nausea and poor health; most passengers go about as if out of their minds and in great torment—some longer than others, and a few for the entire voyage. There is very little desire to eat, and sweet things do not go down well; there is an incredible thirst, sharpened by a diet of hardtack and salt beef. The water ration is half an *azumbre* daily; if you want wine you must bring your own. There are infinite numbers of lice, which eat men alive, and you cannot wash clothing because the sea water shrinks it. There is an evil stink, especially below deck, that becomes intolerable throughout the ship when the pump is working—and it is going more or less constantly, depending on how the ship sails. On a good day the pump runs four or five times, to drain the foul-smelling bilge water.

These and other hardships are common on board ship, but we felt them more because they were so foreign to our usual way of living. Furthermore, even when you are enjoying good health there is no place where you can study or withdraw for a little while, and you have to sit all the time, because there is no room to walk about.... The most disturbing thing of all is to have death constantly staring you in the face; you are separated from it by only the thickness of one board joined to another with pitch.

6. THE GREAT FAIR AT PORTOBELLO

After 1584, the chief port of entry for legal commerce with South America was the little town of Portobello on the Isthmus of Panama. For a few weeks during the year a brisk trade, strictly supervised by royal officials, was plied in the town square. In the 1730s, when the Portobello fair was visited by two youthful Spanish scientists and naval officers, Jorge Juan (1713–1773) and Antonio de Ulloa (1716–1795), it had long passed its heyday, principally because of the growing influx of foreign interlopers into colonial trade. But it still presented a scene of considerable business activity.

The town of Porto Bello, so thinly inhabited, by reason of its noxious air, the scarcity of provisions, and the soil, becomes, at the time of the galleons, one of the most populous places in all South America. Its situation on the isthmus betwixt the south and north sea, the goodness of its harbor, and its small distance from Panama, have given it the preference for the rendezvous of the joint commerce of Spain and Peru, at its fair.

On advice being received at Carthagena that the Peru fleet had unloaded at Panama, the galleons make the best of their way to Porto Bello, in order to avoid the distempers which have their source from idleness. The concourse of people, on this occasion, is such, as to raise the rent of lodging to an excessive degree; a middling chamber, with a closet, lets, during the fair, for a thousand crowns, and some large houses for four, five, or six thousand.

The ships are no sooner moored in the harbor, than the first work is, to erect, in the square, a tent made of the ship's sails, for receiving its cargo; at which the proprietors of the goods are present, in order to find their bales, by the marks which distinguish them. These bales are drawn on sledges, to their respective places by the crew of every ship, and the money given them is proportionally divided.

Jorge Juan and Antonio de Ulloa, *A Voyage to South America*, 2 vols. (London, 1772), 1:103–105.

Whilst the seamen and European traders are thus employed, the land is covered with droves of mules from Panama, each drove consisting of above an hundred, loaded with chests of gold and silver, on account of the merchants of Peru. Some unload them at the exchange, others in the middle of the square; yet, amidst the hurry and confusion of such crowds, no theft, loss, or disturbance, is ever known. He who has seen this place during the *tiempo muerto*, or dead time, solitary, poor, and a perpetual silence reigning everywhere; the harbor quite empty, and every place wearing a melancholy aspect; must be filled with astonishment at the sudden change, to see the bustling multitudes, every house crowded, the square and streets encumbered with bales and chests of gold and silver of all kinds; the harbor full of ships and vessels, some bringing by the way of Rio de Chape the goods of Peru, as cacao, *quinquina*, or Jesuit's bark, Vicuña wool, and bezoar stones; others coming from Carthagena, loaded with provisions; and thus a spot, at all other times detested for its deleterious qualities, becomes the staple of the riches of the old and new world, and the scene of one of the most considerable branches of commerce in the whole earth.

The ships being unloaded, and the merchants of Peru, together with the president of Panama, arrived, the fair comes under deliberation. And for this purpose the deputies of the several parties repair on board the commodore of the galleons, where, in presence of the commodore, and the president of Panama; the former, as patron of the Europeans, and the latter, of the Peruvians; the prices of the several kinds of merchandizes are settled; and all preliminaries being adjusted in three or four meetings, the contracts are signed, and made public, that every one may conform himself to them in the sale of his effects. Thus all fraud is precluded. The purchases and sales, as likewise the exchanges of money, are transacted by brokers, both from Spain and Peru. After this, every one begins to dispose of his goods; the Spanish brokers embarking their chests of money, and those of Peru sending away the goods they have purchased, in vessels called *chatas* and *bongos*, up the river Chagre. And thus the fair of Porto Bello ends.

Formerly this fair was limited to no particular time; but as a long stay, in such a sickly place, extremely affected the health of the traders, his Catholic majesty transmitted an order, that the fair should not last above forty days, reckoning from that in which the ships came to an anchor in the harbor; and that, if in this space of time the merchants could not agree in their rates, those of Spain should be allowed to carry their goods up the country to Peru; and accordingly the commodore of the galleons has orders to reimbark them, and return to Carthagena; but otherwise, by virtue of a compact between the merchants of both kingdoms, and ratified by the king, no Spanish trader is to send his goods, on his own account, beyond Porto Bello: and, on the contrary, those of Peru cannot send remittances to Spain, for purchasing goods there.

7. A FOREIGN VIEW OF THE
SPANISH COMMERCIAL SYSTEM

As the eighteenth century opened, thoughtful Spaniards and foreign observers alike could see that the Spanish commercial policy in the colonies was a dismal failure in terms of Spain's general interests. The English propagandist John Campbell shrewdly analyzed the reasons for this failure.

There is nothing more common than to hear Spain compared to a sieve, which, whatever it receives is never the fuller. How common soever the comparison may be, most certainly it is a very true one; but the means by which all this immense wealth, or at least the far greatest part of it is drawn from the Spaniards, and conveyed to other nations, and in what proportions, is neither so well, nor so generally understood. To account for this shall be our present task. . . .

If after the discovery of the New World, as the Spaniards justly enough called it, the government had encouraged trade or manufactures, there is great probability that the supreme direction of the affairs of Europe would have fallen into the hands of the Catholic Kings. For, if all the subjects of Spain, without restraint, had traded to these far distant regions, this must have created such a maritime force, as no other nation could have withstood. Or, supposing the trade had been restrained as it is at present, yet, if manufactures had been encouraged, so as that the greatest part of the trade of the West Indies had been driven without having recourse to foreigners, such prodigious sums of money must have rested in Spain, as would have enabled its monarchs to have given law to all their neighbors. But, by neglecting these obvious, and yet certain rules for establishing solid and extensive at least, if not universal dominion, her kings had recourse to those refinements in policy, which, however excellent they may seem in theory, have never yet been found to answer in practice. They were for fixing their commerce by constraint, and for establishing power by the sword; the first, experience has shown to be impracticable, and the latter, perhaps was the only method whereby they could have missed that end they used it to obtain. In short, by repeated endeavors to secure the wealth of the Indies to Spain absolutely, they scattered it throughout Europe, and by openly grasping at universal monarchy, they alarmed those they might have subdued; so that in process of time, some of those they intended for slaves became their equals and allies, and some their masters.

Yet the princes that took these steps were not either rash and hasty, or voluptuous and profuse, but, on the contrary, were esteemed by all the world

John Campbell, *The Spanish Empire in America* (London, 1747), pp. 291–299.

the wisest monarchs of their respective times, and, in many things deserved to be so esteemed. They erred, not through want of capacity, or want of application, as their successors did, but for want of considering things in a right light, occasioned purely by their fixing their eyes on that dazzling meteor, universal empire. . . .

From what has been said it is evident, that however wise, however penetrating these princes might be, they certainly overshot themselves in their schemes concerning the Western Indies. Instead of looking upon it as an estate, they seemed to think it only a farm, of which they were to make presently the most they could. In doing this, it must be owned, they acted with skill and vigor, for they drew immense sums from thence, which they wasted in Europe to disturb others, and in the end to destroy their own state. Mr. Lewis Roberts, author of the *Map of Commerce*, an excellent book for the time in which it was written, tells us, that it appeared by the records in the custom-house of Seville, that in the space of seventy-four years, computing backwards from the time in which he wrote, the kings of Spain had drawn into that country from America, two hundred and fifty millions of gold, which make about ninety-one millions sterling. He also observes that . . . Philip II . . . spent more in his reign than all his predecessors in the whole of their respective reigns; though no less than 62 kings had reigned before him. Yet this cunning, this ambitious monarch left his subjects in a manner quite exhausted, and, by establishing a most pernicious system of politics, left the total ruining of his dominions by way of legacy to his successors, a point which with wonderful obstinacy they have pursued ever since.

All who are in any degree acquainted with the history of Europe know, that for a long course of years Spain maintained wars in Flanders, Germany, Italy, and sometimes in Ireland, which created a prodigious expense of treasure and of troops; neither of which from the death of Charles V they were in any condition to spare. As families were reduced by the expense of serving in the army, they were inclined to seek new fortunes in the West Indies: and thus numbers went over thither, not to cultivate the country, or to improve trade, but to strip and plunder those who were there before them. Other great families again concurred with the measures of the crown, in hopes of vice-royalties, and other valuable offices in its conquests: but if ever their schemes were beneficial to their families, which may admit of doubt, certain it is that they contributed more and more to the ruin of the Spanish nation. For, though his Catholic Majesty once possessed Naples, Sicily, Sardinia, Milan, with other territories in Italy, besides all the Low Countries, and some other provinces which are now lost; yet, for want of attending to commerce, and by having no sort of economy, all this turned to his prejudice; and it plainly appeared towards the close of the last century, that with all their boasted sagacity and firmness, the Spaniards had ruined themselves by acquiring too great power, and rendered themselves beggars by misusing their immense riches. With swelling titles and wide dominions, they were despicably weak, and scarce any but copper money was to be seen in a country, which received above twenty millions annually from its plantations.

Before I quit this topic, I must take notice of another thing, which is certainly very extraordinary. This wrong turn in the Spanish policy had a wonderful effect; it made all the enemies of that nation rich, and all its friends poor. Everybody knows that the United Provinces not only made themselves free and independent, but rich and powerful also, by their long war with Spain. Our maritime power was owing to the same cause. If Philip II had not disturbed Queen Elizabeth, our fleet might have been as inconsiderable at the close of her reign as it was at the beginning, when we were pestered with pirates even in the narrow seas. Our plantations abroad were in a great measure owing to expeditions against the Spaniard. Our manufactures at home were the consequence of affording refuge to the king of Spain's protestant subjects. When Queen Elizabeth's successor closed with Spain, he suffered by it, while France, the only country then at war with Spain, was a gainer. I say nothing of Cromwell's breach with Spain, and the advantages he drew from it because the world seems well enough apprized of all I could say on that subject already. . . .

By so long a series of mismanagement the Spaniards have brought their affairs into so wretched a situation that they neither have, nor can have any very great benefit from their vast dominions in America. They are said to be stewards for the rest of Europe; their Galleons bring the silver into Spain, but neither wisdom nor power can keep it there; it runs out as fast as it comes in, nay, and faster; insomuch that the little Canton of Bern is really richer, and has more credit, than the king of Spain, notwithstanding his Indies. At first sight this seems to be strange and incredible; but when we come to examine it, the mystery is by no means impenetrable. The silver and rich commodities which come from the Indies come not for nothing (the king's duties excepted) and very little of the goods or manufactures for which they come, belong to the subjects of the crown of Spain. It is evident, therefore, that the Spanish merchants are but factors, and that the greatest part of the returns from the West Indies belong to those foreigners for whom they negotiate.

8. THE RISE AND FALL OF VILLA RICA

By the last decade of the seventeenth century the sugar cycle of the northeast had about run its course. At this time of acute depression gold was found in Minas Gerais (1690). This discovery gave a new stimulus to Brazil's economic life, led to the first effective settlement of the interior, and shifted the center of economic and political activity from north to south. The story of the rise and fall of the gold mining center of Villa Rica is told by John Mawe (1764–1829), who visited it at the opening of the nineteenth century.

The history of an establishment which, twenty years after its foundation, was reputed the richest place on the globe, was an object of considerable interest to me, and I made many inquiries respecting it from some of the best informed men on the spot. It appears that the first discovery of this once rich mountain was effected by the enterprising spirit of the Paulistas, who, of all the colonists in Brazil, retained the largest share of that ardent and indefatigable zeal for discovery which characterized the Lusitanians of former days. They penetrated from their capital into these regions, braving every hardship, and encountering every difficulty which a savage country, infested by still more savage inhabitants, opposed to them. They cut their way through impervious woods, carrying their provisions with them, and occasionally cultivating small patches of land to afford them food to retreat to, in case of necessity, as well as to keep up a communication with their city, St. Paul's. Every inch of ground was disputed by the barbarous Indians, here called Bootocoodies, who were constantly either attacking them openly or lying in ambush, and but too frequently succeeded in surprising some of them, or their negroes, whom they immediately sacrificed to their horrible appetite for human flesh. They believed the negros to be the great monkeys of the wood. The bones of the unfortunate sufferers were frequently found exposed, shocking testimonies of the barbarity of their murderers, whom the Paulistas, roused to revenge, invariably shot, wherever they met them. These examples of vengeance answered their desired end; the Indians, terrified as well by the noise as by the fatal effect of the fire-arms, fled with precipitation, believing that the white men commanded lightning and thunder.

It does not appear that in exploring this territory they received any assistance whatever from the aborigines; they followed the course of rivers, occasionally finding gold, of which they skimmed the surface, and continued to proceed until they arrived at the mountain which is our present subject. Its riches arrested their course; they immediately erected temporary houses and began their operations. . . . The fame of their success soon reached the city of St. Paul's; fresh adventurers arrived in great numbers, bringing with them all the negros they had means to purchase. Other adventurers went from St. Paul's to Rio de Janeiro to procure more negroes, their own city being drained; and thus the news of the lately discovered gold mountain being made known in the Brazilian capital, men of all descriptions went in crowds to this land of promise by the way of St. Paul's, which was the only route then known. The first settlers might have prevented the exposure of their good fortune, had they been able to moderate their joy, and consented to act in concert; but as gold was in such great abundance, every individual appropriated a lot of ground, and thus became a capitalist. Each strove which should make the most of his treasure in the shortest time, and thus there was

John Mawe, *Travels in the Interior of Brazil* (London, 1747), pp. 171–177.

a continual demand for more negroes, more iron, etc. and, in the general eagerness to obtain them, the secret which all were interested in keeping was disclosed. The Paulistas, independent in spirit, and proud of their wealth, were desirous of giving laws to the newcomers; but the latter determining to oppose this measure, formed themselves into a party under the guidance of Manuel Nuñez Viana, an adventurer of some consequence, who strenuously asserted their claim to equal rights and advantages. Disputes arose on both sides, and were at length aggravated into hostilities, which proved unfavorable to the Paulistas, the great part of whom fled to a considerable station of their own, and there awaited reinforcements. Viana and his followers, without loss of time, went in pursuit of their foes, who they found on a plain near the site of St. João del Rey. The two parties met on the borders of a river, and a sanguinary battle took place, which ended in the defeat of the Paulistas, who afterwards made the best terms they could. The slain were buried on the margin of the river, which, from that circumstance took the name of Rio dos Mortos.

The Paulistas, bent on revenge, but weakened by defeat, appealed to the sovereign, King Pedro, denouncing Viana and his followers as rebels who were attempting to take the district to themselves, and set up an independent government. The King's ministers, apprized of the state of affairs, and learning by report the immense riches of the country, immediately sent a chief, with a competent body of troops, to take advantage of the strife between the two parties; which, in a country tenable by a few men on account of its numerous strongholds, was a most fortunate circumstance. . . . The Paulistas now saw that the riches which they in conjunction with their rivals might have retained, were about to be seized by a third party which would reduce them both to subordination. Disturbances prevailed for some time, but, reinforcements continually arriving from Government, tranquility was at length perfectly established; and in the year 1711 a regular town began to be formed; a government-house, a mint, and a depot for arms were built. A code of laws was enacted for the regulation of the mines; all gold-dust found was ordered to be delivered to officers appointed for that purpose; a fifth in weight was taken for the King, and the remaining four parts were purified, melted into ingots at the expense of Government, then assayed, marked according to their value, and delivered to the owners, with a certificate to render them current. For the greater convenience of trade, gold dust was likewise permitted to circulate for small payments. Notwithstanding these strict regulations, a considerable quantity of the precious metal in its original state found its way to Rio de Janeiro, Bahai, and other ports, clandestinely, without paying the royal fifth, until Government, apprized of this illicit traffic, established registers in various parts for the examination of all passengers, and stationed soldiers to patrol the roads. By these means, gold in immense quantities was seized and confiscated; the persons on whom any was found forfeited all their property, and, unless they had friends of great influence, were sent as convicts to Africa for life. The greatest disgrace was attached to the name of smuggler; and such was the rigor of the law against offenders of this description, that every person quitting the district was obliged to take a certificate stating whither he was going, and what he carried with him. This regulation is still in force, and is rigorously observed.

Villa Rica soon enjoyed a considerable trade with Rio de Janeiro; the returns were negros, iron, woolens, salt, provisions of various kinds, and wine, all which at that time bore amazingly high profits.

About the year 1713, when Dr. Bras de Silvia was appointed governor, the quantity of gold produced was so considerable that the royal fifth amounted to half a million sterling annually. The mountain became pierced like a honeycomb, as the miners worked every soft part they could find, and penetrated as far as they could, conveying the *cascalhão* which they dug out to a convenient place for washing. In rainy weather the torrents of water running down the sides of the mountain, carried away much earthy matter containing delicate particles of gold, which settled in the ground near its base. When the waters abated, this rich deposit gave employment to numbers of the poorer sort of people, who took it away and washed it at their convenience.

Antonio Dias, the person already mentioned as one of the leaders of the Paulistas, who discovered the place, having become extremely rich, built a fine church, and dying soon after, bequeathed to it considerable funds. It still bears his name. Five or six others were begun and soon finished, as neither wood nor stone was wanting, and the inhabitants were all ready to contribute a share of their property, and to employ their negroes in furtherance of these pious works. A law highly creditable to the wisdom of the Portuguese government was now enacted, to prohibit friars from entering the territory of the mines. What treasures were thus saved to the state, and what a number of persons were thus continued in useful labor, who would else have become burthensome to the community!

The town now underwent many improvements; its streets were more regularly built, and some parts of the side of the mountain were leveled to afford more convenient room for the construction of houses, and the laying out of gardens. Reservoirs were formed, from which water was distributed by means of conduits to all parts, and public fountains were erected in the most convenient and central situations. The mint and smelting houses were enlarged, and rendered more commodious for the transaction of business. About this period the inhabitants amounted to twelve thousand or upwards; those who possessed mines were either the first settlers or their descendants, and as the best part of the district was occupied, the new adventurers who continued to arrive from time to time were obliged to enter into the service of the existing owners until they had learned their methods of working, after which they generally went in search of fresh mines, proceeding along the water-courses and ravines, where they sometimes discovered new sources of wealth. Between the years 1730 and 1750 the mines were in the height of their prosperity; the King's fifth during some years of that period is said to have amounted to at least a million sterling annually.

The mines which produced this immense wealth at length became gradually less abundant; and, as the precious metal disappeared, numbers of the miners retired, some to the mother-country, loaded with riches, which tempted fresh adventurers, and many to Rio de Janeiro and other sea-ports, where they employed their large capitals in commerce.

Villa Rica at the present day scarcely retains a shadow of its former splendor. Its inhabitants, with the exception of the shopkeepers, are void of employment; they totally neglect the fine country around them, which, by proper cultivation, would amply compensate for the loss of the wealth which their ancestors drew from its bosom. Their education, their habits, their hereditary prejudices, alike unfit them for active life; perpetually indulging in visionary prospects of sudden wealth, they fancy themselves exempted from that universal law of nature which ordains that man shall live by the sweat of his brow. In contemplating the fortunes accumulated by their predecessors, they overlook the industry and perseverance which obtained them, and entirely lose sight of the change of circumstances which renders those qualities now doubly necessary. The successors of men who rise to opulence from small beginnings seldom follow the example set before them, even when trained to it; how then should a Creolian, reared in idleness and ignorance, feel any thing of the benefits of industry! His negroes constitute his principal property, and them he manages so ill, that the profits of their labor hardly defray the expenses of their maintenance: in the regular course of nature they become old and unable to work, yet he continues in the same listless and slothful way, or sinks into a state of absolute inactivity, not knowing what to do from morning to night. This deplorable degeneracy is almost the universal characteristic of the descendants of the original settlers; every trade is occupied either by mulattoes or negros, both of which classes seem superior in intellect to their masters, because they make a better use of it.

6

COLONIAL POLITICAL AND RELIGIOUS INSTITUTIONS

THE COUNCIL OF THE INDIES, chartered in 1524, stood at the head of the Spanish imperial administration almost to the close of the colonial period. Under the king the council was the supreme legislative, judicial, and executive institution of colonial government. The principal royal agents in the colonies were the viceroys, the captains-general, and the *audiencias*. Viceroys and captains-general had essentially the same functions; these differed only in accordance with the greater importance and size of the territory assigned to the viceroyalty. Each viceroy or captain-general was assisted in the performance of his duties by an *audiencia*, which was the highest court of appeal in its district and also served as the viceroy's council of state.

Provincial administration in the Indies was entrusted to royal officials who governed districts of varying size and importance from their chief towns and were commonly called *corregidores* or *alcaldes mayores*. The only political institution in the Indies that satisfied local aspirations to self-government was the town council, generally known as the *cabildo*. Despite its undemocratic character, inefficiency, and waning prestige and autonomy, the *cabildo* had potential significance. As the only political institution in which the Creoles (American-born Spaniards) were largely represented, it was destined to play an important role in the Creole seizure of power in the coming age of revolution.

The controlling influence of the Catholic Church in the social and spiritual life of the colonies was deeply rooted in the Spanish past. Royal control over ecclesiastical affairs, in both Spain and the Indies, was founded on the institution of the *patronato real* (royal patronage). As applied to the colonies, this patronage consisted in the absolute right of the Spanish kings to nominate all church officials, collect ecclesiastical tithes, and found churches and monasteries in the Americas.

Beginning with Columbus's second voyage, one or more clergymen accompanied every expedition that sailed for the Indies. They converted prodigious numbers of natives, and some championed the rights of the Indians against their Spanish oppressors. But many of the later arrivals preferred a life of ease and profit to one of austerity and service. From first to last, the colonies were a scene of strife between regular and secular clergy about their fields of jurisdiction. The regular clergy were members of the religious orders; the secular clergy made up the ecclesiastical hierarchy from the archbishop to the parish priest. The missionary impulse of the first friars survived longest on the frontier, "the rim of Christendom." The most notable instance of successful missionary effort, at least from an economic point of view, was that of the Jesuit missions in Paraguay.

The Inquisition was established in the Indies by Philip II in 1569. Its independence of other courts, the secrecy of its proceedings, and the dread with which the charge of heresy was regarded made the Inquisition an effective check on "dangerous thoughts," religious, political, or philosophical. Most cases tried by its tribunals, however, concerned offenses against morality or minor deviations from orthodox religious conduct, usually punished with relatively light penalties. Heresy was often punished with burning at the stake and confiscation of property.

The Portuguese crown first governed Brazil through *donatories* or lords—proprietors who were given almost complete authority in their territories in return for assuming the responsibilities of colonization. In 1549, convinced that the system had failed to achieve its ends, the king issued a decree limiting the powers of the *donatories* and creating a central government for all of Brazil. The first captain-general of the colony was Thomé de Souza, and Baía was selected as his capital. Governors, appointed by the king and subordinate to the captain-general, gradually replaced the *donatories* as the political and military leaders of the captaincies.

During the period of the Spanish Captivity (1580–1640), Spain established a Conselho da India for the administration of the Portuguese colonies. After Portugal regained her independence, this body continued to have charge of Brazilian affairs. As the colony expanded, new captaincies or provinces were created. In 1763, the captain-general of Rio de Janeiro replaced his colleague at Baía as head of the colonial administration in Brazil, with the title of viceroy. In practice, however, his authority over the other governors was negligible.

Official inefficiency and corruption seem to have been as common in colonial Brazil as in the Spanish Indies. During the reform administration of the Marquis de Pombal (1756–1777) the situation improved but apparently without lasting effects.

The Brazilian church lacked the immense wealth and influence of its counterpart in the Spanish Indies. By comparison with the Spanish monarchs, the Portuguese kings seemed almost niggardly in their dealings with the Church. But their control over its affairs was equally absolute.

In Brazil, as in the Spanish colonies, the Jesuits carried on intensive missionary work among the Indians. The priests aimed to settle their Indian converts in villages completely isolated from the whites, which led to conflict with the Portuguese landowners, who wanted to enslave the Indians for work on their plantations. The clash of interests was most severe in São Paulo, whose half-breed slave hunters bitterly resented Jesuit interference with their operations.

Like their colleagues in the Spanish colonies, the Brazilian clergy—always excepting the Jesuits and some other orders—were often criticized for their worldly lives and indifference to their charges. Yet such educational and humanitarian establishments as existed were almost exclusively provided by the clergy, and from their ranks came most of the few distinguished names in Brazilian colonial science, learning, and literature.

1. THE STRUCTURE OF COLONIAL GOVERNMENT

The shifting pattern of Spain's administration of the Indies in the sixteenth century reflected the steady growth of centralized rule in Spain itself and the application of a trial-and-error method to the problems of colonial government. By the middle of the century, the political organization of the Indies had assumed the definitive form that it was to retain, with slight variations, until late in the eighteenth century. The Mexican historian and statesman Lucas Alamán (1792–1853) included an informative sketch of colonial governmental institutions in his classic History of Mexico. *His account, although somewhat abstract and idealized, suggests Alamán's sympathy with the old Spanish regime but also reflects his familiarity with the colonial climate of opinion in which he passed his youth and early manhood.*

Among the many kingdoms and lordships that were united in the kings of Spain by inheritance, marriage, and conquest were included the East and West Indies, islands, and Tierra firme of the Ocean Sea, the name given to the immense possessions that these kings held on the continent of America and adjacent islands, the Philippine Islands, and others in the eastern seas. These vast dominions were ruled by special laws promulgated in various

---

Lucas Alamán, *Historia de Méjico*, 5 vols. (México, 1849–1852), 1:31–34, 40–43. Excerpt translated by Benjamin Keen.

times and circumstances and later brought together in a code called the Compilation of Laws of the Kingdoms of the Indies, authorized by King Charles II on May 18, 1680. At the same time the monarch ordered that all the decrees and orders given to the *audiencias* that did not contravene the compiled laws should continue in force, and that where these laws did not suffice those of Castile, known as the Laws of Toro, should apply.

The discovery and conquest of America coincided with the changes that Charles V made in the fundamental laws of Castile and that his son Philip completed by destroying the *fueros* [privileges] of Aragón. The *cortes* of Castile, Aragón, Valencia, and Catalonia, which formerly had met separately, were transformed and gradually declined in importance until they were reduced to a meeting in Madrid of some representatives or deputies of a few cities of Castile and Aragón, solely for the ceremony of acknowledging and taking the oath of allegiance to the heirs to the throne. All the high functions of government, both legislative and administrative, were vested in the councils, of which there were established in Madrid as many as the monarchy had parts. These councils were in no way dependent upon each other, and had no other relation to each other than that of being under a single monarch. Thus there was the Council of Castile, which was called "royal and supreme" and which the kings had always maintained, though in different forms, to aid them with its advice, and with whose concurrence the dispositions of the monarch had the force of laws, as if they were proclaimed in the *cortes*, a phrase that filled the gap caused by the disappearance of these bodies.

There were also Councils of Aragón, Flanders, and Italy, in addition to those which had jurisdiction over particular departments, such as the Council of the Inquisition, over matters of faith; the Council of the Orders, for the towns that belonged to the military orders of knighthood; and that of the *Mesta*, for the problems arising from the migratory herds of sheep. . . . Although these councils were endowed with great powers, they derived their authority entirely from that of the monarch, in whose name they performed all their acts and who was the fountainhead and first principle of all power.

Although the Indies were incorporated in the crown of Castile, "from which they could not be alienated totally or in part, under any condition, or in favor of any person," its government was not on that account made at all dependent on the council established for that kingdom; on the contrary, particular care was taken to establish for the colonies a government entirely independent and separate from the Council of Castile. In 1542 was created "the Council of the Indies," to which were assigned the same exemptions and privileges enjoyed by that of Castile; the same power of making laws in consultation with the king; and the same supreme jurisdiction in the East and West Indies and over their natives, even though resident in Castile, subjecting to it the *audiencia* of the commerce of Seville and expressly forbidding all the councils and tribunals of Spain, except that of the Inquisition, to take cognizance of any question relating to the Indies.

The Council of the Indies, then, was the legislative body in which were framed the laws that governed those vast dominions, it being declared that no law or provision should be obeyed in the colonies that had not passed through the council and had not been communicated by it; it was the supreme court, to which were brought all suits that by reason of the large sums involved could be appealed to this last resort; and, finally, it was the consultative branch of the government in all the weighty matters in which it was judged fitting to hear the Council's opinion. It was also charged with the duty of submitting to the king, through its chamber composed of five councilors, lists of . . . candidates from which were filled the vacant bishoprics, canonates, and judgeships of the *audiencias*. In order to enable it to perform this task more adequately, the viceroys were required to inform the council privately, at stated intervals, concerning residents of the territory under their command who might be worthy of filling these posts. . . .

The first governors [in the colonies] were the conquistadores themselves, either under the terms of their capitulations or agreements with the king, as in the case of Pizarro in Peru, or by choice of their soldiers, later confirmed by the crown, as happened with Cortes in New Spain. Later the governmental authority was transferred to the same bodies that were appointed to administer justice, called *audiencias*. Finally the Emperor Charles V created in Barcelona on November 20, 1542, the two viceroyalties of Mexico and Peru, to which were added in the eighteenth century those of Santa Fe and Buenos Aires, the other provinces remaining under captains-general and presidents, who exercised the same functions as the viceroys and differed from them only in title.

The authority of these high functionaries varied greatly according to the times. In the epoch of the creation of the first viceroyalties it was almost without limits, for the king declared: "In all the cases and affairs that may arise, they may do whatever appears fitting to them, and they can do and dispose just as we would do and dispose . . . in the provinces in their charge . . . saving only what is expressly forbidden them to do. . . ."

In the period we are discussing the power of the viceroys was moderated by prudent compromises, reflected in the participation of other bodies in the different branches of government, although the viceroys retained all the glitter and pomp of their supreme authority. In the arduous and important tasks of public administration . . . they were obliged to consult with the *real acuerdo*, the name given to a sitting of the *audiencia* when it acted as the viceroy's council, although he was not bound to accept the advice of the *oidores* or judges. . . . The viceroy was also subject to the *residencia*, which was a judicial review held immediately at the end of his term of office, and to which the judge who was appointed for this purpose summoned all who desired to complain of some offense or injustice.

From the decision of this judge there was no appeal except to the Council of the Indies. But although all these restrictions had a very laudable object—to limit and bring within the scope of the laws an authority that bordered on the royal—distance and the very extent of the authority frequently made these precautions illusory. A viceroy of Mexico . . . said in this connection: "If he who comes to govern (this kingdom) does not repeatedly remind himself that the most rigorous *residencia* is that which the viceroy must face when he is judged by the divine majesty, he can be more sovereign than the Grand Turk, for there is no evil action that he may contrive for which he will not find encouragement, nor any tyranny that he may practice which will not be tolerated. . . ."

The period of time that a viceroy could remain in office was at first indefinite, and the first two viceroys of New Spain retained their positions for many years. It was later fixed at a period of three years, which was commonly renewed for those who distinguished themselves by their services, or for those who were the objects of the king's favor; finally it was increased to five years. . . .

The authority exercised by the *audiencias* in their respective districts may be likened to that enjoyed by the council over all the Indies. These bodies were held in much respect, not only because they possessed great powers, acted as councils to the viceroys with the name of *acuerdo*, and were supreme tribunals from which there was no appeal (save in particular cases, to the Council of the Indies) but also because of their members' reputation for honesty, their discreet conduct and bearing, and even their distinctive attire on public occasions. . . . This combination of circumstances made these posts very desirable and their holders, objects of envy. Appointments were made according to an established scale, with the judges progressing from less important *audiencias* to those of higher rank.

In order that these magistrates might be entirely independent and devote themselves to the administration of justice without relations of interest, friendship, or kinship in the place where they exercised their functions, they were strictly forbidden to engage in any kind of commerce or business; to borrow or lend money; to own lands, whether vegetable gardens or estates; to pay visits or attend betrothals and baptisms; to associate with merchants; to receive gifts of any kind; or to attend pleasure or gambling parties. These prohibitions also extended to their wives and children. In order to marry they had to obtain a license from the king, on pain of loss of their positions, and if such a license was granted they were generally transferred to another *audiencia*. The number of *oidores* varied according to the rank of the *audiencia*. These tribunals were found not only in the viceregal capitals but wherever else they were necessary.

2. "I Have Seen Corruption Boil and Bubble . . . "

Corruption became a structural element of the government of the Indies in the seventeenth century. Colonial officials, high and low, prostituted their trust in innumerable and ingenious ways. An audacious adventurer who had an intimate knowledge of conditions in the colonies, Gabriel Fernández de Villalobos, marquis of Varinas (1642?–?), showered Charles II with memorials in which he sought to guide the monarch through the bewildering thicket of official misdeeds and warned him that failure to remedy the corruption rampant in colonial government must lead to the loss of the Indies. Villalobos was rewarded for his pains by imprisonment in a North African fortress. The following extract from one of his memorials illuminates the technique of a corrupt viceroy.

I shall assume that your Majesty has everywhere excellent ministers, conscientious and learned, and that the Indies are today and have often before been governed by viceroys and *oidores* [judges] of notable piety and integrity. . . . And certainly some were distinguished by all the virtues; there was one, in particular, of such zeal and integrity that on departing from Mexico City after completing his term of office he received with kindness an Indian who offered him a bouquet of flowers, saying: "This is the first gift I have received in this kingdom." A great viceroy was this, my lord, who died so poor that King Philip II (may he be with God) paid his debts out of the royal treasury. And it may be that these virtues (in addition to the merits of his family) later won for his sons the favor of Philip IV, your Majesty's father.

There were viceroys before and after him who worked in the same righteous spirit. For that reason, in this discourse I shall neither name names nor accuse anyone in particular; I shall speak instead of the evils that I have seen and of the remedies that are necessary. . . .

Your Majesty may assume that a high official driven by an immoderate desire to make his fortune will operate in the following manner:

First, he will utilize or sell (to put it more precisely), for his own profit and at high prices, every kind of judicial office, *alcaldías mayores*, *corregimientos*, commissions, and *residencias*.

Second, he will also sell the rights to *encomiendas*, licenses, and concessions—authorizations to do various things that are forbidden by the laws and ordinances but that the viceroy may allow.

Colección de documentos inéditos . . . de las antiguas posesiones españolas de Ultramar, 25 vols. (Madrid, 1885–1932), 12:226–231. Excerpt translated by Benjamin Keen.

Third, he will dispose in the same way of all kinds of military positions, such as the titles and commissions of lieutenants, captains, generals, recruiting officers, garrison commanders, constables, and many non-existent posts.

Fourth, he will do the same with all that relates to the public finances, selling drafts on the royal treasury (which is the ruin of your Majesty's estate) and disposing of the offices of revenue collectors, of judges appointed to make various investigations, of officials charged with collecting the royal fifth and making financial settlements, of inspectors of the mines and lands, of *alcaldes* with jurisdiction over water rights, and so forth. . . .

Such, my lord, are the articles of faith that your ministers of the Indies observe most diligently.

The minister who does these things, my lord, clearly will be guided not by reason but by his own convenience, and therefore he will surround himself with individuals who will advance his interests; and will encourage these men to commit excesses, while he will always persecute and humiliate the just and virtuous, for these are the only ones he fears.

Such a minister must also seek the good will of superiors as well as inferiors, and share his spoils with them, so that they will write favorably of him to Spain and so that his trickery will be concealed. He must also try to persuade the tribunals to close their eyes to his actions, sometimes through terrorizing them, sometimes by bribing them. . . .

Such viceroys and presidents must also go about in fear and distrust of the people, who see what goes on and murmur, complain, denounce it publicly, and compose satires and squibs. . . .

All these things together, and each one separately, contribute to the total destruction of the Indies, for every item is a source of political offenses and scandalous crimes that cause infinite miseries.

3. THE *CORREGIDOR*: ENEMY OF THE PEOPLE

The provincial governor—or corregidor, *the title he most commonly bore—occupied a key position in the political hierarchy of the Indies. His supreme authority on the local level, under the viceroy from whom he usually bought his position, gave him immense power for good or evil. By common consent, he generally employed that power for bad ends. The worst abuse of his authority arose in connection with the practice of* repartimiento *or* reparto de mercancías, *the requirement that Indians in his district purchase goods from the* corregidor. *The Marquis of Varinas describes in vivid detail the operations of the* repartimiento.

Colección de documentos inéditos, 12:237–239, 245–246, 249–256. Excerpt translated by Benjamin Keen.

This *corregidor* or governor, president or *alcalde mayor*, whose office cost him 10 or 12,000 pesos, must acquire a stock of goods worth 20,000 pesos to sell in his province, in order to make a profit on the money he has expended. . . . He sells this merchandise to his poor subjects at six or eight times its true value, and buys up the products of the Indians and Spaniards at four or five times below the current price of the country, using force and threats . . . to enrich himself and slake his unnatural thirst for money, as soon as he takes up the tasks of government. . . .

The goods that this official receives from the merchants who outfit him, he purchases at steep prices; and he must increase their cost to the Indians accordingly. So the unhappy judge, dragging the chains of his many debts, arrives in his district, which he finds filled with naked Indians and impoverished Spaniards burdened with children and obligations, whose total possessions, if put up at public auction, would not yield 6,000 pesos. Withal, this judge must squeeze out of them more than 30,000 pesos in two years in order to pay his debts, and half as much again if he wishes to make a profit from his office. And if he cannot do this he is beyond salvation (as they say in the Indies), since he is considering only his temporal welfare and forgetting that such a policy may consign him to eternal perdition, as will inevitably ensue if he does not make restitution.

When this judge enters upon his office, his sole concern is to find means of paying off his large debts and to make a profit from his employment; and since time is short, his needs immense, the land exhausted, and his vassals poor, he must use violence and cruelty to attain what equity, moderation, and kindness will not secure.

To this end he must monopolize the products of the land, compelling his miserable vassals to sell all their fruits to him, who, rod in hand, is judge and inspector, merchant, *corregidor*, and interpreter of his own contract. . . .

Let your Majesty's ministers of the Council of the Indies, and your Majesty's confessor, take note that the distribution of goods by the *corregidor*, made to enable him to buy the products of the district, is never carried out by arrangement with the Indians who have to buy this merchandise. The customary practice is for the Spanish governor to turn the goods over to the Indian *alcaldes* and bosses and to fix prices in collusion with them. . . . The Indian bosses never object to the high prices, for they do not have to buy anything; their principal concern is to avoid having to shoulder any part of the burden and to ingratiate themselves with the *corregidores*, so that they may keep their jobs.

Having agreed on prices and received the goods, the Indian bosses, who are stupid and heartless, count the people living in each town; they make no exception of the widows or of the poor, sick, and aged, but treat all alike, and assign to them by heads the payment they must make for these goods. They take the merchandise, according to the assessment made by the *corregidor*, to each one's house, place it before him, and tell him the reckoning; he must pay this in the allotted time or else go to rot in prison. As a clear example of the injustice of his distribution, the Indians are often seen wearing scapularies of various colors . . . which fell to their lot in the distribution and of which they can make no other use. . . .

Your Majesty may imagine from these and similar facts how these Indians fear prison, the threat of which compels the Indian bosses and commoners to submit to their governors; and no wonder, for the Indian prison is a fearful thing. It is a small dark room, without windows or other vent than a very small door. There they must perform their bodily functions, chained by the feet; there are no beds; and as the Indians are brought from other towns, they generally forget to give them any food. They suffer from hunger and thirst and a terrible stench; and since these unhappy beings have been raised in the open country they consider imprisonment worse than death, and therefore many prefer to take their own lives. . . .

At the conclusion of one year, the period for which his office is granted (with a second year possible by way of extension), the judge makes another deal with the superior officer who appointed him, and adds another 1 or 2,000 pesos to the original price, unless this sum was included in the original agreement. If he did not do this he would be completely ruined, for in the first year he was occupied with the distribution of his goods . . . and he must have the second year to collect payment for his merchandise. . . . In any case the judge almost always ends "over-extended" (as they say), with the district owing him for the goods that he distributed—and these debts represent not only the profit that he hoped to make but the sums that he must pay out. On this account the judge resorts to the following expedients, which are all new and greater injustices and injuries to the service of God and of your Majesty:

First, seeing that the end of his term of office and the arrival of a successor are near, the *corregidor* tries to collect payment from Your Majesty's vassals in four days . . . for goods that he had sold on credit for a much longer period.

Second, after his successor has been named he makes a deal with him (if he is the judge of residence), paying him a certain sum; if he is not the judge, he uses this money to have a judge appointed who will absolve him of all guilt.

Third, in any case he will try to obtain a pledge from his successor that he will not permit any inhabitant to lodge any complaints or charges against him in the *residencia*, making it clear to him that whatever befalls the old judge will happen to the new one, since he must of necessity manage his affairs in the same way as his predecessor.

Fourth, since the debt with which he began his term of office—of 10, 12, and 200,000 pesos, with interest added—is so large that his subjects, though exploited with such great severity, simply cannot furnish this sum of money . . . he must choose one of two courses of action. He may remain in the vicinity until he has collected all that is owed him—which is his profit—all the rest having gone to pay his outfitters, his creditors, the official who appointed him, and the judge of residence. In this case Your Majesty's vassals, and the judge who succeeds him, are saddled with a very burdensome and offensive guest who not only obstructs their industry but impoverishes them with his collections. Or he may sell his debts to his successor, taking a partial loss; and since these obligations grow with the passage of time, they come to form an unbearable burden on the Spanish and Indian settlements, so that the people become impoverished and leave their homes, and the district is soon depopulated through these intolerable injuries.

Fifth, the evil ministers often resort to the following expedient: Sometimes, in order to leave no debts outstanding when they quit office, they sell or hire the Indians to owners of workshops to satisfy their debts, using trivial offenses as pretexts. . . . At other times they use for pretexts the arrears in the tribute they owe Your Majesty. In other places they commit still greater offenses and violence for the same cause, compelling the Indians to cultivate fields for them, which gives rise to a mass of injuries more numerous than the seeds of grain gathered from the land, for with this pretext fifty Indians are forced to pay the tributes of five hundred. So these Indians must pass their lives in endless labor, lacking food, clothing, or time in which to plant for themselves and their families. They go about continually harassed—men, women, the aged, boys, widows, young girls, and married women, sowing and plowing with their own hands, unaided by oxen or other animals, and threshing the grain with their feet, all without recompense. . . .

Sixth, since the first question put in the *residencia* asks the witnesses under oath whether the judge engaged in any business dealings on his own account, it becomes necessary to keep from the judge of residence what everybody else knows. Hence, by one means or another—threats or pleas for mercy, or bad conscience—all are made to swear that the *corregidor* engaged in no business dealings, either personally or through intermediaries; and this is sworn to by the same persons to whom the judge forcibly sold and distributed the steers, mules, and other merchandise in which he traded during his term of office, and whose grain and other supplies he monopolized. . . .

Thus, through such perjury and sins of sacrilege on the part of the persons he suborned, the *corregidor* obtains an acquittal and quits his office—one which he secured through bribery and fraud, which he entered with usury and oppression, whose duties he performed with violence and injury, and which he left committing sacrilege, bearing false witness before God concerning his actions.

4. "THESE LAWS ARE OBEYED AND NOT ENFORCED"

A striking feature of colonial political life was the frequent nonobservance of Spanish colonial law. Such nonobservance could be legitimated by use of the formula "obedezco pero no cumplo" ("I obey but do not carry out"), employed by a viceroy to set aside unrealistic or unenforceable legislation. Nonobservance of the law was especially frequent in the case of Indian protective legislation, which was systematically flouted. The crown often closed its eyes to such violations, not only because it wished to avoid confrontation with powerful colonial elites but because these laws sometimes collided with the crown's own pressing need for revenue. Hence the contradiction between that protective legislation, so often cited by defenders of Spain's work in America, and the reality of Indian life and labor in the colonies. A Spanish judge of rare integrity, Alonso de Zorita (1511?–1585), who retired to an honorable poverty in 1566 after nineteen years holding office in the Indies, calls attention to that contradiction in the following excerpt from his report to the crown.

Who shall tell the sum of the miseries and hardships these poor unfortunate people suffer, without help or succor from any quarter! Who does not turn his face against them, who does not persecute and vex them, who does not rob them and live by their sweat! Since I cannot tell all, but have told enough to make clear the need for a remedy, let me be silent concerning the innumerable crimes that I have personally seen and verified or that I have heard of from trustworthy persons.

The ancient kings and lords never ruled in this way, never took the Indians from their towns, never disrupted their way of life and labor. I cannot believe that Your Majesty or the members of Your Majesty's Council know or have been informed about what is taking place. If they knew of it, they would surely take steps to preserve Your Majesty's miserable vassals and would not allow the Indians to be entirely destroyed in order to gratify the wishes of the Spaniards. If the Indians should die out (and they are dying with terrible rapidity), those realms will very quickly become depopulated, as has already happened in the Antilles, the great province of Venezuela, and the whole coast of northern South America and other very extensive lands that have become depopulated in our time. The wishes of Your Majesty and his Royal Council are well known and are made very plain in the laws that are issued every day in favor of the poor Indians and for their increase and preservation. But these laws are obeyed and not enforced, wherefore there is no end to the destruction of the Indians, nor does anyone care what Your Majesty decrees. How many decrees, *cédulas*, and letters were sent by our lord, the Emperor, who is in glory, and how many necessary orders are sent by Your Majesty! How little good have all these orders done! Indeed, the more laws and decrees are sent, the worse is the condition of the Indians by reason of the false and sophistical interpretation that the Spanish officials give these laws, twisting their meaning to suit their own purposes. It seems to me that the saying

Alonso de Zorita, *Life and Labor in Ancient Mexico: The Brief and Summary Relations of the Lords of New Spain*, ed. and trans. Benjamin Keen (New Brunswick, N.J.: Rutgers University Press, 1963), pp. 216–218. The notes that appeared in the original publication have been removed.

of a certain philosopher well applies to this case: Where there is a plenty of doctors and medicines, there is a plenty of ill health. Just so, where there are many laws and judges, there is much injustice.

We have a multitude of laws, judges, viceroys, governors, *presidentes*, *oidores*, *corregidores*, *alcaldes mayores*, a million lieutenants, and yet another million *alguaciles*. But this multitude is not what the Indians need, nor will it relieve their misery. Indeed, the more such men there are, the more enemies do the Indians have. For the more zeal these men display against the Indians, the more influence do they wield; the Spaniards call such men Fathers of their Country, saviors of the state, and proclaim them to be very just and upright. The more ill will such men show against the Indians and friars, the more titles and lying encomiums are heaped upon them. But let an official favor the Indians and the religious (who are bound together, one depending upon the other), and this alone suffices to make him odious and abhorrent to all. For the Spaniards care for one thing alone, and that is their advantage; and they give not a rap whether these poor and miserable Indians live or die, though the whole being and welfare of the country depend upon them.

God has closed the eyes and darkened the minds of these Spaniards, so that they see with their eyes what is happening, yet do not see it, so that they perceive their own destruction, yet do not perceive it, and all because of their callousness and hardheartedness. I have known an *oidor* to say publicly from his dais, speaking in a loud voice, that if water were lacking to irrigate the Spaniards' farms, they would have to be watered with the blood of Indians. I have heard others say that the Indians, and not the Spaniards, must labor. Let the dogs work and die, said these men, the Indians are numerous and rich. These officials say such things because they have not seen the Indians' sufferings and miseries, because they are content to sit in the cool shade and collect their pay. They also say these things to win the good will and gratitude of the Spaniards, and also because they all have sons-in-law, brothers-in-law, relatives, or close friends among them. These friends and relatives are rich in farms, ranches, and herds; and the officials control a major part of this wealth. That is what blinds them and makes them say what they say and do what they do.

In the old days the Indians had few laws, so few that all knew them by heart, as is told of the Lacedaemonians and the Scythians, and none dared to break those laws. They were well governed, their numbers increased, and they lived happily and peacefully. They were masters of their poor little properties. They did not have to leave their native surroundings to support themselves, but enjoyed the company of their wives, children, and kindred by day and night. They paid their tribute without hardship or undue exertion.

I could say much more on this subject, but to tell it all would weary the reader. Indeed, I think it unnecessary, speaking to a Prince so upright, just, and Christian, to enlarge on what is so notorious and glaring that no man attached to the service of God and Your Majesty will deny it.

5. City Government in the Spanish Indies

The colonial city was born just as the freedom and authority of the communes or towns of Spain was passing away. As a result, from the outset the right of the king to appoint municipal officials was accepted without question. Philip II began the practice—which later became general—of selling posts in the town councils to the highest bidders, with the right of resale or bequest of the offices, on condition that a certain part of their value be paid to the crown at each transfer. Gonzalo Gómez de Cervantes, a leading citizen of Mexico, criticized the practice and suggested reforming it in a 1599 memorial addressed to a member of the Council of the Indies.

It is well known and understood that Mexico is the head of all this kingdom and that all the other cities, towns, and places of this New Spain acknowledge it as such. All the more reason, then, that its *regidores* (councilmen) should be outstanding men, of quality, experience, and mature judgment. And the lack of such men has been a cause of many different things that show a serious weakness. The proof of this is that the majority of the *regidores* are youths who even twenty years from now will not have enough experience to govern a city; and it is a sorry thing to see those who have not yet left off being children, already made city fathers.

This evil arises from the permission granted by His Majesty for the sale of these offices—whereby they go to those who can pay the most for them, and not to those who would render the best honor and service to the commonweal. It is shameful that such youths should be preferred for the posts of *regidores* and other important positions over mature and eminent men who should occupy those offices. Truly, it would redound much more to the service of His Majesty and to the increase of his kingdom, if he gave these council seats to qualified persons, descendants of conquistadores, and others who have served him; they would regard their king and country with greater love, if His Majesty rewarded them for their merits and services, and would be inspired to serve him still more.

It is not seemly that those who yesterday were shopkeepers or tavern keepers, or engaged in other base pursuits, should today hold the best offices in the country while gentlemen and descendants of those who conquered and won the land go about poor, dejected, degraded, and neglected. And it is the city that suffers most from this injustice, because the fixing of market prices, the supervision of weights and measures in the markets, and other very important matters are in a state of great disorder. It would be a very efficacious remedy, if his Majesty were to add a dozen council seats and give them to

---

Gonzalo Gómez de Cervantes, *La vida económica y social de Nueva España al finalizar el siglo XVI*, ed. Alberto María Carreño (México, 1944), pp. 93–94. Excerpt translated by Benjamin Keen.

men of quality, maturity, wisdom, and merit—not by way of sale, but as gifts—and if he were to do the same with the seats that fall vacant. If such a policy were adopted, everything pertaining to his royal estate and the preservation of this realm would be greatly served and advanced.

6. THE SOURCES OF CATHOLIC POWER

By the last decades of the colonial era clerical discipline had relaxed, and the Church was rent by unseemly squabbles between monastic and secular clergy and between Creole and peninsular priests. Yet the Church's influence in colonial society, except among a tiny handful of converts to the new materialistic doctrines of the Enlightenment, remained undiminished. In the following excerpt the Mexican historian Alamán explains the sources of Catholic power.

The immense influence of the Church rested on three foundation stones: respect for religion, remembrance of its great benefactions, and its immense wealth. The people, poorly instructed in the essentials of religion, tended to identify it in large part with ceremonial pomp; they found relief from the tedium of their lives in the religious functions, which, especially during Holy Week, represented in numerous processions the most venerated mysteries of the redemption. The festivals of the Church, which should have been entirely spiritual, were thus transformed into so many profane performances, marked by displays of fireworks, dances, plays, bullfights and cockfights, and even such forbidden diversions as cards and the like, in order to celebrate at great cost the festivals of the patron saints of the towns, into which the Indians poured the greater part of the fruits of their labor. It was this vain pomp, attended by little true piety, that led the viceroy whom I have frequently cited [the Duke of Linares] to remark that "in this realm all is outward show, and though their lives are steeped in vices, the majority think that by wearing a rosary about their necks and kissing the hand of the priest they are made Catholics, and that the Ten Commandments can be replaced by ceremonies."

The Indians continued to regard the regular clergy with the respect that the first missionaries had justly gained by protecting them against the oppression and violence of the conquistadores and by instructing them not only in religion but in the arts necessary for subsistence. This respect, which grew to be a fanatical veneration, presented no dangers as long as it was accorded to men of admirable virtue, and the government, to which they were very devoted and obedient, found in these exemplary ecclesiastics its firmest support;

Alamán, *Historia de Méjico*, 1:64–70. Excerpt translated by Benjamin Keen.

but it could become highly dangerous if a clergy of debased morals wished to abuse this influence for its own ends. This danger to the government was made still greater by the very precaution that Archbishop Haro had advised to avoid it, for since the high Church positions were entrusted to Europeans, the Americans, who generally enjoyed only the less important posts and benefices, exerted greater influence over the people with whom they were placed in more immediate contact.

The wealth of the clergy consisted not so much in the estates that it possessed, numerous though they were (especially the urban properties in the principal cities like Mexico City, Puebla, and others), as in capital invested in quitrent mortgages on the property of individuals; the traffic in mortgages and the collection of interest made of every chaplaincy and religious brotherhood a sort of bank. The total property of the clergy, both secular and regular, in estates and loans of this kind, certainly was not less than half of the total value of the real estate of the country.

The town council of Mexico City, seeing the multitude of monasteries and nunneries that were being founded, and the large number of persons destined for the ecclesiastical profession, together with the great sums devised to pious foundations, petitioned King Philip IV in 1644 "that no more convents of nuns or monks be established, since the number of the former was excessive, and the number of their woman servants even greater; that limits be placed upon the estates of the convents and that they be forbidden to acquire new holdings, complaining that the greater part of the landed property of the land had come into the hands of the religious by way of donations or purchases, and that if steps were not taken to remedy the situation they would soon be masters of all; that no more religious be sent from Spain, and that the bishops be charged not to ordain any more clerics, since there were already more than six thousand in all the bishoprics without any occupation, ordained on the basis of tenuous chaplaincies; and, finally, that there should be a reform in the excessive number of festivals, which increased idleness and gave rise to other evils." The *cortes* assembled in Madrid at that period petitioned the king to the same effect, and similar reforms were earlier proposed by the Council of Castile, but nothing was done, and things continued in the same state. . . .

In addition to the revenues derived from these estates and loans, the secular clergy had the tithes, which in all the bishoprics of New Spain amounted to some 1,800,000 pesos annually, although the government received a part of this sum. . . . In the bishopric of Michoacán the tithes were farmed out; this made their collection more rigorous and oppressive, since private interest devised a thousand expedients to burden even the least important products of agriculture with this assessment.

The clergy had a privileged jurisdiction, with special tribunals, and a personal *fuero* which in former times had been very extensive but had greatly diminished with the intervention of the royal judges in criminal cases and with the declaration that the secular courts had jurisdiction in cases involving both principal and interest of the funds of the chaplaincies and pious foundations. The viceroy decided conflicts between ecclesiastical and civil courts, and this prerogative was one of those that gave the greatest luster to his authority.

From the instructions of the Duke of Linares to his successor and from the secret report made by Don Jorge Juan and Don Antonio Ulloa to King Ferdinand VI, it appears that the customs of the clergy had declined at the beginning of the eighteenth century to a point of scandalous corruption, especially among the friars charged with the administration of the curacies or doctrines. In the epoch of which I speak this corruption was particularly notable in the capitals of some bishoprics and in smaller places, but in the capital of the realm the presence of the superior authorities enforced more decorum. Everywhere, it should also be said, there were truly exemplary ecclesiastics, and in this respect certain religious orders stood out. The Jesuits, above all others, were remarkable for the purity of their customs and for their religious zeal, a notable contrast, appearing in the above-cited work by Juan and Ulloa between their comments on the Jesuits and their references to other orders. Their expulsion left a great void, not only in the missions among the barbarians whom they had in charge but in the matter of the instruction and moral training of the people. . . . No less commendable were the friars of the order of Saint James, those of the order of Saint Philip, whose oratories had largely replaced those of the Jesuits, and among the hospitaller orders the Bethlehemites, who devoted themselves to primary education and the care of hospitals.

Into these religious orders the rivalry of birth had also penetrated, excepting always the Jesuits, who had no chapters or tumultuous elections and whose prelates were named in Rome by the general of the order, with regard only to the merit and virtue of individuals. Not only did there prevail in some of them the strife between "gachupines and creoles," but there were entire communities composed almost exclusively of one or the other element.

7. THE ADMINISTRATION OF COLONIAL BRAZIL

The government of Portuguese Brazil broadly resembled that of the Spanish Indies in its spirit, structure, and vices. Henry Koster, an astute observer of Brazilian life in the early nineteenth century, describes the political and financial administration of the important province of Pernambuco.

Henry Koster, *Travels in Brazil*, 2 vols. (London, 1816), 1:46–50.

The *captaincies-general* or provinces of the first rank, in Brazil, of which Pernambuco is one, are governed by captains-general, or governors, who are appointed for three years. At the end of this period, the same person is continued or not, at the option of the supreme government. They are, in fact, absolute in power: but before the person who has been nominated to one of these places can exercise any of its functions, he is under the necessity of presenting his credentials to the *Senado da Câmara*, the chamber or municipality of the principal town. This is formed of persons of respectability in the place. The governor has the supreme and sole command of the military force. The civil and criminal causes are discussed before, and determined by, the *Ouvidor* and *Juiz de Fora*, the two chief judicial officers, whose duties are somewhat similar: but the former is the superior in rank. They are appointed for three years, and the term may be renewed. It is in these departments of the government that the opportunities of amassing large fortunes are most numerous; and certain it is, that some individuals take advantage of them in a manner which renders justice but a name. The governor can determine in a criminal cause without appeal; but if he pleases, he refers it to the competent judge. The *Procurador da Coroa*, attorney-general, is an officer of considerable weight. The *Intendente da Marinha*, port admiral, is likewise consulted on matters of first importance; as are also the *Escrivão da Fazenda Real*, chief of the treasury, and the *Juiz da Alfândega*, comptroller of the customs. These seven officers form the Junta, or council, which occasionally meets to arrange and decide upon the affairs of the captaincy to which they belong.

The ecclesiastical government is scarcely connected with that above mentioned; and is administered by a bishop and a dean and chapter with his vicar-general etc. The governor cannot even appoint a chaplain to the island of Fernando de Noronha, one of the dependencies of Pernambuco; but acquaints the bishop that a priest is wanted, who then nominates one for the place.

The number of civil and military officers is enormous; inspectors innumerable—colonels without end, devoid of any objects to inspect—without any regiments to command; judges to manage each trifling department of which the duties might all be done by two or three persons. Thus salaries are augmented; the people are oppressed; but the state is not benefited.

Taxes are laid where they fall heavy upon the lower classes: and none are levied where they could well be borne. A tenth is raised in kind upon cattle, poultry, and agriculture, and even upon salt; this in former times appertained, as in other Christian countries, to the clergy. All the taxes are farmed to the highest bidders, and this among the rest. They are parceled out in extensive districts, and are contracted for at a reasonable rate; but the contractors again dispose of their shares in small portions: these are again retailed to other persons: and as a profit is obtained by each transfer the people must be oppressed, that these men may satisfy those above them and enrich themselves.

The system is in itself bad, but is rendered still heavier by this division of the spoil. . . .

Now, although the expenses of the provincial governments are great, and absorb a very considerable proportion of the receipts, owing to the number of officers employed in every department, still the salaries of each are, in most instances, much too small to afford a comfortable subsistence. Consequently peculation, bribery, and other crimes of the same description, are to be looked for: and they become so frequent as to escape all punishment or even notice; though there are some men whose character is without reproach. The governor of Pernambuco receives a salary of 4,000,000 *reis*, or about 1000 £ per annum. Can this be supposed to be sufficient for a man in his responsible situation, even in a country in which articles of food are cheap? His honour, however, is unimpeached; not one instance did I ever hear mentioned of improper conduct in him. But the temptation and the opportunities of amassing money are very great, and few are the persons who can resist them.

8. LOCAL GOVERNMENT: THE *CAPITÃO-MÔR*

Away from the few large towns, local government in colonial Brazil in effect meant government by the great landowners, or fazendeiros. In the câmaras, or municipal councils, the power of these rural magnates was sometimes checked by representatives of the crown or of urban interests, but on their vast estates they were absolute lords. To their personal influence the great planters often joined the authority of office, for the royal governors invariably appointed the capitães-môres, *or district militia officers, from among them. Armed with unlimited power to command, arrest, and punish, the* capitão-môr *(captain-major) became a popular symbol of despotism and oppression. The following selection from Koster's book illustrates his comment that "the whole aspect of the government of Brazil is military."*

The *Capitães-môres*, captains-major, are officers of considerable power. They have civil as well as military duties to perform, and ought to be appointed from among the planters of most wealth and individual weight in the several *Termos*, boundaries or districts. But the interest of family or of relations about the Court, have occasioned deviations from this rule; and persons very unfit for these situations, have been sometimes nominated to them. The whole aspect of the government in Brazil is military. All men between the

Koster, *Travels in Brazil*, 1:252–255.

ages of sixteen and sixty, must be enrolled either as soldiers of the line, as militiamen, or as belonging to the body of *Ordenanças*. Of the regular soldiers, I have already spoken in another place. Of the second class, each township has a regiment, of which the individuals, with the exception of the major and adjutant, and in some cases the colonel, do not receive any pay. But they are considered as embodied men; and as such are called out upon some few occasions, in the course of the year, to assemble in uniform, and otherwise accoutered. The expense which must be incurred in this respect, of necessity, precludes the possibility of many persons becoming members of this class, even if the government were desirous of increasing the number of militia regiments. The soldiers of these are subject to their captains, to the colonel, and to the governor of the province. The colonels are either rich planters, or the major or lieutenant-colonel of a regiment of the line is thus promoted to the command of one of these; in this case, and in this case only, he receives pay. I am inclined to think, that he ought to possess some property in the district, and that any deviation from this rule is an abuse; but I am not certain that the law so ordains. The majors and the adjutants are likewise occasionally promoted from the line; but whether they are regularly military men or planters, they receive pay; as their trouble, in distributing orders, and in other arrangements connected with the regiment, is considerable.

The third class, that of the *Ordenanças*, consisting of by far the largest portion of the white persons, and of free mulatto men of all shades, have for their immediate chiefs, the *Capitães-môres*, who serve without pay: and all the persons who are connected with the *Ordenanças*, are obliged likewise to afford their services gratuitously. Each district contains one *Capitão-môr*, who is invariably a person possessing property in the part of the country to which he is appointed. He is assisted by a major, captains, and *alferes*, who are lieutenants or ensigns, and by sergeants and corporals. The duties of the *Capitão-môr* are to see that every individual under his command has in his possession some species of arms; either a firelock, a sword, or a pike. He distributes the governor's orders through his district; and can oblige any of his men to take these orders to the nearest captain, who sends another peasant forward to the next captain, who sends another peasant forward to the next captain, and so forth; all which is done without any pay. A *Capitão-môr* can also imprison for twenty-four hours, and send under arrest for trial a person who is accused of having committed any crime, to the civil magistrate of the town to which his district is immediately attached. Now, the abuses of this office of *Capitão-môr* are very many; and the lower orders of free persons are much oppressed by these great men, and by their subalterns, down to the corporals. The peasants are often sent upon errands which have no relation to public business; for leagues and leagues these poor fellows are made to travel, for the purpose of carrying some private letter of the chief, of his captains, or of his lieutenants, without any remuneration. Indeed, many of these men in place, seldom think of employing their slaves on these occasions, or of paying the free persons so employed. This I have witnessed times out of number; and have heard the peasants in all parts of the country complain: it is a most heavy grievance. Nothing so much vexes a peasant as the consciousness of losing his time and trouble in a service which is not required by his sovereign. Persons are sometimes confined in the stocks for days together, on some trifling plea; and are at last released without being sent to the civil magistrate, or even admitted to a hearing. However, I am happy to say, that I am acquainted with some men, whose conduct is widely different from what I have above stated; but the power given to an individual is too great, and the probability of being called to an account for its abuse too remote, to insure the exercise of it in a proper manner.

The free mulattos and free negros, whose names are upon the rolls, either of the militia regiments which are commanded by white officers, or by those of their own class and color, are not, properly speaking, subject to the *Capitães-môres*. These officers, and the colonels of militia, are appointed by the supreme government: and the subaltern officers are nominated by the governor of each province.

9. THE JESUIT INDIAN POLICY

The Jesuits early established their leadership in the work of Indian conversion and in the religious and educational life of Brazil in general. They aimed to settle their Indian converts in aldeas, *or villages, where they would live under the tutelage of the priests, completely segregated from the white colonists. The Jesuit Indian program led to many clashes with the Portuguese planters, who wanted the natives to work as slaves on their estates. The planters charged that the Indians in the Jesuit villages "were true slaves, who labored as such not only in the* colegios *but on the so-called Indian lands, which in the end became the estates and sugar mills of the Jesuit Fathers." Replying to these and other accusations, Fr. Joseph de Anchieta explained the Jesuit Indian policy.*

Every day, in the morning the Fathers teach the Indians doctrine and say mass for those who want to hear it before going to their fields; after that the children stay in school, where they learn reading and writing, counting, and other good customs pertaining to the Christian life; in the afternoon they

Joseph de Anchieta, *Cartas, informaçoes, fragmentos históricos e sermões do Padre Joseph de Anchieta, S.J. (1554–1594)* (Rio de Janeiro, 1933), pp. 381–382. Excerpt translated by Benjamin Keen.

conduct another class especially for those who are receiving the sacred sacraments. Daily the Fathers visit the sick with certain Indians assigned for this purpose, and if they have some special needs they attend to them, and always administer to them the necessary sacraments. All this they do purely for love of God and for no other interest or profit, for the Fathers get their food from the *colegio*, and they live with the Indians solely because of love of their souls, which have such great need of them. The Fathers make no use of them on plantations, for if the *colegio* needs them for certain tasks, and they come to help, they work for wages, . . . and not through force but of their own free will, because they need clothing or implements. For although it is their natural tendency to go about naked, all those who have been raised in the Jesuit schools now wear clothes and are ashamed to go about naked. It is not true, as some say, that the Fathers are the lords of the villages.

When the Portuguese come to the villages in search of Indian labor, the Fathers help them all they can, summoning one of the Indian headmen to take the Portuguese to the houses of the natives to show them the goods they have brought, and those who wish to go they permit to leave without impediment. If the Fathers object at times, it is because the Indians have not finished their farm work, and they have to do this for the sake of their wives and children. In other cases, the Indians are not getting along with their wives, and once they leave for the homes of the Portuguese they never return; such Indians the Father also restrains from going, so that they may continue living with their wives. . . .

The Indians are punished for their offenses by their own magistrates, appointed by the Portuguese governors; the only chastisement consists in being put in the stocks for a day or two, as the magistrate considers best; they use no chains or other imprisonment. If some Indian who went to work for the Portuguese returns before completing his time, the Father compels him to return to work out his time, and if the Indian cannot go for some good reason the Father arranges matters to the satisfaction of his employer.

The Fathers always encourage the Indians to cultivate their fields and to raise more provisions than they need, so that in case of necessity they might aid the Portuguese by way of barter; in fact, many Portuguese obtain their food from the villages. Thus one could say that the Fathers are truly the fathers of the Indians, both of their souls and of their bodies.

PART FOUR

COLONIAL SOCIETY AND CULTURE

7

COLONIAL SOCIETY

THE SOCIAL ORDER that arose in the Spanish colonies on the ruins of the old Indian societies, like that of Spain, was based on feudal principles. All agricultural and mechanical labor was regarded as degrading. The various races and racial mixtures were carefully distinguished, and a trace of black or Indian blood legally sufficed to deprive an individual of the rights and privileges of white men, including the right to hold public office or enter the professions. In practice, racial lines were not so strictly drawn. For a stipulated sum a wealthy *mestizo* or mulatto could often purchase from the Spanish crown a certificate placing him in the category of whites.

Wealth, not gentle birth or racial purity, was the true distinguishing characteristic of the colonial aristocracy. Legally, Creoles and peninsular Spaniards were equal. In practice, during most of the colonial period the former suffered from a system of discrimination that denied them employment in the highest Church and government posts and in large-scale commerce. In the first half of the eighteenth century their situation improved, and Creoles came to dominate the prestigious *audiencias* of Mexico City and Lima. But in the second half of the century a reaction took place, and high-ranking Creoles were removed from positions in the imperial administration. The cleavage in the colonial upper class grew wider with the passage of time and must be considered a major cause of the Creole wars of independence.

The *mestizo* caste had its main origin in a multitude of irregular unions between Spaniards and native women, although mixed marriages were not uncommon, especially in the early period. The masses of mixed blood were consigned to an inferior social status by their poverty and illegitimate birth. The *mestizo* caste tended to become a lower middle class of artisans, overseers, shopkeepers, and the like.

By contrast with the *mestizo*, no ambiguity marked the position of the Indian in the social scale. Aside from a small and privileged group of hereditary chiefs and their families, the Indians formed a distinct servile class, burdened with many tribute and labor obligations. They lived apart from the whites in their own communities of pre-Conquest origin, or in towns established by the Spaniards. In many regions they preserved their ancestral social organization, language, and other cultural traits. On numerous occasions they rose against their oppressors in revolts that were generally crushed with great severity.

The virtual disappearance of the native population of the Antilles and the rapid growth of sugar cane cultivation led colonists to demand black slave labor. A large black and mixed population came into being in the regions of plantation culture, notably in the West Indies and on the coasts of Mexico and Venezuela. Smaller populations were found in all the large colonial towns, where they were chiefly used as household servants.

Black slavery in the Spanish colonies has been described as patriarchal and humane by comparison with the system in the English and French colonies, but this judgment, based in considerable part on the Spanish eighteenth-century slave code, has recently been subjected to sharp criticism. Emancipation was legal and occurred with some frequency during the colonial period. Whether slaves or freemen, blacks occupied the lowest position in the social scale. Unless redeemed by wealth or singular talents, blacks, mulattos, and other racial mixtures shared this disfavor. Many found employment in the mines, in the mechanical trades, as confidential servants, and in the colonial militia, where they formed separate units under the command of white officers.

Race mixture played a decisive role in the formation of the Brazilian people. The scarcity of white women in the colony, the lack of puritanical attitudes among the Portuguese, and the despotic power of the great planters over their Indian and black slave women all gave impetus to miscegenation. Color lines were drawn less sharply than in the Spanish Indies, and in colonial Brazil the possession of wealth more easily expunged the "taint" of black skin.

Slavery played as important a role in the social organization of colonial Brazil as race mixture did in its ethnic makeup. The social consequences of the system were entirely negative. Slavery corrupted both master and slave, fostered harmful attitudes with respect to the dignity of labor, and retarded the economic development of Brazil. The virtual monopolization of labor by slaves sharply limited the number of socially acceptable occupations in which whites or free mixed bloods could engage. This gave rise to a large class of vagrants, beggars, "poor whites," and other degraded or disorderly elements who would not or could not compete with slaves in agriculture and industry.

The nucleus of Brazilian social as well as economic organization was the large estate; this centered about the Big House and constituted a patriarchal community that included the owner and his family, his chaplain and overseers, his slaves, and his *agregados*, or retainers—freemen of low social status who received the landowner's protection and assistance in return for a variety of services. In the sugar-growing northeast the great planters became a distinct aristocratic class that maintained family traditions and took pride in name and blood.

By contrast with the decisive importance of the *fazenda*, or large estate, most of the colonial towns were mere appendages of the countryside, dominated politically and socially by the rural magnates. But in a few large cities, such as Baía and Rio de Janeiro, other social groups that disputed or shared power with the great landowners existed: high officials of the colonial administration; dignitaries of the Church; wealthy professional men, especially lawyers, and the large merchants, almost exclusively peninsulars, who monopolized the export-import trade and financed the industry of the planters.

1. THE STRUCTURE OF CLASS AND CASTE

The population of the Spanish colonies formed a melting pot of races, white, red, and black. Their progressive amalgamation was slowed but not halted by a caste system that assigned different social values to the respective races and mixtures. Spanish officials Jorge Juan and Antonio de Ulloa describe the complicated structure of class and caste of a colonial town—the Caribbean port of Cartagena.

The inhabitants may be divided into different castes or tribes, who derive their origin from a coalition of Whites, Negroes, and Indians. Of each of these we shall treat particularly. The Whites may be divided into two classes, the Europeans, and Creoles, or Whites born in the country. The former are commonly called *Chapetones*, but are not numerous; most of them either return into Spain after acquiring a competent fortune, or remove up into inland provinces in order to increase it. Those who are settled at Carthagena, carry on the whole trade of that place, and live in opulence; whilst the other inhabitants are indigent, and reduced to have recourse to mean and hard labor for subsistence. The families of the White Creoles compose the landed interest; some of them have large estates, and are highly respected, because their ancestors came into the country invested with honorable posts, bringing their families with them when they settled here. Some of these families, in order to keep up their original dignity, have either married their children to their equals in the country, or sent them as officers on board the galleons; but others have greatly declined. Besides these, there are other Whites, in mean

Jorge Juan and Antonio de Ulloa, *Voyage to South America*, 2 vols. (London, 1772), 1:29–32.

circumstances, who either owe their origin to Indian families, or at least to an intermarriage with them, so that there is some mixture in their blood; but when this is not discoverable by their color, the conceit of being Whites alleviates the pressure of every other calamity.

Among the other tribes which are derived from an intermarriage of the Whites and the Negroes, the first are the Mulattoes. Next to these the *Tercerones*, produced from a White and a Mulatto, with some approximation to the former, but not so near as to obliterate their origin. After these follow the *Quarterones*, proceeding from a White and a *Terceron*. The last are the *Quinterones*, who owe their origin to a White and *Quarteron*. This is the last gradation, there being no visible difference between them and the Whites, either in color or features; nay they are often fairer than the Spaniards. The children of a White and *Quinteron* are also called Spaniards, and consider themselves as free from all taint of the Negro race. Every person is so jealous of the order of their tribe or cast, that if, through inadvertence, you call them by a degree lower than what they actually are, they are highly offended, never suffering themselves to be deprived of so valuable a gift of fortune.

Before they attain the class of the *Quinterones*, there are several intervening circumstances which throw them back; for between the Mulatto and the Negro, there is an intermediate race, which they call *Sambos*, owing their origin to a mixture between one of these with an Indian, or among themselves. They are also distinguished according to the class their fathers were of. Betwixt the *Tercerones* and the Mulattoes, the *Quarterones* and the *Tercerones*, etc. are those called *Tente en el Ayre*, suspended in the air, because they neither advance nor recede. Children, whose parents are a *Quarteron* or *Quinteron*, and a Mulatto or *Terceron*, are *Salto atras retrogrades*; because, instead of advancing towards being Whites, they have gone backwards towards the Negro race. The children between a Negro and *Quinteron* are called *Sambos de Negro, de Mulatto, de Terceron*, etc.

These are the most known and common tribes or *Castas*; there are indeed several others proceeding from their intermarriages; but, being so various, even they themselves cannot easily distinguish them; and these are the only people one sees in the city, the *estancias*, and the villages; for if any Whites, especially women, are met with, it is only accidental, these generally residing in their houses; at least, if they are of any rank or character.

These castas, from the Mulattoes, all affect the Spanish dress, but wear very slight stuffs on account of the heat of the climate. These are the mechanics of the city; the Whites, whether Creoles or *Chapetones*, disdaining such a mean occupation follow nothing below merchandise. But it being impossible for all to succeed, great numbers not being able to procure sufficient credit, they become poor and miserable from their aversion to those trades they follow in Europe, and, instead of the riches which they flattered themselves with possessing in the Indies, they experience the most complicated wretchedness.

The class of Negroes is not the least numerous, and is divided into two parts; the free and the slaves. These [last] are again subdivided into Creoles and *Bozales*, part of which are employed in the cultivation of the haciendas or estancias. Those in the city are obliged to perform the most laborious services, and pay out of their wages a certain quota to their masters, subsisting themselves on the small remainder. The violence of the heat not permitting them to wear any cloths, their only covering is a small piece of cotton stuff about their waist; the female slaves go in the same manner. Some of these live at the *estancias*, being married to the slaves who work there; while those in the city sell in the markets all kind of eatables, and cry fruits, sweet-meats, cakes made of the maize, and cassava, and several other things about the streets. Those who have children sucking at their breast, which is the case of the generality, carry them on their shoulders, in order to have their arms at liberty; and when the infants are hungry, they give them the breast either under the arm or over the shoulder, without taking them from their backs. This will perhaps appear incredible; but their breasts, being left to grow without any pressure on them often hang down to their very waist, and are not therefore difficult to turn over their shoulders for the convenience of the infant.

2. THE COLONIAL CITY: MEXICO CITY

Mexico City and Lima were the two great centers of urban civilization in colonial Spanish America. In each an unbridgeable chasm separated the world of the white upper class, flaunting its wealth in gay apparel, richly ornamented dwellings, and colorful pageants, from that of the sullen Indian, black, and mixed-blood working class, living in wretched huts amid incredible squalor. The renegade English priest Thomas Gage paints a vivid picture of Mexico City in 1625.

At the rebuilding of this city there was a great difference betwixt an inhabitant of Mexico, and a Conqueror; for a Conqueror was a name of honor, and had lands and rents given him and to his posterity by the King of Spain, and the inhabitant or only dweller paid rent for his house. And this hath filled all those parts of America with proud Dons and gentlemen to this day; for every one will call himself a descendant from a Conqueror, though he be as poor as Job; and ask him what is become of his estate and fortune; he will answer that

---

Thomas Gage, *The English–American: A New Survey of the West Indies*, ed. A. P. Newton (London, 1946), pp. 89–92.

fortune hath taken it away, which shall never take away a Don from him. Nay, a poor cobbler, or carrier that runs about the country far and near getting his living with half-a-dozen mules, if he be called Mendoza, or Guzman, will swear that he descended from those dukes' houses in Spain, and that his grandfather came from thence to conquer, and subdued whole countries to the Crown of Spain, though now fortune have frowned upon him, and covered his rags with a threadbare cloak.

When Mexico was rebuilt, and judges, aldermen, attorneys, town clerks, notaries, scavengers, and sergeants with all other officers necessary for the commonwealth of a city were appointed, the fame of Cortez and majesty of the city was blown abroad into far provinces, by means whereof it was soon replenished with Indians again, and with Spaniards from Spain, who soon conquered above four hundred leagues of land, being all governed by the princely seat of Mexico. But since that first rebuilding, I may say it is now rebuilt the second time by Spaniards, who have consumed most of the Indians; so that now I will not dare to say there are a hundred thousand houses which soon after the Conquest were built up, for most of them were of Indians.

Now the Indians that live there, live in the suburbs of the city, and their situation is called Guadalupe. In the year 1625, when I went to those parts, this suburb was judged to contain five thousand inhabitants; but since most of them have been consumed by the Spaniards' hard usage and the work of the lake. So that now there may not be above two thousand inhabitants of mere Indians, and a thousand of such as they call there *mestizos*, who are of a mixed nature of Spaniards and Indians, for many poor Spaniards marry with Indian women, and others that marry them not but hate their husbands, find many tricks to convey away an innocent Uriah to enjoy his Bathsheba. The Spaniards daily cozen them of the small plot of ground where their houses stand, and of three or four houses of Indians built up one good and fair house after the Spanish fashion with gardens and orchards. And so is almost all Mexico new built with very fair and spacious houses with gardens of recreation.

Their buildings are with stone, and brick very strong, but not high, by reason of the many earthquakes, which would endanger their houses if they were above three stories high. The streets are very broad, in the narrowest of them three coaches may go, and in the broader may go six in the breadth of them, which makes the city seem a great deal bigger than it is. In my time it was thought to be of between thirty and forty thousand inhabitants— Spaniards, who are so proud and rich that half the city was judged to keep coaches, for it was a most credible report that in Mexico in my time there were above fifteen thousand coaches. It is a byword that at Mexico there are four things fair, that is to say, the women, the apparel, the horses, and the streets. But to this I may add the beauty of some of the coaches of the gentry, which do exceed in cost the best of the Court of Madrid and other parts of Christendom; for there they spare no silver, nor gold, nor precious stones, nor cloth of gold, nor the best silks from China to enrich them. And to the gallantry of their horses the pride of some doth add the cost of bridles and shoes of silver.

The streets of Christendom must not compare with those in breadth and cleanness, but especially in the riches of the shops which do adorn them. Above all, the goldsmiths' shops and works are to be admired. The Indians, and the people of China that have been made Christians and every year come thither, have perfected the Spaniards in that trade. The Viceroy that went thither the year 1625 caused a popinjay to be made of silver, gold, and precious stones with the perfect colors of the popinjay's feathers (a bird bigger than a pheasant), with such exquisite art and perfection, to present unto the King of Spain, that it was prized to be worth in riches and workmanship half a million of ducats. There is in the cloister of the Dominicans a lamp hanging in the church with three hundred branches wrought in silver to hold so many candles, besides a hundred little lamps for oil set in it, every one being made with several workmanship so exquisitely that it is valued to be worth four hundred thousand ducats; and with such-like curious works are many streets made more rich and beautiful from the shops of goldsmiths.

To the by-word touching the beauty of the women I must add the liberty they enjoy for gaming, which is such that the day and night is too short for them to end a *primera* when once it is begun; nay gaming is so common to them that they invite gentlemen to their houses for no other end. To myself it happened that passing along the streets in company with a friar that came with me that year from Spain, a gentlewoman of great birth knowing us to be *chapetons* (so they call the first year those that come from Spain), from her window called unto us, and after two or three slight questions concerning Spain asked us if we would come in and play with her a game at *primera*.

Both men and women are excessive in their apparel, using more silks than stuffs and cloth. Precious stones and pearls further much their vain ostentation; a hat band and rose made of diamonds in a gentleman's hat is common, and a hat band of pearls is ordinary in a tradesman; nay a blackamoor or tawny young maid and slave will make hard shift but she will be in fashion with her neck chain and bracelets of pearls, and her ear-bobs of some considerable jewels. The attire of this baser sort of people of blackamoors and mulattoes (which are of a mixed nature, of Spaniards and blackamoors) is so light, and their carriage so enticing, that many Spaniards even of the better sort (who are too too prone to venery) disdain their wives for them.

Their clothing is a petticoat of silk or cloth, with many silver or golden laces, with a very broad double ribbon of some light color with long silver or golden tags hanging down before, the whole length of their petticoat to the ground, and the like behind; their waistcoats made like bodices, with skirts, laced likewise with gold or silver, without sleeves, and a girdle about their body of great price stuck with pearls and knots of gold (if they be any ways well esteemed of), their sleeves are broad and open at the end, of Holland or fine China linen, wrought some with colored silks, some with silk and gold, some with silk and silver, hanging down almost unto the ground; the locks of their heads are covered with some wrought coif, and over it another of net-work of silk bound with a fair silk, or silver, or golden ribbon which crosseth the upper part of their forehead, and hath commonly worked out in letters some light and foolish love posy; their bare, black, and tawny breasts are covered with bobs hanging from their chains of pearls.

And when they go abroad, they use a white mantle of lawn or cambric rounded with a broad lace, which some put over their heads, the breadth reaching only to their middle behind, that their girdle and ribbons may be seen, and two ends before reaching to the ground almost; others cast their mantles only upon their shoulders, and swaggers-like, cast the one end over the left shoulder that they may the better jog the right arm, and show their broad sleeve as they walk along; others instead of this mantle use some rich silk petticoat to hang upon their left shoulder, while with their right arm they support the lower part of it, more like roaring boys than honest civil maids. Their shoes are high and of many soles, the outside whereof of the profaner sort are plated with a list of silver, which is fastened with small nails of broad silver heads.

Most of these are or have been slaves, though love have set them loose at liberty to enslave souls to sin and Satan. And there are so many of this kind both men and women grown to a height of pride and vanity, that many times the Spaniards have feared they would rise up and mutiny against them. And for the looseness of their lives, and public scandals committed by them and the better sort of the Spaniards, I have heard them say often who have professed more religion and fear of God, they verily thought God would destroy that city, and give up the country into the power of some other nation. . . .

Great alms and liberality towards religious houses in that city commonly are coupled with great and scandalous wickedness. They wallow in the bed of riches and wealth, and make their alms the coverlet to cover their loose and lascivious lives. From hence are the churches so fairly built and adorned. There are not above fifty churches and chapels, cloisters and nunneries, and parish churches in that city; but those that are there are the fairest that ever my eyes beheld, the roofs and beams being in many of them all daubed with gold, and many altars with sundry marble pillars, and others with brazil-wood stays standing one above another with tabernacles for several saints richly wrought with golden colors, so that twenty thousand ducats is a common price of many of them. These cause admiration in the common sort of people, and admiration brings on daily adoration in them to those glorious spectacles and images of saints.

It is ordinary for the friars to visit their devoted nuns, and to spend whole days with them, hearing their music, feeding on their sweetmeats, and for this purpose they have many chambers which they call *locutorios*, to talk in, with wooden bars between the nuns and them, and in these chambers are tables for the friars to dine at; and while they dine the nuns re-create them with their voices. Gentlemen and citizens give their daughters to be brought up in these nunneries, where they are taught to make all sorts of conserves and preserves, all sorts of needlework, all sorts of music, which is so exquisite in that city that I dare be bold to say that the people are drawn to their churches more for the delight of the music than for any delight in the service of God. More, they teach these young children to act like players, and to entice the people to their churches make these children to act short dialogues in their choirs, richly attiring them with men's and women's apparel, especially upon Midsummer Day, and the eight days before their Christmas, which is so gallantly performed that many factious strifes and single combats have been, and some were in my time, for defending which of these nunneries most excelled in music and in the training up of children. No delights are wanting in that city abroad in the world, nor in their churches, which should be the house of God, and the soul's, not the sense's delight.

The chief place in the city is the market-place, which though it be not as spacious as in Montezuma his time, yet is at this day very fair and wide, built all with arches on the one side where people may walk dry in time of rain, and there are shops of merchants furnished with all sorts of stuffs and silks, and before them sit women selling all manner of fruits and herbs; over against these shops and arches is the Viceroy his palace, which taketh up almost the whole length of the market with the walls of the house and of the gardens belonging to it. At the end of the Viceroy his palace is the chief prison, which is strong of stone work. Next to this is the beautiful street called *La Plateria*, or Goldsmiths Street, where a man's eyes may behold in less than an hour many millions' worth of gold, silver, pearls, and jewels. The street of St. Austin is rich and comely, where live all that trade in silks; but one of the longest and broadest streets is the street called Tacuba, where almost all the shops are of ironmongers, and of such as deal in brass and steel, which is joining to those arches whereon the water is conveyed into the city, and is so called for that it is the way out of the city to a town called Tacuba; and this street is mentioned far and near, not so much for the length and breadth of it, as for a small commodity of needles which are made there, and for proof are the best of all those parts. For stately buildings the street called *del Aquila*, the Street of the Eagle, exceeds the rest, where live gentlemen, and courtiers, and judges belonging to the Chancery, and is the palace of the Marques del Valle from the line of Ferdinando Cortez; this street is so called from an old idol an eagle of stone which from the Conquest lieth in a corner of that street, and is twice as big as London stone.

The gallants of this city show themselves daily, some on horseback, and most in coaches, about four of the clock in the afternoon in a pleasant shady field called *la Alameda*, full of trees and walks, somewhat like unto our Moor-fields, where do meet as constantly as the merchants upon our exchange about two thousand coaches, full of gallants, ladies, and citizens, to see and to be seen, to court and to be courted, the gentlemen having their train of blackamoor slaves some a dozen, some half a dozen waiting on them, in brave and gallant liveries, heavy with gold and silver lace, with silk stockings on their black legs, and roses on their feet, and swords by their sides; the ladies also carry their train by their coach's side of such jetlike damsels as before have been mentioned for their light apparel, who with their bravery and white mantles over them seem to be, as the Spaniard saith, *mosca en leche*, a fly in milk. But the train of the Viceroy who often goeth to this place is wonderful stately, which some say is as great as the train of his master the King of Spain. At this meeting are carried about many sorts of sweetmeats and papers of comfits to be sold, for to relish a cup of cool water, which is cried about in curious glasses, to cool the blood of those love-hot gallants. But many times these their meetings sweetened with conserves and comfits have sour sauce at the end, for jealousy will not suffer a lady to be courted, no nor sometimes to be spoken to, but puts fury into the violent hand to draw a sword or dagger and to stab or murder whom he was jealous of, and when one sword is drawn thousands are presently drawn, some to right the party wounded or mur-dered; others to defend the party murdering, whose friends will not permit him to be apprehended, but will guard him with drawn swords until they have conveyed him to the sanctuary of some church, from whence the Viceroy his power is not able to take him for a legal trial.

3. THE *MESTIZO*: SEED OF TOMORROW

The mestizo *arose from a process of racial fusion that began in the first days of the Spanish conquest and has continued to the present. The Spanish jurist Juan de Solórzano Pereira (1575–1655) discusses the status of the* mestizo *in colonial law and opinion.*

Turning now to the persons called *mestizos* and mulattos, of whom there are great numbers in the Indies, first let me say that the name *mestizo* was assigned to the former because they represent a mixture of blood and nationality. . . .

As for the mulattos, although for the same reason they belong in the class of *mestizos*, yet as the offspring of Negro women and white men, or the re-

Juan de Solórzano Pereira, *Política indiana*, 5 vols. (Madrid, 1930), 1:445–448. Excerpt translated by Benjamin Keen.

verse, which is the most strange and repulsive mixture of all, they bear this specific name which compares them to the species of the mule. . . .

If these men were born of legitimate wedlock and had no other vices or defects, they could be regarded as citizens of those provinces and could be admitted to honor and office in them, as is argued by Victoria and Zapata. I am of the opinion that such an intention was the basis of certain royal decrees that permit *mestizos* to take holy orders and *mestizas* to become nuns, and admit *mestizos* to municipal offices and notaryships.

But because they are most often born out of adultery or other illicit unions, since few Spaniards of honorable position will marry Indian or Negro women . . . , they bear the taint of illegitimacy and other vices which they take in, as it were, with their milk. And these men, I find by many other decrees, are forbidden to hold any responsible public office, whether it is that of Protector of the Indians, councilman, or notary public, unless they acknowledge this defect at the time of application and receive special dispensation from it; and those who have gained office in any other way are not allowed to keep it.

There are other decrees that forbid them to take holy orders, unless by special dispensation.

I shall content myself for the present with saying that if these *mestizos* (especially those in the Indies) possess recognized and assured virtue, and sufficient ability and learning, they could be extremely useful in matters relating to the Indians, being, as it were, their countrymen, and knowing their languages and customs. . . .

But returning to the question of curacies, although for the reason given above it would be convenient to entrust them to *mestizos*, great care must be taken with this, for we see that the majority of them come from a vicious and depraved environment, and it is they who do the most harm to the Indians. . . . And for this reason many decrees forbid them to visit or live in the Indian towns, and compel them to live in the Spanish towns, or in such towns as may be formed and populated by *mestizos* and mulattos. These same decrees order that *mestizas* married to Spaniards, if charged with adultery, shall be tried and punished like Spanish women.

There are other decrees, of later date, issued in 1600 and 1608, directed to the viceroys of Peru Don Luis de Velasco and the marquis of Montes Claros, saying that the king had learned that the number of *mestizos*, mulattos, and *zambahigos* (the children of Negro men and Indian women, or the reverse) was increasing sharply, and ordering them to take appropriate measures that men of such mixtures, vicious in their majority, should not cause injury and disturbances in that kingdom—a thing always to be feared from such people, especially if to the sins that arise from their evil birth are added those that spring from idleness and poor upbringing.

For this reason, although by the ordinances of the viceroy of Peru, Don Francisco de Toledo, they are exempt from paying tribute, by later decrees of the years 1600, 1612, 1619, by the celebrated decrees concerning personal service of 1601 and 1609, and by many others that have been successively promulgated, it is ordered that they pay tribute. And the same decrees command the viceroys to see that the *mestizos* and mulattos, like the Indians, are made to labor in the mines and fields. . . .

For it does not appear just that this labor [of the mines], which requires such physical strength . . . should be assigned entirely to the wretched Indians, while the *mestizos* and mulattos, who are of such evil caste, race, and character, are left to idleness; this contravenes the rule that lewdness should not be more favored than chastity, and that the offspring of legitimate marriage should be more privileged than the illegitimate, as is taught by Saint Thomas and other authorities. . . .

From this abuse results the fact that many Indian women desert their Indian husbands and neglect the children that they have by them, seeing them subject to tribute-payments and personal services, and desire, love, and spoil the children that they have out of wedlock by Spaniards or even by Negroes, because they are free and exempt from all burdens—a condition that plainly should not be permitted in any well-governed state.

4. THE INDIAN TOWN

Among the various races and mixtures that composed the population of the Spanish empire in the Americas, the Indians formed a nation apart. Most of them lived in their own self-governing communities in which Spaniards other than the village priest were forbidden to reside. In many regions they maintained their ancient clan or tribal organization, language, dress, and customs. Thomas Gage, who spent twelve years as a priest in Guatemala and amassed a tidy fortune from the piety and credulity of his native parishioners, describes the life of the Indian town.

Their ordinary clothing is a pair of linen or woolen drawers broad and open at the knees, without shoes (though in their journeys some will put on leather sandals to keep the soles of their feet) or stockings, without any doublet, a short coarse shirt, which reacheth a little below their waist, and serves more for a doublet than for a shirt, and for a cloak a woolen or linen mantle (called *aiate*) tied with a knot over one shoulder, hanging down on the other side almost to the ground, with a twelvepenny or two shilling hat, which after one good shower of rain like paper falls about their necks and eyes; their bed

Gage, *The English-American*, pp. 234–247.

they carry sometime about them, which is a woolen mantle wherewith they wrap themselves about at night, taking off their shirt and drawers, which they lay under their head for a pillow; some will carry with them a short, slight, and light mat to lie, but those that carry it not with them, if they cannot borrow one of a neighbor, lie as willingly in their mantle upon the bare ground as a gentleman in England upon a soft down-bed, and thus do they soundly sleep, and loudly snort after a day's work, or after a day's journey with a hundred-weight upon their backs.

Those that are of the better sort, and richer, and who are not employed as *tamemez* to carry burdens, or as laborers to work for Spaniards, but keep at home following their own farms, or following their own mules about the country, or following their trades and callings in their shops, or governing the towns, as *alcaldes*, or *alguaziles*, officers of justice, may go a little better apparaled, but after the same manner. For some will have their drawers with a lace at the bottom, or wrought with some colored silk or crewel, so likewise the mantle about them shall have either a lace, or some work of birds on it; some will wear a cut linen doublet, others shoes, but very few stockings or bands about their necks; and for their beds, the best Indian Governor or the richest, who may be worth four or five thousand ducats, will have little more than the poor *tamemez*; for they lie upon boards, or canes bound together, and raised from the ground, whereon they lay a board and handsome mat, and at their heads for man and wife two little stumps of wood for bolsters, whereon they lay their shirts and mantles and other clothes for pillows, covering themselves with a broader blanket than is their mantle, and thus hardly would Don Bernabé de Guzman the Governor of Petapa lie, and so do all the best of them.

The women's attire is cheap and soon put on; for most of them also go barefoot, the richer and better sort wear shoes, with broad ribbons for shoe strings, and for a petticoat, they tie about their waist a woolen mantle, which in the better sort is wrought with divers colors, but not sewed at all, pleated, or gathered in, but as they tie it with a list about them; they wear no shift next their body, but cover their nakedness with a kind of surplice (which they call *guaipil*) which hangs loose from their shoulders down a little below their waist, with open short sleeves, which cover half their arms; this *guaipil* is curiously wrought, especially in the bosom, with cotton, or feathers. The richer sort of them wear bracelets and bobs about their waists and necks; their hair is gathered up with fillets, without any coif or covering, except it be the better sort. When they go to church or abroad, they put upon their heads a veil of linen, which hangeth almost to the ground, and this is that which costs them most of all their attire, for that commonly it is of Holland or some good linen brought from Spain, or fine linen brought from China, which the better sort wear with a lace about. When they are at home at work they commonly take off their *guaipil*, or surplice, discovering the nakedness of their breasts and body. They lie also in their beds as do their husbands, wrapped up only with a mantle, or with a blanket.

Their houses are but poor thatched cottages, without any upper rooms, but commonly one or two only rooms below, in the one they dress their meat in the middle of it, making a compass for fire, with two or three stones, without any other chimney to convey the smoke away, which spreading itself about the room filleth the thatch and the rafters so with soot that all the room seemeth to be a chimney. The next unto it is not free from smoke and blackness, where sometimes are four or five beds according to the family. The poorer sort have but one room, where they eat, dress their meat, and sleep. Few there are that set any locks upon their doors, for they fear no robbing nor stealing, neither have they in their houses much to lose, earthen pots, and pans, and dishes, and cups to drink their chocolate being the chief commodities in their house. There is scarce any house which hath not also in the yard a stew, wherein they bathe themselves with hot water, which is their chief physic when they feel themselves distempered.

Among themselves they are in every town divided into tribes, which have one chief head, to whom all that belong unto that tribe do resort in any difficult matters, who is bound to aid, protect, defend, counsel, and appear for the rest of his tribe before the officers of justice in any wrong that is like to be done unto them. When any is to be married, the father of the son that is to take a wife out of another tribe goeth unto the head of his tribe to give him warning of his son's marriage with such a maid. Then that head meets with the head of the maid's tribe, and they confer about it. The business commonly is in debate a quarter of a year; all which time the parents of the youth or man are with gifts to buy the maid; they are to be at the charges of all that is spent in eating and drinking when the heads of the two tribes do meet with the rest of the kindred of each side, who sometimes sit in conference a whole day, or most part of a night. After many days and nights thus spent, and a full trial being made of the one and other side's affection, if they chance to disagree about the marriage, then is the tribe and parents of the maid to restore back all that the other side hath spent and given. They give no portions with their daughters, but when they die their goods and lands are equally divided among their sons. If anyone want a house to live in or will repair and thatch his house anew, notice is given to the heads of the tribes, who warn all the town to come to help in the work, and everyone is to bring a bundle of straw, and other materials, so that in one day with the help of many they finish a house, without any charges more than of chocolate, which they minister in great cups as big as will hold above a pint, not putting in any costly materials, as do the Spaniards, but only a little anis seed, and chili, or Indian pepper; or else they half fill the cup with *atole*, and pour upon it as much chocolate as will fill the cup and color it.

In their diet the poorer sort are limited many times to a dish of *frijoles*, or Turkey beans, either black or white (which are there in very great abundance, and are kept dry for all the year) boiled with chili; and if they can have this, they hold themselves well satisfied; with these beans, they make also dumplings, first boiling the bean a little, and then mingling it with a mass of maize, as we do mingle currents in our cakes, and so boil again the *frijoles* with the dumpling of maize mass, and so eat it hot, or keep it cold; but this and all whatsoever else they eat, they either eat it with green biting chili, or else they dip it in water and salt, wherein is bruised some of that chili. But if their means will not reach to *frijoles*, their ordinary fare and diet is their tortillas (so they call thin round cakes made of the dough and mass of maize) which they eat hot from an earthen pan, whereon they are soon baked with one turning over the fire; and these they eat alone either with chili and salt, and dipping them in water and salt with a little bruised chili. When their maize is green and tender, they boil some of those whole stalks or clusters, whereon the maize groweth with the leaf about, and so casting a little salt about it, they eat it. I have often eat of this, and found it as dainty as our young green peas, and very nourishing, but it much increaseth the blood. Also of this green and tender maize they make a furmety, boiling the maize in some of the milk which they have first taken out of it by bruising it. The poorest Indian never wants this diet, and is well satisfied as long as his belly is thoroughly filled.

But the poorest that live in such towns where flesh meat is sold will make a hard shift but that when they come from work on Saturday night they will buy one half real, or a real worth of fresh meat to eat on the Lord's day. Some will buy a good deal at once, and keep it long by dressing it into *tasajos*, which are bundles of flesh, rolled up and tied fast, which they do when, for example's sake, they have from a leg of beef sliced off from the bone all the flesh with the knife, after the length, form, and thinness of a line, or rope. Then they take the flesh and salt it (which being sliced and thinly cut, soon takes salt) and hang it up in their yards like a line from post to post, or from tree to tree, to the wind for a whole week, and then they hang it in the smoke another week, and after roll it up in small bundles, which become as hard as a stone, and so as they need it they wash it, boil it and eat. This is America's powdered beef, which they call *tasajo*.. . .

As for drinking, the Indians generally are much given unto it; and drink if they have nothing else of their poor and simple chocolate, without sugar or many compounds, or of *atole*, until their bellies be ready to burst. But if they can get any drink that will make them mad drunk, they will not give it over as long as a drop is left, or a penny remains in their purse to purchase it. Among themselves they use to make such drinks as are in operation far stronger than wine; and these they confection in such great jars as come from Spain, wherein they put some little quantity of water, and fill up the jar with some molasses or juice of the sugar-cane, or some honey for to sweeten it; then for the strengthening of it, they put roots and leaves of tobacco, with other kind of roots which grow there, and they know to be strong in operation, and in some places I have known where they have put in a live toad, and so closed up the jar for a fortnight, or month's space, till all that they have put in him be thoroughly steeped and the toad consumed, and the drink well strengthened, then they open it and call their friends to the drinking of it (which commonly they do in the night time, lest their priest in the town should have notice of them in the day), which they never leave off until they be mad and raging drunk. This drink they call *chicha*, which stinketh most filthily, and certainly is the cause of many Indians' death, especially where they use the toad's poison with it. . . .

And thus having spoken of apparel, houses, eating and drinking, it remains that I say somewhat of their civility, and religion of those who lived under the government of the Spaniards. From the Spaniards they have borrowed their civil government, and in all towns they have one, or two, *alcaldes*, with more or less *regidores* (who are as aldermen or jurats amongst us) and some *alguaziles*, more or less, who are as constables, to execute the orders of the *alcalde* (who is a mayor) with his brethren. In towns of three or four hundred families, or upwards, there are commonly two *alcaldes*, six *regidores*, two *alguaziles mayores*, and six under, or petty, *alguaziles*. And some towns are privileged with an Indian Governor, who is above the *alcaldes* and all the rest of the officers. These are changed every year by new election, and are chosen by the Indians themselves, who take their turns by the tribes or kindreds, whereby they are divided. Their offices begin on New Year's Day, and after that day their election is carried to the city of Guatemala (if in that district it be made) or else to the heads of justice, or Spanish governors of the several provinces, who confirm the new election, and take account of the last year's expenses made by the other officers, who carry with them their townbook of accounts; and therefore for this purpose every town hath a clerk, or scrivener, called *escribano* who commonly continueth many years in his office, by reason of the paucity and unfitness of Indian scriveners who are able to bear such a charge. This clerk hath many fees for his writings and informations, and accounts, as have the Spaniards, though not so much money or bribes, but a small matter, according to the poverty of the Indians. The Governor is also commonly continued many years, being some chief man among the Indians, except for his misdemeanors he be complained of, or the Indians in general do all stomach him.

Thus they being settled in a civil way of government they may execute justice upon all such Indians of their town as do notoriously and scandalously offend. They may imprison, fine, whip, and banish, but hang and quarter they may not; but must remit such cases to the Spanish governor. So likewise if a Spaniard passing by the town, or living in it, do trouble the peace, and misdemean himself, they may lay hold on him, and send him to the next Spanish justice, with a full information of his offences, but fine him, or keep him about one night in prison they may not. This order they have against

Spaniards, but they dare not execute it, for a whole town standeth in awe of one Spaniard, and though he never so heinously offend, and be unruly, with oaths, threatenings, and drawing of his sword, he maketh them quake and tremble, and not presume to touch him; for they know if they do they shall have the worst, either by blows, or by some misinformation which he will give against them. . . .

Amongst themselves, if any complaint be made against any Indian, they dare not meddle with him until they call all his kindred, and especially the head of that tribe to which he belongeth; who if he and the rest together find him to deserve imprisonment, or whipping, or any other punishment, then the officers of justices, the *alcaldes* or mayors, and their brethren the jurats inflict upon him that punishment which all shall agree upon. But yet after judgment and sentence given, they have another, which is their last appeal, if they please, and that is to their priest and friar, who liveth in their town, by whom they will sometimes be judged, and undergo what punishment he shall think fittest.

5. THE WORLD OF THE SUGAR PLANTATION

The Jesuit priest João Antonio Andreoni (1650–1715), who went to Brazil in 1667 and spent the rest of his life there, wrote a valuable account of the agricultural and mineral resources of the colony. The following excerpts from Andreoni's book illustrate Brazilian anthropologist Gilberto Freyre's point that "the Big House completed by the slave shed represents an entire economic, social, and political system."

If the plantation owner must display his capacity in one thing more than another, it is in the proper choice of persons to administer his estate. . . .

The first choice that he must make with care, on the basis of secret information concerning the conduct and knowledge of the person in question, is that of a chaplain to whom he must entrust the teaching of all that pertains to the Christian way of life. For the principal obligation of the planter is to teach, or have taught, his family and slaves. This should be done not by some slave born in Brazil, or by some overseer who at best can only teach them their prayers and the laws of God and the Church by word of mouth, but by one who can explain to them what they should believe and what they must do, and how they must do it, and how they are to ask God for what they need.

André João Antonil (João Antonio Andreoni), *Cultura e opulencia do Brazil por suas drogas e minas*, ed. Affonso de E. Taunay (São Paulo, 1923), pp. 77–83, 91–102. Excerpts translated by Benjamin Keen.

And for this reason, if he must pay the chaplain a little more than is customary, the planter should understand that he could not put the money to better use. . . .

The chaplain should live outside the planter's house; this is best for both, because he is a priest and not a servant, a familiar of God and not of men. He should not have any woman slave in his house, unless she be of advanced years, nor should he trade in anything, either human or divine, for all this is opposed to his clerical state and is prohibited by various Papal orders.

It is customary to pay a chaplain, when he is free to say masses during weekdays, forty or fifty thousand *reis* a year, and with what he gains from the saying of masses during the week he can earn a respectable salary—and well earned too, if he does all the things described above. If he is expected to teach the children of the plantation owner, he should receive a just additional compensation. . . .

On the day that the cane is brought to be ground, if the plantation owner does not invite the Vicar, the chaplain blesses the mill and asks God to grant a good yield and to guard those who work in it from all misfortune. When the mill stops grinding at the end of the harvest, he sees to it that all give thanks to God in the chapel. . . .

The arms of the plantation owner, on which he relies for the good governance of his people and estate, are his overseers. But if each should aspire to be the head, it would be a monstrous government and would truly resemble the dog Cerberus, to whom the poets fancifully ascribe three heads. I do not say that the overseers should not possess authority, but I say that this authority must be well ordered and subordinate, not absolute, so that the lesser are inferior to the greater, and all to the master whom they serve.

It is fitting that the slaves should understand that the chief overseer has power to command and reprove them, and to punish them when necessary, but they should also know that they have recourse to the master and that they will be heard as justice requires. Nor must the other overseers suppose that their powers are unlimited, especially in what concerns punishment and seizure. The plantation owner, therefore, must make very clear the authority given to each, and especially to the chief overseer; and if they exceed their authority he should check them with the punishment that their excesses deserve—but not before the slaves, lest another time they rise against the overseer, and so that he may not bear the shame of being reproved before them and hence not dare to govern them. It will suffice if the master lets a third party make known to the injured slave, and to some of the oldest slaves on the estate, that the master was much displeased with the overseer for the wrong that he had committed, and that if he did not amend his ways he would be immediately dismissed.

The overseers must on no account be permitted to kick slaves—in particular to kick pregnant slave women in the belly—or to strike slaves with a stick, because blows struck in anger are not calculated, and they may inflict a mortal head wound on some valuable slave that cost a great deal of money. What they may do is to scold them and strike them a few times on the back with a liana whip, to teach them a lesson. To seize fugitive slaves and any who fight and slash each other and get drunk, so that the master may have them punished as they deserve, is to show a diligence worthy of praise. But to tie up a slave girl and lash her with a liana whip until the blood runs, or to place her in the stocks or in chains for months at a time (while the master is in the city) simply because she will not go to bed with him, or to do the same to a slave who gave the master a faithful account of the overseer's disloyalty, violence, and cruelty, and to invent pretended offenses to justify the punishment—this may not be tolerated on any account, for it would be to have a ravening wolf rather than a well-disposed and Christian overseer.

It is the obligation of the chief overseer of the plantation to govern the people, and to assign them to their tasks at the proper time. It is his duty to learn from the master who should be notified to cut their cane, and to send them word promptly. He should have the boats and carts ready to go for the cane and should prepare the forms and fuel. He should apprise the master of everything that is needed to equip the sugar-mill before the start of grinding, and when the season is over he should put everything away in its place. He must see that each performs his task, and if some disaster occurs he should hasten to the scene to give what help he can. . . .

The slaves are the hands and feet of the plantation owner, for without them you cannot make, preserve, and increase a fortune, or operate a plantation in Brazil. And the kind of service they give depends on how they are treated. It is necessary, therefore, to buy a certain number of slaves each year and assign them to the cane fields, the manioc fields, the sawmills, and the boats. And because they are usually of different nations, and some more primitive than others, and differ greatly in physical qualities, the assignments should be made with great care. Those who come to Brazil are the Ardas, Minas, Congos, others from S. Thomé, Angola, Cape Verde, and some from Mozambique, who come in the India ships. The Ardas and Minas are robust. Those who come from Cape Verde and S. Thomé are weaker. The slaves from Angola, raised in Loanda, are more capable of acquiring mechanical skills than those who come from the other regions that I have named. Among the Congos there are also some who are quite industrious, and good not only for work in the cane fields but for mechanical tasks and housework.

Some arrive in Brazil very barbarous and dull witted, and continue so throughout their lives. Others in a few years become clever and skillful, not only in learning Christian doctrine but in mastering trades, and they can be used to handle a boat, carry messages, and perform any other routine task. . . . It is not well to remove a slave against his will from the plantation where he has been raised since childhood, for he may pine away and die.

Those slaves who were born in Brazil, or were raised from infancy in the homes of whites, form an affection for their masters and give a good account of themselves; one of these who bears his captivity well is worth four slaves brought from Africa.

The mulattos are even more apt for every task; but many of them, taking advantage of the favor of their masters, are haughty and vicious and swagger about, always ready for a brawl. Yet they and the mulatto women commonly have it best of all in Brazil, because the white blood in their veins (sometimes that of their own masters) works such sorcery that some owners will tolerate and pardon anything they do; not only do they not reprove them, but it seems that all the caresses fall to their share. It is hard to say whether the masters or the mistresses are more at fault in this respect, for there are some of both sexes who permit themselves to be ruled by mulattos, and not those of the best sort, either, thus verifying the proverb that says that Brazil is the Hell of the Negroes, the Purgatory of the Whites, and the Paradise of the mulattos—but let some distrust or feeling of jealousy change love into hatred, and it comes forth armed with every kind of cruelty and severity. It is well to make use of their capabilities, if they will make good use of them (as some do, to be sure), but they should not be treated with such intimacy that they lose respect, and from slaves turn into masters. To free mulatto women of loose habits is surely an iniquitous thing, because the money with which they purchase their freedom rarely comes out of any other mines than their own bodies, and is gained with repeated sins; and after they are freed they continue to be the ruination of many.

Some masters are opposed to the marriage of male and female slaves, and they not only are indifferent to their living as concubines but consent and actually encourage them to live in that state, saying; "You, so-and-so, will in due time marry so-and-so"; and after that they permit them to live together as if they were already man and wife. It is said that the reason why masters do not marry such couples off is because they fear that if they tire of the match they may kill each other with poison or witchcraft, for among them there are notable masters of this craft. Others, after marrying off their slaves, keep them apart for years as if they were unwed, and this they cannot do in good conscience. Others are so negligent in what concerns the salvation of the slaves that they keep them for a long time in the cane fields or at the sugar mill without baptism. Furthermore, of those who have been baptized, many do not know who is their Creator, what they should believe, what law they should observe, how to commend themselves to God, why Christians go to Church, why they adore the Church, what to say to the Father when they kneel before him and when they speak into his ear, whether they have souls and if these souls die, and where they go when they leave the body. . . .

In what concerns food, clothing, and rest from labor, clearly these things should not be denied them, for in all fairness the master should give a servitor sufficient food, medicine for his sicknesses, and clothing so that he may be decently covered and not go about half-naked in the streets; he should also regulate their labor so that it is not beyond their strength and endurance. In Brazil they say that the slaves must have the three P's, namely, a stick, bread, and a piece of cloth (*páo, pão, e panno*). And though they make a bad beginning, commencing with the stick, which stands for punishment, yet would to God that the bread and clothing were as abundant as the punishment! For it is frequently inflicted for some offense not wholly proved, or else invented, and with instruments of great severity (even if the crimes were proved), such instruments as are not used on brute beasts. To be sure, some masters take more account of a horse than of a half dozen slaves, for the horse is cared for, and has a groom to find him hay, and wipe his sweat away, and a saddle, and a gilded bridle. . . .

Some masters have the custom of giving their slaves one day a week to plant for themselves, sometimes sending the overseer along to see that they do not neglect their work; this helps to keep them from suffering hunger or from daily milling about the house of the master to beg him for a ration of flour. But to deny them both flour and a day for planting, and to expect them to work in the fields by day, from sunrise to sundown, and in the sugar mill by night, with little rest from labor—how shall such a master escape punishment before the Tribunal of God? If to deny alms to one who needs it is to deny it to Christ our Lord, as the Good Book says, what must it be to deny food and clothing to one's slaves? And how shall that master justify his conduct, who gives woolens and silks and other fineries to her who works his perdition and then denies four or five yards of cotton, and a few more of woolen cloth, to the slave who dissolves in sweat to serve him, and barely has time to hunt for a root and a crab-fish for his meal? And if on top of this the punishment is frequent and excessive, the slaves will either run away into the woods or commit suicide, as is their custom, by holding their breath or hanging themselves—or they will try to take the lives of those who do them such great evil, resorting, if necessary, to diabolical arts, or they will clamor so loudly to the Lord that he will hear them and do to their masters what he did to the Egyptians when they vexed the Jews with extraordinary labor, sending terrible plagues against their estates and sons, as we read in the Sacred Scripture. . . .

Not to punish their excesses would be a serious fault, but these offenses should first be verified, so that innocent people may not suffer. The accused should be given a hearing, and if the charges are proved the culprits should be chastised with a moderate lashing, or by placing them in chains or in the stocks for a short period. But to punish them over hastily, with a vengeful spirit, with one's own hand, with terrible instruments, and perhaps to burn them with fire or heated sealing wax, or to brand the poor fellows in the face—why, this is intolerable in barbarians, to say nothing of Christian Catholics. . . . And if, having erred by reason of their frailty, they themselves come to beg the master's pardon, or find sponsors (*padrinhos*) to accompany them, in such cases it is customary in Brazil to pardon them. And it is well for them to know that this will obtain them forgiveness, for otherwise they may one day flee to some fugitive slave settlement (*mucambo*) in the forest, and if they are captured they may kill themselves before the master can lash them, or some kinsman will take it upon himself to avenge them by the use of witchcraft or poison. Completely to deny them their festivities, which are their only consolation in their captivity, is to condemn them to sadness and melancholy, to apathy and sickliness. Therefore masters should not object if they crown their kings and sing and dance decently for a few hours on certain days of the year, or if they amuse themselves in proper ways of an afternoon, after having celebrated in the morning the holiday of Our Lady of the Rosary, of Saint Benedict, and of the patron-saint of the plantation chapel. . . .

Since the management of a sugar plantation requires so many large outlays, as described above, it is plain that the owner must carefully watch the expenses of his household. . . .

It is a poor thing to have the reputation of being a miser, but it is no credit to bear the name of a prodigal. He who decides to assume the burdens of a plantation must either retire from the city, shunning its diversions, or maintain two houses—which is notably deleterious to the one from which he is absent and also doubly expensive. To keep one's sons on the plantation is to create country bumpkins who can only talk of dogs, horses, and cattle. To leave them in the city is to permit them to fall into vicious habits and contract shameful diseases that are not easily cured. To avoid both extremes, the best course is to place them in the household of some responsible and honorable relative or friend, where they will have no opportunity to make a false step— a friend who will faithfully keep the parent informed of their good or bad conduct and of their improvement or neglect of their studies. The lad's mother should not be permitted to send him money or to send secret orders for that purpose to the father's correspondent or cashier; nor must it be forgotten that money requested for the purchase of books can also be used for gambling. The father should therefore instruct his attorney or agent not to give the boy anything without his order. For these young fellows can be very ingenious in their pleas for money, and can devise all manner of plausible reasons and pretexts, especially when they are supposed to be engaged in some course of studies. They are perfectly willing to spend three years of pleasant life at the expense of their father or uncle, who is in his sugarcane fields and has no idea of what goes on in town. So when a father boasts that he has an Aristotle in the Academy, it may be that he really has an Asinius or an Apricius in the city. But if the father decides to keep his children at home, content to let them learn to read, write, and count, together with some knowledge of events or history, to enable them to converse in company, he should not fail to watch over them, especially when they reach a certain age. For the broad countryside is also a place of much freedom, and can breed thistles and thorns. And if one constructs a fence for cattle and horses to keep them from leaving the pasture, why should one not keep children within bounds, both inside and outside the house, if experience proves that it is necessary? . . . The good example of the father, however, is the best lesson in conduct; and the surest means of achieving peace of mind is to marry off the girls, and the boys as well, at the proper time. If they are content to marry within their station, they will find houses where they can make good matches and receive their rewards.

6. THE FREE POPULATION

Freemen and slaves formed the two great legal categories into which the Brazilian colonial population was divided. However, not all freemen belonged to the master class. Perhaps the most hopeful feature of Brazilian colonial life was the gradual blurring of the color line through race mixture—a circumstance that gave free mulattos and other mixed bloods a greater social mobility than was possible in any other slave society of modern times.

In the Portuguese South American dominions, circumstances have directed that there should be no division of castes, and a very few of those degrading and most galling distinctions which have been made by all other nations in the management of their colonies. That this was not intended by the mother country, but was rather submitted to from necessity, is to be discovered in some few regulations, which plainly show that if Portugal could have preserved the superiority of the whites, she would, as well as her neighbors, have established laws for that purpose. The rulers of Portugal wished to colonize to an unlimited extent: but their country did not contain a population sufficiently numerous for their magnificent plans. Emigrants left their own country to settle in the New World, who were literally adventurers; for they had not any settled plans of life, and they were without families. Persons of established habits, who had the wish to follow any of the ordinary means of gaining a livelihood, found employment at home; neither could Portugal spare them, nor did they wish to leave their native soil. There was no superabundance of population: and therefore every man might find occupation at home, if he had steadiness to look for it. There was no division in political or

Henry Koster, *Travels in Brazil*, 2 vols. (London, 1816), 2:167–187.

religious opinion. There was no necessity of emigration, save that which was urged by crimes. Thus the generality of the men who embarked in the expeditions which were fitted out for Brazil, were unaccompanied by females: and therefore, naturally, on their arrival in that country, they married, or irregularly connected themselves with Indian women, and subsequently with those of Africa. It is true that orphan girls were sent out by the government of Portugal: but these were necessarily few in number. In the course of another generation, the colonists married the women of mixed castes, owing to the impossibility of obtaining those of their own color: and the frequency of the custom, and the silence of the laws upon the subject, removed all idea of degradation, in thus connecting themselves. Still the European notions of superiority were not entirely laid aside: and these caused the passing of some regulations, by which white persons were to enjoy certain privileges. Thus, although the form of trial for all castes is the same, in certain places only, can capital punishment be inflicted upon the favored race. The people of color are not eligible to some of the chief offices of government: nor can they become members of the priesthood.

From the mildness of the laws, however, the mixed castes have gained ground considerably. The regulations which exist against them are evaded, or rather they have become obsolete. Perhaps the heroic conduct of Camarã o and Henrique Dias, the Indian and negro chieftains, in the famous and most interesting contest, between the Pernambucans and the Dutch, and the honors subsequently granted by the crown of Portugal to both of them, may have led to the exaltation of the general character of the much-injured varieties of the human species of which they were members. Familiarity between the chieftains of the several corps must be the consequence of their embarkation in the same cause, when the war is one of skirmishes, of ambuscades, of continual alarm, of assistance constantly afforded to each other; a patriotic war, against a foreign invader, in which difference of religion exists, and each party mortally hates the other. On these occasions all men are equal; or he only is superior whose strength and whose activity surpasses that of others. The amalgamation of castes which is caused by this consciousness of equality could not have had a fairer field for its full accomplishment, than the war to which I have alluded: and the friendships which were formed under these circumstances would not easily be broken off. Although the parties who had been so united might have been in their situations in life very far removed from each other, still the participation of equal danger must render dear the companions in peril, and make the feelings, which had been roused on these occasions, of long duration; they would continue to act, long after the cessation of the series of occurrences which had called them forth.

The free population of Brazil at the present time consists of Europeans; Brazilians, that is, white persons born in Brazil; mulattos, that is, the mixed caste between the whites and blacks, and all the varieties into which it can branch; *mamalucos*, that is, the mixed castes between the whites and Indians, and all its varieties; Indians in a domesticated state, who are called generally *Tapuyas*; negroes born in Brazil, and manumitted Africans; lastly, *mestizos*, that is, the mixed caste between the Indians and negroes. Of slaves, I shall speak by and by more at large; these are Africans, creole negroes, mulattos, and *mestizos*. The maxim of the Civil law, *partus sequitur ventrem*, is in force here as well as in the colonies of other nations.

These several mixtures of the human race have their shades of difference of character as well as of color. First we must treat of the whites. The Europeans who are not in office, or who are not military men, are, generally speaking, adventurers who have arrived in that country with little or no capital. These men commence their career in low situations of life, but by parsimony and continual exertion directed to one end, that of amassing money, they often attain their object, and pass the evening of their lives in opulence. These habits fail not, oftentimes, to give a bias to their dispositions, which is unallied to generosity and liberality. They look down upon the Brazilians, or rather they wish to consider themselves superior to them; and until lately the government took no pains to remove the jealousy which existed between the two descriptions of white persons; and even now, not so much attention is paid to the subject as its great importance seems to require. [The majority of the clergy of Pernambuco, both regular and secular, are of Brazilian parentage. The governor is an European, and so are the major part of the chief officers, civil, military, and ecclesiastical but the bishop is a Brazilian, and so is the *ouvidor*.]

The Brazilian white man of large property, who draws his descent from the first Donatory of a province, or whose family has for some generations enjoyed distinction, entertains a high opinion of his own importance, which may sometimes appear ridiculous; but which much oftener leads him to acts of generosity—to the adoption of liberal ideas—to honorable conduct. If he has been well educated and has had the good fortune to have been instructed by a priest whose ideas are enlightened, who gives a proper latitude for difference of opinion, who tolerates as he is tolerated, then the character of a young Brazilian exhibits much to admire. Surrounded by numerous relatives, and by his immediate dependents living in a vast and half-civilized country, he is endued with much independence of language and behavior, which are softened by the subordination which has been imbibed during his course of education. That this is general, I pretend not to say. Few persons are instructed in a proper manner; and again, few are those who profit by the education which they have received; but more numerous are the individuals who now undergo necessary tuition, for powerful motives have arisen to urge the attainment of knowledge.

I have heard it often observed, and I cannot help saying, that I think some truth is to be attached to the remark, in the country of which I am now treating, that women are usually less lenient to their slaves than men: but this doubtless proceeds from the ignorant state in which they are brought up. They scarcely receive any education; and have not the advantages of obtaining instruction from communication with persons who are unconnected with their own way of life; of imbibing new ideas from general conversation. They are born, bred, and continue surrounded by slaves without receiving any check, with high notions of superiority, without any thought that what they do is wrong. Bring these women forward, educate them, treat them as rational, as equal beings, and they will be in no respect inferior to their countrymen. The fault is not with the sex, but in the state of the human being. As soon as a child begins to crawl, a slave of about its own age, and of the same sex, is given to it as a playfellow, or rather as a plaything. They grow up together: and the slave is made the stock upon which the young owner gives vent to passion. The slave is sent upon all errands, and receives the blame of all unfortunate accidents;—in fact, the white child is thus encouraged to be overbearing, owing to the false fondness of its parents. Upon the boys the effect is less visible in after-life, because the world curbs and checks them: but the girls do not stir from home, and therefore have no opportunities of wearing off these pernicious habits. It is only surprising that so many excellent women should be found among them, and by no means strange that the disposition of some of them should be injured by this unfortunate direction of their infant years.

As vegetation rapidly advances in such climates, so the animal sooner arrives at maturity than in those of less genial warmth; and here again education is rendered doubly necessary to lead the mind to new ideas, to curb the passions, to give a sense of honor, and to instill feelings of that species of pride which is so necessary to a becoming line of conduct. The state of society, the climate, and the celibacy of the numerous priesthood, cause the number of illegitimate children to be very great. But here the *roda dos engeitados*, and a custom which shows the natural goodness of the people, prevent the frequent occurrence of infanticide, or rather render it almost unknown. An infant is frequently during the night laid at the door of a rich person; and on being discovered in the morning is taken in, and is almost invariably allowed to remain: it is brought up with the children of the house (if its color is not too dark to admit of this), certainly as a dependent, but not as a servant. However, a considerable tinge of color will not prevent it from being reared with the white children. These *engeitados*, or rejected ones, as individuals who are so circumstanced are called, are frequently to be met with: and I heard of few exceptions to the general kindness with which they are treated. Public feeling is much against the refusing to accept and rear an *engeitado*. The owner of a house, who is in easy circumstances, and yet sends the infant from his own door to the public institution which is provided for its reception, is generally spoken of in terms of indignation. Sometimes a poor man will find one of these presents at his door: and he will generally place it at the land-holder's threshold on the following night. This is accounted excusable and even meritorious; for at the Great House the child has nearly a certainty of being well taken care of.

I have observed that, generally speaking, Europeans are less indulgent to their slaves than Brazilians. The former feed them well: but they require from the poor wretches more labor than they can perform, whilst the latter allow the affairs of their estates to continue in the way in which they have been accustomed to be directed. This difference between the two descriptions of the owners is easily accounted for. The European has probably purchased part of his slaves on credit; and has, during the whole course of his life, made the accumulation of riches his chief object. The Brazilian inherits his estate: and as nothing urges him to the necessity of obtaining large profits, he continues the course that has been pointed out to him by the former possessors. His habits of quietude and indolence have led him to be easy and indifferent: and although he may not provide for the maintenance of his slaves with so much care as the European, still they find more time to seek for food themselves. That avaricious spirit which deliberately works a man or a brute animal until it is unfit for farther service, without any regard to the well-being of the creature, which is thus treated as a mere machine, as if it was formed of wood or iron, is, however, seldom to be met with in those parts of the country which I visited. Instances of cruelty occur (as has been, and will yet be seen), but these proceed from individual depravity, and not from systematic, cold blooded, calculating indifference to the means by which a desired end is to be compassed.

Notwithstanding the relationship of the mulattos on one side to the black race, they consider themselves superior to the *mamalucos*. They lean to the whites; and from the light in which the Indians are held, pride themselves upon being totally unconnected with them. Still the mulattos are conscious of their connection with men who are in a state of slavery, and that many persons, even of their own color, are under these degraded circumstances. They have therefore always a feeling of inferiority in the company of white men, if these white men are wealthy and powerful. This inferiority of rank is not so much felt by white persons in the lower walks of life: and these are more easily led to become familiar with individuals of their own color who are in wealthy circumstances. Still the inferiority which the mulatto feels, is more that which is produced by poverty than that which his color has caused; for he will be equally respectful to a person of his own cast, who may happen to be rich. [The term of *Senhor* or *Senhora* is made use of to all free persons, whites, mulattos, and blacks: and in speaking to a freeman of whatever class or color the manner of address is the same.] The degraded state of the people of color in the British colonies is most lamentable. In Brazil, even the trifling regulations which exist against them, remain unattended to. A mulatto enters into holy orders, or is appointed a magistrate, his papers stating him to be a white man, but his appearance plainly denoting the contrary. In conversing on one occasion with a man of color who was in my service, I asked if a certain *Capitão-môr* was not a mulatto man: he answered, "he was, but is not now." I begged him to explain, when he added, "Can a *Capitão-môr* be a mulatto man?" I was intimately acquainted with a priest, whose complexion and hair plainly denoted from whence he drew his origin. I liked him much. He was a well-educated and intelligent man. Besides this individual instance, I met with several others of the same description. . . .

Marriages between white men and women of color are by no means rare; though they are sufficiently so to cause the circumstance to be mentioned when speaking of an individual who has connected himself in this manner. But this is not said with the intent of lowering him in the estimation of others. Indeed the remark is only made if the person is a planter of any importance, and the woman is decidedly of dark color; for even a considerable tinge will pass for white. If the white man belongs to the lower orders, the woman is not accounted as being unequal to him in rank, unless she is nearly black. The European adventurers often marry in this manner, which generally occurs when the woman has a dower. The rich mulatto families are often glad to dispose of their daughters to these men, although the person who has been fixed upon may be in indifferent circumstances; for the color of the children of their daughters is bettered; and from the well-known prudence and regularity of this set of men, a large fortune may be hoped for even from very small beginnings. Whilst I was at Jaguaribe, I was in the frequent habit of seeing a handsome young man, who was a native of the island of St. Michael's. This person happened to be with me on one occasion when the commandant from the Sertão was staying at my house. The commandant asked him if he could read and write: and being answered in the negative, said, "then you will not do": and turning to me added, "I have a commission from a friend of mine to take with me back to the Sertão a good-looking young Portuguese of regular habits, who can read and write, for the purpose of marrying him to his daughter." Such commissions (*encommendas*) are not unusual.

Still the Brazilians of high birth and large property do not like to intermarry with persons whose mixture of blood is very apparent: and hence arise peculiar circumstances. A man of this description becomes attached to a woman of color; connects himself with her; and takes her to his home, where she is in a short time visited even by married women. She governs his household affairs: acts and considers herself as his wife; and frequently after the birth of several children, when they are neither of them young, he marries her. In connections of this nature, the parties are more truly attached than in marriage between persons who belong to two families of the first rank; for the latter are entered into from convenience rather than from affection. Indeed the parties, on some occasions, do not see each other until a few days before the ceremony takes place. It often occurs, that inclination, necessity, or convenience induces or obliges a man to separate from the person with whom he is connected. In this case, he gives her a portion; and she marries a man of her own rank, who regards her rather as a widow than as one whose conduct has been incorrect. Instances of infidelity in these women are rare. They become attached to the men with whom they cohabit: and they direct the affairs of the houses over which they are placed with the same zeal that they would display if they had the right of command over them. It is greatly to the credit of the people of that country, that so much fidelity should be shown on one side; and that this should so frequently as it is, be rewarded by the other party, in the advancement of those who have behaved thus faithfully, to a respectable and acknowledged situation in society. It should be recollected too that the merit of moral feelings must be judged of by the standard of the country, and not by our own institutions. I have only spoken above of what occurs among the planters; for in large towns, man is pretty much the same everywhere.

The *mamalucos* are more frequently to be seen in the Sertão than upon the coast. They are handsomer than the mulattos: and the women of this cast particularly surpass in beauty all others of the country. They have the brown tint of mulattos: but their features are less blunt, and their hair is not curled. I do not think that the men can be said to possess more courage than the mulattos. But whether from the knowledge which they have of being of free birth on both sides, or from residing in the interior of the country where the government is more loose, they appear to have more independence of character, and to pay less deference to a white man than the mulattos. When women relate any deed of danger that has been surmounted or undertaken, they generally state that the chief actor in it was a large *mamaluco, mamalucão*; as if they thought this description of men to be superior to all others. *Mamalucos* may enter into the mulatto regiments; and are pressed into the regiments of the line as being men of color, without any regard to the sources from which their blood proceeds.

Of the domesticated Indians I have already elsewhere given what accounts I could collect, and what I had opportunities of observing. The wild Indians are only now to be met with at a great distance from the coast of Pernambuco: and although they are very near to Maranhão, and are dreaded neighbors, I had no means of seeing any of them.

I now proceed to mention that numerous and valuable race of men, the creole negros; a tree of African growth, which has thus been transplanted, cultivated, and much improved by its removal to the New World. The creole negros stand alone and unconnected with every other race of men: and this circumstance alone would be sufficient, and indeed contributes much to the effect of uniting them to each other. The mulattos, and all other persons of mixed blood, wish to lean towards the whites, if they can possibly lay any claim to relationship. Even the *mestizo* tries to pass for a mulatto, and to persuade himself and others, that his veins contain some portion of white blood, although that with which they are filled proceeds from Indian and negro sources. Those only who have no pretensions to a mixture of blood, call themselves negroes, which renders the individuals who do pass under this denomination, much attached to each other, from the impossibility of being mistaken for members of any other cast. They are of handsome persons, brave and hardy, obedient to the whites, and willing to please. But they are easily affronted: and the least allusion to their color being made by a person of lighter tint, enrages them to a great degree; though they will sometimes say, "a negro I am, but always upright." They are again distinct from their brethren in slavery, owing to their superior situation as free men.

7. THE SOCIAL CONSEQUENCES OF SLAVERY

A forerunner of the Brazilian abolitionists of a later day, Luiz dos Santos Vilhena, Regius Professor of Greek in Baía from 1787 to 1798, boldly assailed the system of slave labor on which the sugar culture of his province was based. Slavery, not an enervating tropical climate, he affirmed, was responsible for the dissolute manners and idleness of the Portuguese living in Brazil. The following excerpt from his book on Brazil, written in the form of letters to a Portuguese friend, illustrates the vigor and forthrightness of his attack.

The Negro women and a majority of the mulatto women as well, for whom honor is a delusion, a word signifying nothing, are commonly the first to corrupt their master's sons, giving them their first lessons in sexual license, in which from childhood on they are engulfed; and from this presently arises a veritable troop of little mulattos whose influence on family life is most pernicious. But it often happens that those who are called the old masters, to distinguish them from their sons, are the very ones who set a bad example for their families through their conduct with their female slaves, giving pain to their wives and perhaps causing their death. Frequently their black favorites contrive to put the legitimate children out of the way, to avoid any difficulties in the event of the master's death.

There are other men who never marry, simply because they cannot get out of the clutches of the harpies in whose power they have been since childhood. There are ecclesiastics, and not a few, who from old and evil habit, for-

---

Luiz dos Santos Vilhena, *Recopilação de noticias soteropolitanas e brasilicas*, ed. Braz do Amaral, 2 vols. (Baía, 1921–1922), 1:138–142. Excerpt translated by Benjamin Keen.

getting their character and station, live a disorderly life with mulatto and Negro women, by whom they have sons who inherit their property; in this and other ways many of the most valuable properties of Brazil pass into the hands of haughty, arrogant vagabond mulattos, to the great detriment of the State. This is a matter well deserving of His Majesty's attention, for if these sugar mills and great plantations are not prevented from falling into the hands of these mulattos, who ordinarily are profligate and set little store by these splendid properties, having come by them so easily, in due time they will all fall into their hands and be ruined, as has happened to the greater part of those that came into the possession of such owners.

You must also know that the passion for having Negroes and mulattos in the house is so strong here that only death removes them from the household in which they were born; there are many families that have sixty, seventy, and more superfluous persons within their doors. I speak of the city, for in the country this would not be remarkable. All this black brood, whether mulattos or Negroes, are treated with the greatest indulgence, and that is why they are all vagabonds, insolent, bold, and ungrateful. . . .

The Negroes are harmful in still another way to the State of Brazil. For since all the servile labors and mechanical arts are in their charge, few are the mulattos, and fewer still the white men, who will deign to perform such tasks. . . .

It has been observed that he who comes here as servant to some public official continues to be a good servant until he realizes that the work he does for his master is performed in other households by Negroes and mulattos, whereupon he begins to plead with his master to find him some public employment not open to Negroes. Some masters yield to their entreaties, finding themselves so badgered and badly served that they are driven to distraction. But if they delay in finding them jobs, their servants leave them, preferring to be vagabonds and go about dying from hunger, or to become soldiers and sometimes bandits, to working for an honored master who pays them well and supports and cherishes them—and this only to avoid having to do what Negroes do in other households.

The same occurs with the serving women who accompany the ladies that come to Brazil. The same prejudice induces them to take to the streets; they prefer suffering all the resulting miseries to living in a home where they are honored and sheltered.

The girls of this country are of such disposition that the daughter of the poorest, most abject individual, the most neglected little mulatto wench, would rather go to the scaffold than serve a Duchess, if one were to be found in this country; that is the reason for the great number of ruined and disgraced women in this city.

The whites born in this land must either be soldiers, merchants, notaries, clerks, court officials, judges, or Treasury officials or else hold some other public occupation that is barred to Negroes, such as surgeon, apothecary, pilot, shipmaster or sea-captain, warehouse clerk (*caxeiro do trapiche*), and so forth. A few others are employed as sculptors, goldsmiths, and the like.

Many used to attend the school established by His Majesty in this city, a school that once boasted of excellent students who prepared for the Church and other learned professions. But when their fathers saw that the school was the fixed target at which the recruiting officers and soldiers aimed their shots, and that their sons were being snatched away for garrison duty, against which their immunities, privileges, and exemptions availed them nothing, they became convinced that the State had no further need of ecclesiastics or members of other learned professions . . . and decided that they would not sacrifice their sons by exposing them to the enmity of autocratic and thoughtless soldiers. . . .

Is it not obvious that the inactivity of the whites is the reason for the laziness of the blacks? Why should a man not dig the ground in Brazil who in Portugal lived solely by his hoe? Why should one not labor here who in Portugal knew nothing more than to put one hand to the plough handle and another to the goad?

Why should a man go about here with his body upright who came here bent with labor?

Why should he who knows only obedience want only to command? Why should he who was always a plebeian strut about with the air of a noble?

How plentifully would these blessed lands produce, dear friend, if they were cultivated by other hands than those of savage Negroes, who do no more than scratch their surface!

What great profits they would yield if cultivated by sensible and intelligent men, and if sound views of political economy changed the prevailing system!

No land could boast of greater opulence and plenty than Baía if it were ruled wisely, and if henceforth admittance were denied to slaves, the causes of its backwardness and poverty.

8

＇＇

COLONIAL CULTURE

COLONIAL CULTURE in most of its aspects was a projection of contemporaneous Spanish culture and only faintly reflected Native American influences. Colonial culture thus suffered from all the infirmities of its parent but lacked the breadth and vitality of Spanish literature and art, the product of a much older and more mature civilization.

The Church enjoyed a virtual monopoly of colonial education on all levels. Poverty condemned the great majority of the natives and mixed castes to illiteracy. The universities of Lima and Mexico City, both chartered in 1551, were the first permanent institutions of higher learning. Because they were modeled on Spain's University of Salamanca, their organization, curriculum, and method of instruction were medieval.

Within the limits imposed by official censorship and their own backgrounds, colonial scholars, especially those of the sixteenth and early seventeenth centuries, made impressive contributions in the fields of history, anthropology, linguistics, geography, and natural history. The second half of the seventeenth century saw a decline in the quantity and quality of scholarly production. Nevertheless, in this period two remarkable men, Carlos Sigüenza y Góngora in Mexico and Pedro de Peralta Barnuevo in Peru, foreshadowed the eighteenth-century Enlightenment by the universality of their interests and by their concern with the practical uses of science.

Colonial literature, with some notable exceptions, was a pallid reflection of prevailing literary trends in Spain. Among a multitude of poetasters towered a strange and rare genius, one of the greatest poets of the New World, Sor Juana Inés de la Cruz. Sor Juana could not escape the pressures of her environment. Rebuked by the bishop of Puebla for her worldly interests, she ultimately gave up her books and scientific instruments and devoted the remainder of her brief life to religious devotion and charitable works.

Colonial high culture could boast of only an occasional genius like Sor Juana. Popular culture, however, was thriving—at least to judge from the rare glimpses afforded by the documentary record. Elites may have felt isolated by their distance from European cultural centers and daunted by the prestige of European models, but further down the social ladder, the turbulent mixture of New World and Old World cultures was producing vibrant hybrid or *mestizo* cultures that were uniquely American. At the time, colonial authorities tended to view these *mestizo* cultures with suspicion because their supposedly transgressive nature threatened to undermine established social and cultural hierarchies. Nor were indigenous cultures eradicated despite concerted (if sporadic) efforts by colonial civil and religious authorities. Indigenous knowledge still surfaced from time to time in contemporary accounts to disturb the tranquility of the colonial social order.

1. THE COLONIAL UNIVERSITY

The colonial university was patterned on similar institutions in Spain and faithfully reproduced their medieval organization, curriculum, and method of instruction. Indifference to practical or scientific studies, slavish respect for the authority of the Bible, Aristotle, the Church Fathers, and certain medieval schoolmen, as well as a passion for hairsplitting debate of fine points of theological or metaphysical doctrine, were among the features of colonial academic life. In the following selection a Spanish friar describes the University of Lima in the first quarter of the seventeenth century.

The University with its royal schools is so renowned that it need envy no other in the world, thanks to its founders, the emperor Charles V and later Phillip II, both of glorious memory, who enlarged, ennobled, and enriched it with the same privileges as the University of Salamanca [the most prestigious and oldest university in Spain]. . . . There are chairs [professorships] in Scholastic theology, scripture, law, cannon law, . . . institutes, codes, decrees, three in philosophy, and one in the Indian language for the training of the priests who will serve as parish priests or doctrinal instructors for the Indians— before they are commissioned, they are tested and certified by the language professor.

The professors are for the most part native to the Indies and especially to this city. It would seem that [Lima's] skies, like those of the Indies in general, produce ingenious pilgrims, gifted with wit and facility, such that they are

Antonio Vásquez de Espinosa, *Compendio y descripción de las Indias Occidentales*, 2 vols. (1636), 2:606–608. Excerpt translated by the editors.

generally very able and lively intellects, as is evident from the chairs that they occupy and from the pulpits that they illuminate with great subjects, in particular, the sciences and religious sermons. They are unfortunate, however, in being far from the eyes of Your Majesty, because after having worked so hard—as the chairs are few, the subjects many, and not all can be lawyers—after having worked and excelled and spent 3,500 pesos getting their degrees, and having no way to make a living, they are dismayed to see themselves without prospects. Thus many clerics procure benefices and curacies among the Indians in order to make a living, with the result that many leave their books and studies behind and never finish their degrees.

The Cloister [Faculty] of this University is distinguished because it has more than eighty doctors and masters as well as members of the Royal Audiencia [Supreme Court] who join them because at the end of the year the gratuities [fees] are considerable. The lecture halls in the schools are very good and the chapel is elegant ... but the most remarkable is the amphitheater where they hold public ceremonies and commencement exercises which are very large and majestic as are all the graduation ceremonies because the city's nobility are invited to take part. They gather together at the doctoral candidate's house. A banner bearing the coats of arms of the University and of the graduate hangs from a window over a canopy and a crimson velvet cushion and these are also placed in the theater set up in the Cathedral under the Royal Coat of Arms. The sound of trumpets, flutes, and bugles alert and call together the special guests and the doctors who had formed the previous evening's escort. The nobility follow the banner, followed by the Beadles with their silver maces, and then the masters and doctors with their insignia by order of seniority, and ending with the dean of the Faculty and the graduate. In that fashion they proceed to the Rector's house, where the members of the Royal Audiencia, with the Rector in their center and arranged by order of seniority, wait to join them. In this same order, the following day, they proceed to the Cathedral where the theater and stage have been made ready with decorations and chairs. They hear Mass and, when it is finished, the newest member of the Faculty makes some sarcastic remarks and the head master gives him his degree as is done at Salamanca.

2. THE TENTH MUSE

The conditions of colonial life did not favor the development of a rich literature. Isolation from foreign influences, the strict censorship of all reading matter, and the limited audience for writing of every kind made literary creation difficult. Amid "a flock of jangling magpies," as one literary historian describes the Gongorist versifiers of the seventeenth century, appeared an incomparable songbird, known to her admiring contemporaries as the tenth muse—Sor Juana Inés de la Cruz (1651–1695), who wrote under the pseudonym of Sor Filotea. Rebuked by the bishop of Puebla for her interest in secular learning, Sor Juana replied in a letter that is both an important autobiographical document and an eloquent defense of the rights of women to education and intellectual activity.

I was less than three years old when my mother sent an older sister to be taught reading at a school for small children, of the kind called *Amigas*. Moved by sisterly affection and by a mischievous spirit, I followed her; and seeing her receive instruction, I formed such a strong desire to read that I tried to deceive the schoolmistress, telling her that my mother wanted her to give me lessons. She did not believe me, since it was incredible; but to humor me she acquiesced. I continued to come and she to teach me, no longer in jest but in earnest; and I learned so quickly that I already knew how to read by the time my mother heard about the lessons from the teacher, who had kept them secret in order to break the pleasant news to her and receive her reward all at once. I had concealed it from my mother for fear that I would be whipped for acting without permission. The lady who taught me still lives— God keep her—and can testify to this.

I remember that at that time, although I had the healthy appetite of most children of that age, I would not eat cheese because I heard that it made one dull-witted, and the desire to learn prevailed more with me than hunger, so powerful in children. Later, at the age of six or seven, when I already knew how to read and write, as well as to sew and do other women's tasks, I heard that in Mexico City there was a university, and schools where the sciences were taught. No sooner had I heard this than I began to badger my mother with pleas that she let me put on men's clothing and go to Mexico City, where I could live with some relatives and attend the university. She would not do it, and quite rightly, too, but I satisfied my desire by reading in a large number of books that belonged to my grandfather, and neither punishments nor rebukes could stop me. Hence when I came to Mexico City men wondered not so much at my intelligence as at my memory and knowledge, at an age when it seemed I would do well to know how to talk.

I began to study Latin, in which I had barely twenty lessons; and so intense was my application that although women (especially in the flower of their youth) naturally cherish the adornment of their hair, I would cut it off four or six fingers' length, making it a rule that if I had not mastered a certain subject by the time it grew back, I would cut it off again ... for it did not seem right to me that a head so empty of knowledge, which is the most desir-

Sor Juana Inés de la Cruz, *Carta atenagórica, Respuesta a Sor Filotea*, ed. E. Abreu Gómez (México, 1934), pp. 54–58, 66–70. Excerpt translated by Benjamin Keen.

able adornment of all, should be crowned with hair. I became a nun, for although I knew that the religious state imposed obligations (I speak of incidentals and not of the fundamentals) most repugnant to my temperament, nevertheless, in view of my total disinclination to marriage, it was the most becoming and proper condition that I could choose to ensure my salvation. To achieve this I had to repress my wayward spirit, which wished to live alone, without any obligatory occupation that might interfere with the freedom of my studies or any conventual bustle that might disturb the restful quiet of my books. These desires made me waver in my decision, until, having been told by learned persons that it was temptation, with divine favor I conquered and entered the state which I so unworthily occupy. I thought that I had fled from myself, but—wretched me! I brought myself with me and so brought my greatest enemy, that thirst for learning which Heaven gave me—I know not whether as a favor or chastisement, for repress it as I might with all the exercise that the conventual state offers, it would burst forth like gunpowder; and it was verified in me that *privatio est causa appetitus* [deprivation is the cause of appetite].

I renewed or rather continued (for I never truly ceased) my labors (which were my rest in all the leisure time that my duties left me) of reading and more reading, of studying and more studying, with no other teacher than the books themselves. You will readily comprehend how difficult it is to study from these lifeless letters, denied the living voice and explanation of a teacher, but I joyfully endured all this labor for love of learning. Ah, if it had been for love of God, as was fitting, how worthy it would have been! True, I sought to direct it as much as possible to His service, for my aspiration was to study theology, since it seemed a notable defect to me, as a Catholic, not to know all that can be learned in this life about the Divine Mysteries; and since I was a nun, and not a lay person, it seemed to me an obligation of my state to study literature. . . . So I reasoned, and convinced myself—though it could well be that I was only justifying what I already wanted to do. And so, as I have said, I directed the steps of my studying toward the heights of Sacred Theology; it seemed to me that in order to arrive there I should climb the stairway of the human sciences and arts; for how should I understand the language of the Queen of Sciences if I did not know that of her handmaidens? . . .

At one time my enemies persuaded a very saintly and guileless prelate, who believed that study was a matter for the Inquisition, to forbid me to study. I obeyed her (for the three months or so that she had power over me) in what concerned my reading, but as for the absolute ban on study, this was not in my power to obey, for although I did not study in books, I studied everything that God created, and all this universal machine served me as a textbook. I saw nothing without reflecting upon it; everything I heard moved me to thought. This was true of the smallest and most material things, for since there is no creature, however lowly, in which one does not recognize the *me fecit Deus* [God made me], so there is no object that will not arouse thought, if one considers it as one should. Thus I looked at and wondered about everything, so that even the people I spoke to, and what they said to me, aroused a thousand speculations in me. How did such a variety of temperaments and intellects come about, since we are all of the same species? What could be the hidden qualities and traits that caused these differences? If I saw a figure I would consider the proportion of its lines and measure it in my mind and reduce it to other figures. Sometimes I would walk about in the front part of a dormitory of ours (a very spacious room); I noticed that although the lines of its two sides were parallel and the ceiling was level, the lines seemed to run toward each other and the ceiling seemed to be lower at a distance than it was close by—from which I inferred that visual lines run straight but not parallel, forming a pyramidal figure. And I speculated whether this could be the reason that caused the ancients to wonder whether the world was a sphere or not. Because although it appeared spherical, this might be an optical illusion, presenting concavities where they perhaps did not exist. . . .

This habit is so strong in me that I see nothing without reflecting upon it. I noticed two little girls playing with a top, and I had hardly seen the movement and the object when I began, with my usual madness, to consider the easy motion of the spherical form—and how the impulse, once given, continued independently of its cause, for there was the top dancing at a distance from the girl's hand—the motive cause. Not content with this, I had some flour brought and strewn on the floor, in order to learn whether the top's motion described perfect circles or not; and I discovered that they were only spiral lines that gradually lost their circular character as the impulse diminished. Other children were playing at pins (which is the most infantile game known to children). I began to study the figures they formed, and seeing by chance, that three pins formed a triangle, I set about joining one to the other, remembering that this is said to have been the figure of the mysterious ring of Solomon, in which were depicted some shadowy hints and representations of the most Sacred Trinity, by virtue of which it worked many miracles; it is said that David's harp had the same figure and that for this reason Saul was healed by its sound; the harps we use today have almost the same shape.

But what shall I say, my lady, of the secrets of nature that I have discovered while cooking? I observe that an egg coheres and fries in butter or oil but breaks up in sugar syrup; that to keep sugar fluid it is sufficient to pour on it a little water containing a quince or some other sour fruit; that the yolk and white of an egg are so opposed that each one separately will mix with sugar, but not both together. I shall not weary you with such trifles, which I mention only to give you an adequate notion of my character and which, I am sure, will make you laugh; but, my lady, what can we women know except kitchen philosophy? Lupercio Leonardo aptly said: "It is possible to philosophize while preparing dinner." And I often say, observing these trifles: "If Aristotle had been a cook, he would have written much more." . . .

Although I had no need of examples, I have nevertheless been aided by the many that I have read about, in both divine and profane writings. For I have seen a Deborah giving laws, both military and political, and governing a people in which there were so many learned men. I read of that sage Queen of Sheba, so learned that she dared to test with enigmas the wisdom of the wisest of men, and suffered no reproof for it but instead was made the judge of unbelievers. I observe so many illustrious women—some adorned with the gift of prophecy, like Abigail; others, with that of persuasion, like Esther; others with piety, like Rahab; others with perseverance, like Anna, mother of Samuel; and an infinite number of others, endowed with still other kinds of graces and virtues.

If I turn my gaze to the pagans, I first encounter the Sibyls, chosen by God to prophesy the principal mysteries of our faith, in verses so learned and elegant that they arouse our wonder. I see the Greeks adore as goddess of learning a woman like Minerva, daughter of the first Jupiter and teacher of all the wisdom of Athens. I see a Bola Argentaria, who aided her husband Lucan to write the great "Battle of Pharsalia." I see a Zenobia, Queen of Palmyra, as wise as she was brave. An Aretea, the most learned daughter of Aristippus. A Nicostrata, inventor of Latin letters and most learned in Greek. An Aspasia of Miletus, who taught philosophy and rhetoric and was teacher of the philosopher Pericles. A Hypatia, who taught astronomy and studied for a long time in Alexandria. A Leontia, of Greek birth, who wrote against the philosopher Theophrastus and convinced him. A Jucia, a Corinna, a Cornelia, and finally all that multitude of women who won renown under the names of Greeks, Muses, Pythonesses and in the end were nothing more than learned women, regarded and venerated as such by the ancients. Not to mention an infinite number of others of whom the books tell, such as the Egyptian Catherine, who not only read but overcame in debate the wisest sages of Egypt. I see a Gertrude study, write, and teach. And there is no need to wander far afield, for I see a holy mother of my own order, Paula, learned in Hebrew, Greek, and Latin, and most skillful in interpreting the Scriptures—so much so, in fact, that her biographer, the great and saintly Jerome, declared himself unequal to his task. He said, in his usual serious, forceful way: "If all the members of my body were tongues, they would not be enough to proclaim the wisdom and virtue of Paula." He bestowed the same praise on the widow Blesilla and the illustrious virgin Eustoquio, both daughters of the same Paula; for her learning the latter won the name "Prodigy of the World." Fabiola, a Roman lady, was also most learned in the Sacred Scripture, Proba Falconia, a Roman matron, wrote an elegant work in Virgilian measures about the mysteries of our sacred faith. It is well known that our Queen Isabel, wife of Alfonso XII, wrote on astronomy. And . . . in our own time there flourishes the great Christina Alexandra, Queen of Sweden, as learned as she is brave and magnanimous, and there are also the excellent Duchess of Abeyro and the Countess of Vallambrosa.

3. ON THE FOOLISHNESS OF MEN

As the previous excerpt reveals, Sor Juana was capable of both psychological subtlety and intellectual virtuosity. She was also a brilliant satirist, especially on the topic of male hypocrisy. Her famous "Philosophical Satire" mercilessly ridicules the "inconstancies in the desires and censures of men who blame women for things they cause themselves." Of particular interest is her subversion of the long-standing idea that men are more rational than women. The poem—like her response to the bishop of Puebla—displays Sor Juana's mastery of Greek, Roman, and Christian classics. This time she includes a tongue-in-cheek comparison of two female archetypes from classical antiquity: the infamous Greek courtesan Thaïs, who followed Alexander the Great on his conquests, and the legendary Roman matron Lucretia, who committed suicide to preserve her family's honor after she was raped by the Etruscan tyrant Tarquin. In Dante's Divine Comedy, *Thaïs is consigned to the ring of hell reserved for flatterers, who are forced to spend eternity up to their necks in excrement. In contrast, Lucretia's noble self-sacrifice and the revenge that her father and husband exact on her rapist give birth to the Roman Republic. Erudition aside, Sor Juana was a poet of remarkable versatility and skill. In contrast, the following translation seeks to convey the sense of the poem with as little deviation from the original meaning as possible and makes no attempt to reproduce its ingenious formal characteristics (including an ABBA rhyme scheme). The original poem along with more poetic translations are readily available in literature anthologies and on the web.*

Foolish men, you thoughtlessly
cast the blame on women,
not seeing in yourselves the cause
of the very things you fault:

if with boundless desire
you solicit their disdain,
¿why wish them to behave
if you incite them to sin?

Sor Juana Inés de la Cruz, "Sátira filosófica," in *Obras completas*, 4 vols. (México: Fondo de Cultura Económica, 1951–1957), 1:228–229. Excerpt translated by the editors.

You break down their resistance
and then solemnly declare
the cause to be their flightiness
rather than your persistence.

In seeking out the courage to act
you drive yourselves insane,
like the child who conjures up the boogeyman
and then fears its own creation.

You wish, with foolish presumption,
to find in the one you seek,
a sultry Thaïs while you woo her,
a steadfast Lucrecia once she's wed.

¿What behavior could be stranger
than that by which, without a thought,
the very one who smears the mirror,
complains when it's no longer clear?

Whether women favor or disdain you
your attitude never changes,
you protest if they treat you badly,
you mock them if they love you well.

Your esteem, no woman can ever gain;
since however cautious she might be,
if she refuses to admit you, she's ungrateful,
and if she lets you in, she's shameless.

In a constant frenzy you scurry about,
judging them with weighted scales,
one woman you condemn as cruel
and the other damn as wanton.

¿How then can she be steadfast,
the woman who would win your love,
if when ungrateful, she offends you,
and when easy, makes you angry?

Caught between the anger and anguish
which shape the stories that you tell,
she does well who loves you not
and who cares nothing for your sad complaints.

Your desperate pleas give wings
to the liberties women allow,
then once you've made them bad
you wish to find them pure and good.

¿Which one commits the greater fault
in a passion gone astray:
she who falls to constant pleading,
or he that pleads with her to fall?

¿Or who is most to blame
though both have done their share:
she that sins for pay,
or he that pays to sin?

¿Why then are you so frightened
of the error of your ways?
wish that women be the way you make them
or else make them as you wish.

Were you to quit entreating women so
then later on, with much more cause,
you could blame the woman
when she came to seek you out.

Thus with many weapons I expose
your arrogant and evil ways,
for in both word and deed
you bind devil, flesh, and world.

4. GAUCHO ENTERTAINMENT

World-class intellects like Sor Juana, writing primarily for transatlantic cultural
elites, were not the only ones to combine New World sensibilities and European cul-
tural forms into a uniquely American hybrid or mestizo *culture. In 1775–1776,*
Alonso Carrió de la Vandera, a disappointed colonial bureaucrat from Lima writ-
ing under the pseudonym Concolorcorvo, published his sardonic El lazarillo de ciegos caminantes (Guide for Blind Travelers), *a picaresque travelogue of an*
overland journey from Uruguay to Peru. This excerpt, a "laconic description of Tu-
cumán province along the mail road," provides a rare glimpse into the rural culture
of Argentina—a culture that would later become renowned for its fierce gauchos (cow-

boys) and heated poetry contests. The translation of the poem in this excerpt approximates the original rhyme scheme in order to convey some sense of the mixing of cultural forms that the author found so noteworthy.

A small number of settlers are content to live rustic lives; maintaining themselves on a piece of beef and drinking *aloja*—a mildly alcoholic drink made from fermented carob and honey which they often make in backwoods regions—while sitting in the shade of the carob trees. There they have their bacchanals, telling each other stories, one gaucho to another or to their rustic entourage. Accompanied by the sound of badly strung and out-of-tune guitars, they sing and throw out verses that seem more like dirty jokes. If decency permitted, I would repeat some of the more extravagant ones on love—each clever in its own way—that they sing after warming themselves with *aloja* and then re-heating themselves with a post-*aloja* (although this custom is not common among the younger folks). The openings of their songs are well harmonized in a barbaric and crude sort of way because the verses are conceived and composed beforehand in the head of some witty scoundrel.

One afternoon, the district inspector, who wished to go horseback riding, guided us to a thick grove inhabited by a numerous band of gauchos of both sexes. He warned us that we should laugh with them but without taking sides, so as to avoid inciting them to violence. The inspector, as the most experienced among us, went up to the leader of the assembly, gave him the customary greeting, and asked permission for us to rest awhile in the shade of those leafy trees as we were tired out from riding in the sun. They received all of us graciously and handed us gourds of *aloja*. The inspector drank from the brew and we all did the same, reassured by his good faith and trustworthiness. Four of the rustic lads gallantly surrendered us their log seat. Two robust young women were swinging from two ropes lashed to two thick trees. Other women, perhaps a dozen, entertained themselves brewing *aloja*, preparing mate [tea], and slicing watermelons. Two or three men busied themselves heating pieces of partly dried meat and some marrow bones on the hot coals. Others tried to get their guitars in order by rubbing on the scuffed-up strings. An old man—who seemed about sixty years old but who had enjoyed life for one hundred and four years—rested at the foot of a shady beech tree, from where he gave his orders. Seeing that it was now time for the meal to begin, he sat down and asked the women when they expected to feed the guests. The young women replied that they were waiting for some cheeses and honey for the dessert to be brought from the house. The old man said that that seemed very good to him.

Concolorcorvo (Alonso Carrió de la Vandera), *El lazarillo de ciegos caminantes* (Madrid: Ediciones Atlas, 1943), pp. 95–98. Excerpt translated by the editors.

The inspector, who was feeling a bit impatient, promptly told the old man that to him [the inspector] it seemed very bad "and so Mr. Gorgonio would you mind asking the young women and men to sing us a few of their favorite verses to the sound of their tuneful instruments." "If it will make you happy," said the venerable old man, "and the first to sing will be Cenobia and Saturnina with Espiridión and Horno de Babilonia." They came briskly forward and asked the venerable old man if they should repeat the verses that they had sung earlier that day or if they should improvise others off the top of their heads. Here the inspector interjected: "the latter are the ones I'd prefer since they're likely to be quite salty." They had sung nearly twenty stanzas—which the venerable old man pronounced "awful"—when mother Nazaria with her daughters Capracia and Clotilde arrived [with food from the house] and the company welcomed with great pleasure Pantaleón and Torcuato who brought along the grilled meat. The inspector had already taken out his watch twice, by which we all understood that he wanted to leave. But the old man, who realized what was going on [with the inspector], ordered Rudesinda and Nemesio to sing three or four little stanzas from those that the friar had made when he had come by a week or so ago. The inspector alerted us to be attentive and that each one of us should commit to memory the verse that pleased us most. The first verses they sang, truth be told, were of little consequence. The last four seem to me worthy of setting down in print because of their extravagant nature, so I'm going to record them here for posterity:

> Lady: *I know too well your vile acts,*
>   *and your low life as a felon.*
>   *You eat the finest melon,*
>   *and then give us rabbits for cats.*
> Suitor: *That's quite enough of settling scores;*
>   *there's much worse that I've been called.*
>   *It seems I've scraped my belly bald,*
>   *from so much walking on all fours.*
> Lady: *You really are a brazen lout;*
>   *only moonshine makes your heart pine.*
>   *Then at swallow number sixty nine,*
>   *you let your hidden demons out.*
> Suitor: *Out to the square with all that herd;*
>   *out with that macho bag of gas.*
>   *And out with all who want to go,*
>   *so I can wipe my stinking a_ _!*

"Well the weather is starting to clear up," said the inspector, "and before it starts raining *bolas* [lariats attached to rocks and used to trip up cattle]—

since there aren't any cobblestones—we should get going." And so we took our leave, although with some regret because the younger men wanted to stay to the end of the fiesta even if it lasted all night. The inspector, however, thought it was a bad idea to wait until swallow number sixty nine. The joke about rabbits for cats seemed to us to be the friar's invention but the inspector told us that although it wasn't used much in Tucumán, the saying was common in Paraguay and on the pampas of Buenos Aires. [Editor's note: This common saying is backwards here: the usual substitution is cats for rabbits. Rabbits are often eaten while cats are not, but a cat's dressed carcass resembles a rabbit's closely enough to fool an unsuspecting consumer. It's not clear from the excerpt if the author is confused himself or clueing his readers into the "backward" state of rural culture. Given the tongue-in-cheek tone of this anecdote, it's probably a deliberate "mistake."] The other ingenious verses were as good as those sung by the Arcadian shepherds of antiquity minus the cultured embellishments of Garcilaso and Lope de Vega [Spanish "golden age" writers who composed pastoral poems in the classical Roman style during the sixteenth and early seventeenth centuries]. We were also amazed by the extravagant names of the men and women. The old man told us that they were taken from the names of new saints introduced by Dr. Cosme Bueno in his almanac, and that, in general, new saints performed more miracles than old ones who had grown tired of asking God to intercede on behalf of men and women. This outrageous statement made us all laugh but we made no attempt to dissuade them because the inspector made the sign of the cross with his index finger in front of his mouth. Although the young men addressed each other and any passerby as "macho," we didn't think much about it; but it seemed improper to us that they called the women "macha." The inspector, however, told us that in this manner of expressing themselves they followed in the footsteps of the renowned Quevedo [another Spanish golden age writer], who said with much propriety and grace: "pobres y pobras [poor men and poor women]"—just as they use "macho" and "macha," although only when referring to young men and women.

These folks, who make up the greater part of Tucumán's population, would be the happiest in the world if only their customs were better attuned to evangelical precepts; because the country has a delightful climate and the earth is made extremely fruitful with very little work. Wood is in such abundance that houses constructed from it could contain the populations of the two largest kingdoms of Europe along with arable lands for their sustenance. The only thing missing is stone for strong buildings, as well as navigable waterways and commercial ports spaced at regular intervals to facilitate the movement of commodities. The biggest lack, however, is that of settlers; such an extensive and fertile province has scarcely 100,000 inhabitants according to the best estimates.

5. Indians and the Environment

Although vigorously suppressed by Spanish colonial political and religious authorities, indigenous culture continued to thrive well into the colonial period, especially on the periphery. In this excerpt from El Orinoco ilustrado: Historia natural, civil y geográfica de este gran río (The Illustrated Orinoco: Natural, Civil, and Geographic History of this Great River), *published in 1741, Jesuit missionary priest José Gumilla acknowledges both the persistence and depth of indigenous knowledge of the natural world. The book's mixture of scientific curiosity and religious conviction (in another place Fr. Gumilla defends the notion that the Indians were descended from the ten lost tribes of Israel) is typical of the period.*

The Caberre—the most inhuman, brutal, and bloodthirsty of the Indian nations that inhabit the Orinoco river—controls the supply and manufacture of the most violent poison, as I see it, in the whole world. This nation alone retains the secret of its making and garners a fat profit from the rest of those [Indian] nations, that directly or through third persons, eagerly purchase *curare*, as it is called. It is sold in small clay pots or flasks, the largest of which contains four ounces of the poison, which is very similar in color to caramel just before it boils. It has no particular taste or odor. It can be put in the mouth and drunk without any risk or danger as long as there are no bloody wounds on the gums or other parts of the mouth. That is because all its action and strength affects the blood to such a degree that contact with just a drop causes all the blood in the body to coagulate all of a sudden with the speed of a lightening bolt. It is marvelous to see that when a man is wounded lightly with an arrowhead dipped in curare, although it be no more than a pinprick, all his blood congeals and he dies so instantaneously that he can scarcely utter "Jesus" three times. . . .

Having seen the novel strength and efficacy of *curare*, we move on to examine its peculiar production. It should be known that all the poison of *curare* derives from a root of the same name, a root so singular and unique that it is nothing more than a root, never throwing out leaves or stalks. Although it does grow, it always stays hidden as if it were fearful of revealing its occult malignancy. And, in order to better hide itself, it sought out (or was assigned by the creator) not the common land of the rest of the plants but the rotten and corrupted slime of stagnant lagoons whose waters are drunk only when absolutely necessary because they are murky, of bad color, worse taste, and corresponding smell. In this corrupted slime covered with those pestiferous

José Gumilla, *El Orinoco ilustrado: Historia natural, civil y geográfica de este gran río*, 2 vols. (Bogotá: Biblioteca Popular de Cultura Colombiana, 1944), 2:121–131. Excerpt translated by the editors.

waters, the curare root is born and grows, legitimate offspring of all that mass of filth. The Caberre harvest these brownish roots and after washing them and cutting them into pieces, they mash them and put them in big pots over a low fire. For this task, they search out the most useless old woman of the tribe and when she falls dead from the violent stench of the pots, as usually happens, then they substitute another old woman of the same type in her place. They never refuse this work nor does the community or the family take it badly because she and they know that this is the ultimate fate of old women. As the water cools down, the old woman concocts her death while she goes from pot to pot stirring and squeezing out the juice of that mashed root so that it expel its toxin more easily thus tinting the lukewarm water until it takes the color of clear caramel. Then the preparer, with all the force that a woman of her age can muster, squeezes and presses the liquid into the pot and discards the wrung-out roots. She then adds firewood and quickly brings the liquid to a boil. Shortly after the poisonous pots begin to boil, she falls down dead and a second old woman takes her place. The second women sometimes escapes and sometimes doesn't.

When the concoction finally cooks down to a third of the pot, the unlucky cook gives a shout and the *cacique* [chief] with his captains and the rest of the people of village come over to examine the curare to see if it's ready. (And this is the most marvelous part of this strange process). The *cacique* wets the point of a stick in the *curare*, and at the same time one of the young men makes a wound on his knee, thigh, or arm (wherever he pleases) with the sharp end of a bone. Just as the blood begins to emerge from the mouth of the wound, the *cacique* moves the point of the *curare* stick close to the wound. But he doesn't touch it or put the *curare* too close to the blood, because even if he just touched and withdrew it, the *curare* would spread throughout the veins and the patient would die. If the blood that was about to emerge from the wound retreats, then the poison is ready. If the blood stops cold but doesn't retreat, then the poison is almost ready. But if the blood continues to flow naturally, the poison needs more heat. Then, they order the sad old woman to continue in imminent danger of death until the necessary proofs are made: the natural antipathy that causes the blood to retreat violently from its opposite manifests itself and the *curare* reaches its full strength.

If some famous botanist had encountered this root and made known its occult malignancy, there would be little cause for wonder. If the famous Tritemio or Borri or one of the learned inventors of chemistry, on the strength of experiments and scholarly inquiries, had finally come up with this singular process, they would be worthy of great praise and no one would doubt that it was the product of very cultivated intellects. But that all this be the invention of the coarsest and most barbaric nation of the Orinoco River: Who could believe it, without confessing that the entire process, from the finding of the root until the end, was dictated by the devil? I'm persuaded that this is indeed what happened. . . .

It is no less important to know the duration of this poison, that is to say the obstinacy with which it maintains its potency and vigor until it has been completely used up. The Indians do nothing to preserve it, not even stopping up the little pots they buy it in, but it doesn't evaporate or lose any of its deadly efficiency. This is something in itself, but since the *curare* is kept together and concentrated, it's not so surprising that it maintains its strength. What is unique and admirable is that once the *curare* is applied to a batch of arrowheads, though it be only a daub, even in these small quantities, it maintains and holds on to its strength for many years, for as long as it takes the quiver's owner to use his arrows. . . . I only noticed one thing in various trips through those jungles. And that was, that when the Indians take the arrows from their quiver, whether to kill monkeys or peccaries or in response to surprise attacks, they hold the poisoned arrow in their hands, turn the poison arrowhead around, and put it in their mouths. When I asked them the reason for this . . . they always responded that the heat of the mouth and humidity of the saliva, improved the shot and activated the *curare*—a reaction that seemed instinctual to me.

6. SEXUAL AND RACIAL POLITICS

The New World experience had a profound effect on social relations, whether between men and women or among different races and classes. This gossipy tale of witchcraft and female intrigue from Juan Rodríguez Freyle (1566–1636?), a well-connected member of the Colombian gentry, gives some sense of just how fluid social relations could become (or were perceived to be), especially in the first decades of colonial rule. Rodríguez Freyle's version of this story was probably written in the 1620s and 1630s, but the events narrated in the story are part of a chapter on the foundation of religion in Bogotá in 1550. The comadre *relationship that binds the women in the story refers to the traditional practice of* compadrazgo *(god parentage), a form of real or fictive kinship that involves mutual aid and reciprocal obligations. It is still common today in Latin America. Stories of Africans flying off of hilltops (and presumably back to Africa) were common throughout the Americas.*

On a ship of the fleets that came and went from Castile [Spain] . . . embarked a resident of this city [Bogotá, Nueva Granada] to seek his fortune.

Juan Rodríguez Freyle, *El Carnero: Conquista y descubrimiento del nuevo reino de Granada* (Caracas: Biblioteca Ayacucho, 1979), pp. 211–214. Excerpt translated by the editors.

He was a married man with a young and beautiful wife who had no wish to waste her beauty by not taking advantage of it while her husband was away. She was careless and ended up with a big belly [pregnant]. She was thinking that she could get rid of the child in time. But before the birth could occur, a knock on the door alerted her to the fleet's arrival in Cartagena [Nueva Granada's principal port]. Shocked, she tried desperately to abort the unborn child, but to no avail.

She decided to take her problem to her *comadre* Juana García, a free black woman that had come to these parts with the governor Don Alonso Luis de Lugo. Juana had two daughters that went around the city trailing lots of silk, gold, and even men. This black woman was something of a witch, as it turned out. The pregnant woman consulted with her *comadre*. She told her the problem and begged for some remedy for the situation. Her *comadre* asked her: "Who told you that your husband was with the fleet?" The woman replied that he himself had said that he would come without fail as soon as he could. The *comadre* responded: "If that's how it is, wait, don't do anything, because I want to check out the news about the fleet myself and find out if your husband is with it. Tomorrow, I'll come see you and tell you what to do. Meanwhile, stay in God's care."

The next day the Juana returned. She had made some hasty overnight inquiries and arrived well informed about the truth of the situation. She told the pregnant woman: "My esteemed *comadre*, I have done my best to find out about my *compadre* [the absent husband]: The truth is that the fleet is in Cartagena, but I heard no news of your husband or of anyone who said that he sailed with it." The pregnant woman became quite agitated and pleaded with her godmother to give her something to get rid of the unborn child to which Juana responded: "Don't do anything rash until we know the truth, whether he's coming or not. What you can do is . . . do you see that green bowl over there?" The woman answered, "yes." "Well, *comadre*, fill it with water, put it in your room, and prepare a meal for me and my daughters. I'll bring them tonight and we'll have a good time while we come up a remedy for your problem." With this Juana said goodbye to her *comadre*, went to her house to alert her daughters, and—night having already arrived—they set out for the house of the pregnant woman, who had not failed to comply with the instructions regarding the green bowl.

Juana and her daughters also invited some other young women from their neighborhood who came to pass the time with the pregnant woman that night. They all got together, and while the young women were singing and dancing, the hostess said to her *comadre*: "My stomach is really hurting. Would you please look at it for me?" Her *comadre* responded: "Yes, I'll do it. Take one of these lights and we'll go into your room." The pregnant woman took the candle and they went in. After they entered and the door was closed, she said to Juana: "*Comadre*, the bowl with water is over there." Juana responded: "Well then take this candle and look if you can see something in the water." That she did, and as she was looking she said: "*Comadre*, here I see a land I don't recognize, and there's this guy, my husband, seated in a chair, and a woman is next to a table, and a tailor with scissors in his hands, who wants to cut a scarlet dress." The *comadre* replied: "Well wait, I want to see this too." Then she went over to the bowl and saw all that had been described. The woman asked her: "*Comadre*, what land is this?" And she responded: "It's the island of Hispaniola." With this the tailor wielded his scissors, cutting out a sleeve and throwing it over his shoulder. The *comadre* said to the pregnant woman: "Would you like me to take that sleeve from the tailor?" And she responded: "How are you going to do that?" And Juana replied: "If you wish it, I'll take it from him." The pregnant woman said: "Take it from him then, my *comadre*, on your life." She had scarcely finished the request when Juana said: "Well here it is," and handed her the sleeve.

They were there a while until the dress was cut, which the tailor quickly did, and then everything vanished and nothing was left but the bowl and the water. The *comadre* said to the wife: "I have now seen how slow your husband is; you could well say goodbye to this stomach, and even make another." The pregnant woman was very happy. She threw the scarlet sleeve in a chest that stood next to her bed and with that left for the room where the young women were celebrating. They set the table, enjoyed their dinner, and then returned to their homes.

Let's pause for a second. It's well known that the devil was the author of this trap and that he's very discerning when it comes to the sons of men. But he can't reach inside [to their souls] because that belongs solely to God. Instead, the devil achieves his goals by stratagems that follow the lead of man. I'm not going to jump to conclusions about what was shone in the water to these women except to note that he who dared take Christ, Our Lord, and carry him off to a high mountain, and show him all the kingdoms of the world . . . was the author of a fantastic vision, just like the one shown to the women in bowl of water. I am going to emphasize the rapidity with which the sleeve was snatched, because scarcely had the one said: "Well, take it *comadre*," when the other replied: "Well here it is." I would also say that devil knows well the path these women were taking and was ready for them. And with this said, let's return to the woman's husband, who was the one that uncovered all this witchcraft.

He had arrived at the city of Sevilla [Spain's principal port], just at the moment some family and friends had arrived there from the island of Hispaniola. They told him about the riches that were there and advised him to invest his money and return with them to that island. The man did as they advised: he went to Hispaniola and did very well. He returned to Castile, reinvested his money, and made a second trip to Hispaniola. This second trip was when the scarlet dress was cut. The merchandise was sold, he returned to

Spain, and invested again. And with this investment, he returned to New Granada at a time when the baby had grown up and was being raised in the house as an orphan.

The husband and wife received each other graciously, and for some days they went around very content and agreeable until she persisted in asking for some bauble or other. In the midst of these requests, hints of jealousy began to intrude, in such a way that the husband became vexed; meals went from bad to worse, because the woman from time to time would chide him for the love affairs that he'd had on Hispaniola. From these comments, the husband began to suspect that some friend of his, one of those that had been with him on that island, had said something to his wife. In the end, he hid his suspicions and regaled his wife, to see if he could find out who had betrayed him.

Later on, as the two were dining contentedly, his wife asked him to give her an embroidered green skirt. The husband wasn't pleased with the idea and made some excuses to which she responded: "By the faith if you could give it to the lady from Santo Domingo [the capital of Hispaniola], the way you gave her the scarlet dress, you wouldn't make excuses." With this the husband was forced to give in, but his suspicions were confirmed. And in order to find out what was going on, he regaled her further, giving her the skirt she asked for, and other baubles, which made her very happy.

Finally, after a pleasant afternoon together, the husband said to his wife: "Sister, won't you tell, on your life, who told you that I dressed a woman from Hispaniola in scarlet cloth?" The wife replied: "Well, if you're not going to deny it, tell me the truth and I'll tell you who told me." The husband did as she asked and said: "Dear wife, it's the truth because a man, absent from his home and in foreign lands, has to have some entertainment. I gave that dress to a lady." She said: "Well tell me, when they were cutting it, what was missing?" He responded: "Nothing was missing." The woman replied, saying: "What a liar you are! Wasn't there a sleeve missing?" The husband searched his memory and said: "It's true that the tailor forgot to cut it and had to get more scarlet cloth for it." Then the wife said: "If I showed you the sleeve would you recognize it?" The husband replied: "Well do you have it?" She responded: "Yes, come with me and I'll show it to you." They went together to her room and she took the sleeve from the bottom of the trunk, saying: "Is this the missing sleeve?" The husband said: "That's it: but I swear to God that we have to know who brought it from Hispaniola to Bogotá." And with this, he took the sleeve and went with it to the bishop, who was an Inquisition judge, and informed him about the case.

His holiness reacted swiftly. He had the woman brought before him and took her statement. She readily confessed to all that had happened with the bowl of water. Then he had the black woman, Juana García, and her daughters arrested. She admitted to everything . . . and testified against several other women as is often the case in these situations. Once the evidence was gathered, the bishop sentenced all the culprits. The news spread quickly: many had fallen into the net and that included some very important people.

In the end, Governor Don Gonzalo Jiménez de Quesada, Captain Céspedes, Juan Tafur, Juan Ruiz de Orejuela, along with other dignitaries, went to the bishop. They begged him not to carry out the sentence in this case, arguing that theirs was a new land and association with the case would stain its reputation.

They pressured his holiness so much that he dismissed the case. Only Juana García was punished. She was made to do penance in Santo Domingo during high mass on a scaffold with a noose around her neck and a lighted candle in her hand, where she said, crying: "We all did it, but only I have to pay." They exiled her and her daughters from the kingdom [Nueva Granada]. In her confession she said that when she went to Bermuda . . . she took flight from a hill that's on the shoulders of Our Lady of the Snows, where one of the crosses is. A long time later, they named it Juana García or the hill of Juana García.

PART FIVE

LATE COLONIAL DEVELOPMENTS

9

THE BOURBON REFORMS

IN THE EIGHTEENTH CENTURY, Spain made a remarkable recovery from the state of abject weakness into which it had fallen under the last Hapsburg kings. This revival is associated with the reigns of three princes of the Houses of Bourbon: Philip V (1700–1746), grandson of Louis XIV of France, and his two sons, Ferdinand VI (1746–1759) and Charles III (1759–1788).

The work of national reconstruction reached its peak under Charles III. During his reign, Spanish industry, agriculture, and trade made marked gains. Clerical influence suffered a setback when the Jesuits were expelled from the Americas in 1767 and decrees were enacted that restricted the authority of the Inquisition. Under the cleansing influence of able and honest ministers, a new spirit of austerity and service began to appear among public officials.

In the field of colonial reform the Bourbons moved slowly and cautiously, since powerful vested interests were identified with the old order of things. The *Casa de Contratación*, or House of Trade, was gradually reduced in importance until it finally disappeared in 1790. A similar fate overtook the venerable Council of the Indies, although it was not abolished until 1854. Most of its duties were entrusted to a colonial minister appointed by the king. The Bourbons alternately suspended and tried to rehabilitate the fleet system of sailing, but in the end it was abandoned, the Portobello fleet disappearing in 1740, the Veracruz fleet in 1789. The Portobello and Veracruz fairs vanished contemporaneously. In the same period the trading monopoly of Cádiz was gradually eliminated. The success of the free trade policy was reflected in a spectacular increase in the value of Spain's commerce with Spanish America.

The eighteenth century witnessed a steady growth of agricultural, pastoral, and mining production in Spanish America. By contrast with these signs of progress, the once flourishing colonial handicrafts industry declined, owing to the influx of cheap European wares with which the native products could not compete. Contraband trade, never completely eliminated under the Bourbons, reached vast proportions during the frequent intervals of warfare in which British naval power swept Spanish shipping from the seas.

The most important Bourbon political reform was the transfer to the colonies, between 1782 and 1790, of the intendant system, already introduced in Spain from France. The intendants (provincial governors) were expected to relieve the overburdened viceroys of many of their duties, especially in financial matters, and to develop agriculture, industry, and commerce and generally to promote the welfare of their respective districts. Many of the viceroys and intendants of the reform period were able and progressive men, devoted to the interests of the crown and their subjects. But the same cannot be said of the majority of their subordinates, who, like their predecessors, the *corregidores*, soon became notorious for their oppressive practices. Following the triumph of reaction in Spain after 1788, the familiar evils of administrative corruption, mismanagement, and indifference to the public interest reappeared on a large scale in the colonies, as in Spain.

The Creole upper class enjoyed greater opportunities for material and cultural enrichment in the Bourbon era, but the same was not true of Indians, *mestizos*, and other laboring groups. The intolerable conditions of the common people led to major revolutionary outbreaks in Peru, Bolivia, and Colombia (1780–1783) that were sternly suppressed by Spanish arms.

1. THE BOURBON COMMERCIAL REFORMS

The Bourbon reforms in the field of colonial trade represented a supreme effort to recover for Spain a dominant position in the markets of Spanish America. The reform program provided for a stricter enforcement of the laws against contraband; more importantly, it included a series of measures designed to liberalize the commerce between Spain and its colonies while retaining the principle of peninsular trade monopoly. The Bourbon reforms, combined with a rising European demand for Spanish American products, helped expand colonial trade and prosperity in the last half of the eighteenth century. The Mexican historian Lucas Alamán surveys the beneficial effects of these reforms on the commerce of New Spain.

Commerce with Spain, the only one that was permitted, was restricted until 1778 to the port of Cadiz, where were assembled, under the inspection of the *audiencia* and the House of Trade of Seville, all the goods bound for

---

Lucas Alamán, *Historia de Méjico*, 5 vols. (México, 1849–1852), 1:109–110, 110–113. Excerpt translated by Benjamin Keen.

America. They were carried there in the fleets, which departed each year and whose routes were minutely prescribed by the laws, and in the interval there was no other communication than that of the dispatch boats and the store-ships coming with quicksilver. On the arrival of the fleets a great fair was held at Panama, for all South America, and another in Jalapa for New Spain, whence this town acquired the name of Jalapa of the Fair.

This order of things gave rise to a double monopoly: that enjoyed by the houses of Cadiz and Seville which made up the cargoes and that which was secured at the fairs by the American merchants, who made agreements among themselves whereby particular merchants acquired complete control over certain lines of goods. Since the supply of these goods was not renewed for a long time, it was in their power to raise prices at will, whence arose the high prices of some commodities, especially when maritime war prevented the arrival of the fleets for several years. This condition gave occasion for the arbitrary measures of certain viceroys in fixing retail prices in favor of the consumer, as was done by the second Duke of Albuquerque in 1703.

Commerce with Asia was reduced to a single vessel, known as the "China-ship," which was sent once a year from Manila and, passing in sight of San Blas, arrived at Acapulco, to which came the buyers for the fair that was held there; after the fair it sailed again, carrying the cash proceeds of the sale of the goods that it had brought, the subvention with which the royal treasury of Mexico aided that of Manila, the criminals condemned to serve time in those islands, and those dissipated youths whom their families had consigned to this kind of exile as a disciplinary measure, called "being sent to China." Commerce between New Spain and Peru, Guatemala, and New Granada by way of the Pacific was prohibited for a variety of reasons.

By the ordinance of October 12, 1778, all this system of commerce with Europe was changed. The fleets ceased to come, the last being the one that arrived at Vera Cruz in January of that year, under the command of Don Antonio de Ulloa, so celebrated for his voyage to Peru and his secret report to the king on the state of that kingdom. Commerce thus became free for all Spanish ships sailing from habilitated ports in the peninsula, but it could only be carried on in New Spain through the port of Vera Cruz, and European goods could not be introduced from Havana or any other American place but must be brought directly from Spain.

The results of this change were very important, not only because of the abundance of goods and price reductions that it yielded but also because it ended the monopoly and the vast profits acquired with little labor by the *flotistas*, the name given to the monopolists. These men, finding it impossible to continue their former practices, retired from commerce and invested their capital in agriculture and mining, which they greatly stimulated, especially the latter. Their places were taken by a larger number of individuals, who in order to prosper had to display much activity, and thus instead of a few large capitals there arose many small ones, which, distributed among all the towns, contributed largely to their betterment.

In this same period were lifted the odious restrictions on commerce among the provinces or kingdoms of America; and a royal decree of January 17, 1774, promulgated in the Prado, conceded freedom of trade in the Pacific, though only in the goods and productions of the respective provinces. Later declarations broadened this freedom, removing the restrictions imposed by the aforementioned order in regard to European and Asiatic goods. . . .

The exclusive colonial system of Spain provided great and valuable compensations for the prohibitions that it imposed. If one glances at the balance of trade of Vera Cruz, the only port habilitated in that period for trade with Europe and the West Indies, for the year 1803, one of the last years of peace with England, it will be seen that of the total exports to Spain, worth 12,000,000 pesos, more than a third, or 4,500,000, were in the form of produce, including not only 27,000 *arrobas* of cochineal of a value of 2,200,000 pesos but also 150,000 pounds of indigo, worth 260,000 pesos, and 500,000 *arrobas* of sugar of the value of 1,500,000 pesos, besides 26,600 *quintales* of logwood and 17,000 *quintales* of cotton. Among the exports to various points in America one notes 20,000 *tercios* of flour, 14,700 *varas* of coarse frieze, 1,300 *varas* of baize, 1,760 boxes of soap, and 700 boxes of ordinary Puebla chinaware; all this, with other minor articles, comes to a value of more than 600,000 pesos a year.

The effect of these exports was to give a great value to the sugarcane plantations, while the flour of Puebla, flowing down to Vera Cruz to satisfy not only the needs of that place but also those of Havana, the other islands, and Yucatan, left the provisioning of the markets of Mexico City to the wheat fields of Querétaro and Guanajuato, adding to their value and bringing prosperity to the wheat farmers of those provinces. All this active traffic infused animation and life into our internal commerce. Mexican agriculture today would gladly exchange the sterile freedom to cultivate vines and olives for an exportation of 500,000 *arrobas* of sugar and 20,000 *tercios* of flour.

2. THE REVIVAL OF MINING

The eighteenth century saw a revival of the silver mining industry in the Spanish colonies. Peru and Mexico both shared in this advance, but the Mexican mines, where production had been rising quite consistently since the sixteenth century, forged far ahead of their Peruvian rivals in the Bourbon era. As with agriculture, the increase in production did not result from improved technique but rather the opening of many new as well as old mines and the growth of the labor force. Although the Bourbon kings and their colonial agents exerted themselves to overcome the backwardness of the mining industry, their efforts were largely frustrated by the traditionalism of the mine owners and a lack of capital to finance necessary changes.

Since the brilliant period of the reign of Charles V, Spanish America has been separated from Europe, with respect to the communication of discoveries useful to society. The imperfect knowledge which was possessed in the 16th century relative to mining and smelting, in Germany, Biscay, and the Belgic provinces, rapidly passed into Mexico and Peru, on the first colonization of these countries; but since that period, to the reign of Charles III, the American miners have learned hardly anything from the Europeans, but the blowing up with powder those rocks which resist the pointrole. This King and his successor have shown a praiseworthy desire of imparting to the colonies all the advantages derived by Europe from the improvement in machinery, the progress of chemical science, and their application to metallurgy. German miners have been sent at the expense of the court to Mexico, Peru, and the kingdom of New Granada; but their knowledge has been of no utility, because the mines of Mexico are considered as the property of the individuals, who direct the operations, without the government being allowed to exercise the smallest influence. . . .

After the picture which we have just drawn of the actual state of the mining operations, and of the bad economy which prevails in the administration of the mines of New Spain, we ought not to be astonished at seeing works, which for a long time have been most productive, abandoned whenever they have reached a considerable depth, or whenever the veins have appeared less abundant in metals. We have already observed, that in the famous mine of Valenciana, the annual expenses rose in the space of fifteen years from two millions of francs to four millions and a half. Indeed, if there be much water in this mine, and if it require a number of horse *baritels* to draw it off, the profit must, to the proprietors, be little or nothing. The greatest part of the defects in the management which I have been pointing out, have been long known to a respectable and enlightened body, the Tribunal de Minería of Mexico, to the professors of the school of mines, and even to several of the native miners, who without having ever quitted their country, know the imperfection of the old methods; but we must repeat here, the changes can only take place very slowly among a people who are not fond of innovations, and in a country where the government possesses so little influence on the works which are generally the property of individuals, and not of shareholders. It is a prejudice to imagine, that

―――――

Alexander von Humboldt, *Political Essay on the Kingdom of New Spain*, 4 vols. (London, 1822–1823), 3:231–246.

the mines of New Spain on account of their wealth, do not require in their management the same intelligence and the same economy which are necessary to the preservation of the mines of Saxony and the Hartz. We must not confound the abundance of ores with their intrinsic value. The most part of the minerals of Mexico being very poor, as we have already proved, and as all those who do not allow themselves to be dazzled by false calculations very well known, an enormous quantity of gangue impregnated with metals must be extracted, in order to produce two millions and a half of marcs of silver. Now it is easy to conceive that in mines of which the different works are badly disposed, and without any communication with one another, the expense of extraction must be increased in an alarming manner, in proportion as the shifts (*pozos*) increasing in depth, and the galleries (*cañones*) become more extended.

The labor of a miner is entirely free throughout the whole kingdom of New Spain; and no Indian or *Mestizo* can be forced to dedicate themselves to the working of mines. It is absolutely false, though the assertion has been repeated in works of the greatest estimation that the court of Madrid sends out galley slaves to America, to work in the gold and silver mines. The mines of Siberia have been peopled by Russian malefactors; but in the Spanish colonies this species of punishment has been fortunately unknown for centuries. The Mexican miner is the best paid of all miners; he gains at least from 25 to 30 *francs* per week of six days, while the wages of laborers who work in the open air, husbandmen for example, are seven *livres* sixteen *sous*, on the central table land, and nine *livres* twelve *sous* near the coast. The miners, *tenateros* and *faeneros* occupied in transporting the minerals to the place of assemblage (*despachos*) frequently gain more than six *francs* per day, of six hours. Honesty is by no means so common among the Mexican as among the German or Swedish miners; and they make use of a thousand tricks to steal very rich specimens of ores. As they are almost naked, and are searched on leaving the mine in the most indecent manner, they conceal small morsels of native silver, or red sulphuret and muriate of silver in their hair, under their arm-pits, and in their mouths; and they even lodge in their anus, cylinders of clay which contain the metal. The cylinders are called *longanas*, and they are sometimes found of the length of thirteen centimeters (five inches). It is a most shocking spectacle to see in the large mines of Mexico, hundreds of workmen, among whom there are a great number of very respectable men, all compelled to allow themselves to be searched on leaving the pit or the gallery. A register is kept of the minerals found in the hair, in the mouth, or other parts of the miners' bodies. In the mine of Valenciana at Guanaxuato, the value of these stolen minerals, of which a great part was composed of the *longanas*, amounted between 1774 and 1787, to the sum of 900,000 francs.

3. THE NEW EXPERIMENTAL SCIENCES AND
CATHOLIC EDUCATION

In colonial Spanish America the Enlightenment was, to a great extent, received through its Spanish translation and exportation. Despite Catholic censorship, the Bourbon monarchs and their advisers encouraged the dissemination and practical implementation of new ideas, particularly those pertaining to economic and scientific development. Contrary to most histories of the period, colonial Catholicism was not entirely averse to this change. In fact, the Spanish American Enlightenment was a unique combination of the new and the old: a "Catholic Enlightenment." Members of the higher clergy were often familiar with the new thought, and some even promoted it through teaching and debate. According to priests like Fray José Sullivan, rector of the University of Córdoba (in the viceroyalty of Río de la Plata), authorities should consider finding a place for new science in the curriculum instead of rejecting it out of hand. His arguments in this excerpt were developed as part of a promotion for the purchase of a machine for scientific experimentation by this very traditional Catholic University.

Most excellent sir: the physics machines suggested by me to Don Martín José de Altolaguirre, under the conditions detailed in this file, for the use and improvement of the sciences in the University and Royal College of Montserrat in Córdoba under my supervision, must be bought without further delay, given the usefulness resulting from the more thorough instruction of students there, in all sciences and endeavors, and given its inexpensive price. . . .

The benefit that the students (in particular) or the state (in general) should realize from the use of these machines is sufficiently demonstrated in practice. Thus, I think it unnecessary to digress any further in my address to this wise government and its knowledgeable magistrate. He knows from experience, better than myself, the extraordinary advancements that these famous new inventions have produced in the sciences, even abstract sciences, that are leading man toward God through the greater knowledge of His wonderful works of creation, knowledge which is distributed among persons following various careers—letters, mining, agriculture and other forms of knowledge found in society. These advancements, in particular and in general, are much needed in this country, so vast and rich in untapped primary resources. . . .

"Informe del Rector de la Universidad de Córdoba, Fray José Sullivan, en el expediente sobre la compra de un laboratorio de física experimental, Buenos Aires, 28 de septiembre de 1802," in Fray Zenón Bustos, *Anales de la Universidad de Córdoba, segundo período (1795–1807)*, 3:347–348. Excerpt translated by the editors.

In the preceding report, the Illustrious Cabildo of Córdoba has argued that the purchase is not convenient since the university does not offer studies in physics, particularly in machinery or other areas related to its uses or purposes; that there is no special professor, intelligent and capable of providing his knowledge, or capable of repairing any defect or accident; that the purchase of such machines goes against the spirit of the founder, and does not fit the curriculum approved by His Majesty, a curriculum in which the acquisition of technological science, the increase of scholarships, the purchase of a much-needed library, and the repair of the university are addressed. All of these reasons, enthusiastically offered without knowledge and with little regard toward my person, are, in my opinion, easily refuted. Not offering studies in experimental physics, and not having the special, intelligent tutor capable of using the machines both follow from the fact that we have not had, until this day, any way to use them. Without altering the plan or present distribution of studies, we could substitute syllogisms with the demonstration of the truth, which is the method so justly ordered by our sovereign. Ancient philosophy would be abolished—it has filled the heads of those educated by it with terms of little significance, causing constant contradiction while never advancing toward the truth; in a word, it has made men so spoiled that they are held in contempt by society. This is what the Cabildo of Córdoba endorsed, with the argument that ancient philosophy facilitates a talent for discourse, and that experimental practice is not useful for the possession of theological science as the founder of this University would have wanted. According to this view, our admiring of God through knowledge of the marvels, the greatness, and the power of His creation, through the practical examination of His works, should be neglected because it is more useful to know Him by arguing over doubtful, or even false concepts—concepts never rising to the level of ideas, since true ideas are not permitted by the greatness of the maker. . . .

I conclude by insisting on this purchase as useful, advantageous, and necessary. I remind Your Excellency that my religious status, my character, the trials I have endured in my religious life, and in the administration of this institution, place me above selfish interests, since I am promoting the greater prestige of the university. Your Excellency will resolve what he considers most convenient and in keeping with his superior judgment.

4. Colonial Industry in Decline

In the last half of the eighteenth century, colonial manufacturing, after a period of long and steady growth, began to decline as an influx of cheap European wares displaced domestic products. Internal trade also fell off in some areas, as Spanish Ameri-

can economic life became increasingly geared to the export of agricultural and pastoral products and the import of European finished goods. Alexander von Humboldt's account of his visits to Mexican manufacturing centers clearly reveals the weakness and backwardness of colonial industry.

The oldest cloth manufactories of Mexico are those of Tezcuco. They were in great part established in 1592 by the viceroy Don Louis de Velasco II, the son of the celebrated constable of Castille, who was second viceroy of New Spain. By degrees, this branch of national industry passed entirely into the hands of the Indians and *mestizos* of Querétaro and Puebla. I visited the manufactories of Querétaro in the month of August 1803. They distinguish there the great manufactories, which they call *obrajes*, from the small, which go by the name of *trapiches*. . . .

On visiting these workshops, a traveler is disagreeably struck, not only with the great imperfection of the technical process in the preparation for dyeing, but in a particular manner also with the unhealthiness of the situation, and the bad treatment to which the workmen are exposed. Free men, Indians, and people of color, are confounded with criminals distributed by justice among the manufactories, in order to be compelled to work. All appear half naked, covered with rags, meager, and deformed. Every workshop resembles a dark prison. The doors, which are double, remain constantly shut, and the workmen are not permitted to quit the house. Those who are married are only allowed to see their families on Sunday. All are unmercifully flogged, if they commit the smallest trespass on the order established in the manufactory.

We have difficulty in conceiving how the proprietors of the *obrajes* can act in this manner with free men, as well as how the Indian workman can submit to the same treatment with the galley slaves. These pretended rights are in reality acquired by stratagem. The manufacturers of Querétaro employ the same trick, which is made use of in several of the cloth manufactories of Quito, and in the plantations, where from a want of slaves, laborers are extremely rare. They choose from among the Indians the most miserable, but such as show an aptitude for the work, and they advance them a small sum of money. The Indian, who loves to get intoxicated, spends it in a few days, and having become the debtor of the master, he is shut up in the workshop, under the pretence of paying off the debt by the work of his hands. They allow him only a real and a half, or 20 *sous tournois* per day of wages; but in place of paying it in ready money, they take care to supply him with meat, brandy, and clothes, on which the manufacturer gains from fifty to sixty per cent; and in

Humboldt, *Political Essay on the Kingdom of New Spain*, 3:462–469.

this way the most industrious workman is forever in debt, and the same rights are exercised over him which are believed to be acquired over a purchased slave. I knew many persons in Querétaro, who lamented with me the existence of these enormous abuses. Let us hope that a government friendly to the people, will turn their attention to a species of oppression so contrary to humanity, the laws of the country, and the progress of Mexican industry.

With the exception of a few stuffs of cotton mixed with silk, the manufacture of silks is at present next to nothing in Mexico. In the time of Acosta, towards the conclusion of the sixteenth century, silk worms brought from Europe were cultivated near Panuco, and in la Misteca, and excellent taffeta was there manufactured with Mexican silk.

On my passage through Querétaro, I visited the great manufactory of cigars (*fábrica de puros y cigarros*), in which 3000 people, including 1900 women, are employed. The halls are very neat, but badly aired, very small, and consequently excessively warm. They consume daily in this manufacture 130 reams (*resmas*) of paper, and 2770 pounds of tobacco leaf. . . .

The manufacture of hard soap is a considerable object of commerce at Puebla, Mexico, and Guadalaxara. The first of these towns produces nearly 200,000 *arrobas* per annum; and in the intendancy of Guadalaxara, the quantity manufactured is computed at 1,300,000 *livres tournois*. The abundance of soda which we find almost everywhere at elevations of 2000 or 2500 meters, in the interior table land of Mexico, is highly favorable to this manufacture. . . .

The town of Puebla was formerly celebrated for its fine manufactories of delf ware (*loza*) and hats. We have already observed that, till the commencement of the eighteenth century, these two branches of industry enlivened the commerce between Acapulco and Peru. At present there is little or no communication between Puebla and Lima, and the delf manufactories have fallen so much off, on account of the low price of the stone ware and porcelain of Europe imported at Vera Cruz, that of 446 manufactories which were still existing in 1793, there were in 1802 only sixteen remaining of delf ware, and two of glass.

5. POLITICAL REFORM: THE INTENDANT SYSTEM

The intendant reform was made by Charles III in the interests of greater administrative efficiency and increased royal revenues from the colonies. Among their many duties, the intendants were expected to further the economic development of their districts by promoting the cultivation of new crops, improving mining, building roads and bridges, and establishing consulados (chambers of commerce) and economic societies. The historian Alamán gives a glowing account of the favorable consequences of the es-

tablishment of the intendant system in New Spain and of the accomplishments of two model intendants.

The principal source of profit of the *alcaldes mayores* consisted in the traffic they carried on under the pretext of getting the Indians to work, as was recommended by the laws. They assigned them certain tasks and purchased the product at low prices, paying for it in necessary articles of dress and food that were overpriced. Having all authority in their hands, they compelled the Indians to fulfill these contracts with great punctuality, and reaped large profits thereby. This was particularly true in those districts where there was some valuable product, such as cochineal in Oaxaca, which constituted a monopoly for those officers and for the merchants who equipped them with capital and goods. Meanwhile the Indians were cruelly oppressed. A miserable system of administration was this, in which the pecuniary advantage of the governors was rooted in the oppression and misery of the governed! The Duke of Linares, in his vigorous and concise style, characterized it in a few words: "Although the jurisdiction of the *alcaldes mayores* is most extensive, I can define it very briefly, for it amounts to this: They are faithless to God from the time they enter upon their employment, by breaking the oath they have taken; they are faithless to their king, because of the *repartimientos* they engage in; and they sin against the common Indians, by tyrannizing over them as they do."

The whole order of things, so unjust and oppressive, ceased with the promulgation of the Ordinance of Intendants, published by Minister [José de] Gálvez on December 4, 1786, and limited at that time to New Spain alone, but later extended, with appropriate modifications, to all Spanish America. In it, under the titles of "the four departments of justice, police, finance, and war," were set forth the most comprehensive rules for the administration of the country in these spheres and for the encouragement of agriculture, industry, and mining. The whole territory of the vice-royalty, including Yucatán and the *provincias internas*, was divided into twelve intendancies, which took the names of their capitals. The *corregimiento* of Querétaro was retained for civil and judicial matters, but it was made financially dependent on the intendancy of Mexico. To the posts of intendants were appointed men of integrity and intelligence in the performance of their functions. Among those who distinguished themselves by their special merit were the intendants of Guanajuato and Puebla.

Minister Gálvez, at the time when he was in power, sought to place all his relatives in high posts, and their actions justified this preference. Don Matías, his brother, and Don Bernardo, his nephew, succeeded each other as viceroys

---

Alamán, *Historia de Méjico*, 1:73–76. Excerpt translated by Benjamin Keen.

of Mexico. . . . At the time of the creation of the intendancies, the former was assigned that of Valladolid, where he remained only a short time, being transferred immediately to the more important one of Guanajuato; and Flon was placed over that of Puebla.

The strict and honorable Flon reformed great abuses, encouraged all the branches of industry in his province, and notably beautified its capital. Riaño, of equal integrity but of a mild and affable disposition, had served in the royal navy, and to a knowledge of mathematics and astronomy, natural in that profession, united a taste for literature and the fine arts. These interests, and in particular his delight in architecture, he introduced to Guanajuato; through his influence there were erected, not only in the capital but in all the province, magnificent structures, whose building he himself supervised, even instructing the stonecutters in the art of hewing stone. He promoted the study of the Latin classics of the best Spanish writers; it was owing to his influence that the young men of Guanajuato devoted themselves to the study of the Castilian tongue and to its correct pronunciation.

French, the native tongue of his wife, was spoken in their home, and he introduced among the youth of the provincial capital a taste for that language and its literature, together with an elegance of manners unknown in other cities of the province. He was also responsible for the development of interest in drawing and music and for the cultivation of mathematics, physics, and chemistry in the school that had formerly been maintained by the Jesuits. To that end he zealously patronized Don José Antonio Rojas, professor of mathematics in that school and a graduate of the School of Mines. He also established a theater, promoted the cultivation of olives and vines, and diligently fostered the mining industry, the chief wealth of that province, by encouraging the rich citizens of Guanajuato to form companies for the exploitation of old and abandoned mines as well as new ones.

6. THE MORE THINGS CHANGE . . .

"Plus ça change, plus c'est la même chose" could be fairly applied to Spain's Indian policy. The Ordinance of Intendants *promised to inaugurate a new and better day for the Indian by abolishing the offices of* corregidor *and* alcalde mayor *and forbidding their successors, the subdelegates, to engage in the infamous* reparto de mercancías. *Despite Alamán's contention (see the previous selection) that the old order of things, "so unjust and oppressive, ceased with the promulgation of the* Ordinance of Intendants," *other observers came to different conclusions. In Mexico an enlightened prelate, Bishop Manuel Abad Queipo of Michoacán, denounced the entire system of subjugation and segregation of the Indians and mixed castes and flatly stated that the natives were worse off than they had been before the intendant reform.*

The population of New Spain is composed of some four and a half million inhabitants, who can be divided into three classes: Spaniards, Indians, and castes. The Spaniards number one tenth of the total population but possess almost the entire population or wealth of the kingdom. The other two classes, forming the other nine tenths, can be divided into two parts castes, the other part pure Indians. The Indians and castes are employed in domestic service, agricultural labors, and the ordinary tasks of commerce and industry—that is to say, they are servants and day-laborers for the Spaniards. Consequently there arises between them and the Spaniards that opposition of interests and views that is typical of those who have nothing and those who have everything—between superiors and inferiors. Envy, theft, and unwilling service are the traits of the latter; arrogance, exploitation, and harsh treatment, the qualities of the former. These evils are to a certain extent common to all the world. But in America they are immeasurably greater because there are no gradations or intermediate states: all are either rich or wretched, noble or infamous.

In effect, the two classes of Indians and castes are sunk in the greatest abasement and degradation. The color, ignorance, and misery of the Indians place them at an infinite distance from a Spaniard. The ostensible privileges which the laws accord them do them little good and in most respects injure them greatly. Shut up in a narrow space of six hundred *varas*, assigned by law to the Indian towns, they possess no individual property and are obliged to work the communal lands. This cultivation is made all the more hateful by the fact that in recent years it has become increasingly difficult for them to enjoy any of the fruits of their labor. Under the new intendant system they cannot draw on the communal funds [*caja de comunidad*] without special permission from the office of the royal exchequer [*junta superior de la real hacienda*] in Mexico City.

Forbidden by law to commingle with the other castes, they are deprived of the instruction and assistance that they should receive from contact with these and other people. They are isolated by their language, and by a useless, tyrannical form of government. In each town there are found eight or ten old Indians who live in idleness at the expense of their fellows and artfully try to perpetuate their ancient customs, usages, and gross superstitions, ruling them like despots. Incapable, by law, of making a binding contract or of running into debt to the extent of more than five pesos—in a word, of any dealings at all—they cannot learn anything or better their fortune or in any way raise themselves above their wretched condition. Solorzano, Fraso, and other Spanish authors have wondered why the privileges granted them have

---

José María Luis Mora, *Obras sueltas*, 2 vols. (Paris, 1837), 1:55–57. Excerpt translated by Benjamin Keen.

redounded to their injury; but it is greater cause for wonder that such men as these should have failed to understand that the source of the evil lies in these very privileges. They are an offensive weapon employed by the white class against the Indians, and never serve to defend the latter. This combination of causes makes the Indians indifferent to their future and to all that does not excite the passions of the moment.

The castes are declared infamous by law, as descendants of Negro slaves. They are subject to the payment of tribute, which is punctiliously recorded; as a result, this obligation has become a brand of slavery which neither the passage of time nor the mixture of successive generations can ever obliterate. There are many of these who in their color, physiognomy, and conduct could pass for Spaniards if it were not for this impediment, which reduces them all to the same state. . . .

The Indians as well as the castes are governed directly by magistrates of districts [*justicias territoriales*] whose conduct has measurably contributed to the situation in which they find themselves. The *alcaldes mayores* considered themselves not so much justices as merchants, endowed with the exclusive privilege . . . of trading in their province and of extracting from it in a five-year term of office from thirty to two hundred thousand pesos. Their usurious and arbitrary *repartimientos* caused great injuries. But despite this state of affairs two favorable circumstances commonly resulted, one being that they administered justice with impartiality and rectitude in cases in which they were not parties, the other being that they fostered agriculture and industry, in their own interests.

The Spanish government undertook to put an end to these abuses by replacing the *alcaldes mayores* with the subdelegates. But since the latter were not assigned any fixed salary, the remedy proved much worse than the evil. If they adhere to the schedule of fees, among a wretched folk who litigate only against each other, they will inevitably perish of hunger. They must of necessity prostitute their posts, swindle the poor, and traffic in justice. For the same reason it is extremely difficult for the intendants to find suitable individuals to fill these posts. They are sought, therefore, only by bankrupts or by those whose conduct and talents unfit them for success in the other walks of life. Under these conditions, what benefits, what protection, can these ministers of law dispense to the abovementioned two classes? How can they attract their good-will and respect, when extortion and injustice are virtually their livelihood?

10

❦

WINDS OF CHANGE

IN THE EIGHTEENTH CENTURY, Spanish America roused from its medieval sleep. A lively contraband in unorthodox ideas accompanied the growing trade between the colonies and non-Spanish lands. Spain, now under the sway of the enlightened Bourbon kings, contributed to the intellectual renovation of the colonies. Spanish or foreign scientific expeditions to Spanish America, authorized and sometimes financed by the crown, stimulated the growth of scientific interests. The expulsion of the Jesuits (1767) removed the ablest exponents of scholasticism and cleared the way for modest projects of educational reform. But the most significant cultural activity took place outside academic halls—in economic societies organized for the promotion of useful knowledge; in private gatherings and coffeehouses, where young men ardently discussed the advantages of free trade and the rights of men; and in the colonial press, which gave articulate expression to the new secular and critical spirit.

In addition to this intellectual ferment among the literate classes, popular resistance to colonial authority accelerated under the Bourbons as imperial attempts to centralize political authority and modernize the colonial economy began to take their toll on social relations. While the Creole upper classes often enjoyed greater opportunities for material and cultural enrichment in the Bourbon era (if less political influence), the same was not true of Indians, *mestizos*, blacks, and other laboring groups. Intolerable conditions among the common people led to major revolutionary outbreaks in Peru, Bolivia, and Colombia (1780–1783) that were sternly suppressed by Spanish arms. In Brazil and the Caribbean, endemic revolts reflected ongoing tension produced by reliance on slave labor. The 1804 overthrow of the French colonial regime in Haiti—the most productive of the sugar-producing islands in the Caribbean—by armies of former slaves was the most dramatic and successful of these revolts.

1. Colonial Journalism in Action

Colonial newspapers and reviews played a significant part in the development of a critical and reformist spirit and a nascent sense of nationality among the educated Creoles of Spanish America. These periodicals appeared in increasing numbers after 1780. More important than the routine news items they carried were the articles they included on scientific, economic, and social questions. The Semanario del Nuevo Reino de Granada, *edited between 1808 and 1811 by the distinguished Colombian scientist Francisco José de Caldas (1771–1816), was notable for the high quality of its content. Caldas himself contributed many of the articles in the* Semanario, *including a brilliant essay on the geography of New Granada, from which the following excerpt is taken.*

Whether we look north or south, whether we examine the most populous or the most deserted places in this colony, everywhere we find the stamp of indolence and ignorance. Our rivers and mountains are unknown to us; we do not know the extent of the country in which we were born; and the study of our geography is still in the cradle. This capital and humiliating truth should shake us out of our lethargy; it should make us more attentive to our interests; it should draw us to every corner of New Granada to measure, examine, and describe it. This truth, engraved in the hearts of all good citizens, will bring them together in order to collect information, donate funds, and recruit men of learning, sparing neither labor nor expense to obtain a detailed reconnaissance map of our provinces. I am not speaking now of an ordinary map; reduced scales and economy must disappear from the minds of our countrymen. Two square inches, at least, should represent a league of terrain. Here should appear the hills, mountains, pastures, forests, lakes, marshes, valleys, rivers, their turns and velocities, straits, cataracts, fisheries, all settlements, all agricultural activities, mines, and quarries—in fine, everything above the surface of our land. These features, brought together, will produce a superb map, worthy of New Granada. The statesman, the magistrate, the philosopher, the businessman, will come to look at it to obtain information needed in the performance of their duties; the traveler, the botanist, the mineralogist, the soldier, and the agriculturist will see their concerns depicted in majestic strokes. . . . Each province will copy its own section and will guard it religiously. Our youth will be trained in the study of these sections, and in a few years we shall have men capable of conceiving and carrying out great plans. Everywhere we shall hear only of projects; projects of roads, navigation canals, new branches of industry, naturalization of foreign plants; the flame of patri-

---

Francisco José de Caldas, *Semanario del Nuevo Reino de Granada*, 3 vols. (Bogotá, 1942), 1:51–54. Excerpt translated by Benjamin Keen.

otism will be lighted in every heart; and the ultimate result will be the glory of our monarch and the prosperity of this colony.

If a geographical-economic expedition were formed to survey the whole viceroyalty, composed of an astronomer, a botanist, a mineralogist, a zoologist, and an economist, with two or more draftsmen; if all the provinces contributed toward a fund set up by the wealthy, and especially by the landowners; if the merchants did the same in view of their financial interest in the project; if the Chamber of Commerce [*Consulado*] of Cartagena supported the enterprise as actively as it promotes other projects of the same nature; if the governmental leaders supported it with all their authority—there is no doubt that in a few years we would have the glory of possessing a masterpiece of geographical and political knowledge, and would have laid the foundations of our prosperity.

If this project presents difficulties, there remains no other recourse than to improve our educational system. If instead of teaching our youths trifles . . . we gave them some acquaintance with the elements of astronomy and geography, and taught them the use of some easily-mastered instruments; if practical geometry and geodesy were substituted for certain metaphysical and useless subjects; if on finishing their courses they knew how to measure the earth, make a survey, determine a latitude, use a compass—then we would have reason to hope that these youths, dispersed throughout the provinces, would put into practice the principles they had learned in school, and would make a map of their country. Six months devoted to these interesting studies would qualify a young man to work on the great enterprise of the geography of this colony. I ask the persons responsible for our public education to consider and weigh whether it is more profitable to the State and Church to spend many weeks in sustaining airy systems and all that heap of futile or merely speculative questions than to devote this time to the study of the globe and the land that we inhabit. What do we care about the dwellers on the moon? Would it not be better to learn about the dwellers on the fertile banks of the Magdalena?

The religious orders who have in their charge the missions of the Orinoco, Caqueta, Andaquies, Mocoa, and Maynas should educate the young missionaries in these important subjects. These apostolic men would bring to the barbarians both the light of salvation and that of the useful sciences. Zealous imitators of Fathers Fritz, Coleti, Magnio, and Gumilla, they would leave us precious monuments of their activity and learning. Exact maps, geographical determination, descriptions of plants and animals, and important information about the customs of the savages whom they are going to civilize would be the fruits of these studies. They would serve them as a relief from the tedium and weariness that are inseparable from their lofty ministry.

The rudiments of arithmetic, plane geometry, and trigonometry, of which we possess good compendiums; the use of the graphometer, the gnomon, the quadrant (with some knowledge of how to draw a meridian), and the use of the barometer and the thermometer qualify a young man to assist in the advance of our geographical knowledge.

We have two chairs of mathematics, and that of philosophy offers some instruction in these sciences; thanks to the wise and generous Mutis, we already have an astronomical observatory, where practical experience can be obtained in the use of certain instruments; we have books, and we lack nothing necessary to working for the good of our country. My love for the fatherland dictated these relations. If they are useful to my countrymen, I am already rewarded for the labor they cost me; if not, they will pardon me, taking into account the purity of my intentions.

2. A COLONIAL FREETHINKER

The circulation and influence of forbidden books among educated colonials steadily increased in the closing decades of the eighteenth century and the first years of the nineteenth. Enlightenment influence is strongly evident in the work of the Mexican writer José Joaquín Fernández de Lizardi (1776–1827), whose stormy life spanned the declining years of the colony and the first years of its independence. His masterpiece, El periquillo sarniento *(The Itching Parrot), the first true Spanish American novel, depicted with harsh realism and biting satire the conditions of Mexican life in the late colonial period. The following episode from* El periquillo sarniento, *set in Manila, illustrates Lizardi's emphatic dissent from social folly and prejudice of every kind.*

I said before that a virtuous man has few misfortunes to relate. Nevertheless, I witnessed some strange affairs. One of them was as follows: One year, when a number of foreigners had come from the port to the city for reasons of trade, a rich merchant who happened to be a Negro went down a street. He must have been bound on very important business, because he strode along very rapidly and distractedly, and in his headlong progress he inadvertently ran into an English officer who was paying court to a rich young creole lady. Such was the shock of the collision that if the girl had not supported him the officer would have fallen to the ground. As it was, his hat fell off and his hair was disheveled.

The officer's pride was greatly wounded, and he immediately ran toward the Negro, drawing his sword. The poor fellow was taken by surprise, and since he carried no arms he probably believed that it was all up with him. The young lady and the officer's companions restrained him, but he raged at the

José Joaquín Fernández de Lizardi, *El periquillo sarniento*, 2 vols. (México, 1897), 2:3–7. Excerpt translated by Benjamin Keen.

Negro for some time, protesting a thousand times that he would vindicate his injured honor.

So much abuse did he heap on the innocent black that the latter finally said to him in English: "Sir, be quiet; tomorrow I shall be waiting in the park to give you satisfaction with a pistol." The officer accepted, and there the matter rested.

I, who witnessed this incident and knew some English, having learned the hour and place assigned for the duel, took care to be there punctually to see how the affair would end.

At the appointed time both men arrived, each accompanied by a friend who acted as his second. As soon as they met the Negro drew two pistols, presented them to the officer, and said to him: "Sir, I did not intend yesterday to offend you; my running into you was an accident. You heaped abuse on me and even wished to wound or kill me. I had no arms with which to defend myself against you. I knew that a challenge to a duel was the quickest means of quieting you, and now I have come to give you satisfaction with a pistol, as I said I would."

"Very well," said the Englishman, "let's get on. It gives me no satisfaction to fight with a Negro, but at least I shall have the pleasure of killing an insolent rascal. Let's choose our pistols."

"All right," said the Negro, "but you should know that I no more intend to offend you today than I did yesterday. It seems to me that for a man of your position to decide to kill a man for such a trifle is not a matter of honor but a mere caprice. But if the explanation I gave you means nothing, and only killing will do, I don't propose to be guilty of murder or to die without cause, as must happen if your shot or my shot finds its target. So let luck decide who has justice on his side. Here are the pistols; one of them is loaded with two balls and the other is empty. Look them over, give me the one you don't want, and let us take our chances."

The officer was surprised by this proposal. The others said that it was highly irregular—that both must fight with the same weapons; and they offered other arguments that did not convince the Negro, who insisted that the duel must take place on his terms, so that he might have the consolation of knowing that if he killed his opponent it was because Heaven had ordered it or especially favored him—and if he were killed, it would be no fault of his but pure chance, as when a ship is wrecked at sea. He added that since the arrangement favored neither party, since no one knew who would get the loaded pistol, refusal to accept his proposal could only be attributed to cowardice.

No sooner had the ardent young man heard this than he took up the pistols, selected one, and gave the other to the Negro.

The two men turned their backs to each other, walked a short distance, and then turned to face each other. At that moment the officer fired at the Negro—but in vain, for he had chosen the empty pistol.

He stood there as if stunned, believing with the others that he would be the defenseless victim of the Negro's wrath. But the latter, with the greatest generosity, said to the officer: "Sir, we have both come out with whole skins; the duel is over; you had to accept it with the conditions I imposed, and I could wage it on no other terms. I could fire at you if I wished but if I never sought to offend you before, how could I do it now, seeing you disarmed? Let us be friends, if you consider yourself satisfied; but if only my death can appease you, take the loaded pistol and aim it at my breast."

Saying this, he presented the horrible weapon to the officer. The latter, moved by this extraordinary generosity, took the pistol and fired it in the air. Approaching the Negro with outstretched arms, he embraced him, saying with the greatest tenderness:

"Yes, friends we are and friends we shall be eternally; forgive my vanity and madness. I never believed that Negroes were capable of such greatness of soul." "That prejudice still has many followers," said the Negro, warmly embracing the officer.

We who witnessed this incident were eager to strengthen the bonds of this new friendship, and I, who knew them least of all, hastened to introduce myself to them as their friend, and to beg them to take a glass of punch or wine with me at the nearest coffeehouse.

3. A PLAN FOR DEMOCRATIC EDUCATION

As the influential tutor of Simón Bolívar, Simón Rodríguez (1769–1854) helped introduce Enlightenment thinking into the education of this independence hero. Before taking that memorable job, Rodríguez had been a teacher in a public elementary school in Caracas, where he acquired firsthand experience of the realities of colonial education. His thoughts reflect the concern of educated Creoles and Spaniards that the persistence of traditional scholastic education and the lack of official involvement in public education were hampering the introduction of new ideas into the schools. In this aptly titled tract, "On the Need to Improve Education," Rodríguez articulates the central lessons in his lifelong struggle for the betterment and modernization of education in the newly independent societies. Rodríguez's ideas won him some powerful enemies and he spent most of his life in exile.

[School] does not enjoy the esteem it deserves. It is sufficient to observe the limited state that [the school] is reduced to and the scarcity in which it sustains itself to know the truth of this. Most everyone needs it—because

Simón Rodríquez, *Obras completas*, vol. 1 (Caracas: Universidad Simón Rodríquez, 1975). Excerpt translated by the editors.

without acquiring basic literacy man is blind to all other knowledge. Its aims are the most praiseworthy, the most interesting: to predispose the minds of the children to be imprinted with the most valuable knowledge, in order to make them capable of all undertakings. For the sciences, for the arts, for commerce—it is indispensable for all occupations in life. And yet, compared to other things that contribute to progress and betterment, it is buried in such oblivion. So many men deem the more private and less useful employment as more distinguished; so many regard this ministry as an annex for the aged and the luckless; and so many are loath to dedicate themselves to its promotion and improvement!

Few appreciate its usefulness.   When a good thing is not appreciated, it is for one of two reasons: recklessness or ignorance. The former cannot be true in this case, because it seems impossible that there could exist men of such [low] character. Thus, this fatal state of affairs must be the result of the latter, and this is how I understand it.

The absence of formal schooling has made it necessary for many to resort to private study with an individual, resulting in a difference in tastes, depending on the whim of the teacher. Each one teaches and supports the rules, the precepts, and the distinctions, that he himself received. He is satisfied that his was the best method. His error is not verifying this by observation. He criticizes novelty. Few are those who are aware of their shortcomings.

It is necessary to admit, that among this great number of men, few have tried to correct themselves, and the errors they perpetuate, with new and careful study. In the first place, [this is because] at a mature age few are free from responsibilities to the state, and can devote themselves to the task. In the second place, it requires a natural inclination, and not everyone has it. He who doesn't have it regards the matter with indifference, since he can find at every step along the way so many other identical examples of those who are governed by the same poor letter: So many who ignore arithmetic naturally see elementary education (the proper venue of such teaching) as of little use, thinking they can manage without it.

This opinion was quite commonplace in another time—and it still is today—that the study of penmanship and arithmetic is only deemed necessary for clerks.

Some think that artisans, farmers, and common people know enough if they can sign their names, and that it is an unremarkable fault if they cannot; that those who are to undertake careers in letters do not need arithmetic; that it is enough to know how to shape characters in any manner so as to make yourself understood, because they won't make a living with the pen; that everything children learn at school is later forgotten; that they lose the good penmanship that they learned; that it's better that they learn these things when they are older and have better judgment, etc. So, in their view, it is necessary to show contempt for everything that has been written on the matter;

to consider its authors to be preoccupied with erroneous ideas; and to put down the schools because of their uselessness, leaving the children to their play.

Artisans and farmers are the kinds of men that need to be attended upon, just like their occupations. The State's interest in them is well-known, and thus does not require proof.

Everything is subject to rules. Each day skilled men send to press new works on the discoveries that are made in agriculture and the arts, and they circulate throughout Kingdom for the benefit of those who can use them. If those who study ignore the indispensable principles of reading, writing and counting, they will never be able to make use of these discoveries. They will remain in the darkness, though surrounded by lights that should be illuminating their way. They will make no progress, and the public will complain about being poorly served unnecessarily.

In this town, and even in the whole province, skill in the mechanical arts is confined to *pardos* and *morenos* [blacks and mulattos]. They have no one to instruct them, [since] they cannot attend the white children's school. Poverty sends them to work at an early age. Acquiring practice but not technique, they proceed haphazardly in all things. Some become masters of others, though never having been apprentices themselves. I make exception for those who, due to their utmost dedication and hard work, have been able to instruct themselves.

What progress can these men make, what models for improvement will they have if they are kept in complete ignorance? I do not think them any less deserving of education than white children. First, because they are not deprived of Society. And second, since the Church makes no qualitative distinction for the observance of religion, there shouldn't be any in its teaching. If some people must contribute to the good of the Fatherland by taking political and military posts, entering the ecclesiastical ministry, etc., others must contribute with their manual skills, which are no less important. For the same reason they should be equally served in their primary education. They would be viewed more favorably and there would be less complaints about their behavior if pains were taken to instruct them in a school with whites, although separately. . . .

Schools can function with any available resources.   The school's unfortunate fate over so many years has put it in the position of having to make due with what has been given it. Its value forgotten, it has suffered from utter abandon, with well-known consequences. Even to this day it feels, in many places, the pitiful effects of its misfortune.

It's enough to turn your attention to the hair salons and barber shops that serve as schools to see proof of this. Without stopping to examine its methods, or the ability of its teachers, find out with what authority they have established themselves, who their students are, and what progress they make.

And you will see that it has been an ancient custom for old artisans to retire from their professions with the honors of elementary school teachers, with the respect that white hair confers, the intelligence of Catechism, the deserved gratitude of many parents for the education of their children—that many, even today, create their public schools of reading and combing, or writing and shaving, with open admission for any unqualified applicant that appears, and [that] you never see anyone come out of them who is a credit to the school.

Any book, any pen, inkpot or paper that a child carries is too good for its purpose, since having something to read or something to write with is an accident that turns out one way or another, and that will have to be mended later on. [This is] quite typical of these schools. It would not hurt if they remained; but the pity is that they take the place of the true schools, and make their task difficult.

When a man who knows only [this kind of school] has a son at [a proper] school, and he is asked [to provide] high quality books, paper or pens, it surprises him. He laughs and calls the teacher too meticulous and overly concerned with materials—which is why the teacher is forced to teach the Flos Sanctorum to some, and the Guide for Foreigners to others.

They don't understand that reading properly requires the knowledge of written characters, the clear understanding of texts, and that a teacher cannot teach without having on hand proper copies of the reading material; that in order to give instruction on the methods and rules for shaping letters, the teacher also needs materials in good condition, that will facilitate the student's learning proper execution and provide him with models to which he can aspire.

It is regularly assumed that meditation books or spiritual discourses are the only ones a child needs at School, and they are given to them without further thought. Holy purposes, no doubt, are involved in this. But this is not the only subject that is studied in the world. It is necessary to know how to read in all respects, and to give each expression its own worth. A child that only learns in dialogue will only know how to ask or tell, if he just uses a historical sense. The same with writing and everything else related to teaching. The vice or limitation of the beginning is hard to mend, and the damage is always visible.

Reform is indispensable.   Attentive reading, without further reflection, of the [...] preceding articles, would be enough to deduce such an unavoidable conclusion. But I want to call attention to yet another consideration.

The Primary School of Madrid could never look like the one in this town, no matter how deplorable its state, since the Court is there to provide for its perfection. We see a complete transformation in its method: in terms of its teachers and in the subjects it teaches. There is an ongoing publication of several works geared toward reform and toward freeing it from the mistakes and abuses that used to hinder it. Men of very distinguished class and status are promoting this matter, holding back none of their substantial effort and resources. Some are writing a treatise on arithmetic; others are devoting themselves to a new technique to facilitate the forming of letters. Some personally direct the children, making an effort to reward merit.

What argument can be made, then, to avoid yielding to the force of such a powerful example? If, at the instigation of the Court, the Primary School has had to improve [in Madrid], why should it not have to improve here? Ours is a copy of that one—and for that reason it must follow all the changes of its original if it will conform to it.

This example commands the attention of many men throughout the Kingdom. Wherever we turn our eyes, we find not one or two cities, but entire provinces that are enjoying the finest methods and order in their schools, in imitation of the main schools. And can it be possible that this one—rich in so many qualities and being blessed by many extraordinary students, outstanding leaders, love and, above all, a fervent desire for its improvement— will fail to achieve something so necessary and indispensable, and thus be obliged to cede the advantage to those that have no such benefits? This cannot be: our school is regarded by many as a model, and its honor consists in the fact that others respect it as a leader.

4. THE PLAN OF TUPAC AMARU

The general causes of the great revolt of 1780–1781 in Peru are sufficiently clear. More obscure are the precise aims that the rebel leader, Tupac Amaru (José Gabriel Condorcanqui), set for himself. The fiscal *(prosecuting attorney) of the viceroyalty of Buenos Aires offers a shrewd and convincing argument in favor of the thesis that the rebel leader aimed at independence.*

What is worthy of attention in this affair is not so much the pitiful death of the *corregidor* Don Antonio de Arriaga, the theft of his fortune, the seizure of the arms that he had in his house, or the outrages committed by the perfidious Tupac Amaru, as the astuteness, the painstaking care, and the

---

"Visita del fiscal del virreinato de Buenos Aires, enero 15 de 1781," in *Documentos históricos del Perú*, ed. Manuel de Odriozola (Lima, 1863), pp. 132–133. Excerpt translated by Benjamin Keen.

deceptions with which he managed to perform them and to subvert that and other provinces, preparing them to carry out his reprehensible secret designs.

It appears that in order to seize the *corregidor* Arriaga, in his own house, he arranged a banquet for his victim. In order to summon the military chiefs, caciques, and Indians of the province, he compelled the unhappy *corregidor* to issue or sign orders to that effect. In order to drag him to the gallows in the presence of the multitude with no disturbance, he published a decree, pretending that he acted on His Majesty's orders. On the same pretext, after this horrible deed, he departed for the neighboring province of Quispicanchi, in order to perpetrate similar atrocities on the *corregidor* and as many Spaniards as he could find, and as soon as he had returned to his town of Tungasuca issued orders to the caciques of neighboring provinces to imitate his example.

And although in the provinces of Azangaro and Carabaya, which belonged to this viceroyalty of Buenos Aires, his wicked designs failed to bear fruit, thanks to the loyalty with which his commissioner Don Diego Chuquiguanca (the cacique and governor of the town of Azangaro) and his sons turned over the dispatches, of which copies are found in the file on this case, the fact is that the province of Quispicachi, since the flight of Don Fernando Cabrera, its present *corregidor*, is under the sway of the rebel Tupac Amaru; and he himself asserts in one of the papers written at Chuquiguanca that four more provinces obey his orders. And, knowing as he did the natives' great respect for the orders of the king and their hatred of the *corregidores* and their European associates, he probably did not find it difficult to incite them to execute the supposed orders of the king.

But the essence of the careful planning and perfidy of the traitor Tupac Amaru consists in this, that after speaking so often of the royal orders which authorized him to proceed against the *corregidores* and other Europeans, in his orders, letters, and messages, and in the edicts which he dispatched to Don Diego Chuquiguanca, in order to revolutionize the province and Carabaya, he now says nothing about the orders of the king, and proceeds as the most distinguished Indian of the royal blood and principal line of the Incas to liberate his countrymen from the injuries, injustices, and slavery which the European *corregidores* had inflicted on them, while the superior courts turned a deaf ear to their complaints. From which it follows that he repeatedly used the name of the king—in a vague way, not specifying our present ruler, Charles III—only to secure the acquiescence of the natives of those provinces in the violence done to Arriaga and to induce them to do the same to other *corregidores*. And considering these aims partially achieved, he transforms himself from a royal commissioner into a redeemer from injustices and burdens, moved only by pity for his compatriots, preparing the way for them to acclaim him as king, or at least to support their benefactor with arms, until they have raised him to the defunct throne of the tyrannical pagan kings of Peru, which is doubtless the goal of his contrivances.

Actually, he has already succeeded in assembling a large number of Indians, as noted by Colonel Don Pedro la Vallina (who was his prisoner) in a letter contained in the file on this case—and with their aid, it is stated, he defeated and slew some 300 men who came out to halt his advance on Cuzco, and took their weapons to arm the rebels who follow him. He took these first successful steps in his titanic enterprise after certain other things had occurred: the rising that took place in Arequipa as a result of the establishment of a customs house; the rioting that with less cause broke out in the city of La Paz; the disturbances that occurred in the provinces of Chayanta for the same reason; and the rumors that the natives in other provinces were somewhat restless. When one considers that the rebel Tupac Amaru, informed of these events, offers the natives freedom, not only from customs' house duties but from sales taxes, tributes, and forced labor in the mines, it must be admitted that he offers them a powerful inducement to follow him, and that there is imminent danger that the party of rebellion will progressively increase unless the most energetic effort is made to slay this insolent rebel, the prime mover of this conspiracy, so that others may be deterred from joining the rebellion and abandoning their loyalty to their legitimate monarch and natural lord, to the detriment of themselves and their commonwealth.

5. A HEROINE OF THE TUPAC AMARU REVOLT

Indian and mestiza *women played distinguished military roles in the 1780–1781 Tupac Amaru uprising in Peru, the greatest in the wave of native revolts that shook the Spanish empire in the last decades of the eighteenth century. The rebel leader's wife, Micaela, served as his principal adviser from the beginning, and in his absence assumed full direction of the movement. After an initial victory over a small Spanish force sent from Cuzco, she strongly advised an immediate advance on the city, taking advantage of the chaos and panic that reigned there. The capture of Cuzco, ancient capital of the Inca empire and center of Spanish power in the Andean highlands, would have been a stroke of the greatest moral and military significance. However, Tupac Amaru decided to invade the provinces to the south, promising to return immediately and advance on Cuzco—a promise he failed to keep. By the time he returned, Spanish reinforcements had reached Cuzco from Lima and the golden opportunity had vanished. The bitterness of Micaela's letter to Tupac Amaru reflects her appreciation of the immensity of his blunder. Despite her harsh approach, her letters to Tupac Amaru contain notes of profound and laconic tenderness ("Chepe" was an affectionate nickname for her husband).*

Dear Chepe:

You are causing me mortal concern. While you saunter through the villages, wasting two days in Yauri, showing no sense of urgency, our soldiers are rightly becoming bored, and are leaving for their homes.

I simply cannot endure all this any longer, and I am ready to give myself up to the Spaniards and let them take my life when I see how lightly you regard this serious matter that threatens the lives of all of us. We are surrounded by enemies and constantly insecure; and on your account the lives of all my sons, and of all our people, are in danger.

I have warned you again and again not to dally in those villages, where there is nothing to do—but you continue to saunter, ignoring the fact that the soldiers are running short of food. They are receiving their pay, but the money will not last forever. Then they will all depart, leaving us to pay with our lives, because you must have learned by this time that they came only for reasons of self-interest, and to get all they could out of us. They are already beginning to desert; they are frightened by the rumor spread by Vargas and Oré that the Spaniards of Lampa, united with those of other provinces and Arequipa, are going to surround you, and so they want to get away, fearing the punishment that might befall them. Thus we will lose all the people that I have gotten together for the descent on Cuzco, and the forces at Cuzco will unite with the soldiers from Lima, who have been on the march for many days.

I must tell you all this, though it pains me. If you want to ruin us, continue to sleep and commit such follies as that of passing along through the streets of Yauri, and even climbing to the church tower—actions certainly out of place at this time, and that only dishonor you and gain you disrespect.

I believed that you were occupied day and night with arranging these affairs, instead of showing an unconcern that robs me of my life. I am already a shadow of myself and beside myself with anxiety, and so I beg you to get on with this business.

You made me a promise, but henceforth I shall not heed your promises, for you did not keep your word.

I do not care for my life, but for the lives of my poor children, who need all my help. If the enemy comes from Paruro, as I suggested in my last letter, I am prepared to march to meet them, leaving Fernando in a secure place, for the Indians are not capable of acting by themselves in these perilous times.

I gave you plenty of warnings to march immediately on Cuzco, but you took them all lightly, giving the Spaniards time to prepare as they have done, placing cannon on Picchu Mountain, and devising other measures so dangerous that

"Micaela Bastidas to José Gabriel Tupac Amaru, December 6, 1780," in *Martires y heroinas*, ed. Francisco A. Loayza (Lima, 1945), pp. 48–51. Excerpt translated by Benjamin Keen.

you are no longer in a position to attack them. God keep you many years. Tungasuca, December 6, 1780.

I must also tell you that the Indians of Quispicanchi are tired of serving as guards so long a time. In fine, God must want me to suffer for my sins. Your wife.

After I had finished this letter, a messenger arrived with the definite news that the enemy from Paruro is in Acos; I am going forward to attack them, even if it costs me my life.

6. A CHARTER OF LIBERTY

Although attributable to the same causes, the rising of the Comuneros *in New Granada was a relatively peaceful affair by contrast with the vast upheaval in Peru. Its reformist spirit was reflected in the insurgent slogan: "Viva el rey y muera el mal gobierno!" (Long live the king, and down with the rotten government!) But in view of its organization and its effort to form a common front of all colonial groups with grievances against Spanish authority (excepting only the black slaves), the revolt of the* Comuneros *marked an advance over the chaotic course of events to the south. The popular basis of the* Comunero *movement is evident from the terms that the rebel delegates presented to the Spanish commissioners, which they signed and later repudiated. A number of important or typical articles follow.*

1. The tax entitled Armada de Barloventol must be abolished so completely that its name shall never again be heard in this kingdom. . . .
4. In view of the poverty of this kingdom, stamped paper shall circulate only in sheets of half *real*, for the use of ecclesiastics, religious, Indians, and poor people, and in sheets of two *reales* for the legal titles and lawsuits of persons of some wealth; and no other stamped paper shall circulate. . . .
5. The new tax on tobacco shall be completely abolished. . . .
7. Considering the miserable state of all the Indians, who go about more poorly clothed and fed than hermits, and whose small knowledge, limited faculties, and meager harvests prevent them from paying the high tribute which the *corregidores* exact with such severity, not to mention the stipends assigned to their curates. The total annual tribute of the Indians shall be only four pesos, and that of mulattoes subject to tribute shall be two pesos. The curates shall not collect from the Indians

Manuel Briceño, *Los comuneros* (Bogotá, 1880), Appendix, pp. 122–132. Excerpt translated by Benjamin Keen.

any fee for the administration of holy oils, burials, and weddings, nor shall they compel them to serve as *mayordomos* at their saints' festivals. The cost of these festivals shall (except when some pious person offers to bear them) be borne by the brotherhood. . . . Furthermore, those Indians who have been removed from their towns but whose lands have not been sold or transferred shall be returned to their lands of immemorial possession; and all the lands which they at present possess shall be theirs, not only for their use but as their property, which they may use as the owners thereof. . . .

9. The *alcabala*, henceforth and forever, shall be two per cent of all fruits, goods, cattle, and articles of every kind when sold or exchanged. . . .

10. Since the cause of the widespread commotions in this kingdom and in that of Lima has been the imprudent conduct of the *visitadores*, who tried to squeeze blood out of stones and destroy us with their despotic rule, until the people of this kingdom, ordinarily so docile and submissive, were made desperate by their growing extortions and could no longer tolerate their tyrannical rule. . . . we demand that Don Juan Gutierrez de Piñeres, *visitador* of the royal *audiencia*, be expelled from this kingdom to Spain, where our Catholic Monarch, reflecting on the results of his arbitrary conduct, shall do with him as he thinks best. And never again must officials be sent us who would treat us so severely and unwisely, for in such a case we shall again join together to repel any oppression that may be directed against us on any pretext whatever. . . .

18. All the officers on the present expedition, with the ranks of commander-general, captains-general, territorial captains, lieutenants, ensigns, sergeants, and corporals, shall retain their respective appointments, and shall be obliged to assemble their companies on Sunday afternoon of each week to train them in the use of arms, both offensive and defensive, against the event that an effort be made to break the agreements that we are now making in good faith, and also to aid His Majesty in resisting his enemies. . . .

21. In filling offices of the first, second, and third classes, natives of America shall be privileged and preferred over Europeans, who daily manifest their antipathy toward us . . . for in their ignorance they believe that they are the masters and that all Americans of any kind are their inferiors and servants. And so that this irrational view may disappear, Europeans shall be employed only in case of necessity and according to their ability, good will, and attachment to the Americans, for since we are all subjects of the same king and lord we should live like brothers, and whoever strives to lord it over others and advance himself against the rule of equality must be removed from among us. . . .

32. The order greatly reducing the number of grocery stores has had the result that the stores licensed in each town are owned by the wealthiest

or most favored individuals. We therefore ask, as a matter of public benefit, that the right to establish stores be granted to all inhabitants of the kingdom, as was formerly the case, without limitation as to their number.

7. BRAZILIAN SLAVES RESIST

Slave revolts were common in Brazil and Spanish America, despite being brutally repressed by colonial authorities. Often slaves escaped into the hinterlands to form settlements of their own. The most famous of these settlements or quilombos—*as they were called in Brazil—was the seventeenth-century "kingdom" of Palmares, which had its own ruler, Gangasuma. He even managed to negotiate a peace treaty with the Portuguese governor which ensured that all children born in Palmares would be considered free. Colonial authorities reneged on the treaty and destroyed Palmares in 1694. The following documents from a 1789 slave revolt at Engenho Santana plantation, south of Bahia in Brazil, suggest that the Palmares episode had not been forgotten by Brazilian slaves. In the first document, a colonial official describes the revolt and the punishment of the runaways. The second is a "treaty of peace" drawn up by the runaway slaves, which included the conditions under which they agreed to return to work.*

Part 1

Illustrious and most Excellent Sir:

The Supplicant Gregório Luís, a *cabra* finds himself a prisoner in the jail of this High Court where he was sent by his master, Captain Manoel da Silva Ferreira, resident on his *engenho* [estate] called Santana in the district of the Town of Ilhéus; there coming at the same time with him, as I remember, some fifteen or sixteen other slaves. These were sent to the merchant José da Silva Maia, his commercial agent, so that he could sell them in Maranhão while the Supplicants came with the recommendation that he could be given exemplary punishment. Taking a preliminary investigation of the Supplicant, I have determined the following facts. The above mentioned Manoel da Silva Ferreira being master and owner of the aforesaid *engenho* with three hundred slaves, including some of the Mina nation discovered the majority of them in the rebellion refusing to recognize their subordination to their master. And, the principal leader of the disorder was the Supplicant who began to incite among them the partisan spirit against their master and against the Sugar

---

Cited in Stuart B. Swartz, "Resistance and Accommodation in Eighteenth-Century Brazil: The Slaves' View of Slavery," *Hispanic American Historical Review* 57 (1977): 69–81. Used by permission of the *Hispanic American Historical Review*.

Master. The Supplicant was able with a few of his followers to kill the latter and until now none know where they buried him. Taking control of part of the *engenho*'s equipment, they fled to the forest refusing not only to give their service or to obey their master, but even placing him in fear that they would cruelly take his life. For this reason the *engenho* has remained inactive for two years with such notable damage that its decadence is dated from that time forward, and, moreover, these damages added to the danger that the rest of the slaves might follow the terrible example of those in rebellion. Thus the majority of the slaves persisted divided into errant and vagabond bands throughout the territory of the *engenho*, so absolute and fearless that the consternation and fright of their master increased in consideration that he might one day fall victim to some disaster.

Matters being in this situation, the rebels sent emissaries to their Master with a proposal of capitulation contained in the enclosed copy (see Document II) to which he showed them that he acceded: some came and others remained. The Supplicant as the most astute was able to extort from him a letter of Manumission which was granted at the time without the intention that it have any validity, at the same time he the Supplicant sought the District Judge who entering the *engenho* with eighty-five armed men sought out the house of his Master: The latter who could not now confide in the principal leaders of that uprising took advantage of a stratagem of sending the Supplicant Gregorio and fifteen others with a false letter to the Captain major of the militia, João de Silva Santos, who was in the Vila of Belmonte, telling them that they would receive from him cattle and manioc flour for the *engenho*. Arriving at the said Vila all were taken prisoner with handcuffs despite the great resistance that they made almost to the point of much bloodshed. They were finally conducted to the jail of his High Court as I have said, that is, the Supplicant as the prime mover to be held until his charges were seen and the others with orders to the aforementioned merchant to be sold to Maranhão as they were.

Twice there has been required from this court an order to be sent the investigation or any other charges against the Supplicant and until now they have not arrived.

I must also tell Your Excellency that the Master of the said *Engenho* has on repeated occasions recommended with the greatest insistence that the Supplicant not be released from the prison except by a sentence that exiles him far away because if he is freed he will unfailingly return to the *engenho* to incite new disorders, that may be irreparable.

That which is reported here seems to me enough to give Your Excellency a sufficient idea concerning the Supplicant and the reasons for his imprisonment. God Protect Your Excellency.

Bahia 22 of January of 1806.

The Desembargador Ouvidor geral do Crime,
Claudio José da Costa

Part 2

My Lord, we want peace and we do not want war; if My Lord also wants our peace it must be in this manner, if he wishes to agree to that which we want.

In each week you must give us the days of Friday and Saturday to work for ourselves not subtracting any of these because they are Saint's days.

To enable us to live you must give us casting nets and canoes.

You are not to oblige us to fish in the tidal pools not to gather shellfish, and when you wish to gather shellfish send your Mina blacks.

For your sustenance have a fishing launch and decked canoes, and when you wish to eat shellfish send your Mina blacks.

Make a large boat so that when it goes to Bahia we can place our cargoes aboard and not pay freightage.

In the planting of manioc we wish the men to have a daily quota of two and one-half hands and the women, two hands.

The daily quota of manioc flour must be of five level *alqueires*, placing enough harvesters so that these can serve to hang up the baskets.

The daily quota of sugarcane must be of five hands rather than six and of ten canes in each bundle.

On the boat you must put four poles, and one for the rudder, and the one at the rudder works hard for us.

The wood that is sawed with a hand saw must have three men below and one above.

The measure of firewood must be as practiced here, for each measure a woodcutter and a woman as the wood carrier.

The present oversees we do not want, choose others with our approval.

At the milling rollers there must be four women to feed in the cane, two pulleys, and a *caranha*.

At each cauldron there must be one who tends the fire and in each series of kettles the same, and on Saturday there must be without fail work stoppage in the mill.

The sailors who go in the launch beside the baize shirt that they are given must also have a jacket of baize and all the necessary clothing.

We will go to work the cane field of Jabirú this time and then it must remain as pasture for we cannot cut cane in a swamp.

We shall be able to plant our rice wherever we wish, and in any marsh, without asking permission for this, and each person can cut jacaranda or any other wood without having to account for this.

Accepting all the above articles and allowing us to remain always in possession of the hardware, we are ready to serve you before because we do not wish to continue the bad customs of the other *engenhos*.

We shall be able to play, relax and sing any time we wish without your hindrance nor will permission be needed.

PART SIX

INDEPENDENCE
AND
ITS AFTERMATH

11

╰◦╯

THE STRUGGLE
FOR INDEPENDENCE

MANY FACTORS COMBINED to cause the Latin American wars of independence. The discontent of the Creole class with Spanish restrictions on its economic and political activity, the influence of French and English liberal doctrines, the powerful example of the American and French revolutions, and foreign interest in the liquidation of the Spanish empire in the Americas—all played a part in producing the great upheaval.

The immediate cause of the Spanish American revolutions was the occupation of Spain by French troops in 1808. Napoleon's intervention provoked an uprising of the Spanish people, headed by juntas—local governing committees. Creole leaders in the colonies soon took advantage of Spain's distress. Professing loyalty to "the beloved Ferdinand VII," a prisoner in France, they forced the removal of allegedly unreliable Spanish officials and formed governing juntas to rule in the name of the captive king. Their claims of loyalty did not convince the Spanish authorities, and fighting soon broke out between patriots and loyalists.

Simón Bolívar led the struggle for independence in northern South America, and José de San Martín directed the military efforts of the patriots to the south. In 1822, the enigmatic San Martín resigned command of his army, leaving to Bolívar the task of completing the conquest of Peru, the last Spanish stronghold in the New World. The battle of Ayacucho, won by Sucre, virtually ended the war. Brazil achieved a relatively peaceful separation from Portugal in 1822, under the leadership of Prince Pedro and his adviser José Bonifacio de Andrada.

The Mexican Revolution, initiated in 1810 by the Creole priest Miguel Hidalgo, was continued after his death by another liberal curate, José María

Morelos. These men attempted to combine the Creole ideal of independence with a program of social reform in behalf of the Indian and mixed-blood masses. The radicalism of Hidalgo and Morelos alienated many Creole conservatives, who joined the royalist forces to suppress the revolt. Later, fearing the loss of their privileges as a result of the liberal revolution of 1820 in Spain, the same conservative coalition schemed to bring about a separation from Spain. They found an agent in the ambitious Creole officer Agustín de Iturbide. His Plan of Iguala offered a compromise solution temporarily acceptable to liberals and conservatives, to Creoles and many Spaniards. Slight loyalist opposition was swiftly overcome, and in September 1822, a national congress proclaimed the independence of the Mexican empire.

1. THE CLEAVAGE WITHIN

By the close of the colonial period the Creoles and peninsular Spaniards had become two mutually hostile castes, with different occupations and ideas. The Spaniards justified their privileged status by reference to the alleged indolence and incapacity of the natives. The Creoles vented their spleen by describing the Europeans as mean and grasping parvenus. The pro-Spanish historian Lucas Alamán offers many revealing details of the cleavage within the colonial upper class in his classic History of Mexico.

The number of peninsular Spaniards who resided in New Spain in 1808 was in the neighborhood of 70,000. They occupied nearly all the principal posts in the administration, the Church, the judiciary, and the army; commerce was almost exclusively in their hands; and they possessed large fortunes, consisting of cash, which they employed in various lines of business and in all kinds of farms and properties. Those who were not officeholders had generally left their country at a very early age, belonged to poor but honest families, especially those who came from the Basque provinces and the mountains of Santander, and were for the most part of good character. Since they aimed to make their fortune, they were ready to gain it by every kind of productive labor; neither great distances, perils, nor unhealthy climates frightened them. Some came to serve in the house of some relative or friend of the family; others were befriended by their countrymen. All began as clerks, subject to a severe discipline, and from the first learned to regard work and thrift as the only road to wealth. There was some relaxation of manners in Mexico City and Vera Cruz, but in all the cities of the interior, no matter

Lucas Alamán, *Historia de Méjico*, 5 vols. (México, 1849–1852), 1:8–14. Excerpt translated by Benjamin Keen.

how rich or populous, the clerks in each house were bound to a very narrow and almost monastic system of order and regularity. This Spartan type of education made of the Spaniards living in America a species of men not to be found in Spain herself, and one which America will never see again.

As their fortunes improved or their merits won recognition, they were often given a daughter of the house in marriage, particularly if they were relatives—or they might set up their own establishments; but all married creole girls, for very few of the women there had come from Spain, and these were generally the wives of officeholders. With financial success and kinship to the respectable families of the town came respect, municipal office, and influence, which sometimes degenerated into absolute dominance. Once established in this manner, the Spaniards never thought of returning to their country, and they considered that their only proper concerns were the furthering of their business affairs, the advancement of their communities, and the comfort and dignity of their families. Thus every wealthy Spaniard came to represent a fortune formed for the benefit of the country, a prosperous family rooted in Mexican soil, or, if he left no family, a source of pious and beneficial foundations designed to shelter orphans and succor the needy and disabled—foundations of which Mexico City presents so many examples. These fortunes were formed through the arduous labors of the field, the long practice of commerce, or the more risky enterprise of the mines. Although these occupations did not usually permit rapid enrichment, the economy practiced by these families, who lived frugally, without luxurious furniture or clothing, helped them to attain this goal. Thus all the towns, even the less important ones, included a number of families of modest fortunes, whose parsimony did not prevent the display of liberality on occasions of public calamity or when the needs of the state required it. . . .

The creoles rarely preserved these economical habits or pursued the professions that had enriched their fathers. The latter, amid the comforts that their wealth afforded, likewise failed to subject their sons to the severe discipline in which they themselves had been formed. Wishing to give their sons a more brilliant education, suitable to their place in society, they gave them a training that led to the Church or to the practice of law, or left them in a state of idleness and liberty that was deleterious to their character. Some sent their sons to the seminary of Vergara, in the province of Guipuzcoa in Spain, after the institution had won renown as a school providing general instruction, and if this practice had become general it not only would have contributed greatly to the diffusion of useful knowledge in America but would have aided in formation of more durable bonds between Spanish America and the mother country. From the other and pernicious kind of rearing resulted this state of affairs: The European clerks, married to the master's daughters, carried on his business and became the principal support of the family, increasing their wives' inheritances, whereas the creole sons wasted their substance and in a few years were ruined—at which time they looked about for some trifling desk job that would barely keep them alive in preference to an active and laborious life that would assure them an independent existence. The classical education that some of them had received, and the aristocratic manner that they affected in their days of idleness and plenty, made them scornful of the Europeans, who seemed to them mean and covetous because they were economical and active; they regarded these men as inferiors because they engaged in trades and occupations which they considered unworthy of the station to which their own fathers had raised them. Whether it was the effect of this vicious training or the influence of a climate that conduced to laxity and effeminacy, the creoles were generally indolent and negligent; of sharp wits, rarely tempered by judgment and reflection; quick to undertake an enterprise but heedless of the means necessary to carry it out; giving themselves with ardor to the present, but giving no thought to the future; prodigal in times of good fortune and resigned and long-suffering in adversity. The effect of these unfortunate propensities was the brief duration of their wealth; the assiduous efforts of the Europeans to form fortunes and pass them on to their children may be compared to the bottomless barrel of the Danaïdes, which no amount of water could fill. It resulted from this that the Spanish race in America, in order to remain prosperous and opulent, required a continuous accretion of European Spaniards who came to form new families, while those established by their predecessors fell into oblivion and indigence.

Although the laws did not establish any difference between these two classes of Spaniards, or indeed with respect to the *mestizos* born to either class by Indian mothers, a distinction came to exist between them in fact. With it arose a declared rivalry that, although subdued for a long time, might be feared to break out with the most serious consequences when the occasion should offer. As has been said, the Europeans held nearly all the high offices, as much because Spanish policy required it as because they had greater opportunity to request and obtain them, being near the fountainhead of all favors. [Of the one hundred and seventy viceroys who governed in America until 1813, only four had been born there—and that by chance, as the sons of officeholders. Of the six hundred and two captains-general and presidents, fourteen had been creoles.] The rare occasions on which creoles secured such high posts occurred through fortunate coincidences or when they went to the Spanish capital to solicit them. Although they held all the inferior posts, which were much more numerous, this only stimulated their ambition to occupy the higher posts as well. Although in the first two centuries after the Conquest the Church offered Americans greater opportunities for advancement, and during that period many obtained bishoprics, canonships, pulpits, and lucrative benefices, their opportunities in this sphere had gradually been curtailed. . . . [Of the seven hundred and six bishops who held office in Spanish America until 1812, one hundred and five were creoles, although few held miters of the first class.] The Europeans also dominated the cloisters, and in order to avoid the frequent disturbances caused by the rivalry of birth some religious orders had provided for an alternation of offices, electing European prelates in one election and Americans in the next; but as a result of a distinction introduced between the Europeans who had come from Spain with the garb and those who assumed it in America, the former were favored with another term, resulting in two elections of Europeans to one of creoles. If to this preference in administrative and ecclesiastical offices, which was the principal cause of the rivalry between the two classes, are added the fact that . . . the Europeans possessed great riches (which, though the just reward of labor and industry, excited the envy of the Americans . . .); the fact that the wealth and power of the *peninsulares* sometimes gained them more favor with the fair sex, enabling them to form more advantageous unions; and the fact that all these conditions combined had given them a decided predominance over the creoles—it is not difficult to explain the jealousy and rivalry that steadily grew between them, resulting in a mortal enmity and hatred.

2. THE FORGING OF A REBEL

In his brief but valuable autobiography, Manuel Belgrano (1770–1821), one of the fathers of Argentine independence, describes the influences and events that transformed a young Creole of wealth and high social position into an ardent revolutionary. The French Revolution, disillusionment with Bourbon liberalism, the English invasions, and finally the events of 1808 in Spain all played their part in this process.

The place of my birth was Buenos Aires; my parents were Don Domingo Belgrano y Peri, known as Pérez, a native of Onella in Spain, and Doña María Josefa González Casero, a native of Buenos Aires. My father was a merchant, and since he lived in the days of monopoly he acquired sufficient wealth to live comfortably and to give his children the best education to be had in those days.

I studied my first letters, Latin grammar, philosophy, and a smattering of theology in Buenos Aires. My father then sent me to Spain to study law, and I began my preparation at Salamanca; I was graduated at Valladolid, continued my training at Madrid, and was admitted to the bar at Valladolid. . . .

Since I was in Spain in 1789, and the French Revolution was then causing a change in ideas, especially among the men of letters with whom I associated,

Los sucesos de mayo contados por sus actores, ed. Ricardo Levene (Buenos Aires, 1928), pp. 60–71. Excerpt translated by Benjamin Keen.

the ideals of liberty, equality, security, and property took a firm hold on me, and I saw only tyrants in those who would restrain a man, wherever he might be, from enjoying the rights with which God and Nature had endowed him. . . .

When I completed my studies in 1793 political economy enjoyed great popularity in Spain; I believe this was why I was appointed secretary of the *consulado* of Buenos Aires, established when Gardoqui was minister. The official of the department in charge of these matters even asked me to suggest some other well-informed persons who could be appointed to similar bodies to be established in the principal American ports.

When I learned that these *consulados* were to be so many Economic Societies that would discuss the state of agriculture, industry, and commerce in their sessions, my imagination pictured a vast field of activity, for I was ignorant of Spanish colonial policy. I had heard some muffled murmuring among the Americans, but I attributed this to their failure to gain their ends, never to evil designs of the Spaniards that had been systematically pursued since the Conquest.

On receiving my appointment I was infatuated with the brilliant prospects for America. I had visions of myself writing memorials concerning the provinces so that the authorities might be informed and provide for their well-being. It may be that an enlightened minister like Gardoqui, who had resided in the United States, had the best of intentions in all this. . . .

I finally departed from Spain for Buenos Aires; I cannot sufficiently express the surprise I felt when I met the men named by the king to the council which was to deal with agriculture, industry, and commerce and work for the happiness of the provinces composing the vice-royalty of Buenos Aires. All were Spanish merchants. With the exception of one or two they knew nothing but their monopolistic business, namely, to buy at four dollars and sell for eight. . . .

My spirits fell, and I began to understand that the colonies could expect nothing from men who placed their private interests above those of the community. But since my position gave me an opportunity to write and speak about some useful topics, I decided at least to plant a few seeds that some day might bear fruit. . . .

I wrote various memorials about the establishment of schools. The scarcity of pilots and the direct interest of the merchants in the project presented favorable circumstances for the establishment of a school of mathematics, which I obtained on condition of getting the approval of the Court. This, however, was never secured; in fact, the government was not satisfied until the school had been abolished, because although the peninsulars recognized the justice and utility of such establishments, they were opposed to them because of a mistaken view of how the colonies might best be retained.

The same happened to a drawing school which I managed to establish without spending even half a real for the teacher. The fact is that neither these nor other proposals to the government for the development of agriculture, industry, and commerce, the three important concerns of the *consulado*, won its official approval; the sole concern of the Court was with the revenue that it derived from each of these branches. They said that all the proposed establishments were luxuries, and that Buenos Aires was not yet in a condition to support them.

I promoted various other useful and necessary projects, which had more or less the same fate, but it will be the business of the future historian of the *consulado* to give an account of them; I shall simply say that from the beginning of 1794 to July 1806, I passed my time in futile efforts to serve my country. They all foundered on the rock of the opposition of the government of Buenos Aires, or that of Madrid, or that of the merchants who composed the *consulado*, for whom there was no other reason, justice, utility, or necessity than their commercial interest. Anything that came into conflict with that interest encountered a veto, and there was nothing to be done about it.

It is well known how General Beresford entered Buenos Aires with about four hundred men in 1806. At that time I had been a captain in the militia for ten years, more from whim than from any attachment to the military art. My first experience of war came at that time. The Marqués de Sobremonte, then viceroy of the provinces of La Plata, sent for me several days before Beresford's disastrous entrance and requested me to form a company of cavalry from among the young men engaged in commerce. He said that he would give me veteran officers to train them; I sought them but could not find any, because of the great hostility felt for the militia in Buenos Aires. . . .

The general alarm was sounded. Moved by honor, I flew to the fortress, the point of assembly; I found there neither order nor harmony in anything, as must happen with groups of men who know nothing of discipline and are completely insubordinate. The companies were formed there, and I was attached to one of them. I was ashamed that I had not the slightest notion of military science and had to rely entirely on the orders of a veteran officer—who also joined voluntarily, for he was given no assignment.

This was the first company, which marched to occupy the Casa de las Filipinas. Meanwhile the others argued with the viceroy himself that they were obliged only to defend the city and not to go out into the country; consequently they would agree only to defend the heights. The result was that the enemy, meeting with no opposition from veteran troops or disciplined militia, forced all the passes with the greatest ease. There was some stupid firing on the part of my company and some others in an effort to stop the invaders, but all in vain, and when the order came to retreat and we were falling back I heard someone say: "They did well to order us to retreat, for we were not made for this sort of thing."

I must confess that I grew angry, and that I never regretted more deeply my ignorance of even the rudiments of military science. My distress grew when I saw the entrance of the enemy troops, and realized how few of them there were for a town of the size of Buenos Aires. I could not get the idea out of my head, and I almost went out of my mind, it was so painful to me to see my country under an alien yoke, and above all in such a degraded state that it could be conquered by the daring enterprise of the brave and honorable Beresford, whose valor I shall always admire.

[A resistance movement under the leadership of Santiago Liniers drives the British out of Buenos Aires. A second English invasion, commanded by General John Whitelocke, is defeated, and the entire British force is compelled to surrender. B.K.]

General Liniers ordered the quartermaster-general to receive the paroles of the officer prisoners; for this reason Brigadier-General Crawford, together with his aides and other high officers, came to his house. My slight knowledge of French, and perhaps certain civilities that I showed him, caused General Crawford to prefer to converse with me, and we entered upon a discussion that helped to pass the time—although he never lost sight of his aim of gaining knowledge of the country and, in particular, of its opinion of the Spanish Government.

So, having convinced himself that I had no French sympathies or connections, he divulged to me his ideas about our independence, perhaps in the hope of forming new links with this country, since the hope of conquest had failed. I described our condition to him, and made it plain that we wanted our old master or none at all; that we were far from possessing the means required for the achievement of independence; that even if it were won under the protection of England, she would abandon us in return for some advantage in Europe, and then we would fall under the Spanish sword; that every nation sought its own interest and did not care about the misfortunes of others. He agreed with me, and when I had shown how we lacked the means for winning independence, he put off its attainment for a century.

How fallible are the calculations of men! One year passed, and behold, without any effort on our part to become independent, God Himself gave us our opportunity as a result of the events of 1808 in Spain and Bayonne. Then it was that the ideals of liberty and independence came to life in America, and the Americans began to speak frankly of their rights.

3. MAN OF DESTINY

There is no more controversial figure in Latin American history than Simón Bolívar (1783–1830). To his admirers or worshipers he is the Liberator of a continent; to his critics he is the proverbial "man on horseback," an ambitious schemer who sacrificed

San Martín to his passion for power and glory. Louis Perú de Lacroix, a French member of Bolívar's staff, wrote the following description of the Liberator in a diary that he kept during their stay at Bucaramanga in 1828.

The General-in-Chief, Simón José Antonio Bolívar, will be forty-five years old on July 24 of this year, but he appears older, and many judge him to be fifty. He is slim and of medium height; his arms, thighs, and legs are lean. He has a long head, wide between the temples, and a sharply pointed chin. A large, round, prominent forehead is furrowed with wrinkles that are very noticeable when his face is in repose, or in moments of bad humor and anger. His hair is crisp, bristly, quite abundant, and partly gray. His eyes have lost the brightness of youth but preserve the luster of genius. They are deep-set, neither small nor large; the eyebrows are thick, separated, slightly arched, and are grayer than the hair on his head. The nose is aquiline and well formed. He has prominent cheekbones, with hollows beneath. His mouth is rather large, and the lower lip protrudes; he has white teeth and an agreeable smile. . . . His tanned complexion darkens when he is in a bad humor, and his whole appearance changes; the wrinkles on his forehead and temples stand out much more prominently; the eyes become smaller and narrower; the lower lip protrudes considerably, and the mouth turns ugly. In fine, one sees a completely different countenance: a frowning face that reveals sorrows, sad reflections, and somber ideas. But when he is happy all this disappears; his face lights up, his mouth smiles, and the spirit of the Liberator shines over his countenance. His Excellency is clean-shaven at present. . . .

The Liberator has energy; he is capable of making a firm decision and sticking to it. His ideas are never commonplace—always large, lofty, and original. His manners are affable, having the tone of Europeans of high society. He displays a republican simplicity and modesty, but he has the pride of a noble and elevated soul, the dignity of his rank, and the amour-propre that comes from consciousness of worth and leads men to great actions. Glory is his ambition, and his glory consists in having liberated ten million persons and founded three republics. He has an enterprising spirit, combined with great activity, quickness of speech, an infinite fertility in ideas, and the constancy necessary for the realization of his projects. He is superior to misfortunes and reverses; his philosophy consoles him and his intelligence finds ways of righting what has gone wrong. . . .

He loves a discussion, and dominates it through his superior intelligence; but he sometimes appears too dogmatic, and is not always tolerant enough with those who contradict him. He scorns servile flattery and base adulators.

Louis Perú de Lacroix, *Diario de Bucaramanga, estudio crítico*, ed. Monseñor Nicolás E. Navarro (Caracas, 1935), pp. 327, 329–331. Excerpt translated by Benjamin Keen.

He is sensitive to criticism of his actions; calumny against him cuts him to the quick, for none is more touchy about his reputation than the Liberator. . . .

His heart is better than his head. His bad temper never lasts; when it appears, it takes possession of his head, never of his heart, and as soon as the latter recovers its dominance it immediately makes amends for the harm that the former may have done. . . .

The great mental and bodily activity of the Liberator keeps him in a state of constant moral and physical agitation. One who observes him at certain moments might think he is seeing a madman. During the walks that we take with him he sometimes likes to walk very rapidly, trying to tire his companions out; at other times he begins to run and leap, to leave the others behind; then he waits for them to catch up and tells them they do not know how to run. He does the same when horseback riding. But he acts this way only when among his own people, and he would not run or leap if he thought that some stranger was looking on. When bad weather prevents walking or riding, the Liberator rocks himself swiftly back and forth in his hammock or strides through the corridors of his house, sometimes singing, at other times reciting verses or talking with those who walk beside him. When conversing with one of his own people, he changes the subject as often as he does his position; at such times one would say that he has not a bit of system or stability in him. How different the Liberator seems at a private party, at some formal gathering, and among his confidential friends and aides-de-camp! With the latter he seems their equal, the gayest and sometimes the maddest of them all. At a private party, among strangers and people less well known to him, he shows his superiority to all others by his easy and agreeable ways and good taste, his lively and ingenious conversation, and his amiability. At a more formal gathering, his unaffected dignity and polished manners cause him to be regarded as the most gentlemanly, learned, and amiable man present. . . .

In all the actions of the Liberator, and in his conversation, as I have already noted, one observes an extreme quickness. His questions are short and concise; he likes to be answered in the same way, and when someone wanders away from the question he impatiently says that that is not what he asked; he has no liking for a diffuse answer. He sustains his opinions with force and logic, and generally with tenacity. When he has occasion to contradict some assertion, he says: "No, sir, it is not so, but thus. . . ." Speaking of persons whom he dislikes or scorns, he often uses this expression: "That (or those) c***." He is very observant, noting even the least trifles; he dislikes the poorly educated, the bold, the windbag, the indiscreet, and the discourteous. Since nothing escapes him, he takes pleasure in criticizing such people, always making a little commentary on their defects. . . .

I have already said that the Liberator can assume an air of dignity when among persons who do not enjoy his full confidence or with whom he is not on terms of familiarity; but he throws it off among his own people. In church he carries himself with much propriety and respect, and does not permit his companions to deviate from this rule. One day, noticing that his physician, Dr. Moore, sat with his legs crossed, he had an aide-de-camp tell him that it was improper to cross one's legs in church, and that he should observe how he sat. One thing that His Excellency does not know, when at Mass, is when to kneel, stand up, and sit down. He never crosses himself. Sometimes he talks to the person beside him, but only a little, and very softly.

The ideas of the Liberator are like his imagination: full of fire, original, and new. They lend considerable sparkle to his conversation, and make it extremely varied. When His Excellency praises, defends, or approves something, it is always with a little exaggeration. The same is true when he criticizes, condemns, or disapproves of something. In his conversation he frequently quotes, but his citations are always well chosen and pertinent. Voltaire is his favorite author, and he has memorized many passages from his works, both prose and poetry. He knows all the good French writers and evaluates them competently. He has some general knowledge of Italian and English literature and is very well versed in that of Spain.

The Liberator takes great pleasure in telling of his first years, his voyages, and his campaigns, and of his relations and old friends. His character and spirit dispose him more to criticize than to eulogize, but his criticisms or eulogies are never baseless; he could be charged only with an occasional slight exaggeration. I have never heard his Excellency utter a calumny. He is a lover of truth, heroism, and honor and of the public interest and morality. He detests and scorns all that is opposed to these lofty and noble sentiments.

4. THE ARMY OF THE ANDES

For Argentines the figure of José de San Martín has the same heroic and legendary quality that Bolívar possesses for the peoples of northern South America. Modest and reserved, San Martín was something of an enigma to his contemporaries, and we lack a description as revealing of the man as Perú de Lacroix's sketch of Bolívar. From the military point of view, San Martín's chief claim to greatness is his masterful campaign of the Andes, prelude to the decisive attack on Peru. To this day the standard biography of San Martín is the classic life by Bartolomé Mitre (1821–1906), distinguished Argentine soldier, historian, and statesman. Mitre describes San Martín's painstaking preparations for the passage of the Andes.

Bartolomé Mitre, *Historia de San Martín y de la emancipación sudamericana*, 2 vols. (Buenos Aires, 1944), 1:319–334. Excerpt translated by Benjamin Keen.

San Martín tried to convince the enemy that he planned to invade Chile in the south, whereas he actually intended to strike in the center. This was a fixed major objective of his "war of nerves," and that is why he deceived friend and enemy alike with misleading communications and incomplete confidences, guarding his secret until the last moment. In order to confirm Marcó, the Spanish governor of Chile, in his mistaken views, he devised a new stratagem, which, like all his ruses, bore the stamp of novelty and of a brain fertile in expedients.

Since 1814, San Martín, as governor of Cuyo, had cultivated friendly relations with the Pehuenche Indians, then masters of the eastern slopes of the cordillera south of Mendoza, in order to ensure the safe transit of his secret Chilean agents through the passes they dominated, and to have them on his side in case of an enemy invasion. At the time he assembled his army in the encampment of Plumerillo he decided to renew these relations, with the double object of deceiving the enemy with respect to his true plans, and of giving greater security and importance to the secondary operations which he planned to carry out by way of the southern passes. For this purpose he invited them to a general parley in the Fort of San Carlos, above the boundary line of the Diamond River, with the ostensible object of seeking permission to pass through their lands. He sent ahead trains of mules loaded with hundreds of barrels of wine and skins filled with *aguardiente*; with sweets, bright-colored cloths, and glass beads for the women; and, for the men, horse gear, foodstuffs of all kinds, and all the old clothes that the province could supply, in order to dazzle the allies. On the appointed day the Pehuenches approached the fort with barbaric pomp, blowing their horns, flourishing their long plumed lances, and followed by their women. The warriors were naked from the waist up and wore their long hair untied; all were in fighting trim. Each tribe was preceded by a guard of mounted grenadiers, whose correctly martial appearance contrasted with the savage appearance of the Indians. On approaching the esplanade of the fort, the women went to one side, and the men whirled their lances about by way of greeting. There followed a picturesque sham fight in Pehuenche style, with the warriors riding at full speed around the walls of the redoubt, from whose walls a gun fired a salvo every five minutes, to which the braves responded by striking themselves on the mouth and whooping with joy.

The solemn meeting that followed was held on the parade ground of the fort. San Martín asked permission to pass through the lands of the Pehuenches in order to attack the Spaniards through the Planchón and Portillo passes. The Spaniards, he told them, were foreigners, enemies of the American Indian, whose fields and herds, women and children, they sought to steal. The Colo-colo of the tribes was a white-haired ancient called Necuñan. After consulting the assembly and obtaining their opinions with suitable gravity, he told the general that with the exception of three *caciques*, with whom they could deal later, all accepted his proposals, and they sealed the treaty of alliance by embracing San Martín, one after another. In proof of their friendship they immediately placed their arms in the keeping of the Christians and gave themselves up to an orgy that lasted for eight consecutive days. On the sixth day the general returned to his headquarters to await the result of these negotiations, whose object he kept secret from even his most intimate confidants.

The creole diplomat had foreseen that the Indians, with their natural perfidy—or the dissident *caciques*, at any rate—would report his pretended project to Marcó, as actually happened. But just in case they should not do so, he hastened to communicate it to the Spanish leader directly by means of one of his characteristic ruses, in which he was aided by a coincidence that he had also foreseen. During the reorganization of his army he had cut the supposed communications of the Spaniards of Cuyo with Marcó, and the latter, ignorant of everything that was taking place east of the Andes, sent emissaries to obtain information from the individuals whom he believed to be his official correspondents. Such was San Martín's vigilance that for two years not a single royalist spy had been able to penetrate into Cuyo without being captured in the cordillera by patriot guards who had been warned by secret agents in Chile. The last letters of the Spanish governor met the same fate. With these letters in his possession, San Martin summoned the supposed correspondents to his presence—among them was Castillo de Albo—showed them the incriminating letters, and with pretended anger (it is said that he even threatened them with a pistol that he had on his desk) forced them to write and sign replies that he dictated. In these replies he announced that "about the 15th of October" a squadron was preparing to leave Buenos Aires for an unknown destination. It was "composed of a frigate, three corvettes, two brigantines, and two transports, all under the command of the Englishman Teler [Taylor]." "San Martín," they added, "has held a general parley with the Pehuenche Indians. The Indians have agreed to everything; we shall see how they carry out their pledges; caution and more caution; for lack of it our people have suffered imprisonment and depredations. Everything is known here." In another he said that a French engineer had left Mendoza in order to construct a bridge over the Diamond River. San Martín's letters, sent by an emissary who played the role of a double spy, were delivered to Marcó, who believed everything in them, lost his head entirely, and turned the whole province upside down to guard against a double invasion. At the same time San Martín informed the government of Buenos Aires that the purpose of the parley was to get the Indians "to assist the passage of the army with livestock and horses at the stipulated prices," while to his confidant, Guido, he wrote: "I concluded with all success my great parley with the Indians of the south; they not only will aid the army with livestock but are committed to take an active part against the enemy." As can be seen, San Martín was a well of large and small mysteries, with the naked truth hidden at the bottom.

Marcó, disheartened by the alarming news from his supposed correspondents in Cuyo, and by the simultaneous rising of the guerrillas of Manuel Rodríguez, who extended their excursions between the Maule and the Maipo and made armed assaults on villages in the very vicinity of the capital, dictated a series of senseless and contradictory measures that revealed the confusion in his mind and the fear in his heart. He ordered the ports to be fortified and attempted to convert some of them into islands with the object of preventing a disembarkation; at the same time he equipped a squadron to act against the imaginary fleet of Buenos Aires. He commanded that trenches should be thrown up in the pass of Uspallata, that the southern provinces of the kingdom should be mapped and that the entrances to the Maule and Planchón passes should be surveyed; but before these tasks had been completed he ordered strengthening of the guards at all the passes of the cordillera, from north to south. First he concentrated his troops and then he dispersed most of them again, moving them about in empty space. Finding no inspiration in himself, after jerking about like a puppet manipulated by San Martín, he finished by reproducing the man's very gestures, like a monkey; in imitation of the patriot general he held a parley with the Araucanian Indians, but failed to devise a rational plan of defense.

The objective of the astute Argentine leader was fulfilled: the captain-general of Chile sought to defend all its land and sea frontiers simultaneously; consequently he dispersed his army and thus became weak everywhere, never suspecting the point of the true attack. To crown his confusion, the spies he sent to obtain accurate information either did not return or served San Martín by bringing back false reports that led him to commit new errors. Some of his advisers urged him to take the offensive; others, that he persevere in his absurd waiting plan; and only one of them, his secretary, Dr. Judas Tadeo Reyes, the least knowledgeable in warfare, suggested the plan he should have followed: concentrate the 50,000 veteran troops in the capital, disperse the militia troops about the country, and await the invasion in that posture. However, by this time Marcó was so distraught that good and bad counsels were equally useless. He himself graphically depicted his deplorable morale at this time (February 4, 1817): "My plans are reduced to continual movements and variations according to developments and news of the enemy, whose astute chief at Mendoza, kept informed of my situation by his innumerable lines of communication and the disloyal spies who surround me, seeks to surprise me."

But it was not only the threat of impending invasion that made Marcó uneasy. His resources were scanty, and as a result of the stupid system of taxation established by Osorio and continued and intensified by himself, the very sources of further contributions were exhausted. In order to defray the public expenses he levied a tax on exports of grain and flour and imports of wine and sugar; simultaneously he decreed a forced loan of 400,000 pesos to be collected from individuals with an annual income of 1,000 pesos, not excluding civil and military officers, and payable in cash. The sole result of these measures was the spread of demoralization and discontent, which fanned the sparks of insurrection lighted by the agents of San Martín, who announced his immediate arrival at the head of a powerful liberating army. . . .

The situation was quite different in the encampment at Mendoza: here there was a methodical activity, an automatic obedience coupled with an enthusiasm born of understanding. A superior will, that knew what it wanted and what it was doing, directed all, inspiring the soldiers with the feeling that victory was certain. In Mendoza it was known what Marcó did, thought, or was going to do, whereas Marcó did not even know what he wanted to do. Everyone worked, each performing the task assigned to him, and they all trusted in their general. Pack mules and war horses were assembled; thousands of horseshoes were forged for the animals; packsaddles were made for the beasts of burden; fodder and provisions were stored; and herds of cattle were rounded up for the passage of the cordillera. Leaders, officers, and soldiers devoted themselves to their respective duties and positions. The arsenal turned out hundreds of thousands of cartridges. The forges blazed day and night, repairing arms and casting projectiles. The indefatigable Father Luis Beltran supervised the construction of new machines by means of which, as he put it, the cannon would fly over the tops of the mountains like condors. The ingenious friar had invented, or rather adapted, a kind of narrow carriage (called *zorra*) of rude but solid construction which, mounted on four low wheels and drawn by oxen or mules, replaced the mounts of the cannon; the guns themselves would be carried on the backs of mules along the narrow, tortuous paths of the cordillera until they reached the plain on the other side. As a precaution, long slings were made in which the carriages and cannon would be hoisted over rough places between mules, as if in litters, one after the other; sleds of hide were also prepared in which heavy objects might be hauled up by hand or by a portable winch when the gradients were too steep for the mules.

Meanwhile the general-in-chief, silent and reserved, planned for everyone, inspected everything, and provided for all contingencies in the most minute detail, from food and equipment for men and beasts to the complicated machines of war, even seeing the cutting edge of his soldiers' sabers.

The army needed a healthful and nourishing food that would restore the soldiers' strength and would be suited to the frigid temperatures through which they must pass. San Martín found this in a popular dish called *charquican*, composed of beef dried in the sun, roasted, ground to powder, mixed with fat and chili pepper, and well pounded. A soldier could carry enough of this in his knapsack to last him eight days. Mixed with hot water and roasted maize meal it made a nutritious and appetizing porridge. . . . After providing for his soldiers' stomachs, San Martin took thought for their feet—the vehicles of victory. In order to obtain footwear without burdening the treasury, he asked the *cabildo* of Mendoza to collect and send to the camp the scraps of cowhide discarded every day by the slaughterhouses of the city. From these pieces he had the soldiers make *tamangos*, a kind of closed sandal often used by the Negroes. . . . He carried economy to extreme lengths in order to show, in his own words, that great enterprises can be accomplished with small means. An order of the day, made public to the sound of drums, asked the people to bring to special depots old woolen rags that could be used to line the *tamangos*, because, San Martín declared, "the health of the soldiers is a powerful machine that if well directed can bring victory; and our first concern is to protect their feet." The horns of slaughtered cattle were used to make canteens, necessary in crossing the waterless stretches of the cordillera. Another decree ordered all the cloth remnants in the stores and tailor shops of the city to be collected, and San Martín distributed them to the soldiers to make into straps for their knapsacks.

The sabers of the mounted grenadiers had lost their sharpness; San Martín had them given a razor-like edge and placed them in the hands of his soldiers, saying they were for cutting off Spanish heads. It was not enough to sharpen swords; arms had to be trained to use them; and martial instruments were needed to nerve the soldiers and to take the place of the officer's voice in battle. San Martín chose the trumpet, an instrument rarely used by American cavalry at that time. The army had only three trumpets. San Martin had some made out of tin, but they were mute. In his application to the government San Martín wrote: "The trumpet is as necessary for the cavalry as is the drum for the infantry. . . ."

The general gave the matter of horseshoes his closest attention. Before making a decision he held conferences with veterinarians, blacksmiths, and muleteers; after carefully listening to them, he adopted a model of a horseshoe which he sent to the government telling the officer who carried it to guard it as if it were made of gold and to present it to the Minister of War. . . . The army needed thirty thousand horseshoes with a double set of nails. In two months they were forged by artisans who toiled day and night in the shops of the arms factory in Buenos Aires and in the forges of Mendoza.

How was the army to cross the deep ravines and torrents that lay before it? How were the heavy materials of war to ascend and descend the steep slopes of the mountains? And finally, how were the carriages and their loads to be rescued from the depths into which they might fall? These were problems that had to be solved. For river passages a rope bridge of a given weight and length (60 *varas*) was devised, and the piece of cable which was to be shown to the government as a model was entrusted to an officer with the same solemnity as the horseshoe. "It is impossible to transport the artillery and other heavy objects over the narrow defiles and slopes of the cordillera, or to rescue material fallen from the path," wrote San Martín, "without the aid of two anchors and four cables, of a weight that can be transported on muleback." With this apparatus, moved by a winch, the difficulties of the passage were overcome. . . .

Amid this official correspondence concerning the movement of men, materials, and money, an exchange of letters of mixed character took place between the two protagonists of our story: General San Martín and Pueyrredón, Director of the United Provinces of La Plata. Passionately devoted to the same cause, they aided and comforted each other, until they and their mission became one. . . .

"You don't ask for much," the Director would write San Martín, "and I feel bad because I don't have the money to get these things for you; but I shall do my best, and by the beginning of October I shall have gotten together thirty thousand pesos for the use of the army." But hardly had Pueyrredón assumed direction of the government and began to make good his promises when there broke out in Córdoba a confused anarchical revolt that threatened to throw the entire Republic into chaos. . . .

When the brief uprising of Córdoba had been crushed, the general of the Andes renewed his insistent urging, as has been shown from the official correspondence. The Director provided everything, and when he had satisfied all demands he took up his pen and wrote with humorous desperation and comradely forthrightness: "I am sending official letters of thanks to Mendoza and the other cities of Cuyo. I am sending the officers' commissions. I am sending the uniforms you asked for and many more shirts. I am sending 400 saddles. I am sending off today by post two trumpets—all I could find. In January I shall send 1387 *arrobas* of dried beef. I am sending the 200 spare sabers that you asked for. I am sending 200 tents or pavilions; that's all there are. I am sending the world, the flesh, and the devil! I don't know how I shall get out of the scrape I'm in to pay for all this, unless I declare bankruptcy, cancel my accounts with everyone, and clear out to join you, so that you can give me some of the dried beef I'm sending you. Damn it, don't ask me for anything else, unless you want to hear that they found me in the morning dangling from a beam in the Fort! . . . "

When everything was ready the general of the expedition asked for instructions concerning his military and political courses of action. The government, inspired by the same lofty aims as the general, drew up instructions infused with a broad, generous, and resolute spirit, in harmony with San Martín's continental plan; and formulated, in words which deeds were to make good, the liberation policy of the Argentine Revolution in respect to the other peoples of South America, on the basis of independence and liberty for each one of them. "The consolidation of American independence" (said Article I) "and the glory of the United Provinces of South America are the only motives of this campaign. The general will make this clear in his proclamations; he will spread it through his agents in every town, and will propagate it by every possible means. The army must be impressed with these principles. Care must be taken that not a word is said of pillage, oppression, conquest, or retaining possession of the liberated country. . . ."

With these instructions in his portfolio, all decisions made, and the army poised at the eastern entrances to the Andes, San Martín, one foot already in the stirrup, wrote (January 24, 1817) his last letter to his most intimate confidant: "This afternoon I set out to join the army. God grant me success in this great enterprise."

5. HIDALGO: TORCHBEARER OF THE MEXICAN REVOLUTION

Miguel Hidalgo (1753–1811), the scholarly, white-haired priest of the town of Dolores and onetime rector of the college of San Nicolás Valladolid, hardly seemed fitted by background and disposition to head a revolution. It was Hidalgo, nevertheless, who overcame the wavering of his associates when their conspiracy was discovered and transformed what had been planned as an upper-class Creole revolt into a rising of the masses. Alamán, historian and bitter enemy of the revolution—who knew Hidalgo in the peaceful years before the great upheaval—describes the curate of Dolores.

Don Miguel Hidalgo, being neither austere in his morals nor very orthodox in his opinions, did not concern himself with the spiritual administration of his parish, which he had turned over, together with half the income of his curacy, to a priest named Don Francisco Iglesias. Knowing French—a rather rare accomplishment at the period, especially among churchmen—he formed a taste for technical and scientific books and zealously promoted various agricultural and industrial projects in his parish. He considerably furthered viticulture, and today that whole region produces abundant harvests of grapes; he also encouraged the planting of mulberry trees for the raising of silkworms. In Dolores eighty-four trees planted by him are still standing, in the spot called "the mulberry trees of Hidalgo," as well as the channels that he had dug for irrigating the entire plantation. He established a brickyard and a factory for the manufacture of porcelain, constructed troughs for tanning hides, and promoted a variety of other enterprises.

All this, plus the fact that he was not only generous but lavish in money matters, had won him the high regard of his parishioners—especially the Indians, whose languages he had mastered. It also gained him the esteem of all

Alamán, *Historia de Méjico*, 1:352–354. Excerpt translated by Benjamin Keen.

who took a sincere interest in the advancement of the country, men like Abad y Queipo, the bishop-elect of Michoacán, and Riaño, the intendant of Guanajuato. It seems, however, that he had little basic knowledge of the industries which he fostered, and even less of that systematic spirit which one must have to make substantial progress with them. Once, being asked by Bishop Abad y Queipo what method he used for picking and distributing the leaves to the silkworms according to their age, and for separating the dry leaves and keeping the silkworms clean—concerning which the books on the subject give such elaborate instructions—he replied that he followed no particular order, that he threw down the leaves as they came from the tree and let the silkworms eat as they wished. "The revolution," exclaimed the bishop, who told me this anecdote, "was like his raising of silkworms, and the results were what might be expected!" Nevertheless, he had made much progress, and obtained enough silk to have some garments made for himself and for his stepmother. He also promoted the raising of bees, and brought many swarms of bees to the hacienda of Jaripeo when he bought that estate.

He was very fond of music, and not only had it taught to the Indians of his parish, where he formed an orchestra, but borrowed the orchestra of the provincial battalion of Guanajuato for the frequent parties that he gave in his home. Since his residence was a short distance from Guanajuato, he often visited the capital and stayed there for long periods of time. This gave me an opportunity to see him and to know him. He was fairly tall and stoop-shouldered, of dark complexion and quick green eyes; his head bent a little over his chest and was covered by sparse gray hair, for he was more than sixty years old. [Hidalgo was actually fifty-eight years old in 1810.] He was vigorous, though neither swift nor active in his movements; short of speech in ordinary conversation but animated in academic style when the argument grew warm. He was careless in dress, wearing only such garb as small town curates commonly wore in those days.

6. THE REFORMS OF HIDALGO

Hidalgo and Morelos attempted to combine the Creole ideal of independence with a program of social justice for the oppressed classes of the Mexican population. The following decrees of Hidalgo, issued after his capture of Guadalajara, help explain why many conservative Creoles fought on the Spanish side against the patriots.

Alamán, *Historia de Méjico*, 2:25–26. Excerpt translated by Benjamin Keen.

Don Miguel Hidalgo y Costilla, generalissimo of America, etc. By these presents I order the judges and justices of the district of this capital to proceed immediately to the collection of the rents due to this day by the lessees of the lands belonging to the Indian communities, the said rents to be entered in the national treasury. The lands shall be turned over to the Indians for their cultivation, and they may not be rented out in the future, for it is my wish that only the Indians in their respective towns shall have the use of them. Given in my headquarters of Guadalajara, December 5, 1810. . . .

Don Miguel Hidalgo y Costilla, generalissimo of America, etc. From the moment that the courageous American nation took up arms to throw off the heavy yoke that oppressed it for three centuries, one of its principal aims has been to extinguish the multitude of taxes that kept it in poverty. Since the critical state of our affairs does not permit the framing of adequate provisions in this respect, because of the need of the kingdom for money to defray the costs of the war, for the present I propose to remedy the most urgent abuses by means of the following declarations. First: All slave owners shall set their slaves free within ten days, on pain of death for violation of this article. Second: The payment of tribute by all the castes that used to pay it shall henceforth cease, and no other taxes shall be collected from the Indians. Third: In all judicial business, documents, deeds, and actions, only ordinary paper shall be used, and the use of sealed paper is abolished.

7. THE PLAN OF IGUALA

Ironically, the work begun by Hidalgo and Morelos was consummated by a Creole officer, Agustín de Iturbide (1783–1824), who for nine years had fought the insurgents with great effectiveness. Behind Iturbide were conservative churchmen, army officers, and officials, who preferred separation from Spain to submission to the liberal Constitution of 1812, which the army imposed on Ferdinand VII. Lorenzo de Zavala (1788–1836), a brilliant Mexican statesman, publicist, and historian, describes the origin and triumph of the Plan of Iguala.

Popular revolutions present anomalies whose origin or causes are unknowable. Men who have followed one party, who have fought for certain principles, who have suffered for their loyalty to certain views or persons, suddenly change and adopt a completely different line of conduct. Who would ever have thought that the Mexican officer who had shed the blood of

---

Lorenzo de Zavala, *Ensayo histórico de las revoluciones de México*, 2 vols. (México, 1918), 1:69–79. Excerpt translated by Benjamin Keen.

so many of his compatriots to maintain his country in slavery was destined to place himself at the head of a great movement that would destroy forever the Spanish power? What would have been thought of a man's sanity if in 1817 he had said that Iturbide would occupy the place of Morelos or would replace Mina? Yet the astonished Mexicans and Spaniards saw this happen.

Don Agustín de Iturbide, colonel of a battalion of provincial troops and a native of Valladolid de Michoacán, was endowed with brilliant qualities, and among his leading traits were uncommon bravery and vigor. To a handsome figure he united the strength and energy necessary to endure the great exertions of campaigning, and ten continuous years of this activity had fortified his natural qualities. He was haughty and domineering, and it was observed that to stay in favor with the authorities he had to remain at a distance from those who were in a position to give him orders. Every time that he came to Mexico City or other places where there were superiors, he gave indications of his impatience. . . . It is said that he was involved in a plan hatched at Valladolid in 1809 for the achievement of independence but withdrew because he was not placed in command, though his rank at the time did not qualify him for leadership. Be that as it may, there is no doubt that Iturbide had a superior spirit, and that his ambition was supported by that noble resolution that scorns dangers and does not retreat before obstacles of every kind. He had faced danger and difficulty in combat; he had learned the power of Spanish weapons; he had taken the measure of the chiefs of both parties—and one must confess that he did not err in his calculations when he set himself above all of them. He was conscious of his superiority, and so did not hesitate to place himself at the head of the national party, if he could only inspire the same confidence in his compatriots. He discussed his project with men whose talents would be useful to him in the political direction of affairs, and henceforth he threw himself heart and soul into forming a plan that would offer guarantees to citizens and monarchists and at the same time would remove all cause for fear on the part of the Spaniards.

Anyone who examines the famous *Plan of Iguala* (so called because it was made public in that town for the first time), bearing in mind the circumstances of the Mexican nation at the time, will agree that it was a masterpiece of politics and wisdom. All the Mexicans desired *independence*, and this was the first basis of that document. The killings of Spaniards that had taken place, in reprisal for those that the Spaniards had committed during the past nine years, required a preventive, so to speak, to put an end to such atrocious acts, which could not fail to arouse hostility among the 50,000 Spaniards who still resided in the country. It was necessary to make plain the intentions of the new chief in this respect. Accordingly, he seized upon the word *union* as expressing the solidarity that should exist between creoles and Spaniards, regarded as citizens with the same rights. Finally, since the Catholic religion is the faith professed by all Mexicans, and since the clergy has a considerable influence in the country, the preservation of this church was also stated to be a fundamental basis, under the word *religion*. These three principles, *independence*, *union*, and *religion*, gave Iturbide's army its name of "the Army of the Three Guarantees." The representative monarchical system was established, and various articles stated the elementary principles of this form of government and the individual rights guaranteed to the people. Finally, the Spaniards were given freedom to leave the country with all their property. The expeditionary forces were offered the privilege of returning to Spain at the expense of the public treasury; those who chose to stay would be treated like Mexican soldiers. As can be seen, the plan reconciled all interests, and, raising New Spain to the rank of an independent nation, as was generally desired, with its immense benefits it silenced for the time being the particular aspirations of those who wanted the *republic* on the one hand and the *absolute monarchy* on the other. All the sons of the country united around the principle of *nationality*, putting aside for the moment their different ideals. We shall soon see the sprouting of these germs of ideas, as yet enveloped in mists or suppressed by the great matter of the common cause.

Don Agustín de Iturbide made all these preparations in the greatest secrecy, and to conceal his projects more effectively he entered or pretended to enter the church of San Felipe Neri to take part in religious exercises. There, it is said, was framed the document I mentioned. This display of piety, and the prudence and reserve with which he managed the affair, inspired the viceroy, who also was devout, to entrust him with the command of a small division assigned to pursue Don Vicente Guerrero, whose forces had increased considerably after the arrival of the news of the Spanish revolution. At the end of the year 1820 Colonel Iturbide set out from Mexico City, charged with the destruction of Guerrero but actually intending to join him at the first opportunity to work with him for the achievement of national independence. A few days after his departure from the capital, Iturbide drew near to Guerrero's camp. The latter had routed Colonel Berdejo, also sent out in his pursuit, in a minor clash, and this provided Iturbide with an opportunity to send Guerrero a letter inviting the patriot leader to abandon the enterprise that had cost the country so much futile bloodshed: "Now that the King of Spain has offered liberal institutions and confirmed the social guarantees of the people, taking an oath to support the Constitution of 1812, the Mexicans will enjoy a just equality, and we shall be treated like free men." He added: "The victories that you have recently gained over the government forces should not inspire you with confidence in future triumphs, for you know that the fortunes of war are mutable, and that the government possesses great resources."

This letter was written very artfully, for at the same time that it suggested a desire to enter into agreements and relations with the insurgents it aroused no suspicion in the viceroy, who interpreted it as reflecting the same policy that had been so useful to him in pacifying the country. Presumably the persons employed by Iturbide to deliver these letters carried private instructions explaining his intentions. General Guerrero replied, with the energy that he always showed in defending the cause of independence and liberty, that he was resolved "to continue defending the national honor, until victory or death"; that he was "not to be deceived by the flattering promise of liberty given by the Spanish constitutionalists, who in the matter of independence [hold] the same views as the most diehard royalists; that the Spanish constitution [offers] no guarantees to the Americans." He reminded Iturbide of the exclusion of the castes in the Cadiz constitution; of the diminution of the American representatives; and, finally, of the indifference of the viceroys to these liberal laws. He concluded by exhorting Iturbide to join the national party, and invited him to take command of the national armies, of which Guerrero himself was then the leader. The vigorous tone of this letter, the sound observations that it contained, the convincing logic of its judgments, produced an astounding effect upon the Mexicans. Iturbide needed no persuasion; we have seen him depart from Mexico City with the intent of proclaiming the independence of the country, and the only matter left unsettled was the precise method of beginning the work, with himself as the leader of the daring enterprise.

He received this letter in January 1821, and replied to General Guerrero, in a few lines, that he wished to "confer with [him] about the means of working together for the welfare of the kingdom" and hoped that he (Guerrero) "would be fully satisfied concerning his intentions." An agreement was reached for an interview between the two men. [Historians are not in agreement concerning the time of the first meeting between Iturbide and Guerrero.] General Guerrero himself supplied me with details of what took place at this meeting. The conference was held in a town in the State of Mexico. . . . The two chiefs approached each other with some mutual distrust, although that of Guerrero was plainly the more justified. Iturbide had waged a cruel and bloody war on the independents since 1810. The Spanish leaders themselves hardly equaled this unnatural American in cruelty; and to see him transformed as if by magic into a defender of the cause that he had combated, would naturally arouse suspicions in men like the Mexican insurgents, who had often been the victims of their own credulity and of repeated betrayals. Nevertheless, Iturbide, though sanguinary, inspired confidence by the conscientiousness with which he proceeded in all matters. He was not believed capable of an act of treachery that would stain his reputation for valor and noble conduct. For himself, he had very little to fear from General Guerrero, a man distinguished from the beginning for his humanity and for his loyalty to the cause he was defending. The troops of both leaders were within cannon shot of each other; Iturbide and Guerrero met and embraced. Iturbide was the first to speak: "I cannot express the satisfaction I feel at meeting a patriot who has supported the noble cause of independence and who alone has survived so many disasters, keeping alive the sacred flame of liberty. Receive this just homage to your valor and to your virtues." Guerrero, who also was deeply moved, replied: "Sir, I congratulate my country, which on this day recovers a son whose valor and ability have caused her such grievous injury." Both leaders seemed to feel the strain of this memorable event; both shed tears of strong emotion. After Iturbide had revealed his plans and ideas to Señor Guerrero, that leader summoned his troops and officers, and Iturbide did the same. When both armies had been joined, Guerrero addressed himself to his soldiers, saying: "Soldiers: The Mexican who appears before you is Don Agustín de Iturbide, whose sword wrought such grave injury for nine years to the cause we are defending. Today he swears to defend the national interests; and I, who have led you in combat, and whose loyalty to the cause of independence you cannot doubt, am the first to acknowledge Señor Iturbide as the chief of the national armies. Long live independence! Long live liberty!" From that moment everyone acknowledged the new leader as general-in-chief, and he now dispatched to the viceroy a declaration of his views and of the step he had taken. Iturbide sent General Guerrero to seize a convoy of Manila merchants bound for the port of Acapulco with 750,000 pesos; he himself set out for the town of Iguala, forty leagues to the south of Mexico City, where he published the plan which I have outlined. The Spanish troops began to leave Iturbide's division, but the old patriot detachments began to reassemble everywhere to come to his aid.

All Mexico was set in motion by the declaration of Iguala. Apodaca immediately ordered General Liñán to march with a large division against the new leader, to strangle in its cradle this movement of threatening aspect. But this was not the tumultuous cry of Dolores of 1810; the viceroy was not dealing with a disorderly mob of Indians armed with sickles, stones, and slings and sending up the confused cry "Death to the *gachupines*, long live Our Lady of Guadalupe!" He faced a chief of proven bravery, who, supported by the national will and followed by trained leaders, spoke in the name of the people and demanded rights with which they were well acquainted. . . . While this chief was making extraordinary progress in the provinces, the capital was in the greatest confusion. The Spaniards residing in Mexico City attributed the successes of Iturbide to the ineptitude of Apodaca, who a short time before, according to them, had been the peacemaker, the tutelar angel, of New Spain; now this same man suddenly turned into an imbecile incapable of governing. They stripped him of his command, replacing him with the Brigadier Francisco Novella. This fact alone suffices to give an idea of the state of confusion in which the last defenders of the Spanish government found themselves. Reduced to the support of the expeditionary forces, the dying colonial regime immediately revealed the poverty of its resources. . . . Of the 14,000 soldiers sent to defend the imaginary rights of the Spanish government, only

6,000, at the most, remained—and what could they do against the Mexican army, which numbered at least 50,000 men? Arms, discipline—everything was equal except morale, which naturally was very poor among troops suddenly transported to a strange land, two thousand leagues away from their country. . . . Was it surprising that they surrendered, in view of the situation? Thus, between the end of February, when Iturbide proclaimed his plan of Iguala, and September 27, when he made his triumphant entry into Mexico City, only six months and some days elapsed, with no other memorable actions than the sieges of Durango, Querétaro, Córdoba, and the capital. It was at this time that General Antonio López de Santa-Anna, then lieutenant-colonel, began to distinguish himself.

8. A LETTER TO DOM PEDRO

Brazil made a swift and relatively bloodless transition to independence. The immediate causes of separation were the efforts of a jealous Portuguese cortes to revoke the liberties and concessions Brazilians had won since 1808 and to force the prince regent, Dom Pedro, out of Brazil. Messages of support from juntas throughout the country, such as the following from the junta of São Paulo, encouraged the prince to defy the Lisbon government and to issue his famous "fico" (I remain).

We had already written to Your Royal Highness, before we received the extraordinary gazette of the 11th instant, by the last courier: and we had hardly fixed our eyes on the first decree of the *Cortes* concerning the organization of the governments of the provinces of Brazil, when a noble indignation fired our hearts: because we saw impressed on it a system of anarchy and slavery. But the second, in conformity to which Your Royal Highness is to go back to Portugal, in order to travel incognito only through Spain, France, and England, inspired us with horror.

They aim at no less than disuniting us, weakening us, and in short, leaving us like miserable orphans, tearing from the bosom of the great family of Brazil the only common father who remained to us, after they had deprived Brazil of the beneficent founder of the kingdom, Your Royal Highness's august sire. They deceive themselves; we trust in God, who is the avenger of injustice; He will give us courage, and wisdom.

If, by the 21st article of the basis of the constitution, which we approve and swear to because it is founded on universal and public right, the deputies

Maria Graham, *Journal of a Voyage to Brazil, and Residence There, During Part of the Years 1821, 1822, and 1823* (London, 1824), pp. 174–177.

of Portugal were bound to agree that the constitution made at Lisbon could then be obligatory on the Portuguese resident in that kingdom; and, that, as for those in the other three parts of the world, it should only be binding when their legitimate representatives should have declared such to be their will: How dare those deputies of Portugal, without waiting for those of Brazil, legislate concerning the most sacred interest of each province, and of the entire kingdom? How dare they split it into detached portions, each isolated, and without leaving a common centre of strength and union? How dare they rob Your Royal Highness of the lieutenancy, granted by Your Royal Highness's august father, the King? How dare they deprive Brazil of the privy council, the board of conscience, the court of exchequer, the board of commerce, the court of requests, and so many other recent establishments, which promised such future advantage? Where now shall the wretched people resort in behalf of their civil and judicial interests? Must they now again, after being for twelve years accustomed to judgment at hand, go and suffer, like petty colonists, the delays and chicanery of the tribunals of Lisbon, across two thousand leagues of ocean, where the sighs of the oppressed lose all life and all hope? Who would credit it, after so many bland, but deceitful expressions of reciprocal equality and future happiness!

In the session of the 6th of August last, the deputy of the *Cortes*, Pereira do Carmo, said (and he spoke the truth) that the constitution was the social compact, in which were expressed and declared the conditions on which a nation might wish to constitute itself a body politic: and that the end of that constitution is the general good of each individual who is to enter into that social compact. How then dares a mere fraction of the great Portuguese nation, without waiting for the conclusion of this solemn national compact, attack the general good of the principal part of the same, and such is the vast and rich kingdom of Brazil; dividing it into miserable fragments, and, in a word, attempting to tear from its bosom the representative of the executive power, and to annihilate by a stroke of the pen, all the tribunals and establishments necessary to its existence and future prosperity? This unheard-of despotism, this horrible political perjury, was certainly not merited by the good and generous Brazil. But the enemies of order in the *Cortes* of Lisbon deceive themselves if they imagine that they can thus, by vain words and hollow professions, delude the good sense of the worthy Portuguese of both worlds.

Your Royal Highness will observe that, if the kingdom of Ireland, which makes part of the United Kingdom of Great Britain, besides that it is infinitely small compared to the vast kingdom of Brazil, and is separated from England but by a narrow arm of the sea, which is passed in a few hours, yet possesses a governor-general or viceroy, who represents the executive power of the King of the United Kingdom, how can it enter the head of anyone who is not either profoundly ignorant, or rashly inconsiderate, to pretend, that the vast kingdom of Brazil, should remain without a center of activity, and without a representative of the executive power; and equally without a power to direct our troops, so as that they may operate with celerity and effect, to defend the state against any unforeseen attack of external enemies, or against internal disorders and factions, which might threaten public safety, or the reciprocal union of the province!

We therefore entreat Your Royal Highness with the greatest fervor, tenderness, and respect to delay your return to Europe, where they wish to make you travel as a pupil surrounded by tutors and spies: We entreat you to confide boldly in the love and fidelity of your Brazilians, and especially of your Paulistas, who are all ready to shed the last drop of their blood, and to sacrifice their fortunes, rather than lose the adored Prince in whom they have placed their well-founded hopes of national happiness and honor. Let Your Royal Highness wait at least for the deputies named by this province, and for the magistracy of this capital, who will as soon as possible present to Your Highness our ardent desires and firm resolutions; and deign to receive them, and to listen to them, with the affection and attention, which your Paulistas deserve from you.

May God preserve your Royal Highness's august person many years.

12

❦

SEARCHING FOR A NEW ROAD

THE SPANISH AMERICAN WARS of independence inspired sharp rhetorical attacks on Spain's work in America. Bolívar, for example, claimed that Las Casas had seen America bathed "with the blood of more than twenty million victims." After independence the Spanish colonial legacy became a major issue in the political struggles of the new states. Liberals condemned Spanish tyranny, obscurantism, and backwardness and insisted on the need to liquidate the colonial heritage; conservatives, who often recalled the old social order with nostalgia, offered at least a partial defense of Spain's colonial rule.

These differences among Spanish American elites produced a long, uphill struggle to achieve stable societies. The new states lacked a strong middle class, experience in self-government, and the other advantages the United States enjoyed at independence. The result was an age of violence, dictatorship, and revolution. Its symbol was the *caudillo*, or "strong man," whose power was always based on force, no matter what the constitutional form (although *caudillos* generally displayed some regard for republican ideology and institutions). The *caudillos* played a crucial mediating role in the struggles between political parties, usually called Conservative and Liberal, which were active in most of the new states. Conservatism drew its main support from the landed aristocracy, the Church, and the military; liberalism attracted the merchants, provincial landowners, and professional men of the towns. Regional conflicts often cut across the lines of social cleavage, complicating the political picture.

As a rule, the Conservatives favored a highly centralized government and the social arrangements of the colonial era; the Liberals, inspired by the success of the United States, advocated a federal form of government, guarantees of individual rights, lay control of education, and an end to special privileges for the clergy and the military. Neither party displayed much interest in the problems of the landless, debt-ridden peasantry that formed the majority of almost every nation.

Independent Brazil made a relatively easy and rapid transition to a stable political order. The troubled reign of Dom Pedro I (1822–1831) and the stormy years of the Regency (1831–1840) were followed by the long and serene reign of Dom Pedro II (1840–1889). Brazil's ruling class of great landowners deliberately sacrificed "liberty with anarchy for order and security," in the words of Professor Manchester, and vested the young emperor, called to rule at the age of fifteen, with virtually absolute power. The generally upward movement of Brazilian economic life and the tact, wisdom, and firmness of the emperor contributed to the success with which the system functioned for half a century.

1. THE FATAL LEGACY

In the decades after independence, Latin American leaders debated which road their countries should take to reach the goals of economic progress and political stability. Liberals looked to the United States, England, and France as models of dynamic advance; conservatives proposed to remain in the safe, familiar way of their fathers and retain those features of the colonial regime not incompatible with the new republican order: the supremacy of the Catholic Church, clerical control of education, a hierarchical society with special privileges for the clergy and military, and the like. In 1844 two ardent liberals startled the staid aristocratic society of Santiago with their contributions to the debate. Francisco Bilbao (1823–1865) threw a bombshell with his famous essay on "The Nature of Chilean Society," in which he declared, "Slavery, degradation: that is the past. . . . Our past is Spain. Spain is the Middle Ages. The Middle Ages are composed, body and soul, of Catholicism and feudalism." Bilbao was tried and condemned for blasphemy, sedition, and immorality; he lost his university chair, and his book was officially burned by the public hangman. José Victorino Lastarria (1817–1888), more moderate and scholarly, caused a lesser stir with his address "Investigations on the Social Influence of the Conquest and the Colonial System of the Spaniards in Chile." Despite an occasional factual error—such as the statement that Spain forbade the printing and sale of books of every kind in America—it remains an effective summary of the liberal case against the Spanish colonial regime.

It is well known that the Spaniards who conquered America drenched its soil in blood, not in order to colonize it but to acquire the precious metals it

---

José Victorino Lastarria, "Investigaciones sobre la influencia social de la Conquista i del sistema colonial de los españoles en Chile," in *Obras completas*, vol. 7 (Santiago de Chile, 1909), pp. 45–69. Excerpt translated by Benjamin Keen.

yielded so abundantly. Torrents of adventurers flowed over the New World; they were obsessed by the hope of gaining immense wealth at little cost, and to this end they directed all their activity, sparing no means or violence in order to achieve it. At last reality dispelled their illusions, and the conquistadors, convinced by their own experience that the fertility of the American mines was not as great as they had hoped, gradually abandoned their daring speculations and began to devote themselves to agricultural and commercial enterprises. But this new direction of their ambitions did not yield the benefits that might have been expected, given the potential wealth of the American soil, for they had neither the inclination nor the intelligence to exploit this new source of riches; and their government, for its part, with its absurd economic system, stopped up the very sources of economic progress.

When Spain established her colonies in America, she transplanted thither all the vices of her absurd system of government, vices that multiplied infinitely through causes that had their origin in the system itself. . . .

A single leading idea dominated all the decisions of the Spanish Court and its agents in the colonies: this was the idea of maintaining America forever in a blind dependence on Spain, in order to exploit it exclusively, at the cost of the very existence and development of the colonies, and to extract from its possession all possible advantages. From this point of view, the metropolis had a system, a spirit that gave unity to its decisions and sanctified all means necessary to achieve those ends, no matter how unjust and unworthy they might be. For Spain the New World was a very rich mine that should be exploited and whose fruits should be consumed, no matter what devastation the process produced or what effects it might have on future productivity.

To this end Spain subjected the natives to the grossest, most humiliating servitude, declaring them slaves in certain cases and masking their slavery in others with a pretended, ironic respect for their liberty, even as it subjected them to the *mita*, the *repartimiento*, and other oppressive burdens. The tax laws were precisely calculated to benefit the royal treasury and to extract from the colonies all the wealth possible, even at the expense of the very elements of production. Commerce was monopolized for the benefit of Spain, manufacturing and agriculture were surrounded with a thousand restrictions and burdened with so many taxes that there clearly emerged the intention of impeding their future development. . . . Communication and commerce with foreign powers were forbidden so strictly that not only was it made a crime to maintain such relations but a pretended sovereignty of the seas was invoked, as in a royal *cédula* (1692) that ordered governors "to treat as an enemy ship every foreign ship sailing in American waters without license from this government, even if the vessel belongs to an allied nation."

For the rest, the laws and orders dictated to prevent the intellectual development of the Americans testify to the perverse intention of maintaining them in the most brutal and degrading ignorance, to make them perpetually bow their necks to the yoke of their *natural sovereign* and of all the governors who derived from him all their authority. It was forbidden under severe penalties to sell and print in America books of any kind, even books of devotion; and to introduce books a license was necessary from the Council of the Indies or some other authority anxious to prevent the light of intelligence from penetrating the New World. The few universities and colleges, established and regulated by law, were entirely designed to keep true knowledge from men; to use the happy expression of one American, they were "a monument of imbecility." Entirely subject to the rule of monks, intellectual and moral education was frustrated with the utmost diligence; care was taken to turn out only clergymen or, at most, lawyers and physicians, but all were taught false doctrines. They became accustomed to juggle metaphysical subtleties and the most extravagant theories, and according to the formulas of their useless science they were made to adopt a grotesque and high-sounding style. Thus the Spanish government managed by means of its laws and orders to lead the minds of Americans astray and direct them into anti-social studies that subjected their minds to a perfect slavery and were designed to blind their reason so that they should see "in the king of Spain their absolute lord, who knew no superior or restraint on his power on the face of the earth, whose power derived from God Himself, a king whose person was sacred and in whose presence all should tremble."

In making this rapid survey of the colonial legislation with the aim of investigating its social influence, I must, however, prove my impartiality by noting that the tedium caused by perusal of this monstrous compilation is sometimes relieved by the reading of some provisions that prove the merciful sentiments of their authors. But only "merciful sentiments," mind you, for one does not discover in those provisions, any more than in the rest, that common sense, that foresight, that result from philosophic analysis of the facts—qualities that are salient traits of the wise legislator. In effect, we note various laws designed to regulate the service of the natives in the mines, *encomiendas*, and *repartimientos* to which they were subject, and others that assessed their tributes so that they should not prove too burdensome. There are special laws designed to protect the liberty of the Chilean Indians and grant them more privileges and exemptions than were enjoyed by the Indians of other colonies, doubtless with the aim of attracting the Chilean Indians and ending their wars by means of these mild and protective measures. Undoubtedly these are the laws that have fascinated the defenders of the colonial legislation, who have assumed their good faith and deduced from them arguments to prove the wisdom of Spain and to eulogize the protection that she dispensed to her colonies. But if we recall what was said above concerning the spirit of that code and the system of the metropolis, what were those laws, at most, but the expression of an isolated goodwill, or perhaps a cover with which a corrupt and reactionary Court wished to mask its true intentions and opinions vis-à-vis the unhappy natives of the New World? Be that as it may, those protective laws were a mute and ineffective exception, a dead letter, since their execution, interpretation, and even the right to modify them were in the hands of the colonial governors. . . .

This was the dominant thought, the aspirations, the concentrated essence, of the civilization of the sixteenth-century Spaniard: his king and his interest, God, and the glory of war. . . .

That civilization, then, was the element that conditioned all the exploits of that remarkable people; it was the origin of all its aberrations and determined the direction of its inclinations; it gave form to its customs. I believe, therefore, that when we examine the civil and political laws that molded our society, we must consider them the logical result of that civilization and always keep in mind that the foundations of our social structure were laid by fanatical, warlike Spain; that the basis of the administrative system of our colony was the omnipotence of Charles V; and that our religion had for its base the terrorism of the Inquisition.

2. IN DEFENSE OF SPAIN

Conservative ideologists of the postindependence period, who had lived under Spanish rule and sometimes participated in its overthrow, rarely offered an unqualified defense of the colonial regime. More often, conceding its errors and abuses, they countered the liberal attack by stressing the period's benefits: the long Pax Hispanica, *the relative mildness of Spanish rule, and the like. A review of Lastarria's "Investigations" by Andrés Bello (1781–1865), the distinguished Venezuelan scholar and educator who, as rector of the National University of Chile, gave Lastarria the opportunity to make his address, illustrates the thought of an enlightened conservative on the subject. Observe how Bello, conceding the cruelties of the conquest, diminishes Spanish guilt by shifting responsibility to a flawed human nature, to a universal law by which the strong oppress the weak in all times and places. This line of defense has often been employed by apologists for Spanish imperialism and imperialism in general.*

The vassals of Isabella, Charles I, and Philip II were the premier nation of Europe; their knightly spirit, the splendor of the Spanish Court, Spain's magnificent and proud nobility, the skill of its captains, the ability of its ambassadors and ministers, the bravery of its soldiers, their daring enterprises, momentous discoveries, and conquests, made Spain a target of detractors

---

Andrés Bello, review of Lastarria's "Investigaciones," in *Obras completas*, vol. 19 (Caracas, 1957), pp. 161–166. Excerpt translated by Benjamin Keen.

because it was an object of envy. The memoirs of that age present horrible scenes to our eyes. The Spaniards abused their power, oppressed, committed outrages, not impudently as Señor Lastarria claims—for one need not be impudent to do what everyone else does in the measure of his power—but with the same regard for humanity, the same respect for the rights of men, that powerful states have always displayed in their dealings with the weak, dealings of which our own moral and civilized time presents too many examples.

If we compare the practice, as opposed to theory, of international law in modern times with that of the Middle Ages and antiquity, beneath insubstantial differences of form and method we find a basic similarity. . . . Among the great masses of men that we call nations the savage state in which brute force rules has not ended. Men pay a superficial homage to justice by reference to the commonplaces of security, dignity, protection of national interests, and other equally vague clichés—premises from which a modicum of skill can derive all imaginable consequences. The horrors of war have been partly mitigated, not from greater respect for humanity but because material interests are better calculated, and as a result of the very perfection to which the art of destruction has been brought. It would be madness to enslave the conquered when there is greater profit in making them tributaries and forced suppliers of the conqueror's industry. The pillagers of old have been transformed into merchants, but merchants whose counters display the motto: *Vae victis* (woe to the vanquished). Colonization no longer brings death to the native inhabitants: why kill them, when it is enough to drive them from forest to forest, from prairie to prairie? In the long run deprivation and famine will achieve the work of destruction without noisy scandal. . . .

I do not accuse any nation, but rather human nature. The weak invoke justice, but let them grow strong, and they will prove as unjust as their oppressors.

The picture that Señor Lastarria paints of the vices and abuses of Spain's colonial system he generally supports with documents of irrefutable authenticity and veracity: laws, ordinances, histories, the *Memorias Secretas* of Jorge Juan and Antonio de Ulloa. But profuse shadows appear in the picture; there is something about it that detracts from the impartiality required of the advocate, an impartiality not incompatible with the energetic tone of reproof with which the historian, advocate of the rights of man and interpreter of moral sentiments, should pronounce judgment on corrupting institutions.

To the dominant idea of perpetuating the tutelage of her colonies, Spain sacrificed not only the interests of her colonies but her own; in order to keep them dependent and submissive she made herself poor and weak. While American treasure inundated the world, the Spanish treasury grew empty and her industry remained in swaddling clothes. Colonies served to stimulate the growth of population and the arts in other countries; for Spain they were a cause of depopulation and backwardness. Spain displayed no industrial life or wealth, save in a few emporia that served as intermediaries in the trade between the two hemispheres, emporia in which the accumulated wealth of monopoly flaunted itself amid the general misery.

But we must be just: Spain's was not a *ferocious* tyranny. It chained the arts, clipped the wings of thought, stopped up the very sources of agricultural fertility, but its policy was one of obstacles and restraints, not of blood and torture. The penal laws were laxly administered. In punishing sedition it was not extraordinarily severe; it was as severe as despotism has always been, but no more, at least as concerns its treatment of the Spanish race and until the time of the Revolution that brought freedom to the Spanish dominions.

The prototype of Spanish despotism in America was that of the Roman emperors. There was the same ineffective benignity on the part of the supreme authority, the same pretorian arbitrariness, the same divinization of the Throne, the same indifference to industry, the same ignorance of the great principles that vivify and make fecund human associations, the same judicial organization, the same fiscal privileges. But to compensate for these negative qualities there were others of a different character. That civilizing mission which moves, like the sun, from east to west, and of which Rome was the most powerful agency in the antique world, Spain performed in a more distant, vaster world. No doubt the elements of this civilization were destined to amalgamate with others that should improve it, just as Roman civilization was modified and improved in Europe by foreign influences. Perhaps I deceive myself, but it seems to me that none of the nations that emerged from the ruins of the Empire preserved a more pronounced stamp of the Roman genius: the very language of Spain preserves better than any other the character of that spoken by the masters of the world. Even in material things Spain's colonial administration displayed a touch of the imperial Roman style. To the Spanish government America owes all that is grand and splendid in its public buildings. Let us confess it with feelings of shame: We have hardly been able to maintain the structures erected under the viceroys and captains-general. Remember, too, that Crown revenues were liberally spent for their construction, and that Spain did not impose the taxes and forced labors with which Rome burdened her imperial subjects for the building of roads, aqueducts, amphitheaters, hot baths, and bridges.

3. Bolívar's Ideal Republic

Like Lastarria, Simón Bolívar was critical of the Spanish colonial legacy. At the same time, like Bello, he acknowledged both the importance and difficulty of maintaining public order once the Spanish empire had been replaced by new independent nations. In this "Address Delivered at the Inauguration of the Second National Congress of Venezuela in Angostura, February 15, 1819," Bolívar goes to great pains to balance

the pressing need for strong executive authority and the compelling desire for demo-
cratic political institutions. The many historical references underscore his sense of the
world-historical importance of Latin American independence and the great perils that
lay ahead for its fledgling democracies.

Fortunate is the citizen, who, under the emblem of his command, has convoked this assembly of the national sovereignty so that it may exercise its absolute will! I, therefore, place myself among those most favored by Divine Providence, for I have had the honor of uniting the representatives of the people of Venezuela in this august Congress, the source of legitimate authority, the custodian of the sovereign will, and the arbiter of the Nation's destiny. . . .

America, in separating from the Spanish monarchy, found herself in a situation similar to that of the Roman Empire when its enormous framework fell to pieces in the midst of the ancient world. Each Roman division then formed an independent nation in keeping with its location and interests; but this situation differed from America's in that those members proceeded to reestablish their former associations. We, on the contrary, do not even retain the vestiges of our original being. We are not Europeans; we are not Indians; we are but a mixed species of aborigines and Spaniards. Americans by birth and Europeans by law, we find ourselves engaged in a dual conflict: we are disputing with the natives for titles of ownership, and at the same time we are struggling to maintain ourselves in the country that gave us birth against the opposition of the invaders. Thus our position is most extraordinary and complicated. But there is more. As our role has always been strictly passive and our political existence nil, we find that our quest for liberty is now even more difficult of accomplishment; for we, having been placed in a state lower than slavery, had been robbed not only of our freedom but also of the right to exercise an active domestic tyranny. Permit me to explain this paradox.

In absolute systems, the central power is unlimited. The will of the despot is the supreme law, arbitrarily enforced by subordinates who take part in the organized oppression in proportion to the authority that they wield. They are charged with civil, political, military, and religious functions; but, in the final analysis, the satraps of Persia are Persian, the pashas of the Grand Turk are Turks, and the sultans of Tartary are Tartars. China does not seek her mandarins in the homeland of Genghis Khan, her conqueror. America, on the contrary, received everything from Spain, who, in effect, deprived her of the experience that she would have gained from the exercise of an active tyranny by not allowing her to take part in her own domestic affairs and ad-

Simón Bolívar, *Selected Writings of Bolívar*, comp. Vicente Lecuna, ed. Harold A. Bierck Jr., trans. Lewis Betrand, 2 vols. (New York: Banco de Venezuela/Colonial Press, 1951), 1:173–197. Reprinted by permission of the Banco de Venezuela.

ministration. This exclusion made it impossible for us to acquaint ourselves
with the management of public affairs; nor did we enjoy that personal consideration, of such great value in major revolutions, that the brilliance of power
inspires in the eyes of the multitude. In brief, Gentlemen, we were deliberately kept in ignorance and cut off from the world in all matters relating to
the science of government.

Subject to the threefold yoke of ignorance, tyranny, and vice, the American people have been unable to acquire knowledge, power, or civic virtue.
The lessons we received and the models we studied, as pupils of such pernicious teachers, were most destructive. We have been ruled more by deceit
than by force, and we have been degraded more by vice than by superstition.
Slavery is the daughter of Darkness: an ignorant people is a blind instrument
of its own destruction. Ambition and intrigue abuse the credulity and experience of men lacking all political, economic, and civic knowledge; they adopt
pure illusion as reality; they take license for liberty, treachery for patriotism,
and vengeance for justice. This situation is similar to that of the robust blind
man who, beguiled by his strength, strides forward with all the assurance of
one who can see, but, upon hitting every variety of obstacle, finds himself unable to retrace his steps.

If a people, perverted by their training, succeed in achieving their liberty,
they will soon lose it, for it would be of no avail to endeavor to explain to
them that happiness consists in the practice of virtue; that the rule of law is
more powerful than the rule of tyrants, because, as the laws are more inflexi-
ble, everyone should submit to their beneficent austerity; that proper morals,
and not force, are the bases of law; and that to practice justice is to practice
liberty. Therefore, Legislators, your work is so much more the arduous, inas-
much as you have to reeducate men who have been corrupted by erroneous
illusions and false incentives. Liberty, says Rousseau, is a succulent morsel,
but one difficult to digest. Our weak fellow-citizens will have to strengthen
their spirit greatly before they can digest the wholesome nutriment of freedom. Their limbs benumbed by chains, their sight dimmed by the darkness
of dungeons, and their strength sapped by the pestilence of servitude, are
they capable of marching toward the august temple of Liberty without falter-
ing? Can they come near enough to bask in its brilliant rays and to breathe
freely the pure air which reigns therein?

Legislators, mediate well before you choose. Forget not that you are to
lay the political foundation for a newly born nation which can rise to the
heights of greatness that Nature has marked out for it if you but proportion
this foundation in keeping with the high plane that it aspires to attain. Unless
your choice is based upon the peculiar tutelary experience of the Venezuelan
people—a factor that should guide you in determining the nature and form
of government you are about to adopt for the well-being of the people—and,
I repeat, unless you happen upon the right type of government, the result of
our reforms will again be slavery. . . .

Only democracy, in my opinion, is amenable to absolute liberty. But what democratic government has simultaneously enjoyed power, prosperity, and permanence? On the other hand, have not aristocracy and monarchy held great and powerful empires together century after century? Is there any government older than that of China? What republic has lasted longer than Sparta or Venice? Did not the Roman Empire conquer the earth? Has not France had fourteen centuries of monarchy? Is there any nation greater than England? Yet these nations have been or still are aristocracies and monarchies?

Despite these bitter reflections, I experience a surge of joy when I witness the great advances that our Republic has made since it began its noble career. Loving what is most useful, animated by what is most just, and aspiring to what is most perfect, Venezuela, on breaking away from Spain, has recovered her independence, her freedom, her equality, and her national sovereignty. By establishing a democratic republic, she has proscribed monarchy, distinctions, nobility, prerogatives, and privileges. She has declared for the rights of man and freedom of action, thought, speech, and press. These eminently liberal acts, because of the sincerity that has inspired them, will never cease to be admired. The first Congress of Venezuela has indelibly stamped upon the annals of our laws the majesty of the people, and, in placing its seal upon the social document best calculated to develop the well-being of the nation, that Congress has fittingly given expression to this thought. . . .

The more I admire the excellence of the federal Constitution of Venezuela, the more I am convinced of the impossibility of its application to our state. And, to my way of thinking, it is a marvel that its prototype in North America endures so successfully and has not been overthrown at the first sign of adversity or danger. Although the people of North America are a singular model of political virtue and moral rectitude; although that nation was cradled in liberty, reared on freedom, and maintained by liberty alone; and—I must reveal everything—although those people, so lacking in many respects, are unique in the history of mankind, it is a marvel, I repeat, that so weak and complicated a government as the federal system has managed to govern them in the difficult and trying circumstances of their past. But, regardless of the effectiveness of this form of government with respect to North America, I must say that it has never for a moment entered my mind to compare the position and character of two states as dissimilar as the English-American and Spanish American. Would it not be most difficult to apply to Spain the English system of political, civil, and religious liberty? Hence, it would be even more difficult to adapt to Venezuela the laws of North America. Does not [French political theorist Montesquieu's *Spirit of the Laws*] state that laws should be suited to the people for whom they are made; that it would be a major coincidence if those of one nation could be adapted to another; that laws must take into account the physical conditions of the country, climate, character of the land, location, size, and mode of living of the people; that they should be in keeping with the degree of liberty that the Constitution can sanction respecting the religion of the inhabitants, their inclination, resources, number, commerce, habits, and customs? This is the code we must consult, not the code of Washington! . . .

The first Congress, in its federal Constitution, responded more to the spirit of the provinces than to the sound idea of creating an indivisible and centralized republic. In this instance, out legislators yielded to the ill-considered pleadings of those men from the provinces who were captivated by the apparent brilliance of the happiness of the North American people, believing that the blessings they enjoy result exclusively from their form of government rather than from the character and customs of the citizens. In effect, the United States' example, because of their remarkable prosperity, was one too tempting not to be followed. Who could resist the powerful attraction of full and absolute enjoyment of sovereignty, independence, and freedom? Who could resist the devotion inspired by an intelligent government that has not only blended public and private rights but has also based its supreme law respecting the desires of the individual upon common consent? Who could resist the rule of a beneficent government which, with a skilled, dexterous, and powerful hand always and in all regions, directs its resources toward social perfection, the sole aim of human institutions?

But no matter how tempting this magnificent federative system might have appeared, and regardless of its possible effect, the Venezuelans were not prepared to enjoy it by immediately casting off their chains. We were not prepared for such good, for good, like evil, results in death when it is sudden and excessive. Our moral fiber did not then possess the stability necessary to derive benefits from a wholly representative government; a government so sublime, in fact, that it might more nearly befit a republic of saints. . . .

Permit me to call the attention of the Congress to a matter that may be of vital importance. We must keep in mind that our people are neither European nor North American; rather, they are a mixture of African and the Americans who originated in Europe. Even Spain herself has ceased to be European because of her African blood, her institutions, and her character. It is impossible to determine with any degree of accuracy where we belong in the human family. The greater portion of the native Indians has been annihilated; Spaniards have mixed with Americans and Africans, and Africans with Indians and Spaniards. While we have all been born of the same mother, our fathers, different in origin and in blood, are foreigners, and all differ visibly as to the color of their skin: a dissimilarity which places upon us an obligation of the greatest importance.

Under the Constitution, which interprets the laws of Nature, all citizens of Venezuela enjoy complete political equality. Although it may not have been the political dogma of Athens, France or North America, we must consecrate it here in order to correct the disparity that apparently exists. My opinion, Legislators, is that the fundamental basis of our political system hinges directly and exclusively upon the establishment and practice of equality in Venezuela. Most wise men concede that men are born with equal rights to share the benefits of society, but it does not follow that all men are born equally gifted to attain every rank. All men should practice virtue, but not all do; all ought to be courageous, but not all are; all should possess talents, but not everyone does. Herein are the real distinctions which can be observed among individuals even in the most liberally constituted society. If the principle of political equality is generally recognized, so also must be the principle of physical and moral inequality. Nature makes men unequal in intelligence, temperament, strength, and character. Laws correct this disparity by so placing the individual within society that education, industry, arts, services, and virtues give him a fictitious equality that is properly termed political and social. The idea of a classless state, wherein diversity increases in proportion to the rise in population, was an eminently beneficial inspiration. By this step alone, cruel discord has been completely eliminated. How much jealousy, rivalry, and hate have thus been averted!

Having dealt with justice and humanity, let us now give attention to politics and society, and let us resolve the difficulties inherent in a system so simple and natural, yet so weak that the slightest obstacle can upset and destroy it. The diversity of racial origin will require an infinitely firm hand and great tactfulness in order to manage this heterogeneous society, whose complicated mechanism is easily damaged, separated, and disintegrated by the slightest controversy.

The most perfect system of government is that which results in the greatest possible measure of happiness and the maximum of social security and political stability. The laws enacted by the first Congress gave us reason to hope that happiness would be the lot of Venezuela; and, through your laws, we must hope that security and stability will perpetuate this happiness. You must solve the problem. But how, having broken all the shackles of our former oppression, can we accomplish the enormous task of preventing the remnants of our past fetters from becoming liberty-destroying weapons? The vestiges of Spanish domination will long be with us before we can completely eradicate them: the contagion of despotism infests the atmosphere about us, and neither the fires of war nor the healing properties of our salutary laws have purified the air we breathe. Our hands are now free, but our hearts still suffer the ills of slavery. When man loses freedom, said Homer, he loses half his spirit.

Venezuela had, has, and should have a republican government. Its principles should be the sovereignty of the people, division of powers, civil liberty, proscription of slavery, and the abolition of monarchy and privileges. We need equality to recast, so to speak, into a unified nation, the classes of men, political opinions, and public customs. . . .

I recommend to you, Representatives, the study of the British Constitution, for that body of laws appears destined to bring about the greatest possible good for the peoples that adopt it; but, however perfect it may be, I am by no means proposing that you imitate it slavishly. When I speak of the British government, I only refer to its republican features; and, indeed, can a political system be labeled a monarchy when it recognizes popular sovereignty, division and balance of powers, civil liberty, freedom of conscience and of press, and all that is politically sublime? Can there be more liberty in any other type of republic? Can more be asked of any society? I commend this Constitution to you as that most worthy of serving as model for those who aspire to the enjoyment of the rights of man and who seek all the political happiness which is compatible with the frailty of human nature.

Nothing in our fundamental laws would have to be altered were we to adopt legislative power similar to that held by the British Parliament. Like the North Americans, we have divided national representation into two chambers: that of Representatives and the Senate. The first is very wisely constituted. It enjoys all its proper functions, and it requires no essential revision, because the Constitution, in creating it, gave it the form and powers which the people deemed necessary in order that they might be legally and properly represented. If the Senate were hereditary rather than elective, it would, in my opinion, be the basis, the tie, the very soul of our republic. In political storms this body would arrest the thunderbolts of the government and would repel any violent popular reaction. Devoted to the government because of a natural interest in its own preservation, a hereditary senate would always oppose any attempt on the part of the people to infringe upon the jurisdiction and authority of their magistrates. It must be confessed that most men are unaware of their best interests and that they constantly endeavor to assail them in the hands of their custodians—the individual clashes with the mass, and the mass with authority. It is necessary, therefore, that in all governments there be a neutral body to protect the injured and disarm the offender. To be neutral, this body must not owe its origin to appointment by the government or to election by the people, if it is to enjoy a full measure of independence which neither fears nor expects anything from these two sources of authority. The hereditary senate, as a part of the people, shares its interests, its sentiments, and its spirit. For this reason it should not be presumed that a hereditary senate would ignore the interests of the people or forget its legislative duties. The senators in Rome and in the House of Lords in London have been the strongest pillars upon which the edifice of political and civil liberty has rested.

At the outset, these senators should be elected by Congress. The successors to this Senate must command the initial attention of the government, which should educate them in a *colegio* designed especially to train these guardians and future legislators of the nation. They ought to learn the arts, sciences, and letters that enrich the mind of a public figure. From childhood they should understand the career for which they have been destined by Providence, and from earliest youth they should prepare their minds for the dignity that awaits them.

The creation of a hereditary senate would in no way be a violation of political equality. I do not solicit the establishment of a nobility, for, as a celebrated republican has said, that would simultaneously destroy equality and liberty. What I propose is an office for which the candidates must prepare themselves, an office that demands great knowledge and the ability to acquire such knowledge. All should not be left to chance and the outcome of elections. The people are more easily deceived than is Nature perfected by art; and, although these senators, it is true, would not be bred in an environment that is all virtue, it is equally true that they would be raised in an atmosphere of enlightened education. Furthermore, the liberators of Venezuela are entitled to occupy forever a high rank in the Republic that they have brought into existence. I believe that posterity would view with regret the effacement of the illustrious names of its first benefactors. I say, moreover, that it is a matter of public interest and national honor, of gratitude on Venezuela's part, to honor gloriously, until the end of time, a race of virtuous, prudent, and persevering men who, overcoming every obstacle, have founded the Republic at the price of the most heroic sacrifices. And if the people of Venezuela do not applaud the elevation of their benefactors, then they are unworthy to be free, and they will never be free.

A hereditary senate, I repeat, will be the fundamental basis of the legislative power, and therefore the foundation of the entire government. It will also serve as a counterweight to both government and people; as a neutral power it will weaken the mutual attacks of these two eternally rival powers. In all conflicts the calm reasoning of a third party will serve as the means of reconciliation. Thus the Venezuelan senate will give strength to this delicate political structure, so sensitive to violent repercussions; it will be the mediator that will lull the storms and it will maintain harmony between the head and the other parts of this political body.

No inducement could corrupt a legislative body invested with the highest honors, dependent only upon itself, having no fear of the people, independent of the government, and dedicated solely to the repression of all evil principles and to the advancement of every good principle—a legislative body that would be deeply concerned with the maintenance of a society, for it would share the consequences, be they honorable or disastrous. It has rightly been said that the upper house in England is invaluable to that nation because it provides a bulwark of liberty; and I would add that the Senate of Venezuela would be not only a bulwark of liberty but a bastion of defense rendering the Republic eternal.

The British executive power possesses all the authority properly appertaining to a sovereign, but he is surrounded by a triple line of dams, barriers, and stockades. He is the head of the government, but his ministers and subordinates rely more upon law than upon his authority, as they are personally responsible; and not even decrees of royal authority can exempt them from this responsibility. The executive is commander in chief of the army and navy; he makes peace and declares war; but Parliament annually determines what sums are to be paid to these military forces. While the courts and judges are dependent on the executive power, the laws originate in and are made by Parliament. To neutralize the power of the King, his person is declared inviolable and sacred; but, while his head is left untouched, his hands are tied. The sovereign of England has three formidable rivals: his Cabinet, which is responsible to the people and to Parliament; the Senate *sic,* which, representing the nobility of which it is composed, defends the interests of the people; and the House of Commons, which serves as the representative body of the British people and provides them with a place in which to express their opinions. Moreover, as the judges are responsible for the enforcement of the laws, they do not depart from them; and the administrators of the exchequer, being subject to prosecution not only for personal infractions but also for those of the government, take care to prevent any misuse of public funds. No matter how closely we study the composition of the English executive power, we can find nothing to prevent its being judged as the most perfect model for a kingdom, for an aristocracy, or for a democracy. Give Venezuela such an executive power in the person of a president chosen by the people or their representatives, and you will have taken a great step toward national happiness.

No matter what citizen occupies this office, he will be aided by the Constitution, and therein being authorized to do good, he can do no harm, because his ministers will cooperate with him only insofar as he abides by the law. If he attempts to infringe upon the law, his own ministers will desert him, thereby isolating him from the Republic, and they will even bring charges against him in the Senate. The ministers, being responsible for any transgressions committed, will actually govern, since they must account for their actions. The obligation which this system places upon the officials closest to the executive power, that is, to take a most interested and active part in governmental deliberations and to regard this department as their own, is not the smallest advantage of the system. Should the president be a man of no great talent or virtue, yet, notwithstanding his lack of these essential qualities, he will be able to discharge his duties satisfactorily, for in such a case the ministry, managing everything by itself, will carry the burdens of the state.

Although the authority of the executive power in England may appear to be extreme, it would, perhaps, not be excessive in the Republic of Venezuela. Here the Congress has tied the hands and even the heads of its men of state. This deliberative assembly has assumed a part of the executive functions, contrary to the maxim of Montesquieu, to wit: A representative assembly should exercise no active function. It should only make laws and determine whether or not those laws are enforced. Nothing is as disturbing to harmony among the powers of government as their intermixture. Nothing is more dangerous with respect to the people than a weak executive; and if a kingdom has deemed it necessary to grant the executive so many powers, then in a republic these powers are infinitely more indispensable.

If we examine this difference, we will find that the balance of power between the branches of government must be distributed in two ways. In republics the executive should be the stronger, for everything conspires against it; while in monarchies the legislative power should be superior, as everything works in the monarch's favor. The people's veneration of royal power results in a self-satisfaction that tends greatly to increase the superstitious respect paid to such authority. The splendor inherent in the throne, the crown, and the purple; the formidable support that it receives from the nobility; the immense wealth that a dynasty accumulated from generation to generation; and the fraternal protection that kings grant to one another are the significant advantages that work in favor of royal authority, thereby rendering it almost unlimited. Consequently, the significance of these same advantages should serve to justify the necessity of investing the chief magistrate of a republic with a greater measure of authority than that possessed by a constitutional prince.

A republican magistrate is an individual set apart from society, charged with checking the impulse of the people toward license and the propensity of judges and administrators toward abuse of the laws. He is directly subject to the legislative body, the senate, and the people: he is the one man who resists the combined pressure of the opinions, interests, and passions of the social state and who, as Carnot states, does little more than struggle constantly with the urge to dominate and the desire to escape domination. He is, in brief, an athlete pitted against a multitude of athletes.

This weakness can only be corrected by a strongly rooted force. It should be strongly proportioned to meet the resistance which the executive must expect from the legislature, from the judiciary, and from the people of a republic. Unless the executive has easy access to all the administrative resources, fixed by a just distribution of powers, he inevitably becomes a nonentity or abuses his authority. By this I mean that the result will be the death of the government, whose heirs are anarchy, usurpation, and tyranny. Some seek to check the executive authority by curbs and restrictions, and nothing is more just; but it must be remembered that the bonds we seek to preserve should, of course, be strengthened, but not tightened.

Therefore, let the entire system of government be strengthened, and let the balance of power be drawn up in such a manner that it will be permanent and incapable of decay because of its own tenuity. Precisely because no form of government is so weak as the democratic, its framework must be firmer, and its institutions must be studied to determine their degree of stability. Unless this is done, we must plan on the establishment of an experimental rather than a permanent system of government; and we will have to reckon with an ungovernable, tumultuous, and anarchic society, not with a social order where happiness, peace, and justice prevail. . . .

The formation of a stable government requires as a foundation a national spirit, having as its objective a uniform concentration on two cardinal factors, namely, moderation of the popular will and limitation of public authority. The extremes, which these two factors theoretically establish, are difficult to define in practice; but it can be well conceived that the maxim that must guide them is mutual limitation and concentration of power, in order that there may be the least possible friction between the popular will and the constituted public authority. The science of achieving this balance is acquired almost imperceptibly, through practice and study. Progress in the practice of this science is hastened by progress in the enlightenment of the people, and integrity of mind and spirit needs the progress of enlightenment.

Love of country, love of law, and respect for magistrates are the exalted emotions that must permeate the soul of a republic. The Venezuelans love their country, but they cannot love her laws, because these, being sources of evil, have been harmful; neither can they respect their magistrates, as they have been unjust, while the new administrators are scarcely known in the calling which they have just entered. Unless there is a sacred reverence for country, laws, and authority, society becomes confused, an abyss—an endless conflict of man versus man, group versus group.

All our moral powers will not suffice to save our infant republic from this chaos unless we fuse the mass of the people, the government, the legislation, and the national spirit into a single united body. Unity, unity, unity must be our motto in all things. The blood of our citizens is varied: let it be mixed for the sake of unity. Our Constitution has divided the powers of government: let them be bound together to secure unity. Our laws are but a sad relic of ancient and modern despotism. Let this monstrous edifice crumble and fall; and, having removed even its ruins, let us erect a temple to Justice; and, guided by its sacred inspiration, let us write a code of Venezuelan laws. Should we wish to consult the monuments of legislation, those of Great Britain, France, and the United States of North America afford us admirable models.

Popular education should be the primary concern of the paternal love of Congress. Morality and enlightenment are the foundations of a republic; morality and enlightenment constitute our primary needs. From Athens let us take her Areopagus and her guardians of custom and law; from Rome, her censors and domestic tribunals; and, having effected a holy alliance of these moral institutions, let us revive in the world the idea of a people who, not content to be free and strong, desire also to be virtuous. From Sparta let us take her austere institutions; and, when from these three springs we have made a fountain of virtue, let us endow our republic with a fourth power having jurisdiction over the youth, the hearts of men, public spirit, good customs, and republican ethics. Let us establish an Areopagus to watch over the education of our youth and to promote national enlightenment, in order that it may purify every instance of corruption in the Republic and denounce ingratitude, selfishness, indifferent love of country, and idleness and negligence on the part of the citizens, that it may judge the first signs of corruption and of evil example, using moral penalties to correct violation of customs, even as criminals are punished by corporal penalties. Such action should be taken not only against that which conflicts with customs, but also against that which mocks them; not only against that which attacks them, but also against that which weakens them; not only against that which violates the Constitution, but also against that which outrages public decency. The jurisdiction of this truly sacred tribunal should be effective with respect to education and enlightenment, but advisory only with regard to penalties and punishments. But its annals or registers containing its acts and deliberations, which will, in effect, record the ethical precepts and the actions of citizens, should be the public books of virtue and vice. These books would be consulted for guidance by the people in elections, by the magistrates in their decisions, and by the judges in rendering verdicts. Such an institution, chimerical as it may appear, is infinitely more feasible than others which certain ancient and modern legislators have established with less benefit to mankind. . . .

I pray you, Legislators, receive with indulgence this profession of my political faith, these innermost yearnings of my heart, these fervent pleas, which, on behalf of the people, I venture to place before you. I pray you, grant to Venezuela a government preeminently popular, preeminently just, preeminently moral; one that will suppress anarchy, oppression, and guilt—a government that will usher in the reign of innocence, humanity, and peace; a government wherein the rule of inexorable law will signify the triumph of equality and freedom.

Gentlemen: you may begin your labors, I have finished mine.

4. THE AGE OF VIOLENCE

"There is no good faith in America," wrote Bolívar in 1829, "nor among the nations of America. Treaties are scraps of paper; constitutions, printed matter; elections, battles; freedom, anarchy; and life, a torment." Many Spanish American observers echoed Bolívar's cry of despair during the chaotic half century that followed independence. A fiery Chilean liberal, Francisco Bilbao (1823–1865), subjected republican government in Latin America to a penetrating critique in his essay America in Danger, *written in 1862.*

The conquest of power is the supreme goal. This leads to the immoral doctrine that "the end justifies the means. . . ." But since there are constitutional provisions that guarantee everyone his rights, and I cannot violate them, I invoke the system of "preserving the form."

If the Constitution declares: "Thought is free," I add: "within the limits established by law"—and since the law referred to is not the constitutional provision but one that was issued afterwards, I inscribe in it the exceptions of Figaro. "Thought is free," but there can be no discussion of dogma or exposition of systems that attack morality. And who is to judge? A commission or jury named in the last analysis by the authorities. And we have the colonial "censorship" reestablished under the guise of the freest institution of all, the jury. Sublime victory of duplicity! "But the form has been preserved."

The electoral power is the only power exercised by the "sovereign people," and it exercises this power not to make the laws but to select the persons who will make them. Very well. The majority vote, then is the expression . . . of the popular will.

That is the basis of republican power, and that is why free and legitimate elections establish the legitimacy of power.

The election is free, it is said; but what if I control the election returns? What if I, the established power, name the inspector of the election returns, if the law permits one to vote twenty times a day in the same election? What if I dominate the elections and frighten my opponents away with impunity?

What happens then? Why, the government is perpetuated in office, and the popular will is flouted and swindled.

But "the form has been preserved," and long live free elections!

"The domicile is inviolable," but I violate it, adding: "save in the cases determined by law." And the "cases" are determined in the last analysis by the party in power.

"The death penalty in political cases is abolished," but I shoot prisoners because I consider that these are not "political cases"; and since I am the infallible authority I declare that these political prisoners are bandits, and "the form has been preserved."

The Executive can be accused before the Chamber of Deputies and is subject to impeachment for one year after leaving office.

But that Chamber has been selected by me, and functions for one year after my departure. The persons who must judge me are my employees, my protégés, my creatures, my accomplices. Will they condemn me? No. Nor will they dare to accuse me. I am vindicated, and the "form" has saved me. Montt smiles over the bodies of his eight thousand victims. [The reference is

Francisco Bilbao, *La América en peligro* (Santiago de Chile, 1941), pp. 34–40. Excerpt translated by Benjamin Keen.

to the Chilean Liberal revolt of 1851, crushed by the administration of President Montt with a heavy loss of life.]

"The press is free." But I name the jury, and, backed by the authority of that free institution, I can accuse, harass, persecute; I can silence free speech. Then there reigns, absolute and sovereign, the opinion of one party. I spread the shroud of infamy over the corpse of the vanquished and cry: "The press is free!"

All liberal publicists, it can be said, accept the doctrine of "the separation of powers," as indispensable for the safety of the Republic.

But if the Executive has the power to name the judges; if the Executive participates in the framing of the laws; if the Executive can use the electoral law to name the members of Congress, what remains, in the last analysis, of the famous separation of powers?

"The guarantees established by this constitution cannot be suspended." But if I have the power to declare a province or the Republic in a state of siege, authorized to do so, as in Chile, by a "Council of State" appointed by the President, what security can a citizen have?

This miserable Machiavellianism has "preserved the forms" at the cost of plunging Chile into bloodshed and reaction for a space of thirty years.

There is discussion, the press is free; citizens come together, for they have the right of assembly; an enlightened public opinion almost unanimously clamors for reforms; preparations are made for elections that will bring to power representatives of the reform movement; and then the Executive Power declares the province or the Republic in a state of siege, and the suspended guarantees soar over the abyss of "legal" dictatorship and constitutional despotism!

And then? Either resignation or despair, or civil war, etc., etc. Then revolution raises its terrible banner, and blood flows in battles and on scaffolds. Respect for law and authority is lost, and only force holds sway, proclaiming its triumph to be that of liberty and justice. . . .

We have seen that our republican constitutions bear in themselves the germ of "legal despotism," a monstrous association of words that well describes the prostitution of the law. And since despotism, being "legal," is vindicated, the result is that the sentiment of justice is erased from the consciences of men.

Its place is taken by sophistry, duplicity, and intrigue, used to win power at all cost, for power legitimizes everything. . . .

Experience proves that in the legal combat of the parties the party in power always gains the victory. Experience shows that the party that conducts itself loyally is swindled and routed. What can be the result of this state of affairs? That justice is forgotten, and success becomes justice. To win, then, is the supreme desideratum.

Then the debased conscience alters even the countenances of men, and their words, in the expression of Talleyrand, serve only "to mask their thought."

Then chaos emerges. Words change their meaning, the tongues of men become as twisted as serpents, their speech grows pompous and hollow, the language of the press is like the tinsel thrown on a grave to adorn "a feast of worms," and the prostitution of the word crowns the evolution of the lie.

The conservative calls himself a progressive.

The liberal protests that he is a loyal Catholic.

The Catholic swears by liberty.

The democrat invokes dictatorship, like the rebels in the United States, and defends slavery.

The reactionary asserts that he wants reform.

The educated man proclaims the doctrine that "all is for the best in the best of all possible worlds."

The "civilized man" demands the extermination of the Indians or of the gauchos. [An ironic reference to D. F. Sarmiento's book, *Civilization and Barbarism: The Life of Juan Facundo Quiroga*; see next excerpt.]

The "man of principles" demands that principles yield to the principle of the public good. There is proclaimed, not the sovereignty of justice, presiding over the sovereignty of the people, but the sovereignty of "the end"— which legitimizes every "means."

The absolutist proclaims himself the savior of society.

And if it governs with coups d'état, states of siege, or permanent or transitory dictatorships, while the constitutional guarantees are flouted, mocked, or suppressed, the party in power will tell you: civilization has triumphed over barbarism, authority over anarchy, virtue over crime, truth over the lie. . . .

We have behind us a half century of independence from Spain. How many years of true liberty have any of the new nations enjoyed?

That is difficult to say; it is easier to reckon the years of anarchy and despotism that they have endured.

Shall Paraguay be the "model" with its forty years of dictatorship?

Or shall it be the Argentine Republic, with its provincial and national dictatorships, culminating in the twenty-year tyranny of Rosas?

And who knows what is to come?

Shall it be Chile, beginning with the dictatorship of O'Higgins and continuing with an intermittent dictatorship of thirty consecutive years?

Shall it be Bolivia, with its terrifying succession of sanguinary dictatorships?

Shall it be Peru, which has had more dictators than legal presidents?

Shall it be Ecuador, with its twenty years of the dictatorship of Flores?

Shall it be New Granada? And there one almost finds the exception, but Obando, the liberal legal president, was "overthrown for being a dictator."

Shall it be Venezuela, with its twenty years of Monagas?

Shall it be the little republics of Central America, and even Mexico? But this will suffice.

And these dictatorships have proclaimed all the principles.

The *pelucones* [or "bigwigs," the nickname given to Chilean conservatives by their liberal opponents in the period after the winning of independence], the conservatives, the reds, the liberals, the democrats, the Unitarians, the Federalists, all have embraced dictatorship. With the best of intentions the parties genially proclaim: "dictatorship in order to do good."

That is to say: despotism in order to secure liberty.

Terrible and logical contradiction!

5. FACUNDO: BARBARIAN *CAUDILLO*

The caudillo *appeared in many guises. A common type in the first period after independence was the barbarian chieftain, whose rule represented dictatorship in its crudest, most lawless form. A specimen of this breed was Juan Facundo Quiroga, master under Juan Manuel Rosas of the Argentine province of San Juan and the terrible hero of a memorable book by Domingo Faustine Sarmiento (1811–1888).*

Facundo, as he was long called in the interior, or General Don Facundo Quiroga, as he afterwards became, when society had received him into its bosom and victory had crowned him with laurels, was a stoutly built man of low stature, whose short neck and broad shoulders supported a well-shaped head, covered with a profusion of black and closely curling hair. His somewhat oval face was half buried in this mass of hair and an equally thick black, curly beard, rising to his cheek-bones, which by their prominence evinced a firm and tenacious will. His black and fiery eyes, shadowed by thick eyebrows, occasioned an involuntary sense of terror in those on whom they chanced to fall, for Facundo's glance was never direct, whether from habit or intention. With the design of making himself always formidable, he always kept his head bent down, to look at one from under his eyebrows, like the Ali Pacha of Monovoisin. The image of Quiroga is recalled to me by the Cain represented by the famous Ravel troupe, setting aside the artistic and statuesque attitudes, which do not correspond to his. To conclude, his features were regular, and the pale olive of his complexion harmonized well with the dense shadows which surrounded it.

The formation of his head showed, not withstanding this shaggy covering, the peculiar organization of a man born to rule. . . . Such natures develop according to the society in which they originate, and are either noble leaders

---

D. F. Sarmiento, *Life in the Argentine Republic in the Days of the Tyrants: Or Civilization and Barbarism*, trans. Mrs. Horace Mann (New York, 1868), pp. 76–90.

who hold the highest place in history, ever forwarding the progress of civilization, or the cruel and vicious tyrants who become the scourges of their race and time.

Facundo Quiroga was the son of an inhabitant of San Juan, who had settled in the Llanos of Lo Rioja, and there had acquired a fortune in pastoral pursuits. In 1779, Facundo was sent to his father's native province to receive the limited education, consisting only of the arts of reading and writing, which he could acquire in its schools. After a man has come to employ the hundred trumpets of fame with the noise of his deeds, curiosity or the spirit of investigation is carried to such an extent as to scent out the insignificant history of the child, in order to connect it with the biography of the hero: and it is not seldom that the rudiments of the traits characteristic of the historical personage are met amid fables invented by flattery. . . .

Many anecdotes are now in circulation relating to Facundo, many of which reveal his true nature. In the house where he lodged, he could never be induced to take his seat at the family table; in school he was haughty, reserved, and unsocial; he never joined the other boys except to head their rebellious proceedings or to beat them. The master, tired of contending with so untamable a disposition, on one occasion provided himself with a new and stiff strap, and said to the frightened boys, as he showed it to them, "This is to be made supple upon Facundo." Facundo, then eleven years old, heard this threat, and the next day he tested its value. Without having learned his lesson, he asked the headmaster to hear it himself, because, as he said, the assistant was unfriendly to him. The master complied with the request. Facundo made one mistake, then two, three, and four; upon which the master used his strap upon him. Facundo, who had calculated everything, down to the weakness of the chair in which the master was seated, gave him a buffet, upset him on his back, and, taking to the street in the confusion created by this scene, hid himself among some wild vines where they could not get him out for three days. Was not such a boy the embryo chieftain who would afterwards defy society at large? . . .

Facundo reappears later in Buenos Aires, where he was enrolled in 1810 as a recruit in the regiment of Arribeños, which was commanded by General Ocampo, a native of his own province, and afterwards president of Charcas. The glorious career of arms opened before him with the first rays of the sun of May; and doubtless, endowed with such capacity as his, and with his destructive and sanguinary instincts, Facundo, could he have been disciplined to submit to civil authority and ennobled in the sublimity of the object of the strife, might some day have returned from Peru, Chile, or Bolivia, as a General of the Argentine Republic, like so many other brave gauchos who began their careers in the humble position of a private soldier. But Quiroga's rebellious spirit could not endure the yoke of discipline, the order of the barrack, or the delay of promotion. He felt his destiny to be to rule, to rise at a single leap, to create for himself, without assistance, and in spite of a hostile and civilized society, a career of his own, combining bravery and crime, government and disorganization. He was subsequently recruited into the army of the Andes, and enrolled in the Mounted Grenadiers. A lieutenant named Garcia took him for an assistant, and very soon desertion left a vacant place in those glorious files. Quiroga, like Rosas, like all the vipers that have thriven under the shade of their country's laurels, made himself notorious in after-life by his hatred for the soldiers of Independence, among whom both the men above named made horrible slaughter.

Facundo, after deserting from Buenos Aires, set out for the interior with three comrades. A squad of soldiery overtook him; he faced the pursuers and engaged in a real battle with them, which remained undecided for awhile, until, after having killed four or five men, he was at liberty to continue his journey, constantly cutting his way through detachments of troops which here and there opposed his progress, until he arrived at San Luis. He was, at a later day, to traverse the same route with a handful of men to disperse armies instead of detachments, and proceed to the famous citadel of Tucumán to blot out the last remains of Republicanism and civil order.

Facundo now reappears in the Llanos, at his father's house. At this period occurred an event which is well attested. Yet one of the writers whose manuscripts I am using, replies to an inquiry about the matter, "that to the extent of his knowledge Quiroga never attempted forcibly to deprive his parents of money," and I could wish to adopt this statement, irreconcilable as it is with unvarying tradition and general consent. The contrary is shocking to relate. It is said that on his father's refusal to give him a sum of money which he had demanded, he watched for the time when both parents were taking an afternoon nap to fasten the door of the room they occupied, and to set fire to the straw roof, which was the usual covering of the building of the Llanos! [The author afterwards learned that Facundo related this story to a company of ladies, and one of his own early acquaintances testified to his having given his father a blow on one occasion.]

But what is certain in the matter is that his father once requested the governor of La Rioja to arrest him in order to check his excesses, and that Facundo, before taking flight from the Llanos, went to the city of La Rioja, where that official was to be found at the time, and coming upon him by surprise, gave him a blow, saying as he did so, "You have sent, sir, to have me arrested. There, have me arrested now!" On which he mounted his horse and set off for the open country at a gallop. At the end of a year he again showed himself at his father's house, threw himself at the feet of the old man whom he had used so ill, and succeeded amid the sobs of both, and the son's assurances of his reform in reply to the father's recriminations, in reestablishing peace, although on a very uncertain basis.

But no change occurred in his character and disorderly habits; races, gambling parties, and expeditions into the country were the occasions of new acts of violence, stabbings, and assaults on his part, until he at length made himself intolerable to all, and rendered his own position very unsafe. Then a great thought which he announced without shame got hold of his mind. The deserter from the Arribeños regiment, the mounted grenadier who refused to make himself immortal at Chacabuco or Maipú, determined to join the *montonera* of Ramírez, the off shoot from that led by Artigas, whose renown for crime and hatred for the cities on which it was making war, had reached the Llanos, and held the provincial government in dread. Facundo set forth to join those buccaneers of the pampa. But perhaps the knowledge of his character, and of the importance of the aid which he would give to the destroyers, alarmed his fellow provincials, for they informed the authorities of San Luis, through which he was to pass, of his infernal design. Dupuis, then (1818) governor, arrested him, and for some time he remained unnoticed among the criminals confined in the prison. This prison of San Luis, however, was to be the first step in his ascent to the elevation which he subsequently attained. San Martín had sent to San Luis a great number of Spanish officers of all ranks from among the prisoners taken in Chile. Irritated by their humiliations and sufferings or thinking it possible that the Spanish forces might be assembled again this party of prisoners rose one day and opened the doors of the cells of the common criminals, to obtain their aid in a general escape. Facundo was one of these criminals, and as soon as he found himself free from prison, he seized an iron bar of his fetters, split the skull of the very Spaniard who had released him, and passing through the group of insurgents, left a wide path strewn with the dead. Some say that the weapon he employed was a bayonet, and that only three men were killed by it. Quiroga, however, always talked of the iron bar of the fetters, and of fourteen dead men. This may be one of the fictions with which the poetic imagination of the people adorns the types of brute force they so much admire; perhaps the tale of the iron bar is an Argentine version of the jaw-bone of Samson, the Hebrew Hercules. But Facundo looked upon it as a crown of glory, in accordance with his idea of excellence, and whether by bar or bayonet, he succeeded, aided by other soldiers and prisoners whom his example encouraged, in suppressing the insurrection and reconciling society to himself by this act of bravery, and placing himself under his country's protection. Thus his name spread everywhere, ennobled and cleansed, though with blood, from the stains which had tarnished it.

Facundo returned to La Rioja covered with glory, his country's creditor: and with testimonials of his conduct, to show in the Llanos, among gauchos, the new titles which justified the terror his name began to inspire; for there is something imposing, something which subjugates and controls others in the man who is rewarded for the assassination of fourteen men at one time. . . .

Something still remains to be noticed of the previous character and temper of this pillar of the Confederation. An illiterate man, one of Quiroga's companions in childhood and youth, who has supplied me with many of the above facts, sends me the following curious statements in a manuscript describing

Quiroga's early years: "His public career was not preceded by the practice of theft; he never committed robbery even in his most pressing necessities. He was not only fond of fighting, but would pay for an opportunity, or for a chance to insult the most renowned champion in any company. He had a great aversion to respectable men. He never drank. He was very reserved from his youth, and desired to inspire others with awe as well as with fear, for which purpose he gave his confidants to understand that he had the gift of prophecy, in short a soothsayer. He treated all connected with him as slaves. He never went to confession, prayed, or heard mass; I saw him once at mass after he became a general. He said of himself that he believed in nothing." The frankness with which these words are written prove their truth. . . .

Facundo is a type of primitive barbarism. He recognized no form of subjection. His rage was that of a wild beast. The locks of his crisp black hair, which fell in meshes over his brow and eyes, resembled the snakes of Medusa's head. Anger made his voice hoarse, and turned his glances into dragons. In a fit of passion he kicked out the brains of a man with whom he had quarreled at play. He tore off both the ears of a woman he had lived with, and had promised to marry, upon her asking him for thirty dollars for the celebration of the wedding; and laid open his son Juan's head with an axe, because he could not make him hold his tongue. He violently beat a beautiful young lady at Tucumán, whom he failed either to seduce or to subdue, and exhibited in all his actions a low and brutal yet not a stupid nature, or one wholly without lofty aims. Incapable of commanding noble admiration, he delighted in exciting fear; and this pleasure was exclusive and dominant with him to the arranging [of] all his actions so as to produce terror in those around him, whether it was society in general, the victim on his way to execution, or his own wife and children. Wanting ability to manage the machinery of civil government, he substituted terror for patriotism and self sacrifice. Destitute of learning, he surrounded himself with mysteries, and pretended to a foreknowledge of events which gave him prestige and reputation among the commonalty, supporting his claims by an air of impenetrability, by natural sagacity, an uncommon power of observation, and the advantage he derived from vulgar credulity.

The repertory of anecdotes relating to Quiroga, and with which the popular memory is replete, is inexhaustible; his sayings, his expedients, bear the stamp of an originality which gives them a certain Eastern aspect, a certain tint of Solomonic wisdom in the conception of the vulgar. Indeed, how does Solomon's advice for discovering the true mother of the disputed child differ from Facundo's method of detecting a thief in the following instances:

An article had been stolen from a band, and all endeavors to discover the thief had proved fruitless. Quiroga drew up the troop and gave orders for the cutting of as many small wands of equal length as there were soldiers; then, having had these wands distributed one to each man, he said in a confident voice, "The man whose wand will be longer than the others tomorrow morning is the thief." Next day the troop was again paraded, and Quiroga proceeded to inspect the wands. There was one whose wand was, not longer but shorter than the others. "Wretch!" cried Facundo, in a voice which over-powered the man with dismay, "it is thou!" And so it was; the culprit's confusion was proof of the fact. The expedient was a simple one; the credulous gaucho, fearing that his wand would really grow, had cut off a piece of it. But to avail one's self of such means, a man must be superior in intellect to those about him, and must at least have some knowledge of human nature.

Some portions of a soldier's accoutrements having been stolen and all inquiries having failed to detect the thief, Quiroga had the troops paraded and marched past him as he stood with crossed arms and a fixed, piercing, and terrible gaze. He had previously said, "I know the man," with an air of assurance not to be questioned. The review began, many men had passed, and Quiroga still remained motionless, like the statue of Jupiter Tonans or the God of the Last Judgment. All at once he descended upon one man, and said in a curt and dry voice, "Where is the saddle?" "Yonder, sir," replied the other, pointing to a thicket. "Ho! four fusileers!" cried Quiroga. What revelation was this? that of terror and guilt made to a man of sagacity.

On another occasion, when a gaucho was answering to charges of theft which had been brought against him, Facundo interrupted him with the words, "This rogue has begun to lie. Ho, there! a hundred lashes!" When the criminal had been taken away, Quiroga said to someone present, "Look you, my master, when a gaucho moves his foot while talking, it is a sign he is telling lies." The lashes extorted from the gaucho the confession that he had stolen a yoke of oxen.

At another time he was in need of a man of resolution and boldness to whom he could entrust a dangerous mission. When a man was brought to him for this purpose, Quiroga was writing; he raised his head after the man's presence had been repeatedly announced, looked at him and returned to his writing with the remark, "Pooh! that is a wretched creature. I want a brave man and a venturesome one!" It turned out to be true that the fellow was actually good for nothing.

Hundreds of such stories of Facundo's life, which show the man of superior ability, served effectually to give him a mysterious fame among the vulgar, who even attribute superior powers to him.

6. MEXICO CITY UNDER SANTA ANNA

Most descriptions of caudillo *rule stress the brutality and instability of the period. In this 1841 letter, the Scottish-born wife of the Spanish ambassador, Frances Calderón de la Barca, provides an unexpected glimpse into the rich cultural and institutional life of Mexico City under Santa Anna. The practice of upper-class women touring and even sponsoring charitable institutions was an old one that transcended the political feuding and periodic* pronunciamientos *(revolts) that occupied their male counterparts. Toward the end of the excerpt, the letter refers to Santa Anna's wooden leg. Lost in battle against foreign invaders, the leg was a symbol, at least to the* caudillo's *loyal followers, of his sacrifice for the nation.*

A great *función* was given in the opera in honor of his excellency [Santa Anna]. The theatre was most brilliantly illuminated with wax lights. Two principal boxes were thrown into one for the president and his suite, and lined with crimson and gold, with draperies of the same. The staircase leading to the second tier where this box was, was lighted by and *lined* all the way up with rows of footmen in crimson and gold livery. A crowd of gentlemen stood waiting in the lobby for the arrival of the hero of the fête. He came at last in regal state, carriages and outriders at full gallop; himself, staff and suite, in splendid uniform. As he entered, Señor Roca presented him with a libretto of the opera, bound in red and gold. We met the great man *en face*, and he stopped, and gave us a cordial recognition. Two years have made little change in him in appearance. He retains the same interesting, resigned, and rather melancholy expression; the same quiet voice, and grave but agreeable manner; and surrounded by pompous officers, he alone looked quiet, gentlemanly, and high bred. The theatre was crowded to suffocation; boxes, pit, and galleries. There was no applause as he entered. One solitary voice in the pit said "Viva Santa Anna!" but it seemed checked by a slight movement of disapprobation, scarcely amounting to a murmur.

The generals, in their scarlet and gold uniforms, sat like peacocks surrounding Santa Anna, who looked modest and retiring, and as if quite unaccustomed to the public gaze! The boxes were very brilliant—all the diamonds taken out for the occasion. His Excellency is by no means indifferent to beauty—*tout au contraire*; yet I dare say his thoughts were this night of things more warlike and less fair.

Let all this end as it may, let them give everything whatever name is most popular, the government is now a military dictatorship. Señor ____ calls this revolution "the apotheosis of egotism transformed into virtue"; and it must be confessed, that in most of the actors, it has been a mere calculation of personal interests.

The following day we visited . . . the *Hospital de Jesus*.. . .

The establishment, as an hospital, is much finer, and the building infinitely handsomer than the other. The director, a physician, led us first into his own apartments, as the patients were dining, and afterwards showed us

Frances Calderón de la Barca, "Letter the Forty-Seventh," in *Life in Mexico, During a Residence of Two Years in That Country* (London: Chapman & Hall, 1843).

through the whole establishment. The first large hall, into which we were shown, is almost entirely occupied by soldiers, who had been wounded during the *pronunciamiento*. One had lost an arm, another a leg, and they looked sad and haggard enough, though they seemed perfectly well attended to, and, I dare say, did anything but *bless* the revolutions that brought them to that state, and with which they had nothing to do; for your Mexican soldier will lie down on his mat at night, a loyal man, and will waken in the morning and find himself a *pronunciado*. Each one had a separate room, or at least a compartment divided by curtains from the next; and in each was a bed, a chair, and a small table; this on one side of the long hall. The other was occupied by excellent hot and cold baths. We then visited the women's apartment, which is on a similar plan. Amongst the patients is an unfortunate child of eight years old, who in the *pronunciamiento* had been accidentally struck by a bullet, which entered her left temple and came out below the right eye, leaving her alive. The ball was extracted, and a portion of the brain came out at the wound. She is left blind, or nearly so, having but a faint glimmering of light. They say she will probably live, which seems impossible. She looks like a galvanized corpse—yet must have been a good-looking child. Notwithstanding the nature of her wound, her reason has not gone, and she sat upright in her little bed, with her head bandaged, and her fixed and sightless eyes, she answered meekly and readily to all the questions we put to her. Poor little thing! she was shocking to look at; one of the many innocent beings whose lives are to be rendered sad and joyless by this revolution. The doctor seemed very kind to her.

We went in the evening to visit the *Cuna*, which is not a fine building, but a large, healthy, house. At the door, where there are a porter and his wife, the babies are now given in. Formerly they were put in at the *reja*, at the window of the porter's lodge; but this had to be given up, in consequence of the tricks played by boys or idle persons, who put in dogs, cats, or dead animals. As we were going upstairs, we heard an old woman singing a cheerful ditty in an awfully cracked voice, and as we got a full view of her before she could see us, we saw a clean, old body sitting, sewing and singing, while a baby rolling on the floor in a state of perfect ecstasy, was keeping up a sort of crowing duet with her. She seemed delighted to see these ladies, who belong to the *Junta*, and led us to a large hall where a score of nurses and babies were performing a symphony of singing, hushing, crying, lullabying, and other nursery music. All along the room were little green painted beds, and both nurses and babies looked clean and healthy. The _____s knew every baby and nurse and directress by name. Some of the babies were remarkably pretty, and when he had admired them sufficiently, we were taken into the next hall, occupied by little girls of two, three, and four years old. They were all seated on little mats at the foot of their small green beds; a regiment of the finest and healthiest children possible; a directress in the room sewing. At our entrance, they all jumped up simultaneously, and surrounded us with the noisiest expressions of delight. One told me in a confidential whisper, that "Manuelita had thumped her own head, and had a pain in it"; but I could not see that Manuelita seemed to be suffering any acute agonies, for she made more noise than any of them. One little girl sidled up to me, and said in a most insinuating voice, "*Me llevas tu?*" "Will you take me away with you?" [F]or even at this early age they begin to have a glimmering idea that those whom the ladies choose from amongst them are particularly favored. We stayed some time with them, and admired their healthy, happy and well-fed appearance; and then proceeded to the apartment of the boys; all little things of the same age, sitting ranging in a row like senators in congress, and, strange to say, much quieter and graver than the female babies; but this must have been from shyness, for before we came away, we saw them romping in great style. The directresses seem good respectable women, and kind to the children, who, as I mentioned before, are almost all taken away and brought up by rich people, before they have time to know that there is anything peculiar or unfortunate in their situation. After this adoption, they are completely on a level with the other children of the family—an equal portion is left them, and although their condition is never made a secret of, they frequently marry as well as their adopted brothers and sisters.

Those who are opposed to this institution, are so on the plea that it encourages and facilitates vice. That the number of children in the hospital is a proof that much vice and much poverty do exist, there is no doubt; that by enabling the vicious to conceal there guilt, or by relieving the poor from their burden, it encourages either vice or idleness, is scarcely probable. But even were it so, the certain benefits are so immense, when laid in the balance with the possible evils, that they cannot be put in competition. The poor mother who leaves her child at the *Cuna*, would she not abandon it to a worse fate, if this institution did not exist? If she does so to conceal her disgrace is it not seen that a woman will stop at no cruelty, to obtain this end? as exposure of her infant, even murder? and that, strong as maternal love is, the dread of the world's scorn has conquered it? If poverty be the cause, surely the misery must be great indeed, which induces the poorest beggar or the most destitute of the Indian women (whose love for their children amounts to a passion) to part with her child; and though it is suspected that the mother who has left her infant at the *Cuna*, has occasionally got herself hired as a nurse, that she may have the pleasure of bringing it up, it seems to me that no great evil can arise, even from that.

These orphans are thus rescued from the contamination of vice, from poverty, perhaps from the depths of depravity; perhaps their very lives are saved, and great sin prevented. Hundreds of innocent children are thus placed under the care of the first and best ladies in the country, and brought up to be worthy members of society.

Another day we devoted to visiting a different and more painful scene—the *Acordada*, or public jail; a great solid building, spacious, and well ventilated. For this also there is *Junta*, or society of ladies of the first families, who devote themselves to teaching the female malefactors. It is painful and almost startling to see the first ladies in Mexico familiarly conversing with and embracing women who have been guilty of the most atrocious crimes; especially of murdering their husbands; which is the chief crime of the female prisoners. There are no bad faces amongst them; and probably not one who has committed a premeditated crime. A moment of jealousy during intoxication, violent passions without any curb, suddenly aroused and as suddenly extinguished, have led to these frightful results. We were first shown into a large and tolerably clean apartment, where were the female prisoners who are kept apart as being of a more *decent family*, than the rest. Some were lying on the floor, others working—some were well dressed, others dirty and slovenly. Few looked sad; most appeared careless and happy, and *none* seemed ashamed. Amongst them were some of the handsomest faces I have seen in Mexico. One good-looking common woman, with a most joyous and benevolent countenance, and lame, came up to salute the ladies. I inquired what she had done. "Murdered her husband, and buried him under the brick floor!" Shade of Lavater! It is some comfort to hear that their husbands were generally such brutes, they deserved little better! Amongst others confined here is the wife, or rather the widow, of a governor of Mexico, who made away with her husband. We did not see her, and they say she generally keeps out of the way when strangers come. One very pretty and coquettish little woman, with a most intellectual face, and very superior-looking, being in a fact a relation of Count ____'s, is in jail on suspicion of having poisoned her lover. A beautiful young creature, extremely like Mrs. ____, of Boston, was among the prisoners. I did not hear what her crime was. We were attended by a woman who has the title of *Presidenta*, and who, after some years of good conduct, has not the charge of her fellow-prisoners—but she also murdered her husband! We went upstairs, accompanied by various of the distinguished criminals, to the room looking down upon the chapel, in which room the ladies give them instruction in reading, and in the Christian doctrine. With the time which they devote to these charitable offices, together with their numerous devotional exercises, and the care which their houses and families require, it cannot be said that the life of a Mexican señora is an idle one; nor, in such cases, can it be considered a useless one.

We then descended to the lower regions, where, in a great, damp, vaulted gallery, hundreds of unfortunate women of the lowest class, were occupied in *travaux forces* [forced labor]—not indeed of a very hard description. These were employed in baking tortillas for the prisoners. Dirty, ragged, and miserable-looking creatures there were in the dismal vaults, which looked like purgatory, and smelt like—Heaven knows what! But, as I have frequently had occasion to observe in Mexico, the sense of smell is a doubtful blessing. Another large hall near this, which the prisoners were employed in cleaning and sweeping, has at least fresh air, opening on one side into a court, where poor little children, the saddest sight there, were running about—the children of the prisoners.

Leaving the side of the building devoted to the women, we passed on to another gallery, looking down upon several hundreds of male prisoners, unfortunately collected together without any reference to the nature of their crime; the midnight murderer with the purloiner of a pocket-handkerchief; the branded felon with the man guilty of some political offence, the debtor with the false coiner; so that many a young and thoughtless individual whom a trifling fault, the result of ignorance or of unformed principles, has brought hither, must leave this place wholly contaminated and hardened by bad example and vicious conversation. Here there were indeed some ferocious, hardened-looking ruffians—but there were many mild, good-humored faces; and I could see neither sadness not a trace of shame on any countenance; indeed they all seemed much amused by seeing so many ladies. Some were stretched full-length on the ground, doing nothing; other were making rolls for hats, of different colored beads, such as they wear here, of little baskets for sale; whilst others were walking about alone, or conversing in groups. This is the first prison I ever visited, therefore I can compare it with no other; but the system must be wrong which makes no distinction between different degrees of crime. These men are the same *forçats* [forced laborers] whom we daily see in chains, watering the Alameda or Paséo, or mending the streets. Several hundreds of prisoners escaped from the Acordada in the time of the *pronunciamiento*—probably the worst amongst them—yet *half the city* appears to be here now. We were shown the rows of cells for criminals whom it is necessary to keep in solitary confinement, on account of disorderly behavior—also the apartments of the directors.

In passing downstairs, we came upon a group of dirty-looking soldiers, busily engaged in playing at cards. The *alcalde*, who was showing us through the jail, dispersed them all in a great rage, which I suspected was partly assumed for our edification. We then went into the chapel, which we had seen from above, and which is handsome, and well kept. In the sacristy is a horrid and appropriate image of the bad thief. We were also shown a small room off the chapel, with a confessional, where the criminal condemned to die spends three days preceding his execution with a padre chosen for that purpose. What horrid confessions what lamentations and despair that small dark chamber must have witnessed! There is nothing in it but an altar, a crucifix, and a bench. I think the custom is a very humane one.

We felt glad to leave this palace of crimes, and to return to the fresh air.

The following day we went to visit *San Hipólito*, the insane hospital for men, accompanied by the director, a fine old gentleman, who has been a great deal abroad, and who looks like a French marquis of the *ancien régime*. I was astonished, on entering, at the sweet and solitary beauty of the large stone courts, with orange trees and pomegranates now in full blossom, and the large fountains of beautifully clear water. There must be something soothing in such a scene to the senses of these most unfortunate of God's creatures. They were sauntering about, quiet and for the most part sad; some stretched out under the trees, and others gazing on the fountain; all apparently very much under the control of the administrator, who was formerly a monk, this *San Hipólito* being a dissolved convent of that order. The system of giving occupation to the insane is not yet introduced here.

On entering, we saw rather a distinguished-looking, tall and well-dressed gentleman, whom we concluded to be a stranger who had come to see the establishment, like ourselves. We were therefore somewhat startled when he advanced towards us with long strides, and in an authoritative voice shouted out, "Do you know who I am? I am the Deliverer of Guatemala." The administrator told us he had just been taken up, was a Frenchman, and in a state of furious excitement. He continued making a tremendous noise, and other madmen seemed quite ashamed of him. One unhappy-looking creature, with a pale, melancholy face, and his arms stretched out above his head, was embracing a pillar, and when asked what he was doing, replied that he was "making sugar."

We were led into the dining-hall, a long airy apartment, provided with benches and tables, and from thence into a most splendid kitchen, high vaulted, and receiving air from above, a kitchen that might have graced the castle of some feudal baron, and looked as if it would most surely last as long as men shall eat and cooks endure. Monks at *San Hipólito*! how many a smoking dinner, what viands steaming and savory must have issued from this noblest of kitchens to your refectory next door.

The food for the present inmates, which two women were preparing, consisted of meat and vegetables, soup and sweet things; excellent meat, and well-dressed *frijoles*. A poor little boy, imbecile, deaf and dumb, was seated there cross-legged, in a sort of wooden box; a pretty child, with a fine color, but who has been in this state from his infancy. The women seemed very kind to him, and he a placid, contented expression on his face; but took no notice of us when we spoke to him. Strange and unsolvable problem, what ideas pass through the brain of that child!

When we returned to the dining-hall, the inmates of the asylum, to the number of ninety or a hundred, were all sitting at dinner, ranged quietly on the benches, eating with wooden spoons out of wooden bowls. The poor hero of Guatemala was seated at the lower end of the table, tolerably tranquil. He started up on seeing us, and was beginning some furious explanations, but was prevented by his neighbor, who turned round with an air of great superiority, saying, "He's mad!" at which the other smiled with an air of great contempt, and looking at us said, "He calls me mad!" The man of the pillar was eyeing his soup, with his arms as before, extended above his head. The director desired him to eat his soup, upon which he slowly and reluctantly brought down one arm, and ate a few spoonfuls. "How much sugar have you made to-day?" asked the director. "Fifty thousand kingdoms!" said the man. . . .

The director then led us to the gallery above, where are more cells, and the terrible "*Cuarto Negro*," the Black Chamber; a dark, round cell, about twelve feet in circumference, with merely a slit in the wall for the admission of air. The floor is thickly covered with straw, and the walls are entirely covered with soft stuffed cushions. Here the most furious madman is confined on his arrival, and whether he throws himself on the floor, or dashes his head against the wall, he can do himself no injury. In a few days, the silence and the darkness soothe his fury, he grows calmer, and will eat the food that is thrust through the aperture in the wall. From this he is removed to a common cell, with more light and air; but until he has become tranquil, he is not admitted into the court amongst the others.

From this horrible, though I suppose necessary den of suffering, we went to the apartments of the administrator, which have a fine view of the city and the volcanoes, and saw a virgin, beautifully carved in wood, and dressed in white satin robes, embroidered with small diamonds. On the ground was a little dog, dying, having just fallen off from the *azotea*, an accident which happens to dogs here not infrequently. We then went up to the *azotea*, which looks into the garden of San Fernando and of our last house, and also into the barracks of the soldiers, who, as _____ observed, are more dangerous madmen than those who are confined. Some rolled up in their dirty yellow cloaks, and others standing in their shirt-sleeves, and many without either; they were as dirty-looking a set of military heroes as one would wish to see. When we came downstairs again, and had gone through the court, and were passing the last cell, each of which is only lighted by an aperture in the thick stone wall, a pair of great black eyes glaring through, upon a level with mine, startled me infinitely. The eyes, however, glared upon vacancy. The face was thin and sallow, the beard long and matted, and the cheeks sunken. What long years of suffering appeared to have passed over that furrowed brow! I wish I had not seen it. . . .

Having stopped in the carriage on the way home, at a shoemaker's, we saw *Santa Anna's leg* lying on the counter, and observed it with due respect, as the prop of a hero. With this leg, which is fitted with a very handsome boot, he reviews his troops next Sunday, putting his *best foot foremost*; for generally he merely wears an unadorned wooden leg. The shoemaker, a Spaniard, whom I can recommend to all customers as the most impertinent individual I ever encountered, was arguing, in a blustering manner, with a gentleman who had brought a message from the general, desiring some alteration in the boot: and wound up by muttering, as the messenger left the shop, "He shall either wear it as it is, or review the troops next Sunday without his leg!"

7. DOM PEDRO II: A POLITICAL PORTRAIT

Historians and biographers of Dom Pedro II (1825–1891) have written sufficiently concerning his amiable, democratic traits, his patronage of arts and letters, and his scholarly tastes and accomplishments. But Dom Pedro's best claim to fame is the skill with which he guided the Brazilian ship of state for almost half a century. Joaquim Nabuco (1849–1910), famous Brazilian abolitionist, diplomat, and historian, paid tribute to the emperor's political wisdom in his monumental biography of his own statesman-father, first published in 1897.

The commanding figure of the Second Empire was that of the Emperor himself. To be sure, he did not govern directly and by himself; he respected the Constitution and the forms of the parliamentary system. But since he determined the fate of every party and every statesman, making or unmaking ministries at will, the sum of power was effectively his. Cabinets had short and precarious lives, holding office only as long as it pleased the Emperor. Under these conditions there was but one way to govern, and that was in agreement with him. To oppose his plans, his policies, was to invite dismissal. One or another minister might be ready to quit the government and the office on whose duties he had just entered, but cabinets clung to life, and the party imposed obedience to the royal will from love of offices, of patronage. So the ministers passively assented to the role that the Emperor assigned to them. The senate, the council of state, lived by his favor and grace. No leader wished to be "incompatible." He alone represented tradition and continuity in government. Since cabinets were short-lived and he was permanent, only he could formulate policies that required time to mature. He alone could wait, temporize, continue, postpone, sowing in order to reap in due season. Whenever he needed to display his own unquestioned authority he shunted the most important statesmen away from the throne. . . . Having these examples before them, younger men learned that without the Emperor's confidence and approval they were nothing. . . .

On one point he had strong feelings and was very sensitive: He must not be suspected of having favorites. . . . No one but he knew what the next day

---

Joaquim Nabuco, *Um estadista do imperio: Nabuco de Araujo, sua vida, suas opiniões, sua epoca*, 2 vols. (São Paulo, 1936), 2:374–385. Excerpt translated by Benjamin Keen.

would bring. He set the course of administration, now steering in one direction, now in another; and only he knew the true course of the ship of state. . . .

The work of government was carried on in this fashion; what are the Emperor's wishes, what does the emperor not wish? The statesman who would not adjust to these conditions condemned himself to complete failure. For this reason the advocates of a new idea accomplished nothing until they had awakened the interest of the Emperor and gained his sympathy. Once that was attained, all parties and governments followed the Emperor's lead like an avalanche. So it was with everything, especially in the great question of his reign, slavery; the pronouncements of Rio-Branco in 1871, of Dantas in 1884, of Cotegipe in 1885, only came after Dom Pedro had been won over to their point of view. In 1888 Cotegipe took advantage of the absence of the Emperor to carry out immediate abolition, but if the Emperor had been in the country he also would have been summoned to solve the problem, though in another way.

His power, however, was a spontaneous, natural phenomenon, the result of our social and political condition. If that power had no check it was not because of the Emperor, but because it was impossible to have free elections with a people like the Brazilian, and because free elections would only have made the electorate more attached to the government, whatever it might be—that is, to the power that had the right to make appointments. That is why his power was indestructible. In effect, there was only one means—short of a republican revolution—of compelling him to surrender his personal power: to confront the omnipotent Crown with independent chambers. But that was just the impossibility; that was the great illusion of the propagandists for direct elections, and afterward of the statesmen who expected direct elections to bring about a regeneration of the representative system. . . . When, after long resisting the project, the Emperor, who in the end always let himself be conquered—but professing to be only conquered and not convinced— yielded . . . what were the consequences? That as a result of the first experiment in honest elections anarchy and corruption prevailed everywhere; that the parliament came to reflect the general sickness of the localities—the thirst for jobs and influence, the dependence on the government. . . .

The Emperor always exercised his power: (1) within the limits of the Constitution; (2) in accord with the fictions and usages of the English parliamentary system as adapted by our own parties; and (3) yielding always to public sentiment and opinion. "The honor of my reign can only consist in complying with the Constitution which I swore to obey." The distinguishing feature of his government was the sacrament of form; from the day on which his majority was proclaimed to that of his abdication he never abandoned his role of constitutional monarch. Then, too, the progress of affairs in his reign was not his work; he was only the clock, the regulator, that marked the time or gave the rhythm. In matters of politics, to be sure, the minister never proposed and the chambers never approved any measure that he had not sanctioned; it was he who sounded both sides of the channel that was being navigated. But the origin of his inspirations was to be found elsewhere. If everything that was deliberate and personal in his reign reflected the Emperor's directing will and consciousness, the march of events always proceeded ahead of the wishes of the imperial mover or moderator. Every day, everywhere, his individual action was annulled by the action of social forces over whose agents, reactions, and collisions he had no control. . . .

The Emperor inspired and directed, but he did not govern. He might check on every nomination, every decree, every word of his ministers, but the responsibility for their actions was theirs. He rarely intervened in the political and administrative machinery—the parties with their adherents and official hierarchies, their personnel and transactions. He did not even wish to know about the internal life of the parties, nor did he establish direct and personal relations with them, but only with the leaders who one day would be presidents of the council. We have seen how he proceeded with the latter: he always reserved the right to dismiss them when he chose; that right he always possessed. All ministries had their elements of disintegration. He could impede or facilitate the process of dissolution, as he pleased; there was always an anxious opposition party at his orders, awaiting a summons; within the ministerial camp itself there were rivalries to be used; and he always had at hand the instrument of dissolution. Throughout his reign, from 1840 to 1889, all the statesmen who served under him were conscious that their mandates were not final, their positions uncertain and dependent. . . . But even if their mandates were precarious, even if they entered upon their duties knowing that the first serious disagreement with the monarch must lead to their dismissal, nevertheless the Emperor scrupulously respected the sphere of ministerial action. Nor could the ministers complain of the observations made by the Emperor in the council, for in his role of devil's advocate he elucidated questions, clarified his nominations, deduced precedents, compared the reports brought to him from all quarters . . . lending to each administration the prestige of his high position and the assistance of his vast experience. At the same time he left to the ministers the political patronage, the distribution of jobs among their partisans, and the administration of affairs, including the realization of the ideas they had advocated while in the opposition. In many branches he hardly intervened at all—in the fields of justice and finance, for example.

That is why the most eminent men of the period were proud to hold those positions and competed for them, despite their uncertain tenure and the qualified nature of their mandates. It was from their number, from a small circle in parliament, that the Emperor always made his choices. He was, in fact, free only to alternate the parties, to pass from one group to the group in opposition, on the same conditions, choosing from what was always a league of chieftains the name that best pleased him at that juncture. Thus they were not royal ministers, creatures of the Palace; they were parliamentary ministers, like those of France in the reign of Louis Philippe, not like those of England in the reign of Queen Victoria. The Emperor could dismiss them, as the electorate dismisses them in the United Kingdom, but aside from this difference—that there was no electoral power capable of sustaining its representatives in the case of an appeal to the country—the ministerial mandate was the same. Yet to aspire to hold office, under existing conditions, was both honorable and legitimate. The Emperor was not to blame for the absence of free elections; the parties were infinitely more responsible for this condition than he, who had almost nothing to do with the abuses that corrupted the elections. The monarch did not degrade his ministers; he respected them, treated them with dignity. As a governor he sought only one glory for himself: to make Brazil a model of liberty among the nations. The truth about his reign is summed up in the epigram attributed to Ferreira Vianna: "The Emperor passed fifty years in maintaining the pretense that he ruled over a free people"—that is, in upholding Brazil's reputation before the world, concealing the general indifference of its citizenry toward public affairs, toward their rights and liberties; in practicing and cherishing the cult of the Constitution as the political divinity of the Empire.

If the Constitution was Brazil's Palladium, Parliament was its Forum; it was for seventy years the center of the political life of the country, the scene of struggles for power and liberty. It was not a great historical theater, to be sure, but Brazilians of the old colonial stocks—whatever the feelings of the new nationalities that may in time replace them—will always regard its ruins with veneration. Nothing would have been impossible there for a true political genius, endowed with real ambition and capable of making his ideals come true; unhappily, we never had a statesman who united to genius the qualities of ambition, independence, and will power. Had one existed, he would have found no obstacle in Dom Pedro II. *He* was not responsible for the degeneration of the political spirit of the chambers, in which once had risen men like Villela Barbosa, Vasconcellos, Alves Branco, and Paula Souza. It is absurd, when one observes that the majority of these men evolved from Conservatives into Liberals, in some cases, and from Liberals into Conservatives, in others, to suppose that it was the Emperor who determined these regular movements of opinion from one to another social pole. He was not the source of that skepticism, or indifference, or political lukewarmness, that replaced the ancient fervor, seriousness, and persistence of the epoch of solid and austere character. . . .

As with parliament, so with the council of state. A grand political conception was this council of state, one that even England might envy us, heard in all the great questions, guardian of the political traditions of the Empire, in which the opposition was called to collaborate in the wise government of the country, where the opposition had to reveal its plans, its alternatives, its mode of attacking the great problems whose solution fell to the lot of the ministry. This admirable product of the Brazilian genius, which complemented the other and equally admirable device of the Moderative Power, taken from Benjamin Constant, united about the Emperor the finest political talents of both sides, with all their accumulated experience, whenever it was necessary to confer about some serious public issue. It made the opposition, up to a certain point, a participant in the government of the country, the superintendent of its interests, the depository of the secrets of state.

That was the system of the Empire from 1840 to 1889. Political life went on in the chambers, in the press, in the provinces, as in England—but the parties did not display moderation, would not resign themselves to free elections; and as a result the last word belonged, willy-nilly, to the power that named the ministers, and not to the chambers from which they came. But the difference was hardly apparent, because the Emperor did not upset situations abruptly or capriciously, being always guided by public opinion or necessity. The fact is that this dual mechanism, monarchical-parliamentary, in which the monarch, as well as parliament, was a director, instead of being a kind of automaton moved by the chambers, ensured the tranquility and security of the country for four generations. Had the Emperor not had supreme direction, had he not been the independent arbiter of the parties, had he been limited to signing the decrees presented to him, had he been helpless to change the situation except through the effect of elections, his reign would very likely have been nothing more than a continuation of the regency or an anticipation of the Republic, and the imperial power, slave and instrument of the oligarchy, would have disappeared in a few years in the whirlpool of factions. Men intellectually superior to the Emperor, governing in his name, statesmen of greater capacity than his own, dispensing with his intervention and accustoming the country to regard the throne as vacant, would only have unleashed the forces of anarchy against themselves—while he, by the sagacious and moderate exercise of his role of constitutional emperor, kept his authority intact for half a century, whereas his father, the founder of the Empire, had only managed to stay in power for nine years, and the three regencies for four, two, and three years. . . .

There was much that was noble about this imperial policy, a policy of always pushing down the road that seemed straight to him, scorning the resistance that must be overcome, heedless of the resentments that might one day cut off his retreat. It was a decided and resolute policy that sought to prevent the formation of *maires du palais*, of personalities that might put him in the shade; that sought to extinguish the old revolutionary foci of the First Empire and of the Regency, military and political; that worked to extirpate feudalism, defiant of justice, superior to the law, an asylum for outlaws; that

struck down with one blow the powerful slave traffic; that later carried the
Five Years' War to the last stronghold of López in the Aquidaban; that attempted to achieve the gradual extinction of slavery in his realm; that sought
to subject the Church to the temporal power. But the inner and profound
characteristic of the royal policy was its indifference to the interests of the
throne. . . .

At bottom, Dom Pedro II had the same attitude toward the throne as
Dom Pedro I. Neither would maintain himself in power by bloodshed; they
would be emperors only as long as the country wanted them, only as long as
everyone wanted them; they would not haggle with the people. The one willingly made the sacrifice of May 13, 1822, when he implicitly renounced for
love of Brazil the crown of Portugal and its Empire; the other did not regret
years of self-abnegation and sacrifice for his country. Deposed, he went into
exile, burdened with debts which were nothing compared with the charities
that he had provided out of his civil list. And he paid these debts, in what was
perhaps the only case of its kind in the history of monarchy, by selling the
furniture and jewels of his palace at public auction, leaving to the State his library, his only wealth. . . .

The Emperor's persistent policy of indifference toward consequences was
thus a policy of tacit renunciation. It was not the policy of a sovereign convinced that the monarchy was necessary to the country and determined to regard it as his primary political interest. If they dismissed him, the fault would
not be his; an honorable settlement of this kind would do for him. In one of
his notes the Emperor wrote: "If the mistaken conduct of the monarchical
parties should give victory to the republicans, what will that prove? The
monarch will not on that account cease to be an honest and disinterested
man—disinterested in all that does not touch the welfare of his country,
which for him cannot exist outside the Constitution."

This voluntary dependence of his on the good will of the country was so
strong that, deposed from the throne, he did not once affirm his right to rule
by virtue of any of the old pacts—that of the Independence, of the Constitution, of April 7, of his majority, and much less by virtue of his traditional Portuguese right.

His was a policy entirely independent of circumstances, indifferent to the
personal consequences of his actions. It did not lean on any class, corporation, or party; it presumed the general good will; it rested on the spirit of
progress, on trust in his rectitude, on the movement imparted to society by
new reforms, on confidence in the general good sense, on disinterested support that would frustrate the intrigues of private interests and assure the
unimpeded progress of the nation. . . . If the result should prove the contrary,
the royal stoic would resign his throne without a murmur, regretting only for
love of Brazil—perhaps his only passion—that he must die in a foreign
land. . . .

PART SEVEN

CONSTRUCTING THE NATION-STATE

13

∾

REAL AND IMAGINED

COMMUNITIES

AFTER THE GREAT UPHEAVALS of the revolutionary period, followed by the long era of civil war and economic uncertainty, the second half of the nineteenth century witnessed a gradual consolidation of the newly independent nations. The cycle of dictatorship and revolution continued in many lands, but the revolutions became less frequent and less devastating. Old party lines dissolved as both Conservatives and Liberals united under the banner of progress. To a great extent, this much-delayed change of course was possible because Latin America had found a place in the international economic system. In the context of the neocolonial compact that defined the terms of the international division of labor, the export sectors of these economies expanded, with each country specializing in the production of a few primary products for the European market—guano in Peru, sugar in the Caribbean, beef and grain in Argentina, sugar and coffee in Brazil, copper in Chile, and so on. Free trade policies were almost unanimously adopted. A flood of foreign investment and an increase in available credit allowed for the modernization of the economic infrastructure of this system. New ports and, perhaps more importantly, new railways closed distances and transformed landscapes everywhere. However, Latin America's place in the international economic system directly depended on the price of its raw materials and foodstuffs, a fact that would have serious consequences for its future development.

The relative prosperity brought by growing trade with Europe allowed for greater political stability, an indispensable component of a new economic order that demanded peace and continuity. As the civil wars ended and the power of the *caudillos* ebbed, new political elites found a more receptive context for the long postponed projects of liberalism. In Mexico, where political instability lasted longer than in most other nations, the conservative tide gave way to a liberal one, allowing Benito Juárez to lead a *Reforma* [reform movement] that sought to install modern capitalism and a constitution that would protect civil liberties. Legislation on communal land was passed in areas where collective ownership (whether Indian or ecclesiastical) was an obstacle to private landownership. Juan B. Alberdi—an opponent of Rosas's dictatorship in the 1830s—became the inspiration for the new Argentine leadership in its promotion of immigration, education, and an economic system increasingly focused on the export of foodstuffs. European immigrants arrived in Brazil as well, attracted by the strong incentives offered by the government. As in other societies, port cities grew steadily, generating urban middle and lower classes that acquired increasingly demanding habits of consumption.

Yet these new winds of optimism, material progress, and liberal politics were at odds with certain harsh realities. Slavery continued in Brazil and Cuba, and its legacy would haunt these societies long after abolition. Indians were under oppression in Peru, Mexico, and many other societies. Indeed, the situation of rural villages worsened with the loss of communal land, exposing rural workers to the worst kind of debt peonage. The modern, educated, industrious communities (modeled on European or North American ideals) that Latin American liberal elites imagined for their nations were directly contradicted by structural elements of these societies. Despite the changes of the time, the challenges brought by the persistent gap between the communities as imagined and the realities of Latin American nations would remain.

1. ROADS TO THE FUTURE

Another important struggle between Spanish American liberalism and conservatism took place in Argentina between 1830 and 1852. Against the tyranny of Juan Manuel Rosas, representing the narrow interests and views of the great cattlemen of the province of Buenos Aires, the cultured youth of the capital rose in romantic but ineffective revolt. In 1852 Rosas fell, buried under the weight of the many enmities, domestic and foreign, that his policies had aroused. On the eve of the convention of 1853, summoned to draft a new constitution for Argentina, a book by Juan Bautista Alberdi (1810–1884) appeared, entitled Bases and Points of Departure for the Political Organization of the Argentine Republic, *which strongly influenced the work of the delegates. The following selections from this book illustrate the optimistic, "civilizing," and pragmatic temper of Argentine liberalism in the age of Alberdi, Mitre, and Sarmiento.*

Our youth should be trained for industrial life, and therefore should be educated in the arts and sciences that would prepare them for industry. The South American type of man should be one formed for the conquest of the great and oppressive enemies of our progress: the desert, material backwardness; the brutal and primitive nature of this continent.

We should therefore endeavor to draw our youth away from the cities of the interior, where the old order with its habits of idleness, conceit, and dissipation prevails, and to attract them to the coastal towns so that they may obtain inspiration from Europe, which extends to our shores, and from the spirit of modern life.

The coastal towns, by their very nature, are better schools than our pretentious universities. . . .

Industry is the grand means of promoting morality. By furnishing men with the means of getting a living you keep them from crime, which is generally the fruit of misery and idleness. You will find it useless to fill the minds of youths with abstract notions about religion if you leave them idle and poor. Unless they take monastic vows they will be corrupt and fanatical at the same time. England and the United States have arrived at religious morality by way of industry; Spain has failed to acquire industry and liberty by means of religion alone. Spain has never been guilty of irreligion, but that did not save her from poverty, corruption, and despotism. . . .

The railroad offers the means of righting the topsy-turvy order that Spain established on this continent. She placed the heads of our states where the feet should be. For her ends of isolation and monopoly this was a wise system; for our aims of commercial expansion and freedom it is disastrous. We must bring our capitals to the coast, or rather bring the coast into the interior of the continent. The railroad and the electric telegraph, the conquerors of space, work this wonder better than all the potentates on earth. The railroad changes, reforms, and solves the most difficult problems without decrees or mob violence.

It will forge the unity of the Argentine Republic better than all our congresses. The congresses may declare it "one and indivisible," but without the railroad to connect its most remote regions it will always remain divided and divisible, despite all the legislative decrees.

Without the railroad you will not have political unity in lands where distance nullifies the action of the central government. Do you want the government, the legislators, the courts of the coastal capital to legislate and judge concerning the affairs of the provinces of San Juan and Mendoza, for example? Bring the coast to those regions with the railroad, or vice versa; place those widely separated points within three days' travel of each other, at least.

Juan Bautista Alberdi, *Bases y puntos de partida para la organización política de la República Argentina* (Buenos Aires, 1951), pp. 62–63, 85–88, 90–92, 240–245. Excerpts translated by Benjamin Keen and the editors.

But to have the metropolis or capital a twenty days' journey away is little better than having it in Spain, as it was under the old system, which we overthrew for presenting precisely this absurdity. Political unity, then, should begin with territorial unity, and only the railroad can make a single region of two regions separated by five hundred leagues.

Nor can you bring the interior of our lands within reach of Europe's immigrants, who today are regenerating our coasts, except with the powerful aid of the railroads. They are or will be to the life of our interior territories what the great arteries are to the inferior extremities of the human body: sources of life. . . .

The means for securing railroads abound in these lands. Negotiate loans abroad, pledge your national revenues and properties for enterprises that will make them prosper and multiply. It would be childish to hope that ordinary revenues may suffice for such large expenditures; invert that order, begin with expenditures, and you will have revenues. If we had waited until we had sufficient revenues to bear the cost of the War of Independence against Spain, we would still be colonists. With loans we obtained cannons, guns, ships, and soldiers, and we won our independence. What we did to emerge from slavery, we should do to emerge from backwardness, which is the same as slavery; there is no greater title to glory than civilization.

But you will not obtain loans if you do not have national credit—that is, a credit based on the united securities and obligations of all the towns of the state. With the credits of town councils and provinces you will not secure railroads or anything notable. Form a national body, consolidate the securities of your present and future revenues and wealth, and you will find lenders who will make available millions for your local and general needs; for if you lack money today, you will have the means of becoming opulent tomorrow. Dispersed and divided, expect nothing but poverty and scorn. . . .

The great rivers, those "moving roads," as Pascal called them, are yet another means of introducing the civilizing action of Europe into the interior of our continent by means of her immigrants. But rivers that are not navigated do not, for practical purposes, exist. To place them under the exclusive domination of our poor banners is to close them to navigation. If they are to achieve the destiny assigned to them by God of populating the interior of the continent, we must place them under the law of the sea—that is, open them to an absolute freedom of navigation. . . .

Let the light of the world penetrate every corner of our republics. By what right do we maintain our most beautiful regions in perpetual brutality? Let us grant to European civilization what our ancient masters denied. In order to exercise their monopoly, the essence of their system, they gave only one port to the Argentine Republic; and we have preserved the exclusivism of the colonial system in the name of patriotism. No more exclusion or closure, whatever be the pretext that is invoked. No more exclusivism in the name of the Fatherland. . . .

What name will you give a land with 200,000 leagues of territory and a population of 800,000? A desert. What name will you give the constitution of that country? The constitution is a desert. Very well, the Argentine Republic is that country—and whatever its constitution, for many years it will be nothing more than the constitution of a desert.

But what constitution best fits a desert? One that will help to make it disappear: one that will enable it in the shortest possible time to cease being a desert and become a populated country. This, then, should and must be the political aim of the Argentine constitution and in general of all South American constitutions. The constitutions of unpopulated countries can have no other serious and rational end, at present and for many years to come, than to give the solitary and abandoned countryside the population it requires, as a fundamental condition for its development and progress.

Independent America is called upon to complete the work begun and left unfinished by the Spain of 1450. The colonization, the settlement of this world, new to this day despite the three hundred years that have passed since its discovery, must be completed by the sovereign and independent American states. The work is the same; only its authors are different. At that time Spain settled our lands; today we settle them ourselves. All our constitutions must be aimed at this great end. We need constitutions, we need a policy of creation, of settlement, of conquest of the solitude and the desert. . . .

The end of constitutional policy and government in America, then, is essentially economic. In America, to govern is to populate. . . .

How will the vivifying spirit of the European civilization come to our land? The same way it came in all periods: Europe will bring us its new spirit, its habits of industry, its practices of civilization, in the immigrations it will send to us.

Each European that comes to our shores brings us more civilization in the habits that he communicates to our inhabitants than are contained in many books of philosophy. Perfection that cannot be seen or touched is hard to understand. A laboring man is the most edifying catechism.

Do we want to plant and adapt in America, English freedom, French culture, the industriousness of the man of Europe and the United States? Let us bring living pieces of them in the customs of their inhabitants, and let's settle them here.

Do we want habits of order, discipline, and industry to prevail in our America? Let's fill it with people who will have those deep habits. They communicate; next to the European industrial attitude, the American industrial attitude will soon emerge. The plant of civilization doesn't spread from seeds. It's like the vine; it grows from a torn-off branch.

This is the only way America, today a desert, will turn into an opulent world in a short time. Reproduction alone is a very slow way.

If we want to see our states become bigger in a short time, let's bring from outside its element already formed and prepared.

Without big populations, there is no development of culture, no meaningful progress; everything is mean and small. Nations with half a million inhabitants, they may be according to their expanse of territory; but according to their population they'll be provinces, villages; and all of their things will carry the mean stamp of the province.

Important notice to South American men of state: primary schools, high schools, universities, are, in themselves, very poor ways to progress without the big enterprises of production—children of the great portions of men.

The population—the South American need that represents all the others— is the exact measure of the capacity of our governments. The minister of state who doesn't double the census of these peoples every ten years, has wasted his time in trifles and trivialities.

Make the *roto*, the *gaucho*, the *cholo*, the elemental unit of our popular masses, go through all the transformations of the best system of instruction; but in a hundred years you won't make out of him an English worker, who labors, consumes and lives with dignity and comfort. Put the million inhabitants that constitute the average population of these Republics, in the best possible place for education . . . will you have a great and flourishing state as a result? Certainly not: a million men in a territory that can accommodate 50 million, is that anything other than a pitifully small population?

This argument is made: educating our masses, we'll have order: having order the foreign population will come.

I'll tell you that this argument reverses the true method of progress. It will produce neither order nor popular education except through the influx of masses with deep seeded habits of order and good education.

Multiply the serious population, and you'll see those vain agitators, disregarded and alone, with their plans for frivolous revolts, in the middle of a world absorbed with grave occupations.

2. THE GUANO BOOM

During the second half of the tumultuous nineteenth century, many Latin American nations experienced a series of economic booms and busts. One of the earliest and longest of these booms was in guano, the manure of sea birds found in huge quantities on islands off the coast of Peru. The Peruvian guano boom lasted from the mid-1840s to around 1880 and, as the following excerpt from 1845 demonstrates, it sparked tremendous optimism, speculation, and corruption in both the public and private sectors. This "exposition" to the Peruvian congress by two disgruntled speculators also reveals some of the international economic implications (and pitfalls) of a classic boom cycle. Despite (and probably because of) the incredible profits generated by these booms, they contributed significantly to the region's seemingly chronic political, economic, and social instability—and, paradoxically, to its economic underdevelopment vis-à-vis western Europe and the United States.

Don Francisco Quiros and Don Aquiles Allier, both businessmen of this Capital [Lima], with due respect, present ourselves to Congress and declare: That it is today unquestionable that the idea of applying the use of guano from the [Pacific] islands to European agriculture will be a source of incalculable benefits for Peru and that in the near future, thanks to this idea, the Republic will be able to count on vast resources taken exclusively from a sector that had in the past always been sterile and unproductive for the national treasury.

His Excellency the President of the Republic did Peru a distinct service when, disregarding uniformed concerns, he agreed to admit the proposals that Don Francisco Quiros made to the government with the object of launching into the world of commerce this commodity hitherto unknown outside our coastal region. And it is now commonly acknowledged that this fertilizer enjoys wide acceptance in countries where it has been tried and in particular in Great Britain. It is impossible to calculate the immense profits that Peru will realize from a source of wealth over which it has almost exclusive control. . . .

While the African deposits supply the foreign markets, the extraction of Peruvian guano will remain largely paralyzed but will resume operations with vigor and benefit as soon as the strength and power of its adversary diminishes; such that Peru in probably a very short time will come to see itself in an advantageous position relative to African guano, which meanwhile will have spread the use of guano and made it one of the necessities of foreign agriculture.

Adopting for ourselves the prudent and measured approach that the English have established in Ceylon [Sri Lanka] for the extraction of cinnamon, and that General Santa Cruz established in Bolivia for that of cascarilla [a tree bark used as a popular tonic], it is undeniable that Peruvian guano will reach the highest price that agriculturalists can pay, and that with the extraction of several tons, small in comparison with what is currently taken from Africa to consumer markets, the Government will realize the double advantage of not squandering the nation's resources by using them up and of taking out sufficient resources to cover its necessary expenses.

Looking at the guano business in the immediate future, it seems beyond doubt that those who initiated this business and had the idea to give value to a commodity that until then was of no use to the Nation have rendered Peru a real service of some importance.

Francisco Quiros and Aquiles Allier, "Exposición que don Francisco Quiros y don Aquiles Allier elevan al soberano congreso" (Lima: Imprenta del Correo Peruano, 1845). Excerpt translated by the editors.

The men who have rendered this service are Don Francisco Quiros and Don Aquiles Allier, and Congress should know what has happened to them as a result.

The first thing to note it that when the lease for the guano deposits was agreed upon, neither we nor anyone else knew the price guano would bring in Europe. We had no idea that it would reach anything like the price of the first sales. Thus, when we received a letter, dated May 1841, from William Joseph Meyers and Company of Liverpool, advising us that given the appearance of the vegetation of some plants fertilized with a small quantity of guano, they hoped to sell the first shipment at twelve pounds sterling [per ton], Don Aquiles Allier wrote a letter to his Excellency President Don Agustin Gamarra, then in Lampa, to give him the unexpected news, adding that if these hopes were realized, our intention was that the Government would share in the profits of the transaction.

Having made know the circumstances, in order to show that we never intended to entrench ourselves behind a solemn contract, executed by a Government of undisputed constitutionality, or were so blinded by our rights, that we did not know that justice, equity, and our own consciences, obliged us to turn over to the Government the greater part of a contract whose profits reached a level that we had not calculated nor could have calculated at the time we negotiated it, and therefore, it was unnecessary with us to use arbitrariness or violence.

These are the circumstances that Don Aquiles Allier referred to when he said in an issue of "Comercio" published on that date, that there were written proofs that it had never been our intention to keep all the profits from the deal once the extent of that they would reach was made known. And we stand by our belief that if his Excellency President Gamarra had not met the honorable death that to Peru's misfortune ended his presidency, today we would not have to deplore the loss of our investment, the enormous damages we have suffered, and our notable reverse of fortune, but would have been celebrating a new just and rational contract that would take into account both the legitimate interests of the State and the respect that public agreement deserve and should maintain.

As soon as it was known in Lima from the Liverpool correspondence that arrived on the English ship "Dyron" that the guano had been sold for nearly 120 pesos per ton, a veritable fever took control of everyone's brain. We were attacked with considerable violence and Mr. Colmenares, the public prosecutor for the Supreme Court, even went to the extreme of asking for an embargo of Don Francisco Quiros's assets for having resorted to deceit and fraud, cheating the government in the contract they had negotiated with him.

Meanwhile, His Excellency Mr. Menendez had sent for Don Francisco Qiuros to work out with him an alteration of the lease, and in effect an agreement was reached with the President and Mr. Cano, the Finance Minister, for a new contract according to which the lease continued under the condition that the Government would take two thirds of the new profit of the guano and the other part would go to the contractors. They drew up a draft of this new contract and ordered a final version to be signed and published. Under these circumstances, his Excellency Mr. Menendez told Don Francisco Quiros that since the deal had been arranged and concluded, and the Government was now a business partner, it seemed natural and in order that they know as much about it as we did, and they hoped that we would allow them to review the correspondence on the matter that we had received from Europe.

Although the contract had not yet been signed, seeing that his Excellency Mr. Menendez asked us for the correspondence, and under the assumption that the deal was arranged and concluded as agreed upon, we believed it would be an insult to the President of the Republic to doubt his good faith and suspect him capable of reneging on the gentlemen's agreement, so we turned over all our correspondence.

In it, his Excellency Mr. Menendez and his Ministers, saw the notice given us by Messrs. William Joseph Meyers and Company verifying the sale of seven million tons of guano as soon as it arrived, two million at the price of eighteen pounds sterling, (or ninety pesos) and the other five thousand at a floating and conditional price subject to the market value of the commodity.

Reading the notice of these sales must have made a tremendous impression on his Excellency Mr. Menendez since far from signing the contract agreed upon the day before, which he had considered arranged and concluded, he sent for us two days after having read the correspondence and, in the palace, in the presence of his Ministers, he told us that the public was convinced that we had received the contract in exchange for a gift of five thousand pesos, and that, finding his reputation damaged by such rumors, he had resolved not to get involved in this business and would pass it along to the Supreme Court for a ruling. That said he returned our correspondence.

Its Excellency, the Council of State, also found itself possessed by the same vertigo that had afflicted everyone else. Some members proposed authorizing the Executive to dispose of one or two million pesos worth of guano as soon as possible, and since this meant annulling our lease, the council passed an unprecedented resolution.

What we had expected from what was said and written came to pass: everyone clamored for the annulment of our contract, reneging on earlier offers of great benefit to the treasury. When the Government realized that no one was coming forward with acceptable offers, they called for bidders in the official newspaper. When this did not work out, they acknowledged that their treatment of us had been unjust and imprudent. His Excellency Mr. Menendez sent for Don Francisco Quiros and General Ladez sent for Don Aquiles Allier in order that we work things out with the Government and resume our guano deal under the conditions previously agreed upon. We resisted at first because it seemed that after what had happened, we were exposing ourselves to new worries and hardships, but we finally capitulated. His Excellency Mr. Menendez, when he received our verbal acquiescence from Don Francisco Quiros, seized his hand, held it firmly in his own, and said that he would never forget the service we were rendering to the Government and to himself in particular by lifting from his shoulder the weight of this affair that had so overwhelmed him.

By virtue of our acquiescence, we met that same night in the home of the Finance Minister, Dr. Cano, and there we agreed to the terms of a contract which stipulated that we would give up thirty of the forty thousand that we had turned over for rights to the first four years of the lease on the guano deposits, of which only one year had transpired, and that we would advance the Government 287,000 pesos on account against its share of the profits. We would receive in return a five-year lease to export guano internationally. As a result of this agreement, we turned over the 87,000 pesos of the first installment, having been assured by the Minister that his Excellency would sign it and that the decree would appear in the next issue of "El Peruano" [the official newspaper].

Much was our surprise, when we saw that instead of publishing the contract, agreed upon and stipulated with us, it was published with notable alterations which had never been mentioned to us, stating instead of five years, *one obligatory and four optional years* for [exportation to] Europe rather than internationally. . . .

The next day following the publication of the decree of 8 December 1841, three contractors from the Capital, presented themselves, asking to submit proposals with better conditions than ours as the law allowed them to do. The pretense of legality was maintained and a ruling of the Public Prosecutor of the Supreme Court invalidated the offers of the aforementioned contractors, but before the decision was reached, his Excellency Mr. Menendez attached a verbal condition to the resolution in which we agreed to donate to the State the uniforms and equipment for a cavalry regiment at a cost to us of eight thousand dollars.

Notwithstanding the verbal assurances that his Excellency Mr. Menendez had given us on various occasions, we saw published in the 29 December issue of "El Peruano," that is to say ten days after our contract was signed and ratified, some proposals which offered to advance the Government 150,000 pesos for the four optional years of our concession and extending it to include international sales in place of Europe. The upshot of these proposals was that we, whose hands had been shaken so gratefully and whose services would never be forgotten, saw ourselves threatened with having paid for the privilege of exporting guano to Europe and for just one year. . . .

The publication of this proposal, in addition to seeming to us offensive to the honor and probity of the Government, naturally alarmed us, because in the mere fact of allowing it to be published in the official newspaper, the Government let it be known that it considered the proposal admissible. We returned again to the house of his Excellency Mr. Menendez, who again reassured us, saying that he wanted everything related to guano out in the open and he had order published any and all proposals to the Government, but that none would be allowed to affect our contract, of whose finality we should rest assured.

After so many and such repeated assurances from his Excellency Mr. Menendez, one can imagine our surprise when a few days after this conversation, obeying an invitation that we received to meet at seven at night in the house of his Excellency, the President of the Council of State, charged with executive power, his Excellency declared in the presence of his Ministers, that the Government had resolved to dispose of the four optional years of our contract, and had called for a meeting of interested contractors so that we could reach an agreement on the matter.

We were so surprised by the turn of events, after what had happened with his Excellency Mr. Menendez, that we left instantly without waiting for the other contractors, distrustful that in our understandable anger some expression might escape us that would fail to show due respect to the authority of the Government in whose presence we found ourselves. Then, we proceeded to lodge a protest against these unexpected and unheard of proceedings.

Seeing finally, that the Government had resolved to dispose of our property against the express tenor of a contract signed and ratified just days before, and whose ink had scarcely had time to dry, we knew that we had no means of salvation other than joining together with our competitors because it was materially impossible for us after a sacrifice of 38,000 pesos, as a forced gift, and given the obligation to advance 287,000 pesos, and adding in the new advance of 200,000 pesos that these gentlemen [our competitors] had offered in order to conquer the scruples of his Excellency Mr. Menendez and his Ministers, and since failing to join with them was going to result in our inevitable ruin thanks to the impossibility of extracting enough guano to cover our advances in the one year of European export left to us, since our competitors had already assembled a fleet of ships with the purpose of preventing us from assembling the means to supply the market that would otherwise remain open and would become theirs at year's end. As a result of this meeting, the current contract was approved on 19 February 1842.

While they despoiled us here of our legitimately acquired rights, in England the business had suffered a disastrous setback. The heat of enthusiasm had been followed by the ice of disappointment. MacDonald and Company had purchased the seven thousand tons in the belief that their name alone would inspire enough confidence in farmers that they would decide to use guano without having experimented with it first, because they [MacDonald and Co.] had been the first to introduce nitrates from Tarapacá as a fertilizer.

But when the time came for consumer sales, that is to say the months of February, March, and April, MacDonald and Company were disappointed and realized that the farmers, unwilling to accept their word as guarantee, far from switching to guano, only bought the minimum amount necessary in order to make tests. Then, these speculators realized the imprudence of having purchased an unknown commodity at such a high price, and this operation would have cost them a huge part of their investment if, opportunely for them, the news had not arrived in England that the Government of Peru had annulled our lease and called for bidders to make proposals for the extraction of guano.

MacDonald and Company took advantage of this news to notify Messrs. William Joseph Meyers and company that since our concession was cancelled, they saw no reason to go forward with the purchases of guano because they had agreed to the purchases with the understanding that this commodity could be obtained from only one source but that since now there were various sources, they repudiated their contract and refused to accept delivery of the guano.

Messrs. William Joseph Meyers and Company received this declaration from MacDonald and Company almost at the same time that we informed them of the new contract with Government which obliged us to advance 287,000 pesos which we hoped to draw against the proceeds of the sales which they had informed us about in their earlier letters.

The coincidence of such unexpected events filled Messrs. William Joseph Meyers and Company with dismay, the Government's annulment of a contract to which they were party seemed to them outside the practice followed in other countries and undermined their confidence in the new agreement into which we had entered, and they were determined to protest all of our bills of exchange, which they in fact did. The bill holders here went before Trade Court which went so far as to seal the doors of our warehouses and offices which delivered us an affront that we did not deserve and reduced us, Quiros to suspending his business deals and mortgaging his farms, and Allier to stopping all business transactions in order to avoid a massive bankruptcy of his estate and factory, and both to suffering incalculable losses.

This has been the recompense that we have received for services rendered to the Government of Peru up until this point, that is to say enormous setbacks and obstacles, the exclusive doing of his Excellency Mr. Menendez. . . .

[Members of Congress], we humbly request that you address our complaint, granting us the reward and indemnity that you think that we deserve, and that we request under the present circumstances only because it in no way harms the Treasury or deprives it of ready resources. On the contrary, evident and positive advantages would accrue to the State from this act of equity and justice that we hope to receive from a magnanimous nation.

3. FLORA TRISTAN:
PIONEER FEMINIST AND SOCIALIST

Not all upper- or middle-class Latin American women in the nineteenth century obeyed the conventions or rules of conduct propounded by social conservatives. One rebel against such rules was Flora Tristan (1803–1844), daughter of a Peruvian aristo-cratic landowner and officer and a French mother. Her short, stormy life has drawn increasing attention from students of the early history of feminism and socialism. Al-though she spent most of her life in France, she is regarded by Peruvian feminists and leftists as one of their own. A woman of striking beauty, she separated early on from her husband and became active in French feminist and socialist circles about 1835. In 1835, she published a novel, Méphis, *which proposed the transformation of society ac-cording to feminist and socialist principles, and in 1840,* Promenades in London, *a description of the monstrous contrasts between wealth and poverty in the English me-tropolis. In her last book,* The Workers' Union *(1844), she called for "the working men and women of the world" to unite, anticipating by four years Marx's appeal in the Communist Manifesto. Her writings are dotted with other striking statements: "The most oppressed male can oppress another human being who is his own wife. Woman is the proletariat of the proletariat." And "the liberation of women is the nec-essary condition for the liberation of men." In her* Promenades in London *she de-scribes the vast extent of prostitution in the city and reflects on its causes.*

Prostitution is the most horrible plague produced by the unequal distri-bution of goods in this world. This infamy withers mankind and is a greater assault on society than crime.

Prejudice, misery, and slavery combine their disastrous effects to produce this appalling degradation. If women were not persuaded that chastity is a virtue—a virtue that is not obligatory for men—society would not reject them for having yielded to the feelings of their hearts, and women who are seduced, deceived, and abandoned would not be reduced to prostitution. If women were permitted to have the same education and engage in the same employments and professions as men, they would not be more prone than men to live in misery. If women were not exposed to all the abuses of power by the despotism of *patria potestas* [the father's complete control over his fam-ily] and the indissoluble nature of marriage, they would not always have to choose between the alternative of suffering oppression or infamy.

Virtue or vice assume the freedom to do good or evil, but what can be the morality of a woman who is not mistress of herself, has no means of her own, and whose whole life has prepared her to either escape from a man's arbitrary

---

Flora Tristan, *Ensayos escogidos*, intro. and ed. Eduardo Nuñe (Lima: Ediciones Persa, 1974), pp. 157–159. Excerpt translated by Benjamin Keen.

conduct by use of her wits or be coerced by seduction? And when she is tortured by misery, when she sees that men enjoy all the good things of life, will not the art of pleasing in which she has been educated lead her inevitably to prostitution?

It follows that society is to blame for this monstrosity and that women must be absolved of it. As long as women are subject to the yoke of men or prejudice, as long as they do not receive the most minimum professional education and are deprived of their civil rights, no moral law can exist for them. As long as they can only have access to possessions by appealing to the passions of men, as long as they cannot have title to anything and can be despoiled by their husbands of the property they acquired by their labor or by inheritance from their fathers, as long as they can only be secure in their possessions or liberty by being celibate, no moral law exists for them. It can be said that until women are emancipated, prostitution will continue to grow.

4. Reform by Revolution

Mexico and Argentina were the main battlefields of the struggle between liberalism and conservatism in nineteenth-century Latin America. The movement to which Mexican historians give the name La Reforma *represented an ambitious effort to transform backward Mexico into a progressive middle-class state. The movement's climactic moments were the implementation of the Reform Laws (including laws named after future president Benito Juárez and prominent jurist Miguel Lerdo de Tejada noted here) and the adoption of the Constitution of 1857, which ushered in the War of the Reform, which was swiftly followed by the French Intervention. Justo Sierra (1848–1912), brilliant Mexican historian and educator, records the movement of events that led to the outbreak of the War of the Reform.*

The Juárez Law organized the administration of justice and set in it the foundation stone of the Reform. Excitement ran high; the conservative newspapers raised the cry of alarm against every effort at innovation; the liberal newspapers with equal insistence demanded a program of struggle, not of peace. . . . In November, 1855, appeared the Juárez Law; Article 42 suppressed the special tribunals (there still were many—of commerce, the treasury, etc.) and exempted from this suppression the ecclesiastical and military tribunals. But they were only to continue temporarily. The first (until the passage of a law that should definitively regulate the ecclesiastical privileges) would have jurisdiction only over common offenses of members of the clergy.

Justo Sierra, *Obras completas*, vol. 12, *Juárez, su obra y su tiempo* (México, 1948), pp. 87–113. Excerpt translated by Benjamin Keen.

Civil affairs were to be under the exclusive control of the common courts. Moreover, ecclesiastics were given the right to reject trial by ecclesiastical courts of a penal character. With respect to the military, something very similar was provided; jurisdiction over civil affairs was also taken away from the military courts, and it was retained only for purely military or mixed offenses, and only if the responsible parties were soldiers.

A true daughter of the Revolution of Ayutla, the Juárez Law was a revolutionary law; given by an authority which had the revolution for its sole source of power, it declared that as a general (federal) law the states could neither modify nor change it. The uproar was great but had been anticipated; [President Ignacio] Comonfort made common cause with his cabinet; and the protests of the bishop who sought to have the point referred to the judgment of the Pope and the Supreme Court (which objected to an organic court law framed without consulting its opinion) did not deter Juárez from putting the law into immediate effect. In a short time it had assumed the character of a *res adjudicata*, as the jurists say, and so it has been down to our time, because the conquests of the Reform had this peculiarity: once established in law they have been converted into enduring facts; they have been enlarged, but never altered or revoked. . . .

The clergy and the army felt the blow of the formidable adversary that rose before them and prepared for combat. Their protests and complaints were the agitated whirlpool that shows on the surface; below was the danger, the permanent conspiracy, the conspiracy that united in intimate contact soldiers and churchmen, that now expanded until it became international, now convulsively contracted to center about the curacies of the mountains, the larger towns, from which sparks constantly flew up, presaging the imminent conflagration. . . .

. . . war raised its threatening visage everywhere: a rising in Guanajuato, where Doblado, an individual of many expedients and few scruples, had raised the banner of Comonfort with no plausible motive, was crushed by a piece of paper—a very sensible, worthy, and biting letter from Juan Álvarez— and Doblado bowed his head; the mountains of Querétaro burned with religion and *fueros*; the indefatigable Mejía was on the war path; Uraga sought to take advantage of the discontent of the "old army" with the Juárez Law; Jalisco and the whole North were restless, and bands of outlaws roamed the country in search of spoil. In the Bajío the situation was returning to normal. In Puebla, on the other hand, there broke out a blaze which had to be isolated and smothered before it could spread to the entire country.

The Bishop of Puebla (Don Pelagio Antonio de Labastida y Dávalos, future Archbishop of Mexico) had acquired by his merits, fine intelligence, and social graces, an immense prestige in Puebla society. From the highest to the lowest, that society lived in the Church and by the Church; the aristocratic families were all petrified, embalmed in devotion and mysticism about this canon, that curate, such-and-such a friar, and at the foot of one or another image of Christ or of Our Lady. Life there consisted of pious exercises, of saints' festivals, of processions, of novenas. As for mortal sin, a microbe which pullulated at the bottom of the most angelic beatitudes, it did not show on the transparent surface of that life, as clear as water; high-powered microscopes had not yet come into use. And the populace, vicious and dirty, but much less so than the rabble of the capital, only lived by what it obtained from the convents, by the crumbs of the Church, by the protection and charity of the priests.

And that is why all that concerned the Church touched them to the quick, reached the innermost recesses of their beings, of their interests, of their loves and hates. And with slight shades of difference it was the same everywhere in the Republic, with the exception of some coastal towns, where the salty sea air diluted somewhat the influence of the clergy. The bishops, like Señor Labastida, publicly affirmed that they did not mix in political affairs, that they reproved armed revolts, and that they counseled obedience to the government as long as its dispositions were not in conflict with the Catholic conscience; and what they affirmed they doubtless believed and practiced. This was least of all true, however, of the Bishop of Puebla, who shortly after the events that unfolded in his diocese in the year 1856 showed very plainly what an ardent politician he was. . . .

Given the national character, however, even if the bishops had not prompted or desired the revolt it inevitably followed from their protests. These protests affirmed that the Church was suffering grave offenses, unjust attacks that were causing irreparable injury to national Catholicism; the Juárez Law . . . they proclaimed to be a rude assault on the most obvious rights of the Church. But how could the clergy resist the attack except by defending themselves, and what better defense than to overthrow the government? All this was clear, and the Catholic populace proceeded with more logic than its prelates, though with less understanding of the situation.

Taking advantage of the feverish atmosphere of Puebla, large groups of the permanent army—on whose support Comonfort, clinging tenaciously to his illusions, still counted—false to their commitments, to their honor, to their oaths, seized the city, which all the spokesmen for military and clerical reaction had made their headquarters. The president determined to atone for his naiveté by striking a hard blow, during the very days when the Constituent Assembly was gathering. The campaign, very prudently and energetically directed, once again placed in bold relief the distinguished soldierly traits of the leader of the Revolution of Ayutla: a desire to spare his soldiers' blood, respect for the advice of experts in the technical aspects of war, and a serene bravery that gave him a kind of heroic aura. The soldiers of the national guard adored him.

Once master of Puebla, where the populace, ever ready to cheer the victor, gave him a friendly reception, the President returned to Mexico City in a better position to sustain two great struggles—one against the clergy, ordering the confiscation of the property of the bishopric of Puebla, and the second against the permanent army, humiliating, degrading, and irritating the officer class. Bishop Labastida, who resisted the orders of the government, was exiled; it was a sound political measure. Clearly, in a city like Puebla the funds of the Church, with or without the wishes of its head, only served to foment conspiracies; it was necessary to deprive the fire of oil, and to give the proof of energy for which the Liberal Party loudly clamored by putting a hand on the most rebellious of the prelates. Away to Europe to conspire went the bishop; he conspired furiously, incessantly, from that moment. Thereby he revealed what lay at the bottom of his heart; Comonfort had not been mistaken.

The degradation of the officers, on the other hand, produced contrary effects. These men thought of nothing but revenge, of settling scores, and they thought about it with pleasure. The future General Sostenes Rocha, who at the time was a petty officer in the Sappers and who was one of the officers stripped of their ranks and confined to towns south of Puebla, relates in his colorful memoirs (as yet unpublished) the ruses to which all these culprits, who naturally regarded themselves as heroes, resorted in order to keep alive.... One by one they succeeded in escaping from their confinements, drawn to the counter-revolutionary center in Mexico City or called to military posts in certain states (as happened with Rocha), and it is clear that the stages of their flight were from convent to convent, and from curacy to curacy. It would have been better for the country and for Comonfort to have shot three or four of the principal officers and to have imprisoned the rest for two or three years; such energy would have spared the country a great deal of suffering. The writer of these lines cannot forget that as a student, representing the School of Law, he went to plead with President Juárez to spare the life of a great impenitent revolutionary, captured almost in *flagrante delicto* while assaulting a treasure-train under government convoy. The prisoner had a name intimately linked to a glorious date. "It is well," replied Señor Juárez to my petition, "I had already decided to pardon him. But do not forget, and let your friends know, that by pardoning a man of this kind, who thinks that politics signifies disorders and barrack-room revolts, I am sentencing to death many hundreds of innocent people." Perhaps these words could be applied to the perennial clemency of Comonfort....

The Juárez Law was the lighted fuse, and its first result the explosion of Puebla, a tremendous rising with its train of sanguinary combats, a costly and difficult campaign, the military degradation of the old army, the confiscation of Church property in that priestly city, and the exile of Bishop Labastida. Comonfort gave constant proofs of his private religiosity, as if to match the professions of obedience made by the clergy each time it questioned the right of the government to subject all social classes to its jurisdiction.... The attitude taken by the Church, its decision to struggle for its privileges by appealing to religious sentiments (exciting them not against the government but in favor of the Church) gave the sessions of Congress a certain solemn and religious tone. When one heard Zarco, Mata, and Arriaga speak of the fundamental conformity between the Constitution and the Gospel, when they discussed religious tolerance, the Constituent Assembly resembled an assembly of Puritans on the eve of the great English religious wars. All this raised to the highest pitch the political fever of the country. And the press with its immense clamor echoed the tribune and the pulpit; the time of Religious Wars appeared to be drawing near for Mexico. Comonfort meditated— that is to say, he vacillated. Later he sent an agent to Rome in search of reconciliation and an agreement; as might be expected, the Pope would not receive him. Pius IX, a great heart filled with all the fire of apostolic zeal, a warrior and martyr by nature but of small intelligence when compared with his successor, dismissed the Mexican minister from the pontifical throne with the same wrathful and tremulous hand that hurled anathema against the Reform. Very logical, perhaps, but infinitely imprudent and improvident. Heads grew heated in Mexico on receipt of this news, and when an undecided person had made up his mind, he was no longer a simple friend of the civil power but a resolute enemy of the Church. To this attitude of the Pontiff must be ascribed the anti-Catholic tone of the reform press and the iconoclastic and "War-to-the-friar" character of the Three Years' War. . . .

Comonfort, no Mirabeau, Napoleon, or Cromwell, yielded here and yielded there, and believed that he was advancing in zigzag fashion; in reality he was zigzagging into the abyss. With the sword of Damocles over the head of the press (the Lafragua Law), he was stern toward the conservative journals and excessively timid with the revolutionary ones. . . . He attached the property of the bishopric of Puebla and exiled the bishop; this show of energy frightened the high clergy, but some months later its effect was nullified by the suspension of the process of seizure. . . . The suppression of the Company of Jesus caused a profound uproar, intensified by the feverish excitement with which the people followed the discussions of the Constituent Congress. . . . When the Bishop of Puebla, awaiting in Havana the possible revocation of his exile, learned of the suppression of the Company, he understood that the fight had just begun, and departed for Rome.

Arriving in Spain, he found even greater cause for despair. The Lerdo Law had been promulgated in June (1856). With a severe preamble that summarized the economic reasons justifying the law, and which could be reduced to the necessity of putting in circulation an almost unproductive mass of wealth, the minister of the treasury set forth in articles as clear as his character and intellect the conditions under which disentail should take place. The law left in the hands of the actual possessors the estates or urban properties belonging to civil (philanthropic, public educational) or ecclesiastical corporations. Calculating the value of the property by the rent or lease at 6 percent, the resulting sum should constitute a mortgage on the disentailed estate, which was to pay 6 percent interest to the corporation. This species of mortgage could on no condition result in a return of the estate to the corporation, but under certain conditions enumerated in the law it could be put up at auction. . . .

During the days that Congress discussed the article of the draft constitution that related not to freedom of worship but to religious toleration, the capital, and before long the whole Republic, lived in an atmosphere saturated with the electric tension that presages combat. All upper-class Mexico, the governing classes en masse, arose as one man and presented to the Congress eloquent memorials pleading that it vote down the Satanic article. This work of the devil, claimed to be a source of evils compared with which the Deluge was child's play, declared: "There shall not be promulgated any law or order that prohibits or impedes the exercise of any religious cult; but since the Roman, Catholic, Apostolic Faith has been the exclusive religion of the Mexican people, the Congress of the Union shall seek to protect it by means of just and prudent laws, providing they do not injure the interests of the people or the rights of national sovereignty." The authors of the project could be criticized for not having dared to carry their thinking to its logical conclusion by proclaiming complete freedom of worship, without any privileged religion, as a consequence of the separation of Church and State. However, the tremendously excited state of public opinion probably intimidated them . . . [and] it was badly beaten in the breach, and under the formidable pressure of the government and popular opinion (the bourgeoisie and the illiterate class), the article disappeared from the draft. . . .

The constitution was voted; the great promise of Ayutla, in the words of the members, was fulfilled. Trembling with horror, the society that lived in the shadow of the belfry saw the ancient [former liberal President Valentín] Gómez Farías, the founder of the reform government, take an oath of loyalty to the new law on bended knees, his hand on the Bible; then the whole country was summoned to take the same oath. The Church, with some hesitation (some bishops and ecclesiastical dignitaries swore loyalty), because it understood that upon its attitude depended peace or war, loosened the folds of its long mantle and chose war, like the Roman senator in Carthage. The nation, placed under a kind of interdict, displayed nervousness, almost epilepsy. Some refused to swear; others retracted their oaths; all who swore fell under the ban of excommunication. The crisis was at the very base of society; in the family; in the home; in the terrible anguish of the public official wavering between his religious duty and the prospect of misery; in the sobs, the appeals, the reproaches of mothers and wives; in the homes of the liberals themselves. . . .

Comonfort, terribly moved by this social crisis, daily confronted by the mute and tearful pleading of his mother, was content at the time he took the oath to ask for immediate reform of the constitution: a really senseless action.

His indecision was immense. One idea had taken hold of his brain: it was impossible to govern with the constitution. The Executive, he believed, was made so impotent in the face of the action of a unitary Congress and the right of intervention—which could be incessant—of the judicial power, that only an uninterrupted succession of extraordinary powers could enable the President to govern; and these powers, painful experience told him, were usually denied, so that authority might remain in revolutionary hands.

Yet special powers were indispensable. The whole interior of the country was up in arms. Puebla witnessed a new revolt, a new siege, a new victory of the government, a new waste of blood and money that exhausted the resources of the treasury at a time when the foreign horizons darkened. The question of the Spanish claims became increasingly urgent and alarming. . . . In fine, the foreign intervention that Paredes had asked for, that Santa Anna had demanded, was in the air of the Mexican Gulf. Money and more money was needed to conjure away the storm. Where was it to come from? The proceeds of the tax on disentails were negligible or nil; the clergy had stopped with its interdict a movement that might have saved both it and the government of Comonfort.

[Under these conditions elections are held for the first congress and president under the Constitution of 1857, and for the members of the Supreme Court, whose president was also to be Vice President. Comonfort is elected President; Juárez becomes his Vice President. Comonfort's requests for special powers and a revision of the Constitution are rejected by the Liberal majority in the Congress. In November, 1857, General Félix Zuloaga, an instrument of conservative military and clerical groups, "pronounces" for a Comonfort dictatorship, dismisses Congress, and arrests Juárez.]

The Plan of Tacubaya repealed the Constitution of 1857 as unsuited to the usages and manners of the country, placed dictatorial powers in the hands of Comonfort, and referred to a future constituent assembly whose decisions were to be reviewed by the people (ad referendum). Comonfort adhered to the Plan two days later. Never did a more modest Caesar, or one with less confidence in himself and his future, pronounce "the die is cast"; he pronounced it almost inaudibly. This man, who was no longer at peace with himself, was to bring peace to the Republic!

Zuloaga was a conservative four-square; if he had joined the Liberal ranks it was from personal loyalty to Comonfort and nothing more. Now, brought to the fore, he was surrounded by counter-revolutionaries who hemmed him in, brought pressure upon him. What did they want? The Constitution no longer existed. There was talk of a grouping or coalition of certain states of the interior, of forces that came and went, of Parodi, of Degollado, of Arteago, of Doblado. True, the Archbishop had declared for the Plan of Tacubaya, and the priest Valdovinos had blessed it. The Church had joyfully "pronounced" in its favor! But this was not enough; the Council of Conservatives, *moderados* [moderates], and *puros* [radicals] formed by Comonfort no longer gave satisfaction. He must go on to destroy the coalition, and above all and before all else he must repeal the Juárez Law; and above all and right away he must repeal the Lerdo Law, the law of disentail; he must return everything to the Church—but quickly, quickly!

The unhappy Comonfort said: "But this law has created new interests, new rights, new positions, and all under my pledge, my signature, my protection!" "What would you do if you were in my position?" the President asked the conservative leader José M. Cuevas. "Repeal the Lerdo Law and put myself in the hands of the conservatives," replied the lawyer. "And if you were in my place, with my background, my ideas, would you do it?" the anxious Comonfort asked. "Not I," replied the reactionary gentleman. "Thanks," Comonfort concluded, "I shall never do it." The next day Zuloaga's brigade "Re- pronounced," disavowing Comonfort as President. And Comonfort, gathering the few forces left to him, declared the Constitution of 1857 reestablished. It was a tragic retraction. Twenty days later, standing on the stern of an American ship as it steamed out of Veracruz, he watched the Mexican coasts recede in the distance, and his political dreams merged with the clouds, with the shadows. . . .

On the day of Zuloaga's second "pronouncement" (January 11, 1858), Juárez was released by order of Comonfort. The two old friends probably did not speak to each other. Juárez could not recognize Comonfort as President, despite his repentance. Comonfort had accused, judged, and sentenced himself. Juárez, president of the Supreme Court, replaced him, according to the Constitution. It was Comonfort's last service to the liberal cause, though not to his country, for which he died obscurely six years later. The effort to achieve reform by way of persuasion and clemency had failed. The tremendous Three Years' War had begun.

5. A MEXICAN RADICAL

Nineteenth-century conservatives and liberals gave little or no attention in their programs to the land problem—the growing concentration of land ownership, with all its negative economic, social, and political consequences. In Mexico, however, where the problem of land monopoly had become increasingly acute, and where a social revolutionary tradition existed since the time of Hidalgo, left-wing liberals raised the land question in the Constitutional Convention of 1856–1857. The chief spokesman for this small band of Mexican radicals was Ponciano Arriaga. In a speech remarkable for its modern socioeconomic ideas, Arriaga pungently described the effects of the land monopoly but offered a relatively moderate solution: the state should seize and auction off uncultivated estates more than fifteen square leagues in extent. Arriaga's prophetic insistence that the agrarian reform must sooner or later prevail would be verified by the events of the Mexican Revolution of 1910.

One of the most deeply rooted evils of our country—an evil that merits the close attention of legislators when they frame our fundamental law—is the monstrous division of landed property.

While a few individuals possess immense areas of uncultivated land that could support millions of people, the great majority of Mexicans languish in a terrible poverty and are denied property, homes, and work.

Such a people cannot be free, democratic, much less happy, no matter how many constitutions and laws proclaim abstract rights and beautiful but impracticable theories—impracticable by reason of an absurd economic system.

There are Mexican landowners who occupy (if one can give that name to a purely imaginary act) an extent of land greater than the area of some of our sovereign states, greater even than that of one or several European states.

In this vast area, much of which lies idle, deserted, abandoned, awaiting the arms and labor of men, live four or five million Mexicans who know no other industry than agriculture, yet are without land or the means to work it, and who cannot emigrate in the hope of bettering their fortunes. They must either vegetate in idleness, turn to banditry, or accept the yoke of a landed monopolist who subjects them to intolerable conditions of life.

How can one reasonably expect these unhappy beings to escape from their condition of abject serfs through legal channels, or hope that the magic power of a written law will transform them into free citizens who know and defend the dignity and importance of their rights?

We proclaim ideas and forget realities; we launch on discussions of rights and turn away from stubborn facts. The constitution should be the law of the land, but we do not regulate or even examine the state of the land. . . .

How can a hungry, naked, miserable people practice popular government? How can we proclaim the equal rights of men and leave the majority of the nation in conditions worse than those of helots or pariahs? How can we condemn slavery in words, while the lot of most of our fellow citizens is more grievous than that of the black slaves of Cuba or the United States? When will we begin to concern ourselves with the fate of the proletarians, the men we call Indians, the laborers and peons of the countryside, who drag the heavy chains of serfdom established not by Spanish laws—which were so often flouted and infringed—but by the arbitrary mandarins of the colonial regime? Would it not be more logical and honest to deny our four million poor Mexicans all share in political life and public offices, all electoral rights,

Francisco Zarco, *Historia del congreso estraordinario constituyente de 1856 y 1857*, 2 vols. (México, 1857), 1:546–555. Excerpt translated by Benjamin Keen.

and declare them to be things, not persons, establishing a system of government in which an aristocracy of wealth, or at most of talent, would form the basis of our institutions?

For one of two things is inevitable: either our political system will continue to be dominated for a long time to come by a de facto aristocracy—no matter what our fundamental laws may say—and the lords of the land, the privileged caste that monopolizes the soil and profits by the sweat of its serfs, will wield all power and influence in our civil and political life; or we will achieve a reform, shatter the trammels and bonds of feudal servitude, bring down all monopolies and despotisms, end all abuses, and allow the fruitful element of democratic equality, the powerful element of democratic sovereignty—to which alone authority rightfully belongs—to penetrate the heart and veins of our political institutions. The nation wills it, the people demand it; the struggle has begun, and sooner or later that just authority will recover its sway. The great word "reform" has been pronounced, and it is vain to erect dikes to contain those torrents of truth and light. . . .

Is it necessary, in an assembly of deputies of the people, in a congress of representatives of that poor, enslaved people, to prove the unjust organization of landed property in the Republic, and the infinite evils that flow from it? . . . In the realm of a purely ideal and theoretical politics, statesmen discuss the organization of chambers, the division of powers, the assignment of jurisdictions and attributes, the demarcation of sovereignties, and the like. Meanwhile other, more powerful men laugh at all that, for they know they are the masters of society, the true power is in their hands, they exercise the real sovereignty. With reason the people think that constitutions die and are born, governments succeed each other, law codes pile up and grow ever more intricate, "pronouncements" and "plans" come and go, but after all those changes and upheavals, after so much disorder and so many sacrifices, no good or profit comes to the masses who shed their blood in the civil wars, who swell the ranks of the armies, who fill the jails and do forced labor on the public works, who, in fine, suffer all the misfortunes of society and enjoy none of its benefits. . . .

With some honorable exceptions, the rich landowners of Mexico (who rarely know their own lands, palm by palm), or the administrators or majordomos who represent them, resemble the feudal lords of the Middle Ages. On his seignorial land, with more or less formalities, the landowner makes and executes laws, administers justice and exercises civil power, imposes taxes and fines, has his own jails and irons, metes out punishments and tortures, monopolizes commerce, and forbids the conduct without his permission of any business but that of the estate. The judges or officials who exercise on the hacienda the powers attached to public authority are usually the master's servants or tenants, his retainers, incapable of enforcing any law but the will of the master.

An astounding variety of devices are employed to exploit the peons or tenants, to turn a profit from their sweat and labor. They are compelled to work without pay even on days traditionally set aside for rest. They must accept rotten seeds or sick animals whose cost is charged to their miserable wages. They must pay enormous parish fees that bear no relation to the scale of fees that the owner or majordomo has arranged beforehand with the parish priest. They must make all their purchases on the hacienda, using tokens or paper money that do not circulate elsewhere. At certain seasons of the year they are assigned articles of poor quality, whose price is set by the owner or majordomo, constituting a debt which they can never repay. They are forbidden to use pastures and woods, firewood and water, or even the wild fruit of the fields, save with the express permission of the master. In fine, they are subject to a completely unlimited and irresponsible power.

6. BLACK SLAVERY UNDER THE EMPIRE

Under the empire, as in colonial times, black slavery formed the massive base of virtually all of Brazil's significant economic activity. The condition and prospects of the black people in Brazil aroused the lively interest of foreign visitors. Two North American travelers present a summary view of the situation.

The subject of slavery in Brazil is one of great interest and hopefulness. The Brazilian Constitution recognizes, neither directly nor indirectly, color as a basis of civil rights; hence, once free, the black man or the mulatto, if he possess energy and talent, can rise to a social position from which his race in North America is debarred. Until 1850, when the slave-trade was effectually put down, it was considered cheaper, on the country-plantations, to use up a slave in five or seven years and purchase another, than to take care of him. This I had, in the interior, from intelligent native Brazilians, and my own observation has confirmed it. But, since the inhuman traffic with Africa has ceased, the price of slaves has been enhanced, and the selfish motives for taking greater care of them have been increased. Those in the city are treated better than those on the plantations: they seem more cheerful, more full of fun, and have greater opportunities for freeing themselves. But still there must be great cruelty in some cases, for suicides among slaves—which are almost unknown in our Southern States—are of very frequent occurrence in the cities of Brazil. Can this, however, be attributed to cruelty? The Negro of the United States is the descendant of those who have, in various ways, ac-

D. P. Kidder and J. C. Fletcher, *Brazil and the Brazilians* (Philadelphia, 1857), pp. 132–138.

quired a knowledge of the hopes and fears, the rewards and punishments, which the Scriptures hold out to the good and threaten to the evil; to avoid the crime of suicide is as strongly inculcated as to avoid that of murder. The North American Negro has, by this very circumstance, a higher moral intelligence than his brother fresh from the wild freedom and heathenism of Africa; hence the latter, goaded by cruelty, or his high spirit refusing to bow to the white man, takes that fearful leap which lands him in the invisible world.

In Brazil everything is in favor of freedom; and such are the facilities for the slave to emancipate himself, and, when emancipated, if he possess the proper qualifications, to ascend to higher eminences than those of a mere free black, that *fuit* will be written against slavery in this Empire before another half-century rolls around. Some of the most intelligent men that I met with in Brazil—men educated at Paris and Coimbra—were of African descent, whose ancestors were slaves. Thus, if a man have freedom, money, and merit, no matter how black may be his skin, no place in society is refused him. It is surprising also to observe the ambition and the advancement of some of these men with Negro blood in their veins. The National Library furnishes not only quiet rooms, large tables, and plenty of books to the seekers after knowledge, but pens and paper are supplied to such as desire these aids to their studies. Some of the closest students thus occupied are mulattoes. The largest and most successful printing establishment in Rio—that of Sr. F. Paulo Brito—is owned and directed by a mulatto. In the colleges, the medical, law, and theological schools, there is no distinction of color. It must, however, be admitted that there is a certain—though by no means strong— prejudice existing all over the land in favor of men of pure white descent.

By the Brazilian law, a slave can go before a magistrate, have his price fixed, and can purchase himself; and I was informed that a man of mental endowments, even if he had been a slave, would be debarred from no official station, however high, unless it might be that of Imperial Senator.

The appearance of Brazilian slaves is very different from that of their class in our own country. Of course, the house-servants in the large cities are decently clad, as a general rule; but even these are almost always barefooted. This is a sort of badge of slavery. On the tables of fares for ferry-boats, you find one price for persons wearing shoes (*calçadas*), and a lower one for the *descalças*, or without shoes. In the houses of many of the wealthy Fluminenses you make your way through a crowd of little woolly-heads, mostly guiltless of clothing, who are allowed the run of the house and the amusement of seeing visitors. In families that have some tincture of European manners, these unsightly little bipeds are kept in the background. A friend of mine used frequently to dine in the house of a good old general of high rank, around whose table gamboled two little jetty blacks, who hung about their "pai" [father] (as they called him) until they received their portions from his hands, and that, too, before he commenced his own dinner. Whenever the lady of the house drove out, these pets were put into the carriage, and were as much offended at being neglected as any spoiled only son. They were the children of the lady's nurse, to whom she had given freedom. Indeed, a faithful nurse is generally rewarded by manumission.

The appearance of the black male population who live in the open air is anything but appetizing. Their apology for dress is of the coarsest and dirtiest description. Hundreds of them loiter about the streets with large round wicker baskets ready to carry any parcel that you desire conveyed. So cheaply and readily is this help obtained, that a white servant seldom thinks of carrying home a package, however small, and would feel quite insulted if you refused him a *preto de ganho* to relieve him of a roll of calico or a watermelon. These blacks are sent out by their masters, and are required to bring home a certain sum daily. They are allowed a portion of their gains to buy their food, and at night sleep on a mat or board in the lower purlieus of the house. You frequently see horrible cases of elephantiasis and other diseases, which are doubtless engendered or increased by the little care bestowed upon them.

7. THE ANTISLAVERY IMPULSE

Black slavery was the great domestic issue of Dom Pedro's reign, and after 1880 the abolitionist movement assumed the character of a popular crusade. In Joaquim Nabuco, son of a distinguished liberal statesman of the empire, Brazilian abolitionism found a leader of towering intellectual and moral stature. His eloquent indictment of slavery, O Abolicionismo *(1883), made a profound impression in Brazilian intellectual circles. In one chapter of this book, Nabuco examines the social and political consequences of slavery in Brazil.*

History knows no example of free government founded on slavery. The governments of antiquity were not based on the same principles of individual liberty as modern states; they represented a very different social order. Since the French Revolution there has been only one notable case of democracy combined with slavery—the United States; but the southern states of the Union never were free governments. American liberty, taking the Union as whole, actually only dates from Lincoln's Proclamation freeing the millions of slaves in the South. Far from being free, the states south of the Potomac were societies organized on the basis of the violation of all human rights.

Joaquim Nabuco, *O Abolicionismo* (São Paulo, 1938), pp. 167–195. Excerpt translated by Benjamin Keen.

American statesmen like Henry Clay or Calhoun, who compromised or identified themselves with slavery, did not properly calculate the force of the antagonism that was later to prove so formidable. The ensuing course of events—the rebellion in which the North saved the South from committing suicide through the formation of a separate slave power, and the manner in which the rebellion was crushed—proves that in the United States slavery did not affect the social constitution as a whole, as is the case with us. The superior part of the organism remained intact, and even strong enough to bend the hitherto dominant section of the country to its will, despite all its complicity with that section.

Among us there is no dividing line. There is no section of the country that differs from another. Contact is synonymous with contagion. The whole circulatory system, from the great arteries to the capillaries, serves as a channel for the same impurities. The whole body—blood, constituent elements, respiration, force and activity, muscles and nerves, intelligence and will, not only the character but the temperament, and above all the energy—is affected by the same cause. . . .

In the southern states of the American Union a social color line was drawn. The slaves and their descendants did not form part of society. Race mixture took place on a very small scale. Slavery devastated the soil, obstructed industrial growth, prepared the way for economic bankruptcy, impeded immigration—produced, in fine, all the results of that kind that we know in Brazil; but American society was not formed from units created in that process. . . .

In Brazil just the opposite occurred. Brazilian slavery, though based on the difference between the two races, never developed a prejudice against dark skin, and was infinitely more sagacious in that respect. The contacts between the races, from the first colonization by the *donatories* until today, have produced a mixed population; and the slave who receives his certificate of freedom simultaneously acquires the rights of citizenship. Thus there are no perpetual social castes among us; there is not even a fixed division into classes. The slave, as such, practically does not exist for society, for he may not even have been registered by his master, who in any case can alter the registration at will. For the rest, registration in itself means nothing, since the government does not send inspectors to the *fazendas*, nor are the masters obliged to account for their slaves to the authorities. This being, who enjoys no more right of protection by society than any other piece of personal property, on the day after he has gained his freedom becomes a citizen like any other, with full political rights. Furthermore, in the very shadow of his own captivity he can buy slaves, perhaps—who knows?—some child of his old master. This proves the confusion of classes and individuals, and the unlimited extent of social crossings between slaves and free men, which make the majority of Brazilian citizens political mixed-bloods, so to speak, in whom two opposed natures struggle: that of the master by birth and that of the domesticated slave.

Our slavery extended its privileges to all without distinction: white man and black, *ingenuos* and freedmen, slaves, foreigners and natives, rich and poor; and in this way it acquired a redoubled capacity for absorption and an elasticity incomparably greater than it would have had if there were a racial monopoly of the institution, as in the South of the United States. In 1845, the year of the Aberdeen Bill [A bill, much resented by Brazilians that empowered the British government to take unilateral measures to suppress the Brazilian slave trade], Macaulay said in the House of Commons: "I think it not improbable that the black population of Brazil will be free and happy within eighty or a hundred years. I do not see a reasonable prospect of a like change in the United States." He appears to have been as correct in his insight into the relative happiness of the Negro race in the two countries as he was wrong in his belief that the United States would lag behind us in the emancipation of its slaves. What deceived the great English orator in this case was his assumption that the color line was a social and political force in favor of slavery. On the contrary, its chief strength consists in banishing race prejudice and opening the institution to all classes. But for this very reason the greatest possible ethnic chaos prevailed among us, and the confusion that reigns in the regions where the process of national unity is working itself out with all those heterogeneous elements reminds one of the proud disorder of the incandescent stars.

Athens, Rome, and Virginia were, to draw an analogy from chemistry, simple mixtures in which the different elements retained their individual properties; Brazil, on the other hand, is a compound in which slavery represents the causal affinity. The problem that awaits solution is how to make a citizen of this compound of master and slave. The problem of the American South was very different, because there the two species did not mix. Among us slavery did not exert its influence exclusively below the Roman line of *libertas*; it also exerted it within and above the sphere of *civitas*; it leveled all the classes, except the slaves, who always live in the social depths; but it leveled them by degrading them. Hence the difficulty, in analyzing its influence, of discovering some feature in the temperament of the people, or in the aspect of the country, or even in the social heights most distant from the slave huts, which should not be included in the national synthesis of slavery. Consider our different social classes. They all present symptoms of retarded or impeded development, or what is worse, of artificial, premature growth. . . .

An important class whose development is impeded by slavery comprises the cultivators who are not landowners and the dwellers in the countryside and the hinterlands in general. We have already seen the unhappy state of this class, which constitutes nearly our entire population. Since they lack all independence and are dependent on another man's whims, the words of the

Lord's Prayer, "Give us this day our daily bread," have for the members of this class a concrete and real significance. Their plight is not that of workers, who, dismissed from one factory, can find work in another establishment, or of day laborers who can go to the labor market to offer their services, or of families which can emigrate; they constitute a class without means or resource— taught to consider work a servile occupation, having no market for its products, and far removed from a region of wage labor (if there is such an *El Dorado* in our country)—a class that consequently must resign itself to living and raising its children in dependency and misery.

This is the picture which a compassionate sugarmill owner presented of a section—the most fortunate section—of this class at the Agricultural Congress held in Recife in 1878:

> The cultivator who is not a sugarmill owner leads a precarious life; his labor is not remunerated; his personal dignity is not respected; he is at the mercy of the sugarmill owner on whose land he lives. There is not even a written contract to bind the interested parties; everything is based on the absolute will of the sugarmill owner. In exchange for a dwelling, often of the most wretched kind, and for permission to cultivate a patch of manioc, invariably situated in the most unproductive land—in return for this the sharecropper divides equally with the sugarmill owner the sugar obtained from his crop. The owner also gets all the syrup and rum derived from the sugarcane; all the refuse—an excellent fuel for the manufacture of sugar; and all the sugarcane leaves, which provide a succulent food for his cattle. Thus the landowner receives the lion's share—all the more unjustly when it is remembered that the sharecropper bears all the expense of planting, cultivation, cutting, and preparation of the cane, and of its transport to the sugarmill.

And this is a favored class, that of the sharecroppers, below which there are others who have nothing of their own, tenants who have nothing to sell the landowner and who lead a nomadic existence, having no obligations to society and denied all protection by the State.

Consider now the other classes whose development is retarded by slavery— the working and industrial classes, and the commercial classes in general.

Slavery does not permit the existence of a true working class, nor is it compatible with the wage system and the personal dignity of the artisan. The artisan himself, in order to escape the stigma with which slavery brands its workers, attempts to widen the gulf that separates him from the slave, and becomes imbued with a sense of superiority that is based in one who himself emerged from the servile class or whose parents were slaves. For the rest, there can be no strong, respected, and intelligent working class where the employers of labor are accustomed to order slaves about. As a result, the workers do not have slightest political influence in Brazil.

Slavery and industry are mutually exclusive terms, like slavery and colonization. The spirit of the former, spreading through a country, kills every one of the human faculties from which industry springs—initiative, inventiveness, individual energy, and every one of the elements that industry requires—the formation of capital, an abundance of labor, technical education of the workers, confidence in the future. Agriculture is the only Brazilian industry that has flourished in native hands. Commerce has prospered only in the hands of foreigners. . . . The advent of industry has been singularly retarded in our country, and it is barely making its entrance now.

Brazilian large-scale commerce does not possess the capital available to foreign commerce, in either the export or the import trade; and retail trade, at least as concerns its prosperous sector, with its own life, is practically a foreign monopoly. At various times in our history this has provoked popular demonstrations, proclaiming that retail commerce must become Brazilian, but this cry was characteristic of the spirit of exclusivism and hatred of competition, no matter how legitimate, in which slavery reared our people. More than once it was accompanied by uprisings similar in character but actuated by religious fanaticism. Those who supported the program of closure of Brazilian ports, and of annulling all the progress made since 1808, were unaware that if we took retail commerce away from foreigners it would not pass into native hands but would simply create a permanent shortage of goods—because it is slavery, not nationality, that prevents any significant development of Brazilian retail trade.

In relation to commerce, slavery proceeds in this fashion: It shuts off to trade, whether from distrust or from a spirit of routine, all of the interior except the provincial capitals. Aside from the towns of Santos and Campinas in São Paulo, Petropolis and Campos in Rio de Janeiro, Pelotas in Rio Grande do Sul, and a few other cities, outside the capitals you will not find a business establishment that is more than a little shop selling articles necessary for life, and these are generally crudely made or adulterated. Just as you will find nothing that betokens intellectual progress—neither bookstores nor newspapers—so will you find no trace of commerce except in the ancient rudimentary form of the store-bazaar. Consequently, aside from the articles that are ordered directly from the capital, all commercial transactions take the form of barter, whose history is the history of our whole interior. Barter, in fact, is the "pioneer" of our commerce, and represents the limits within which slavery is compatible with local exchange.

Yet commerce is the fountainhead of slavery, and its banker. A generation ago it supplied plantation agriculture with African slaves; many rural properties fell into the hands of slave traders; and the fortunes made in the traffic (for which counterfeit money sometimes had a great affinity), when not converted into town and country houses, were employed in assisting agriculture by way of loans at usurious rates. At present the bond between commerce and slavery is not so dishonorable for the former, but their mutual dependence continues to be the same. The princes of commerce are slave owners; coffee always reigns on the exchanges of Rio and Santos; and commerce, in the absence of industry and free labor, can function only as an agent of slavery, buying whatever it offers and selling whatever it needs. That is why in Brazil commerce does not develop or open new perspectives for the country; it is an inactive force, without stimuli, and conscious that it is merely an extension of slavery, or rather the mechanism by which human flesh is converted into gold and circulates, within and outside the country, in the form of letters of exchange. Slavery distrusts commerce, as it distrusts any agency of progress, whether it is a businessman's office, a railroad station, or a primary school; yet slavery needs commerce—and so the latter tries to live with it on the best possible terms. But so long as slavery endures, commerce must always be the servant of a class, and not an independent national agent; it cannot thrive under a régime that will not permit it to enter into direct relations with consumers, and will not allow the population of the interior to rise into that category.

Of the classes whose growth slavery artificially stimulates, none is more numerous than that of government employees. The close relation between slavery and the mania for officeholding is as indisputable as the relation between slavery and the superstition of the All-Providing State. . . . Take at random any twenty or thirty Brazilians in any place where our most cultured society is to be found; all were, or are, or will be government employees—if not they, then their sons.

Officeholding is . . . the asylum of the descendants of formerly rich and noble families that have squandered the fortunes made from slavery, of which it can be said, as a rule, as of fortunes made by gambling, that they neither last nor bring happiness. But officeholding is also our political olive tree, that shelters all those young men of brains and ambition but no money who form the great majority of our talented people. Draw up a list of distinguished Brazilian statesmen who solved their personal problem of poverty by marrying wealth (which meant, in the great majority of cases, becoming humble clients of the slaveowners); make up another list of those who solved that problem by acquiring government jobs; in those two lists you will find the names of virtually all our outstanding politicians. But what this means is that the national horizons are closed in all directions—that fields that might offer a livelihood to men of other than commercial talents, such as literature, science, journalism, and teaching, are severely restricted, while others that might attract men of business ability are so many closed doors, thanks to lack of credit, to the narrow scope of commerce, to the rudimentary structure of our economic life. . . .

But can we have this consolation, that having degraded the various professions and reduced the nation to a proletariat, slavery at least succeeded in making the landowners a superior class, prosperous, educated, patriotic, worthy of representing the country intellectually and morally?

As concerns wealth, we have already seen that slavery ruined a generation of farmers whose place was taken by slave labor. From 1853 to 1857, when the obligations formed during the period of the slave traffic should have been in the process of liquidation, the mortgage debt of the city and province of Rio de Janeiro rose to sixty-seven thousand *contos*. The present generation has been no more fortunate. A large part of its profits was converted into human flesh, at a high price, and if an epidemic were to devastate the coffee plantations today, the amount of capital that the agriculture of the whole Empire could raise for new plantings would horrify those who believe it to be in a flourishing state. On top of this, for the past fifteen years there has been talk of nothing but "aid to agriculture." In 1868 appeared a little work by Sr. Quintino Bocayuva, *The Crisis of Agriculture*, in which that notable journalist wrote: "Agriculture can only be revived by the simultaneous application of two types of aid that cannot be longer delayed: the establishment of agricultural credit and the procurement of labor." The first measure was to be "a vast emission" based on the landed property of the Empire, which would thus be converted into ready money; the second should be Chinese colonization.

For fifteen years we have heard on all sides the cry that agriculture is in crisis, in need of aid, in agony, facing imminent bankruptcy. The government is daily denounced for not making loans and increasing the taxes in order to enable the *fazendeiros* to buy still more slaves. A law of November 6, 1875, authorized the government to give its guarantee to the foreign bank—no other could make its notes circulate in Europe—which would lend money to the planters at a rate lower than that of the domestic money market. In order to have sugar centrals and improve their product, the landowners must have the nation build them at its expense. The same favor has been asked for coffee. On top of sugar centrals and money at low interest rates, the great planters demand railroad freight rates set to their liking, official expositions of coffee, Asiatic immigration, exemption from any direct tax, and an employment law that would make the German, English, or Italian colonist a white slave. Even the native population must be subjected to a new agricultural recruitment in order to satisfy certain Chambers of Commerce; and, above all, the rate of exchange, by an economic fallacy, must be kept as low as possible so that coffee, which is paid for in gold, may be worth more in paper money. . . .

As concerns its social functions, a landed aristocracy can serve its country in different ways: by working to improve the condition of the surrounding population of the countryside in which its estates are situated; by taking the direction of the progress of the nation into its own hands; by cultivating or protecting art and literature; by serving in the army and the navy or distinguishing itself in a variety of careers; by becoming the embodiment of all that is good in the national character, of the superior qualities of the people—of all that merits being preserved as tradition. We have already seen what our landed aristocracy achieved in each of these respects, when we noted what the slave system over which it presides has done to the land and the people, to the masters and the slaves. Since the class for whose profit it was created and exists is not an aristocracy of money, birth, intelligence, patriotism, or race, what is the permanent role in Brazil of a heterogeneous aristocracy that cannot even maintain its identity for two generations?

When we turn from the different classes to social institutions, we see that slavery has either turned them to its own interests, when of compromising tendency, or created a vacuum about them, when hostile, or hampered their formation, when incompatible with the slavery system.

Among the institutions that have identified themselves with slavery from the start, becoming instruments of its pretensions, is the Church. Under the system of domestic slavery, Christianity became mixed with fetishism, just as the two races mixed with each other. Through the influence of the wet nurse and the house slaves on the training of the children, the mumbo-jumbo terrors of the converted fetishist exert . . . the most depressing influence on the minds of the young. The faith, the religious system that results from this fusion of African traditions with the antisocial ideal of the fanatical missionary is a jumble of contradictions that only a total lack of principle can seek to reconcile. What is true of religion is true of the Church.

Our bishops, vicars, and confessors do not find the sale of human beings repugnant; the Bulls that condemn it have become obsolete. Two of our prelates were sentenced to imprisonment at hard labor for declaring war on Freemasonry; none, however, was willing to incur the displeasure of the slavocracy. . . .

Take another social force that slavery has appropriated in the same way—patriotism. The slavocracy has always exerted itself to identify Brazil with slavery. Whoever attacks it immediately falls under suspicion of connivance with foreigners, of hostility toward the institutions of his own country. Antonio Carlos de Andrada was accused by the slave power of being un-Brazilian. To attack monarchy in a monarchical country, to attack Catholicism in a Catholic country, is perfectly proper, but to attack slavery is national treason and felony. . . .

But as with all the moral forces that it subjugated, slavery degraded patriotism even as it bent it to its will. The Paraguayan War offers the best illustration of what it did to the patriotism of the slaveowning class, to the patriotism of the masters. Very few of them left their slaves to serve their country; many freed a few blacks in order to win titles of nobility. It was among the humblest strata of our population, descendants of slaves for the most part—the very people that slavery condemns to dependence and misery—among the illiterate proletarians whose political emancipation slavery indefinitely postponed—that one felt beating the heart of a new *patria*. It was they who produced the soldiers of the Volunteer Battalions. With slavery, said José Bonifacio de Andrada in 1825, "Brazil will never form, as she must form, a spirited army and a flourishing navy"—because with slavery there can be no true patriotism, but only a patriotism of caste or race; that is, a sentiment that should unite all the members of society is used to divide them. . . .

Among the forces of progress and change around which slavery has created a vacuum as hostile to its interests, the press is notable—and not only the newspaper but the book, and everything that concerns education. To the credit of our journalism, the press has been the great weapon of struggle against slavery, the instrument for the propagation of new ideas; efforts to found a "black organ" have always collapsed. Whether insinuated timidly or affirmed with energy, the dominant sentiment in all our journalism, from North to South, is emancipation. But in order to create a vacuum around the newspaper and the book, and around all that could foster abolitionist sentiment, slavery has instinctively repelled the school and public education, maintaining the country in ignorance and darkness—the milieu in which it can prosper. The slave hut and the school are poles that repel each other.

The state of public education under a slave system interested in universal ignorance is well illustrated by the following excerpt from a notable report by Sr. Ruy Barbosa, reporter for the Commission on Public Instruction of the Chamber of Deputies:

> The truth—and your Commission wants to be very explicit on this point, displease whom it may—is that our public instruction is as backward as is possible in a country that regards itself as free and civilized; that decadence and not progress prevails; that we are a people of illiterates, and that the rate of illiteracy is declining at an intolerably slow rate if it is declining at all; that our academic instruction is infinitely below the scientific level of the age; that our youth leave the secondary schools more and more poorly prepared for advanced study; and that popular education, in the capital as in the provinces, is merely a desideratum. . . .

Among the forces whose emergence slavery has impeded is public opinion, the consciousness of a common destiny. Under slavery there cannot exist that powerful force called public opinion, that simultaneously balances and offers a point of support to the individuals who represent the most advanced thought of the country. Just as slavery is incompatible with spontaneous immigration, so will it prevent the influx of new ideas. Itself incapable of invention, it will have nothing to do with progress. . . .

And because we lack this force of social change, Brazilian politics are the sad and degrading struggle for spoils that we behold; no man in public life means anything, for none has the support of the country. The president of the council lives at the mercy of the Crown, from which he derives his power; even the appearance of power is his only when he is regarded as the Emperor's lieutenant and is believed to have in his pocket the decree of dissolution—that is, the right to elect a chamber made up of his own henchmen. Below him are the ministers, who live by the favor of the president of the council; farther down still, on the third plane, are found the deputies, at the mercy of the ministers. The representative system, then, is a graft of parliamentary forms on a patriarchal government, and senators and deputies only take their roles seriously in this parody of democracy because of the personal advantages they derive therefrom. Suppress the subsidies, force them to stop using their positions for personal and family ends, and no one who had anything else to do would waste his time in such *skimaxai*, such shadow boxing, to borrow a comparison from Cicero.

Ministers without support from public opinion, who when dismissed fall into the limbo of forgotten things; presidents of the council who spend their days and nights seeking to fathom the esoteric thinking the Emperor; a Chamber of Deputies conscious of its nullity and wanting only to be left alone; a Senate reduced to being a *prytaneum*; political parties that are nothing more than employment agencies and mutual benefit societies for their members. All these ostensible evidences of a free government are preserved by national pride like the consular dignity in the Roman Empire, but what we really have is a government of primitive simplicity in which responsibilities are infinitely divided while power is concentrated in the hands of one man. He is the chief of State. When some leader seems to have effective authority and power, individual prestige, it is because at that particular moment he happens to be standing in the light cast by the throne. Let him take one step to the right or left away from that sphere of light, and he vanishes for ever into the darkness. . . .

This so-called *personal government* has been explained by the absurd theory that the Emperor corrupted an entire people; that he demoralized our politicians by means of supreme temptations after the manner of Satan; that he stole the virtue of parties which never had ideas or principles, save as a field of exploitation. The truth is that this government is the direct result of the practice of slavery in our country. A people accustomed to slavery does not prize liberty or learn to practice self-government. Hence the general abdication of civic functions, the distaste for the obscure and anonymous exercise of personal responsibility, without which no people can be free, since a free people is only an aggregate of free individuals. These are the causes that have resulted in the supremacy of the only permanent and perpetual element—the monarchy.

8. ON RACIAL MISCEGENATION IN BRAZIL

In Brazil, the process of nation building was linked to debates that were specific to the national context. The late overthrow of monarchy (1889) and the establishment of a republic, for example, turned the opposition between the two into an expression of modernity and tradition. Another central issue of the period was the link between racial miscegenation and modern nation building. Like many of his contemporaries, Euclides Da Cunha (1866–1909) was deeply influenced by European evolutionist ideas of race, and adopted their pessimistic views on race mixture. The rebellion of Canudos in the backlands provided him with the opportunity to reflect on racial and geographical determinism. Da Cunha's famous book Os Sertões *(1902)—like Sarmiento's* Facundo—*is an essay on national interpretation and, to a great extent, a reflection on Brazilian national character. While condemning the military repression of the Canudos uprising and denouncing the brutal inequalities behind the utopia of the modern nation, Da Cunha exposes, in the excerpt below, the concern of many turn-of-the-century intellectuals over the racial instability of the typical* sertões, *a mixture of Indian and African ethnicities.*

An intermingling of races highly diverse is, in the majority of cases, prejudicial. According to the conclusions of the evolutionist, even when the influence of a superior race has reacted upon the offspring, the latter shows vivid traces of the inferior one. Miscegenation carried to an extreme means retrogression. The Indo-European, the Negro, and the Brazilian-Guarany or the Tapuia represent evolutionary stages in confrontation; and miscegenation, in addition to obliterating the pre-eminent qualities of the higher race, serves to stimulate the revival of the primitive attributes of the lower; so that the *mestizo*—a hyphen between the races, a brief individual existence into which are compressed age-old forces—is almost always an unbalanced type. Fovel compares them in a general way to hysterics, but the nervous disequilibrium in such a case is incurable; there in no therapeutic for this clash of antagonistic tendencies on the part of races of a sudden brought together and fused in an isolated organism. It is not to be understood how, after they have diverged so extremely for long ages—ages compared to which history is but a moment—two or three peoples can suddenly come together and combine their mental constitutions, thus annulling within a short space of time those distinctions which have resulted from a long, slow, laborious process of selection. As in algebraic sums, the qualities of the juxtaposed elements are not increased, subtracted from, or destroyed by the positive and negative signs that are present. The *mestizo*—mulatto, *mameluco*, or *cafuso*—rather than an intermediary type, is a degenerate one, lacking the physical energy of his savage ancestors and without the intellectual elevation of his ancestors on the other side. In contrast to the fecundity which he happens to possess, he shows extraordinary cases of moral hybridism: a brilliant mind at times, but

Euclides Da Cunha, *Rebellion in the Backlands (Os Sertões)*, intro. and trans. Samuel Putman (Chicago: University of Chicago Press, 1944), pp. 84–86. Reprinted by permission of the publisher.

unstable, restless, inconstant, flaring one moment and the next moment extinguished, victim of the fatality of biologic laws, weighted down to the lower plane of the less favored race. Important when it comes to forming any bonds of solidarity between the opposed forebears from whom he sprang, he can reflect only their various dominant attributes in a permanent play of antitheses. And when, as not infrequently happens, he shows himself capable of broad generalizations and of grasping the most complex abstract relationships, all this mental vigor (saving those exceptional cases which merely go to prove the rule) will be found to rest upon a rudimentary morality in which is present the impulsive automatism of the lower races.

The fact is that in the marvelous competition of peoples, all of them evolving in a struggle that knows no truce, with selection capitalizing those attributes which heredity preserves, the *mestizo* is an intruder. He does not struggle; he does not represent an integration of forces; he is something that is dispersive and dissolvent, suddenly springing up without characteristics of his own and wavering between the opposing influences of a discordant ancestry. The tendency toward a regression to the primitive race is a mark of his instability. It is an instinctive tendency toward a situation of equilibrium. The very play of natural laws would appear to extinguish little by little the anomalous product which violates those laws, by sending it back to its own generative sources. The mulatto, then, has an irresistible contempt for the Negro and seeks with a most anxious tenacity such intermarriages as may extinguish in his progeny the stigma of the dark brow; the *mameluco* becomes the inexorable *bandeirante* and hurls himself fiercely on the conquered native villages.

This tendency is significant. In a manner of speaking, it picks up the thread of evolution which miscegenation has severed. The superior race becomes the remote objective toward which the depressed *mestizos* tend; and the latter, in seeking this objective, are merely obeying their own instinct of self-preservation and defense. The laws of evolution of species are inviolable ones; yet, if all the subtlety of the missionaries was impotent when it came to winning the mind of the savage to the simplest conceptions of a superior mental state; if there is no force capable of causing the African, under the tutoring of the best masters, to approximate at least the intellectual average of the Indo-European—for every man, is above everything else, an integration of racial forces, and his brain is a heritage—if all this is true, how then account for the normality of an anthropologic type which suddenly makes its appearance, combining tendencies that are so opposed?

14

~

MODERNITY AND THE
EMERGENCE OF THE
NATION-STATE

As they consolidated their place as producers of raw materials and food-stuffs during the last quarter of the nineteenth century, Latin American economies further consolidated their path toward modernity. Argentina was probably the most spectacular case. With every indicator of economic expansion skyrocketing, hundreds of thousands of European immigrants arrived every year to settle permanently. But a similar tendency was evident everywhere else on the continent. Key areas of the export economy were in foreign hands—particularly those that were technologically complex. Railways carried commodities from the producing areas to the ports, sugar mills, refrigerated meatpacking plants, and grain storage silos. Some countries—particularly in Central America and the Caribbean—saw the development of foreign enclaves that grew increasingly isolated from neighboring zones as they modernized their infrastructure and developed according to the demands of foreign markets. Prosperity, however, did not mean economic stability, since the oscillations of the international market could quickly lead these dependent national economies from feverish growth to total collapse in short periods of time.

This general context of export-led prosperity, however, allowed political elites to consolidate their power, as the dominant climate of ideas shifted gradually from midcentury liberalism toward a more conservative—even authoritarian—conception of politics. A new type of "progressive" *caudillo*—Díaz in Mexico, Núñez in Colombia, Guzmán Blanco in Venezuela, Barrios in Guatemala—symbolizes this era of pragmatic liberalism. The phrase "Order and Progress," a motto used by political leaders, encapsulates the importance attached to both the concentration of power in the hands of the executive branch and to material prosperity. Traditional liberal claims for civil liberties and constitutional methods of government were no longer central to liberalism. Regional revolts did not disappear completely, but they became increasingly rare as states, in pursuit of a monopoly on violence, centralized and professionalized their armed forces. Material prosperity also allowed states to expand and streamline their bureaucracies, a fact reflected in the imposing state buildings that multiplied throughout the capital cities. Political discourse took a decidedly positivistic turn. The prestige of science persuaded leaders to associate their administrations with the languages and views of reform provided by medicine and biology.

As the century drew to a close, dissatisfied urban middle- and working-class groups combined to form parties that challenged the political establishments in a number of countries. Interestingly, the economic systems of these countries remained beyond major ideological challenge until the first decades of the following century. Democratic or radical parties, quite moderate in their demands, challenged the political elites on moral grounds. While the first socialist groups arose in Chile and Argentina as early as the 1890s, their historical moment would come later.

1. POLITICAL STABILITY AND ECONOMIC DEVELOPMENT

The year 1880 represents a turning point in the process of state and nation building in Argentina. The end of the "Indian problem," officially settled with the Campaign of the Desert (as the final stages of the war against the Indians were called), eliminated one of the main barriers to economic expansion, opening up vast tracts of new land and subjugating about 14,000 Indians. Thanks to the prestige he gained as the military leader of this undertaking (1879–1880) and to the endorsement by a broad coalition of governors and Buenos Aires political factions, Julio A. Roca won the presidential election. One of the most contentious issues—it caused an uprising after Roca's electoral triumph—was the location of the nation's capital (later resolved with the federalization of Buenos Aires and the foundation of La Plata, a new capital for the province of Buenos Aires). Delivered in this unsettled context, Roca's presidential inauguration speech exhibits a concern for civil order and asserts the legitimacy of the state's use of violence over dissident groups, which had been contested ever since the promulgation of the Constitution in 1853. In Roca's view, the consolidation of state authority would bring order and peace. Material progress would naturally follow.

General Julio A. Roca, "Discurso ante el Congreso al asumir la presidencia," *La Prensa*, October 13, 1880. Excerpt translated by the editors.

When it comes to the freedom and betterment of peoples, nothing great, nothing stable or durable can be achieved in the world without supreme effort and painful sacrifice. The hard tests that the Argentine Republic has been through should not surprise us, especially when we contemplate the rapid progress and compare the conquests made in our half-century of national life with the slow march of the governments of the most advanced societies. We live at a quick pace, and in our feverish impatience to one day reach the level that other peoples have achieved after centuries of work and bloody trials, we are surprised by, and unprepared for, many of the larger problems of our political and social organization.

The Congress of 1880 has complemented the system of representative, federal Government, and it can be said that only as of today has the rule of the Constitution been fully established. The law that you have just passed, establishing the definitive capital of the Republic, marks the beginning of a new era in which the government will be able to freely deploy its force, unfettered by the daily and depressing challenges to its authority that it had to face as it defended its rights against the invasive pretensions of subaltern functionaries. This law responds to the highest aspiration of the people, because it means the consolidation of the union, and the establishment of peace for many years to come. Its achievement was an inevitable necessity, and having so faithfully interpreted its support will entitle you to the gratitude of the Republic.

From now on, free from the worries and internal commotion that threatened everything, including the very integrity of the Republic, at each step the government will now be able to devote itself to the task of administration and to the labors of fruitful peace. The revolutionary era, which has continually hindered our regular march, is closed forever, and we will shortly harvest the fruits of your wise choice and integrity.

In assuming the general administration of the country, two main concerns prevail over all others: the army and the communication routes.

The army and the navy, which secure the integrity and protection of the motherland in the exterior as well as its internal peace and order, must claim the preferential attention of Congress and the new government. The Republic can count on an army that is exemplary in its self-abnegation, resilient, brave in combat, loyal, and faithful to its flag. But it lives at the mercy of arbitrariness, devoid of rules or laws that organize it under a regular and systematic plan. I will devote my greatest efforts to the reforms that are needed in this area, in order to avoid the dangers of militarism—in other words, the possibility of the suppression of liberty at some point in the future, and to turn the army into a true institution, which both the Constitution and modern progress require. In this way, immune from the movement of political parties, and exalted as it already is in the eye of the Republic, it will be able, if the rights of the Republic were ever to be compromised, to develop insuperable strength. This task will also have an economic purpose: keeping down useless expenses that weigh heavily on public funds, thanks to the inability of previous governments to found an efficient civil and military administration of the army.

As to the communication routes, they represent for me an imperious and inescapable need that cannot be delayed without doing harm to the common good. It is indispensable that the railways reach in the shortest possible time their natural terminals in the north, the east and the west, with their adjunct branches completing the communication system and linking in their material interests all the provinces with each other. He who has followed with attention the course of this country has noticed, as have you, the deep economic, social and political revolution that the iron road and the telegraph generate as they penetrate the interior. With these powerful agents of civilization, national unity has been consolidated, the spirit of *montonera* [localism] has been defeated and exterminated, and the solution of a seemingly unsolvable problem has been made possible, at least for the moment. Rich and fertile provinces await only the arrival of the railway, and the ease with which it will carry their diverse and high quality products to the markets and ports of the coast, in order to increase their productive capacity. As for me, I will consider it the greatest glory of my government if, in three years, counting from this day, we can salute with the locomotive whistle the towns of San Juan and Mendoza, the region of vines and olives; Salta and Jujui, the region of coffee, sugar and other tropical products, also opening the doors of commerce of Bolivia, which will bring the metals of its rich and inexhaustible mines. I count on your support, and that of the whole country, to undertake these works without delay—works that will neither strain nor surpass our resources, if only we can maintain peace.

The other realms of the administration—such as immigration, public instruction, the spread of education in all social classes, the due protection of religion, commerce, the arts and industry—are normal duties that no government can neglect.

I must, however, make special mention of the need to people the desert territories, formerly inhabited by savage tribes, and today open for settlement by numerous populations, as the most efficient way of securing its domination. I will continue the military operations in the south and north of the current frontier lines, until the submission of the Indians of Patagonia and Chaco is complete, in order to erase forever the military frontiers, so that there won't be an inch of Argentine land that won't be subjected to the laws of the nation. Let us free completely those vast and fertile territories of their traditional enemies, those that have represented a barrier to the development of our pastoral wealth. Let us offer guarantees to the life and property of those who go with their capital and their labor to fertilize them. Thus we'll soon see a multitude of men from all countries and races go there; and from the depths of those regions, today so desolate, we'll see the emergence of new provinces that will increase the power and greatness of the Republic.

When a young and vital people like ours unites its territorial extension and the liberalism of its institutions to a fertile land and a privileged climate, it need not envy the prodigies that, in similar conditions, have frequently appeared in the history of human societies. We are the promise of a great nation, destined to exert powerful influence in the civilization of America and the world. But in order to make the picture complete and perfect in all its details, it is necessary to step firmly on the path of the regular life of a people, similarly to those we have adopted as model. In other words, we need durable peace, stable order, and permanent freedom.

With this in mind, I declare loudly from this high stage, so that the whole Republic can hear: I will employ all the resources and means with which Constitution has endowed the nation's Executive, to avert, smother, and repress any attempt against public peace. Wherever in the Argentine territory a fratricidal arm is raised, or a subversive movement against established authority erupts, the whole power of the nation will be there to repress it. I hope, however, that this won't be necessary, because no one—neither men nor political parties—is strong enough to stop the wagon of the Republic's progress with the crime of civil war.

In contrast, the freedoms and rights of the citizen will be religiously respected. As long as political parties don't leave their constitutional orbit and don't degenerate into revolutionary parties, they can rest assured that their activities will not be limited or restricted by my government. All parties and noble ambitions can fit through the wide door of the Constitution and the law. Does anyone doubt that the party that has twice in six years made the mistake of attempting to repair with weapons its electoral defeat could today be legitimately leading the destiny of the nation, had it not resorted to such heinous extremes? . . .

I finish here, Honorable Sirs, with a brief statement of my approach to government: Sincere intentions; firm will to defend the nation's executive branch and to have our laws be strictly enforced; great humility in my own abilities; deep faith in the future greatness of the Republic; a spirit of tolerance of all opinions, as long as they are not revolutionary; and the healing of all the wounds that are inflicted and received during the electoral process— such are the personal qualities that I bring to the first office of my country. Fortunately, at this moment there is not one Argentine who does not understand the secret of our prosperity: that it depends upon keeping the peace and maintaining an absolute respect for the Constitution; and the outstanding qualities of superior men are certainly not needed to make straight, honest, progressive government. I can say, truly and without boasting, that the banner of my government will be: Bread and Administration. In order to achieve this, I will rely upon the protection of holy providence (that is never invoked in vain), the help of your insights, and the support of the national consensus that has brought me to this office, and of all honest men living in our land.

2. BUENOS AIRES: FIRST IMPRESSIONS

At the turn of the nineteenth century, the French newspaper Le Figaro *commissioned journalist Jules Huret (1864–1915) to travel to several European and American countries. As part of this mission, Huret visited Buenos Aires, and in 1911 he published his views on the prosperous Argentine capital. His impressions largely coincide with those of most foreign observers of that period: a new cosmopolitan nation in the midst of a frenetic race toward progress with many signs of a bright future ahead.*

We arrived in Buenos Aires one lovely winter morning. It was the month of July, and for the disembarking, all of the Argentine ladies had put on, with charming coquettishness, the most beautiful and most modern toilettes which they had brought from Paris.

This was demanded by fashion and the fevered impatience of those who were waiting for them. One of our traveling companions, who wept with emotion when she saw her mother (whom she had not seen for some time) on the pier, crossed the ramp and had barely reached dry land when I saw her surrounded by friends and relatives circling around her. With one hand holding her handkerchief, moist with tears, she opened with the other hand her fur coat, as if it to show its lining, which was as beautiful as the coat itself. She had barely dried her tears and was already smiling to welcome their congratulations.

From the pier, one single structure commands the view of the city. It is the most recently constructed hotel—the Plaza Hotel, a seven story building whose whiteness stands in sharp contrast to the blue of the sky. Thus, there is little similarity between the arrival in Buenos Aires and the arrival in New York—nothing of the monumental sight of North American cities, as certain comparative descriptions have claimed. Quite the contrary. The first impression one experiences is that of arriving in a great European city. That impression is due to the fact that nothing extraordinary claims our attention. It is true that streets are laid out as a chess board, and that many houses have no more than a first floor, but one is distracted from these idiosyncrasies by the city's bustling streets.

What town does Buenos Aires remind us of? Properly speaking, none. Perhaps London, for its narrow streets full of houses, its match vendors, and the black helmets of its policemen; Vienna, for its two-horse Victoria carriages; Spain, in general, because of its houses with plain facades, grated windows, and for the griminess of some of the more marginal streets; New York,

Jules Huret, *De Buenos Aires al Gran Chaco* (Buenos Aires: Hysamérica, 1988), pp. 26–29. Excerpt translated by the editors.

for its shoe-shine boys; Paris, for its beautiful Avenida de Mayo, its spacious sidewalks, and cafés with terraces.

I did not experience, at first, any of the impressions of the traveler who finds himself far from his center, none of the exoticness that great distances suggest, instilling in us a sense of being far away. Nevertheless, if you disembark on one of those sunny winter days that are not uncommon in Argentina, you will be seduced by the sweetness of the atmosphere and the idyllic purity of the sky. There are palm trees everywhere, and in the woods of Palermo, where you will take your first stroll, the great eucalyptus, the pepper and bamboo trees will make you understand that you are in a country with a wonderful climate, in an enchanted Riviera where life must be abundant and easy.

Between the pier where the boat lands and the center of town, you are surprised by the liveliness and activity everywhere. In the face of that enormous town, that immense unknown that has been growing in silence for twenty years without its Latin sisters noticing, I was not immune from the general surprise that I later observed in all those who had disembarked.

That vast port, with its ample piers, as clean as those of a German port, crowded with ships in three and four abreast; the orderliness of the disembarking; the politeness of the functionaries; the comfort of the Customs waiting-rooms; the luxurious cars driving you to the hotels through the main arteries; the bustling streets in the commercial district; Florida Street, so narrow, with its Parisian stores; the traffic in nearby streets, 25 de Mayo, Bartolomé Mitre, and Reconquista; the great offices and the teeming Banks, showing off their logos in white porcelain and sending your imagination wandering to the sites of London or Hamburg; all of that, taken separately or as a whole, makes up this great European town, a mixture of the capitals and commercial metropolis of Europe.

Nothing indigenous or typically local dilutes this impression. Where are the gauchos arriving from the countryside, the beggars on horseback or the powdered Cármenes I expected to see? To what far away neighborhood do I have to go to hear serenades outdoors by night? I saw nothing but elegant women wearing toilettes from Rue de la Paix, and young men dressed in Piccadilly suits, promenading in their carriages.

The impression of wealth is soon matched by that of activity. The luxury of the carriages and automobiles parading down the avenues; the general look of passers-by, elegant, polished, with fashionable ties, shoes with half boots as shiny as crystal—all of these reinforce the impression of prosperity suggested by the port and commercial streets.

I search in vain for people with red ties, buttons made with large diamonds or bombastic trinkets. I see people like you and me, perhaps a bit more elegant, with a British correctness (slightly out of place, because what suits the English and their affected rigidity, their stiffness and phlegm, does not suit the vivacious and spontaneous Latins). One certainly finds shinier shoes here than in any part of Europe. One notices their taste for polish and the cleanliness of their feet, whether varnished or polished, remind me of those of Athenians and Spaniards.

The impression of prosperity and luxury grows even more if one visits the western neighborhoods, as sumptuous as our Passy or our Plaine-Monceau, though with greater variety and even more private hotels, some quite exquisite. In certain areas, they remind one of Berlin or, even better, Charlottenburg, Schoeneberg, or Wilmersdorf with its new streets of houses, only more stylish and elegant.

The tidiness of the streets, the regularity and frequency with which they are cleaned, also reminds one of German towns. Men with small brooms and shovels work constantly in the busiest streets, cleaning and sweeping all day.

3. A DIFFERENT MODEL OF ECONOMIC DEVELOPMENT: A NEW PROGRAM FOR CHILE

The formula for Argentine development advocated by Alberdi (see Chapter 13), with its stress on opening the country to European capital, commerce, and immigrants, may be described as the classic nineteenth-century developmental model and was accepted by most Latin American countries and flourished from about 1870 to 1914. It came to be based on the exchange of a few staples, foodstuffs, and raw materials for European and North American finished goods. This exchange brought greater political stability and some prosperity to the area, but in the long run it created serious problems of dependency (neocolonialism) and underdevelopment. This model was not, however, the only possible or inevitable model for the area. Between 1811 and 1866, a state-directed program of autonomous economic development turned Paraguay into one of the most progressive and prosperous states in South America. This progress was destroyed by the terrible Paraguayan War of 1865–1870, which pitted Paraguay against Argentina and Brazil. In Chile, in the 1880s, President José Manuel Balmaceda offered a nationalistic program for a many-sided economic development that included the promotion of native industry and the Chileanization of the British-dominated nitrate industry. His program provoked a revolt by conservative forces, supported by British interests, that led to Balmaceda's defeat and suicide in 1891. The following excerpts from his speeches suggest the main thrust of his program.

Economic developments of the last few years prove that, while maintaining a just balance between expenditures and income, we can and should un-

---

José de Balmaceda, *El pensamiento de Balmaceda*, ed. Fernando Silva Vargas (Santiago de Chile, 1974), pp. 67–68. Excerpt translated by Benjamin Keen.

dertake productive national works that will nourish, more especially, our public education and our national industry.

And since I speak of our national industry, I must add that it is weak and uncertain because of lack of confidence on the part of capital and because of our general resistance to opening up and utilizing its beneficial currents.

If, following the example of Washington and the great republic of the North, we preferred to consume our national production, even if it is not as finished and perfect as the foreign production; if the farmer, the miner, and the manufacturer constructed their tools and machines whenever possible in our country's workshops; if we broadened and made more varied the production of our raw materials, processing and transforming them into objects useful for life or personal comfort; if we ennobled industrial labor, increasing wages in proportion to the greater skill of our working class; if the state, while maintaining a balance between revenues and expenditures, devoted a portion of its resources to the protection of national industry, nourishing and supporting it during its first trials; if the state, with its resources and legislation, and all of us together, collectively and singly, applied ourselves to producing more and better and consuming what we produce, then a more vigorous sap would circulate through the industrial organism of the Republic, and increased wealth and well-being would give us the possession of that supreme good of an industrious and honorable people: the capacity to live and clothe ourselves by our own unaided efforts.

The extraction and processing of nitrate must be left to the free competition of the industry itself. But the question of the privately owned and government-owned nitrate properties is a matter for serious meditation and study. The private properties are almost all foreign owned, and effectively concentrated in the hands of individuals of a single [British] nationality. It would be preferable that these properties belonged to Chileans as well; but if our national capital is indolent or fearful, we must not be surprised if foreign capital fills, with foresight and intelligence, the void in the progress of this region [Tarapaca] left by the neglect of our compatriots. . . .

The importance of nitrate in agriculture and industry and the growing tempo of its production counsel the legislator and the statesman not to delay the solution of the problem, and to resolve it by effectively protecting the interests of our nationals. It is true that this must not be done in such a way as to effectively stifle free competition and production of nitrate in Tarapaca, but neither should we allow that vast and rich area to become a mere foreign enclave. We cannot ignore the very real and serious fact that the peculiar nature of the industry, the manner in which the nitrate properties came into being, the absorption of small properties by foreign capital, and even the temper of the races that dispute the dominion of that vast and fertile region, demand a special legislation, based on the nature of things and the special needs of our economic and industrial existence. This question has such profound consequences for the future that upon its solution will in large part depend the development of our private wealth, today removed from that fecund center of labor and general prosperity.

4. PORFIRIO DÍAZ ASSESSES HIS LEGACY

For nearly thirty-five years (1876–1911), Mexico was under the effective control of one man, General Porfirio Díaz. According to the regime's propagandists, this prolonged period of relative stability provided a much needed respite from contentious politics and a golden opportunity for economic development under the expert guidance of Díaz's cadre of loyal científicos *(technocrats). Economic development, in turn, was promoting the growth of democratic sensibilities in the Mexican people through expanded educational and employment opportunities. Much of that economic development would come from increased foreign investment drawn by generous financial incentives and guarantees of security. In this famous 1908 interview with American journalist James Creelman, Porfirio Díaz demonstrates his understanding of this developmentalist agenda as well as his mastery of public relations. The promise of free elections in the upcoming presidential campaign, probably intended for American rather than Mexican readers, encouraged the development of a political opposition that would eventually put an end to Díaz's authoritarian rule.*

"It is a mistake to suppose that the future of democracy in Mexico has been endangered by the long continuance in office of one President," he said quietly. "I can say sincerely that office has not corrupted my political ideals and that I believe democracy to be the one true, just principle of government, although in practice it is possible only to highly developed peoples." ...

"I received this Government from the hands of a victorious army at a time when the people were divided and unprepared for the exercise of the extreme principles of democratic government. [Díaz came to power in a military coup in 1876 after a disputed election.] To have thrown upon the masses the whole responsibility of government at once would have produced conditions that might have discredited the cause of free government."

"Yet, although I got power at first from the army, an election was held as soon as possible and then my authority came from the people. I have tried to leave the Presidency several times, but it has been pressed upon me and I remained in office for the sake of the nation which trusted me. The fact that the price of Mexican securities dropped eleven points when I was ill at Cuer-

James Creelman, "President Díaz, Hero of the Americas," *Pearson's Magazine* 19, no. 3 (March 1908): 234–245.

navaca indicates the kind of evidence that persuaded me to overcome my personal inclination to retire to private life."

"We preserved the republican and democratic form of government. We defended the theory and kept it intact. Yet we adopted a patriarchal policy in the actual administration of the nation's affairs, guiding and restraining popular tendencies, with full faith that an enforced peace would allow education, industry and commerce to develop elements of stability and unity in a naturally intelligent, gentle and affectionate people."

"I have waited patiently for the day when the people of the Mexican Republic would be prepared to choose and change their government at every election without danger of armed revolutions and without injury to the national credit or interference with national progress. I believe that day has come." . . .

"It is commonly held true that democratic institutions are impossible in a country which has no middle class," I [Creelman] suggested.

President Díaz turned, with a keen look, and nodded his head.

"It is true," he said. "Mexico has a middle class now; but she had none before. The middle class is the active element of society, here as elsewhere."

"The rich are too much preoccupied in their riches and in their dignities to be of much use in advancing the general welfare. Their children do not try very hard to improve their education or their character."

"On the other hand, the poor are usually too ignorant to have power."

"It is upon the middle class, drawn largely from the poor, but somewhat from the rich, the active, hard-working, self-improving middle class, that a democracy must depend for its government. It is the middle class that concerns itself with politics and with the general progress."

"In the old days we had no middle class in Mexico because the minds of the people and their energies were wholly absorbed in politics and war. Spanish tyranny and misgovernment had disorganized society. The productive activities of the nation were abandoned in successive struggles. There was general confusion. Neither life nor property was safe. A middle class could not appear under such conditions." . . .

"The future of Mexico is assured," he said in a clear voice. "The principles of democracy have not been planted very deep in our people, I fear. But the nation has grown and it loves liberty. Our difficulty has been that the people do not concern themselves enough about public matters for a democracy. The individual Mexican as a rule thinks much about his own rights and is always ready to assert them. But he does not think so much about the rights of others. He thinks of his privileges, but not of his duties. Capacity for self-restraint is the basis of democratic government, and the self-restraint is possible only to those who recognize the rights of their neighbors."

"The Indians, who are more than half of our population, care little for politics. They are accustomed to look to those in authority for leadership instead of thinking for themselves. That is a tendency they inherited from the Spaniards, who taught them to refrain from meddling in public affairs and rely on the Government for guidance."

"Yet I firmly believe that the principles of democracy have grown and will grow in Mexico."

"But you have no opposition party in the Republic, Mr. President. How can free institutions flourish when there is no opposition to keep the majority, or governing party, in check?"

"It is true there is no opposition party. I have so many friends in the Republic that my enemies seem unwilling to identify themselves with so small a minority. I appreciate the kindness of my friends and the confidence of my country; but such absolute confidence imposes responsibilities and duties that tire me more and more."

"No matter what my friends and supporters say, I retire when my present term of office ends, and I shall not serve again. I shall be eighty years old then."

"My country has relied on me and it has been kind to me. My friends have praised my merits and overlooked my faults. But they may not be willing to deal so generously with my successor and he may need my advice and support; therefore I desire to be alive when he assumes office so that I may help him."

He folded his arms over his deep chest and spoke with great emphasis.

"I welcome an opposition party in the Mexican Republic," he said. "If it appears, I will regard it as a blessing, not as an evil. And if it can develop power, not to exploit but to govern, I will stand by it, support it, advise it and forget myself in the successful inauguration of complete democratic government in the country."

"It is enough for me that I have seen Mexico rise among the peaceful and useful nations. I have no desire to continue in the Presidency. This nation is ready for her ultimate life of freedom." . . .

"The railway has played a great part in the peace of Mexico," he continued. "When I became President at first there were only two small lines, one connecting the capital with Vera Cruz, the other connecting it with Querétaro. Now we have more than nineteen thousand miles of railways. Then we had a slow and costly mail service, carried on by stage coaches, and the mail coach between the capital and Puebla would be stopped by highwaymen two or three times in a trip, the last robbers to attack it generally finding nothing left to steal. Now we have a cheap, safe and fairly rapid mail service throughout the country with more than twenty-two hundred post-offices. Telegraphing was a difficult thing in those times. Today we have more than forty-five thousand miles of telegraph wires in operation."

"We began by making robbery punishable by death and compelling the execution of offenders within a few hours after they were caught and condemned. We ordered that wherever telegraph wires were cut and the chief officer of the district did not catch the criminal, he should himself suffer; and in case the cutting occurred on a plantation the proprietor who failed to prevent it should be hanged to the nearest telegraph pole. These were military orders, remember."

"We were harsh. Sometimes we were harsh to the point of cruelty. But it was all necessary then to the life and progress of the nation. If there was any cruelty, results have justified it."

The nostrils dilated and quivered. The mouth was a straight line.

"It was better that a little blood should be shed that much blood should be saved. The blood that was shed was bad blood; the blood that was saved was good blood."

"Peace was necessary, even an enforced peace, that the nation might have time to think and work. Education and industry have carried on the task begun by the army." . . .

"And which do you regard as the greatest force for peace, the army or the schoolhouse?" I asked.

The soldier's face flushed slightly and the splendid white head was held a little higher.

"You speak of the present time?"

"Yes."

"The schoolhouse. There can be no doubt of that. I want to see education throughout the Republic carried on the national Government. I hope to see it before I die. It is important that all citizens of a republic should receive the same training, so that their ideals and methods may be harmonized and the national unity intensified. When men read alike and think alike they are more likely to act alike."

"And you believe that the vast Indian population of Mexico is capable of high development?"

"I do. The Indians are gentle and they are grateful, all except the Yacquis [Yaquis] and some of the Myas [Maya]. They have the traditions of an ancient civilization of their own. They are to be found among the lawyers, engineers, physicians, army officers and other professional men."

Over the city drifted the smoke of many factories.

"It is better than cannon smoke," I said.

"Yes," he replied, "and yet there are times when cannon smoke is not such a bad thing." . . .

5. Porfirio Díaz, Viceroy of Mexico

The Age of Díaz (1867–1911) enriched a favored few at the expense of Mexico's millions. Shortly after the dictator fell from power, a cultured Mexican exile wrote the following appraisal of the Díaz regime.

A popular maxim said, "Mexico is the mother of foreigners and the step-mother of Mexicans." This saying, which passed from mouth to mouth and even appeared in books by foreigners, summed up in a few words the financial, administrative, domestic, and foreign policies of General Díaz. And nothing explains better why, while foreign countries showered decorations on Díaz and his sons, nephews, kinsmen, and lackeys and exalted him as the greatest statesman of Latin America, the Mexican people, outside the circle of his adoring favorites, heaped curses on him and waited impatiently for death to snatch him from the Presidency of the Republic or for some man to arise and topple him from his pinnacle of power. . . .

The object of every national government is to improve the social and political condition of its people. A good government does not reject foreign aid, for that would be absurd and even impossible in the present state of civilization, but it insists that this cooperation always be subordinated to the national interest. Immigration is only desirable when the immigrant represents a civilizing force and joins his interests to those of the country in which he makes his residence.

Only colonial governments of the worst type have for their sole object the unrestrained, senseless, and disorderly exploitation of the national resources for the benefit of foreigners and the enslavement or extermination of the natives. The government of General Díaz belongs in this unhappy category. . . .

The dazzling prosperity of the Díaz era was due in very large part to the exploitation of certain resources—of minerals, above all—on a greater scale than ever before. The export of these commodities, as well as that of certain tropical products in great demand abroad, increased in an astounding way. In only twenty years of Díaz' rule the export of minerals rose from a value of 36 million pesos (in 1890) to more than 111 million (in 1910). In the same period the export of henequen increased from a value of less than 6 million to more than 20 million pesos, and the export of other tropical products, such as fine woods, tobacco, coffee, etc., also rose sharply.

But aside from henequen, coffee, and some other products of particular regions, this prosperity was based on the exploitation of exhaustible resources owned by foreigners who did not even reside in Mexico. The lion's share of the 120 million pesos of exported minerals went into dividends for foreign stockholders; only the extremely low wages paid to the workers remained in the country. As in colonial times, ships sailed from Mexico with treasure drawn from the bowels of the earth by enslaved Indians, for the benefit of

Luis Lara y Pardo, *De Porfirio Díaz a Francisco Madero* (New York, 1912), pp. 81–97. Excerpt translated by Benjamin Keen.

foreign masters who never set eyes on the places where those riches were produced.

As in colonial times, around these mines arose populous and hastily built centers. But again as in colonial times, the day had to come when the veins would be exhausted and the people would depart with empty purses, leaving only skeleton cities, vast cities of the dead like Zacatecas, Guanajuato, Taxco, that retain only the vestiges of their ancient splendor.

The same happened with our agricultural exports, except for henequen and coffee. . . . As concerns the exploitation of the fine woods, it is well known that it was carried on in such a destructive way that whole forests were ravaged without seeding a single useful plant in the looted soil.

Meanwhile agricultural production for the internal market, the cultivation of the grains on which our people live, remained stationary or even declined in relation to the population; year after year it was necessary to import North American corn and wheat to fill the needs of the internal market.

Equally dismal are the statistics for industry: There were 123 textile factories in 1893; eighteen years later the number was 146. And only the fact that the textile industry, almost entirely monopolized by Spaniards and Frenchmen, enjoyed privileges that closed the door to similar foreign articles and compelled the people to buy high-priced articles of inferior quality, made this achievement possible. The tobacco and liquor industries, on the other hand, advanced by leaps and bounds. There were 41 factories manufacturing cigarettes and cigars in 1893; in 1909 their number had increased to 437—that is, ten times. The production of rum reached 43 million liters in 1909.

The panegyrists of General Díaz proclaim his greatness as an administrator. They base their claim above all on the construction of more than 20,000 kilometers of railroads. I have already explained the open-handed generosity of Díaz in granting concessions to American capitalists for the construction of railroads. Each of these concessions was a gift, made directly to the capitalist involved or through the mediation of some favorite that he had bribed. All Mexico knows that many families owe their present wealth to concessions secured from General Díaz and sold to foreign capitalists. In the ministry of communications there were employees who defrauded the state of millions of pesos, taking bribes from individuals who obtained concessions and subventions for the construction of railways. It is no mystery that many of those roads were not constructed with the aim of favoring commerce or of meeting the needs of particular regions. . . .

The official statistics maintain a profound silence concerning the nationality of the directors of the mining companies, the great agricultural enterprises, and of the manufacturing industries of Mexico. But everyone knows that more than 75 percent of them are foreign; as for the railroads, their foreign character is so marked that English has been the official language of the majority of lines.

In order to explain and justify this situation, which became so acute during the rule of General Díaz that it caused almost a crisis of "antiforeignism," some say that our lack of enterprise, our apathy, and our ignorance render us unfit to exploit our own resources, and that these must inevitably pass into the hands of foreigners.

I do not deny that from lack of education and on account of the social conditions in our country the Mexican people suffer from such defects. Nor do I make the mistake of attributing this state of affairs to General Díaz, or of demanding that he explain why the national character did not experience a radical change under his rule.

But this is not the only reason that Mexico is absolutely dominated by foreigners at present; furthermore, the government of General Díaz made not the slightest effort to keep the foreign invasion within the limits of fair dealing and the national interest. The monopolization of business by foreigners would have been legitimate and beneficial for the country if it had been the result of free competition between the natives and the immigrants—if the latter, through their capital and their spirit of enterprise, employed within just and legal limits, had emerged victorious. . . .

But for every property legitimately acquired, for every dollar, or franc, or mark, or pound sterling invested in enterprises that yielded benefits to the country, how many monopolies, servitudes, ruinous and truly iniquitous contracts did the government of General Díaz not leave behind it!

Not apathy and ignorance but tyranny deprived the Mexicans of the possession and exploitation of their own resources. If a Mexican sought the grant of a waterfall, a forest, a piece of land, a mine, or a deposit of coal or oil, his petition had to be supported and endorsed by some minion of the President who secured at an exorbitant price the favor of having the matter attended to with fair dispatch. Frequently the Mexican, having purchased in this manner the services of public officials, would receive a round "No" for an answer; and in a little while he would see in the Official Daily the announcement that the favor he was applying for had been graciously granted—to none other than the person whose intercession he had sought!

And if this happened to Mexicans on a social level close to that of the privileged class, what must have been the condition of laborers, small farmers, and artisans! Pity the unhappy peasant who, loving the soil he had inherited from his forefathers and seized with a sudden passion for progress, undertook to irrigate his inheritance, to buy machines and use fertilizers, and who by means of patient and painful effort succeeded in obtaining the best yields and in attracting the attention of the neighborhood to his land! From that moment was awakened the rapacity of the *jefe político*, of the military commander, of the secretary of the state government, or of the curate, canon, or archbishop, who would not rest until they had despoiled him of his property;

and if he defended it with the admirable tenacity with which the Indian defends his land, he would land in the barracks, condemned to the slavery of the soldier-convict, or a group of soldiers would take him out of jail and shoot him in the back while on the march.

In the court archives of Mexico there are thousands of episodes of this kind. I have seen many of them; I know in detail histories that would fill books—stories of people dragged from their farms by soldiers in order to satisfy the greed of the governor, or the local commander, or the foreigner, supported by General Díaz.

In 1863 President Juarez, wishing to promote agriculture, issued the law of vacant lands (*terrenos baldíos*), by which public lands were ceded to whoever would locate, survey, and exploit them, paying for them at a fixed price and receiving a part gratis in return for his engineering services. Basing itself on this law, the government of General Díaz committed the greatest iniquities. Documents published in Mexico show that time and time again certain magnates, seized by the fever of speculation in lands called "vacant," despoiled not only individuals but entire towns that had worked and made their living from those lands for centuries.

Among the many notions that certain sociological theories proclaim, and that serve to justify robbery by conquest, there is a fine-sounding doctrine that dazzles even educated and thoughtful persons. It affirms that if the owner of a source of wealth does not exploit it he may rightly be despoiled whenever there appears a claimant capable of making better use of it.

It would not have been so bad if this doctrine had really inspired and justified all these iniquities. One would have less cause for complaint if the natives had changed from the class of owners to that of tenants, or even to that of employees, peons, day laborers of the new owner, and if land once barely cultivated had begun to produce in abundance with the aid of irrigation, the plow, fertilizer. If all the square kilometers of land seized from their legitimate owners during the reign of Don Porfirio were now in production, even at the extremely low level of production typical of Mexican agriculture, all the granaries of the Republic would now be filled, and from our ports would depart ships loaded with wheat, flour, corn, and the many other products that the benign climate of Mexico yields.

But that is not what happened; in the great majority of cases the inhabitants were simply expelled and the lands closed to exploitation, awaiting the coming of some Yankee prospector in search of vast tracts—to be used in bamboozling his countrymen through the organization of one of many fraudulent agricultural companies. In official newspapers of the States I have seen the orders given by the authorities to inhabitants of villages and towns to abandon their homes and give up their lands to avaricious claimants. And those unhappy Indians, whose only crime was that they lacked a written title to the lands on which their forefathers had peacefully lived since long before the birth of Columbus, frequently preferred to die hunted down like wild beasts, or to rot in jail, to leaving voluntarily what for them was their only patria. . . .

Governmental expenditures during the thirty-five years' reign of Don Porfirio amounted to more, much more, than 2 billion pesos. This vast sum was entirely at his disposal; it was tribute paid by the country that General Díaz could have invested in bettering the social condition of Mexico. But of this immense sum of money not a cent was ever invested in irrigating or fertilizing the land on which 12 million Indians passed their lives in struggle for a handful of grain with which to sate their hunger. Nor was any part of it used to bring to these people—the largest social class, the only class devoted to the cultivation of the soil—some notion of justice or some education that would enable them to take a step toward civilization. Not the least effort was made to liberate the rural population from the slavery that made its life almost intolerable. Calling itself paternal, his government made not the slightest effort to rescue this enormous mass of people from the clutches of alcoholism, which a rapacious master class injected into the veins of the people the better to ensure its domination.

That is why at the end of those thirty-five years the rural population of Mexico continues under a régime of true slavery, receiving a daily wage of a few cents, sunk in ignorance, without hope of redemption. And since the monopolies have greatly raised the cost of living, the situation of the people in general is much worse than when General Díaz rose to power. Above that great oppressed mass arose a wealthy, brutal, splendid caste—but when has the wealth of a master class served any other purpose than to oppress and degrade the serfs? Has it ever served to liberate them?

The influence of General Díaz was as disastrous and corrupting on the political as on the social life of Mexico. Arrived at the pinnacle of power, he could and should have modified his system without danger to himself in such a way that the people could gradually have been educated in the exercise of their rights. . . .

But instead his policy of extermination, degradation, and prostitution was directed toward the concentration of power, and all the important changes that he made in the Mexican constitution were highly lethal to liberty and rendered the people increasingly incapable of governing itself. Thus, his most important reforms were designed to restrict the sphere of action of the town councils. Not even in the capital of the Republic—the center of culture, where the district action of the federal government was greatest—did he permit the existence of an elected council that would have charge of municipal taxation. On the contrary, he stripped the council of all its powers, converting it into an ornamental body, and put the municipal administration in the hands of the ministries. Another of his important reforms was to restrict trial by jury, and later he reformed the ley de amparo to the point where it was made inapplicable in civil cases. . . .

These were the salient features of the political system of General Díaz, and they justify my affirmation that his government was a viceroyalty, bringing a peace of extermination and oppression; pompous, brilliant, and profitable to foreigners, but productive of ills to the patria that future generations may be unable to cure.

6. A Popular Perspective on Modernity

The prints of José Guadalupe Posada (1852–1913), especially his skeletal calaveras, have become perhaps the best known example of Mexico's rich popular culture and an inspiration to generations of Mexican (and Mexican American) artists eager to develop a distinctive national (or ethnic) style. Posada did his most important work as an illustrator for a Mexico City broadsheet publisher, Antonio Vanegas Arroyo, and for the capital's lively turn-of-the-century penny press. The Vanegas Arroyo broadsheets were single pages (sometimes on brightly colored paper), with an illustration, often by Posada, at the top and explanatory text at the bottom. The subject matter varied widely—death, oddities of nature, bullfights, religious images, sensational crimes, bandit escapades, executions, political commentary, battles (especially during the revolutionary years), macho men, and heartless women—anything the publisher thought would sell. While the broadsides functioned primarily as tabloids, the penny press specialized in political and social satire. Intended for a working-class audience that bore the brunt of Porfirio Díaz's obsession with order, the penny press mocked vain women, corrupt politicians, Yankee interlopers, capitalist exploiters, upper-class pretensions, and ignorant policemen. The four images included here reflect popular attitudes toward the Díaz administration's attempts at modernization: "Great Electric Skeleton" uses traditional Day of the Dead imagery and humor to expose the often violent side of modern conveniences like electric streetcars—violence that in the case of Mexico City was both symbolic and real. "The American Mosquito" is a humorous example of long-standing popular complaints about the encroachment of capital and culture from the United States, often in conjunction with the railroads. "New and Entertaining Verses of a Brave Man from Bajío" contrasts the rough, traditional masculinity of a provincial cowboy from north-central Mexico with the smoother, more modern style of his urban counterparts. "Feminism Imposes Itself" reflects urban male anxieties about the emasculating effects of modern civilization. The number 41 refers to the scandalous 1901 arrest of forty-one men, half of them dressed as women, at a private party in downtown Mexico City—an incident that turned the number 41 into a popular code for male homosexuality.

José Guadalupe Posada, "Gran Calavera Eléctrica."
Courtesy of the Department of Special Collections,
Stanford University Libraries.

Title:	Great Electric Skeleton
Full Title:	Great Electric Skeleton presents a very sharp looking *calavera*
	[Day of the Dead image] of pure electricity.
Subheading:	The first of November,
	Like devils will run
	The electric street cars
	That go out to Dolores [cemetery in Mexico City].
Verse 4:	The electricity will be
	Of the strongest, *señores*,
	There will be dead folks and skeletons
	On their crop-tailed horses.
Verse 10:	Into the light of many lamps
	Lit by our electricity
	The dead there [at Dolores Cemetery] will emerge,
	From their tombs to dance.
Verse 24 :	The electric street cars
(next to the	¡So many people they'll bring
last verse)	To turn them into skeletons
	With pure electricity!

366

José Guadalupe Posada, "El Mosquito Americano."
Courtesy of the Department of Special Collections,
Stanford University Libraries.

Title: The American Mosquito
Subheading: The American Mosquito
Has just now arrived;
They say that it came to walk around
On our Mexican soil.

Verse 1: They say it started on Sunday
Over there in Laredo, Texas,
Biting on the ears
Of some old women at the Station.
It made them run around
Until it made them sweat
This inhuman beast:
The American Mosquito.

Verse 2: It proceeded on to Guanajuato,
This is a laughable thing,
It never made it to the center of town,
But it was in Marfil.
Now they suffer no more
Such a rude and haughty thing,
Why it bit an old soldier
Right on his behind.
Because it's really very crude
The American Mosquito.

Verse 3: It went off toward Irapuato
And passed through Pénjamo;
From there it returned
Through the village of Uriagato,
The hacienda of Villachato
It left all in shambles;
All the people frightened
As their buddy Mariano found them,
Grandma Emeteria shouted:
The American Mosquito.

Verse 4: Through the ports of San Juan
Piedra Gorda and la Sandía,
An old woman said:
"Jesus, what a ferocious beast!"
Tell me Don Pascual
Has the Mosquito arrived?
They say it's really tiny,
And also very beastly;
What does it say papa Pachito
The American Mosquito?

NUEVOS Y DIVERTIDOS VERSOS
DE UN VALIENTE DEL BAJIO
A SUS VALEDORES.

Aquí estoy por que ya vine,
Por que quiero y por que sí,
Vengo á ver si encuentro uno
Que pueda igualarse á mí

Soy de Ranchería de Amoles
De la pura Sierra soy......
Y soy de lo más hombrote
Y á cualquiera parte voy.

Traigo mi caballo prieto;
Buena silla de montar;
Una rechulona cuarta
Y espuelas de apuntillar.

Suave reata, buen machete
Y mis pistolas de á par,
Mi jorongo potosino;
Mi charrito del Palmar.

Toquilla de *cieriopelo*,
Barbiquejo de juglar,
Ando forrado de cuero
Como charro caporal.

Porque me dá la real gana
Y á ningun cuerno le vá....
Con mis tacos de baqueta
Que á mi retebién me están.

Al pinto que no le cuadre
Que se vaya á rebuznar,
Y sabrá lo que es la leche
Que se toma en mi corral,

Yo he lidiado toros bravos
No gatos de garbanzal......
Nomás no regüelvan la agua
Porque así la han de tragar.

He bajado por el pueblo,
Porque los vengo á tantear;
Buscando á los jugadores
Que juegan tan bien billar.
Mi machetito es el taco.
Las ganas me han de sobrar;
La mesa el purito campo
Donde hemos de juguetear.
No le hace que sean grandotes
¡Si no los he de cargar!......
Y si se encuentran muy débiles
Gordas llevo en mi costal!
No crean que de hambre estoy flaco
Mis carnes así han de estar;
No por que me ven chaparro,
Crean que he de reventar....
La ley está en los chaparros
Y se los puedo probar.
Lo único que les encargo:
No se vayan á rajar......
Con ustedes me recreo
Y me los llevo á pasear,
No le hace que se amontonen;
A todos puedo tantear.
Traigan sus viejas si quieren,
Yo las puedo contentar....
Les mantendré á la familia,
Sóy *peche* pá trabajar.
Y itórenle y no reculen
Que no los voy á tragar,
No se espanten con la sangre
Ni se vayan á llamar. . .
Sóy su paracito, chulos,
A quien han de *respetar*....
No más no regüelvan la agua..
Porque así la han de tragar.

José Guadalupe Posada, "Nuevos y divertidos versos
de un valiente del Bajío a sus valedores." Courtesy of the
Harry Ransom Humanities Research Center,
University of Texas–Austin.

Title: New and Entertaining Verses of a Brave Man from Bajío to
       his Buddies

Verse 1: Here I am because I came,
       Because I want to and just because,
       I come to see if there's anyone
       That can measure up to me.

Verse 2: I'm from the Amoles ranch
       A man of the Sierra is what I am. . . .
       And I'm one of the manliest men
       And I go where I please.

Verse 3: I bring my bay [horse];
       A good saddle;
       A really fancy riding crop;
       And my pointed spurs. . . .

Verse 9: I've come down to town,
       To check out how things are;
       To find out about the players
       Who play so well at pool. . . .

Verse 14: I'm going to have some fun with you
       I'll take you out to walk around,
       Just don't let the folks get pushy;
       Everyone will get a chance to see.

Verse 15: Bring your women if you like
       I can make them happy too. . . .
       I'll keep them in the family way
       'Cause I put my back into my work.

Verse 16: So don't choke up and don't back down
       I'm not going to swallow you up,
       Don't let your blood run cold,
       I'm not going to call you out . . .

Verse 17: I'm your papa, hotshots,
       The one you must *respect* . . .
       So don't stir up the water boys . . .
       Because that's the way you'll drink it.

370

José Guadalupe Posada, "El feminismo se impone," *La Guacamaya*, July 25, 1907. Courtesy of the Benson Latin American Collection, University of Texas–Austin.

Title: Feminism Imposes Itself
Verse 1: While the woman goes off
          to the workshop and the office,
          and dresses in cashmere,
          and abandons the home
          and enters freely into bars,
Verse 2: The clean-shaven man
          stays [at home] making breakfast
          he sews, irons, and cares for the baby,
          and all of them with great affection (?)
          they call forty-one.

7. "THE OLD ORDER CHANGETH . . . "

The abolition of slavery in 1888, followed the next year by the establishment of the re-
public, consummated a long evolution in Brazil's economic and social life. Eminent
Brazilian historian Pedro Calmon interprets these important developments.

In Brazil, the historical and chronological epochs do not coincide. Our sixteenth century began in 1532, with the founding of S. Vicente; the seventeenth, in 1625, with the restoration of Bahia; the eighteenth, in 1694, with the discovery of the mines; the nineteenth, in 1808, with the arrival of the Portuguese Court. Our twentieth century began in 1888–89, with the abolition of slavery, which transformed the economy, and the foundation of the Republic, which changed the political face of the country.

The Revolution of 1888–1889 was profound and general in its consequences.   More than a government fell before the advance of the new conditions of national life, before Federalism and revolutionary, Americanist liberalism. To the hierarchical and respectable society of the Empire succeeded a different society. The skillful, conciliatory formulas of Dom Pedro's parliamentary regime had long put off or concealed the collapse of the equilibrium between the old antagonisms of Brazilian society—the capital and the provinces, agriculture and industry, French and American models, order and idealism, the barons of the monarchy and the lawyers, traditional stability and rapid progress. But the machine went off its course amid the tumults of the eighties; there was the abolitionist campaign, the military question, the skepticism of the disgruntled parties (the Liberal Party, whose idealism had lost it the elections of 1881 and 1884, and the Conservative Party, which won empty victories in its exhausting struggle against erupting reforms), and the weight of years and illness pressing upon the Emperor.

A new generation demanded new laws.   The provinces of the South wanted tariff protection for industry; the North demanded protection for its decaying agriculture, credits, and free trade.

The sudden emancipation of the slaves inaugurated the epoch of immigration. High prices for coffee enabled São Paulo to bear the blow of abolition without disruption of its aristocratic plantation system. The *fazendeiros* could pay for labor and thus retain the workers they had acquired in recent years from the slave traders. Foreign colonists (beginning in 1888, 100,000 entered each year through the port of Santos!) swelled the ranks of the labor force.

Pedro Calmon, *História social do Brasil*, vol. 3, *A época republicana* (São Paulo, 1939), pp. 1–6. Excerpt translated by Benjamin Keen.

But in the province of Rio de Janeiro and in the Recôncavo, agriculture languished and withered because of unfavorable conditions: an exhausted soil, ancient and divided estates of scanty yield, the patriarchal character of the economy, kept alive only by class spirit and the historic ties of the great families to the land on which they had lived for three centuries. The *usina*, the great sugar factory, destroyed the sugar mill of colonial type and swallowed up the properties of the old nobility. . . . The axis of wealth, and with it the axis of power, shifted from the Recôncavo to the South. In 1887 the political poles were Cotegipe and Antonio Prado, or Paulino and Silveira Martins. The cycle of sugar against that of coffee and cattle. The binomial of the nineteenth century (sugar and coffee), perhaps the agricultural formula of the unity of the Empire in the epoch of the aristocratic *latifundio* and the baron-colonels, was shattered. Coffee could survive without the slave, and withstood the blow of abolition. But sugar, blockaded in Brazil by the terrific development of other sugar-producing centers, could not endure that shock. Sugar gave Brazil its independence in 1822. Coffee made the Republic in 1889.

Not that the conservative coffee planters were anti-monarchical by conviction and temperament. On the contrary, until 1888 they regarded the monarchy as their chief point of support. But they were tied to the mentality of a swift-moving civilization. They belonged to a time of audacious enterprises.

The divergence between the two economic zones was essentially a contrast in rhythms. Sugar moved slowly, coffee at a dizzy pace; one was a fixed, static culture, the other was extensive and expansive. The vertical line (sugar) combined with the horizontal (coffee) to define the "dynamism" of Brazil: solid and unstable, paralyzed in a conquest, the structural Brazil of the North, the polymorphic Brazil of the South. . . .

The coffee planters and a climate of liberalism, well suited to the pursuit of individual and unlimited prosperity, arose together. They had no use for the maturity and serenity of that other agriculture, the slow-moving culture of the cane, which crystallized its social types in the shadow of the colonial sugar-mill, gaining in deep, sentiment-steeped roots what the coffee planter gained in new horizons. . . .

If one word can sum up the political confusion of that phase of transition from one regime to another, that word is—impatience.

The effect of abolition was as great in the minds of men as in the material realm.

Three days had sufficed to bring crashing down the infamous system that had lasted three centuries. If total reforms were so easy, why hesitate to illuminate the land with the ardent new lights of the time? Federation in American style; a republic *à la française*; a strong government as taught by Auguste Comte; industries, factories, companies, banks, inflation, business, as in the United States—and away with senile caution!

The movement of ideas that brought the *coup d'état* of November 15 was freighted with that formless impatience as the summer wind is freighted with the tepidity of the earth, the fire of space. . . . There arose a vague crusade against dogmas. A spiritual insurrection against the past, against consecrated values. A change of symbols, of principles, of ends. Instead of political continuity, the revolution; instead of monarchical ruralism, republican citizenship; no more national *unity*, but *union* of autonomous States; strong government, and not weak cabinet governments; speeches in the streets, not in Parliament; a "Jacobin" and lyrical nationalism, as in 1831, but with different models— democratic equality, a clamor of popular demands, and, in place of the ancient Emperor, a President-marshal. Let the giant learn to walk . . . urged the liberal propagandists. Let a democracy of labor replace patriarchal customs; let the States place no impediment in the way of prosperity; let the citizen not feel the restraining hand of government upon his new-found liberty, cut to the patterns of Gambetta and Castelar.

The army removed the barrier of the Empire from that road. . . . The army precipitated the transformation; most important of all, it insured external peace, the appearance of transition without disorder. In the paralysis of the constitutional parties, of the old governing class, with its sense of organization it gave discipline and order to the nascent federation. An officer assumed the government of the province; supported by its garrison, he kept the officials at their posts, protected the magistrates in the performance of their duties. Anarchy was thus avoided.

Indeed, the least dramatic revolution was the political: the overthrow of the throne by the second brigade of Rio de Janeiro, commanded by Marshal Manoel Deodoro da Fonseca. It was Brazilian society that experienced change from top to bottom. No superficial tempest, this; all social strata were affected by the upheaval. It was not so much a new régime as a new century that arose. Republic? Say, rather, the twentieth century.

Aristides Lobo, correspondent of the *Diario Popular* of São Paulo, wrote for his readers a letter that has the revealing quality of a portrait, on November 15, 1889:

"For the time being the aspect of the government is purely military, and so it should be. Theirs was the work, only theirs, because the action of civilian elements was practically nil. The people looked on, stupefied, astonished, dumbfounded without an inkling of what it all meant. Many honestly believed that they were watching a parade."

8. ". . . Yielding Place to New"

In the wake of the revolution came a flurry of modernization, with changes in manners, values, and even the physical appearance of some of Brazil's great urban centers. These changes were most marked in the federal capital, made into a beautiful and healthful city through the initiative and efforts of Prefect Pereira Passos and the distinguished scientist Oswaldo Cruz.

Eighteen-ninety was a year of rash gaiety, of a revolution in manners more intense and profound than the political revolution. Gone were the restraints of the hierarchy, of the polished and sober bon ton of the Empire. Rio de Janeiro was transformed from top to bottom. The new "republican equality" cut off its peaks; the new police force of Sampaio Ferraz cleansed its roots. The Great Boom, the *Encilhamento*, subverting economic values and making wealth a common and dominant ideal, suddenly destroyed the moderate and elegant conception of life that had long prevailed and that had been inherent and implicit in the monarchical system, with its lifetime Senate, the honors of the Court, the tradition that statesmen should grow poor in the public service instead of enriching themselves, the radiant, fastidious honesty of the Palace of São Cristovão. Barons with recently acquired titles jostled each other in the corridors of the Stock Exchange or in the Rua da Alfândega, buying and selling stocks; the tilburies that filled the length of São Francisco Street were taken by a multitude of millionaires of recent vintage—commercial agents, bustling lawyers, promoters of all kinds, politicians of the new generation, the men of the day. They were shunned with dignity by the nonconformists, members of the old nobility, politicians of the Empire who held aloof; another year, and their number would be swollen by the disillusioned. But the Republic was not simply a movement against "Your Excellencies" in the name of plain "you." It took strong measures against hooliganism, against the disorders of the popular wards. In the very first days of the regime, Sampaio Ferraz cleaned out the vagabonds who had infested the city for a hundred years. . . . The gangs and the "young gentlemen of quality" went out together. The symbol of the new governing class was the horse car—leaving from the corner of Gonçalves Dias Street—whose "bourgeois benches" united all the citizens in perfect equality.

Pleasure—easy, commercial, exotic—held sway. The coffee-houses were full, the Rua do Ouvidor thronged, the horse cars crowded. Roulette-wheels were installed in private houses; the club became a business center; the vicissitudes of the Great Boom were discussed at the tables of the confectionary shops where literati, financiers, gamblers, and courtesans congregated and astounded, dazzled provincials looked on. "City of vice and pleasure" was how the annoyed Anselmo Coelho Neto described "the Federal Capital." . . .

Calmon, *História social de Brasil*, pp. 143–145, 164–169. Excerpt translated by Benjamin Keen.

The Epidemic.   That Federal Capital, refulgent in spirit and quivering with civic excitement, had its fashionable season and its season of gloom. The carioca unquestionably grew accustomed to yellow fever. He came to regard it as a cyclical scourge, his summer ailment, recurring each year between December and April and terrible at the start, especially for foreigners; but that soon ceased to disturb the routine life of the great city, which solved the problem as best it could. The people went to the mountains. They fled to the high spots of the surrounding countryside. They returned to nature, abandoning the city—and with it those who could not get away—to its periodic tragedy. There remained only the poor, the merchants, the officials. Petropolis offered its charms of a European city to the invaders of the upper class. It was even more imperial under the Republic, more opulent, more desired, but now without the examples of sobriety, the lessons in modesty, of Dom Pedro II.

In connection with the commemoration of the fiftieth anniversary of the arrival of the Sisters of Notre Dame de Sion in Brazil (they landed at Rio on October 9, 1888), their "diary" was published, with its disillusioned impressions of the plague-ridden Rio summer, of the horror inspired by the fever. . . . One of the nuns, Mother Felix, soon died, and the others left for Petropolis. They were ordered to remain there, together with their school for girls, which, between 1889 and 1892, functioned part of the year in Rio and the rest of the time in the mountains. A teacher who kept his pupils in the city during the period of the epidemic, that is, during the summer, would have committed a crime. The capital became uninhabitable, particularly for foreigners. The obituary lists caused terror. Hundreds died each month.

The Renovation of Rio de Janeiro.   Oswaldo Cruz and Prefect Passos were the powerful arms that awoke the sleeping city. It awoke with a start at the sight of the gangs of workmen that began to demolish the old Rio. . . .

The monarchy fell in effigy in 1889.

The past really fell in 1904, with the passing of the narrow streets in the center of the city, with the widening of the city's heart, with the construction of modern avenues that would permit the free movement of a people fascinated by the civilization which thus made its triumphant entrance.

If the duel between sanitation and popular distrust had its trying aspects, from cold incredulity to armed resistance, the struggle of the city planner with the spirit of routine was no less dramatic and difficult. Both men could count on the absolute solidarity of the Federal Government; Cruz and Passos would not accept their dangerous missions on any other terms. The law of December 29, 1902, placed in the authoritarian hands of the Prefect almost dictatorial powers. Article 25, for example, authorized him to remove the occupants of condemned dwellings with the aid of the police and without judicial appeal. He got everything he asked for. Recalcitrants who beat at the doors of justice found themselves escorted away by armed soldiers. Passos was arbitrariness itself. It was a terribly lawless situation, in which a single man, absorbed in the mysteries of his plans, decided the fate of a city. But it was effective and necessary. A loan of six million pounds sterling that the Prefecture was empowered to float failed in Europe: Rio's business community covered it to the amount of four million pounds. Force and money—Passos' iron will would do the rest. That will did not weaken.

Cruz and Passos, working in concert, cultivated an ungrateful soil.

Hygiene depended on remodeling the city, on doing away with the cesspools and dissolving the ancient filth; and the old Rio could be made over only by conquering yellow fever. Each in his own field, the two dictators of public improvement encountered the same hostility. Oswaldo Cruz fought the battle of convictions—his struggle was the more abstract. Pereira Passos confronted a league of vested interests—his fight was more concrete. He faced the hostility of business, the property owners, the stubbornly, solidly conservative classes. The passivity of tenants, the force of habit, the new liberalism that taught the inviolability of the home, the old customs. . . .

Had he attempted to realize partial reforms, like those carried out at the end of the Empire, like the opening of Gonçalves Dias (1854) and Senador Dantas streets or the ward of Vila Isabel, he would have met with universal applause. But his program, just like the hygienist's, was total and brusque.

Since 1871, as a member of the commission named by Minister João Alfredo, Passos had meditated on his grand project. He kept it to himself until 1902. In 1882, together with Teixeira Soares, he had obtained the franchise for the construction of the Corcovado Railroad. . . . Now his plan consisted in tearing down the old buildings, in rectifying with rectilinear and tree-covered designs the tortuous colonial plan. No more unlighted hovels and big old houses falling into ruins, no more dirty streets and discolored façades, no more repellent odors of pestilent alleys, no more oppressive atmosphere of the colonial city. He used his engineering equipment like a broom. He had to sweep away the filth of a commercial city that had grown too fast within the small area that housed its asphyxiated prosperity and its slums, its plenty and its poverty, its warehouses and its congested society that gasped for breath within the narrow bounds of its historic walls. Passos attacked the problem as a whole. He dislodged without pity the merchants affected by the condemnations, and took for their basis the low declarations of value made for tax purposes. He gave the construction of the new arteries the appearance of a catastrophe. . . . He worked with great haste. He knew that without drive and energy, without closing his eyes to cases of individual hardship, he could not carry his plan through. And the worst of all would be to leave the job half done, the houses torn down, the avenues still unopened, all buried in the rubble of the demolitions, with nothing to show for the destruction he had wrought. He had to be adamant in order to be efficient. On all sides he met with resistance. The newspapers hurled insults at him; the merchants whose interests were affected opposed him. He would be handed a court summons by day and by that night began leveling the walls. The controversy increased as endless points of law were invoked—but meanwhile the pickaxes did not stop. Without that useful and massive violence he would have failed at the very start—he and Oswaldo Cruz. His heroism consisted in making himself insensible to all protests. President Rodrigues Alves armed himself with the same stoicism. The tactic was a skillful one: first tear down, then be free to rebuild at will. . . .

The first section of the new port at Rio de Janeiro was inaugurated November 8, 1906.

That year electric lights bathed the city in their luminous glow.

The Prefect wanted Rio to be the best illuminated city in the world.

It was the touch of magic needed to make the prodigy visible; from the deep ruins of the year of devastations emerged the modern outlines of the rejuvenated city.

"Rio is becoming civilized," sang the minstrels of the people. The patriarchal city that on other nights, dimly lit by gas lamps, had resounded with their languid serenades, was fleeing before their eyes. The hills of Rio, the Santo Antonio, the Castelo, the Conceição, the Favela, now ceased to be the refuges of poverty. Down below, swarms of workers advanced over the clouds of dust raised by the demolitions. And from the rubble emerged the shining tracks of the tilbury and the newly-arrived automobile. . . .

9. OUR AMERICA

For Cuban nationalists chafing under Spanish colonial rule and observing the growing imperial ambitions of the United States, the confidence and optimism of turn-of-the-century liberal oligarchs in places like Argentina, Mexico, and Brazil seemed a bit naive. In this 1891 call to arms, exiled Cuban poet José Martí critiques the cosmopolitan pretensions of Latin American elites, calls for a new Latin American solidarity and self-awareness, and sings the praises of "Our America." He also issues an ominous warning about the need for Latin American countries to join ranks to meet the challenge of the "giants with seven league boots," in particular the United States. The annexation of Cuba, Puerto Rico, and the Philippines by the United States in the wake of the 1898 Spanish-American War—or from Martí's perspective, the U.S. intervention in the Cuban War of Independence—followed by a rash of early-twentieth-century interventions in the Caribbean basin suggests that his warning was timely (if generally unheeded).

José Martí, *Nuestra América* (New York, 1891). Excerpt translated by the editors.

The vain villager believes that the entire world is his village. And as long as he can remain the mayor or humiliate the rival that stole his sweetheart or augment the savings in his strong box, he sees the universal order as good, knowing nothing of the giants in seven league boots that might crush him underfoot or the celestial battle of the comets that pass through the still air, devouring worlds. What remains of the village in America must awaken. . . .

Peoples who know nothing of each other had better learn quickly—if they are to fight together. Those that shake their fists at each other like jealous brothers who both want the same piece of land, or the same small house, or that envy those with better houses, must join together, their two hands becoming one. Those that hide behind a criminal tradition in order to carve off, with a saber stained with the blood of their own veins, the land of the conquered brother already punished far beyond his crimes, if they don't want the people to call them thieves: Let them return their brother's lands. Debts of honor are not paid in money as so much a slap. We can no longer be a people of leaves that live suspended in air, our treetops in full bloom, snapping or rustling in response to the caress of capricious light or the whippings and beatings of tempests. The trees must join ranks so that the giant with the seven league boots cannot pass! It is the time for gathering and marching together, and we must proceed in tight formation, like the silver in the roots of the Andes.

Only the prematurely born are lacking in valor. . . . Because they lack valor, they deny it to others. Because the spindly arm, the arm with painted nails and bracelets, the arm of Madrid or of Paris, cannot climb the difficult tree, they say it cannot be climbed. Ships should be filled with these dangerous insects that gnaw the bones of the motherland that nurtures them. . . . These sons of carpenters who are ashamed that their father was a carpenter! These sons born in America who are ashamed of the mother that bore them because she wears an Indian apron and who renounce—the scoundrels!—their ailing mother and leave her alone on her sickbed! So who is the real man? He who stays to help cure his sick mother, or he who puts her to work where she can't be seen and who lives from her sustenance in the decaying lands with his worm of a necktie, cursing the womb that carried him, displaying a traitor's sign on the back of his fancy dress coat? These sons of our America that can only save itself through its Indians and that is improving; these deserters that enlist in armies of a North America that drowned its Indians in blood and that is getting worse! These delicate ones, who are men and don't want to do men's work! . . .

In what homeland can a man have more pride than in our long-suffering American republics, raised up by the bloody arms of a hundred apostles, among the mute Indian masses, the din of the struggle between the book and the [religious] candle? Never before in history, have such advanced and united nations been created from such disjointed elements. The arrogant man believes that the earth was made to serve as his pedestal, because he has a facile pen or colorful words, and he accuses his native republic of being in-capable or unredeemable because its jungles don't provide him the means to travel the world like a great lord, riding ponies in Persia and dispensing champagne. Incapacity is not in the nascent country which seeks suitable forms and useful grandeur but in those that would rule unique peoples of sin-gular and violent dispositions with laws derived from three centuries of free-dom in the United States or from ten centuries of monarchy in France. . . . Which is to say: to govern [in these republics] one must take care to govern well. And the good governor in America is not he that knows how they gov-ern in Germany or France, but he that knows what elements his country is made of and how to bring them together in order to arrive at—through methods and institutions born in the country itself—that desirable state in which each man knows and exerts himself, and where everyone enjoys the abundance that nature gave to all the people that they might make it fertile with their labor and defend it with their lives. The government must be born of the country. The spirit of government must be of the country. The form of government must derive from the proper constitution of the country. Gov-ernment is nothing more than the balance of the natural elements of the country.

For that reason the imported book has been vanquished in America by the natural man. Natural men have vanquished artificial letters. The native *mes-tizo* has vanquished the exotic creole. There is no battle between civilization and barbarism but between false erudition and a state of nature. Natural man is good and respects and prizes superior intelligence as long as it doesn't take advantage of his submission to harm him or offend him by treating him as in-consequential, which is something natural man never forgives, disposed as he is to recover by force the respect of whomever would wound his susceptibility or go against his interests. By pandering to these disdained natural elements, American tyrants have risen to power; and have fallen when they betray them. [American] republics have paid in tyranny for their unwillingness to get to know the true elements of the country, to derive from them the [ap-propriate] form of government, and to govern with them. "Governor," in a new nation, is to say "creator."

In nations composed of cultured and uncultured elements, the uncultured will govern through their practice of attacking and resolving doubts with their hands in those places where the cultured don't learn the art of gover-nance. The uncultured mass is lazy and fearful of intellectual endeavors, and it wants to be governed well. But if the government harms them, they shake it off and govern themselves. How are universities to produce governors if there is no American university where they teach the rudiments of the art of governance—which is the analysis of the particular characteristics of the American peoples? The young go out in the world to discover these things with Yankee or French eyeglasses and aspire to govern a people they do not know. Entrance into a political career should be denied to those ignorant of the rudiments of politics. Prizes should not be given for the best ode but for the best study of the country's characteristics. The newspaper, the faculty, the academy should advance the study of the country's real characteristics. To know them is enough, without blinders or ambiguities; because he that willfully or negligently sets aside a part of the truth falls in the end for the lack of that truth which grows if neglected and tears down what was erected without knowledge of it. . . . To know is to resolve. To know the country and govern it according to that knowledge is the only way to free it of tyrannies. The European university must give way to the American university. The history of America, from the Incas forward, must be taught in detail even if it means not teaching about the archons [leaders] of Greece. Our Greece is preferable to the Greece that is not ours. Ours is more necessary. National politics must replace exotic politics. Let us graft the world onto our republics; but the trunk must be our republics. And let us silence the vanquished pedant: there is no homeland of which a man could be more proud than of our long-suffering American republics. . . .

The continent—thrown out of alignment for three centuries by a regime that denied men the use of their reason, then ignored and turned a deaf ear to the ignorant multitude that had helped redeem it—introduced a government based on reason; an all-encompassing reason and not the academic reason of one side over the peasant reason of the others. The problem with independence wasn't the change of forms but the change of spirit. Common cause was needed with the oppressed to ensure a system that opposed the interests and practices of the oppressor's regime. The [colonial] tiger, frightened by the clash, returns at night for its prey. It dies shooting flames from its eyes and clawing the air. Its going is silent; it comes on velvet paws. When the prey awakes, the tiger is on top of it. The colony continues living in the republic; and our America is saving itself from its great mistakes—from the arrogance of the capital cities, from the blind triumph of the despised peasants, from the excessive importation of foreign ideas and formulas, from the iniquitous and impolitic disdain for the aboriginal race—for the greater virtue, paid for by necessary blood, of the republic that fights against the colony. The tiger waits behind each tree, crouching on each corner. It will die, clawing the air, shooting flames from its eyes. . . .

These countries will save themselves because a moderate temperament that comes from the harmonious serenity of nature seems to prevail in the continent of light and because the influx of a critical philosophy [positivism] from Europe has replaced the guesswork and utopianism that saturated the previous generation. A real man for real times is being born in America.

We were a vision, with the chest of an athlete, hands of a dandy, and forehead of a child. We were a mask, with English trousers, Parisian vest, North American jacket, and Spanish cap. The Indian—mute—circled around us and went off to the mountain, to the mountain peak, to baptize his children. The black—indolent—sang his heartfelt night songs, alone and unseen, between the surf and the wild beasts. The peasant—creator—aroused himself, blind with indignation, against the disdainful city, against his child. We were men of epaulets and robes in countries that came to the world with sandals on their feet and headdresses on their heads. The mark of genius would have been in joining together, with the charity of the heart and the daring of the founders, the headdress and the robe, in empowering the Indian, in incorporating the competent black, in bringing liberty to the bodies that rose up and conquered for it. Instead, we ended up with the general, the scholar, and the sinecure. Angelic youth, caught in the arms of an octopus, launched themselves into the sky, only to fall back in sterile glory, their heads crowned with clouds. The natural people, pushed by instinct and blinded by triumph, overwhelmed the golden staffs [of Spanish imperial government]. Neither the European book nor the Yankee book held the key to the Hispanic American enigma. Hate was tried, and each year the countries were worse off. Tired of useless hate, of the struggle of the book against the lance, of reason against the candle, of the city against the countryside, of the impossible dominion of the divided urban classes over the natural nation (tempestuous or inert), an attempt is being made, almost without realizing it, to try love. Nations stand up and greet each other. "How are we?" they ask, and with one another they talk about how they are. . . . The youth of America roll up their sleeves, sink their hands in the dough, and raise it up with the yeast of their sweat. "Create" is the password of this generation. The wine is plantain wine; and even if it comes out bitter: it is our wine! . . . [T]o be viable, liberty must be sincere and full. And if the republic fails to open its arms to everyone and move forward with everyone, the republic dies. The tiger within enters through the cracks, so does the tiger from without. The general makes the cavalry march at the pace of the infantry because if the infantry is left behind the enemy will surround the cavalry. [In Spanish the word *infantes* can mean both infantry and infants.] Strategy is politics. The nations must go on criticizing each other and themselves because criticism is healthy but with a single breast and a single mind. Let us reach down to the unfortunate ones and raise them in our arms! Let us melt a frozen America with the fire in our hearts! Let us send up, bubbling and ricocheting through the veins, the natural blood of the country! On their feet, with the happy eyes of workers, they greet each other, one people to another, the new American men. The natural statesmen arise from the direct study of nature. They read in order to apply but not to copy. The economists study the problems at their roots. Orators moderate their speeches. Playwrights bring native characters to the stage. Academics discuss viable subjects. Poetry cuts off its flowing locks and hangs its blushing vest on the glorious tree. Prose, sparkling and discerning, goes forth charged with ideas. The governors in the Indian republics learn Indian. . . .

But perhaps our America runs another risk that comes not from within but from the difference in origins, methods, and interests between the two continental factors. And soon an enterprising and energetic nation that dismisses and disdains [our America] will approach demanding intimate relations. And like all virile nations that have made something of themselves with shotguns and laws, they only love other virile nations. . . . The urgent duty of our America is to reveal itself as it is, united in soul and intent, swift conqueror of a suffocating past, stained only with fertile blood drawn from our hands by the struggle to clear away the ruins and from our veins by the pricks of our masters. The disdain of the formidable neighbor that does not know us is the greatest danger to our America. And because visiting day is at hand, it is urgent that our neighbor know us, and soon, so that it does not disdain us. Through ignorance, it would covet us. Through respect—once it knows us—it would release us from its grasp.

PART EIGHT

CONSOLIDATING THE NATION-STATE

15

❧

THE RISE OF MASS
POLITICS AND CULTURE

THE FIRST DECADES of the twentieth century witnessed the appearance of a new conception of politics that allowed for the increasing visibility and participation of the masses in several Latin American countries. The foundations of the neocolonial system, after being repeatedly undermined by international crises, were finally destroyed by the Great Depression. Meanwhile, political exclusion gave way to an era of mass politics and great charismatic leaders, who maintained the legitimacy of their rule by means of periodic political rituals—rallies, demonstrations, and so on. A growing consensus over the increased role of the state in the regulation of the economy, in the development of national industry, and in the organization of labor was at the root of most of the national and regional efforts during this era of mass politics.

The first major movement against the existing economic system (characterized by large plantations, peonage, and foreign control over national resources) and in favor of raising the living standards of the masses was the 1910 Mexican Revolution. Its first leader, Francisco Madero, emphasized political rather than social objectives. But popular pressure forced his successors to accept a social reform program. Even after peace returned in 1920, reform proceeded slowly and uncertainly. By 1928, many revolutionary leaders, now grown wealthy and corrupt, had abandoned their reformist ideals. Popular discontent with the rule of the "millionaire socialists" produced an upsurge of change in the administration of President Lázaro Cárdenas (1934–1940), when the agenda of the Mexican Revolution resumed its course and the material and cultural conditions of the majorities began to improve. In the context of a positive reassessment of state intervention in social and economic arenas, Cárdenas distributed land to the villages and made efforts to improve agricultural productivity. He also strengthened urban labor by replacing the old, corrupt leadership. Foreign economic influence was weakened in 1938, when the oil industry was nationalized. Like other leaders of his time, Cárdenas was interested in national control of strategic industries but was not opposed to private ownership in most instances.

In Brazil, the shift to populist politics was directly linked to the Great Depression and the collapse of the coffee industry. The establishment of a republic in 1889 had not threatened the dominance of the coffee producers and cattle ranchers of São Paulo and Minas Gerais. The sugar industry, seriously affected by the abolition of slavery in 1888, had already declined in importance. The problem of overproduction and falling prices for coffee led to official efforts to maintain prices at an artificially high level. After 1920, this chronic crisis diverted workers and capital to the manufacturing sector, which experienced considerable growth in São Paulo, Rio de Janeiro, and other urban centers. The collapse of the coffee industry in 1929, combined with bitter interprovincial rivalries, enabled Getúlio Vargas, a shrewd *caudillo* from Rio Grande do Sul, to seize power through a coup d'état. The Vargas years (1930–1945) saw sweeping centralization of power by the federal government, government assistance for the new industrialists as well as for agriculture, and a drastic silencing of all opposition. At the same time, his politics of wealth redistribution and legal protection of urban workers brought him enormous popularity as the "father of the poor."

In Argentina, the era of mass politics and culture was linked to the expansion of the urban population due to an influx of clerical and industrial workers (either native Argentines or recent European immigrants). In this more mobile society, the public education system played a key role, helping assimilate the children of these recent arrivals, increasing the literacy rate of the urban masses, and creating rising expectations of upward social mobility and political participation. Changes in the electoral legislation led to the first triumph of Hipólito Yrigoyen, the "radical" leader who opposed the oligarchic regime that had held power since 1880. Although Yrigoyen did little to challenge the economic preeminence of the landowning elite, his quasi-religious leadership style, combined with the plebeian tone of his administration, did much to alienate the conservative opposition. After fourteen years of radical rule, Yrigoyen was ousted by a military coup, inaugurating what would become a long sequence of military interventions in Argentine politics. Ironically, it was from the ranks of the army that the next charismatic leader would emerge. In 1943, Colonel Juan Perón participated in another military coup—this time against an unpopular conservative administration—and soon showed himself to be the strong man of the regime. Perón's popularity came from the great support he garnered from industrial workers, who greatly benefited from the social policies he inaugurated. He became president in 1946 and was reelected in 1951. His government combined authoritarian measures against political opponents with nationalist economic policies, and a powerful appeal to a working class that would remain ever faithful to its leaders, Perón and Evita. Although he was ousted by another coup in 1955, to this day the political identity of the Argentine working classes is decidedly Peronist.

1. FOR LAND AND LIBERTY

In his Plan of San Luis Potosí, *which was a call for revolution, Francisco Madero had emphasized political objectives, only lightly touching on the subject of land reform. But in the mountainous southern state of Morelos, where the Indian communities had long waged a losing struggle against the encroaching sugar haciendas, the revolution, led by Emiliano Zapata, began under the slogan "Tierra y Libertad" (Land and Liberty). When Zapata became convinced that Madero did not intend to carry out his promise to restore land to the villages, he revolted and issued his own program, the* Plan of Ayala, *for which he continued to battle until the great guerrilla fighter was slain by treachery in 1919. Zapata's principled and tenacious struggle and the popularity of his ideas among the landless peasantry contributed to the adoption of a bold program of agrarian reform in the Constitution of 1917. Important provisions of the* Plan of Ayala *follow.*

The Liberating Plan of the sons of the State of Morelos, members of the insurgent army that demands the fulfillment of the *Plan of San Luis Potosí,* as well as other reforms that it judges convenient and necessary for the welfare of the Mexican nation.

We, the undersigned, constituted as a Revolutionary Junta, in order to maintain and obtain the fulfillment of the promises made by the revolution of November 20, 1910, solemnly proclaim in the face of the civilized world . . . so that it may judge us, the principles that we have formulated in order to destroy the tyranny that oppresses us. . . .

1. Considering that the President of the Republic, Señor Don Francisco I. Madero, has made a bloody mockery of Effective Suffrage by . . . entering into an infamous alliance with the *científicos,* the *hacendados,* the feudalists, and oppressive caciques, enemies of the Revolution that he proclaimed, in order to forge the chains of a new dictatorship more hateful and terrible than that of Porfirio Díaz . . . For these reasons we

"Plan de Ayala," in Gildardo Magaña, *Emiliano Zapata y el agrarismo en México,* 2 vols. (México, 1934–1937), 1:126–130. Excerpt translated by Benjamin Keen.

declare the said Francisco I. Madero unfit to carry out the promises of the Revolution of which he was the author. . . .

4. The Revolutionary Junta of the State of Morelos formally proclaims to the Mexican people:

5. That it endorses the *Plan of San Luis Potosí* with the additions stated below for the benefit of the oppressed peoples, and that it will defend its principles until victory or death. . . .

6. As an additional part of the plan we proclaim, be it known: that the lands, woods, and waters usurped by the *hacendados*, *científicos*, or *caciques* through tyranny and venal justice henceforth belong to the towns or citizens who have corresponding titles to these properties, of which they were despoiled by the bad faith of our oppressors. They shall retain possession of the said properties at all costs, arms in hand. The usurpers who think they have a right to the said lands may state their claims before special tribunals to be established upon the triumph of the Revolution. . . .

7. Since the immense majority of Mexican towns and citizens own nothing but the ground on which they stand and endure a miserable existence, denied the opportunity to improve their social condition or to devote themselves to industry or agriculture because a few individuals monopolize the lands, woods, and waters—for these reasons the great estates shall be expropriated, with indemnification to the owners of one third of such monopolies, in order that the towns and citizens of Mexico may obtain *ejidos*, colonies, town sites, and arable lands. Thus the welfare of the Mexican people shall be promoted in all respects.

8. The properties of those *hacendados*, *científicos*, or *caciques* who directly or indirectly oppose the present *Plan* shall be seized by the nation, and two thirds of their value shall be used for war indemnities and pensions for the widows and orphans of the soldiers who may perish in the struggle for this *Plan*.

9. In proceeding against the above properties there shall be applied the laws of disentail and nationalization, as may be convenient, using as our precept and example the laws enforced by the immortal [former President Benito] Juárez against Church property—laws that taught a painful lesson to the despots and conservatives who at all times have sought to fasten upon the people the yoke of oppression and backwardness.

2. THE INDIAN PROBLEM

Peruvian writer and thinker José Carlos Mariátegui (1894–1930) authored many influential essays diagnosing the problems of his society. Despite his background as a Marx-

ist intellectual—evident in his emphasis on economic explanations and periodization—Mariátegui identified the Indian (rather than the industrial worker) as the ultimate oppressed class in Peru. As the following excerpt shows, Mariátegui dismissed traditional ways of conceptualizing the "Indian problem," pointing instead to gamonalismo (the web of local control that attached peons to large landed property) as the explanation. Only its abolition would permit the liberation of the Indian and the regeneration of Peruvian society.

All of the theses on the indigenous problem that ignore it or avoid it as a socioeconomic problem are merely sterile theoretical exercises. . . . Practically speaking, most of them have served only to hide or disfigure the reality of the problem. The socialist critique uncovers it and clarifies it, because it searches for its causes in the economy of the country rather than in its administrative, juridical, ecclesiastical mechanisms, or in the duality or plurality of races, or in its cultural or moral conditions. The Indian question begins with our economy. Its roots are to be found in the system of ownership of the land. Any attempt to solve it with administrative or police measures, with teaching methods or road works will be a superficial or secondary endeavor, as long as the feudal *gamonales* survive.

Gamonalismo inevitably invalidates any law or ordinance to protect the Indian. The landowner, the boss, is a feudal lord. Written law is powerless against his authority, supported by environment and custom. Unpaid work is prohibited by law, and yet, unpaid work (or even forced work) survives on the large property. The judge, the sub-prefect, the commissioner, the teacher, and the tax collector are all vassals to property. The law cannot prevail over *gamonales*. The functionary who insists on enforcing it would be abandoned and sacrificed by central power, around which the influences of *gamonalismo* are all-powerful, operating directly or by way of congress, either way being equally effective.

Thus, the new examination of the indigenous problem is much less concerned with the guidelines of tutelary legislation than it is with the consequences of the regime of agrarian property. . . .

This critique repudiates and disqualifies the various theses that consider the question by means of any of the following exclusive and unilateral criteria: administrative, juridical, ethnic, moral, educational or ecclesiastic.

The oldest and most obvious defeat is, no doubt, that of those who reduce the protection of Indians to a question of mere administration. Since the time of Spanish colonial legislation, the wise and tidy ordinances passed in answer to conscientious investigations have shown themselves to be totally fruitless.

José Carlos Mariátegui, "El problema del indio," in *Siete ensayos de interpretación de la realidad peruana* (Lima: Editorial Minerva, 1944), pp. 25–32. The text was originally published in 1928. Original footnotes have been removed. Excerpt translated by the editors.

Since the days of Independence, the copiousness of the Republic's attempts—by means of decrees, laws and provisions—to protect the Indians against exaction and abuse is not inconsiderable. Today's *gamonal*, like yesterday's *encomendero* has, however, little to fear from administrative theory. He knows that practice is another matter.

The individualistic nature of the Republic's legislation has favored, unquestionably, the absorption of indigenous property by *latifundismo* [the pattern of large land holdings]. In this respect, the situation of the Indian was more realistically contemplated by Spanish legislation. But juridical reform has no more practical value than administrative reform, faced with a feudalism intact in its economic structure. The appropriation of the greatest part of communal and individual Indian property has already been achieved. The experience of all countries that have emerged from their feudal era shows us, on the other hand, that no liberal law can function anywhere without the dissolution of feudalism.

The supposition that the Indian problem is an ethnic problem stems from the oldest repertoire of imperialist ideas. The concept of inferior races helped the white Occident in its project of expansion and conquest. Expecting Indian emancipation from an active mixing of the aboriginal race with white immigrants is an anti-sociological naïveté, only conceivable in the rudimentary mind of an importer of merino lambs. Asiatic peoples, to whom the Indian people are not inferior in the least, have admirably assimilated Western culture in its most dynamic or creative forms, without European blood transfusions. The degeneracy of the Indian is a cheap invention of feudal shysters.

The tendency to consider the indigenous problem as a moral problem embodies a liberal, humanistic, nineteenth-century, enlightenment conception—the very same that in the political order of the West sparks and motivates the "Leagues for the Rights of Man." The conferences and anti-slavery societies that in Europe have denounced (more or less uselessly) the crimes of the colonizers, are born of this tendency, which has always placed too much trust in the moral sense of civilization. . . .

Centuries ago, religion (with great energy, or at least great authority) placed itself in the domain of reason and morality. This crusade, however, amounted to nothing but laws and wisely inspired measures. The fate of the Indians did not vary substantially. . . .

But today, the hope for an ecclesiastical solution is unquestionably the most backward and anti-historical of all. Those who represent it don't even worry, like their distant—how distant!—masters, about obtaining a new declaration of the rights of the Indian, with adequate authority and decrees, but rather about entrusting the missionaries with the function of mediating between the Indian and the *gamonal*. The works that the Church couldn't achieve when its spiritual and intellectual capacity could be measured in friars like father [Bartolomé] las Casas, what elements would it count on to prosper today? The Adventist missions, in this respect, have won the leadership over the Catholic clergy, whose cloisters produce a smaller number of evangelists each day.

The concept that the problem of the Indian is one of education doesn't seem supported by even the most narrow and autonomously pedagogic criteria. Today more than ever, pedagogy takes into account social and economic factors. The modern pedagogue knows perfectly well that education is not merely a question of school and didactic methods. The economic and social milieu inevitably conditions the task of the teacher. *Gamonalismo* is fundamentally opposed to the education of the Indian: its very existence sees the same interest in maintaining his ignorance as it does in encouraging his alcoholism.

The modern school—assuming that within the current circumstances it might grow in proportion to the school-age peasant population—is incompatible with feudal *latifundio*. The mechanics of servitude would totally negate the purpose of the school, even if, by means of some inconceivable miracle in the social status quo, it were able to maintain in the atmosphere of feudalism, its purely pedagogical mission. The most efficient and grandiose school teaching couldn't perform these miracles. The school and the teacher are hopelessly condemned to denaturalize themselves under the pressure of the feudal environment, incompatible as it is with the most elemental progressive or evolutionist conception of things. A partial understanding of this truth leads one to search for the solution in indigenous boarding schools. But the glaring shortcomings of this formula become clear as soon as one considers the insignificant percentage of the Indian school population that can be housed in those schools.

The pedagogic solution, advanced by many in untainted good faith, is dismissed even on the official level. Educators are, I insist, those who can least consider independence from socioeconomic reality. It does not exist, thus, in actuality, but as a vague and amorphous suggestion, that no body and no doctrine claims to itself.

The new way of looking at the problem of the Indian is by searching for its roots in the problem of the land.

3. TEACHING AND TELLING STORIES

Gabriela Mistral (1889–1957), the first Latin American woman to win a Nobel Prize in Literature, was born in Vicuña, a small town in northern Chile. Her talent as a poet, writer, and speaker would turn her into Chile's representative abroad for almost twenty years, a role that included diplomatic missions to the League of Nations and the United Nations. In spite of her international fame as a literary woman and diplomat, Mistral never forgot her passion for teaching—a passion developed during her youth, when she worked as a maestra normal *(public school teacher) near Santiago. (*Maestras normales *were a key figure in the expansion of school systems in Latin America, at a time when states were focusing on education as part of the project of nation building.) In 1922, Mistral was invited by Mexican education secretary José Vasconcelos to work on educational programs for the poor in Mexico. She introduced mobile libraries to rural areas to make access to literature easier for everyone. In 1923, the Chilean government awarded Gabriela Mistral the title of "Teacher of the Nation."*

The art of story-telling, an essential classroom skill seldom taken into account in the assessment of teachers, is undervalued when one has it and is not demanded when one does not. The same occurs with the rare, precious, and happy vocation of being able to foster play among children. Likewise all instances of grace within the business of teaching. (Philistinism lives comfortably everywhere, but it has established itself as patron to the leaders of the teaching trade).

Yet, half the lesson is in the telling. Half of the day and half of the managing of the children is in the telling—when (like an adagio) to tell a story is to enchant, to let the magic in.

I am referring to primary school, naturally, although this also pertains to the first three years of high-school.

Zoology tells the story of the lion-creature, the bird-creature, and the serpent-creature, until one-by-one they walk, fly or climb before the child's eyes, until they get into the child's soul—into that core where the child keeps all of the beings with whom he establishes that lovely animal familiarity that is pure childhood.

Images—all possible images; abundant, numerous images—should be provided first. Without them, the room will be devoid of any real object upon which the child can build knowledge. To this imprint, I would add a colorful adventure or tale—whether an excerpt from a good zoology anthology, or a story about the creature that the teacher might know—describing the animal's habits. Only after receiving this double image of the little creature (one graphic and one oral) would I approach the technical description, keeping it as vigorously lean as the lines of an etcher, because it is always cumbersome for the child. From there I would finally move on to *phyllum* and *genum* (which, being exercises in generalization) are quite unrewarding to the little one.

Gabriela Mistral, "Contar," *Repertorio Americano* (San José, Costa Rica, 1929). Excerpt translated by the editors.

Warmed up with the tale, thrown into the subject like a swimmer plunging headfirst, he finds in the bee-creature or the lion-creature an element that gives him pleasure, and from there he will take the necessary steps within the subject, at least to the extent that narration in conjunction with images has aroused his interest.

Botany involves no less story-telling than zoology, contrary to what some believe. The harvest and elaboration of linen can be told with the same beautiful architecture of a tale. The story of the many wonderful American trees can be told so as to provide the child with the same enchantment as an animal fable: thus-and-so is the bread tree, thus-and-so is the palm tree, and thus-and-so is the Ecuadorian tagua or the Chilean larch—all comprising a kind of vegetal tribe.

For a great geographer, geography is story-telling; for the mediocre, it is all numbers and squares and figures. The admirable Reclus was a rich and expansive story-teller. Swen Hedin and Humboldt were story-tellers. The throngs of authors of geography texts know neither how to tell in their own words nor how to quote generously from the masterful pages of the classics of their field. Hence the ugly and monotonous texts that make up a science which is genuinely beautiful, insofar as her domain is the very panorama.

The American landscape is an untapped source of fine description and narration. [Mexican poet and essayist] Alfonso Reyes began the task a few years ago with *La Visión de Anáhua*, a tour-de-force of lapidary description which should be a model for all Indo-American writers. Our obligation as writers is to give, with integrity and dignity, our native landscape to distant readers. . . .

It is settled, then, that the person who can narrate skillfully has half the battle won.

Now we should clarify what good story-telling is.

I believe that you don't learn this by asking a fable expert (that is, a writer), but rather by recalling those who, when we were children, narrated those important "events" that have remained in our memory for thirty years.

My mother did not know how to tell a story, or did not like to. My father could, but he knew too many things—from his good Latin to his fine decorative drawing. He was an extraordinary man, and I prefer to remember ordinary story-tellers. Two or three elderly men from my village taught me the folklore of Elqui (where I come from), and those tales, along with the bible stories that my teacher sister (instead of the priest) taught me, were all of my childhood literature. Since then I have read many masterpieces of childhood literature from all around the world. I must say that the folk tales I heard at age five and those I came upon later in my passion for folklore are, for me, the best. They are what aesthetics professors call "pure beauty," the most intoxicating of fables, and those I like to call classics above all classics.

The narrator of folklore does not use "floweriness," adding neither pedantic flourishes nor saccharine flourishes, and doesn't employ clever adjectives in order to compel interest. This flows naturally and honestly from the very core of the fable. The folkloric story-teller's vitality comes from his sobriety, which always yields something magical, or at least extraordinary, something charged with creative electricity. With repetition over millennia, the tale (like the good gymnast) has lost the fat of superfluous details and only pure muscle remains. Thus, the folk-tale is not long and is not burdened with digressions. It flies as straight as an arrow to its target and does not tire either the child or the adult. These I think are the main qualities of the popular tale.

And those of the story-teller? Some of them spring from the above.

The storyteller must be simple, even humble, if he is to repeat without additions a master fable that needs no adornment. He should be witty (his words laced with charm, shining with grace), for the child is more receptive to wit than either Goethe or Ronsard. Besides simply narrating, he will have to reduce everything to images, leaving un-tethered to an image only that which cannot be transmuted into one. He will forgo expansiveness, which in narration is an adult taste rather than that of a child. Within the cluster of fables that has formed, he will have to highlight those elements that bear some living relation to his environment: fresh fruit, tree, creature, or landscape. He will try to use facial expressions and gestures as brotherly aids to the fine tale, because the child likes to see the face of the story-teller animated and alive. If his voice is ugly, there are ways to train it, if only a little, in order to squeeze some sweetness out of it. For a pleasant voice, one that yields like silk to the matter at hand, is a gift the listener is grateful for.

If I were Headmistress of a school, I would create a chair in general and regional folklore. And I wouldn't certify as a teacher anyone who does not narrate with agility, joy, freshness, and even a certain fascination.

4. WHAT IS APRA?

Victor Raúl Haya de la Torre (1895–1979) was the founder and leader of APRA (American Popular Revolutionary Alliance), the oldest political party in Peru, and one of the oldest in Latin America. Since its birth in 1924 as an anti-imperialist movement with a continental agenda, APRA struggled through proscription and persecution until finally achieving political success. Peru's President Alan García (first term, 1985–1990; second term, 2006–2011) is Haya de la Torre's political disciple and APRA's current leader. The party's international and economic agenda has, however, become quite moderate, with its revolutionary principles giving way to less ideological, more gradual, and realistic measures and alliances. In contrast, the following selection from APRA's founding principles summarizes Haya de la Torre's diagnosis of the main obstacle to progress in Latin America—U.S. imperialism—and possible ways of fighting it. The first part describes the betrayal by the local bourgeoisie (upper

middle class), which chooses to ally itself with imperialism rather than pursuing na-
tional interests. The second part presents one of the most distinctive features of APRA's
project: a multiclass alliance against imperialism consisting of workers, peasants, and
the middle class—a notion that set it apart from class-based Marxist liberation move-
ments. Finally, the document sketches the outlines of a future anti-imperialist state.

The history of political and economic relations between Latin America
and the United States, especially the experience of the Mexican Revolution,
brings us to the following conclusions:

1. The governing classes of the Latin American countries—big landowners, big businessmen, and the incipient national bourgeoisie—are allied with imperialism.
2. These classes have the governments of our countries in their hands in
   exchange for a policy of concessions, government loans, and other
   deals which the big landowners, bourgeoisie, big businessmen, and the
   groups or *caudillos* [strongmen] who support them, negotiate or share
   with the imperial powers.
3. As a result of this alliance of classes, the natural riches of our countries are mortgaged or sold, the financial policy of our governments
   are reduced to a crazy succession of huge government subsidies, and
   our working classes, who have to produce for the owners, are brutally
   exploited.
4. The progressive economic subordination of our countries to imperialism results in political subjugation, loss of national sovereignty, armed
   invasions by the soldiers and marines of imperialism, the buying off of
   Creole *caudillos*, etc. Panama, Nicaragua. Cuba, Santo Domingo [Do-
   minican Republic], and Haiti are true Yankee colonies or protectorates
   as a consequence of imperialism's "politics of penetration."

As the problem is common to all Latin American countries in which the
dominant classes ally with imperialism in the joint exploitation of our working classes, it is not an isolated or national question, but a huge international
problem that affects all the Latin American republics. Nevertheless, the policies of the governing classes, which cooperate in all the imperial plans of the
United States, encourage divisions among the republics . . . Peru against
Chile, Brazil against Argentina, Ecuador and Colombia against Peru, etc.
Each time that the United States intervenes as an "amicable conciliator" or
"arbitrator" of the great Latin American international questions, the usual

Victor Raúl Haya de la Torre, *El antimperialismo y el APRA* (Santiago de Chile: Ediciones Er-
cilla, 1936), pp. 35–37, 63–70, 137–141. Excerpt translated by the editors.

tactic is to feign pacifism, but always to leave behind the apple of discord. [In Greek mythology, a dispute over awarding the "apple of discord" to the most beautiful goddess set in motion the chain of events that led to the Trojan War.—eds.] . . .

Our historical experience in Latin America . . . shows us that the immense power of Yankee imperialism cannot be confronted without the unity of the Latin American countries. But our governing classes and imperialism, which aids them and guarantees their grip on power, conspire against this unity. . . . Consequently the struggle against our governing classes is indispensable: political power must be captured by the producers [i.e., workers], production must be socialized, and Latin America must be united in a Federation of States. . . .

APRA represents, therefore, a political organization in struggle against imperialism and the Latin American governing classes which its auxiliaries and accomplices. . . . APRA is an autonomous Latin American movement without foreign intervention or influences. It is the result of the spontaneous desire of our people to come together in defense of liberty, vanquishing both internal and external enemies. The experiences of Mexico, Central America, Panama and the Antilles, and the present position of Peru, Bolivia and Venezuela, where the policy of imperial penetration has made itself keenly felt, has determined the organization of APRA on new grounds that promote realistic and effective methods of action. APRA's motto synthesizes beyond the shadow of a doubt the aspirations of twenty endangered peoples [republics]: "Against imperialism, for the Political Unity of Latin America, for the realization of Social Justice." . . .

An anti-imperialist, Indo-American party sensitive to our social reality, cannot be the party of one class alone. Much less a party based on a European model. And much less still, a party subject to foreign direction [i.e., communism]. . . .

And an anti-imperialist, Indo-American party sensitive to our social reality should be a United Front party that brings together all the social classes threatened by imperialism. It must also be a party with its own realistic and efficient program and tactics, and with national jurisdiction. . . .

Imperialism doesn't just threaten the proletariat [working class]. Imperialism, which implies in all of our countries the arrival of the industrial capitalist era under the characteristic forms of economic penetration, brings with it the economic and social phenomena produced by capitalism in the countries where it originated: great industrial and agricultural concentration, monopoly of the production and circulation of wealth, progressive destruction or absorption of small capital, small manufacturing, small property, and small commerce, and the formation of a truly proletarian industrial class.

It is necessary to point out, then, that the class that first suffers the impact of capitalist imperialism in our countries is not the incipient working class, nor the poor peasant, nor the Indian. The worker in small industry and the independent artisan, attracted by a new form of production backed with large amounts of capital, receives a securer and higher wage, temporarily improves his conditions, and realizes certain advantages as he becomes a member of the industrial proletariat. . . . The same thing happens to the poor peasant, the peon, and the Indian serf. Once they become proletarians in a large-scale manufacturing, mining, or agricultural enterprise, they almost always enjoy a temporary improvement in their welfare. They exchange their miserable wage of centavos or in-kind for a higher one paid by their foreign master, always richer and more powerful than the national master. Thus imperialism in newly developing countries is a determining factor in the formation and strengthening of a genuine modern proletariat. This social phenomenon . . . has its characteristic limitations, determined by the conditions and peculiarities of imperialist expansion in backward countries. The industrial proletariat which is being formed is, then, a new, young, and weak class, fascinated with immediate gains, whose collective conscience only appears later to confront the implacable rigor of exploitation under the new system.

Since the great imperial enterprise is based on cheap labor, the wage paid the new worker, although greater than that which he received under previous conditions, is significantly less than that received by a worker in the industrial countries. When imperial capital comes to our countries, it comes like a missionary among savages showing them the spangles and mirrors that attract the passing fancy of the oppressed. . . . the laboring masses who are transformed into a modern proletariat do not perceive the violence of the imperialist exploitation until much later. Modern imperialism, especially the North American variety, so advanced and refined in its methods, offers benefits and progress only in the beginning. . . .

[Along with imperial capitalism's effect on the working classes] the monopoly which imperialism imposes cannot avoid the destruction, stagnation, and regression of what we refer to as the middle class. Industrial capitalism, when it appears in the most highly developed countries, reduces, absorbs, and turns into proletarians most of the petty bourgeoisie [lower middle class] with only a very few able to join the dominant class. Likewise, imperialism subjugates or economically destroys the middle classes of the backward countries it penetrates. The small capitalist, the small industrialist, the small rural and urban proprietor, the small miner, the small merchant, the intellectual, the clerk, etc. form the middle class whose interests are attacked by imperialism. Only a very small segment of this middle class allies itself with imperialism and obtains advantages from its dominion, becoming its collaborators and clients at the national level. Under capitalism's laws of competition and monopoly, the imperialist form—its ultimate expression—destroys the incipient capitalists and proprietors, subjugates them, beats them down, and smothers them among the tentacles of the great trusts or under the yoke of bankers and mortgage brokers. As imperialism advances, the limits it imposes on the possible economic progressive of our middle classes become increasingly apparent. . . . Thus, while imperialist penetration produces an upward movement of the working masses, who pass from semi-slavery and servitude or from elemental forms of free labor to become proletarians, the middle classes suffer the first attacks as their economic institutions are subjected to the imperial reins. They soon realize the situation, and soon react and protest against it. This is the economic explanation for why the first cries against imperialism in our countries have come from the middle classes, which are also the most educated. . . . From their ranks appear the first agitators and the most determined and heroic soldiers of the initial anti-imperialist movement.

It would be pointless to try to explain the historic fact that the Indo-American working classes have not joined with the middle classes in social protest movements against imperialism by citing their lack of pugnacity. It is well known that uprisings by Indo-American workers and peasants have been frequent and have a long history among us. But their protests have been directed for many years against visible exploitation, against the instruments of immediate oppression: the feudal master, the patron, the manager, the *cacique* [boss], the foreman, or the government supporting them. It is only much later, when imperialist exploitation unleashes all its implacable force that our working classes will understand the danger and will discover the true economic enemy. And, then, when imperial oppression is felt in the form of national oppression—through government subsidies, concessions, turning over of public riches—or political subjugation—through interventions, threats, etc.—reality will show them the need to join forces with the middle classes, who have already taken on their historic role in the struggle against imperialism. . . .

The middle classes oppressed and displaced by imperialism want to fight it, but they wish to fight against imperialism in a political way from within the ranks of a party which also seeks to address their interests. The historical task of an anti-imperialist party consists, in the first place, of affirming national sovereignty, freeing it from the oppressors of the nation and capturing power in order to accomplish its libratory objectives. This is a difficult and arduous task for which the aid of the middle classes, who will stand to benefit from this liberating movement, is essential. . . .

Because of the extremely complicated characteristics of the imperialist phenomenon and because of the ignorance of the working people in backward countries—an ignorance that results from the agrarian or feudal nature of their economy—it is necessary to form an alliance with intellectuals in the service of the anti-imperialist movement. . . . All over our America, the work of agitation and the channeling of anti-imperialist currents has been carried out by a new generation of middle-class intellectuals who have clearly seen the gravity of the situation and have shown us the surest ways to confront it.

An anti-imperialist State cannot be a capitalist or bourgeois state as in France, England, or the United States. It is crucial to acknowledge that if, as anti-imperialists, we accept as a post-revolutionary objective the creation of a bourgeois-type State, we will be crushed inexorably by the steamroller of imperialism. The anti-imperialist State must dedicate itself to the defensive struggle against the greatest enemy. Once imperialism is defeated in a given country, the State becomes the sustaining bulwark of the victory, which presumes a certain political and economic structure. Imperialism will not cease its aggression, and its attacks will have to seek a weak point in the new state mechanism erected by the triumphant movement. The anti-imperialist state must be, then, above all a defense State, which opposes imperial capitalism, a new system, distinct from the old, which will seek to proscribe the old oppressive regime. . . . The triumphant anti-imperialist movement will thus organize its defense by establishing a new, scientifically-planned economic system and a new governmental structure which will not be a democratic, "free" State, but a war State, that limits the exercise of economic freedom to ensure that it doesn't work to the benefit of imperialism. . . .

For the anti-imperialist State, the war State engaged in economic self-defense, it is also crucial to limit private initiative and to control production and the circulation of wealth. The anti-imperialist State that is obliged to *direct* the national economy, will have to deny individual or collective economic rights when their use implies an imperialist danger. It is impossible to reconcile—and this is the normative function of the anti-imperialist state—absolute individual liberty in the economic sphere with the struggle against imperialism. The national proprietor of a mine or hacienda, who sells his property or business to a Yankee entrepreneur; is not just carrying out a private contract because that buyer not only invests money in a business, he also *invests sovereignty*, so to speak. Behind the new interest created by this apparently simple economic operation, is political protection, the force of imperialist power that backs—with a perspective that is different from and even opposed to that of the country which receives the investment—the interests of the foreigner. Is this a private deal? Clearly not. The anti-imperialist state will therefore have to limit the concept of individual use and abuse (*jus utendi, jus abutendi*), restrain the economic freedom of the exploiting and middle classes, and increasingly assume, as in case of State capitalism, the control of production and commerce.

If the anti-imperialist State fails to separate itself from the capitalist system and abets the formation of a national bourgeoisie, thereby stimulating individualistic and insatiable exploitation—supported by the tenets of democratic-liberalism—it would get quickly caught up in the imperialist machinery from which no bourgeois national structure can escape. For this reason, a new State of this kind requires the extensive and scientific organization of a nationalized cooperative system and the adoption of a political structure of *a workable democracy based on the categories of labor*. In this way, then, the anti-imperialist state can carry out the work of economic and political education that it needs to consolidate its defensive position. So too will it efficiently and in a coordinated way channel the efforts of the three classes [peasants, industrial workers, middle classes] represented in it. The anti-imperialist state will chart and direct its historic path towards a different kind of economic system that rejects and defends itself from the current one through the progressive control of production and wealth—through the nationalization of the land and industry according to the APRA program. This goal must be the touchstone of Indo-American unity and the effective economic emancipation of our peoples.

5. Cárdenas Speaks

Mexico's struggle for economic sovereignty reached a high point under Lázaro Cárdenas. In 1937, a dispute between U.S. and British oil companies and Mexican unions erupted into a strike, followed by legal battles between the contending parties. When the oil companies refused to accept a Mexican Supreme Court verdict in favor of the unions, Cárdenas intervened. On March 18, 1938—celebrated by Mexicans as marking their declaration of economic independence—the president announced in a radio speech that the properties of the oil companies had been expropriated in the public interest. But the oil nationalization did not set a precedent, and subsequently Cárdenas allowed some 90 percent of the mining industry to remain in foreign hands. An excerpt from his message to the nation follows.

The history of this labor dispute, which culminates in this act of economic emancipation, is the following: In connection with the strike called in 1934 by the various workers' unions in the employ of the Compañía Mexicana de Petróleo "El Águila," the Federal Executive agreed to intervene as arbitrator to secure a conciliatory agreement between both parties.

In June 1934, the resultant Award was handed down and, in October of the same year, this was followed by an explanatory decision establishing ade-

---

Lázaro Cárdenas, *Mexico's Oil* (Mexico, 1940), pp. 878–879.

quate procedure for revising those resolutions which had not already been agreed to.

At the end of 1934 and early in 1936, the Chief of the Labor Department, delegated by me for that purpose, handed down several decisions with respect to wage levels, contractual cases, and uniformity of wages, on the basis of the Constitutional principle of equal pay for equal work.

The same Department, for the purpose of eliminating certain anomalous conditions, called the representatives of the various trade-union groups into a conference at which an agreement was reached on numerous pending cases, others being reserved for subsequent investigation and analysis by commissions composed of labor and employer representatives.

The Union of Oil Workers then issued a call for a special assembly in which they laid down the terms of a collective contract which was rejected by the oil companies on its presentation.

Out of consideration for the wishes of the companies and in order to avert a strike, the Chief of the Labor Department was instructed to secure the acquiescence of both parties to the holding of a worker-employer convention to be entrusted with the task of establishing, by mutual agreement, the terms of the collective contract. The agreement to hold the convention was signed November 27, 1936, and in the meetings the companies presented their counter-proposals. Because of the slow progress being made, it was then decided to divide the clauses of the contract into economic, social, and administrative categories, so that an immediate examination of the first-named group might be undertaken.

The difficulties preventing an agreement between the workers and the companies were clearly revealed by the discussions; their respective points of view were found to be very far apart, the companies maintaining that the workers' demands were exaggerated and the workers, for their part, pointing to the companies' intransigence in refusing to understand their social necessities. As a result of the breakdown of the negotiations, the strike began in May 1937. In response to my appeals, the companies then offered an increase in wages and a betterment of certain other conditions, and the Union of Oil Workers decided to resume work on June 9th, at the same time bringing an economic action against the companies before the Board of Conciliation and Arbitration.

As a result of these events, the Board of Conciliation and Arbitration took jurisdiction in the case and, in accordance with the provisions of the law, a commission of experts, composed of persons of high moral standing and adequate preparation, was designated by the President of the Board.

The commission's report found that the companies could afford to meet the disbursements recommended in it, namely, an annual increase of 26,332,756 pesos, as against the offer made by the seventeen oil companies at the time of the strike in May 1937. The experts specifically stated that the conditions recommended in the report would be totally satisfied with the expenditure of the sum stipulated, but the companies argued that the amount recommended was excessive and might signify an even greater expenditure, which they estimated at a total of 41,000,000 pesos.

In view of these developments, the Executive then suggested the possibility of an agreement between representatives of the Union of Oil Workers and the companies, duly authorized to deal with the dispute, but this solution proved impossible because of the refusal of the companies.

Notwithstanding the failure of this effort, the Public Power, still desirous of securing an extrajudicial agreement between the parties at issue, instructed the Labor Authorities to inform the companies of its willingness to intervene with the purpose of persuading the Labor Unions to accept the interpretations necessary to clarify certain obscure points of the Award which might later lend themselves to misunderstandings, and to assure the companies that in no case would the disbursements ordered by the Award be allowed to exceed the above-mentioned sum of 26,332,756 pesos; but in spite of this direct intervention of the Executive, it was impossible to obtain the results sought.

In each and every one of the various attempts of the Executive to arrive at a final solution of the conflict within conciliatory limits, and which include the periods prior to and following the *amparo* action which has produced the present situation, the intransigence of the companies was clearly demonstrated.

Their attitude was therefore premeditated and their position deliberately taken, so that the Government, in defense of its own dignity, had to resort to application of the Expropriation Act, as there were no means less drastic or decision less severe that might bring about a solution of the problem.

For additional justification of the measure herein announced, let us trace briefly the history of the oil companies' growth in Mexico and of the resources with which they have developed their activities.

It has been repeated *ad nauseam* that the oil industry has brought additional capital for the development and progress of the country. This assertion is an exaggeration. For many years, throughout the major period of their existence, the oil companies have enjoyed great privileges for development and expansion, including customs and tax exemptions and innumerable prerogatives; it is these factors of special privilege, together with the prodigious productivity of the oil deposits granted them by the Nation often against public will and law, that represent almost the total amount of this so-called capital.

Potential wealth of the Nation; miserably underpaid native labor; tax exemptions; economic privileges; governmental tolerance—these are the factors of the boom of the Mexican oil industry.

Let us now examine the social contributions of the companies. In how many of the villages bordering on the oil fields is there a hospital, or school or social center, or a sanitary water supply, or an athletic field, or even an electric plant fed by the millions of cubic meters of natural gas allowed to go to waste?

What center of oil production, on the other hand, does not have its company police force for the protection of private, selfish, and often illegal interests? These organizations, whether authorized by the Government or not, are charged with innumerable outrages, abuses, and murders, always on behalf of the companies that employ them.

Who is not aware of the irritating discrimination governing construction of the company camps? Comfort for the foreign personnel; misery, drabness, and insalubrity for the Mexicans. Refrigeration and protection against tropical insects for the former; indifference and neglect, medical service and supplies always grudgingly provided, for the latter; lower wages and harder, more exhausting labor for our people.

The tolerance which the companies have abused was born, it is true, in the shadow of the ignorance, betrayals, and weakness of the country's rulers; but the mechanism was set in motion by investors lacking in the necessary moral resources to give something in exchange for the wealth they have been exploiting.

Another inevitable consequence of the presence of the oil companies, strongly characterized by their anti-social tendencies, and even more harmful than all those already mentioned, has been their persistent and improper intervention in national affairs.

The oil companies' support to strong rebel factions against the constituted government in the Huasteca region of Veracruz and in the Isthmus of Tehuantepec during the years 1917 to 1920 is no longer a matter for discussion by anyone. Nor is anyone ignorant of the fact that in later periods and even at the present time, the oil companies have almost openly encouraged the ambitions of elements discontented with the country's government, every time their interests were affected either by taxation or by the modification of their privileges or the withdrawal of the customary tolerance. They have had money, arms, and munitions for rebellion, money for the anti-patriotic press which defends them, money with which to enrich their unconditional defenders. But for the progress of the country, for establishing an economic equilibrium with their workers through a just compensation of labor, for maintaining hygienic conditions in the districts where they themselves operate, or for conserving the vast riches of the natural petroleum gases from destruction, they have neither money, nor financial possibilities, nor the desire to subtract the necessary funds from the volume of their profits.

Nor is there money with which to meet a responsibility imposed upon them by judicial verdict, for they rely on their pride and their economic power to shield them from the dignity and sovereignty of a Nation which has generously placed in their hands its vast natural resources and now finds itself unable to obtain the satisfaction of the most elementary obligations by ordinary legal means.

As a logical consequence of this brief analysis, it was therefore necessary to adopt a definite and legal measure to end this permanent state of affairs in which the country sees its industrial progress held back by those who hold in their hands the power to erect obstacles as well as the motive power of all activity and who, instead of using it to high and worthy purposes, abuse their economic strength to the point of jeopardizing the very life of a Nation endeavoring to bring about the elevation of its people through its own laws, its own resources, and the free management of its own destinies.

With the only solution to this problem thus placed before it, I ask the entire Nation for moral and material support sufficient to carry out so justified, important, and indispensable a decision.

The Government has already taken suitable steps to maintain the constructive activities now going forward throughout the Republic, and for that purpose it asks the people only for its full confidence and backing in whatever dispositions the Government may be obliged to adopt.

Nevertheless, we shall, if necessary, sacrifice all the constructive projects on which the Nation has embarked during the term of this Administration in order to cope with the financial obligations imposed upon us by the application of the Expropriation Act to such vast interests; and although the subsoil of the country will give us considerable economic resources with which to meet the obligation of indemnification which we have contracted, we must be prepared for the possibility of our individual economy also suffering the indispensable readjustments, even to the point, should the Bank of Mexico deem it necessary, of modifying the present exchange rate of our currency, so that the whole country may be able to count on sufficient currency and resources with which to consolidate this act of profound and essential economic liberation of Mexico.

It is necessary that all groups of the population be imbued with a full optimism and that each citizen, whether in agricultural, industrial, commercial, transportation, or other pursuits, develop a greater activity from this moment on, in order to create new resources which will reveal that the spirit of our people is capable of saving the nation's economy by the efforts of its own citizens.

And, finally, as the fear may arise among the interests now in bitter conflict in the field of international affairs that a deviation of raw materials fundamentally necessary to the struggle in which the most powerful nations are engaged might result from the consummation of this act of national sovereignty and dignity, we wish to state that our petroleum operations will not depart a single inch from the moral solidarity maintained by Mexico with the democratic nations, whom we wish to assure that the expropriation now decreed has as its only purpose the elimination of obstacles erected by groups who do not understand the evolutionary needs of all peoples and who would themselves have no compunction in selling Mexican oil to the highest bidder, without taking into account the consequences of such action to the popular masses and the nations in conflict.

6. ON THE PROTECTION OF THE BRAZILIAN WORKER

In September 1937, Getúlio Vargas, president of Brazil since 1930, led a coup that canceled the upcoming elections, dissolved Congress, and turned his government into a dictatorship. In many respects, the Estado Novo *(New State), as the regime was called, mirrored the program of European fascism. Strongly authoritarian, it persecuted the opposition and censored the press. At the same time, the state vigorously expanded its social and economic capacities, promoting industry and offering workers numerous specific gains. Vargas became a symbolic figure—the workers' guardian. The excerpt below is one of the many state documents publicizing the social achievements of the regime.*

Since 1930, the Brazilian Government has been undertaking a social policy whose main goal is to protect the working classes through the betterment of their working conditions, elevating their standard of life and extending the social security system. This plan has been uninterrupted. Indeed, the 1937 Constitution proclaims that work is a social duty and establishes that it is the Government's responsibility to guarantee the fulfillment of this duty, securing favorable conditions and protecting work—whether intellectual, technical, or manual. To secure the enforcement of this principle, the Constitution established certain rules that must be observed by social legislation. In this way, the Constitution guarantees the right of organization, recognizes the current unions as representatives of the workers and authorizes the signing of collective-bargaining agreements. Salaries are protected and must function to provide a minimum standard of life. The workday is eight hours long, and there is one mandatory day of rest. Paid vacations are mandatory. Workers are protected against unjustified dismissal. Minors under 14 years old are not allowed to work; neither are those 16 years old allowed to work night shifts; women and men under 18 years old cannot work in unhealthy work-sites. Regarding social welfare and assistance, the Constitution establishes that the state must provide medical assistance to the workers and it must protect maternity and create insurance against old age, as well as disability. It also compels professional associations to provide assistance to its members. In order to enforce these principles, the Constitution anticipates the creation of a Work Tribunal whose goal will be to arbitrate in all work-related litigation.

The Enforcement of Constitutional Principles. The Constitutional declaration of the rights of the working classes is not a mere theoretical

Legislación social brasilera y principios constitucionales en la protección al trabajo. Official publication of the Brazilian Government, 1940. Excerpt translated by the editors.

promise of social justice. This declaration has been implemented by a series of concrete measures the Government is undertaking. They are: laws limiting the workday to eight hours (or less in certain cases, depending on the nature of the work); laws protecting workers against unjustified dismissal, guaranteeing a certain indemnification based on their monthly salary and the number of years of service. Regarding maternity, female workers are protected by law insuring the continued payment of their salaries, and are entitled to subsidies and paid vacation both before and after the delivery.

According to the Constitution, minors under age 14 are not allowed to work, minors under 16 cannot work at night, and unhealthy tasks cannot be fulfilled by women or men below 18. The law of professional association allows them to represent their respective professional classes, and to negotiate with the Government or their bosses about issues concerning the interests of the professions they represent. They can also sign collective-bargaining agreements. All workers have the right to 15 days of paid vacation a year. The minimum-wage law includes measures related to the feeding of workers and establishes what must be considered essential in different regions of the country. Work-related litigation must be solved through a collective arbitration committee and, in certain cases—especially in cases of unjustified dismissal and guarantees of employment, by the National Council for Work. . . .

Social Insurance.   The problem of social security has benefited from the special attention it has received from the Brazilian government. As a result, there are special institutions meant to insure workers against the risks of handicap, old age and death. . . . Social security is also extended to all public employees, through the Institute of Pensions for the Public Employee, that sets pensions for retirement, death, and social assistance.

Indirect Methods of Protection.   Besides the direct methods of protection to workers, the Brazilian Government is trying to improve the condition of workers through projects to build inexpensive houses, to which effect the social insurance institutions have been authorized to use part of their funds in the construction of houses for its members, who will reimburse them within 15 or 20 years. Attention has also been paid to the nutrition question, in the form of clauses included in the legal definition of minimum wage. Several measures have also been undertaken in the construction of hospitals and the campaign against tuberculosis in the working classes.

Technical and Professional Education.   The Constitution establishes that technical and professional education is a duty of the state. This principle has been undertaken through the construction of new institutes for technical education in all states of the federation, as well as the Model Institute in Rio de Janeiro. Technical instruction is administrated at three levels: the first one is aimed at training specialized workers; the second at training leaders; and the third level at training instructors.

Equality of Rights.   Finally, it must be stressed that Brazilian legislation guarantees equality of rights to all workers, regardless of nationality, color or race. It does so while mandating that industry and commerce employ national workers for at least two thirds of their workforce. But in terms of social protection, foreign workers enjoy the same rights as Brazilians.

7. Perón Appeals to the People

On October 17, 1945, thousands of workers peacefully gathered in the Plaza de Mayo in Buenos Aires. They were calling for the release of the most popular figure of the military regime, Colonel Juan Perón, who had been arrested by a rival government faction. As a result of this unexpected popular mobilization, Perón was indeed released, and the saga ended with a speech given from the balcony of the government house. To this day, this event symbolizes the birth of Peronism. "Saved" by his people, Peron would face his opponents, become a presidential candidate, and win elections in 1946, 1952, and (after eighteen years of exile) in 1974. For the opposition, however, October 17 meant something quite different. On that day, the middle classes of Buenos Aires felt their dearest neighborhoods "invaded" by a class of Argentines who had remained quite invisible until then. The echoes of Sarmiento's "civilization and barbarism" were at the center of their interpretation of this new Peronist reality. In a book of memoirs published in 1955, essayist Martínez Estrada (1895–1964) recalled his impressions of that day in a section titled "The Inhabitants of the Basement."

We had talked a lot about our people. The national anthem mentions them, but we did not know them. Perón revealed to us not the people, but rather an area of the people that seemed positively strange and foreign. On October 17, Perón poured into the central streets of Buenos Aires, a social sediment that no one would have recognized. It seemed like an invasion of people from another country, speaking another language, wearing exotic costumes. And still, they were part of the Argentine people, the people in the National Anthem. Because until then, we had lived in ignorance of a part of the family that made up that people—those low people, those miserable people. Even demagogue politicians had marginalized or forgotten them.

Ezequiel Martínez Estrada, *¿Qué es esto? Catilinaria* (Buenos Aires: Editorial Lautaro, 1956), pp. 26–29. Excerpt translated by the editors.

And Perón had more than goodness and intelligence: he had the ability to make them visible and exhibit them without being ashamed of them—not as a people, but rather as a tremendous and aggressive force that endangered the very foundations of a society built with just a fraction of its human element (that being the chosen people that we had watched parade on national holidays, dressed in their Sunday best). These were the people that we had not taken into account, as I said, but still existed. Not a buried people, like the Inca or Aztec, a living people, yet also a dead people. No. It was a living people that was now on the move. And they were our ragged brothers, our miserable brothers—what could be called, to use a technical term, the *Lumpenproletariät*. They were also the *Mazorca*, since they came out of meat refrigerating plants like the others that came out of the meat salting plants. They were the same troops that had belonged to Rosas, and were now enrolled under Perón's flag, who was at the same time the successor of that older tyrant. Of the same species, and the legal representatives of those masses, they moved through the city, this time without ponchos, in the very bosom of the city without ponchos, but with a knife, the tool of hamstringers, slaughterers, and salters of beef jerky. The country was still a great breeding-ground and slaughterhouse of cattle, as it had been from Echeverría until Hudson. And those sinister demons of the plain that Sarmiento described in Facundo had not perished. They are alive this instant and dedicated to the same task, only this time under a roof, in much larger businesses than those of Rosas, Anchorena, Terrero y Urquiza. On October 17 they came out to ask about their captivity, to demand a place under the sun. And they appeared with their butcher's knives in their belts, threatening a *barrio norte* version of Saint Batholomew's massacre. We felt chills watching them parade in a true silent horde, carrying signs that threatened a terrible revenge.

He didn't just give that *infraproletariat* of poor workers a place in the sun. In many ways he placed them above the employee, the teacher, and even the professional. The liberal middle class and the bureaucracy were left behind and below them. He formed a new class, so to speak, intermediate between the superior class of potentates and their associates, and the middle class, properly speaking. He sketched for it a Peronist sociology, philosophy, and even religion, with its codes and doctrines. He took advantage of the cracks produced during centuries of misery and ignorance, and in them he introduced his cold chisel, reducing "his" people to impotence. How can we reproach the people that did not feel this as a loss of liberty and dignity when they had never had these things to begin with. In taking advantage of their good faith, others had preceded him a long time before.

This is the "obrerismo" [pro-worker attitude] of Perón—how different than Yrigoyen's electoralism, but at the same time how similar to Rosas' government of mulattoes and gauchos.

8. EVA PERÓN: ON WOMEN'S RIGHT TO VOTE

The beginning of the feminist struggle to improve women's place in society dates from the late 1800s. Much as in western Europe, Latin American feminism was associated with urban contexts, and frequently with socialist or anarchist agendas. Although women's suffrage was not the first priority of feminist organizations in Latin America, it was a clearly articulated right at least since the early 1900s. It would take much longer, however, for actual laws to be enacted. In Argentina, the cradle of many important feminist organizations, women would have to wait until 1947 for the right to vote. Paradoxically, this achievement was not the result of long-standing feminist demands, but rather an initiative of the new Peronist government, which at the time was closely associated with the Catholic Church. The appointed leader of the Peronist version of this cause was Eva Perón—then only twenty-seven years old. Her campaign took full advantage of the melodramatic talents developed in her previous career as a radio actress. In one of her first independent political performances, although still a far cry from the radical image of the Evita of the late 1940s and early 1950s, she integrated women's suffrage into a context of traditional values—a context quite different from that put forward by the old leaders of the feminist cause.

Friends and companions,

Once again, I request your attention hoping to be the first Argentine woman to lead her companions, to champion their claims.

Once again, I demand your support, because my struggle—the struggle of all Argentine women—cannot be given up until victory is sure. I address all of you, then, with the deep conviction of speaking a common language, a language that is truthful, patriotic and, above all, profoundly feminine.

Women's anguishes have always been, and will always be mine. I live and breathe women's concerns. Their hopes are mine. They animate me, they are my impulse. They feed my belief in the goodness and justice of our mission. Everything the woman of my country hopes to obtain is part of my program of action. I could never step back or withdraw from the clear and straight road to what is dearest in my people.

I have told you about the conquest of female suffrage, an imminent achievement for our sex. I must reiterate my previous concepts. I must emphasize the need for the Legislature to promulgate this law so women can take the place they deserve in public institutions. A protector of civic faith, a testimony to national responsibility, a credit to public faith in the men that rule—the woman's vote will be the most powerful weapon ever brandished for the decisive conquest of the Argentine soul. It complements and verifies

---

Eva Perón, radio speech, February 26, 1947, Radio del Estado y Red Argentina de Radiodifusión. Excerpt translated by the editors.

the male will, and contributes with the certified logic of another vast human sector. Workers, students, employees, professionals, farmers, women in a thousand towns and a thousand occupations, are having an effect on the complex electoral mechanism. They voice their concerns. They express their will. They introduce themselves decisively into the dynamics of the country. They bring their domestic responsibilities, already engaged as they are in the solution of national problems. They rescue from unjustified forgetfulness on the part of the public the feminine mentality and feeling, what is most intimate and clear about human experience. In short, they contribute to the electoral movement the clarity, the sixth sense, the portentous faculty of intuition, seeing right through the tricks of politicians and the fickle games of human passion.

The Argentine woman, responsible for the Christian nurturing of the family; the Argentine woman, essential foundation of the household, represents, above all else, what is unpolluted and truthful. Life itself, with its endless sequence of judgments, its infinite range of great and small needs, is present in the will of the woman. Women think for their households, which means thinking for their families as well as thinking for their country—the sum of all the families dispersed across the fertile ground of our motherland. Thus, female suffrage will provide civic rights to women already knowledgeable in human rights. In this way, women are attaching a universal stamp to their vote, a vote that will now carry the depth of everyday pain, joy, and concern. We mean to bring to the ballot the hearts of the women of this country. To abstract politics we want to bring human warmth, this breadth of life that is always supporting her man in his struggles, and contributing to the national wealth. The woman of the factory is one with the rural woman; the woman of the laboratory lives under the same sky as the teacher in the far away school; the *porteño* woman [from Buenos Aires] in the street dreams of having a place in Argentine society, just like the sacrificing woman of the rural *pampa*. The hour of the woman has arrived in Argentina, [and will be a] precursor to American rights movements.

However, female suffrage means something else. It means responsibility. It means a sacred commitment—the responsibility and commitment of the example that the exercise of this right involves. Let us not forget that the woman represents the home. In fact, the home is the cradle of the new men, the environment where they develop. It is his education, the exercise of his first public faith, the example of the beginning of the difficult career of citizenship. This is where the weapon of suffrage is extraordinarily valuable for women: the will to choose, to discriminate, to illustrate; the will to deny or consent in the democratic game of the elections of a people.

I believe that we can't speak of an Argentine household that is not a Christian household. The image of the Crosses in the old houses of our ancestors is still fresh. We were conceived under the Cross. . . . Under the

Cross we learned our ABCs and counted on the abacus. Under the Cross we have crossed our hands in the last invocation. Everything of value in our customs is Christian. Dormant or active, the religious sentiment has prevailed over every other sign of non-Argentine ethic. We have told the truth when we have spoken about traditional Catholic faith. And we have lied, or we have made mistakes, when we built upon the foreign atheism that had infiltrated our legislation, or established by surprise in institutions such as education. So when we speak of the Argentine home, and of the woman as the symbol of that home, we speak of the Christian woman and the home based on this solid foundation of traditional morality. In fact, in order to legitimate our hope that every woman vote, we could add that every woman should vote according to her religious sense, that is, according to the measure of her duty as mother, wife or daughter. . . .

Women will defend what is permanent with their vote, better than men will. When choosing, women define themselves in relation to the preservation of the home, the family, the Catholic faith, discarding everything that might be opposed to moral scruples and Argentine values. I think that women will be more than regular citizens at the ballot box: they will be the moral outpost, overcoming the sterility and narrowness of mere electoral politics. The hour of the woman is the hour of public virtue for this country. Her home guarantees her will. Her vote is not just a formal right, but a permanent commitment, along with the daily reality of the home. Being wrong would mean abdicating into strange hands her role as leader of her own. Voting wrongly would be a painful family experiment. The female vote inextricably binds within the community principles of moral order and political order. Women can vote and must vote, as the hope of collective dreams. But they must vote, most of all, as a demand of personal liberation, never more just than today. . . .

9. LETTER TO PRESIDENT PERÓN

Much as Vargas did in Brazil, the Peronist government (Argentina, 1946–1955) greatly expanded the state's capacity to provide services for the working classes. For the first time, workers were explicitly included in the dominant definition of citizenship; to the traditional (political) definition, Peronism added a social component. This change took many forms, both in discourse and action. Not the least important of these changes were the many policies of social inclusion and redistribution of wealth undertaken by a great variety of new official departments. Another innovation was the creation of channels of direct communication between the leaders and their people, channels that went beyond the visible rituals of celebration of October 17. Every week, Evita received in her office a multitude of people (mostly poor women and children), who hoped that her Social Assistance Foundation would help them. Other state offices collected the messages common citizens sent to Perón, in which they asked for favors or offered advice on specific problems. The following letter, written by a group of neighbors hoping to become owners of their houses, reveals many aspects of the connection between these leaders and their people.

Buenos Aires, December 17, 1951
To His Excellency the President of Argentina,
General of the Army, Don Juan D. Perón
. . . Most Excellent Mr. President, about two years ago, approximately, your Wife favored us with the award of one of the prefabricated cabins built by the Ministry of Public Works . . . in Villa Lugano, with the help of the Department of Social Assistance, owner of this neighborhood of houses and land. These houses are inhabited by large families with more than three children each, and they are built on plots that we are requesting to buy. We will pay in installments, according to our resources, either to the National Department of Social Assistance or to whoever is designated by the National Mortgage Bank.

We are humble people who have also dreamed of owning a small part of our dear native soil, and of seeing our children grow up healthy and happy, without the fear of having to abandon the roof over our heads, hoping to establish roots in the modest piece of ground where we live today. We appeal to you, most Excellent Mr. President, and to your *Señora*, our EVITA, the true Guardian Angel of the helpless. In you we place all our faith and trust in the fulfillment of our longings.

We would take this opportunity to thank you endlessly, and also to say to you, "ALL PRESENT, MY COLONEL!" as faithful and loyal soldiers, our eyes on the horizon of the future, much like the watchmen in the old forts, like radar stations, watching for the enemies of the Revolution, always ready for another OCTOBER 17 if necessary, for the good of this blessed motherland, hoping her children can lead her to the place she deserves in the community of nations.

We greet your Most Excellent Mr. President in the name of all the neighbors of the cabins of Villa Lugano. Please accept a manly hug and a strong handshake from those of fervent faith in the cause, and who have had the honor to address Mr. President.
"FOR THE MOTHERLAND AND FOR PERON, EVERYTHING"
Signed, Juan P. Castro
Secretary of the Neighborhood Committee
House No. 69

"Carta de Juan Patrocinio Costa al Presidente Perón," in Rose Aboy, "Viviendas para el pueblo. Espacio urbano y sociabilidad en un barrio peronista: Los Perales, 1946–1955" (MA thesis, Universidad de San Andrés, 2002). Excerpt translated by the editors.

10. OF MAN, WOMAN, AND TIME

In the first half of the twentieth century Latin American women made some strides toward emancipation from political, economic, and legal disabilities. Their struggle to gain the vote began around 1914 and ended successfully when Paraguay finally granted women suffrage in 1961. A pioneer in that struggle was the Chilean Amanda Labarca. In 1922 she became the first woman professor at the University of Chile and in 1931 was named director of secondary education, the highest post ever attained by a woman at that time. In a book published in 1934 she reflected on the gains and the losses in the struggle for women's liberation.

Progress is as tortuous as the advance of the tide. An inviting beach beckons it inland; a rocky shore detains it. So it has been with the wave of feminism. Great Britain, Scandinavia, the Soviet Republics, North America, have incorporated its theses—once regarded as so daring—in their daily life. France and many of the Latin countries only tolerate it in their mental diet, without having fully digested it; and doubtless in more than one secluded valley of the Cauca or the Amur one can still live pleasantly under the omnipotent rod of the patriarchal master. What is true of the horizontal of geography is also true of the vertical of social classes. Conduct that the aristocracy regards as scandalously emancipated is an imperative not even discussed in the classes that live under the lash of poverty. And for the Latin girl of the middle class it is often a tragicomedy.

The first theorists of feminism paid dearly for their apostolate. They consoled themselves, in part, by reflecting that the sorrows they endured would help to fill the cup of happiness of the future. Has their hope been realized? Or, after the solution of certain problems, have not other, unforeseen problems arisen, perhaps more difficult than the old ones? Has not that cup of happiness been dearly paid for? Has feminism brought gains or losses to the Latin-American middle-class girl of today?

Gains. First of all, the consciousness of her own worth in the totality of human progress. Today's girl knows that there are no insurmountable obstacles to the flight of her intelligence; that the question of whether her entire sex is intelligent will not be raised before she is permitted to engage in any intellectual activity; that in the eyes of the majority her womanhood does not mark her with the stigma of irremediable inferiority, and that if she has talent she will be allowed to display it.

The law codes have returned to her, in large part, control over her life and property. She has well-founded hopes of seeing abolished within her lifetime

---

Amanda Labarca Hubertson, *¿A dónde va la mujer?* (Santiago de Chile, 1934), pp. 241–247. Excerpt translated by Benjamin Keen.

the laws that still relegate her, in certain aspects, to the position of a second-class citizen, and that accord her unequal legal treatment.

She has made progress in economic liberty, basis of all independence, whether it be a question of a simple individual or one of nations. Today she is gaining admission into fields of labor forbidden to her mother.

Before her extends an unbounded horizon of opportunities. Hopes! She can live her years of illusions imagining—like every adolescent male—that the whole world awaits her, and that only her own limitations can prevent her from ascending the highest peaks of this world.

She has won liberty, including—it may seem ridiculous to mention it—the liberty of going about without papa or the classic brother at her side. To be sure, I do not speak of a nineteen-year-old Amy Johnson, who cleaves the air in a fantastic flight, without other pilot or mechanic than her youth, her skill, and valor, from England to remote Australia, in a secondhand plane that any established ace would have scorned as useless.

She has lost, in the first place, the respect of the male majority. One might say that formerly consideration for women formed part of good breeding, and it was denied only to one who by her conduct showed that she did not merit it. Today it is the other way around. In general, woman receives no tribute, and she must prove convincingly that she is a distinguished personage before receiving the homage that once was common.

Which has diminished—the respect or the quality of respectability?

It is worth one's while to analyze the point.

Men used to expect of women a stainless virtue, perfect submission—after God, thy husband, orders the epistle of St. Paul—and a life-long devotion to the orbit in which her man revolved. A saint in the vaulted niche of her home, saint to the world, mistress of her four walls, and slave to her man. In exchange for this—respect and devotion. True, the father or husband sometimes played the role of sacristan to the saint. They allowed no one to fail to reverence her, but they themselves took liberties and even mistreated her—conduct that the saint had to bear with resignation . . . she had no recourse. It is also true that there are personalities that break all shackles, and that, with or without laws, ever since the world began there have been women who with the rosy point of a little finger, or armed with a gossamer web, have governed husband, children, home, and estate as they willed. But we are not concerned with male or female exceptions.

It is unnecessary to refer again to the upheavals that the invention of machinery brought to the world, the sharp rise in the cost of living and the pauperization of the household, which from producer was reduced to being a simple consumer. It became impossible for a man of average means to satisfy the needs of all his womenfolk, and women had to enter offices, the professions, and other remunerative employment that had been men's traditional source of income. Woman has gone out into the world, and although this fact in itself is an economic imperative and does not essentially imply the abandonment of any virtue, the ordinary man has denied her his respect. As if it were not much more difficult, and consequently more meritorious, to preserve one's purity, sweetness, and delicacy amid the turmoil of the world than in the secluded garden of the old-time home!

On entering the economic struggle she rubs shoulders with misery. Yesterday she only knew of it by hearsay. Today it bespatters her. The rawness of life surrounds her. Often she must solve the problem of staying in the path of rectitude without the help of, or even defending herself from, the man who is ready to exploit any of her weaknesses. For the ordinary man, woman's freedom is license: her equality, the right to treat her without courtesy.

She has lost in opportunities for marriage, for establishing a household, and for satisfying that yearning for maternity that is her fundamental instinct. The more cultured a woman, the more difficult for her to find a husband, because it is normal for her to seek refuge, understanding, and guidance in a person superior to herself. And the latter do not always prefer cultured women. They imagine that knowledge makes them unfeeling—an absurd notion—that it makes them domineering—which concerns not acquired knowledge but character—or that it makes them insufferably pedantic. I regret to say that here they have a little justice on their side. Knowledge is such a recent attainment of women that the majority make an excessive show of it. We play the role of the *nouveaux-riches* of the world of culture. For their wives men prefer the "old-fashioned" girl.

That is the pathos of the tragedy of middle-class women in the Latin countries. Evolution has taken place in opposition to the fundamental convictions of men, who only tolerate it—in the case of their daughters, for example—because imperious necessity dictates it, and only with profound chagrin. Men—I repeat that I speak of the majority—continue to judge women from the viewpoint of fifty years ago, and if they retain some respect and esteem in their inner beings, they tender it to the woman who remained faithful to the classic type—the woman who has progressed they place very close to those for whom they have no respect.

Men cannot understand that external conditions—culture, profession, liberty—have not radically transformed the classic femininity, the maternal instincts, the impulses of the sweet Samaritan, the yearnings of a noble spirituality. The cases of this kind that he knows about do not convince him; he imagines that they constitute exceptions.

Nor are men of more advanced ideas free from this attitude. And it would be amusing—if it did not have tragic implications—to observe what a socialist, a radical, a communist, proclaims on the public platform and what he praises in the intimacy of his home.

Man and woman. Feared and beloved master; slave, sweetly or tyrannically subjugated; wall and ivy. Today divergent and almost hostile, but not comrades. Woman and man cannot yet be comrades, save in an infinitely small number of cases. The relationship of comrades implies equality, confidence, and the same criteria for judging each other.

"But if she acknowledges her bitter lot, why not turn back?" more than one naive soul asks. Impossible. Time does not turn back. The sharp point of its whirling lance moves on, heedless of shattered lives. New social theories will solve these problems and create new ones on the way to an inscrutable future that human faith—a flame that wavers but that only death can extinguish—imagines must be a better one.

Meanwhile, sisters, let us not preach feminism to women; let us win over the men, in the hope that our daughters may pay less dearly for their cup of happiness.

16

❧

DEMOCRACY, DICTATORSHIP,

AND "DEVELOPMENT"

THE 1954 SUICIDE of Brazilian president Getúlio Vargas, followed by the 1955 military coup that ousted Argentine president Juan Perón, marked in dramatic fashion the end of populist regimes (if not populist politics) in Latin America. The state-directed economic policies of these regimes, especially their emphasis on import substitution industrialization (ISI), had begun to diversify the larger regional economies, making them less obviously dependent on the United States and western Europe for their manufactured goods. The nationalization of strategic industries like railroads, oil, and steel had the same intended effect. Some of these policies had alienated important economic players, especially in older export sectors like commercial agriculture, although ISI continued to attract support from the next generation of national policymakers. The mass mobilization of workers was much more controversial. Thus, by the mid-1950s, a new coalition of traditional elites and the increasingly conservative middle class had come to power determined to control the "revolution of rising expectations" among the working classes.

The fragile nature of this coalition and the continued strength of populist political parties (in the face of frequent bans on their activities) produced cycles of intensifying repression. The decline of social services and government subsidies as Latin American economies, burdened by massive debts, reverted from incipient state welfarism back to dependent capitalism exacerbated popular discontent and prompted various kinds of popular resistance from general strikes to guerrilla activities to social revolution. Most Latin American governments responded with greater repression. Governments in the Southern Cone countries—Chile, Argentina, Uruguay, Brazil—were often directed by military juntas that promised to put an end to civilian politics for an undetermined period of "structural adjustments" to new economic "realities." Governments in Central America—Nicaragua, Guatemala, El Salvador, Honduras—were perhaps less bureaucratic but no less repressive. The Andean countries—Peru, Bolivia, Ecuador—and Mexico were only marginally better. Many of these authoritarian regimes received ideological and practical support from the United States, which benefited from both their rabid anticommunism and their willingness to open national markets to international trade.

These authoritarian regimes, however, proved unable to reform national economies or refrain from politics, much less suppress political life altogether. The Argentine junta even failed to fulfill its basic military function in a disastrous 1981 war with Great Britain over the Malvinas (Falkland) Islands. For whatever reason, during the 1980s, governments throughout Latin America became considerably more democratic despite a series of devastating economic crises in the early 1980s and the imposition of the neoliberal economic "reforms." Demanded by international lenders like World Bank and the International Monetary Fund (IMF) and supported by the United States, these so-called reforms included major cuts in government spending, the opening of national economies to international trade, and drastic austerity plans designed to restore solvency to the region's debt-ridden national economies. The 1990s global economic boom held out hope (at least to policymakers) that the neoliberal project would indeed foster economic development in the region—despite the near collapse of the Mexican economy in 1994. The global economic downturn that inaugurated the new century, however, has neoliberal policies on the defensive as rebels in Chiapas (see Chapter 17), hemispheric protests, the rise of regional trading blocs, and resurgent populism raise disturbing questions about the negative impact of globalization throughout the Americas.

1. THE NEW *LATIFUNDIO*

The Cárdenas land distribution dealt a crushing blow to the traditional semifeudal latifundio (large land holding). From the first, however, the land reform suffered from structural defects. In many cases the peasants received parcels of land that were too small to be economically viable, while aid in the form of seeds, credit, and technical assistance was often inadequate. After Cárdenas left office, moreover, conservative Mexican governments increasingly tended to favor large private farms and to neglect the communally owned landholdings, called ejidos. The result was the rise of a new hacienda, or latifundio, with disastrous social consequences. At the turn of the twenty-first century, by the government's own admission, 35 million Mexicans are malnourished, while production of basic staple foods stagnates, imports of basic grains increase, and more and more acreage and resources are devoted to raising sorghum and other crops used to feed animals in order to satisfy the taste of an affluent minority and to producing fresh vegetables for the American market. Since Arturo Warman wrote the article from which this selection is taken, the very survival of Mexican small farmers has been endangered by the signing of the North American Free Trade Agreement (NAFTA) between the United States and Mexico (1993), which greatly increased importation of cheap corn from the United States, and by a 1992 reform of Article 27 of the Mexican Constitution that allows the lease or sale of ejido lands.

A history can be written in many ways. One possible way of narrating and analyzing the agrarian history of Mexico during the last quarter-century is to write the history of the new *latifundio*, an enterprise, legally nonexistent, that has dominated the development of the country's agriculture. The history that I tell here does not claim to be a formal economic analysis. . . . This account focuses on the qualitative social changes that have taken place in the Mexican countryside and its effects on the country as a whole.

To define the new *latifundio*, even for the limited purposes of this essay, is not easy. It is a kind of monster with a thousand heads and local forms that is protected by a legal fiction that hides or masks it. It does not exist for fiscal purposes and the registries of property titles meticulously deny its possibility. It defies the registries of capitalism even as it enjoys its benefits. This "irregularity" may serve to attempt a provisional and limited definition of the Mexican *latifundio*, conceived and implemented as a pillar of development of the industrial capitalist type. Defined in the most general terms, the new *latifundio* is a capitalist enterprise devoted to the production of agricultural products for sale in a large market with the aim of reproducing its capital and making a profit. Like every other capitalist enterprise, it achieves its aim by its control and accumulation of the means of production and its control over the channels and mechanisms of exchange. What is peculiar about the new *latifundio* is that its control of the means of production does not conform to the classic rules of the system and is not necessarily connected with ownership. This is especially important when the means of production is land, the material basis of agriculture, but it is equally valid for labor, which is acquired through the system of peonage, and for the capital involved, which in good measure is supplied by the state. This "irregularity" of the new *latifundio*, and indeed of the social and institutional framework within which it operates, is the source of its dynamism and efficacy, but is also its Achilles' heel, its limitation, and the origin of its rapid decay and obsolescence, expressed in an agricultural crisis of enormous proportions.

Arturo Warman, "El neolatifundio mexicano: Expansión y crisis de una forma de dominio," in *Ensayos sobre el campesinado en México* (México: Editorial Nueva Imagen, 1979), pp. 39–63. Excerpt translated by Benjamin Keen.

The new *latifundio* began to make its appearance in the Mexican country-side during the Second World War. Its precursor, the great estate, had been liquidated by the revolutionary movement in some parts of the country and in many others by the world crisis of the thirties when foreign markets for its products had collapsed and the internal market could not absorb its output of raw materials. The Cárdenas land reform radically altered the agrarian structure and half of the cultivated area was turned over to the peasants under the *ejido* system. The distributed land was used principally for subsistence crops that were integrated into the national economy through the market. The system was modified to concentrate and transfer the surpluses of the peasant sector to the capitalist enclaves of the country. The great estate had appropriated peasant labor, converting that labor into commercial products, but allowed the peasants to grow the traditional crops for their own subsistence, obviously in order to lower wages, which only supplemented the food grown by peasants for their own use. After the land division it was the peasants' production that was appropriated, and the transfer of their surpluses became dependent on the mechanism of prices and its aids: usury, monopoly, and the ownership of the work animals that were rented to the peasants.

The Cárdenas land reform, in its aspect of a somewhat belated reaction to the international crisis, overlapped with the recovery of foreign markets. Those markets revived under the stimulus of a war economy (1939–1945). The nation, or rather its ruling groups, embarked on an industrialization program, once again found attractive the prospect of selling agricultural products in foreign markets that paid in foreign currency; that is, the prospect of returning to the system of expropriating peasant labor, separated from the means of production. But the land reform was a political fact that had unleashed powerful forces. To undo the land division was an impossibility; even its future suspension was inconceivable. The great estate could not be restored. From this contradiction arose the new *latifundio*.

Although the great estate could not be restored, it was possible to protect its remnants, which could be converted into territorial nuclei of a new type of enterprise. To this end the state took steps to protect and strengthen private landholdings capable of being used for commercial production. Some of these measures had a legal character. Under Cárdenas, for example, a law designed to stimulate cattle exports exempted from division cattle ranches with areas larger than permitted by the existing legislation.

The effects of the legal measures were multiplied by their institutional application. Despotism, bureaucratic inefficiency, and corruption, with results that always favored the large landowners, dominated the public agencies charged with administering agrarian policy. The grave consequences of the "reform" in the agrarian legislation were aggravated by political measures designed to benefit the large landowners. Physical repression of nonconformist peasants gradually revived after the Cárdenas era. One of the most serious steps in this direction was the permission given to the associations of cattle raisers to act as rural police on the pretext of pursuing cattle thieves; this permission was used to legalize the actions of the gunmen employed by the large landowners. Less dramatic, but perhaps more effective, was the creation of a single peasant organization that became a bureaucratic and political appendage of the government and was used for the performance of bureaucratic tasks and the distribution of various sinecures. The management of the organization was placed in the hands of officials named from above who assumed the representation of the peasants in order to control them. This was effectively achieved, thanks to a political measure of very great importance—the continuance of land division.

During the presidency of Ávila Camacho, distribution of land to the peasantry diminished; it reached its lowest point during the presidency of Ruiz Cortines. Under President López Mateos the quantity of distributed land tended to increase and it reached its peak under Díaz Ordaz, who distributed approximately as much land as Lázaro Cárdenas. But the quality of the distributed land steadily grew worse; the proportion of arable land was minuscule and it was almost totally useless for the planting of commercial crops; the rest was deserts, badlands, mountains, or even land under water. Land distribution became a political ritual devoid of any economic significance. Land was distributed to placate political demands, but with the intention of preserving rather than transforming the agrarian structure.

The result of the agrarian reform after Cárdenas has been to polarize the disparity of landholding. Land ownership has steadily become more concentrated; this is shown by a comparison of census data for 1940, 1950, and 1960. It seems clear that when the figures for 1970 are in this tendency will be even more pronounced, and this does not take account of the frauds and shams practiced by the large landowners. But the tendency toward land concentration was not sufficiently intense to achieve the restoration of the great estate as the dominant form of exploitation. The great estate exists and never completely ceased to exist, but it is less important than the new *latifundio*. It is likely that the statistical concentration of ownership reflects the consolidation of the nuclei of the new *latifundio*, which extends its territorial sway through the mechanism of renting land—another legal impossibility.

The rental of *ejido* land is the most common means of increasing production by the new *latifundio*. It has taken different forms: direct rental, illegal and perhaps most frequent; "associations" between sharks and sardines, more subtle but equivalent to direct rent; various forms of credit, in which the lender makes the decisions with respect to crops, harvesting, and sale for the debtor. In the last instance the government plays the most active role as a new *latifundista* while private investors dominate in the others. The renting of land has become so general that there exists a large group of new *latifundistas* who possess no land whatever. With a few agricultural machines, some money, and a lot of connections, they cultivate enormous extents of land rented in lots. Some of them, like migratory peons, wander about according to the different agricultural seasons. Not only *ejidatarios* but many small landowners in the broad sense of the word, lacking the means to engage in commercial agriculture on their own, have been caught in the spider web of rent. Thus the new *latifundio* in its different forms has come to control almost all the land on which it is possible to obtain very high yields with very little risk. . . .

Government policies in the fields of irrigation and road construction also furthered the expansion of the territorial area controlled by the agricultural entrepreneurs. Road construction made it possible for lands with the characteristic desired by the new *latifundistas*, but without access to markets, to join the march of progress. In a certain sense, the new roads were the vanguard of the new *latifundio*. Cotton was sowed in Chiapas, sesame in the hot lands of Guerrero, and rice in Sinaloa, and today a sugar mill is under construction in Chiapas. . . .

The construction of irrigation works, the most sizeable item of public investment in the countryside, was perhaps the most valuable government gift to the new *latifundistas*. Since they did not own land, they were not about to invest to improve lands which did not belong to them. They were caught in a vicious circle; they were able and willing to invest, but outside of their own territorial nuclei they could not invest in land. The state assumed that task for them. The new irrigated lands, owned by *ejidatarios* or poor small landowners who lacked the resources to produce in the quantities demanded by the government in order to recover its investment, passed on their totality to the control of the entrepreneurs who possessed these resources. The advantage was immense, and the new *latifundio*, in return for the payment of a ridiculous rent that frequently did not amount to 5% of the value of the crop, acquired control of an enormous investment made by the state.

Frequently, even the resources used by the new private *latifundistas* to cultivate the lands opened up by the federal investment also came from the government. They obtained these resources through government credit facilities in their multiple forms. A good part of the government credit directed toward the countryside wound up in the hands of the new *latifundistas*, working through legal or illegal channels, again without leaving a statistical trace. They also captured the fruits of agricultural research. They were the beneficiaries of a "green revolution," conceived in entrepreneurial terms, whose techniques could only be applied in the conditions under which the new *latifundistas* operated. Many agricultural entrepreneurs took their capital out of agriculture and transferred it to more secure if less profitable fields, content to employ the government's resources for their own benefit.

The new *latifundio* obtained another enormous benefit from state intervention in control of the market through the establishment of guaranteed official prices for their products. These were fixed, in the 1950s, taking as base the costs and returns of the new *latifundistas*, figured with a juicy margin of profit; this allowed them to operate with complete security. When the prices of their products were frozen or increased much less than those of urban products, for the benefit of the urban sectors of the population, the new *latifundistas* could absorb the relative decline, thanks to the increased yields made possible by the "green revolution." Others, who operated in less favorable zones, could not stand the decline and gradually abandoned their crops, replacing them with others that required higher rates of investment. But all received another benefit in the fact that the price of corn, declining in real terms, remained fixed; since this price regulated wage levels in the countryside, the cost of labor to the new *latifundistas* went down.

All seemed to be going well, splendidly. The new *latifundio* grew and increased its production. Between 1942 and 1964 agricultural and cattle production grew by a healthy 4.6% a year, 1.5% more than the rate of population increase, and between 1945 and 1956, precisely when the most large-scale assistance was being given to the new *latifundio*, it grew at the spectacular rate of 5.9% a year. By the beginning of the 1960s, Mexico had achieved self-sufficiency in agricultural and meat production and adequately satisfied the national demand or under consumption—whatever one wishes to call it. In 1965 great quantities of corn and wheat were exported. More important still, from the viewpoint of industrial development, the export of agricultural products grew at satisfactory rates. In 1960, 22% of agricultural production was exported and accounted for a little more than half of all the country's exports. The exported products were totally produced by the new *latifundio*: cotton (the most important), coffee, sugar, henequen, tomatoes, and meat. The agricultural sector was acquiring foreign exchange to compensate for the enormous deficit created by imports destined for the industrial sector. . . .

From the state's point of view, things were going so well in the countryside that it decided there was no need to invest so much in agriculture when that money was badly needed for industry. Public investment in agriculture was never very great, especially if we consider that it was targeted at half of the population, at least. . . . The abandonment of the countryside, covered up with rhetoric and symbolic distribution of land, had become clear by 1965. Its effects were mitigated by several years of good rainfall. Even so, the decline in agricultural and pastoral production as a proportion of the total national production was evident. In a suicidal manner, these facts were officially interpreted as clear proof of the triumph of industrialization and progress: Mexico was approaching the threshold of development.

Beginning in 1970 the decline accelerated and became clear to all. The crash was provoked by the international economic crisis, the greatest since the 1930s, but its deeper causes cannot be assigned solely to the erratic course of foreign markets or unfavorable meteorological conditions. The imports of corn and wheat, uninterrupted since 1972 and with no prospect of improvement in the short range, certainly the most troublesome aspect of the crisis, basically are caused by internal factors linked to the structure of production in the countryside and its articulation with industrial production and the service sector. The "peculiarity" of the new *latifundio*, its internal structure and its relations with other sectors, can serve as the point of departure for an inquiry into the nature and origin of the agricultural crisis.

For my guiding thread I shall take the results of that separation of the control of land from its possession that in good measure determines the composition of capital in Mexican agriculture and sets limits on its accumulation, though not its reproduction. The only land on which the new *latifundista* can make such improvements as irrigation, leveling, and conditioning of the soil, is that which belongs to him. When such land exists, it forms a small portion in relation to the total area in which the entrepreneur operates and whose control he obtains by renting. He will not invest a cent in the rented area, and only in certain types of enterprises—dairies, for example—will he invest in his own land. Basically his profits depend on the extent of the area which he can cultivate, not on the yields that can be obtained. The new *latifundio* grows horizontally, above all, on land which does not belong to it. The disadvantages of investing in this land determine the fact that the major part of the invested capital goes into operating costs, for the purchase of machinery and to cover the costs of cultivation. Agricultural machinery has great importance for the new *latifundio*, not so much because of its technical or economic advantages but because it is the physical instrument by means of which the entrepreneur takes control of the land during critically short periods of time. Thus the production of the new *latifundio* is generally of the extensive type and cannot be transferred to more intensive types of cultivation that require treatment of the soil or other adaptations. On the other hand, the composition of capital explains, in part, the high rate of profit, sometimes amounting to 100% of the investment and normally exceeding the rate of profit achieved in other activities. . . .

Its limitations as concerns investment in the countryside make the new *latifundio* the most effective instrument for achieving the greatest and most rapid transfer of resources from the countryside to other activities. This effectiveness may help to explain the unlimited assistance that the government has given to the most brutal and rapid agency for despoiling the countryside and its inhabitants. But the effectiveness of the new *latifundio* has a high price: the destruction of natural resources, often nonrenewable. Soils, forests, natural vegetation of economic importance to the peasants are annihilated; meanwhile pests increase, the immoderate use of chemical products becomes indispensable, and salinity and erosion grow. Obviously, this enormous price is not paid by the entrepreneurs, but by the peasants who regain the land after it has become a wasteland from which all good has been extracted, while the entrepreneurs search for or demand from the state new lands for their operations. . . .

2. ECONOMIC DEPENDENCY

As the economic power of the United States expanded after World War II, Latin American economists began to reassess their region's role in the global economy. Founded in 1948, the United Nations Economic Commission for Latin America (ECLA, or CEPAL in Spanish) played a central role in that reassessment. One of the commission's most important contributions was this 1950 critique of the classic liberal economic doctrine of "comparative advantage" in which national and regional economies engaged in "free trade" were encouraged to specialize in the economic activities best suited to their level of economic development and to their available natural and human resources. The report's author, Argentine economist Raúl Prebisch, argued that while these policies had proven extremely beneficial to "central," industrialized economies like the United States and western Europe, they had contributed to the underdevelopment of "peripheral," export-oriented economies other places in the world including Latin America.

In Latin America, reality is undermining the out-dated schema of the international division of labor, which achieved great importance in the nineteenth century and, as a theoretical concept, continued to exert considerable influence until very recently.

Under that schema, the specific task that fell to Latin America, as part of the periphery of the world economic system, was that of producing food and raw materials for the great industrial centers.

There was no place within it for the industrialization of the new countries. It is nevertheless being forced upon them by events. Two world wars in a single generation and a great economic crisis between them have shown the Latin American countries their opportunities, clearly pointing the way to industrial activity.

The academic discussion, however, is far from ended. In economics, ideologies usually tend either to lag behind events or to outlive them. It is true that the reasoning on the economic advantages of the international division of labor is theoretically sound, but it is usually forgotten that it is based upon

Raúl Prebisch, *The Economic Development of Latin America and Its Principal Problems, Economic Commission for Latin America* (Lake Success, N.Y.: United Nations Department of Economic Affairs, 1950).

428 ◌∾ *Part Eight: Consolidating the Nation-State*

an assumption which has been conclusively proved false by facts. According to this assumption, the benefits of technical progress tend to be distributed alike over the whole community, either by the lowering of prices or the corresponding raising of incomes. The countries producing raw materials obtain their share of these benefits through international exchange, and therefore have no need to industrialize. If they were to do so, their lesser efficiency would result in their losing the conventional advantages of such exchange.

The flaw in this assumption is that of generalizing from the particular. If by "the community" only the great industrial countries are meant, it is indeed true that the benefits of technical progress are gradually distributed among all social groups and classes. If, however, the concept of the community is extended to include the periphery of the world economy, a serious error is implicit in the generalization. The enormous benefits that derive from increased productivity have not reached the periphery in a measure comparable to that obtained by the peoples of the great industrial countries. Hence, the outstanding differences between the standards of living of the masses of the former and the latter and the manifest discrepancies between their respective abilities to accumulate capital, since the margin of saving depends primarily on increased productivity.

Thus there exists an obvious disequilibrium, a fact which, whatever its explanation of justification, destroys the basic premise underlying the schema of international division of labor.

Hence, the fundamental significance of the industrialization of the new countries. Industrialization is not an end in itself, but the principal means at the disposal of those countries of obtaining a share of the benefits of technical progress and of progressively raising the standard of living of the masses. . . .

The industrialization of Latin America is not incompatible with the efficient development of primary production. On the contrary, the availability of the best capital equipment and the prompt adoption of new techniques are essential if the development of industry is to fulfill the social objective of raising the standard of living. The same is true of the mechanization of agriculture. Primary products must be exported to allow for the importation of the considerable quantity of capital goods needed.

The more active Latin America's trade, the greater the possibility of increasing productivity by means of intensive capital formation. The solution does not lie in growth at the expense of foreign trade, but in knowing how to extract, from continually growing foreign trade, the elements that will promote economic development.

If reasoning does not suffice to convince us of the close tie between economic development and foreign trade, a few facts relating to the situation today will make it evident. The economic activity and level of employment in the majority of the Latin American countries are considerably higher than before the war. This high level of employment entails increased imports of consumer goods, both non-durable and durable, besides those of raw materials and capital goods, and very often exports are insufficient to provide for them.

This is evident in the case of imports and other items payable in dollars. There are already well known cases of scarcity of that currency in certain countries, despite the fact that the amount of dollars supplied to the rest of the world in payment of its own imports was considerable. In relation to its national income, however, the import coefficient of the United States has, after a persistent decline, arrived at a very low level (not over 3 per cent). It is, therefore, not surprising that, notwithstanding the high income level of the United States, the dollar resources thus made available to the Latin American countries seem insufficient to pay for the imports needed for their intensive development.

It is true that as European economy recovers, trade with that continent can profitably be increased, but Europe will not supply Latin America with more dollars unless the United States increases its import coefficient for European goods.

This, then, is the core of the problem. It is obvious that if the above-mentioned coefficient is not raised, Latin America will be compelled to divert its purchases from the United States to those countries which provide the exchange to pay for them. Such a solution is certainly very dubious, since it often means the purchase of more expensive or unsuitable goods.

It would be deplorable to fall back on the measures of that kind when a basic solution might be found. It is sometimes thought that, by reason of the enormous productive capacity of the United States, that country could not increase its import coefficient for the purpose of providing the basic solution to the world problem. Such a conclusion cannot be substantiated without a prior analysis of the factors that have caused the United States steadily to reduce its import coefficient. These factors are aggravated by unemployment, but can be overcome when it does not exist. One can understand that it is of vital importance, both to Latin America and the rest of the world, that the United States achieve its aim of maintaining a high level of employment.

It cannot be denied that the economic development of certain Latin American countries and their rapid assimilation of modern technology, in so far as they can utilize it, depend to a very large extent upon foreign investment. The implications involved render the problem far from simple. The negative factors include the failure to meet foreign financial commitments during the great depression of the nineteen thirties, a failure which, it is generally agreed, must not be allowed to happen again. Fundamentally the problem is the same as that referred to in the preceding paragraph. The servicing of these foreign investments, unless new investments are made, must be paid for by means of exports in the same currency and, if these do not show a corresponding increase, in time the same difficulties will arise again. They will be the greater if exports fall violently. The question thus arises whether, pending that basic solution, it would not be wiser to direct investments toward such productive activities as would, through direct or indirect reduction of dollar imports, permit the regular servicing of foreign obligations.

Here one must beware of dogmatic generalizations. To assume that the meeting of foreign commitments and the proper functioning of the monetary system depend upon nothing more than a decision to obey certain rules of the game is to fall into an error involving serious consequences. Even when the gold standard was in operation in the great centers, the countries of the Latin American periphery had great difficulty in maintaining it, and their monetary troubles frequently provoked condemnation from abroad. The more recent experiences of the large countries have brought a better understanding of some aspects of the situation. Great Britain, between the two wars, encountered difficulties somewhat similar to those which arose and continue to arise in the Latin American countries, which have never taken kindly to the rigidity of the gold standard. That experience doubtless helps to bring about a better understanding of the phenomena of the periphery.

The gold standard has ceased to function, as in the past, and the management of currency has become even more complex in the periphery. Can all these complications be overcome by a strict application of sound rules in monetary behavior? Sound rules for these countries are still in the making. Here there arises another vital problem; that of utilizing individual and collective experience to find a means of harmoniously fitting monetary action into a policy of regular and intensive economic development. . . .

There is yet another aspect of the problem of dollar exchange. It is true that, as already stated, a high level of employment increases imports. But it is also a fact that an excessive monetary expansion has often unduly increased the pressure on the balance of payments, thus leading to the use of foreign exchange for purposes not always compatible with economic development.

These facts must be taken into account in an objective analysis of the effects of the inflationary increase on the process of capitalization. It must, however, be admitted that, in most of the Latin American countries, voluntary savings are not sufficient to cover the most urgent capital needs. In any case, monetary expansion does not bring about an increase in the foreign exchange reserves necessary for the importation of capital goods; it merely redistributes income. It must now be determined whether it has led to a more active capital formation.

The point is a decisive one. The raising of the standard of living of the masses ultimately depends on the existence of a considerable amount of capital permanently employed in industry, transport and primary production, and on the ability to use it well.

Consequently, the Latin American countries need to accumulate an enormous amount of capital. Several have already shown their capacity to save to the extent of being able to finance a large part of their industrial investments through their own efforts. Even in this case, which is exceptional, capital formation has to overcome a strong tendency towards certain types of consumption which are often incompatible with intensive capitalization.

Nevertheless, it does not appear essential to restrict the individual consumption of the bulk of the population, which, on the whole, is too low, in order to accumulate the capital required for industrialization and for the technical improvement of agriculture. An immediate increase in productivity per man could be brought about by well-directed foreign investments added to present savings. Once this initial improvement has been accomplished, a considerable par of the increased production can be devoted to capital formation rather than to inopportune consumption.

How are sufficient increases in productivity to be achieved? The experience of recent years is instructive. With some exceptions, the rise in employment necessitated by industrial development was made possible by the use of men whom technical progress had displaced from primary production and other occupations, especially certain comparably poorly paid types of personal services, and by the employment of women. The industrial employment of the unemployed, or ill-employed, has thus meant a considerable improvement in productivity and, consequently, where other factors have not brought about a general lowering of productive efficiency, a net increase in national income.

The great scope for technical progress in the field of primary production, even in those countries where it has already been considerable, together with the perfecting of existing industries, could contribute, to national income, a net increase that would provide an ever increasing margin of saving.

All this, however, especially in so far as it is desired to reduce the need for foreign investments, presupposes a far greater initial capitalization than is usually possible with the type of consumption of certain sectors of the community, or the high proportion of national income absorbed, in some countries, by fiscal expenditure, which makes no direct or indirect contribution to national productivity.

It is, in fact, a demonstration of the latent conflict existing in these countries between the desire to assimilate, quickly, ways of life which the technically more advanced countries adopted step by step as their productivity increased, and the need for capitalization without which this increase in productivity could not be achieved.

For the very reason that capital is scarce, and the need for it great, its use should be subjected to a strict standard of efficacy which has not been easy to maintain, especially where industries have developed to meet an emergency. There is, however, still time to correct certain deviations and, above all, to avoid them in the future.

In order to achieve this, the purpose of industrialization must be clearly defined. If industrialization is considered to be the means of attaining an autarchic ideal in which economic considerations are of secondary importance, any industry that can produce substitutes for imports is justifiable. If, however, the aim is to increase the measurable well-being of the masses, the limits beyond which more intensive industrialization might mean a decrease in productivity must be borne in mind.

Formerly, before the great depression, development in the Latin American countries was stimulated from abroad by the constant increase of exports. There is no reason to suppose, at least at present, that this will again occur to the same extent, except under very exceptional circumstances. These countries no longer have an alternative between vigorous growth along those lines and internal expansion through industrialization. Industrialization has become the most important means of expansion.

This does not mean, however, that primary exports must be sacrificed to further industrial development. Exports not only provide the foreign exchange with which to buy the imports necessary for economic development, but their value usually includes a high proportion of land rent, which does not involve any collective cost. If productivity in agriculture can be increased by technical progress and if, at the same time, real wages can be raised by industrialization and adequate social legislation, the disequilibrium between incomes at the centers and the periphery can gradually be corrected without detriment to that essential economic activity.

This is one of the limits of industrialization which must be carefully considered in plans of development. Another concerns the optimum size of industrial enterprises. It is generally found in Latin American countries that the same industries are being attempted on both sides of the same frontier. This tends to diminish productive efficiency and so militates against fulfilling the social task to be accomplished. The defect is a serious one, which the nineteenth century was able to attenuate considerably. When Great Britain proved, with facts, the advantages of industry, other countries followed suit. Industrial development, however, spurred by active competition, tended towards certain characteristic types of specialization which encouraged profitable trade between the various countries. Specialization furthered technical progress and the latter made possible higher incomes. Here, unlike the case of industrial countries by comparison with those producing primary products, the classic advantages of the division-of-labor between countries that are equal, or nearly so, followed.

The possibility of losing a considerable proportion of the benefits of technical progress through an excessive division of markets thus constitutes another factor limiting the industrial expansion of these countries. Far from being insurmountable, however, it is a factor which could be removed with mutual benefit by a wise policy of economic interdependence.

Anti-cyclical policies must be included in any programs of economic development if there is to be an attempt, from a social point of view, to raise real income. The spread of the cyclical fluctuations of the large centers to the

Latin American periphery means a considerable loss of income to these countries. If this could be avoided, it would simplify the problem of capital formation. Attempts have been made to evolve an anti-cyclical policy, but it must be admitted that, as yet, but little light has been thrown on this subject. Furthermore, the present dwindling of metallic reserves in several countries means that, in the event of a recession originating abroad, they would not only be without a plan of defense but would lack means of their own to carry out the measures demanded by the circumstances. . . .

3. "HISTORY WILL ABSOLVE ME"

Fidel Castro made his entrance into history at dawn on July 26, 1953, when he led a tiny force of Cuban patriots, 165 men and 2 women, in an assault on the Moncada barracks in Santiago de Cuba. The quixotic adventure ended in disaster. Nearly half the rebels were killed, many being tortured to death after capture. Those who survived were imprisoned. At his trial the twenty-seven-year-old Castro, a lawyer by profession and the son of a large landowner, made a five-hour defense speech in which he outlined the aims of the uprising. In a general way his speech offers a blueprint of the radical reform program that the Cuban Revolution was to implement, but the whole document bears the stamp of a democratic, romantic ideology that Castro would later abandon in favor of Marxism-Leninism. The title of this selection is taken from the final phrase of Castro's speech: "Condemn me. History will absolve me."

. . . When we speak of the people we do not mean the comfortable ones, the conservative elements of the nation, who welcome any regime of oppression, any dictatorship, and despotism, prostrating themselves before the master of the moment until they grind their foreheads into the ground. When we speak of struggle, the people means the vast unredeemed masses, to whom all make promises and whom all deceive; we mean the people who yearn for a better, more dignified and more just nation; who are moved by ancestral aspirations of justice, for they have suffered injustice and mockery, generation after generation; who long for great and wise changes in all aspects of their life; people, who, to attain these changes, are ready to give even the very last breath of their lives—when they believe in something or in someone, especially when they believe in themselves. In stating a purpose, the first condition of sincerity and good faith, is to do precisely what nobody ever does, that is, to speak with absolute clarity, without fear. The demagogues and professional

Fidel Castro, *Fidel Castro's History Will Absolve Me* (Havana: Impreso por Cooperativa Obrera de Publicidad, 1960), pp. 33–43.

politicians who manage to perform the miracle of being right in everything and in pleasing everyone, are, of necessity, deceiving everyone about everything. The revolutionaries must proclaim their ideas courageously, define their principles and express their intentions so that no one is deceived, neither friend nor foe.

The people we counted on in our struggle were these:

Seven hundred thousand Cubans without work, who desire to earn their daily bread honestly without having to emigrate in search of livelihood.

Five hundred thousand farm laborers inhabiting miserable shacks, who work four months of the year and starve for the rest of the year, sharing their misery with their children, who have not an inch of land to cultivate, and whose existence inspires compassion in any heart not made of stone.

Four hundred thousand industrial laborers and stevedores whose retirement funds have been embezzled, whose benefits are being taken away, whose homes are wretched quarters, whose salaries pass from the hands of the boss to those of the usurer, whose future is a pay reduction and dismissal, whose life is eternal work and whose only rest is in the tomb.

One hundred thousand small farmers who live and die working on land that is not theirs, looking at it with sadness as Moses did the promised land, to die without possessing it; who, like feudal serfs, have to pay for the use of their parcel of land by giving up a portion of their products; who cannot love it, improve it, beautify it or plant a lemon or an orange tree on it, because they never know when a sheriff will come with the rural guard to evict them from it.

Thirty thousand small business men weighted down by debts, ruined by the crisis and harangued by a plague of filibusters and venal officials.

Ten thousand young professionals: doctors, engineers, lawyers, veterinarians, school teachers, dentists, pharmacists, newspapermen, painters, sculptors, etc., who come forth from school with their degrees, anxious to work and full of hope, only to find themselves at a dead end with all doors closed, and where no ear hears their clamor or supplication.

These are the people, the ones who know misfortune and, therefore, are capable of fighting with limitless courage!

To the people whose desperate roads through life have been paved with the brick of betrayals and false promises, we were not going to say: "we will eventually give you what you need, but rather—Here you have it, fight for it with all your might so that liberty and happiness may be yours!"

In the brief of this cause there must be recorded the five revolutionary laws that would have been proclaimed immediately after the capture of the Moncada barracks and would have been broadcast to the nation by radio. It is possible that Colonel Chaviano may deliberately have destroyed these documents, but even if he has done so, I conserve them in my memory.

The First Revolutionary Law would have returned power to the people and proclaimed the Constitution of 1940 the supreme Law of the land, until such time as the people should decide to modify or change it. And, in order to effect its implementation and punish those who had violated it—there being no organization for holding elections to accomplish this—the revolutionary movement, as the momentous incarnation of this sovereignty, the only source of legitimate power, would have assumed all the faculties inherent to it, except that of modeling the Constitution itself: In other words it would have assumed the legislative, executive and judicial powers.

This approach could not be more crystal clear nor more free of vacillation and sterile charlatanry. A government acclaimed by the mass of rebel people would be vested with every power, everything necessary in order to proceed with the effective implementation of the popular will and true justice. From that moment, the Judicial Power, which since March 10th has placed itself against the Constitution and *outside* the Constitution, would cease to exist and we would proceed to its immediate and total reform before it would again assume the power granted to it by the Supreme Law of the Republic. Without our first taking those previous measures, a return to legality by putting the custody of the courts back into the hands that have crippled the system so dishonorably would constitute a fraud, a deceit, and one more betrayal.

The Second Revolutionary Law would have granted property, not mortgageable and not transferable, to all planters, sub-planters, lessees, partners and squatters who hold parcels of five or less "caballerias" of land, and the state would indemnify the former owners on the basis of the rental which they would have received for these parcels over a period of ten years.

The Third Revolutionary Law would have granted workers and employees the right to share 30% of the profits of all the large industrial, mercantile and mining enterprises, including the sugar mills. The strictly agricultural enterprises would be exempt in consideration of other agrarian laws which would have been implemented.

The Fourth Revolutionary Law would have granted all planters the right to share 55% of the sugar production and a minimum quota of forty thousand "arrobas" for all small planters who have been established for three or more years.

The Fifth Revolutionary Law would have ordered the confiscation of all holdings and ill-gotten gains of those who had committed frauds during previous regimes, as well as the holdings and ill-gotten gains of all their legatees and heirs. To implement this, special courts with full powers would gain access to all records of all corporations registered or operating in this country (in order) to investigate concealed funds of illegal origin, and to request that foreign governments extradite persons and attach holdings (rightfully belonging to the Cuban people). Half of the property recovered would be used to subsidize retirement funds for workers and the other half would be used for hospitals, asylums and charitable organizations.

Furthermore, it was to be declared that the Cuban policy in the Americas would be one of close solidarity with the democratic people of this continent, and that those politically persecuted by bloody tyrants oppressing our sister nations would find generous asylum, brotherhood, and bread in the land of Martí. Not the persecution, hunger and treason that they find today. Cuba should be the bulwark of liberty and not a shameful link in the chain of despotism.

These laws would have been proclaimed immediately, as soon as the upheaval was ended and prior to a detailed and far-reaching study, they would have been followed by another series of laws and fundamental measures, such as, the Agrarian Reform, Integral Reform in Education, nationalization of the Utilities Trust and the Telephone Trust, refund to the people of the illegal excessive rates this company has charged, and payment to the Treasury of all taxes brazenly evaded in the past.

All these laws and others would be inspired in the exact fulfillment of two essential articles of our Constitution. One of these orders the outlawing of feudal estates by indicating the maximum area of land any person or entity can possess for each type of agricultural enterprise, by adopting measures which would tend to revert the land to the Cubans. The other categorically orders the State to use all means at its disposal to provide employment to all those who lack it and to insure a decent livelihood to each manual laborer or intellectual.

None of these articles may be called unconstitutional. The first popularly elected government would have to respect these laws, not only because of moral obligation to the nation, but because when people achieve something they have yearned for throughout generations, no force in the world is capable of taking it away again.

The problems concerning land, the problem of industrialization, the problem of housing, the problem of unemployment, the problem of education and the problem of the health of the people; these are the six problems we would take immediate steps to resolve, along with the restoration of public liberties and political democracy.

Perhaps this exposition appears cold and theoretical if one does not know the shocking and tragic conditions of the country with regard to these six problems, to say nothing of the most humiliating political oppression.

Eighty-five percent of the small farmers in Cuba pay rent and live under the constant threat of being dispossessed from the land that they cultivate. More than half the best cultivated land belongs to foreigners. In Oriente, the largest province, the lands of the United Fruit Company and West Indian Company join the north coast to the southern one. There are two hundred thousand peasant families who do not have a single acre of land to cultivate to provide food for their starving children. On the other hand, nearly three hundred thousand "caballerias" of productive land owned by powerful interests remain uncultivated.

Cuba is above all an agricultural state. Its population is largely rural. The city depends on these rural areas. The rural people won the Independence.

The greatness and prosperity of our country depends on a healthy and vigorous rural population that loves the land and knows how to cultivate it, within the framework of a state that protects and guides them. Considering all this, how can the present state of affairs be tolerated any longer?

With the exception of a few food, lumber and textile industries, Cuba continues to be a producer of raw materials. We export sugar to import candy, we export hides to import shoes, we export iron to import plows. Everybody agrees that the need to industrialize the country is urgent, that we need steel industries, paper and chemical industries; that we must improve cattle and grain products, the technique and the processing in our food industry, in order to balance the ruinous competition of the Europeans in cheese products, condensed milk, liquors and oil, and that of the Americans in canned goods; that we need merchant ships; that tourism should be an enormous source of revenue. But the capitalists insist that the workers remain under a Claudian yoke [Claudius Caecus was a repressive Roman emperor.]. . . .

Just as serious or even worse is the housing problem. There are two hundred thousand huts and hovels in Cuba; four hundred thousand families in the country and in the cities live cramped into barracks and tenements without even the minimum sanitary requirements; two million two hundred thousand of our urban population pay rents which absorb between one fifth and one third of their income; and two million eight hundred thousand of our rural and suburban population lack electricity. If the State proposes lowering rents, landlords threaten to freeze all construction; if the State does not interfere, construction goes on so long as the landlords get high rents, otherwise they would not lay a single brick even though the rest of the population should have to live exposed to the elements. The utilities monopoly is no better; they extend lines as far as it is profitable and beyond that point, they don't care if the people have to live in darkness for the rest of their lives. The State folds its arms and the people have neither homes nor electricity.

Our educational system is perfectly compatible with the rest of our national situation. Where the *guajiro* [small farmer] is not the owner of his land, what need is there for agricultural schools? Where there are no industries what need is there for technical or industrial schools? Everything falls within the same absurd logic: there is neither one thing nor the other. In any small European country there are more than 200 technical and industrial arts schools; in Cuba, there are only six such schools, and the boys graduate without having anywhere to use their skills. The little rural schools are attended by only half the school-age children—barefoot, half naked and undernourished—and frequently the teacher must buy necessary materials from his own salary. Is this the way to make a nation great?

Only death can liberate one from so much misery. In this, however—early death—the state is most helpful. Ninety percent of rural children are consumed by parasites which filter through their bare feet from the earth. Society is moved to compassion upon hearing of the kidnapping or murder of one child, but they are criminally indifferent to the mass murder of so many thousands of children who die every year from lack of facilities, agonizing with pain. Their innocent eyes—death already shining in them—seem to look into infinity as if entreating forgiveness for human selfishness, as if asking God to stay his wrath. When the head of a family works only four months a year, with what can he purchase clothing and medicine for his children? They will grow up with rickets, with not a single good tooth in their mouths by the time they reach thirty; they will have heard ten million speeches and will finally die of misery and deception. Public hospitals, which are always full, accept only patients recommended by some powerful politician, who, in turn, demands the electoral votes of the unfortunate one and his family so that Cuba may continue forever the same or worse.

With this background, is it not understandable that from May to December over a million persons lost their jobs, and that Cuba, with a population of five and a half million, has a greater percentage of unemployed than France or Italy with a population of forty million each?

When you judge a defendant for robbery, Your Honors, do you ask him how long he has been unemployed? Do you ask him how many children he has, which days of the week he ate and which he didn't, do you concern yourselves with his environment at all? You send him to jail without further thought. But those who burn warehouses and stores to collect insurance do not go to jail, even though a few human beings should have happened to (be cremated with the property insured). The insured have money to hire lawyers and bribe judges. You jail the poor wretch who steals because he is hungry; but none of the hundreds who steal from the Government have ever spent a night in jail; you dine with them at the end of the year in some elegant place and they enjoy your respect.

In Cuba when a bureaucrat becomes a millionaire overnight and enters the fraternity of the rich, he could very well be greeted with the words of that opulent Balzac character, Taillefer, who, in his toast to the young heir to an enormous fortune, said: "Gentlemen, let us drink to the power of gold! Mr. Valentine, a millionaire six times over, has just ascended the throne. He is king, can do everything, is above everything—like all the rich. Henceforward, equality before the law, before the Constitution, will be a myth for him; for he will not be subject to laws, the laws will be subject to him. There are no courts or sentences for millionaires."

The future of the country and the solution of its problems cannot continue to depend on the selfish interests of a dozen financiers, nor on the cold calculations of profits that ten or twelve magnates draw up in their air-conditioned offices. The country cannot continue begging on its knees for miracles from a few golden calves, similar to the Biblical one destroyed by the fury of a prophet. Golden calves cannot perform miracles of any kind. The problems of the Republic can be solved only if we dedicate ourselves to fight for that

Republic with the same energy, honesty and patriotism our liberators had when they created it. . . .

4. Advice for the Urban Guerrilla

The Minimanual of the Urban Guerrilla, *written by Brazilian activist Carlos Marighella (born in Salvador, Bahia, in 1911), is a guide to strategies for disrupting established authority, with the purpose of creating the conditions for a social revolution. As its title suggests, Marighella considered cities the main cradle of revolutionary movements, distinguishing himself from other 1960s revolutionaries. (Che Guevara, for example, believed that rural areas were better suited for that role.) By that time, Marighella had ended his long career as a prominent member of the Brazilian Communist Party, having served as a legislator and Executive Committee member. He was expelled in 1967 due to his critical views on the leadership's mild, "reformist" policies, and because of his personal commitment to Castro's Cuba. He founded ALN (Ação Libertadora Nacional), a radical organization dedicated to confronting Brazil's military dictatorship (1964–1985) with revolutionary armed struggle. In this context he published his* Minimanual. *Written in 1969, it became an instant classic in underground networks. The following selection describes ways to win over public opinion by exposing (and taking advantage of) the failures of the dictatorship. In November 1969, shortly after publication, Marighella was killed in a police ambush in the streets of São Paulo.*

One of the constant concerns of the urban guerrilla is his identification with popular causes to win public support. Where government actions become inept and corrupt, the urban guerrilla should not hesitate to step in and show that he opposes the government, and thus gain popular sympathy. The present government, for example, imposes heavy financial burdens and excessively high taxes on the people. It is up to the urban guerrilla to attack the dictatorship's tax collection system and to obstruct its financial activities, throwing all the weight of armed action against it.

The urban guerrilla fights not only to upset the tax collection system—the weapon of armed action must also be directed against those government agencies that raise prices and those who direct them as well as against the wealthiest of the national and foreign profiteers and the important property owners. In short, against all those who accumulate huge fortunes out of the high cost of living, the wages of hunger, excessive prices and high rents. Foreign

Carlos Marighella, "Popular Support," in *Minimanual of the Urban Guerrilla*, www.marxists .org/archive/marighella-carlos/1969/06/minimanual-urban-guerrilla/ch38.htm.

industries, such as refrigeration and other North American plants that monopolize the market and the manufacture of general food supplies, must be systematically attacked by the urban guerrillas. The rebellion of the urban guerrilla and his persistence in intervening in political questions is the best way of ensuring popular support for the cause which we defend. We repeat and insist on repeating—it is the way of ensuring popular support. As soon as a reasonable portion of the population begins to take seriously the actions of the urban guerrilla, his success is guaranteed.

The government has no alternative except to intensify its repression. The police networks, house searches, the arrest of suspects and innocent persons, and the closing off of streets make life in the city unbearable. The military dictatorship embarks on massive political persecution. Political assassinations and police terror become routine.

In spite of all this, the police systematically fail. The armed forces, the navy and the air force are mobilized to undertake routine police functions, but even so they can find no way to halt guerrilla operations or to wipe out the revolutionary organization with its fragmented groups that move around and operate throughout the country.

The people refuse to collaborate with the government, and the general sentiment is that this government is unjust, incapable of solving problems, and that it resorts simply to the physical liquidation of its opponents. The political situation in the country is transformed into a military situation in which the "gorillas" [i.e. the authorities] appear more and more to be the ones responsible for violence, while the lives of the people grow worse.

When they see the military and the dictatorship on the brink of the abyss, and fearing the consequences of a civil war which is already well underway, the pacifiers (always to be found within the ruling elite) and the opportunists (partisans of nonviolent struggle) join hands and circulate rumors behind the scenes begging the hangmen for elections, "re-democratization," constitutional reforms, and other tripe designed to fool the people and make them stop the rebellion.

But, watching the guerrillas, the people now understand that it is a farce to vote in any elections which have as their sole objective guaranteeing the survival of the dictatorship and covering up its crimes. Attacking wholeheartedly this election farce and the so-called "political solution," which is so appealing to the opportunists, the urban guerrillas must become even more aggressive and active, resorting without pause to sabotage, terrorism, expropriations, assaults, kidnappings, executions, etc. This action answers any attempt to fool the people with the opening of Congress and the reorganization of political parties—parties of the government and of the positions which the government allows—when all the time parliament and the so-called "parties" only function thanks to the permission of the military dictatorship, in a true spectacle of puppets or dogs on a leash.

The role of the urban guerrilla, in order to win the support of the population, is to continue fighting, keeping in mind the interests of the people and heightening the disastrous situation within which the government must act. These are the conditions, harmful to the dictatorship, which permit the guerrillas to open rural warfare in the middle of an uncontrollable urban rebellion.

The urban guerrilla is engaged in revolutionary action for the people, and seeks the participation of the people in the struggle against the dictatorship and for the liberation of the country. Beginning with the city and the support of the people, the rural guerrilla war develops rapidly, establishing its infrastructure carefully while the urban area continues the rebellion.

5. PRELUDE TO DICTATORSHIP

The 1970 election of an avowed Marxist, Salvador Allende, as president of Chile came as a shock to many conservative Chileans and to the virulently anticommunist U.S. government. Allende's administration quickly embarked on efforts to restructure the Chilean economy by nationalizing the copper mines (mostly owned by U.S. companies) and banks, enacting extensive land reforms, and investing heavily in social services like housing, public health, and education. These major structural changes were attempted without a congressional majority or support from the judiciary, and with considerable resistance from within the armed forces and the police. The Nixon administration opposed Allende's program as well. National Security Adviser Henry Kissinger boldly announced that "I don't see why we have to let a country go Marxist just because its people are irresponsible." With the covert support of the U.S. Central Intelligence Agency, Allende's opponents launched a series of attacks on the fragile Chilean economy that produced soaring inflation rates and growing middle-class opposition. An aborted coup in June 1973, although suppressed by loyal army officers, led to calls for the arming of workers, which further heightened tensions. The following congressional declaration of August 22, 1973, entitled "Grave Breakdown of the Republic's Legal and Constitutional Order," clearly reflects these growing political tensions. Just three weeks later, on September 11, 1973, an armed forces junta led by General Augusto Pinochet overthrew the Allende government and proceeded to jail, torture, and execute thousands of its political enemies. The Pinochet dictatorship promptly banned all political opposition and ruthlessly defended its hold on national politics until 1989.

Declaration of the Chamber of Deputies, "Grave Breakdown of the Republic's Legal and Constitutional Order," August 22, 1973.

Considering:

First: That in order for Rule of Law to exist, public authorities must carry out their activities and discharge their duties within the framework of the Constitution and the laws of the land, with full respect for the principle of reciprocal independence to which they are bound, and that all inhabitants of the country must be allowed to enjoy the guarantees and fundamental rights assured them by the Constitution;

Second: That the legitimacy of the Chilean State lies with the people who, over the years, have invested in this legitimacy the fundamental consensus of their coexistence. To assault legitimacy thus destroys not only the cultural and political heritage of our Nation, but also denies, in practice, all possibility of democratic life;

Third: That the values and principles expressed in article 2 of the Constitution express that the essence of sovereignty resides in the Nation, and that authorities may not exercise more powers than those delegated to them by the Nation. Article 3 further states that any government that arrogates to itself rights not delegated to it by the people commits sedition;

Fourth: That the current President of the Republic was elected by the full Congress, in accordance with a statute of democratic guarantees incorporated in the Constitution for the very purpose of assuring that the actions of his administration would be subject to the principles and norms of the Rule of Law that he solemnly agreed to respect;

Fifth: That it is a fact that the current government of the Republic, from the beginning, has sought to achieve absolute power with the stated purpose of subjecting all citizens to the strictest political and economic control by the state and, in this manner, fulfill [its] goal of establishing a totalitarian system: the absolute opposite of the representative democracy established by the Constitution;

Sixth: That to achieve this end, the administration has committed, not isolated violations of the Constitution and of the law, but rather has made such violations a permanent practice, to such an extreme that it systematically ignores and usurps the proper role of the other branches of government, habitually violates the Constitutional guarantees of all citizens of the Republic, and allows and supports the creation of illegitimate parallel powers that constitute an extremely grave danger to the Nation. By these means it has destroyed essential elements of institutional legitimacy and Rule of Law;

Seventh: That the administration has committed the following assaults on the proper role of the National Congress, seat of legislative power:

A. It has usurped Congress's principle legislative function by adopting various measures of great importance to the country's social and economic life that are indisputably matters of legislation. It has done so through special decrees enacted in abuse of [executive] power or through simple administrative resolutions using "legal loopholes." It is noteworthy that all of this has been done with the deliberate and confessed purpose of substituting the country's institutional structures, as conceived by current legislation, with absolute executive authority and the total elimination of legislative authority;

B. It has consistently mocked the National Congress's oversight role by effectively removing its power to formally accuse Ministers of State who violate the Constitution or laws of the land, or who commit other offenses specified by the Constitution, and;

C. Lastly—in what is the most extraordinarily grave [violation]—it has utterly swept aside the exalted role of Congress as a duly constituted power by refusing to enact the Constitutional reform of three areas of the economy that were approved in strict compliance with the norms established by the Constitution.

Eighth: That it has committed the following assaults on the judicial branch:

A. With the goal of undermining the authority of the courts and compromising their independence, it has led an infamous campaign of libel and slander against the Supreme Court, and it has sanctioned very serious attacks against judges and their authority;

B. It has made a mockery of justice in cases of delinquents belonging to political parties or groups affiliated with or close to the administration, either through the abusive use of pardons or deliberate noncompliance with detention orders;

C. It has violated express laws and utterly disregarded the principle of separation of powers by not carrying out sentences and judicial resolutions that contravene its objectives and, when so accused by the Supreme Court, the President of the Republic has gone to the unheard of extreme of arrogating to himself the right to judge the merit of judicial sentences and to determine when they are to be complied with;

Ninth: That, as concerns the Comptroller General's Office—an independent institution essential to administrative legitimacy—the administration has systematically violated decrees and activities that point out the illegality of the actions of the Executive Branch or of entities dependent on it;

Tenth: That among the administration's constant assaults on the guarantees and fundamental rights established in the Constitution, the following stand out:

A. It has violated the principle of equality before the law through sectarian and hateful discrimination in the protection authorities are required to give to the life, rights, and property of all inhabitants, through activities related to food and subsistence, as well as numerous other instances. It is to note that the President of the Republic himself has made these discriminations part of the normal course of his government by proclaiming from the beginning that he does not consider himself the president of all Chileans;

B. It has grievously attacked freedom of speech, applying all manner of economic pressure against those media organizations that are not unconditional supporters of the government, illegally closing newspapers and radio networks; imposing illegal shackles on the latter; unconstitutionally jailing opposition journalists; resorting to cunning maneuvers to acquire a monopoly on newsprint; and openly violating the legal mandates to which the National Television Network is subject by handing over the post of executive director to a public official not named by the Senate, as is required by law, and by turning the network into an instrument for partisan propaganda and the defamation of political adversaries;

C. It has violated the principle of university autonomy and the constitutionally recognized right of universities to establish and maintain television networks, by encouraging the takeover of the University of Chile's Channel 9, by assaulting that university's new Channel 6 through violence and illegal detentions, and by obstructing the expansion to the provinces of the channel owned by Catholic University of Chile;

D. It has obstructed, impeded, and sometimes violently suppressed citizens who do not favor the regime in the exercise of their right to freedom of association. Meanwhile, it has constantly allowed groups—often armed—to gather and take over streets and highways, in disregard of pertinent regulation, in order to intimidate the populace;

E. It has attacked educational freedom by illegally and surreptitiously implementing the so-called Decree of the Democratization of Learning, an educational plan whose goal is Marxist indoctrination;

F. It has systematically violated the constitutional guarantee of property rights by allowing and supporting more than 1,500 illegal "takings" of farms, and by encouraging the "taking" of hundreds of industrial and commercial establishments in order to later seize them or illegally place them in receivership and thereby, through looting, establish state control over the economy; this has been one of the determining causes of the unprecedented decline in production, the scarcity of goods, the black market and suffocating rise in the cost of living, the bankruptcy of the national treasury, and generally of the economic crisis that is sweeping the country and threatening basic household welfare, and very seriously compromising national security;

G. It has made frequent politically motivated and illegal arrests, in addition to those already mentioned of journalists, and it has tolerated the whipping and torture of the victims;

H. It has ignored the rights of workers and their unions, subjecting them, as in the cases of El Teniente [one of Chile's most important copper mines] and the transportation union, to illegal means of repression;

I. It has broken its commitment to make amends to workers who have been unjustly persecuted, such as those from Sumar, Helvetia, Banco Central, El Teniente, and Chuquicamata; it has followed an arbitrary policy in the turning over of state-owned farms to peasants, expressly contravening the Agrarian Reform Law; it has denied workers meaningful participation, as guaranteed them by the Constitution; it has given rise to the end to union freedom by setting up parallel political organizations of workers.

J. It has gravely breached the constitutional guarantee to freely leave the country, establishing requirements to do so not covered by any law.

Eleventh: That it powerfully contributes to the breakdown of the Rule of Law by providing government protection and encouragement for the creation and maintenance of a number of organizations which are subversive in their exercise of the authority granted to them neither by the Constitution nor the laws of the land, in open violation of article 10, number 16 of the Constitution. These include community commandos, peasant councils, vigilance committees, the JAP, etc.; all designed to create a so-called "popular authority" with the goal of replacing legitimately elected authority and establishing the foundation of a totalitarian dictatorship. These facts have been publicly acknowledged by the President of the Republic in his last State of the Nation address and by all government media and strategists;

Twelfth: That especially serious is the breakdown of the Rule of Law by means of the creation and development of government-protected armed groups which, in addition to threatening citizens' security and rights as well as domestic peace, are headed towards a confrontation with the Armed Forces. Just as serious is that the police are prevented from carrying out their most important responsibilities when dealing with criminal riots perpetrated by violent groups devoted to the government. Given the extreme gravity, one cannot be silent before the public and notorious attempts to use the Armed Forces and Police for partisan ends, to destroy their institutional hierarchy, and to politically infiltrate their ranks;

Thirteenth: That the creation of a new ministry, with the participation of high-level officials of the Armed and Police Forces, was characterized by the President of the Republic to be "for national security" and its mandate "the establishment of political order" and "the establishment of economic order," and that such a mandate can only be conceived within the context of full restoration and validation of the legal and constitutional norms that make up the institutional framework of the Republic;

Fourteenth: That the Armed and Police Forces are and must be, by their very nature, a guarantee for all Chileans and not just for one sector of the Nation or for a political coalition. Consequently, the government cannot use their backing to cover up a specific minority partisan policy. Rather their presence must be directed toward the full restoration of constitutional rule and of the rule of the laws of democratic coexistence, which are indispensable to guaranteeing Chile's institutional stability, civil peace, security, and development;

Fifteenth: Lastly, exercising the role attributed to it by Article 39 of the Constitution,

The Honorable Chamber of Deputies, in exercise of the powers conferred on it by article 39 of the State Political Constitution, agrees:

First: To present the President of the Republic, Ministers of State, and members of the Armed and Police Forces with the grave breakdown of the legal and constitutional order of the Republic, the facts and circumstances of which are detailed in sections 5 to 12 above;

Second: To likewise point out that by virtue of their responsibilities, their pledge of allegiance to the Constitution and to the laws they have served, and in the case of the ministers, by virtue of the nature of the institutions of which they are high-ranking officials and oath they swore upon taking office, it is their duty to put an immediate end to all situations herein referred to that infringe on the Constitution and the laws of the land with the goal of redirecting government activity toward the path of Law and ensuring the constitutional order of our Nation and the essential underpinnings of democratic coexistence among Chileans;

Third: To declare that if so done, the presence of those ministers in the government would render a valuable service to the Republic. To do the contrary, they would gravely compromise the national and professional character of the Armed and Police Forces, openly infringing article 22 of the Constitution and seriously damaging the prestige of their institutions; and

Fourth: To communicate this agreement to His Excellency the President of the Republic, and to the Ministers of Economy, National Defense, Public Works and Transportation, and Land and Colonization.

6. THE DEATH OF VICTOR JARA

The military coup that overthrew the democratic Allende government in September 1973 ushered in a reign of terror without precedent in Chilean history. Many thou-

sands of Allende's followers were tortured and executed. As if aping the Nazis, the fascist junta showed a special hatred for the creators of culture and their works. The junta's soldiers attempted to purify Chilean culture by holding book-burning sprees. They devastated the home of Pablo Neruda, Chile's greatest poet and Nobel Prize winner, as he lay dying of cancer. And they tortured and killed Victor Jara, a beloved composer, folk singer, and theater director, as described in the following account.

Victor Jara was brought to the Chile Stadium, together with the employees and students of the Technical University after the assault on that institution, on Wednesday, September 12. There an officer of the *carabineros* (national police) discovered him: "You're Victor Jara, you son-of-a-bitch." And so began the Calvary of the distinguished composer, folk singer, and stage director. The officer threw himself furiously on Victor and struck him with the butt of his rifle on his stomach, head, everywhere. Victor fell down and another soldier joined in his punishment. They kicked him and hurled insults at him. One kicked him in the face, and an eye filled with blood. They yelled and beat him savagely. Victor curled up, but made no sound.

The head of the "prisoner camp" arrived and said: "Let's cut off the hands of this son-of-a-bitch." He hit Victor with a stick. "Sing now, you bastard; get up!" he ordered. Then they bent him over, with his hands on a sawhorse, and began to beat his hands and wrists until they became a bloody mass. All this took place in a passage of the stadium. There were five thousand prisoners in the stadium and many were able to see the torture. Impotent tears streamed down the faces of all the witnesses. They had also received or were receiving their dose of punishment. Now Victor was down on the ground. They left him for a few minutes and then returned. They showed him off to the fascists who arrived as if he were a trophy of war. Three air force officers arrived and stopped in front of him, insulting and taking turns in kicking him. "Do you want a smoke, bastard?" they asked in a mocking tone. Victor did not respond. They put out a cigarette on one of his hands, a mass of wounds. The torture continued until very late in the afternoon of the twelfth. They left him unconscious all that night and the next day, the thirteenth, of course without food or water.

Then they seemed to forget him. They had other entertainments. Someone ordered that he should be taken away with the other prisoners. Signs of solidarity with Victor came from every corner of the stadium: pieces of bread, a biscuit, a jacket to keep him warm. Victor gradually came to himself. Now he was happy, though he suffered atrocious pain. He spoke of the future, of his wife and children. Meanwhile the stadium resounded with the groans of

Centro de Estudios y Publicaciones, *Chile: Una esperanza aplastada* (Estella, Spain: Editorial Verbo Divino, 1975), pp. 24–25. Excerpt translated by Benjamin Keen.

the victims of fascism. They killed and tortured in the presence of five thousand men. Some prisoners went mad and threw themselves down from the top of the stadium. Others cried and ran, and the lieutenants beat them till they died. From the underground rooms, moans and cries rose day and night. Foreigners, "agents of international communism," suffered special agonies. Victor continued to recover, though his body was one large hematoma, his wounded eye continued to bleed, and his face showed the wounds he had received.

Saturday, the thirteenth, they announced a transfer of prisoners to the national stadium, and all thought that Victor would leave with the rest. It seemed they had finally forgotten him. That morning he began to dictate the verses that he entitled "Chile Stadium." He would never finish them. They took him, together with a group described as "Marxist specialists in explosives" out of the corridors. They took him into one of the rooms converted into torture chambers and the rain of blows began again. They stretched him out on the ground, spread his legs apart, and kicked him in the testicles. They attacked him with savage fury. They would leave and then return to the attack. A student who managed to come out of that inferno alive tells that at the end blood poured from his mouth, nostrils, ears, eyes. Thus died Victor Jara, who had sung of love, tenderness, and hope in the language of the humble. There he died, beaten to death by the irrational hatred of fascism. Afterwards, by way of an example to others, they left him lying in the foyer of the stadium.

7. Open Letter to the Military Junta

Rodolfo Walsh (1927–1977) is considered one of Argentina's most important contemporary writers. Although he is usually associated with politically engaged literature, a substantial part of his earlier work shows a taste for abstract intellectual games, as reflected in his interest in chess, detective fiction, and formal aspects of the short story. In the late 1950s, during Peronism's long proscription from the political arena, Walsh (a former anti-Peronist) became increasingly concerned with the fate of the defeated working class. Operación Masacre (1957), his narrative report on the execution of a group of workers outside Buenos Aires at the hands of the anti-Peronist military government, is both a political and a literary landmark. By combining narrative techniques with sound journalistic investigation, it marks the beginning of the genre of literary nonfiction in Latin America, as well as the beginning of Walsh's personal commitment to the poor, which would lead him to embrace the cause of the Peronist guerrilla group, the Montoneros. By the time the military took power in the coup of 1976, Walsh's commitment to social revolution had long since displaced his focus on literary fiction. By then, he defined his writing as that of a politically committed writer-journalist. In the face of brutal censorship—a tactic of the military regime that Walsh considered one of the main ways of instilling terror—he created ANCLA and

Cadena Informativa, *two clandestine information networks based on word-of-mouth dissemination. His letter to the junta, written on the first anniversary of the coup, was mailed to Argentine newspapers (which could not publish it) as well as to foreign correspondents. Its diagnosis of the nature of the military regime, based on data gathered in the first stages of that regime, is remarkably lucid in the connection it makes between political repression and economic transformation—a link widely acknowledged today but rarely made at the time. Written in desperation, the letter still bears the marks of its author's long commitment to investigative journalism. Rodolfo Walsh was killed on a Buenos Aires street by a military commando on March 25, 1977—one day after writing this letter, his last public utterance.*

1. Press censorship, the persecution of intellectuals, breaking into my home in Tigre, the murder of dear friends and the loss of a daughter who died fighting you: these are some of the facts that force me into this clandestine form of expression, after thirty years of freely and openly making known my views as a writer and journalist.

The first anniversary of this military junta leads me to an assessment of the government's actions, based on its documents and official speeches, in which what you call successes are mistakes, what you admit as mistakes are crimes, and what you omit altogether are calamities.

On March 24, 1976, you overthrew a government of which I was a part, to whose discredit you contributed by carrying on its repressive policies, and whose end was already in sight in the form of elections slated for nine months later. From this perspective, what you brought an end to was not the transitory mandate of Isabel Martínez [Juan Perón's second wife "Isabelita"], but rather all possibility of a democratic process in which the people might remedy the evils that you have continued and aggravated.

Illegitimate from the beginning, the administration that you lead could have legitimized itself by salvaging the program that 80% of argentines supported in the 1973 elections, a program that continues to be the objective expression of the people's will, the only possible meaning of the "national being" that you so often invoke. Reversing this stream, you have restored the current of ideas of defeated minority interests that hinder the development of productive forces, exploit the people, and tear apart the nation. Such policies can only be imposed temporarily—by banning political parties, taking control of unions, silencing the press, and setting into motion the greatest terror that argentine society has ever known.

2. Fifteen-thousand missing, ten-thousand imprisoned, four-thousand dead, tens of thousands in exile: these are the naked statistics of this terror.

Rodolfo Walsh, "Carta abierta de un escritor a la Junta Militar." Translated by the editors. Original footnotes have been removed.

With ordinary jails overwhelmed, you made virtual concentration camps of military garrisons, where no judge, lawyer, journalist or international observer is allowed. The military secrecy of these procedures, which you justify as made necessary by the rigors of investigation, turns most of your detentions into kidnappings, in which unlimited torture and summary execution are permitted.

Over seven thousand writs of habeas corpus have been rejected in the past year. In the cases of thousands of other disappearances, this tool hasn't even been attempted, either because its was known in advance to be futile or because no lawyer would dare to file a writ after fifty or sixty of those who did were themselves abducted.

In this way, you have stripped torture of its time limit. Since the detainee does not exist, there's no possibility of presenting him to the judge after ten days, as is required by a law which has been respected even at the repressive extremes of previous dictatorships.

To the lack of a time limit has been added the lack of limits with regard to methods, a return to the time when pain was inflicted directly on the joints and bowels of the victims, although now with the help of surgical and pharmacological aids that ancient executioners did not have at their disposal. The rack, the "spinning wheel," skinning alive, and the saw of medieval inquisitors all reappear in testimonies, along with contemporary techniques such as the cattle prod and waterboarding.

Arguing that the goal of exterminating the guerrilla justifies any and all means, you have arrived at absolute, timeless, metaphysical torture, in which the original intent of obtaining information goes astray in the unbalanced minds of those who yield to the impulse to crush human substance until broken, until it has lost the dignity already lost by the torturer, the dignity you have yourselves lost.

3. This Junta's refusal to publish the names of prisoners is covering the systematic execution of hostages out in remote wastelands, late at night, under the pretext of staged combat and imaginary attempts to flee. Extremists who distribute pamphlets in the middle of nowhere, who scrawl graffiti in drainage ditches, or who cram themselves into cars that just happen to catch fire—these are the plot-lines of a script that is not intended to be believed, but rather to deceive international observers. Meanwhile, the domestic narrative is all about reprisals in response to guerilla actions.

Seventy people shot after a bomb went off at Federal Security Headquarters, fifty in response to the explosion at the Police Headquarters in La Plata, thirty for the bombing of the Ministry of Defense, forty in the New Year's Eve Massacre that followed the death of Coronel Castellanos, nineteen after the explosion that destroyed the precinct house in Ciudadela: these are just some of the 1,200 executions in 300 so-called battles in which there were no wounded among the opposing forces, and in which the side that reported these numbers had no casualties.

Assigned the kind of collective guilt which has been abolished by all civilized norms of justice, having no influence in the political process resulting in their persecution, many of these hostages are union delegates, intellectuals, relatives of guerilla activists, unarmed dissidents, simple suspects who are killed in order to balance the numbers of casualties, according to the foreign doctrine of "body counting" used by the [Nazi] SS in occupied countries and by the invaders of Vietnam.

Evidence for the cold-blooded shooting of wounded or captured guerrilla militants in real battles comes from the military's own communiques, which in one year counted 600 dead and only 10 or 15 wounded among the guerillas, a ratio unheard of even in the bloodiest of conflicts. This perception is further confirmed by a sample undertaken by the press (and circulated clandestinely) which shows that between the December 18, 1976 and February 3, 1977, in 40 military actions, the legal forces had 23 casualties and 40 wounded, while the guerillas had 63 casualties (and no wounded).

More than one hundred people awaiting trial have also been killed attempting to flee, the official version of which is, again, not directed toward anyone who might believe it, but in order to warn the guerillas and political parties that even well-known inmates can be used as a strategic reserve of reprisals at the disposal of the military commanders, either in the course of combat, as a didactic convenience, or as their mood sees fit.

This is how General Benjamin Menendez, chief of the Third Army Battalion, earned his stripes: first, before March 24, by assassinating Marcos Asatinsky, who was detained in Cordoba; later, through the death of Hugo Vaca Narvaja and fifty other inmates in various episodes involving unlawful flight, enforced without mercy and related without decency. The assassination of Dardo Cabo, detained in April of 1975 and executed on January 6, 1977 with seven other prisoners under the jurisdiction of General Suarez Masson's First Army Battalion, reveals that these episodes are not the isolated outbursts of a few deluded centurions, but rather the expressions of the very policies that you conceive from your high commands, that you discuss in your cabinet meetings, that you impose as commanders of the three branches of the Army, and that you approve, as members of the governing Junta.

4. Between one and three thousand people have been secretly massacred after you prohibited reporting about the finding of cadavers. The information has nevertheless leaked out, either because it has affected other countries, or because of its genocidal magnitude, or because of the horror it has produced within its own forces. Twenty-five mutilated bodies appeared on the shores of Uruguay between March and October of 1976—perhaps a small sample of the many who have been tortured to death in Naval Mechanicals School and then thrown from Navy boats into the River Plate, including

the fifteen-year-old Floreal Avellaneda, his feet and hands tied, "with wounds in the anal region and visible fractures," according to the autopsy.

A veritable underwater cemetery was discovered in August 1976 by a neighbor diving in lake San Roque, Cordoba. His report was not accepted at the police precinct, just as his letters to the newspapers went unpublished.

Thirty-four corpses in Buenos Aires between April 3 and April 9, eight in San Telmo on July 4 and ten the Lujan River on October 9—all leading up to the massacres of August 20, which left a pile of thirty bodies fifteen kilometers from the Campo de Mayo [the military headquarters], and then seventeen more dead in Lomas de Zamora. These facts expose the fiction behind those versions that blame these episodes on right-wing extremist groups, alleged heirs of Lopez Rega's Triple A—as if such groups would be able to cross the country's largest garrison in military trucks, cover the River Plate with dead bodies or throw prisoners into the sea from the planes of the First Brigade without the knowledge of General Videla, Admiral Masseraor Bridadier General Agosti. Today the Triple are the three Armed Forces, and the Junta you preside over is neither the balance between "violence of different stripes," nor the just arbiter between "two terrorisms." It is the very source of terror that has lost direction and can only babble the discourse of death.

The same historical continuity links the assassination of General Carlos Prats, during the previous administration, with the abduction and death of Generals Juan José Torres, Zelmar Michelini Héctor Gutiérrez, along with dozens of refugees, whose deaths it was hoped would also bring the death of the democratic processes of Chile, Bolivia, and Uruguay.

The certain participation of the Department of Foreign Affairs of the Federal Police in these crimes, led by officers trained by the CIA through AID, such as Commissioners Juan Gattei and Antonio Gettor (both acting under the authority of Mr. Gardener Hathaway, Station Chief of the CIA in Argentina), will give rise to future revelations like those shaking the international community right now. As the role of this agency (along with high-ranking military chiefs, led by General Menéndez) in the creation of the Lodge of the Liberators of America (which replaced the Triple A until its role was taken over by the Junta on behalf of the Three Branches), is laid bare, these revelations will only continue.

This picture of extermination does not begin to include the settling of personal accounts, such as the assassination of Captain Horacio Gándara, who had for nearly a decade been investigating the business dealings of the chiefs of the Navy, or the murder of *Prensa Libre* journalist Horacio Novillo, who was stabbed and burned after that newspaper made public the personal connections of Minister Martínez de Hoz with certain international monopolies.

These episodes give a final meaning to the definition of this war, as pronounced by one of its leaders [Lieutenant Colonel Pascarelli]: "Our struggle, recognizing neither moral nor natural limits, takes place beyond good and evil."

5. Shocking as these facts may be to the conscience of the civilized world, they are not however the worst that the Argentine people have been made to suffer, nor the worst violations of human rights you have committed. It is in this government's economic policy where one should look not only for the explanation of these crimes, but also a greater atrocity which afflicts millions of human beings with planned misery.

In just one year you have reduced by 40% the real salary of workers, whose portion of the national income has diminished to 30%. You have increased from six to eighteen the number of hours per day a worker needs to provide his family with basic needs, resuscitating forms of forced labor unknown even in the very last colonial redoubts.

By freezing salaries at gunpoint while prices rise at the point of a bayonet, abolishing all means of collective petition, banning assemblies and internal commissions, extending working hours, bringing unemployment to a record 9% while promising to increase it with another 300,000 layoffs, you have set labor relations back to the beginnings of the industrial era. And when workers have tried to protest, you've called them subversives, abducting entire delegate corps who in some cases later reappeared dead. Others never reappeared at all.

These policies have had catastrophic results. In the first year of this administration, food consumption has decreased by 40%, clothing by more than 50%, while access to medicine has all but disappeared in the poorer sectors of society. In certain areas of Greater Buenos Aires, infant mortality is above 30%, a figure that puts us on a par with Rhodesia, Dahomey, and the Guyanas. Incidence of diseases such as seasonal diarrhea, intestinal parasites, and even rabies is approaching or surpassing worst global levels. As if these were your intended goals, you've reduced the public health budget to less than one third of military expenses, undermining even the free public hospitals, while hundreds of doctors, professionals, and technicians join the exodus provoked by terror, low salaries, and "rationalization."

It's enough just to walk a few hours in Greater Buenos Aires to verify the speed with which this policy has turned the area into a shanty town of ten million. Half-lit cities, entire neighborhoods without water because monopolies have taken control of the aquifers, thousands of city blocks turned into one huge pothole because you only pave military neighborhoods and decorate the Plaza de Mayo, the shores of the world's largest river polluted by the industrial waste produced by associates of Minister Martinez de Hoz, and the only remedy you propose is to ban people from swimming in it.

Nor have you been any more fortunate in your more abstract economic goals, those you identify as "the country": a decline in the GNP of almost 3%, external debt at nearly 600 dollars per capita, annual inflation close to 400%, an increase in currency circulation which only in one week in December reached 9%, a 13% decrease in foreign investment—all world records, strange fruit of cold deliberation and base incompetence.

While all the creative and protective functions of the state are left to atrophy and dissolve into anemia, one thrives autonomous: 1.8 billion dollars (equivalent to half of argentine exports) budgeted for security and defense in 1977, four-thousand new positions created in the Federal Police, twelve-thousand in the Police Department of the Province of Buenos Aires, with salaries doubling those of industrial workers and tripling those of school principals. Meanwhile, your own military salaries are secretly increased by 120%, proving that there is neither stagnation nor unemployment in the kingdom of torture and death, the only field of Argentine activity where production grows and where the rate of guerilla casualties rises faster than the dollar.

6. Dictated by the International Monetary Fund, according to a formula applied without distinction in Zaire or Chile, Uruguay or Indonesia, the Junta's economic policy only benefits the old landed oligarchy, the new oligarchy of speculation, and a select group of international monopolies led by ITT, Esso, the automobile industry, US Steel, Siemens, with whom Minister Martinez de Hoz and all of his fellow cabinet members have personal ties.

A 722% increase in the cost of cattle production in 1976 makes clear the extent to which the oligarchy has been restored under Martinez de Hoz, as does the creed of the Rural Society, as illustrated by its president, Celedonio Pereda: "It is stunning that small but active groups keep demanding that food prices remain low."

The spectacle of a stock exchange where in one week certain people have increased their income by one or two-hundred percent without working, where certain businesses double their capital overnight without producing more than before, the crazy wheel of speculation in dollars and letters of credit, adjustable values, the simple usury that counts interest by the hour— these are rather curious facts under an administration which supposedly came to put an end to the "feast of the corrupt." By means of the denationalization of banks, savings and credit are transferred into the hands of foreign banks. Subsidizing ITT and Siemens, you reward those companies that have defrauded the state. By reopening outlets you increase the profit of Shell and Esso. By lowering customs taxes you create employment in Hong Kong and Singapore, and unemployment in Argentina. Faced with all of these facts, one would do well to wonder about the "stateless" of official communiqués, the mercenaries in the service of foreign interests, the ideology which threatens the "national being."

Were it not for an overwhelming propaganda campaign, a distorted reflection of evil facts—that this Junta wants peace, that General Videla defends human rights, that Admiral Massera loves life—it might still be possible to demand of the Commanders in Chief of the Three Branches that they meditate on the ways in which they are driving the country into an abyss, behind the illusion of winning a war in which, even if they killed the last guerrilla activist, would only start over in new ways, because the causes that have driven the people's resistance for twenty years will not have disappeared, but only been aggravated by the memory of the ravages that resulted, and the revealing of the atrocities committed.

On the first anniversary of your sinister government, these are the thoughts that I've wanted to share with the members of the Junta, without hope of being listened to, certain of being persecuted, but remaining faithful to a commitment I made a long time ago to give testimony in difficult times.

8. MOTHERS OF THE DISAPPEARED

As part of its program of repression of Marxist and Peronist subversive groups, the military dictatorship of Argentina (which took power in 1976) began a systematic campaign of terror. With Argentine civil society paralyzed by fear and kept in the dark by extreme media censorship, illegal groups linked to the army kidnapped thousands of people (the exact figure is still unknown, although human rights organizations mention as many as 30,000). These victims of state terror—students, workers, lawyers, activists, journalists, teenagers, parents, even entire families—vanished into clandestine concentration camps where they were tortured and often murdered. They simply "disappeared." During this dark time, the only form of visible resistance came from a group of mothers—housewives with no previous political experience who were looking for their missing children. The "Madwomen of Plaza de Mayo," as they were labeled by the military leaders, would become a powerful symbol of resistance to dictatorship, a resistance harder to repress because of their status as suffering mothers. In the interview excerpts that follow, they recall the origins of the Mothers of the Plaza de Mayo.

Hebe de Bonafini: When Jorge disappeared my first reaction was to rush out desperately to look for him. I didn't cry. I didn't tear my hair out. Nothing mattered any more except that I should find him, that I should go everywhere, at any time, day or night. I didn't want to read anything about what was happening, just search, search. Then I realized we had to look for all of

---

Jo Fisher, *Mothers of the Disappeared* (Boston: South End, 1989), pp. 52–54. Reprinted by permission of the publisher.

them and that we had to be together because together we were stronger. We had no previous political experience. We had no contacts. We knew no one. We made mistakes at first, but we learned quickly. Every door slammed in our faces made us stop and think, made us stronger. We learned quickly and we never gave up. Everything they said we shouldn't do, that we weren't able to do, we proved we could do.

Dora de Bazze: Our first problem was how we were going to organize meetings if we didn't know each other. There were so many police and security men everywhere that you never knew who was standing next to you. It was very dangerous. So we carried different things so we could identify each other. For example one would hold a twig in her hand, one might carry a small purse instead of a handbag, one would pin a leaf to her lapel—anything to let us know this was a Mother. We used to go to the square and sit on the benches with our knitting or stroll about, whispering messages to each other and trying to discuss what else we could do.

Sometimes we met in churches. Most of us were very religious. At that time I was a believer too, so we went to the churches to pray together 'Our Father' . . . and at the same time we would be passing round tiny pieces of folded paper, like when you're in school, cheating on a test. Then we hid them in the hems of our skirts in case we were searched later. Only the small churches, a long way out, lost in the middle of nowhere, would let us in. The rest closed their doors when they found out we were Mothers.

We tried to produce leaflets as well—we had to do it secretly because it was illegal of course—and little stickers saying "the Mothers will be in such and such a place on such and such a day" and "*¿Dónde están nuestros hijos desaparecidos?*" [Where are our disappeared children?]; or "*Los militares se han llevado a nuestros hijos*" [The military have taken our children]. We went out at night to stick them on the buses and underground trains. And we wrote messages on peso notes so that as many people as possible would see them. This was the only way we could let people know that our children had been taken, and what the military government was doing, because when you told them they always said, "They must have done something." There was nothing in the newspapers. If a journalist reported on us, he disappeared. The television and radio were completely under military control, so people weren't conscious. In the beginning we had no support at all.

María del Rosario: At first we didn't march together in the square. We sat on the benches with our knitting or stood in small groups, trying to disguise the letters we were signing to send to the churches, to government officials, to the military. We had to speak to each other quickly, in low voices so it didn't look as if we were having a meeting. Then, when the police saw what was happening and began pointing their rifles at us and telling us to move on, that we had to disperse, that we couldn't be more than two together, we began to walk in twos around the edge of the square. Two in front, two behind—because we had to keep moving but we also had to be able to speak to each other, to talk about what we were going to do next. Every time it got more difficult to communicate with each other because every week there were more police. Sometimes we met in parks as if we were having an office party and there were a few, very few, priests who let us meet in their churches occasionally, and some of the press agencies helped us. France Press lent us their offices sometimes.

At first we walked around the outside of the square, but because there were so few of us we were hardly noticed—and we had to make sure the public knew we existed. We wanted people to see us, to know we were there, so we began to walk in the centre of the square, around the monument. Even if people supported us they stayed outside the square. It was very dangerous for them to approach us. We were very alone in the beginning.

Aída de Suárez: The headscarves grew out of an idea of our dear Azucena. It was at the time when thousands of people walk to Luján on the annual pilgrimage to pay homage to the Virgin. We decided to join the march in 1977 because many of us were religious and also because we thought it would be a chance for us to talk to each other and organize things. But as some of the Mothers were elderly and wouldn't be able to walk, and we would all be coming from different places, we thought, how will we be able to identify each other amongst all those people, because many thousands go, and how can we make other people notice us? Azucena's idea was to wear as a headscarf one of our children's nappies—because every mother keeps something like this, something which belonged to your child as a baby. It was very easy to spot the headscarves in the crowds and people came up to us and asked us who we were. We'd managed to attract attention, so we decided to use the scarves at other meetings, and then every time we went to Plaza de Mayo together. We all made proper white scarves and embroidered the names of our children on them. Afterwards we put on them "*Aparición con Vida*" [literally, 'Reappearance with life'], because we were no longer searching for just one child but for all of the disappeared.

We used to go to the military regiments together to look for other women like us. The only way we could communicate was by word of mouth and we had to find a way to find other women—not just in Buenos Aires, but women from all over the country. The press was silent. The only one which ever wrote anything about us was the English one, the [Buenos Aires] Herald. I went to ask for information at the Herald offices many times. It was very dangerous for journalists to show any interest in us.

9. THE CHURCH IN THE NICARAGUAN REVOLUTION

A distinctive feature of the Nicaraguan Revolution that overthrew the tyranny of the Somoza dynasty in 1979 was the role played by rank-and-file clergy in the revolutionary

*movement and their later involvement in implementing the goals of the revolution.
On the other hand, the Church hierarchy, headed by Archbishop Miguel Obando y
Bravo, traditionally aligned with the wealthy class and late converts to anti-Somoza
positions, grew increasingly hostile to the Sandinista government. Ernesto Cardenal,
one of Latin America's great poets and minister of culture in the Sandinista government, describes the spiritual road traveled by a Jesuit priest who joined the revolutionary struggle.*

Our people lived for four centuries in conditions of misery, malnutrition,
illiteracy, and abandonment. They worked in unjust and inhuman conditions,
lacking means of communication, schools, or culture. They had no part in
determining the destiny of our country, no possibility of becoming the makers of their own history. Add to these evils the half century of Somoza dictatorship, which inflicted on our country the greatest injustices, lack of
freedom, and a constant and ferocious repression.

Our people have always fought, but only after the founding of the Sandinista Front of National Liberation (FSLN) in 1961 did they struggle in a truly
organized and effective way. Thousands of Nicaraguans were assassinated in
the course of those years. But new heroes always arose, heroes who fought,
offering the last drop of their blood to free our people from slavery, without
fear of Pharaoh.

Our Church lived in peace and tranquility with the oppressors. There are
some significant facts. Nicaraguans will never forget that during the funeral
of General Somoza García, founder of the dynasty, the then archbishop of
Managua gave the dictator the title of Prince of the Church.

In 1967 several leaders of the FSLN were captured and later murdered;
on that occasion the auxiliary bishop of Managua published an article in the
government newspaper in which he practically justified the repression on the
grounds that those young men, according to him, were Communists.

I shall never forget the day, on my return as an ordained priest to
Nicaragua in 1968, when the popular struggle and the repression were growing daily, that I read the first pastoral letter of the bishops of Nicaragua. It offered no theological doctrine for a better understanding of God's will in
those difficult times; it only required priests to wear black cassocks. Not a
word about the black situation of our people. With some glorious exceptions,
the Church maintained an alliance with the dictatorship.

I had to leave the country in 1969 for nine months in order to complete
my religious training by taking the last course required of Jesuits, called the
Last Probation. I asked to take it in the city of Medellín (Colombia), for there

Ernesto Cardenal, "No crean las calumnias sobre la Nicaragua (carta a un amigo)," *Cuadernos
Americanos* 44 (March–April 1985): 23–27. Excerpt translated by Benjamin Keen.

they had moved the site of the course from a lovely four-floor building set among gardens and sport grounds to a poor ward in the "misery belt" around Medellín. The previous year the Second General Conference of Latin American Bishops had been held there. I lived those months among people scourged by hunger, unemployment, illness, with no electric lighting or any other public service or convenience. I came to feel an enormous love for these people and my life with them marked me forever.

My Christian faith, my human feelings, and all that I daily saw and heard brought me to a conclusion that arose from the depths of my being: Things cannot go on in this way! It is not right that such misery should exist! God cannot be neutral toward this situation!

My spiritual experience among those poor people confirmed the conception that I drew from the Bible of a God who was not neutral, who heard the clamor of the oppressed and took their side. Never was the meaning of the Bible clearer to me than when I read it amid the quagmires and misery of that ward.

In mid-1970 I completed the course and returned to my country, but not before making a vow to the dwellers of that ward of Medellín: "I shall dedicate my life to the complete liberation of the poor of Latin America, in the place where I shall be most useful." I began to work in the Central American University (UCA) of Managua as co-director in charge of students. A long night continued to envelope our people: dictatorship, dependency, prison, torture, hunger, malnutrition, fear, death, and violation of all human and civil rights. The official Church continued to live peacefully side by side with that genocidal government. Only some half-dozen priests were attempting to teach the new pastoral that was born from the documents of Medellín. [A reference to the second conference of Latin American bishops, held at Medellín, Colombia, in 1968, whose conclusions resembled those of the so-called "theology of liberation."]

The Sandinista Front of National Liberation (FSLN) was already known to all and had gained the respect and sympathy of the people by its valiant and clean fight for the people and against the dictatorship. Inspired by the documents of Medellín and seeking the complete liberation of man, I and a few other priests began to participate in all the civic struggles of the people for liberation: demonstrations, occupations of churches, hunger strikes, speeches at meetings, articles in newspapers, etc.

We also began to take part in the struggle of the Christian student groups, which were to become so important later on.

The most significant moment in the Christian participation in the popular struggle was the occupation of the cathedral. Three of us, priests, accompanied by nearly a hundred students of the Catholic University, took part in a hunger strike in the Cathedral of Managua in 1970, demanding respect for the lives of all the university students who had been imprisoned in recent days, permission to speak to them and, in conformity with Nicaraguan law, that within two days they be freed or put on trial on specific charges.

The normal thing was for prisoners to be tortured for weeks in the offices of the National Security. The occupation of the cathedral created a nation-wide commotion. The army surrounded the cathedral in a threatening manner. We rang the mourning bells every fifteen minutes, night and day, and announced that we would continue ringing them until justice was done and the law complied with. From the principal parishes of Managua came large groups of people who sat down in the plaza to show their support for us; thousands came, and other thousands passed by, greeting us from cars and buses. In three and a half days we made the dictator yield. For the first time a Christian group had taken part in a forceful political act. Messages of support were published by the Bible Study Classes (*Cursillos de Cristiandad*), the Christian Family Movement, the Christian grass-roots communities (*Comunidades de Base*), etc. In a few days the Bishops' Conference of Nicaragua published a letter condemning our protest. Thousands of Christians signed a respectful letter telling the bishops that the bodies of the students, who were being profaned and tortured in prisons, and not the temple of stone, were the temple of the Holy Spirit. But the most essential part of the letter was that in which the bishops were told that the people of Nicaragua had chosen the path of struggle for justice and that they, the pastors, instead of placing themselves at the head of that people, stood aside and condemned it. Henceforth Christians would be present in all the phases of the popular struggle.

In my talks before Christian groups I would say to them: Latin America is marching toward its transformation. Revolution would soon come to Nicaragua. It was important to be aware that the revolution would be made with the Christians, without the Christians, despite the Christians, or against the Christians. So many years later, people throughout the country have reminded me of that statement.

I knew how important it was that the Church should appear to have a role in this process, that our young people could see that the Church had a program of justice for the exploited; paradoxically, the problem of unity between Christians and revolutionaries did not arise from the latter, but from the Christians. I personally knew the founder of the FSLN, Commander Jose Carlos Fonseca Amador (assassinated in 1976), and knew his receptive attitude and desire for unity with the Christians. I studied the statutes of the FSLN, written by him in 1969, in which he speaks of religious liberty and support for the priests who work for the people. In 1970 I had an interview with Commander Jose Turcios, member of the national directorate of the FSLN (assassinated in 1973). He said to me on that occasion: "What matters is not that you believe there is another life after death and I don't; the basic question is whether we can work together for the construction of a new society."

The Christian grass-roots communities and the young Christians, above all, played an ever larger role in that slow and dangerous march toward liberation. Faith moved thousands of Nicaraguans who committed themselves to that struggle in a natural, spontaneous way. They understood that by fighting for justice and the poor they were following God's cause. Thanks to them, the Nicaraguan Revolution was made with the Christians.

When, in 1973, Commander Eduardo Contreras (assassinated in 1976) asked me to accept an official role in the work of the FSLN, I instantly accepted, remembering the parable of the Good Samaritan, for it seemed obvious that I should not act like that priest and that Levite who went around the injured man. The Samaritans of Nicaragua asked me to help cure our wounded people and, given my Christian faith, I could give only one answer: commitment. I continued to work with students, directing Bible Study Classes, conducting spiritual exercises, and retaining my chair of philosophy at the National Autonomous University of Nicaragua (UNAN), but at the same time collaborated secretly with the FSLN in the struggle for national liberation.

The cry of the oppressed and the realities of my country were forcing me to discover other aspects of my priestly ministry. There was no break with the priesthood; I merely accented more and more its prophetic aspect. It was an option fully compatible with the different aspects of the priesthood, an option based not so much on the elements of the ministry according to the Old Testament as on the prophetic aspects proclaimed by Jesus in the New. My work was daily becoming more dangerous, since the greater part of my revolutionary activities were public. Somoza's authorities expelled me in 1970 from the National Autonomous University. In 1973 I participated actively in forming the Christian Revolutionary Movement (MCR), which formed so many cadres and leaders for the FSLN. The revolutionary leaders sent me to Washington in 1976 to denounce the crimes and violations of human rights by the dictator Somoza before the United States Congress. On my return to Nicaragua the president of the Nicaraguan Senate proposed that I be declared a traitor to my country. At that time we founded the Nicaraguan Commission on Human Rights.

A thousand details of the struggles, fears and hopes of the priests who participated in those years of struggle must remain untold for lack of space. Always inspired by our faith, but sometimes wandering in the dark, wishing to see and follow the Lord of History, when all we saw were crimes and the dictator's smiling face as he emerged victorious from every crisis. Sometimes our hopes faded. Often I was afraid, very much afraid, especially of being tortured. Despite the order of arrest issued against us, we entered Nicaragua July 4, 1978. Before two months had gone by, it became necessary to shift completely to underground work. Then came the September insurrection and the next year the final offensive which led to the triumph of July 19,

1979, won through the heroic sacrifices of 50,000 of my compatriots. We were not the only priests who contributed something to the struggle. Other priests aided the cause by preaching from their pulpits, while many religious men and women collaborated in the most varied ways with the guerrillas. Thousands of Christians fought from every trench and barricade in the fields and cities of Nicaragua. The bishops finally condemned in some of their writings the dictator's violations of human rights and on various occasions took firm positions against Somoza. But all this was accompanied by great contradictions; and right down to the day of victory the bishops wrote not a word in favor of the struggle of the FSLN. What was worse, they often condemned the struggle of the people when they condemned in their writings "violence no matter whence it comes," which placed on the same level the unjust violence of the oppressor and the just, legitimate violence of the oppressed people. Not until one week before the final offensive did the bishops justify the popular insurrection.

It is important for me to make clear that at no time were my decisions the result of a crisis of my priestly condition; they were the result of the spiritual journey of a priest who gradually discovered the prophetic dimension of his priesthood and the demands they imposed in a country like ours. Let me add that all the steps I took in those years were made in consultation with and had the approval of my spiritual superiors and had the approval of my order.

I am profoundly convinced that the Nicaraguan people were the motor that made possible my advance. My only merit was to place myself among them and let myself be pushed forward.

10. Death of the "Mexican Economic Miracle"

The de la Madrid–Salinas neoliberal program of privatization and total trade liberalization, capped by ratification of the North American Free Trade Agreement, gave rise to a hectic financial boom as foreign investors rushed in to take advantage of the sale of virtually all of Mexico's state companies and the speculative opportunities it presented. But the boom, chiefly enriching foreign bankers, multinationals, and their native allies (by 1994, Mexico had twenty-four listed billionaires, just behind the United States, Japan, and Germany), did not promote sustainable economic development and was in fact detrimental to Mexican national industry. It failed to alleviate the plight of the 13 million to 18 million Mexicans who live in what the United Nations calls "extreme poverty." The debt and monetary crisis of December 1994 plunged Mexico into a deep and probably prolonged depression. The Mexican collapse flashed a red light to other Latin American countries with immense foreign debt and economic programs largely based on volatile foreign investment. The following selection analyzes the causes of the disaster and puts the blame squarely on the neoliberal structural adjustment policies of the PRI leadership.

The Salinas government, of which Ernesto Zedillo formed a part, offered us "a happy and prosperous future" based on a neo-liberal economic reform: complete freedom of foreign trade and NAFTA [North American Free Trade Agreement], privatization of state companies in the fields of infrastructure and services, unrestricted foreign investment, a struggle against inflation, strict control of wages and public spending, and the anti-poverty program of PRONASOL. [The National Solidarity Program (PRONASOL), initiated by the Salinas administration, accounted by 1991 for 35 percent of the government's non-debt spending. Ostensibly designed to assist Mexico's poorest classes, it also served PRI's electoral ends by targeting selected communities to receive supplies and equipment for local development projects.] In his election campaign, Cuauhtémoc Cárdenas stressed the continuing crisis, the grave trade deficit, the destruction of our economic base, the speculative character of the foreign capital invested in the stock market and its volatility, the inexorable disappearance of our foreign exchange reserves, and the imminence of devaluation. During 1994, Salinas, PRI, and Zedillo denied these facts, hid from the Mexican people the grave economic reality, aggravated it by the multimillion squandering of their election campaign, and retained power by means of lies and fraud. It took only three weeks of Zedillo's government to prove that the neo-liberal economic policy was not viable and for the promised "growth with stability" to fade away, making inevitable a massive (over fifty percent) devaluation of the peso.

Up to the last moment, the government and its party lied to the Mexican people. The Secretary of the Treasury (previously Secretary of Commerce and now the government's scapegoat) guaranteed to legislators a four percent economic growth rate, a four percent inflation rate, and exchange stability for 1995; when the "band" within which the peso could float was widened, the Pristas [members of the PRI] denied it was a devaluation. And when the Bank of Mexico withdrew from the exchange market and the collapse of the peso in relation to the dollar became evident, the Prista majority in Congress, deaf to the opposition's sound arguments, irresponsibly approved a budget that every first-year economics student knew would have to be completely restructured.

The PRI puts all the blame for the economic "instability" on the murders of Posadas, Colosio, and Ruiz Massieu—murders that the government cannot or does not want to explain; and on the conflict in Chiapas, limited, according to the government, to four townships in the Southeast with an insignificant role in the national economy, whose people barely survive in extreme poverty and are excluded from the games of high finance. The government has prolonged and aggravated that conflict by its lack of proposals and

Emilio Pradilla Cobos, "Zedillo sabe cómo hacerlo" (Primera de dos partes), *La Jornada*, México, January 3 and 9, 1995. Excerpt translated by Benjamin Keen.

effective negotiations, by electoral fraud, and by imposing Governor Robledo in Chiapas (with President Salinas in attendance at his inauguration). Additionally, post-election conflicts show that elections managed by the PRI, that is by the Mexican state, are dishonest, dirty, and not credible to Mexican society. [The author is referring to three highly publicized and still unexplained murders: The 1993 murder of Cardinal Juan José Posadas has been charged to drug traffickers; the 1994 assassinations of PRI presidential candidate Luis Donaldo Colosio and PRI General Secretary José Francisco Ruiz Massieu have been variously attributed to drug traffickers, warring factions within PRI, or a mix of both. Former President Salinas de Gortari's brother, Raúl, was eventually convicted of masterminding Ruiz Massieu's murder.]

The government has concealed the structural reasons for the permanent economic crisis because they form part of the neo-liberal project that Prista governments have applied since 1983. The total, sudden, and uncontrolled opening up of the Mexican market has resulted in an accelerated growth of the trade deficit, due to an avalanche of imports much greater than the increase in exports. This deficit had to be covered at all costs by the indiscriminate entry of foreign capital and by contracting new foreign debts. The foreign debt has not ceased to grow, with the result that a large part of the available foreign exchange has to be devoted to the service of the debt. Today, with the peso's devaluation, a very substantial portion of the gross domestic product is committed to serving the debt. The uncontrolled influx of foreign capital has two objectives. One is speculation on the stock exchange. This speculative capital does not increase the productive base, is highly volatile, and flees at the least sign of a fall in the profit rate. The other objective is control of the industrial, commercial, financial, and service sectors, which send their profits abroad in dollars, without fertilizing the national economy. The destruction of the productive base of small and medium-sized agricultural, industrial, and commercial enterprises that cannot survive international competition or modernize leaves the Mexican consumer dependent on foreign goods. Mexico's almost total technological dependence, due to the absence of a local sector producing capital goods or engaged in research and development, is deepened by the drive to modernize at all cost.

We do not enjoy economic sovereignty; today the economy's direction is determined by a handful of great national and foreign capitalists and their speculative activities on the stock exchange and the money market. Their conservatism is such that they give unconditional support to the ruling party, demand more thorough application of the neo-liberal model, and lament that the government does not have absolute control of the political and economic situation, but their own actions are harmful to the nation's economic and social stability. On December 29, Zedillo partially recognized these facts but not their causes or the responsible parties; consequently they remain without a solution.

Some PRI legislators who form part of the state apparatus and its high bureaucracy claim that the former government, not the present one, is responsible for the devaluation and its costs. Another smoke screen. The key figures in the present government were distinguished members of the Salinas camp and are committed to the neo-liberal policy, whose continuity they proclaimed to the world. Salinas and Zedillo assured us that the macroeconomic adjustment had been successfully completed and it only remained to bring to fruition its "benefits" on the microeconomic level and achieve "wellbeing for the Mexican family." Today it is clear that the first assurance was a lie, and the second was campaign demagogy to win the elections. In the next six years we will have to pay the costs of their fiasco and bear the new lies with which they will try to cover up that fiasco, looking to the elections of 1997 and 2000. No doubt remains: Zedillo knows how to get things done. [A sarcastic reference to Zedillo's campaign slogan.]

Who are the winners and losers by the fiasco of the neo-liberal economic policy of Salinas and Zedillo, made evident by the recent massive devaluation?

The winners, if such there be, are the great national and foreign capitalists, the money barons—the international financial speculators, who consumed the Mexican foreign exchange reserves used to prop up the stock market and the money market and to guarantee the repatriation of their capital when the crisis was imminent, and who have now returned to buy up at bargain prices the shares of the remaining Mexican companies. The great Mexican-American commercial enterprises, which are hiding and marking up their imported and domestic goods. The moneychangers who speculate with foreign exchange. In a word, the handful of beneficiaries of the past and present neo-liberal policy.

The losers are the losers of yesteryear. The small and medium-size agricultural, industrial, commercial, and service enterprises whose market has disappeared as a result of unequal competition with the monopolies and imported merchandise or as a result of the recurring and now aggravated collapse of the domestic market. The enterprises asphyxiated by debts in dollars or pesos—borrowed at high rates of interest, with high bank charges—that have come due, enterprises now menaced by the devaluation and the rise of interest rates. The entrepreneurs who lack liquidity, who cannot replace their equipment or modernize because of the high cost of imported machinery and equipment and who cannot obtain it in the domestic market because of the stagnation of the local capital goods industry.

Hardest hit are the wage earners on all levels, suffering from two decades of wage ceilings and the decline of their real income, and now obliged by a pact between government and employers to accept a ten percent wage increase that only hours later was nullified by a devaluation, decreed by the same government, whose inflationary impact cannot be foretold. Other losers are the new unemployed and the workers in the "informal" sector, who will have fewer clients for their subsistence activities. Will the workers silently accept this new and violent expropriation of their means of subsistence? Will they continue to submit to the iron control of a trade union bureaucracy fused with capital and its authoritarian state? Other losers will be the millions of debtors to banks and credit cards who believed the claims of stability, who went into debt and now must pay at exchange and interest rates much higher than when they contracted their debts. The spoliation of the majority of Mexicans in 1982 is being repeated; then they assured us that thanks to neo-liberalism it could not happen again.

Ahead lie new threats. In the field of politics, the threat of a hardening of authoritarianism in Chiapas, Tabasco, Veracruz, Guerrero, Oaxaca, and the other impoverished and oppressed rural and urban areas whose just demands for justice, democracy, and development may be stifled with repressive violence: The bully boys of the economic and political elite have tried to convince themselves and everybody else that the problems of the economy and the nation stem from "nonconformity." They will make a great mistake to think that all of Mexican society accepts this lie and that they have the support and justification they need to strike an exemplary blow. We must show them that they are wrong, that Mexicans yearn for peace with justice and dignity and will not accept this false solution.

In the field of economics, the PRI government's policy, delineated by Zedillo on December 29, will once again, in the name of "fighting inflation," tighten the screw of wage austerity and public spending in order to transfer all the costs of the crisis to the workers and taxpayers. He spoke of unspecified fiscal measures that will surely affect the welfare of the broad masses and expand the privatization of state companies (the state oil monopoly, Pemex, the state electricity company, and the state railroads may be among them, since very few are left), the infrastructures (roads, transport, communication), and services (Social Security, schools and universities, etc.) in order to cover the approaching fiscal deficit. These measures were foreshadowed in Zedillo's electoral campaign. The national patrimony, constructed with the taxes of all Mexicans, will continue to be auctioned off to the highest foreign or national bidders, transferred for their individual benefit, while we the taxpayers will continue to pay the enormous sumptuary expenses of the bureaucracy and the costs of the crisis of their policy. At the same time we will have to pay twice for public services, a just and lawful payment to the treasury and another to the private entrepreneurs. One more blow to the national sovereignty and the pockets of Mexicans.

Zedillo said nothing about modifying the neo-liberal policy or about a new social policy, or about attacking the structural causes of this new crisis of Mexican capitalism; he spoke of deepening the policy, of purely conjunctural adjustments and more sacrifices for Mexicans. He fired the Secretary of the Treasury, made a scapegoat, but the nature of the government was unchanged. Zedillo's electoral promise of "wellbeing for the Mexican family" (whose family?) revealed its demagogic character only three weeks after he took office. "Zedillo knows how to get things done"; he learned from his neo-liberal teachers in the United States and got his practice in Salinas's government. Because of the characteristics of the Mexican government, we will have to stand six whole years of this political and economic drama. For us there does not exist the possibility, which exists in truly democratic countries, of a change of government.

11. COMMUNIQUÉ FROM SUBCOMANDANTE MARCOS

Disgust with the passage of the North American Free Trade Agreement coupled with constitutional changes that ended land reform in Mexico produced one of the most innovative and durable resistance movements in Latin America. Taking their name from the Mexican revolutionary hero most closely associated with land reform and indigenous rights, the self-styled Zapatistas launched a surprise attack on January 1, 1994, that took over a sizable portion of the southern state of Chiapas, including several major towns. Fearful of appearing too repressive at a delicate international political moment, the Mexican government entered into talks with the rebels. With the government unable and/or unwilling to address Zapatista demands, these on-again, off-again talks have continued (or not). In this communiqué from May 1994, the Zapatistas' charismatic spokesperson, Subcomandante Marcos, demonstrates a mastery of nationalist symbols—in this case a retelling of the origin myth from the Popol Vuh *(see Chapter 1)—that has come to characterize the movement. Carried out in part over the Internet, Marcos's battle over the meaning of nationalist symbols helped undermine the legitimacy of Mexico's ruling party and probably contributed to its defeat in the 2000 presidential election. The wise Native American elder, Old Antonio, is a stock character in Marcos's communiqués and represents the voice of what one Mexican anthropologist has called "México profundo" or deep Mexico.*

We are totally surrounded. We have been "heroically" resisting the avalanche of reactions to the event of May 15. Three days ago, helicopters joined the airplanes that watch us from overhead. The cooks complain that there won't be enough pots to cook all the food we will need if they fall at the same time. The superintendent argues that there is enough firewood to have a barbecue, and that we should invite some Argentine journalist to it because the Argentines know how to barbecue. I think about it, it's useless: The best

---

Subcomandante Marcos, "Communiqué About the End of the Consultations," May 28, 1994.

Argentines are guerrillas (i.e. Che), or poets (i.e. Juan Gelman), or writers (i.e. Borges), or artists (i.e. Maradona), or chroniclers (i.e. Cortázar). There aren't any famous Argentine barbecuers. Some ingenious person proposes that we wait for the improbable hamburgers from the University Student Council. Yesterday we ate radio XEOCH's control console and microphones. They had a rancid taste, like something rotten. The medics are giving out lists of jokes instead of painkillers. They say that laughter is also a cure. The other day I surprised Tacho and Moi as they were crying . . . of laughter. "Why are you laughing?" I asked. They couldn't answer because their laughter had left them short of breath. A medic explained, "It is because they have bad headaches." Day 136 of the military blockade. Sigh.

To top it all off, Toñita asks me to tell a story. I tell her a story as it was told to me by old Antonio, the father of Antonio that appears in "Chiapas: The Southwest in Two Winds, a Storm and a Prophecy":

"In the time before the world came into being, the gods came together and decided to create the world and to create men and women. They thought to make the first people very beautiful and very strong. So they made the first people of gold, and the gods were very content because these people were strong and shining. Then the gods realized that the golden people never moved; they never walked or worked because they were so heavy. So the gods came together again in order to figure out a way to solve the problem. They decided to make another group of people and they decided to make this group of people of wood. The wooden people worked and walked and the gods were again content. Then the gods realized that the golden people were forcing the wooden people to work for them and carry things for them. The gods realized that they had made a mistake, and in order to remedy the mistake, they decided to make people of corn, a good people, a true people. Then the gods went to sleep and they left the corn people to find a solution to the problem. The corn people used the true tongue to reach an agreement among themselves, and they went to the mountains in order to find a path for people . . . "

Old Antonio told me that the golden people were the rich, the white-skinned ones, and the wooden people were the poor, the brown-skinned ones, who forever work for the rich. They are both waiting for the arrival of the corn people. The rich fear their arrival and the poor hope for it. I asked old Antonio what color the skin of the corn people was, and he showed me several types of corn with different colors. He told me that nobody knew exactly, because the corn people don't have faces . . .

Old Antonio has died. I met him 10 years ago in a community deep in the jungle. He smoked like nobody else I knew, and when he was out of cigarettes he would ask me for some tobacco and would make more cigarettes. He viewed my pipe with curiosity, but the one time I tried to loan it to him he showed me the cigarette in his hand, telling me without words that he preferred his own method of smoking. Two years ago, in 1992, I was travelling through the communities attending meetings to decide whether or not we should go to war, and eventually I arrived at the village where old Antonio lived. While the community was discussing whether or not to go to war, old Antonio took me by the arm and led me to the river, about 100 meters from the center of the village. It was May and the river was green. Old Antonio sat on a tree trunk and didn't say anything. After a little while he spoke, "Do you see? Everything is clear and calm. It appears that nothing will happen . . ." "Hmmm," I answered, knowing that he wasn't asking me to answer yes or no. Then he pointed out to me the top of the nearest mountain. The clouds lay gray upon the summit, and the lightning was illuminating the diffuse blue of the hills. It was a powerful storm, but it seemed so far away and inoffensive that old Antonio made a cigarette and looked uselessly around for lighter that he knew he didn't have. I offered my lighter. "When everything is calm here below, there is a strong storm in the mountains," he said after inhaling. "The mountain streams run strongly and flow toward the riverbed. During the rainy season this river becomes fierce, like a whip, like an earthquake. Its power doesn't come from the rain that falls on its banks, but from the mountain streams that flow down to feed it. By destroying, the river reconstructs the land. Its waters will become corn, beans, and bread on our tables here in the jungle.

"Our struggle is the same," the older Antonio told me. "It was born in the mountains, but its effects won't be seen until it arrives here below." He responded to my question about whether he believed the time had come for war by saying, "Now is the time for the river to change color . . ." Old Antonio became quiet and supported himself on my shoulder. We returned to the village slowly. He said to me, "You the Army are the mountain streams and we are the river. You must descend now. . . ." The silence continued and we arrived at his shack as it was growing dark. The younger Antonio returned with the official result of the meeting, and announcement that read, more or less:

We, the men, women, and children of this village met in the community's school in order to see if we believed in our hearts that it is time to go to war for our freedom. We divided ourselves into three groups, one of men, one of women, and one of children to discuss the matter. Later, we came together again and it was seen that the majority believed that it was time to go to war because Mexico is being sold to foreigners and the people are always hungry. Twelve men, twenty-three women and eight children were in favor of beginning the war and have signed this announcement.

I left the village in the early morning hours. Old Antonio wasn't around; he had already gone to the river.

Two months ago I saw old Antonio again. He didn't say anything when he saw me and I sat and began to shuck corn with him. "The river rose," he said to me after a bit. "Yes," I answered. I explained to the younger Antonio what was happening with the consultations and I gave him the documents that outlined our demands and the government's response. We spoke of what had happened in Ocosingo during the offensive, and once again I left the village in the early morning hours. Old Antonio was waiting for me at a turn in the road. I stopped alongside him and lowered my backpack to look for some to-bacco to offer him. "Not now," he said to me as he pushed away the bag of tobacco that I was offering him. He put his arm around me and led me to the foot of a tree. "Do you remember what I told you about the streams and the river?" he asked me. "Yes," I responded, whispering as he had when he had asked me the question. "There is something I didn't tell you," he added, looking at his bare feet. I answered with silence. "The streams . . ." he was stopped by a cough that wracked his entire body. He took a breath and con-tinued, "the streams, when they descend . . ." Once again he was stopped by a cough and I went for a medic. Old Antonio turned down the help of the old *compañero* [comrade] with the Red Cross. The medic looked at me and I made a sign that he should leave. Old Antonio waited until the medic left and then, in the twilight of the dawn, he continued, "The streams . . . when they descend . . . have no way of returning, . . . except beneath the ground." He embraced me rapidly and left. I stayed there watching as he walked away, and as he disappeared in the distance. I lit my pipe and picked up my backpack. As I mounted my horse I thought about what had just occurred. I don't know why, it was very dark, but it seemed that old Antonio was crying.

I just received a letter from the younger Antonio with his village's re-sponse to the government's proposals. He also wrote me that old Antonio had become very ill and that he had died that night. He didn't want anyone to tell me that he was dying. The younger Antonio wrote me that when they in-sisted that I be told, old Antonio said, "No, I have already told him what I had to tell him. Leave him alone, he has much work to do."

When I finished the story that Antonio had told me, six-year-old Toñita solemnly told me that yes, she loves me, but that from now on she won't kiss me because "it itches." Rolando says that when Toñita has to go to the medic's area, she asks if the Sup is there. If she is told that I'm there she doesn't go. "Because the Sup only wants kisses and he itches," says the in-evitable logic of a six year old, which, on this side of the stream, we call "Toñita."

The first rains have begun here. We thought that we should have to wait for the arrival of the anti-riot water cannons in order to have water.

Ana María says that the rain comes from the clouds that are fighting on top of the mountains. They do it this way so that men and women will not see their disputes. On the summits of the mountains, the clouds fight their ferocious battles with what we call lightning. Armed with infinity, the clouds fight for the privilege of dying and becoming rain to feed the land. We Zapatistas are similar to the clouds, without faces, without names, without any payment. Like the clouds we fight for the privilege of becoming a seed for the land.

All right. Health and a raincoat (for the rains and the riots),
From the mountains of the Mexican Southeast,

Subcommander Marcos
May, 1994

P.S.: The majority disguised as the untolerated minority. About all of this whether Marcos is homosexual: Marcos is gay in San Francisco, a black person from South Africa, Asian in Europe, a Chicano in San Isidro, an anarchist in Spain, a Palestinian in Israel, an indigenous person in the streets of San Cristóbal, a gang-member in Neza, a rocker on campus, a Jew in Germany, an ombudsman in the Department of Defense, a feminist in a political party, a communist in the post-Cold War period, a prisoner in Cintalapa, a pacifist in Bosnia, a Mapuche in the Andes, a teacher in the National Confederation of Education, an artist without a gallery or a portfolio, a housewife in any neighborhood in any city in any part of Mexico on a Saturday night, a guerilla in Mexico at the end of the twentieth century, a striker in the CTM, a sexist in the feminist movement, a woman alone in a Metro station at 10 p.m., a retired person standing around in the Zócalo, a *campesino* without land, an underground editor, an unemployed worker, a doctor with no office, a non-conformist student, a dissident against neo-liberalism, a writer without books or readers, and a Zapatista in the Mexican Southeast. In other words, Marcos is a human being in this world. Marcos is every untolerated, oppressed, exploited minority that is resisting and saying, "Enough!" He is every minority who is now beginning to speak and every majority that must shut up and listen. He is every untolerated group searching for a way to speak, their way to speak. Everything that makes power and the good consciences of those in power uncomfortable—this is Marcos.

PART NINE

CHALLENGES TO THE NATION-STATE

17

~

GLOBALIZATION AND

ITS DISCONTENTS

A DECADE HAS ELAPSED since a tidal wave of neoliberal economic reforms swept over Latin America in the 1990s. The extent and intensity of the process—privatization of public companies, dismantling of state controls, and a resigned acceptance of the social costs of economic modernization—led many observers to conclude that the region had given up its long-standing fondness for state intervention (and organized social protest) and was entering the "global era" eager to embrace neoliberal recipes for economic growth. The first decade of the new century, however, reveals a very different Latin America, in which new economic agendas, political identities, and forms of social activism have emerged from the intersection of global trends and local realities.

Perhaps the most visible new direction involves electoral politics. With a few exceptions (e.g., Mexico's controversial 2006 election), Latin American elections have suggested a turning of the ideological tide—a "left turn" as Jorge Casteñeda calls it in his influential essay (see Excerpt 4 below). This ideological shift has produced a new generation of political leaders (and revived a few icons of past social struggles) along with an unprecedented level of political representation for socially marginalized groups. As recently as ten years ago, few observers would have predicted that a union leader (Luiz Inácio Lula da Silva in Brazil), two women (Michelle Bachelet in Chile and Cristina Fernández de Kirchner in Argentina), an indigenous activist (Evo Morales in Bolivia), and a radical Roman Catholic bishop (Fernando Lugo in Paraguay) would ever become president of their respective countries.

This political left turn occurs in an economic context that seems unusually favorable for the region. Increasing global demand for agricultural products coupled with a worldwide energy crisis that has brought the prices of oil and gas to record levels is already benefiting countries like Brazil, Venezuela, Mexico, Bolivia, Chile, and Argentina. The upward trend in commodity prices is not expected to change, at least in the short term, and most economic analysts point to new opportunities for Latin America to increase its presence in world markets—even if this signals a return to the region's traditional role as producer of primary (nonindustrialized) goods. Moreover, these optimistic predictions seem to hold for the whole region. Studies performed in 2007 by the Economic Commission for Latin America and the Caribbean (CEPAL) show steady economic growth for eighteen countries in the region, its strongest performance since the early 1970s. Some analysts have even begun to talk about a Latin American economic boom.

Economic optimism has led to new expectations, including reduced unemployment, increased social inclusion, and better redistribution of wealth. Although employment figures are rising, statistical measures hide the precarious nature of most new jobs. And economic growth inevitably generates new occasions for social conflict as traditional unions regain negotiating power and labor activism takes advantage of new modes of social protest.

Access to advanced communications technologies has made it possible for historically marginalized groups to express their dissent in new ways. A striking example of the intersection between global trends (technological and ideological) and local issues is the expanded opportunity for political expression now available to indigenous societies in the Andean region and Central America. In association with local, national, and international nongovernmental organizations and environmental activists, many indigenous communities are now making their case for cultural, economic, and environmental rights to a much wider audience. In some cases, separatist movements have developed that threaten the very principle of the nation-state. The increasingly popular notion of "plurinational state," in particular, reflects the desire of indigenous peoples to regain control over their land and its natural resources. For example, in Bolivia ethnic separatism (indigenous and nonindigenous) has coincided with economic interests to produce separatist movements that threaten the administration of the region's first indigenous president.

Even with steady macroeconomic growth, the challenges faced by democratically elected governments are daunting. Indeed, translating the advantages of economic renaissance into improvements in governmental institutions and citizens' quality of life is far from easy, as exemplified in the problem of rising urban crime rates, one of the main threats to democracy in Latin America. Statistical data points to an unprecedented rise in everyday violence, even for a region accustomed to high levels of political conflict. Increased trafficking in arms and drugs, set against a background of severe social exclusion in the region's megacities, is generating a level and type of violence that is no longer exclusively the problem of societies such as Colombia, Brazil, Mexico, and Venezuela. Until recently public safety issues were of marginal political importance in countries like Chile, Argentina, and Uruguay; these days, however, opinion polls place security issues at the top of citizen concerns all over Latin America. The impotence of democratic institutions to counteract these threats (whether real or imagined) is a daily reminder of the limits of institutional power and dangerously undermines confidence in democratic institutions, especially the criminal justice system and the police.

Coming years will demonstrate whether or not Latin American societies can take advantage of the region's prominent role in the new global economy. No doubt the future will also reveal new examples of creative adaptation to the cultural and political challenges of globalization. And it will also tell us whether or not these new opportunities and creative adaptations can work to counteract a long history of social inequality and exclusion.

1. LULA SPEAKS OUT

As one economic crisis followed another in Latin America, the relative complacency of the late 1990s gave way to a growing distrust of the neoliberal economic policies demanded by international lenders like World Bank and the International Monetary Fund, with the support of major economic players like the United States, the European Union, and Japan. In 2002 a former autoworker and labor organizer, Luiz Inácio Lula da Silva, was elected president of Brazil, just a few months after the Argentine economy nearly collapsed. The election had profound repercussions throughout the region, especially in Brazil. The popular appeal of Lula's critique of neoliberal economics made him a logical spokesperson for the interests of marginalized peoples and nations throughout the world. Moreover, his political influence in Latin America's largest economy ensured that the developed countries would listen. In this 2003 speech to the World Economic Forum's annual meeting in Davos, Switzerland, Lula lays out an ambitious agenda for Brazil, Latin America, and the world.

As you know, I have come straight from Porto Alegre, where I took part in the World Social Forum and spoke to tens of thousands of people on the same subjects that I intend to address here. The core theme of the Annual Meeting of the World Economic Forum is "Building Trust." I feel very comfortable with this theme.

Lula da Silva, Address to the annual meeting of the World Economic Forum in Davos, Switzerland, January 26, 2003.

The Brazilian people have placed their trust in me, giving me the responsibility of running a country with a population of 175 million, one of the world's biggest industrial economies. But a country that also lives with huge social inequalities. I bring to Davos the feeling of hope that has gripped the whole of Brazilian society. Brazil has rediscovered itself, and this rediscovery is being expressed in its people's enthusiasm and their desire to mobilize to face the huge problems that lie ahead of us.

Here in Davos, it is generally assumed that there is now only one god—the market. But free and secure citizens are one of the main prerequisites for a free market.

I responded calmly and maturely to those who did not trust the commitments we made during the electoral campaign. In my Letter to the Brazilian People, I stressed my willingness to implement deep economic, social and political reforms, whilst showing respect for the country's contracts and securing a balanced economy.

Brazil is working to reduce its social and economic inequalities, deepen its political democracy, guarantee public freedoms and actively promote human rights.

These inequalities are most visible in the more than 45 million Brazilians who live below the poverty line. The most dramatic form of these inequalities is the hunger that affects tens of millions of our brothers and sisters. For this reason, we have made the fight against hunger our top priority. I will never tire from repeating my commitment to ensuring that every Brazilian can have breakfast, lunch and supper every day.

The fight against hunger is not only the government's task; it belongs to the whole of society. Structural changes are a prerequisite for the eradication of hunger. It requires the creation of decent jobs, along with better investments, a substantial increase in domestic savings, expansion of domestic and export markets, high-quality health and education provision, and cultural, scientific and technological development. Brazil must promote agricultural reform and achieve a return to economic growth as a way to distribute income. We are establishing clear, stable and transparent economic rules, and are implacably fighting corruption. Our infrastructure must be developed, and this will involve foreign investment.

We are a hospitable country. The Brazilian people are characterized by tolerance and solidarity. We have a skilled workforce, ready to meet the huge challenges of production in the 21st century. To achieve future growth we need to overcome external constraints. Brazil has to break the vicious circle whereby it takes on new loans to pay existing ones. We need to make an extraordinary effort to expand our international trade, in particular our exports, diversifying into new products and markets, and adding value to what we produce.

The efforts we are making to revive the Brazilian economy in a responsible way will not however be fully realized without major changes in the world economic order. We want free trade, but free trade that is reciprocal. Any export efforts we might make will be worth nothing if the rich countries continue to preach free trade and practice protectionism. The required changes in the world economic order must also involve a greater discipline in capital flows, which move around the world at the mercy of subjective rumors and speculation with no basis in reality. The international community needs to play a role in preventing the illegal flight of capital seeking refuge in tax havens.

Greater discipline in this area is vital if we are to effectively combat international terrorism and crime, both of which are fed by money laundering.

Constructing a new international economic order that is both fairer and more democratic is not only an act of generosity, but also, and principally, a demonstration of political astuteness. More than ten years following the fall of the Berlin Wall, there are still walls separating the well-fed from the hungry, those who have work from the unemployed, those with decent homes from those who live in the street or in miserable slums, those who have access to education and humanity's cultural heritage from those who are submerged in illiteracy and complete alienation.

New ethical standards are also required. It is not enough to proclaim the values of humanism. These values must also prevail in relations between countries and peoples. Our foreign policy is firmly focused on the pursuit of peace and negotiated solutions to international conflicts, and to the uncompromising defense of our national interests.

Peace is not just a moral objective. It is an imperative of reason. This is why we maintain that disputes must be resolved by peaceful means and under the aegis of the United Nations. We have to accept that poverty, hunger and deprivation are very often the breeding ground of fanaticism and intolerance. Protecting national interests is not incompatible with co-operation and solidarity. Our domestic policies are not hostile to foreigners, they are universalist.

We are looking to develop closer relationships with other South American countries and to increase economic, commercial, social and political integration with them. We would also like to develop increasingly positive relationships with the United States, the European Union, and Asia. As the country with the second largest black population in the world, we feel a special affinity for Africa, a continent with which we have very close ethnic and cultural ties.

I would like to invite all of you here today, on this "Magic Mountain" of Davos, to look at the world through different eyes. It is vital that we build a world economic order than can satisfy the yearnings of those billions of people who are today excluded from the extraordinary scientific and technological advances that humankind has achieved. Do not just sit and wait for signals that the time has come for a change of attitude towards my country and the countries in the developing world.

Peoples, like individuals, need opportunities. The nations that are rich today are rich only because of the opportunities they have had in the past. If those nations wish to be true to their past successes, they cannot and must not put barriers in the way of developing countries. On the contrary, they can and must work with us to build a new agenda for shared global development.

Brazil has already started to change, you may be sure of that. Our determination is not only the result of the commitments we made many years ago; it is also fuelled by the hope that is driving our country. I know that contemporary debate is full of divergent opinions and different, even conflicting, world visions. I am president of the entire Brazilian people, not just those who voted for me. We are looking to build a new social contract in which all forces of Brazilian society are represented and heard. To this end, I am seeking dialogue with all sectors, all of which will be represented in the Council for Economic and Social Development. I will be seeking contacts and sources of support for our plans to change Brazilian society, wherever they may be found.

The change we are seeking should not benefit just one social, political or ideological group. But most of all it should benefit the vulnerable, the deprived, and the persecuted, and who now see the possibility of personal and collective redemption. This is a cause we can all adopt. It is a universal cause par excellence.

As the largest and most industrialized country of the southern hemisphere, Brazil feels it has both a right and a duty to call on all those attending the Davos Forum to exercise good sense. We would like to appeal to you to make scientific discoveries universally available, so that their benefits can be enjoyed by all countries of the world.

To this same end, I would like to call upon the Group of Seven nations, with the support of major international investors, to establish a new International Fund to tackle poverty and hunger in the Third World. The road to building a fairer world is a long one, and hunger cannot wait. My greatest desire is that the hope that has overcome fear in my country will help vanquish it around the world. We urgently need to unite around a worldwide pact for peace and against hunger. Brazil will play its part.

2. CITIZENS TALK ABOUT THE POLICE

Everyday violence is one of the most pressing problems faced by Latin American democracies today, a problem that points to enduring social inequality and the fragility of political institutions. The crime problem is particularly acute in large urban centers and especially in Brazil, where fear of crime has divided cities into increasingly segregated territories. Walled neighborhoods with private security dramatically symbolize the separation between the rich and the poor. Crime and victimization are socially differentiated: outside of those walls, the working classes and lower-middle classes are sub-

jected with relative impunity to the violence of family members, criminals, and police. As the following testimonies from São Paulo show, criminals and police are not perceived as separate worlds, at odds with each other. Unprotected citizens share a tacit understanding about police corruption and connections to the world of crime. Most residents fear rather than trust the police.

Look, if someone approaches me and says, "I'm a bandit, I'm going to take you home," I would accept it more than if a guy in a uniform approaches me saying "I'm a policeman, and I'm going to take you home." No, I don't trust the police. I'm afraid of the police.

—Airport janitor, Cidade Júlia, thirty-four, married, with three daughters; her husband is unemployed

You know that the police get confused, or that many times in order to show off, they mindlessly kill an innocent guy accusing him of being a bandit. They put a gun in some poor guy's hands. Look, if you don't have important friends, if you don't have wisdom, your son dies as a bandit without his being a bandit because the police killed him by mistake and said he was a bandit. . . . I know of a student who, because he was not carrying his identity papers, ran away afraid from the police, and he was shot and declared to be a bandit, even though he wasn't.

—Housewife and neighborhood organizer in Jaguaré, thirty-five, with four children; her husband is a skilled worker in a textile factory

The police only arrest those guys who work, workers, heads of households. Those they arrest, beat, do whatever they want. Now, those bandits, they don't [arrest]. . . . If a worker, if a head of a household, forgets his papers at home, he goes to jail. But if it is a bandit, no. . . . The guy steals in the afternoon, they arrest him, divide the money. . . . The world is completely turned upside down.

—Office assistant, eighteen, Jardim das Camélias, lives with his parents, a sister, and two nephews

Most members of the working classes see the actions of the police as arbitrary. Their descriptions of mistaken killings and police cover-ups coincide with the reports of human rights organizations . . . the pattern is well-known. The police mistake workers for criminals, use violence against them, and try to cover up their errors. For the police, as for many people, the boundary between the image of the poor worker and that of the criminal is very thin indeed. As a consequence, members of the working classes can be harassed by the police. Their natural reactions (like running away) may be interpreted as the behavior of criminals. The narratives of working-class people are often

Teresa Pires do Rio Caldeira, *City of Walls: Crime, Segregation, and Citizenship in São Paulo* (Berkeley: University of California Press), pp. 182–189.

punctuated by references to signs that should prove their identities as workers. Central among these signs is the *carteira profissional*, or professional identification, a document that registers a worker's occupational history:
profession, labor contracts, the names of employers, salaries, vacations, social
security entitlements, etc. The *carteira profissional* is the worker's most important proof of citizenship. Other signs are the *marmite*—the lunch container—
and calluses on their hands as proof of manual labor.

Nevertheless, even the clearest signs may be ignored by the police force
that, in popular opinion, may be violent with workers but is soft on criminals.
The reasons workers give for thinking that criminals receive "better treatment"
fall into two categories. On the one hand, they believe the police have monetary interests in crime and criminals; they are corrupt and may be directly involved in crime themselves. On the other, they are convinced that the police
are not well prepared to perform their duties. In both circumstances, the imagery used to describe the criminal may also be used to describe the police.

> Yesterday I was listening to the radio, and the reporter said that three police-
> men and a police chief were arrested because they're stealing. It means that
> policemen themselves are bandits as well. . . . The worst is that Rota [Rondas
> Ostensivas Tobias de Aguiar, a special division of the military police responsi-
> ble for most killings of civilians in metropolitan São Paulo], they sometimes
> kill innocent people. They kill the innocent while bandits are free on the
> streets. Now, why don't they arrest the bandits? Because they give them
> money. I think it is because of that. Because they rob, then they divide up the
> money with them [the policemen], and everything is OK.
> —*Housewife from Jardim das Camélias, thirty-three, four children;*
> *has participated in various social movements and local associations;*
> *her husband is a skilled worker in a small textile factory*

> I don't think of the policemen as state functionaries, I think of them more as
> people who are out there to defend their own interests related to drug traffic,
> to prostitution, to networks of those hotels you rent per hour. And inside the
> police there are many personal interests among them, agglomeration of males,
> I have always thought of that as something tending to deviance. . . . In sum, for
> me the police is also corrupt. Gun licenses, guns, drugs, those things involve a
> lot of money. The police are in charge of apprehending those things; so they
> apprehend and use the money to create capital to buy hotels.
> —*College graduate, twenty-three, Moóca, unemployed, has a degree*
> *in communication with a major in radio, lives with his parents*

Even when the police are not considered corrupt, they are thought to be
under-prepared for the job. In general, the police are said to be close to the

evil elements of the environment of crime: perversion, sickness, prostitution, and bad influences are only a few elements on a long list.

What do I think of the police? Look, I think the following: they're lamentable—in relation to workers like us. It's lamentable that the police today are very unprepared. It's not the police's fault, but once more it is the general structure which is very unprepared.

[The speaker argues that the men who become policemen are very young and lack the necessary training. Because of that, they feel insecure and are afraid of confronting criminals. As a consequence, they use their guns more than necessary to overcome their fear or sometimes just "to show that they are men." Moreover, because they lack training, they do not have the notion that they are out there to serve society, that they are paid with tax money, and that they should not harass ordinary citizens.]

These days, for the policemen, everybody is a bandit, everybody is marginal, everybody deserves to be arrested, and everybody should respect them. It's lamentable, it's lack of training. The police have always been unprepared and are getting worse. They have never been good.

—Bar owner, Moóca, has a law degree but does not work
as a lawyer; single, lives with three roommates

The police are a public disaster! I think this is because of the lack of ability of the policemen. I think that they get anyone to become a policeman, they get anyone who comes there from Paraíba, from Maranhão, from the middle of nowhere, doesn't even know how to read and is already a policeman, a PM! What does a person like that know about things and principally about the law? It must be that. You don't see in the police force people born in São Paulo; all you see are *nortistas*. . . . Any ten *cruzeiros* buy a policeman. They are just to get money. They want money, especially the PM.

—Retired skilled worker, Jardim Marieta, late fifties, married with two children

The police? The police are afraid of facing armed criminals! Only the Rota doesn't hesitate—the Rota is like the Esquadrão da Morte. You know that if you needed to depend on a policeman to defend you, you might as well forget it. Among one thousand you're going to find one, because the rest only think of their families. . . . The police don't have training, they don't have education. Now they are starting to be a little polite with the public, but the majority of them are like horses, animals, and illiterate! . . . If I had to depend on the help of the police, it would be easier to ask the help of a bandit to protect me from another bandit. Because they [policemen] say: "I have a child to raise, I have a household to support, I'm not going to die here, because I don't make enough money for that. That is, we criticize, but we shouldn't criticize the policeman, but their foundation. And what is that? The government. The government

484 Part Nine: Challenges to the Nation-State

should give them more support, both moral and financial, because they are exposed to danger, and we should see this.

—Housewife and neighborhood organizer in Jaguaré, thirty-five,
with four children; her husband is a skilled worker in a textile factory

Even when people may understand the poor and dangerous working conditions of the policemen—many of whom live in their own neighborhoods—and find some justification for their inefficiency, they still criticize them. The police are associated with the stereotypes and elements that compose the image of the criminal: they are considered to be from the northeast, uneducated, animalistic, ignorant of their public role, and so on. In fact, when people talk of crime, the two main characters of the universe of crime—the criminal and the policeman—are not opposed but compared.

Many times, and especially in narratives of the upper classes, the police are described by the same stereotypes used to denigrate the poor ... the arrogance of the policeman (portrayed as someone without education) with a weapon in his hands is described in the same way that an upper-class woman describes the arrogance of a working-class person who buys a new car. This tendency is also revealed in the following comment about the risks involved in the expansion of private security services.

Logically, if you let those guys from firms [of private security] go armed around the city, this is an additional risk. With the police it is already something horrible, imagine if you expand the number of armed people! ... You can even argue that it does not matter if it is public or private, since the guys who are armed are all from the same mentality, from the same social class, and equally unprepared, and equally ready to use the guns for any stupid reason.

—Freelance journalist, forty-three, Morumbi, divorced, with two children

The merging of the images of criminals and policemen, and of both with images of the poor, is frequent in discussions of crime. In all circumstances the confusion can lead to death—of working-class people. As a consequence, not only are people always afraid and uncertain, but they also find it difficult to figure out the right reaction—to run or not to run—when encountering either the police or criminals. In facing criminals, to pretend ignorance is one of the best bets.

Many times, when there is a robbery, the neighbors say, "It was that one, that one." But the police say, "We haven't caught him in the act, so we don't arrest him," and they go away. And what happens? The guy wants vengeance and goes around killing a lot of people, as it happens today. When a crime happens on the street, the population doesn't collaborate with the police because of that ... . It's fear of vengeance, they don't say anything, say they haven't seen anything. If I see a robber killing someone, I won't want to know anything about it. I'll pretend I haven't seen anything. If the police ask me, I'll say, "I haven't seen anything."

If by any chance you're robbed, do you think it is worth reporting it?

I don't think it is worth it. We go to the police to file a claim, we do everything and still go out of there mad, because we know that [when] we turn our back on them, they throw the paper away.

—*Eldest of three brothers who live in Jardim des Camélias,*
twenty-two, an auto mechanic, married

In situations of crime and violence, workers feel powerless. They are paralyzed between fear of the police, fear of criminal's vengeance and, as we shall see, a belief that the justice system in unable to provide justice. Without protection, their *modus vivendi* is to adopt silence as a way of maintaining good relations with criminals they might know personally.

Ironically or not, those views were confirmed by a policeman, a PM who lives in Jardim das Camélias, describes himself as a worker and member of the working classes, and shares many of his neighbor's opinions about crime, including the view that silence is a good tactic for dealing with threats of vengeance.

Long weekends are a disaster. People go traveling, and when they come back on Monday or Sunday night, we get a lot of calls that the house was burglarized, people have taken everything. And the worst is that the neighbors don't see anything. In fact, they see, but they are afraid of calling the police.

Why are they afraid?

Because of the fragility of the laws. People know that if they call the police, either the PM or the civil police, they are not going to have any protection. We cannot provide individual protection if we don't have a superior order. If we're simply passing by and someone says, "There are two bandits inside that house," we go there and arrest the guys, but that person stays at the bandit's mercy. We cannot pass by his house every hour to check if everything is all right . . .

What do you think should change to help your work?

If there were only justice! It's discouraging to take someone to the police station. There is corruption everywhere. I'm not trying to exempt the PM from this, for there are some corrupt policemen. However, in the civil police here in São Paulo it is worse. It's discouraging to take an individual to the station, and the commander—I have already seen that—takes money from the guy and says to him, "Let the PM leave [the building] so that it doesn't look bad, and I'll release you." I have already seen this happening. I left and saw the guy leaving through the back door. . . . The other day I was talking with another PM, saying that Brazil has become a Paraguay. Here, everything works on the basis of money. If you want to get something, you pay. Understand? There are a lot of people out on the street who should be in prison and are free because of corruption. There should also be efficient legislation in relation to corruption. . . . If there were justice, and some legal reform, it wouldn't take much . . .

The PM is ridiculed. I was saying that some time ago it made you proud to go around in uniform. Nowadays, it's a source of shame. If a PM is in uniform, he walks looking to the side, checking if everything is OK. People keep looking at him, and he thinks they are laughing at him. This happens sometimes because of lack of respect, and sometimes because of the brutality of the policemen themselves. Let's not attribute all wrong to society. I think that today the police are not prepared to exercise their duties. Wherever they go, they pull out their badges and say, "I'm police," and so forth. This should not happen. It's an abuse. He likes to take advantage of the uniform, and the fact that he is a policeman, to get what he wants. . . . The people say as much, they don't like the police. I don't know whether it is because of the laws. I don't know, but I know that in a way the people don't like the police. People even are afraid of the police these days.

—*Military policeman, Jardim das Camélias, early thirties, married to a woman who works as a secretary in a factory, one child, works off-duty as a private guard*

In their descriptions of criminals, the people I interviewed always reminded me that it is necessary to be careful with generalizations, that in any category there are both good and bad elements. The same is true of discussions about the police. Even when an officer performs the way he should, popular distrust is so widespread that people prefer to hold on to their negative evaluations and see the instance as an exception. This was the attitude of a woman from Moóca who told me that a policeman had returned three gold chains stolen from her at a traffic light. When the officer called to her, she assumed that he wanted money or was going to harass her. When she realized he was returning the chains, she was so amazed that she wrote a letter to the reader's column of *Folha de São Paulo.* In spite of that incident, however, her general view of the police is unchanged: "This case hasn't convinced me, but even today I admire him."

If one takes into consideration the arbitrariness and violence of the police, the constant confusion (workers mistaken for criminals, policemen mistaken for criminals), the identification of criminals with policemen (both symbolic and material) and of both with poor people—in sum, the context of uncertainty, confusion, and fear of both policemen and criminals—one can only conclude that the police are far from being able to offer a feeling of security to the working and lower middle classes. The population often feels pressed against the wall, without alternatives.

3. SEX AND REVOLUTION

All social revolutions seek to revolutionize social relations and focus in large part on the family. The three great twentieth-century Latin American social revolutions— Mexico (1910–1920), Cuba (1959), Nicaragua (1979)—each made a concerted ef-

fort to produce "new" men and women who would join together to form the revolutionary family, the bedrock of a "new" society committed to the welfare of all its citizens. Revolutionary leaders considered anyone who didn't fit into that family to be a social deviant in immediate need of reeducation or, if that failed, expulsion (or at least severe repression). Of the three revolutions, the Cuban revolution was the most insistent on the need for a national project of radical social transformation and the most rigorous in attempting to carry out that program. In a 1961 speech to Cuban intellectuals, Fidel Castro explained the new order in no uncertain terms: "Inside the Revolution, everything; outside the Revolution, nothing." One group that had no place in Cuba's revolutionary family was openly gay men. During the early 1960s, Che Guevara headed a New Man campaign to tackle the perennial problem of irresponsible machismo grounded in male violence and extreme individualism. Only responsible, mature men, he insisted, could transform Cuba into a socialist paradise. Needless to say, those men would also be heterosexual. As a result, Cuban authorities rigorously persecuted male homosexuals as bourgeois degenerates and enemies of the revolution. Oppressive as Cuban government policies toward homosexuals undoubtedly were, official repression was vigorously resisted by Cuban and international gay rights groups who often turned revolutionary rhetoric about social justice to their own purposes.

Official homophobia has diminished in recent years, pressured by Cuban and international gay rights and human rights activists, and embarrassed by the international publicity generated by exiled writer Reinaldo Arenas's controversial memoir, Before Night Falls. *Renowned Cuban revolutionary filmmaker Tomás Gutiérrez Alea and longtime collaborator Juan Carlos Tabío directed the internationally acclaimed 1993 film* Strawberry and Chocolate, *which provided further evidence of this shift. The film is based on a 1990 short story by Cuban writer Senel Paz, "The Woods, the Wolf, and the New Man," about a straight university student's encounter with and growing acceptance of a cultured (and effeminate) gay man. This trajectory from official homophobia to tolerance is evident in the two pieces included here. The first is a 1965 cartoon from a revolutionary magazine,* Mella, *drawn by prominent cartoonist Virgilio Martínez Gaínza in the early—and most homophobic—days of the revolution. The second is a 2003 interview with Mariela Castro Espín, the director of Cuba's National Center for Sex Education (and daughter of current president Raul Castro). A high-profile educator and psychologist, Mariela Castro has become an outspoken advocate for LGBT rights in Cuba, sponsoring Cuba's first gay marriage ceremony (for two women) and setting up a clinic to provide sexual reassignment surgery for transsexuals at government expense. In another interview, she admits that the revolution made some mistakes in the early years—which she blames in part on mainstream medical science's classification of homosexuality as a mental disorder—but argues that those mistakes have been corrected through the process of revolutionary self-critique and recent advances in medical understandings of human sexuality.*

Virgilio Martínez Gaínza, "Vida y milagros de Florito Volandero," *Mella* (1965): 20–21; and Mariela Castro Espín, interview by Eduardo Jiménez García, "Más relajados, no más tolerantes: La sociedad cubana ante la homosexualidad," *Alma Mater: Revista digital de los universitarios cubanos*, May 23, 2003. Excerpt translated by the editors.

488

Translation for "Vida y milagros de Florito Volandero"

Panel 1: This is Florito . . .

Panel 2: Until recently he lived very tranquilly. He and his pals would get together at his house to listen to the latest hit records sent by one of his friends . . .

Panel 3: When tedium and anguish oppressed his poor, sensitive heart, he suffered . . .

Panel 4: It's true that the world didn't understand him and that people sometimes criticized him, but others understood his problem and they gave him hope . . .

First man: "It's as old as the world . . . just read the history of Greece."

Second man: "I've been assured that Nero too . . . "

Third man: "Sure . . . but since people are narrow-minded and dogmatic they don't know how to take a broad modern view of these problems."

Fourth man: "We're more sensitive and emotional . . . and therefore more artistic . . . "

Panel 5: Florito would pull himself together . . . he'd smile . . . and write a "revolutionary" poem for "The Fountain" . . .
"Cane Cutter"
Coarse cane cutter . . .
Oh, oh, cane cutter!
Oh!
[signed] Florito Voladera
Dedicated to the Salt of the Earth

Panel 6: So it must be taken into account the Florito was a "REVOLUTIONARY" . . .

Florito: " . . . though I might have my weaknesses, I'm very Marxist . . . So there!"

Translation for
"Vida y milagros de Florito Volandero" (continued)

	Nevertheless, with each day that passed he understood less . . . and poor Florito couldn't help but compare:
Column 1:	Cuba:
Panel 1:	[soldiers marching in formation]
Panel 2:	[sign reads] Everyone to the coffee harvest.
Panel 3:	[man with glasses says] ". . . and we must continue the purges . . . We don't want worms [counterrevolutionaries] or degenerates in the university."
Column 2:	The Free World:
Panel 1:	[criminal types on the street]
Panel 2:	[newspaper headline] New York sees publication of a magazine dedicated especially to homosexuals.
Panel 3:	[scene in a gay/lesbian bar]
Bottom left panel:	. . . and Florito finally understood . . .
Bottom right panel:	
Florito:	"Protect me, Johnny! I'm being persecuted by communists!"

Interview with Mariela Castro Espín, "More Relaxed, Not More Tolerant: Cuban Society in the Presence of Homosexuality."

Q: Do you think that the 1990s saw the beginnings of an era of greater social tolerance with respect to homosexuality in Cuba?

A: I think that's right, people are a bit more relaxed about homosexuality in public as well as in the family, but only more relaxed, no more tolerant. There's a lot more work to do in our society so that this "relaxation" becomes real respect with regard to sexual diversity. Sexuality is more complex than science can fathom and we can imagine. So we should be very careful in the decisions we make with regard to it. . . .

I can't provide statistical data or other scientific information that demonstrate greater tolerance because we have no studies of this topic in our country. Nevertheless I can speculate on this phenomenon from a professional and personal perspective. I think that certainly since the 1990s there is a greater acceptance of the presence of homosexual persons as part of the population and in public institutions. This is not to suggest that contradictions between the micro and macro levels of society have been resolved.

At the macro social level, it seems to me that we are in a good position to implement more explicit policies with respect to the defense of the rights of homosexuals of both sexes, in a way will allow us to better confront different manifestations of discrimination around issues of sexual orientation.

As early as the 1970s, thanks to reforms in the Penal Code, the homosexual was no longer considered a criminal; any words or phrases that might have discriminated against homosexuals were modified. That was still not enough, because I believe that our laws ought to reflect, more often and better, the respect that all homosexual persons deserve.

At the micro social level, there is a need for more thorough and more professional work because it involves changing mental structures, modifying the social imaginary. For that reason, I would link a truly humanistic effort to develop greater respect for the rights of persons of homosexual orientation to the larger debates in our society these days. I think that these culture wars and policy battles should include this imperative because [debating homosexual rights] strengthens the Revolution culturally, socially, and ideologically.

Q: Is this an actual proposal?

A: Yes. It's a proposal I made as part of my responsibilities as the director of the National Center for Sex Education. It was made in the appropriate places and I assure you that it has met with a favorable reception. This suggestion is not at all far from the spirit of the Revolution or from the process that has been called the "battle of ideas." It would be marvelous if we could undertake an extensive, inter-sectoral study of the topic to encourage Cuban society to develop a saner, more equitable sexual culture, and to help overcome erroneous beliefs and ancestral prejudices with regard to sexual orientation. Something like this would ensure that the Revolution's humanistic ethic would be even more consequential because the Cuban Revolution was accomplished with the participation of all Cubans, male and female, who identified with the conquests and dreams of this social project; and this includes persons of diverse sexual orientations. So it would be unjust to allow the dignity of homosexuals to be damaged by ancestral taboos. For these reasons I believe that [respect for homosexual rights and sexual diversity] is a crucial task that requires much more work.

Q: How do you think that our laws could better demonstrate respect for the rights of homosexuals?

A: In the Constitution of the Republic all persons are protected regardless of race, sex, age . . . and, obviously, this protection includes homosexual persons although not in an explicit way. . . . Because of this, in my humble opinion, some day, should they decided to amend the Constitution, it would explicitly mention sexual orientation . . . I don't consider this urgent; I do believe, however, that our laws could be clearer, more explicit, about this issue, not only to protect these people from discrimination in public institutions but also within the family, because it is often there that the homosexual is first labeled as a transgressor.

One of the experiences most disorienting for the personality and mental health of the human being is to be rejected by his or her family, and this is especially the case when it occurs for reasons beyond the individual's control, that is to say because of sexual orientation.

Q: Why do you think that the gay community in Cuba has been unable to organize itself as happened in other countries to demand more social spaces and greater respect, among other claims?

A: I think the biggest difficulty is that there isn't a compelling and unifying [gay rights] project because homosexuals are as heterogeneous as heterosexuals. Nevertheless, I don't see in this situation a lack of capacity, but a complex reality. Also, it would require support from the rest of Cuban civil society, a society still deeply permeated by sexual prejudices.

But more than attempting to organize, I believe that gays and lesbians should try a strategy of greater social integration because "organizing" can also lead to a period of self-segregation, of isolation, and not stronger social ties and the acceptance of their sexual condition within society. I think that homosexuals should participate more in the spaces set aside for social and political discussions in Cuba, despite the prejudices, in order to reveal the truth about themselves, their legitimate needs for equality, their beliefs, and to seek out the support of the scientific community with the goal of introducing arguments that would serve to institute necessary and just social changes. I think that this strategy would have a greater effect and would be healthier.

Today, I think we have arrived at a very opportune moment in which persons of homosexual orientation can be better understood and better integrated into different sectors of our society.

4. LATIN AMERICA'S LEFT TURN

Perhaps the most striking political trend in Latin America in the first decade of the twenty-first century has been the resurgence of the political left throughout the region. Leftist politicians have been elected to the presidency in Argentina, Bolivia, Chile, Ecuador, Nicaragua, Paraguay, Peru, Uruguay, and Venezuela (and very nearly Mexico in 2006). In this selection, Jorge Castañeda, Mexico's former secretary of foreign relations (2000–2003), argues that this resurgence has two distinct faces: "right left" and "wrong left." A former leftist university professor and prominent public intellectual, Castañeda shows considerable sympathy for "responsible" leftists like Brazilian president Luiz Inácio Lula da Silva who have transcended their Marxist-Leninist origins and infatuation with Fidel Castro to reach an accommodation of sorts with global capitalism and the United States. (Castañeda was once a member of the Mexican Communist Party and authored a biography of Che Guevara.) In contrast, he has no use for "irresponsible" populists like Venezuela's Hugo Chávez who seek to maintain their power—in Castañeda's view—by bashing free trade agreements, multinational corporations, and U.S. foreign policy. Castañeda's division of Latin American leftists into good guys (former revolutionaries) and bad guys (old-time populists) is a bit simplistic—as many of the examples he includes here suggest—and unabashedly partisan. It does, however, provide a useful framework for understanding the historical complexity behind recent political trends in the region.

Jorge G. Castañeda, "Latin America's Left Turn," *Foreign Affairs* 85, no. 3 (May–June 2006): 28. Reprinted by permission of the Council on Foreign Affairs.

Just over a decade ago, Latin America seemed poised to begin a virtuous cycle of economic progress and improved democratic governance, overseen by a growing number of centrist technocratic governments. In Mexico, President Carlos Salinas de Gortari, buttressed by the passage of the North American Free Trade Agreement, was ready for his handpicked successor to win the next presidential election. Former Finance Minister Fernando Henrique Cardoso was about to beat out the radical labor leader Luiz Inácio Lula da Silva for the presidency of Brazil. Argentine President Carlos Menem had pegged the peso to the dollar and put his populist Peronist legacy behind him. And at the invitation of President Bill Clinton, Latin American leaders were preparing to gather in Miami for the Summit of the Americas, signaling an almost unprecedented convergence between the southern and northern halves of the Western Hemisphere.

What a difference ten years can make. Although the region has just enjoyed its best two years of economic growth in a long time and real threats to democratic rule are few and far between, the landscape today is transformed. Latin America is swerving left, and distinct backlashes are under way against the predominant trends of the last 15 years: free-market reforms, agreement with the United States on a number of issues, and the consolidation of representative democracy. This reaction is more politics than policy, and more nuanced than it may appear. But it is real.

Starting with Hugo Chávez's victory in Venezuela eight years ago . . . a wave of leaders, parties, and movements generically labeled "leftist" have swept into power in one Latin American country after another. After Chávez, it was Lula and the Workers' Party in Brazil, then Néstor Kirchner in Argentina and Tabaré Vázquez in Uruguay, and then, earlier this year, Evo Morales in Bolivia. [Editor's note: Since this article was written several new leftist presidents have come into power in Latin America including former Sandinista revolutionary leader Daniel Ortega in Nicaragua, Peronist Cristina Fernández de Kirchner (wife of Néstor Kirchner) in Argentina, APRA leader Alán García in Perú, "twenty-first century socialist" Rafael Correa in Ecuador, and former Roman Catholic bishop Fernando Lugo in Paraguay.]

The rest of the world has begun to take note of this left-wing resurgence, with concern and often more than a little hysteria. But understanding the reasons behind these developments requires recognizing that there is not one Latin American left today; there are two. One is modern, open-minded, reformist, and internationalist, and it springs, paradoxically, from the hard-core left of the past. The other, born of the great tradition of Latin American populism, is nationalist, strident, and close-minded. The first is well aware of its past mistakes (as well as those of its erstwhile role models in Cuba and the Soviet Union) and has changed accordingly. The second, unfortunately, has not.

The reasons for Latin America's turn to the left are not hard to discern. . . . The first [is] that the fall of the Soviet Union would help the Latin American left by removing its geopolitical stigma. Washington would no longer be able to accuse any left-of-center regime in the region of being a "Soviet beachhead" (as it had every such government since it fomented the overthrow of Jacobo Arbenz's administration in Guatemala in 1954); left-wing governments would no longer have to choose between the United States and the Soviet Union, because the latter had simply disappeared.

The second point [is] that regardless of the success or failure of economic reforms in the 1990s and the discrediting of traditional Latin American economic policies, Latin America's extreme inequality (Latin America is the world's most unequal region), poverty, and concentration of wealth, income, power, and opportunity meant that it would have to be governed from the left of center. The combination of inequality and democracy tends to cause a movement to the left everywhere. This was true in western Europe from the end of the nineteenth century until after World War II; it is true today in Latin America. The impoverished masses vote for the type of policies that, they hope, will make them less poor.

Third, the advent of widespread democratization and the consolidation of democratic elections as the only road to power would, sooner or later, lead to victories for the left—precisely because of the social, demographic, and ethnic configuration of the region. In other words, even without the other proximate causes, Latin America would almost certainly have tilted left.

This forecast became all the more certain once it became evident that the economic, social, and political reforms implemented in Latin America starting in the mid-1980s had not delivered on their promises. With the exception of Chile, which has been governed by a left-of-center coalition since 1989, the region has had singularly unimpressive economic growth rates. They remain well below those of the glory days of the region's development (1940–80) and also well below those of other developing nations—China, of course, but also India, Malaysia, Poland, and many others. Between 1940 and 1980, Brazil and Mexico, for example, averaged six percent growth per year; from 1980 to 2000, their growth rates were less than half that. Low growth rates have meant the persistence of dismal poverty, inequality, high unemployment, a lack of competitiveness, and poor infrastructure. Democracy, although welcomed and supported by broad swaths of Latin American societies, did little to eradicate the region's secular plagues: corruption, a weak or nonexistent rule of law, ineffective governance, and the concentration of power in the hands of a few. And despite hopes that relations with the United States would improve, they are worse today than at any other time in recent memory, including the 1960s (an era defined by conflicts over Cuba) and the 1980s (defined by the Central American wars and Ronald Reagan's "contras").

But many of us who rightly foretold the return of the left were at least partly wrong about the kind of left that would emerge. We thought—perhaps naively—that the *aggiornamento* of the left in Latin America would rapidly and neatly follow that of socialist parties in France and Spain and of New Labour in the United Kingdom. In a few cases, this occurred—Chile certainly, Brazil tenuously. But in many others, it did not.

One reason for our mistake was that the collapse of the Soviet Union did not bring about the collapse of its Latin American equivalent, Cuba, as many expected it would. Although the links and subordination of many left-wing parties to Havana have had few domestic electoral implications (and Washington has largely stopped caring anyway), the left's close ties to and emotional dependency on Fidel Castro became an almost insurmountable obstacle to its reconstruction on many issues. But the more fundamental explanation has to do with the roots of many of the movements that are now in power. Knowing where left-wing leaders and parties come from—in particular, which of the two strands of the left in Latin American history they are a part of—is critical to understanding who they are and where they are going.

The left—defined as that current of thought, politics, and policy that stresses social improvements over macroeconomic orthodoxy, egalitarian distribution of wealth over its creation, sovereignty over international cooperation, democracy (at least when in opposition, if not necessarily once in power) over governmental effectiveness—has followed two different paths in Latin America. One left sprang up out of the Communist International and the Bolshevik Revolution and has followed a path similar to that of the left in the rest of the world. The Chilean, Uruguayan, Brazilian, Salvadoran, and, before Castro's revolution, Cuban Communist Parties, for example, obtained significant shares of the popular vote at one point or another, participated in "popular front" or "national unity" governments in the 1930s and 1940s, established a solid presence in organized labor, and exercised significant influence in academic and intellectual circles.

By the late 1950s and early 1960s, however, these parties had lost most of their prestige and combativeness. Their corruption, submission to Moscow, accommodation with sitting governments, and assimilation by local power elites had largely discredited them in the eyes of the young and the radical. But the Cuban Revolution brought new life to this strain of the left. In time, groups descended from the old communist left fused with Havana-inspired guerrilla bands. There were certainly some tensions. Castro accused the leader of the Bolivian Communist Party of betraying Che Guevara and leading him to his death in Bolivia in 1967; the Uruguayan and Chilean Communist Parties (the region's strongest) never supported the local Castroist armed groups. Yet thanks to the passage of time, to Soviet and Cuban understanding, and to the sheer weight of repression generated by military coups across the hemisphere, the Castroists and Communists all came together—and they remain together today.

The origin of the other Latin American left is peculiarly Latin American. It arose out of the region's strange contribution to political science: good old-fashioned populism. Such populism has almost always been present almost everywhere in Latin America. It is frequently in power, or close to it. It claims as its founders historical icons of great mythical stature, from Peru's Víctor Raúl Haya de la Torre and Colombia's Jorge Gaitán (neither made it to office) to Mexico's Lázaro Cárdenas and Brazil's Getúlio Vargas, both foundational figures in their countries' twentieth-century history, and to Argentina's Juan Perón and Ecuador's José Velasco Ibarra. [Editor's note: See excerpts Haya de la Torre, Cárdenas, Vargas, and Perón.] The list is not exhaustive, but it is illustrative: many of these nations' founding-father equivalents were seen in their time and are still seen now as noble benefactors of the working class. They made their mark on their nations, and their followers continue to pay tribute to them. Among many of these countries' poor and dispossessed, they inspire respect, even adulation, to this day.

These populists are representative of a very different left—often virulently anticommunist, always authoritarian in one fashion or another, and much more interested in policy as an instrument for attaining and conserving power than in power as a tool for making policy. They did do things for the poor—Perón and Vargas mainly for the urban proletariat, Cárdenas for the Mexican peasantry—but they also created the corporatist structures that have since plagued the political systems, as well as the labor and peasant movements, in their countries. They nationalized large sectors of their countries' economies, extending well beyond the so-called commanding heights, by targeting everything in sight: oil (Cárdenas in Mexico), railroads (Perón in Argentina), steel (Vargas in Brazil), tin (Victor Paz Estenssoro in Bolivia), copper (Juan Velasco Alvarado in Peru). They tended to cut sweetheart deals with the budding local business sector, creating the proverbial crony capitalism that was decried much later. Their justifications for such steps were always superficially ideological (nationalism, economic development) but at bottom pragmatic: they needed money to give away but did not like taxes. They squared that circle by capturing natural-resource or monopoly rents, which allowed them to spend money on the *descamisados*, the "shirtless," without raising taxes on the middle class. When everything else fails, the thinking went, spend money.

The ideological corollary to this bizarre blend of inclusion of the excluded, macroeconomic folly, and political staying power (Perón was the dominant figure in Argentine politics from 1943 through his death in 1974, the Cárdenas dynasty is more present than ever in Mexican politics) was virulent, strident nationalism. Perón was elected president in 1946 with the slogan "Braden or Perón" (Spruille Braden was then the U.S. ambassador to Buenos Aires). When Vargas committed suicide in 1954, he darkly insinuated that he was a victim of American imperialism. Such nationalism was more than rhetorical. In regimes whose domestic policy platform was strictly power-driven and pragmatic, it was the agenda.

These two subspecies of the Latin American left have always had an uneasy relationship. On occasion they have worked together, but at other times they have been at war, as when Perón returned from exile in June 1973 and promptly massacred a fair share of the Argentine radical left. In some countries, the populist left simply devoured the other one, although peacefully and rather graciously: in Mexico in the late 1980s, the tiny Communist Party disappeared, and former PRI (Institutional Revolutionary Party) members, such as Cuauhtémoc Cárdenas, Porfirio Muñoz Ledo, and 2006 presidential candidate, Andrés Manuel López Obrador, took over everything from its buildings and finances to its congressional representation and relations with Cuba to form the left-wing PRD (Party of the Democratic Revolution).

More recently, something funny has happened to both kinds of leftist movements on their way back to power. The communist, socialist, and Castroist left, with a few exceptions, has been able to reconstruct itself, thanks largely to an acknowledgment of its failures and those of its erstwhile models. Meanwhile, the populist left—with an approach to power that depends on giving away money, a deep attachment to the nationalist fervor of another era, and no real domestic agenda—has remained true to itself. The latter perseveres in its cult of the past: it waxes nostalgic about the glory days of Peronism, the Mexican Revolution, and, needless to say, Castro. The former, familiar with its own mistakes, defeats, and tragedies, and keenly aware of the failures of the Soviet Union and Cuba, has changed its colors.

When the reformed communist left has reached office in recent years, its economic policies have been remarkably similar to those of its immediate predecessors, and its respect for democracy has proved full-fledged and sincere. Old-school anti-Americanism has been tempered by years of exile, realism, and resignation.

The best examples of the reconstructed, formerly radical left are to be found in Chile, Uruguay, and, to a slightly lesser extent, Brazil. This left emphasizes social policy—education, antipoverty programs, health care, housing—but within a more or less orthodox market framework. It usually attempts to deepen and broaden democratic institutions. On occasion, Latin America's age-old vices—corruption, a penchant for authoritarian rule—have led it astray. It disagrees with the United States frequently but rarely takes matters to the brink.

In Chile, former President Ricardo Lagos and his successor, Michelle Bachelet, both come from the old Socialist Party (Lagos from its moderate wing, Bachelet from the less temperate faction). Their left-wing party has governed for 16 consecutive years, in a fruitful alliance with the Christian Democrats. This alliance has made Chile a true model for the region. Under its stewardship, the country has enjoyed high rates of economic growth;

significant reductions in poverty; equally significant improvements in education, housing, and infrastructure; a slight drop in inequality; a deepening of democracy and the dismantling of Augusto Pinochet's political legacy; a settling of accounts (although not of scores) regarding human rights violations of the past; and, last but not at all least, a strong, mature relationship with the United States, including a free-trade agreement signed by George W. Bush and ratified by the U.S. Congress and Washington's support for the Chilean candidate to head the Organization of American States. U.S.-Chilean ties have continued to prosper despite Chile's unambiguous opposition to the U.S. invasion of Iraq in the UN Security Council in 2003.

In Uruguay, Vázquez ran for president twice before finally winning [in 2004]. His coalition has always been the same: the old Uruguayan Communist Party, the Socialist Party, and many former Marxist Tupamaro guerrillas, who made history in the 1960s and 1970s by, among other things, kidnapping and executing CIA station chief Dan Mitrione in Montevideo in 1970 and being featured in Costa-Gavras' 1973 film *State of Siege*. There was reason to expect Vázquez to follow a radical line once elected—but history once again trumped ideology. Although Vázquez has restored Uruguay's relations with Cuba and every now and then rails against neoliberalism and Bush, he has also negotiated an investment-protection agreement with the United States, sent his finance minister to Washington to explore the possibility of forging a free-trade agreement, and stood up to the "antiglobalization, politically correct" groups in neighboring Argentina on the construction of two enormous wood-pulp mills in the Uruguay River estuary. He refused to attend Morales' inauguration as president of Bolivia and has threatened to veto a bill legalizing abortion if it gets to his desk. His government is, on substance if not on rhetoric, as economically orthodox as any other. And with good reason: a country of 3.5 million inhabitants with the lowest poverty rate and the least inequality in Latin America should not mess with its relative success.

Brazil is a different story, but not a diametrically opposed one. Even before his inauguration in 2003, Lula had indicated that he would follow most of his predecessor's macroeconomic policies and comply with the fiscal and monetary targets agreed on with the International Monetary Fund (IMF). He has done so, achieving impressive results in economic stability (Brazil continues to generate a hefty fiscal surplus every year), but GDP growth has been disappointing, as have employment levels and social indicators. Lula has tried to compensate for his macroeconomic orthodoxy with innovative social initiatives (particularly his "Zero Hunger" drive and land reform). At the end of the day, however, perhaps his most important achievement on this front will be the generalization of the *Bolsa Família* (Family Fund) initiative, which was copied directly from the antipoverty program of Mexican Presidents Ernesto Zedillo and Vicente Fox. This is a successful, innovative welfare program, but as neoliberal and scantly revolutionary as one can get.

On foreign policy, Brazil, like just about every Latin American country, has had its run-ins with the Bush administration, over issues including trade, UN reform, and how to deal with Bolivia, Colombia, Cuba, and Venezuela. But perhaps the best metaphor for the current state of U.S.-Brazilian relations today was the scene in Brasilia last November, when Lula welcomed Bush at his home, while across the street demonstrators from his own party burned the U.S. president in effigy.

The Workers' Party, which Lula founded in 1980 after a long metalworkers' strike in the industrial outskirts of São Paulo, has largely followed him on the road toward social democracy. Many of the more radical cadres of the party, or at least those with the most radical histories (such as José Genoino and José Dirceu), have become moderate reformist leaders, despite their pasts and their lingering emotional devotion to Cuba. (Lula shares this devotion, and yet it has not led him to subservience to Castro: when Lula visited Havana in 2004, Castro wanted to hold a mass rally at the Plaza de la Revolución; instead, Castro got a 24-hour in-and-out visit from the Brazilian president, with almost no public exposure.) Lula and many of his comrades are emblematic of the transformation of the old, radical, guerrilla-based, Castroist or communist left. Granted, the conversion is not complete: the corruption scandals that have rocked Brazil's government have more to do with a certain neglect of democratic practices than with any personal attempt at enrichment. Still, the direction in which Lula and his allies are moving is clear.

Overall, this makeover of the radical left is good for Latin America. Given the region's inequality, poverty, still-weak democratic tradition, and unfinished nation building, this left offers precisely what is needed for good governance in the region. If Chile is any example, this left's path is the way out of poverty, authoritarian rule, and, eventually, inequality. This left is also a viable, sensitive, and sensible alternative to the other left—the one that speaks loudly but carries a very small social stick.

The leftist leaders who have arisen from a populist, nationalist past with few ideological underpinnings—Chávez with his military background, Kirchner with his Peronist roots, Morales with his coca-leaf growers' militancy and agitprop, López Obrador with his origins in the PRI—have proved much less responsive to modernizing influences. For them, rhetoric is more important than substance, and the fact of power is more important than its responsible exercise. The despair of poor constituencies is a tool rather than a challenge, and taunting the United States trumps promoting their countries' real interests in the world. The difference is obvious: Chávez is not Castro; he is Perón with oil. Morales is not an indigenous Che; he is a skillful and irresponsible populist. López Obrador is neither Lula nor Chávez; he comes straight from the PRI of Luis Echeverría, Mexico's president from 1970 to 1976, from which he learned how to be a cash-dispensing, authoritarian-inclined populist. Kirchner is a true-blue Peronist, and proud of it.

For all of these leaders, economic performance, democratic values, programmatic achievements, and good relations with the United States are not imperatives but bothersome constraints that miss the real point. They are more intent on maintaining popularity at any cost, picking as many fights as possible with Washington, and getting as much control as they can over sources of revenue, including oil, gas, and suspended foreign-debt payments.

Argentina's Kirchner is a classic (although somewhat ambiguous) case. Formerly the governor of a small province at the end of the world, he was elected in the midst of a monumental economic crisis and has managed to bring his country out of it quite effectively. Inflation has been relatively controlled, growth is back, and interest rates have fallen. Kirchner also renegotiated Argentina's huge foreign debt skillfully, if perhaps a bit too boldly. He has gone further than his predecessors in settling past grievances, particularly regarding the "dirty war" that the military and his Peronist colleagues waged in the 1970s. He has become a darling of the left and seems to be on a roll, with approval ratings of over 70 percent.

But despite the left-wing company he keeps, Kirchner is at his core a die-hard Peronist, much more interested in bashing his creditors and the IMF than in devising social policy, in combating the Free Trade Agreement of the Americas (FTAA) than in strengthening Mercosur, in cuddling up to Morales, Castro, and Chávez than in lowering the cost of importing gas from Bolivia. No one knows exactly what will happen when Argentina's commodity boom busts or when the country is forced to return to capital markets for fresh funds. Nor does anyone really know what Kirchner intends to do when his economic recovery runs out of steam. But it seems certain that the Peronist chromosomes in the country's DNA will remain dominant: Kirchner will hand out money, expropriate whatever is needed and available, and lash out at the United States and the IMF on every possible occasion. At the same time, he will worry little about the number of Argentines living under the poverty line and be as chummy with Chávez as he can.

Chávez is doing much the same in Venezuela. He is leading the fight against the FTAA, which is going nowhere anyway. He is making life increasingly miserable for foreign—above all American—companies. He is supporting, one way or the other, left-wing groups and leaders in many neighboring countries. He has established a strategic alliance with Havana that includes the presence of nearly 20,000 Cuban teachers, doctors, and cadres in Venezuela. He is flirting with Iran and Argentina on nuclear-technology issues. Most of all, he is attempting, with some success, to split the hemisphere into two camps: one pro-Chávez, one pro-American.

At the same time, Chávez is driving his country into the ground. A tragicomic symbol of this was the collapse of the highway from Caracas to the Maiquetía airport a few months ago because of lack of maintenance. Venezuela's poverty figures and human development indices have deteriorated since 1999, when Chávez took office. A simple comparison with Mexico—which has not exactly thrived in recent years—shows how badly Venezuela is faring. Over the past seven years, Mexico's economy grew by 17.5 percent, while Venezuela's failed to grow at all. From 1997 to 2003, Mexico's per capita GDP rose by 9.5 percent, while Venezuela's shrank by 45 percent. From 1998 to 2005, the Mexican peso lost 16 percent of its value, while the value of the Venezuelan bolivar dropped by 292 percent. Between 1998 and 2004, the number of Mexican households living in extreme poverty decreased by 49 percent, while the number of Venezuelan households in extreme poverty rose by 4.5 percent. In 2005, Mexico's inflation rate was estimated at 3.3 percent, the lowest in years, while Venezuela's was 16 percent.

Although Chávez does very little for the poor of his own country (among whom he remains popular), he is doing much more for other countries: giving oil away to Cuba and other Caribbean states, buying Argentina's debt, allegedly financing political campaigns in Bolivia and Peru and perhaps Mexico. He also frequently picks fights with [former Mexican president Vicente] Fox and Bush and is buying arms from Spain and Russia. This is about as close to traditional Latin American populism as one can get—and as far from a modern and socially minded left as one can be. . . .

What will prove most damaging is that the populist left loves power more than democracy, and it will fight to keep it at great cost. Its disregard for democracy and the rule of law is legendary. Often using democratic means, it has often sought to concentrate its power through new constitutions, take control of the media and the legislative and judicial branches of government, and perpetuate its rule by using electoral reforms, nepotism, and the suspension of constitutional guarantees. Chávez is the best example of this left, but certainly not the only one. . . .

This populist left has traditionally been disastrous for Latin America, and there is no reason to suppose it will stop being so in the future. As in the past, its rule will lead to inflation, greater poverty and inequality, and confrontation with Washington. It also threatens to roll back the region's most important achievement of recent years: the establishment of democratic rule and respect for human rights.

Distinguishing between these two broad left-wing currents is the best basis for serious policy, from Washington, Brussels, Mexico City, or anywhere else. There is not a tremendous amount Washington or any other government can actually do to alter the current course of events in Latin America. The Bush administration could make some difference by delivering on its promises to incumbents in the region (on matters such as immigration and trade), thereby supporting continuity without interfering in the electoral process; in South American nations where there is a strong European presence, countries such as France and Spain could help by pointing out that certain policies and attitudes have certain consequences.

But there is a much bolder course, a more statesmanlike approach, that would foster a "right left" instead of working to subvert any left's resurgence. This strategy would involve actively and substantively supporting the right left when it is in power: signing free-trade agreements with Chile, taking Brazil seriously as a trade interlocutor, engaging these nations' governments on issues involving third countries (such as Colombia, Cuba, and Venezuela), and bringing their leaders and public intellectuals into the fold. The right left should be able to show not only that there are no penalties for being what it is, but also that it can deliver concrete benefits.

The international community should also clarify what it expects from the "wrong left," given that it exists and that attempts to displace it would be not only morally unacceptable but also pragmatically ineffective. The first point to emphasize is that Latin American governments of any persuasion must abide by their countries' commitments regarding human rights and democracy. The region has built up an incipient scaffolding on these matters over recent years, and any backsliding, for whatever reason or purpose, should be met by a rebuke from the international community. The second point to stress is that all governments must continue to comply with the multilateral effort to build a new international legal order, one that addresses, among other things, the environment, indigenous people's rights, international criminal jurisdiction (despite Washington's continued rejection of the International Criminal Court and its pressure on several Latin American governments to do the same), nuclear nonproliferation, World Trade Organization rules and norms, regional agreements, and the fight against corruption, drug trafficking, and terrorism, consensually defined. Europe and the United States have enormous leverage in many of these countries. They should use it.

Finally, Washington and other governments should avoid the mistakes of the past. Some fights are simply not worth fighting: If Morales wants to squabble with Chile over access to the sea, with Argentina over the price of gas, with Peru over border issues and indigenous ancestry, stand aside. . . . If Chávez really wants to acquire nuclear technology from Argentina, let him, as long as he does it under International Atomic Energy Agency supervision and safeguards. Under no circumstances should anyone accept the division of the hemisphere into two camps—for the United States, against the United States—because under such a split, the Americas themselves always lose out. Such a division happened over Cuba in the 1960s and over Central America in the 1980s. Now that the Cold War is over, it should never happen again. So instead of arguing over whether to welcome or bemoan the advent of the left in Latin America, it would be wiser to separate the sensible from the irresponsible and to support the former and contain the latter. If done right, this would go a long way toward helping the region finally find its bearings and, as [Colombian novelist and Nobel Prize winner] Gabriel García Márquez might put it, end its hundreds of years of solitude.

5. WOMEN TAKE CHARGE

Michelle Bachelet became Chile's first female president in March 2006. Her father, a prominent general who supported Salvador Allende's socialist administration, was imprisoned and executed after Augusto Pinochet's military coup in September 1973. She and her mother were also arrested but were subsequently allowed to leave the country as political exiles. After returning to Chile in 1979, Bachelet actively opposed the military dictatorship but remained primarily committed to her work as a pediatrician. When democratic politics were restored in the early 1990s, she emerged as a rising figure in the Socialist Party. Her popularity grew by leaps and bounds during her tenure as health minister and then defense minister in the administration of President Ricardo Lagos (2000–2006). Bachelet succeeded Lagos as leader of the Concertación de Partidos por la Democracia, *the center-left coalition that has ruled Chile since 1989. Early in her tenure as president she faced a number of unexpected challenges, chief among them an unprecedented wave of student protests and a rocky start for the new transportation system in Santiago, Chile's capital city. In this interview, President Bachelet addresses these problems and shares her views on the challenges of being the country's first woman president.*

Q: Do you think *Concertación* retains its historical significance, something that keeps it alive after so many years in power?

A: Of course. I am proud to be part of the *Concertación*, proud of how it was born and what it has accomplished. This coalition has not only been successful from an electoral point of view—we have won fourteen elections!—it has also been socially efficient. We have changed the country in recent decades. Housing, education and consumer goods have expanded. Chilean men and women are better off. Inequality is still our main concern, but we have reduced it. . . . And if we add to the increase in families' real incomes the benefits of social policies, inequality diminishes even further. The *Concertación* has achieved the construction of a powerful majority that includes Social-Christians, Social-Democrats and Liberal Progressives, in support of its main project of transforming the neo-liberal matrix designed by the dictatorship. This long-term goal still unites us, and distinguishes us from the right. . . .

Q: There is a certain perception of disorder in state management, fueled by disputes within your Cabinet and the crisis of *Trasantiago* [Santiago's public transportation system]. Is this impression based on objective reality, or is it simply a result of the heat of political competition?

Michelle Bachelet, interview by Carlos Peña González, *El Mercurio*, August 8, 2007. Excerpt translated by the editors.

A: It is a mixture of all those things. It would be pointless to deny that *Trasantiago* was a severe problem, but I've already said all I had to say about it. I said it on national television: it was a mistake whose costs were paid by the weakest, a public policy mistake that contradicted all the goals of my administration. But those who were supposed to take responsibility did so, and today structural problems are being solved. All governments have problems, make mistakes, good or bad decisions. What is decisive is how they face those problems. As far as I am concerned, I assume my responsibilities in full view of my fellow citizens, and I have already proven that I make the changes that must be made. . . .

Q: And how do you respond to other criticism? I am referring to the lack of autonomy and power of your ministers. . . .

A: That criticism is based on false information. Each minister has clear tasks and responsibilities. And if one of them feels disempowered, it's a sign of his incapacity to perform his functions. Contrary to what certain analysts say, I see my ministers as fundamental advisors. The "second floor" that has also been mentioned [in these criticisms] does the follow-up work. It advises the President, but does not replace ministers.

Q: But these complaints come from your own team. . . .

A: If anyone says or feels this way, I can't help seeing it as an excuse. Those who claim they have not been empowered are lying. I have never ordered anyone not to do what they must do. Each minister has clearly-defined tasks and responsibilities. If anyone assumes or insinuates that he has been disempowered, it's because he lacks the leadership required by his position. I pray that you write it exactly as I say it. There are no ambiguities or lack of power regarding ministers. Nor distrust. Let me tell you that I am surprised at the analyses that one reads in the press. They portray me as a person full of grudges!

Q: Aren't you suspicious?

A: I am not suspicious. But I am realistic: I know who can be trusted and who cannot. By the way . . . no female minister has said that she feels disempowered. It's about gender and power.

Q: Do you perceive gender problems in this matter?

A: It could be that complaints about lack of autonomy are nothing more than symbolic resistance to a woman being in charge. It would not be the first time that analyses of my government have this bias.

Q: You seem resigned to it. . . .

A: No. I am a realist and I don't complain. It will be understood some day that female leadership is not linked with the capacity to make decisions, but rather to a certain style of doing so. I understand that in this respect I symbolize a cultural change of great proportions, an irreversible change. I don't know whether there will be another female president in the future. I hope so. But I am sure of one thing: in the past, girls told me they wanted to be doctors; and now they tell me they want to be president. This will be good for the country. Because I am aware that women's participation is not only fair, but also efficient, I am sponsoring a legal project to foster the participation of women in politics. This law will make more resources available for women's political activity and will generate incentives for those parties undertaking affirmative action.

Q: Gender remains very important to you. . . .

A: I have been very much impressed by gender bias. I am a medical doctor, and this has never been an issue in my profession. In politics, however, being a woman matters. Political parties are *machista* [aggressively male], there is great resistance to leadership being in the hands of a woman. I have experienced this. But I don't complain. It's a patriarchal culture. It would be foolish to deny it.

6. THE NEW POPULISM

Elected president of Bolivia in January 2006, Evo Morales is the first indigenous (Aymara) president in the history of this multicultural indigenous nation. The leader of the coca grower's union, Morales has long been involved in the struggle to protect the right to grow this traditional Aymara and Quechua crop, resisting U.S. pressure to eradicate it—a struggle that made him popular but also led to political persecution and confinement. As the leader of MAS (Movimiento al Socialismo), *Morales promised to reestablish state control over Bolivia's important energy reserves. In addition to strengthening ties with Venezuela and Cuba, he fulfilled this promise shortly after taking power. In this interview, ten months into his tenure as president, Morales describes (for an international audience) what his leadership means for Bolivian indigenous peoples, as he defends their legal and cultural integration in the national community. Inviting capitalist investors to be partners rather than bosses, he assesses the many challenges facing his nationalistic economic agenda and calls for the respect and goodwill of U.S. policies in the region.*

Q: Why did you bring a coca leaf to the United Nations?

A: First of all, thanks very much for the invitation to speak with you today. It's the first time I've been in these lands, the United States.

Evo Morales, interview by Amy Goodman and Juan González, *Democracy Now*, September 22, 2006. Morales's comments translated by the editors.

And as the coca leaf has been permanently accused of being a drug, I brought the leaf to show that coca is not cocaine. The coca leaf is green. It's not white; cocaine is white. So I came to show that the coca leaf is a natural agricultural product that can be beneficial to humanity. That's why I was there at the first ordinary session at the United Nations with a coca leaf. Had it been a drug, cocaine, I would certainly have been detained. We're starting the campaign to bring dignity back to the coca leaf, starting with its international decriminalization.

Q: How is it used for beneficial purposes? Why is it so important to you in Bolivia?

A: The coca leaf is part of culture. Its legal and traditional consumption, which is called the *piccheo* in Bolivia, the *chaccheo* in Peru, *el mambeo* in Colombia, is the traditional chewing of coca. Moreover, this traditional consumption is backed up by scientific research done in universities in Europe and the United States. Four or five years ago, a study came out of Harvard University reporting that it's very nutritious—it's a good source of nutrition, and it recommends not only chewing it, but also eating it. The last study done by the World Health Organization has demonstrated clearly that the coca leaf poses no threat to human health.

And there's also ritual use, including in the Aymara and Quechua cultures, for example, when you ask for someone's hand in marriage, the coca leaf plays an important part in that ritual. We could also talk about a number of pharmaceutical products that come or derive from the coca leaf. The first local anesthetics used in modern medicine were derived from the coca leaf. Up to some five, six, seven years ago, the Agua Exporters del Chapare, in Cochabamba [Morales's region of origin], used to buy coca to be exported for the making of Coca-Cola. And we can think of many industrial products derived from the coca leaf that are beneficial to humanity.

Q: Mr. President, in the United States voters are accustomed to leaders promising much, but when they get into office delivering very little. Since you have become President in Bolivia, you have moved rapidly to make changes. You've cut your own salary. You've raised the minimum wage by 50 percent. What is the message you are trying to send to your own people and to Latin American leaders in general?

A: I never wanted to be a politician. In my country, politicians are seen as liars, thieves, arrogant. In 1997 they tried to get me to run for president. I rejected that idea, even though that brought me problems with my own grassroots organizations—the coca growers of Chapare. I was later obligated to become a member of the lower house of parliament. I didn't want to do that at the time, either. I preferred to be the head of a rat than the tail of a horse. I preferred to be the head of my own union fighting for human rights and social rights, and not getting involved in electoral political processes and wind up not fulfilling promises.

But what I was learning in that period in '95, '96, '97 is that to get involved in politics means taking on the responsibility, a new way of looking at politics as serving the people, because politics means service. Serving the people, and not using the people. And after hearing the broad demands of the indigenous peasant movement and the popular movement, I decided to run for president.

For the last national elections, we had a ten-point program. And of those ten, we've fulfilled six already. In terms of the austerity measures that you mentioned a moment ago, I cut my own salary by more than 50 percent, as we cut the ministers' as well as the members of congress. That money has been redirected to health and education, convinced as I am that being president means serving the people. And we said we were going to do a consultation for a referendum on greater autonomy for the regions, and we've done that. Fifty-eight percent of the population said no to greater autonomy, although it is important to secure more autonomy for the regions and the indigenous communities.

We said we were going to nationalize the gas and oil sector. We did, without expropriating or excluding any of the companies. We said it's important to have partners but not bosses. And we followed this principle. The investor has the right to recoup his investment and make a reasonable profit, but we can't allow for sacking, where only the companies benefit, and not the state. I just came from a meeting with businessmen, and I am quite pleased with their proposals.

The struggle against corruption is a key issue in my country. We're starting that campaign aggressively, starting with members of the executive branch. The judicial branch still is not supportive of this process. And I can talk a lot about the other things we're doing to meet the demands that accumulated over time. For example, the centers for eye treatments and surgery, the literacy work that we're doing.

We've also made advances in terms of providing people with legal documents, something that often indigenous peoples don't have. These are the social problems that my family has experienced. My mother, for example, never had an ID. She didn't know when she was born. There's an anecdote about my father. One day I found his ID, and there was a birthdate on it. I said to my sister Esther, "Okay, let's have a party. We know what my father's birthday is." She was very happy. She said, "Yes, let's do this birthday party." We said to my father, "We're going to throw a party for you." And he said, "But I don't know what my birthday is." We showed him his ID, and we said,

"Here it is. Here's your birthday." And he said very bitterly, "I had to invent that date when I was drafted in the military." My father didn't know when he was born. And when I was in a big political rally in 1999 in the electoral campaign for the municipalities and I asked everybody there to raise their hand, "Who's going to vote?" About two-thirds of the people raised their hands. Another third didn't, and I said, "What's going on here? You're not going to vote for Evo Morales?" And they all said, "We don't have IDs." And one *compañero* came to me almost in tears. He said, "This society thinks I'm only useful for raising my hands or giving assent to something, but I'm not good enough to vote." He was from northern Potosí, from the highlands. He didn't know when he was born. He didn't have a birth certificate. These are the sorts of problems. But with the help of some countries, we're receiving support so we can give people documents to fully incorporate them as citizens. . . .

Q: What is your assessment of President Bush?

A: I hope that we can improve relations with Bush's government. We would like their support in these deep, peaceful, democratic transformations that we're pursuing. We hope that we can count on more systematic support in health programs, but especially that they can accept the structural transformations that the Bolivian people have demanded.

Indigenous cultures are cultures of dialogue and life, not cultures of war. I've said publicly and very respectfully that the United States and other countries should get their troops out of Iraq, because it's not acceptable that the invaded and the invaders continue to die, and especially the innocent. Conflicts should be discussed and debated in places like the United Nations. . . .

The indigenous movement lives in solidarity with fellow humans, and also in harmony with Mother Earth. And we're very worried about global warming that's creating water shortages. In the past we've seen the bodies of water that were up to certain levels are now declining. That means that in a very short time we're going to have very serious problems. Without light, we can live with oil lamps, but without water, we can't live. I was pleased to participate in a forum sponsored by ex-President Clinton yesterday, where a commission is studying these issues of global warming.

Q: I'd like to ask you, in many poor countries around the world, it is said that the most powerful official in the country is the U.S. ambassador. But in your campaign, you actually ran against not just the other opponents, but against the role of the U.S. embassy and the U.S. ambassador in Bolivia. What is the role that the United States has played historically not only in Bolivia but in Latin America, as far as you're concerned?

A: The arrogance of an ambassador or the arrogance of others, including a president, is always an error. This arrogance creates greater rebellion, greater resistance. In 2002, former U.S. ambassador to Bolivia, Manuel Rocha, said, "Don't vote for Evo Morales." And after that, people came out massively to vote for me. I said he was my best campaign chief. And a number of things were said when I came to the presidency: that international cooperation would be reduced, we would no longer have access to markets, and so on, when in fact I've come to the presidency and we've seen a lot more support from other governments. The U.S. embassy tried to criticize the military high command. I said, "That's not going to be changed. That's a sovereign decision." So in this respect, we have obvious differences, but we want to work out those differences. Even though we're an underdeveloped country, we're a sovereign country, a country with dignity. One of the advantages that we have is that we begin to return dignity to the country. The name Bolivia has been elevated. Our peoples need a strong sense of self-esteem. We want relations with all the countries to be based on mutual respect, relations of complementarity, balance, solidarity, and for now cooperation so that we can ensure the changes we're trying to achieve. . . .

Q: You've mentioned on several occasions your indigenous origins in your movement. Throughout Latin America now, five hundred years after the European conquest, the native peoples of Mexico, Peru, Colombia, Bolivia are taking a greater role politically. What is the importance of this movement to Latin America?

A: Those excluded for over five hundred years, exploited, and for a time condemned to extermination, also have the rights of any human being and any full citizen. I mentioned at the United Nations that thirty or forty years ago, my mother didn't have the right to walk through public spaces, on sidewalks, in public plazas. And there are some fascist and racist sectors in Santa Cruz who don't want those people to enter the fairgrounds today. This is a fair of agricultural producers, as well as cattlemen, and it's always been inaugurated by the president. Now they don't want this president, the Aymara president, inaugurating it. So there's this strong feeling of excluded people, discriminated people to unite, not for revenge or to oppress or to subordinate anybody but to recognize we have obligations that our rights be fully respected. The thinking of indigenous peoples is not that of exclusion. I can tell you about the experiences of the Aymara, the Quechua from the highlands and the valleys in Bolivia, of how they welcome people in, not exclude people. This is the sector that's been discriminated against. We've been called everything. We've been called animals. Manuel Rocha once called me the Andean Taliban. But we fundamentally want our rights to be respected. That's our struggle. . . .

7. CHALLENGING THE NATION-STATE

One of the most potent contemporary challenges to the nation-state in Latin America has come from indigenous rights organizations, especially in Andean and Central American countries with large Native American populations. Native resistance to genocide, domination, and exploitation has a long history that dates back to the Conquest era. In recent years, these long-standing grievances have coalesced around issues like territorial sovereignty, control of natural resources, and environmental degradation. In Ecuador, for example, an ongoing, widely publicized lawsuit against oil giant Chevron/Texaco by indigenous peoples from the Amazon region has helped raise political awareness among Native American groups and environmental organizations within Ecuador, throughout Latin America, and around the world. The political and social consequences of indigenous mobilizations like the Chevron lawsuit have been remarkable; protests sparked by Native American concerns and led by indigenous rights groups have even brought down governments in Ecuador and Bolivia. In this declaration from a 2008 international conference on indigenous peoples, plurinational nation-states, and water rights held in Quito, Ecuador, Native American groups from Ecuador, Colombia, Peru, Bolivia, Guatemala, Mexico, Chile, and Argentina voice their demands for a plurinational state in which indigenous cultures are accorded equal respect and indigenous peoples maintain sovereignty over their ancestral homelands, including a share of control over the extraction of natural resources like oil, minerals, and water—resources previously controlled solely by national governments and leased to international corporations like Chevron.

WE CONSIDER:

THAT the impoverished peoples of Latin America have been the object of domination, exploitation, and political, social, economic, and cultural exclusion while a minority, under the auspices of the mono-cultural Nation-States, have benefited from the riches of our lands.

THAT the peoples of Latin America are pushing ahead processes of profound change, demonstrating that "another world is possible" and that we are part of and a path towards this other world, a world in which human beings can live in harmony with Mother Nature. These processes are not easy; the hegemonic sectors of political and economic power that have run our countries seek to destabilize progressive governments and social organizations.

THAT neo-liberalism is not yet defeated and the social conflicts it has provoked are still active. Different neo-liberal governments have granted concessions to millions of *hectares* of land [1 hectar = 2.47 acres], without respect-

---

Confederación de Nacionalidades Indígenas del Ecuador (CONAIE), "Declaración final," Encuentro Internacional: Pueblos Indígenas, Estados Plurinacionales y Derecho al Agua, Quito, Ecuador, March 14, 2008. Excerpt translated by the editors.

ing ancestral territories, for exploitation by mining and oil companies, they have affected hundreds of rivers by allowing the construction of privately owned hydroelectric dams, [and] they have privatized basic services. All this has accomplished nothing but the destruction of national economies and bio-diversity, and it has generated thousands of social conflicts involving indigenous peoples, rural communities, and poor city dwellers.

THAT in the name of development [neoliberal governments] have permanently violated the rights of [indigenous] Nations and Peoples, rural communities, and the impoverished population of our countries, implanting foreign models imposed by multinational corporations who seek to appropriate national resources and concentrate wealth and, to achieve this purpose, introduce practices that persecute and criminalize social movements.

THAT the "powers that be" have refused to hear our voice and acknowledge our aspirations, this being the reason for the permanent confrontation and struggle of our peoples.

THAT at present, [Latin America] lives in an historical moment of great relevance, a moment of profound hope for the great majority of us who fight for the construction of a post-capitalist and post-colonial society, a society that promotes the good life passed down from generation to generation by our ancestors, a society that brings back the teachings of our ancestral peoples, [a moment of profound hope that we] can live in harmony [and] with justice.

WE CONCLUDE that the concept of a Plurinational State is a viable policy proposal for our countries, that derives from the recognition of the diversity of Nationalities, peoples, and cultures, that values them and promotes them, and that seeks unity in diversity, generating intercultural relations that will permit us to build a common future for all.

WE DEFEND the proposal of the Plurinational State because it is the most democratic way to resolve the historical problems that plague our countries, since it is a new form of political, economic, territorial, juridical, cultural, and administrative organization for the State, [proposed] in the spirit of intercultural and direct democracy, equity, and economic justice.

WE PROMOTE a true unity of Latin American peoples and their struggles based on mutual respect and active solidarity as a way to reach the objectives that we have set out; founding a model of justice and equality, a model of plurinational democracy.

WE DEMAND the reversion of all mineral concessions to the State. We oppose medium and large-scale mining and [demand] that the concessions for small-scale artisanal mining be strictly regulated and limited. [We demand] support for agricultural and environmental recuperation of the areas degraded by mining.

WE DEMAND the reversion of private hydroelectric concessions because they are prejudicial to the State and have violated the right to free assembly, the principle of prior consultation, and have ignored collective rights, putting at risk the national food supply by privatizing lands and biodiversity (fragile ecosystems, sources of water, rivers), as well as threatening the integrity of communal lands and territories.

WE DEFEND the legitimacy and legality of the people's struggles in defense of their collective and individual rights, just as we denounce their criminalization.

WE SUPPORT the struggle of . . . all the indigenous movements of the continent in defense of their territories, their natural resources, and their cultural forms. And we reject any attempt on the part of imperialism or its local agents to classify these groups as terrorist organizations and we will be vigilant so that they are not persecuted through accusations of this type.

WE REJECT the carrying out of free trade agreements and treaties . . . that try to impose development models that are foreign to our national realities and that violate the rights of the poorest populations.

WE REJECT the Initiatives of Regional Integration based solely on the market, just as we denounce infrastructure schemes . . . whose only objective is the continued extraction of the wealth of our region to benefit capitalist accumulation in the North [i.e., United States, western Europe, Japan, etc.] and by its national lackeys.

WE REJECT policies that foster agribusiness and the monopolization of lands and water. We oppose the dedication of lands to mono-crop agriculture.

These are the voices of the organizations of indigenous peoples and rural workers of the continent that take part in the struggle for the future of *SUMACK KAWSAY* [the good life] for all men and women.

18

∽

THE TWO AMERICAS

A FEELING OF GREAT ADMIRATION characterized the attitude of Latin American leaders toward Great Britain and especially the United States from the era of independence to the closing years of the nineteenth century. That feeling, explains the Mexican philosopher Leopoldo Zea, "derived from the negative attitude of the Latin American toward his own historical and cultural heritage." But in the case of some, notably among Mexicans, the sentiment of admiration was tempered by resentment and misgivings about past and prospective territorial losses to the young colossus of the north. Others, like the Chilean Francisco Bilbao, already questioned the North American scale of values, setting the Latin love of beauty and spiritual values against alleged Yankee materialism and egotism.

After 1890 the increasingly aggressive foreign policy of the United States toward some of its southern neighbors rapidly depleted the Latin American reservoir of goodwill toward the republic of the north. The Yankeemania of Domingo Faustine Sarmiento turned into Yankeephobia on the part of many Latin American intellectuals. The transition in attitude was strikingly revealed in the writings of José Martí, epic chronicler of the United States from 1880 to 1895, whose reportage, long favorable to the United States, grew increasingly hostile toward the end of his journalistic career (see Chapter 14).

Latin American ill will toward the United States, elicited by many North American acts of intervention, reached a climax in the 1920s. Official awareness of the adverse economic and political effects of this hostility, as well as pressure from an aroused U.S. public, brought a gradual revision of policy toward Latin America and flowered into the Good Neighbor policy under Franklin Delano Roosevelt. Between 1933 and 1945 the old one-sided treaties were abrogated, the right of intervention was completely abandoned, and economic and cultural relations were greatly expanded. The Good Neighbor policy proved its value during the critical years of World War II.

However, in the years that followed the war, rifts began to appear in the New World alliance. Dissatisfaction with U.S. foreign economic policy was one source of friction between the erstwhile good neighbors. Latin American leaders resented the position taken by both the Truman and Eisenhower administrations that Latin American developmental loans must be financed for the most part by private capital rather than intergovernmental loans. A rising wave of nationalism opposed to all foreign-owned enterprises in the area added to U.S. difficulties in Latin America.

Moreover, many Latin Americans accused the United States of supporting right-wing dictatorial regimes, like those of Trujillo in the Dominican Republic and Batista in Cuba that oppressed their own peoples but protected the interests of foreign investors. The same critics charged that the U.S. government and North American business interests sometimes connived with reactionary local groups to destroy Latin American governments seeking to carry out necessary reforms. Widespread accusations of "intervention" and "Yankee imperialism" were raised in Latin America when the Arbenz regime in Guatemala, having launched a sweeping agrarian reform, was overthrown in 1954 by a revolt that received encouragement and assistance from the United States. Protesters were not impressed by U.S. assurances that the Arbenz regime had been "communist-dominated."

The hostile demonstrations against Vice President Richard Nixon during his visit to Latin America in 1958, the riotous outbreaks in the Panama Canal Zone in 1959, and the break in diplomatic relations between Cuba and the United States early in 1961 indicated how far relations between the two Americas had fallen. In April 1961, a force of counter-revolutionary exiles was defeated as it attempted to invade Cuba—an invasion organized by and prepared with the aid of the U.S. Central Intelligence Agency—plunging U.S. prestige in Latin America to new depths. In an apparent response to the threat of yet another and more powerful invasion from the United States, Castro invited the placement of Soviet ballistic missiles in Cuba. World peace hung by a thread in October 1962 when President Kennedy imposed a blockade of Cuba in order to end the buildup of Soviet missile bases on the island. The crisis ended with a compromise: the Soviets agreed to remove their missiles in return for a pledge by the United States not to invade Cuba.

Meanwhile the Kennedy administration had responded to the Cuban challenge by launching the Alliance for Progress, a program that combined large-scale outside aid for Latin America with massive projects of internal reform. But a decade later the program was almost universally pronounced a failure. Following the assassination of President Kennedy in November 1963, Vice President Lyndon Johnson became president and appeared to signal a shift toward a tougher Latin American policy, stressing cooperation with conservative and militarist elements in Latin America to maintain the status quo. In April 1965, President Johnson dispatched a force of marines to the Dominican Republic, allegedly to assist in the safe evacuation of U.S. and other foreign nationals. Critics pointed out that the U.S. intervention effectively served to frustrate the efforts of rebels to overthrow a ruling military junta and return the reform-minded former president Juan Bosch to power. The result was a new wave of anger and bitterness toward the United States in the Dominican Republic and throughout Latin America. The election of Richard Nixon to the presidency portended no basic change in U.S. Latin American policy, as evident from the Rockefeller Report (1969), with its stress on giving support to Latin American police and military forces in their struggle against "subversion."

Under President Jimmy Carter (1977–1981) there was a softening of the Republican hard line toward Latin America, reflected in his stress on human rights issues in dealing with Chile, Argentina, and Brazil, countries whose governments were among the worst violators of human rights. This softening also was reflected in Carter's tentative efforts to reach an accommodation with the new Sandinista government of Nicaragua. In both areas, however, Carter's posture was fluctuating, uncertain. Under his successor, Ronald Reagan (1981–1989), the hard line toward Latin America regained full ascendancy. The undeclared covert war against Sandinista Nicaragua, the invasion of the tiny Caribbean island of Grenada in 1983 on security grounds that were clearly specious, and the decision to support a NATO ally, Great Britain, against Argentina in the 1982 Malvinas-Falklands War were among the major Latin American policy decisions of the Reagan administration. The same hard line was pursued by President George H. W. Bush (1989–1993) against Sandinista Nicaragua and against the Panamanian ruler Manuel Noriega when he displayed an inconvenient independence and ceased to be "our man in Panama." The invasion of Panama in December 1989, resulting in the loss of thousands of Panamanian lives and the capture of Noriega, appeared to mark a return to the discredited policies of gunboat diplomacy.

The Latin American policy of President Bill Clinton (1993–2001) can be summed up as more of the same. Clinton's stand on a series of issues reflected the essential continuity of the Reagan-Bush Latin American policy. The Reagan and Bush administrations, using the massive Latin American foreign debt as a weapon of coercion and enlisting the cooperation of local elites, had imposed on the area a neoliberal economic system based on free trade, austerity, and privatization of state enterprises that nullified the area's past advances toward economic independence and caused large increases in poverty. The logical next step was incorporating the area into a Western Hemisphere common market that would aid the United States in its competition with Japan and the European Community. This was the meaning of the North American Free Trade Agreement (NAFTA) with Canada and Mexico, negotiated by Bush and pushed through Congress by Clinton over the virtually unanimous opposition of the labor movement, which feared a heavy loss of domestic jobs. The same essential continuity was reflected in Clinton's hard-line stand toward Cuba and his pressure on President Jean-Bertrand Aristide of Haiti, ousted by military plotters in 1991, to accept a return to power in 1994 under the control of U.S. intervention forces.

George W. Bush's presidency (2001–2009) saw a further intensification of these trends in U.S. Latin American policy with an escalating regional drug war, especially in Colombia and Mexico, clumsy meddling in Venezuelan politics, further isolation of Castro's Cuba, and a hardening of neoliberal economic policies. But while Clinton was a relatively popular figure in Latin America (during a period of economic growth), the Bush administration's tough talk on these and other issues provoked considerable outrage in the region and dampened the sympathy generated by the September 11, 2001, terrorist attacks on the United States. In recent years, unsuccessful efforts to weaken leftist governments in the region, especially the populist/socialist regime of Hugo Chávez in Venezuela, have done nothing to allay long-standing suspicions about U.S. intentions.

Meanwhile, new light has recently been shed on the darker side of U.S. policy in Latin America. We now know, for example, that the CIA cooperated with Contra drug traffickers during the secret U.S. war against the Sandinistas. After the overthrow and flight of the dictator Alfredo Stroessner, a vast cache of documents—known to Paraguayans as "the archives of terror"—was unearthed in Asunción, Paraguay. The documents illuminate the U.S. role in Operation Condor, a secret plan among the security forces of six military dictatorships, initiated in 1975 by General Manuel Contreras of Chile, to destroy left-wing dissent in their countries. The plan allowed security forces of the six nations to pursue their targets across borders. The *New York Times* (August 11, 1999) commented that the archives, although "sanitized," suggest "that U.S. officials backed Condor nations not only with military aid but with information" concerning the individuals they pursued. A State Department spokesman shrugged off inquiries on the subject, claiming it was "ancient history." Ancient history or not, ongoing efforts to bring former national security adviser and secretary of state Henry Kissinger before an international tribunal for crimes against humanity, along with the work of national "truth and reconciliation" projects, have kept current the issue of U.S. complicity in political repression in the region. If this weren't enough, the same pattern is evident in present U.S. "drug war" policy toward Colombia, the third-largest recipient of U.S. military and financial aid, a country whose military and security forces are notorious for human rights violations.

1. THE VISION OF BOLÍVAR

Bolívar's most grandiose political conception was a league of friendship and mutual assistance uniting all the Latin American states under the leadership and protection of Great Britain. To achieve this project, Bolívar invited these and other nations to a

congress held in Panama in 1826. In the end this assembly proved an almost total fail-
ure. On the eve of the meeting Bolívar wrote down a statement of the advantages to be
gained from the proposed confederacy. This document suggests that fear of the Holy
Alliance, on the one hand, and of black and Indian insurrections, on the other, partly
influenced Bolívar's decision to summon the Congress of Panama.

The Congress of Panama will bring together all the representatives of America and a diplomat-agent of His Britannic Majesty's government. This Congress seems destined to form a league more extensive, more remarkable, and more powerful than any that has ever existed on the face of the earth. Should Great Britain agree to join it as a constituent member, the Holy Alliance will be less powerful than this confederation. Mankind will a thousand times bless this league for promoting its general welfare, and America, as well as Great Britain, will reap from it untold benefits. A code of public law to regulate the international conduct of political bodies will be one of its products.

1. The New World would consist of independent nations, bound together by a common set of laws which would govern their foreign relations and afford them a right to survival through a general and permanent congress.
2. The existence of these new states would receive fresh guarantees.
3. In deference to England, Spain would make peace, and the Holy Alliance would grant recognition to these infant nations.
4. Domestic control would be preserved untouched among the states and within each of them.
5. No one of them would be weaker than another, nor would any be stronger.
6. A perfect balance would be established by this truly new order of things.
7. The power of all would come to the aid of any one state which might suffer at the hands of a foreign enemy or from internal anarchic factions.
8. Differences of origin and color would lose their influence and power.
9. America would have nothing more to fear from that tremendous monster who has devoured the island of Santo Domingo, nor would she have cause to fear the numerical preponderance of the aborigines.
10. In short, a social reform would be achieved under the blessed auspices of freedom and peace, but the fulcrum controlling the beam of the scales must necessarily rest in the hands of England.

Simón Bolívar, *The Selected Writings of Bolívar*, comp. Vicente Lecuna, ed. Harold A. Bierck Jr., trans. Lewis Betrand, 2 vols. (New York: Colonial Press, 1951), 2:561–562. Reprinted by permission of the Banco de Venezuela.

Great Britain would, of course, derive considerable advantage from this arrangement.

1. Her influence in Europe would progressively increase, and her decisions would be like those of destiny itself.
2. America would serve her as an opulent domain of commerce.
3. America would become the center of England's relations with Asia and Europe.
4. British subjects in America would be considered the equals of American citizens.
5. The relations between England and America would in time become those between equals.
6. British characteristics and customs would be adopted by the Americans as standards for their future way of life.
7. In the course of the centuries, there might, perhaps, come to exist one single nation throughout the world—a federal nation.

These ideas are in the minds of many Americans in positions of importance who impatiently await the inauguration of this project at the Congress of Panama, which may afford the occasion to consummate the union of the new states and the British Empire. . . .

2. THE UNITED STATES AS MODEL

Latin American leaders in the nineteenth century, seeking to orient their countries in new and progressive directions, regarded the United States and England as their models. None expressed such passionate attachment for the United States and its institutions as did future Argentine president Domingo Sarmiento, who visited this country in 1847 and again (as Argentine foreign minister) in 1865–1868. The following selection is from his Travels in France, Africa, and America.

Europeans and even South Americans accuse the Yankees of many character flaws. For my part, I look with admiration on these very defects, attributing them to the human race, the times, hereditary predispositions, and the imperfection of the mind. A people composed of all the peoples of the world, as free as consciousness, as free as the air, and without teachers, armies, or prisons, is the product of all human antecedents, Europeans and Christians.

Domingo F. Sarmiento, *Obras de D. F. Sarmiento*, vol. 5, *Viajes por Europa, Africa i América, 1845–1847* (Santiago de Chile: Imprenta Gutenberg, 1886), pp. 361–362. Excerpt translated by the editors.

Their defects, then, must be those of the human race at any given period of its development. But as a nation, the United States is the end result of human logic. They have no kings, nobles, privileged classes, men born to command, or human machines born to obey. Is not this the result of ideas of justice and equality which Christianity accepts in theory? Well-being is more widely distributed [in the United States] than among any other people; population increases at an unparalleled rate; production makes astounding progress. Are these the result of freedom of action and lack of government as Europeans assert? They say that the ready availability of land is the cause of all this prosperity. But why, in South America, where land is just as readily available, or even more so, are neither population nor wealth on the increase, and [why are] cities and even capitals so stagnant that not a hundred new houses have been built in the past ten years? No census has yet been taken on the mental capacity of any nation's residents. Population is counted by number of inhabitants, and, from such figures, the strength and rank of a nation are deduced. Perhaps for war, which sees man as an engine of destruction, such statistical data might be significant, but one peculiarity of the United States invalidates even this calculation. When it comes to killing, one Yankee is worth many men of other nationalities, and therefore the destructive capacity of the United States can be estimated at two hundred million people. The rifle is the national weapon, target shooting is child's play in the forest states, and the practice of knocking squirrels out of trees by shooting their feet off so as not to injure the pelt, produces an astonishing dexterity which all acquire.

Statistics for the United States show that the number of adult males corresponds to a population of twenty million inhabitants: all of them educated, able to read and write, and enjoying political rights, with exceptions that only serve to prove the rule. [The typical Yankee is] the man who owns a home or who is certain to own one someday; the man who is beyond the reach of hunger and despair; the man who can hope for any future that his imagination can conjure up; the man endowed with political understanding and political needs; the man, in sum, who is his own master, who possesses a mind elevated by education and a sense of his own dignity. They say that man is a rational being, and thus capable of the acquisition and exercise of reason; in this sense no other country on earth can count on a greater number of rational beings, even with ten times the inhabitants.

3. THE MONROE DOCTRINE

In the early nineteenth century, the political and economic power of the United States was still relatively modest by international standards. At the time, the initial appearance of the Monroe Doctrine in President James Monroe's annual message to Congress on December 2, 1823, was little more than wishful thinking. Nevertheless, the tacit

support of Great Britain and its powerful navy likely hindered efforts by Spain, Por-
tugal, and France to retake their former colonies, even if it couldn't halt those efforts
altogether. As U.S. power grew, however, the Monroe Doctrine became increasingly
significant for Latin America in two ways. First, it continued to discourage European
colonial expansion in the region. Second, it reminded Latin American countries of
their supposed dependency on U.S. tutelage—a dependency implied in the persistently
unilateral approach the United States takes regarding hemispheric affairs.

At the proposal of the Russian Imperial Government, made through the minister of the Emperor residing here, a full power and instructions have been transmitted to the minister of the United States at St. Petersburg to arrange by amicable negotiation the respective rights and interests of the two nations on the northwest coast of this continent. A similar proposal has been made by His Imperial Majesty to the Government of Great Britain, which has likewise been acceded to. The Government of the United States has been desirous by this friendly proceeding of manifesting the great value which they have invariably attached to the friendship of the Emperor and their solicitude to cultivate the best understanding with his Government. In the discussions to which this interest has given rise and in the arrangements by which they may terminate the occasion has been judged proper for asserting, as a principle in which the rights and interests of the United States are involved, that the American continents, by the free and independent condition which they have assumed and maintain, are henceforth not to be considered as subjects for future colonization by any European powers. . . .

. . . In the wars of the European powers in matters relating to themselves we have never taken any part, nor does it comport with our policy to do so. It is only when our rights are invaded or seriously menaced that we resent injuries or make preparation for our defense. With the movements in this hemisphere we are of necessity more immediately connected, and by causes which must be obvious to all enlightened and impartial observers. The political system of the allied powers is essentially different in this respect from that of America. This difference proceeds from that which exists in their respective Governments; and to the defense of our own, which has been achieved by the loss of so much blood and treasure, and matured by the wisdom of their most enlightened citizens, and under which we have enjoyed unexampled felicity, this whole nation is devoted. We owe it, therefore, to candor and to the amicable relations existing between the United States and those powers to declare that we should consider any attempt on their part to extend their system to any portion of this hemisphere as dangerous to our peace and safety. With the existing colonies or dependencies of any European power we have not interfered and shall not interfere. But with the Govern-

President James Monroe, Annual Message to Congress, December 2, 1823.

ments who have declared their independence and maintain it, and whose independence we have, on great consideration and on just principles, acknowledged, we could not view any interposition for the purpose of oppressing them, or controlling in any other manner their destiny, by any European power in any other light than as the manifestation of an unfriendly disposition toward the United States. In the war between those new Governments and Spain we declared our neutrality at the time of their recognition, and to this we have adhered, and shall continue to adhere, provided no change shall occur which, in the judgment of the competent authorities of this Government, shall make a corresponding change on the part of the United States indispensable to their security.

The late events in Spain and Portugal show that Europe is still unsettled. Of this important fact no stronger proof can be adduced than that the allied powers should have thought it proper, on any principle satisfactory to themselves, to have interposed by force in the internal concerns of Spain. To what extent such interposition may be carried, on the same principle, is a question in which all independent powers whose governments differ from theirs are interested, even those most remote, and surely none of them more so than the United States. Our policy in regard to Europe, which was adopted at an early stage of the wars which have so long agitated that quarter of the globe, nevertheless remains the same, which is, not to interfere in the internal concerns of any of its powers; to consider the government de facto as the legitimate government for us; to cultivate friendly relations with it, and to preserve those relations by a frank, firm, and manly policy, meeting in all instances the just claims of every power, submitting to injuries from none. But in regard to those continents circumstances are eminently and conspicuously different. It is impossible that the allied powers should extend their political system to any portion of either continent without endangering our peace and happiness; nor can anyone believe that our southern brethren, if left to themselves, would adopt it of their own accord. It is equally impossible, therefore, that we should behold such interposition in any form with indifference. If we look to the comparative strength and resources of Spain and those new Governments, and their distance from each other, it must be obvious that she can never subdue them. It is still the true policy of the United States to leave the parties to themselves, in hope that other powers will pursue the same course. . . .

4. THE TWO AMERICAS

The Chilean writer Francisco Bilbao, though not unmindful of the achievements of North American democracy, called attention to certain defects in the North American character and sounded the alarm against U.S. expansionist designs on Latin America. Bilbao wrote the following lines at a time (1856) of aggressive North American

diplomacy and filibustering expeditions designed to secure Cuba, Central America,
and portions of Mexico for the United States.

Today we behold empires reviving the ancient idea of world domination. The Russian Empire and the United States, two powers situated at the geographical as well as political extremes, aspire, the one to extend Russian slavery under the mask of Pan-Slavism, the other to secure the sway of Yankee individualism. Russia is very far away, the United States is near. Russia sheathes its claws, trusting in its crafty snares; but the United States daily extends its claws in the hunting expedition that it has begun against the South. Already we see fragments of America falling into the jaws of the Saxon boa that hypnotizes its foes as it unfolds its tortuous coils. First it was Texas, then it was Northern Mexico and the Pacific that hailed a new master.

Today the skirmishers of the North are awakening the Isthmus with their shots, and we see Panama, that future Constantinople of America, doubtfully suspended over the abyss and asking itself: Shall I belong to the South or to the North?

There is the danger. Whoever fails to see it, renounces the future. Is there so little self-awareness among us, so little confidence in the intelligence of the Latin American race, that we must wait for an alien will and an alien intellect to organize us and decide our fate? Are we so poorly endowed with the gifts of personality that we must surrender our own initiative and believe only in the foreign, hostile, and even overbearing initiative of individualism?

I do not believe it, but the hour for action has arrived.

This is the historic moment of South American unity; the second campaign, that will add the association of our peoples to the winning of independence, has begun. Its motive is the danger to our independence and the threat of the disappearance of the initiative of our race. . . .

The United States of South America has sighted the smoke of the campfires of the United States. Already we hear the tread of the young colossus that with its diplomacy, with that swarm of adventurers that it casts about like seed, with its growing power and influence that hypnotize its neighbors, with its intrigues among our peoples, with its treaties, mediations, and protectorates, with its industry, its merchant marine, its enterprises—quick to note our weaknesses and our weariness, quick to take advantage of the divisions among our republics, ever more impetuous and audacious, having the same faith in its imperial destiny as did Rome, infatuated with its unbroken string of successes—that youthful colossus advances like a rising tide that rears up its waters to fall like a cataract upon the South.

Francisco Bilbao, *América en peligro* (Santiago de Child, 1941), pp. 144–154. Excerpt translated by Benjamin Keen.

The name of the United States—our contemporary, but one that has left us so far behind—already resounds throughout the world. The sons of Penn and Washington opened a new historical epoch when, assembled in Congress, they proclaimed the greatest and most beautiful of all existing Constitutions, even before the French Revolution.

Then they caused rejoicing on the part of sorrowing humanity, which from its torture-bed hailed the Atlantic Republic as an augury of Europe's regeneration. Free thought, self-government, moral freedom, and land open to the immigrant, were the causes of its growth and its glory. It was the refuge of those who sought an end to their misery, of all who fled the theocratic and feudal slavery of Europe; it provided a field for utopias, for all experiments; in short, it was a temple for all who sought free lands for free souls.

That was the heroic moment of its annals. All grew: wealth, population, power, and liberty. They leveled the forests, peopled the deserts, sailed all the seas. Scorning tradition and systems, and creating a spirit that devours space and time, they formed a nation, a particular genius. And turning upon themselves and beholding themselves so great, they fell into the temptation of the Titans. They believed they were the arbiters of the earth, and even rivals of Olympus.

Personality infatuated with itself degenerates into individualism; exaggeration of personality turns into egotism; and from there to injustice and callousness is but a step. They would concentrate the universe in themselves. The Yankee replaces the American; Roman patriotism, philosophy; industry, charity; wealth, morality; and self-interest, justice. They have not abolished slavery in their States; they have not preserved the heroic Indian races—nor have they made themselves champions of the universal cause, but only of the American interest, of Saxon individualism. They hurl themselves upon the South, and the nation that should have been our star, our model, our strength, daily becomes a greater threat to the independence of South America.

Here is a providential fact that spurs us to enter upon the stage of history, and this we cannot do if we are not united.

What shall be our arms, our tactics? We who seek unity shall incorporate in our education the vital elements contained in the civilization of the North. Let us strive to form as complete a human entity as possible, developing all the qualities that constitute the beauty or strength of other peoples. They are different but not antagonistic manifestations of human activity. To unite them, associate them, to give them unity, is our obligation.

Science and industry, art and politics, philosophy and Nature should march in a common front, just as all the elements that compose sovereignty should live inseparable and indivisible in a people: labor, association, obedience, and sovereignty.

For that reason let us not scorn, let us rather incorporate in ourselves all that shines in the genius and life of North America. Let us not despise under the pretext of individualism all that forms the strength of the race.

When the Romans wished to form a navy, they took a Carthaginian ship for their model; they replaced their sword with that of Spain; they made their own the science, the philosophy, and the art of the Greeks without surrendering their own genius; they raised a temple to the gods of the very peoples that they fought, as if in order to assimilate the genius of all races and the power of all ideas. In the same way should we grasp the Yankee axe in order to clear the earth; we should curb our anarchy with liberty, the only Hercules capable of overcoming that hydra; we should destroy despotism with liberty, the only Brutus capable of extinguishing all tyrants. And the North possesses all this because it is free, because it governs itself, because above all sects and religions there is a single common and dominant principle: freedom of thought and the government of the people.

Among them there is no State religion because the religion of the State is the State: the sovereignty of the people. That spirit, those elements, we should add to our own characteristics. . . .

Let us not fear movement. Let us breathe in the powerful aura that emanates from the resplendent star-spangled banner, let us feel our blood seething with the germination of new enterprises; let us hear our silent regions resounding with the din of rising cities, of immigrants attracted by liberty; and in the squares and woods, the schools and congresses, let the cry be repeated with all the force of hope: forward, forward! . . .

We know the glories and even the superiority of the North, but we too have something to place in the scales of justice.

We can say to the North:

Everything has favored you. You are the sons of the first men of modern Europe, of those heroes of the Reformation who crossed the great waters, bringing the Old Testament, to raise an altar to the God of conscience. A knightly though savage race received you with primitive hospitality. A fruitful nature and an infinite expanse of virgin lands multiplied your efforts. You were born and reared in the wooded fields, fired with the enthusiasm of a new faith, enlightened through the press, through freedom of speech—and your efforts were rewarded with abundance.

You received a matchless education in the theory and practice of sovereignty, far from kings, being yourselves all kings, far from the sickly castes of Europe, from their habits of servility and their domesticated manners; you grew with all the vigor of a new creation. You were free; you wished to be independent and you made yourselves independent. Albion [Great Britain] fell back before the Plutarchian heroes that made of you the greatest federation in history. It was not so with us.

Isolated from the universe, without other light than that which the cemetery of the Escorial [Spain's imperial palace] permitted, without other human voice than that of blind obedience, pronounced by the militia of the Pope, the friars, and by the militia of the kings, the soldiers—thus were we educated. We grew in silence, and regarded each other with terror.

A gravestone was placed over the continent, and upon it they laid the weight of eighteen centuries of slavery and decadence. And withal there was word, there was light in those gloomy depths; and we shattered the sepulchral stone, and cast those centuries into the grave that had been destined for us. Such was the power of the impulse, the inspiration or revelation, of the Republic.

With such antecedents, this result merits being placed in the balance with North America.

We immediately had to organize everything. We have had to consecrate the sovereignty of the people in the bosom of theocratic education.

We have had to struggle against the sterile sword that, infatuated with its triumphs, believed that its tangent of steel gave it a claim to the title of legislator. We have had to awaken the masses, at the risk of being suffocated by their blind weight, in order to initiate them in a new life by giving them the sovereignty of the suffrage.

We who are poor have abolished slavery in all the republics of the South, while you who are rich and fortunate have not done so; we have incorporated and are incorporating the primitive races, which in Peru form almost the totality of the nation, because we regard them as our flesh and blood, while you hypocritically exterminate them.

In our lands there survives something of that ancient and divine hospitality, in our breasts there is room for the love of mankind. We have not lost the tradition of the spiritual destiny of man. We believe and love all that unites; we prefer the social to the individual, beauty to wealth, justice to power, art to commerce, poetry to industry, philosophy to textbooks, pure spirit to calculation, duty to self-interest. We side with those who see in art, in enthusiasm for the beautiful (independently of its results), and in philosophy, the splendors of the highest good. We do not see in the earth, or in the pleasures of the earth, the definitive end of man; the Negro, the Indian, the disinherited, the unhappy, the weak, find among us the respect that is due to the name and dignity of man!

That is what the republicans of South America dare to place in the balance opposite the pride, the wealth, and the power of North America.

But our superiority is latent. We must develop it. That of the North is present and is growing. . . .

What nation shone more brilliantly in history than Greece? Possessing in the highest degree all the elements and qualities that man can display in the plenitude of his powers, united for the full development of personality, she succumbed through internal division, and division quenched the light that her heroism had maintained. We are barely born, and in our cradle serpents assault us. Like Hercules, we must strangle them. Those serpents are anarchy, division, national pettiness. The battle summons us to perform the twelve symbolic labors of the hero. In the forest of our prejudices monsters lurk, spying upon the hour and the duration of our lethargy. Today the columns of

Hercules are in Panama. And Panama symbolizes the frontier, the citadel, and the destiny of both Americas.

United, Panama shall be the symbol of our strength, the sentinel of our future. Disunited, it will be the Gordian knot cut by the Yankee axe, and will give the possession of empire, the dominion of the second focus of the ellipses described by Russia and the United States in the geography of the globe.

5. "ON THE UNIQUENESS OF LATIN AMERICAN SPIRIT"

In 1900, Uruguayan writer and philosopher José Enrique Rodó published Ariel, *a brief essay would become enormously influential among contemporary intellectuals. It still stands as a symbol for the defense of what proponents view as humanistic Latin American values against the utilitarian North American model. Written shortly after the Spanish-American War (1898),* Ariel's *defense of Latin American uniqueness carries the flavor of Spain's traumatic defeat by the United States. Although Rodó refused to admit this interpretation, his allegorical conflict between Ariel, the embodiment of beauty and truth, and Caliban, the evil spirit of materialism and positivism (characters from William Shakespeare's* The Tempest), *became a metaphor for the differences between Latin America and the United States. On another level,* Ariel *is the symbol of idealist reaction against positivism. Its views on the "genius of the race" offer a critique of the pessimistic racial thinking of the period.*

Utilitarianism, as a concept of human destiny, and equality in mediocrity, as a norm for social relationships, are inextricably linked in one formula—what in Europe has generally been called the spirit of Americanism. It is impossible to consider either of these inspirations for behavior or social interaction, or to compare them with their opposites, without that association bringing insistently to mind the image of that formidable and productive democracy to our north, whose display of prosperity and power is a dazzling testimony to the efficacy of its institutions and the guidance of its ideas. If it can be said that "utilitarianism" is the word for the spirit of the English, then the United States can be considered the incarnation of that word. And the gospel of that word spreads everywhere, advocating the triumph of its material miracles. In this regard, Spanish America can no longer be rightly qualified as a land of heathens. That powerful federation is undertaking a kind of moral conquest among us. Admiration for its greatness and strength is a sentiment mounting steadily in the minds of our leaders, and, perhaps even more, in that

---

José Enrique Rodó, *Ariel* (Buenos Aires: Edit. Jackson, 1945), pp. 61–65. Excerpt translated by the editors.

of the multitude, which is awed by the appearance of victory. Then, from admiration they make the easy transition to imitation. For the psychologist, admiration and belief are passive modes of imitation. "The seat of the imitative tendency of our moral nature," said [English legal philosopher Walter] Bagehot, "is in that part of the soul where belief resides." Ordinary common sense and experience should in themselves be sufficient to establish this simple relationship. One imitates someone in whose superiority or in whose prestige one believes. This is how the vision of an America de-Latinized of its own volition, without threat of conquest, and reconstituted in the image and likeness of the northern archetype, casts a shadow over the dreams of those who are generally concerned about our future. And this vision, the inspiration behind the most suggestive parallels, manifests itself in constant proposals for innovation and reform. We have our mania for the north. It must be limited by the boundaries that reason and sentiment together dictate.

I do not suggest that these boundaries be an absolute negation. I well understand that one derives inspiration, enlightenment, and teaching from the example given by the strong. Nor am I unaware that intelligent attention to useful and beneficial external events is singularly fruitful for peoples still forming and modeling their national identities.

I understand well that some aspire to correct, by persevering education, those elements of human society which need be brought into line with the new demands of civilization and new opportunities in life, thus balancing an innovating influence with the forces of tradition and custom. But I see neither glory nor purpose in denaturalizing the character of a people—its personality—in order to impose upon it the identification with a foreign model to which it must sacrifice the irreplaceable originality of its spirit. Nor do I see any gain in the ingenuous belief that this might be obtained by artificial or improvised imitation. This mindless transferal of what is natural and spontaneous in one society into the heart of another, where it has neither natural nor historical roots, was for [French historian Jules] Michelet much like attempting to introduce something dead into a living organism by simple implantation. In social relations, as in literature or art, mindless imitation will only corrupt the lines of the model. The delusion of those who think they have reproduced the essential character of a human collectivity, the living forces of its spirit, and the secret of its triumphs and prosperity, reproducing precisely the mechanism of its institutions and the exterior forms of its customs, reminds one of fresh-faced beginners who imagine that they have acquired the genius of the master when in fact they have merely copied his style and techniques.

Furthermore, there is something ignoble in this futile effort. Eager mimicry of the prominent and strong, the winners and the fortunate, might be viewed as a kind of political snobbery, a kind of servile abdication—like that of the snobs condemned for eternity to be satirized in [English novelist William Makepeace] Thackeray's books. Sadly, the futile imitation of the caprices and vagaries of those at society's apex consumes the energies of those spirits not blessed by nature or fortune. Caring for our internal independence—our personality, our judgment—is a basic form of self-respect. Ethical treatises often comment upon one of [Roman philosopher and politician] Cicero's moral precepts, according to which one of our duties as human beings is that each of us zealously protect and nourish the originality of his personal character, whatever determines and differentiates it, while respecting Nature's primary impulse to further the common good by establishing in the world a diverse distribution of its gifts. And the force of this precept seems to me even greater when applied collectively to the character of human societies. Regarding the present ordering of our peoples, one might hear it said that there is no distinctive stamp which, for its permanence and integrity, might be worth striving to maintain. Perhaps what is lacking in our collective character is a sharply defined "personality." But instead of this perfectly differentiated and autonomous quality, we Latin Americans have a heritage of culture, a great ethnic tradition to maintain, a sacred link with the immortal pages of history that relies upon our honor for its continuation. Cosmopolitanism, which we have accepted as a compelling necessity in our formation, excludes neither that sense of loyalty to the past, nor the governing and formative role that the genius of the race must play in the recasting of those elements that constitute the American of the future.

It has been observed more than once that history's great evolutions—the great epochs, the most enlightened and fruitful periods in the unfolding of humanity—are almost always the result of two contemporaneous, yet distinct forces that through concerted opposition, keep life interesting and stimulating, something that would wane in the calm of absolute unanimity. Thus, the two poles of Athens and Sparta formed the axis around which revolved the most genial and civilizing of cultures. At present, America must maintain the original duality of its composition, recreating in history the classic myth of the two eagles simultaneously released at each of the world's poles in order that each might arrive at the limits of its domain at the same time. This genial and competitive diversity does not exclude, but rather tolerates and, in many respects, even favors harmony and solidarity. And if a greater harmony could be glimpsed in the distant future, it would not be based upon unilateral imitation, as [French sociologist Gabriel] Tarde would say, of one culture by another, but rather upon reciprocal influence and the mutually advantageous exchange of those attributes that give each its glory.

6. THE WHITE MAN'S BURDEN

In 1899 British writer Rudyard Kipling, renowned for his children's stories and his enthusiasm for empire, wrote a poem challenging the United States to assume its imperial

The Cuban Melodrama.
THE NOBLE HERO (to the HEAVY VILLAIN):
**"Stand back, there, gol darn ye!—If you force this
thing to a fifth act, remember that's where I git my
work!" (C. Jay Taylor, *Puck*, June 3, 1896).**

These cartoons appear with additional historical background in John J. Johnson, *Latin America in Caricature* (Austin: University of Texas Press, 1980), pp. 81, 95, 125, 127, 163. A lesson plan for these images by Luis Martínez-Fernández is in the *OAH Magazine of History* 12, no. 3 (Spring 1998).

532

"I Come to Buy, Not to Beg, Sir" (William Allen Rogers,
Harper's Weekly, November 7, 1903).

**John Bull [Great Britain]: "It's really extraordinary
what training will do. Why, only the other day I
thought that man unable to support himself"**
(Fred Morgan, *Philadelphia Inquirer*, 1898).

"After the First Mile"
(W. L. Evans, *Cleveland Leader*, 1903).

UNCLE SAM to PORTO RICO: "And to think that bad boy came near to being your brother!" (*Chicago Inter Ocean*, 1905).

responsibility by taking up "the white man's burden" to civilize its "new caught, sullen peoples/Half-devil and half-child." Future president Theodore Roosevelt liked the sentiment behind the poem well enough to copy it for a friend (although he acknowledged that it was "poor poetry"). Kipling had in mind the Philippines, newly acquired in the Spanish-American War, but for political cartoonists in the United States his arguments applied equally well to "liberated" territories in the Caribbean, Cuba, and Puerto Rico. As these cartoons show, U.S. political cartoonists (and presumably their editors and readers) shared Kipling's paternalistic, racist attitudes toward the new U.S. charges. Two cartoons depict Cuba as a young woman: a damsel in distress (before the war) and grateful, polite child (after the U.S. military occupation ended in 1902). The other three cartoons depict Cuba, Puerto Rico, and the other "liberated" territories as dark-skinned savages and/or black children desperately in need of guidance and discipline. The final cartoon from 1905 shows bad boy Cuba abusing its newfound freedom (from U.S. military control) while docile Puerto Rico (which remained a U.S. territory) looks on.

7. COROLLARY TO THE MONROE DOCTRINE

The Monroe Doctrine demonstrated U.S. resolve to prevent European intervention in the Western Hemisphere. In practice, however, the United States continued to tolerate temporary interventions in Latin America by European powers in order to collect debts. U.S. concerns over the 1902–1903 German and British intervention in Venezuela over unpaid debts, coupled with the 1903 U.S. intervention in Colombia and the imminent prospect of an American-controlled canal across the newly created nation of Panama (previously a Colombian province), led President Theodore Roosevelt to reconsider previous practice in his annual message to Congress on December 6, 1904. This Roosevelt Corollary to the Monroe Doctrine would set the tone for a new era of U.S. intervention in Latin America.

The [United States] continues to enjoy noteworthy prosperity. Such prosperity is of course primarily due to the high individual average of our citizenship, taken together with our great natural resources; but an important factor therein is the working of our long-continued governmental policies. The people have emphatically expressed their approval of the principles underlying these policies, and their desire that these principles be kept substantially unchanged, although of course applied in a progressive spirit to meet changing conditions. . . .

It is not true that the United States feels any land hunger or entertains any projects as regards the other nations of the Western Hemisphere save such as

President Theodore Roosevelt, Annual Message to Congress, December 6, 1904.

are for their welfare. All that this country desires is to see the neighboring countries stable, orderly, and prosperous. Any country whose people conduct themselves well can count upon our hearty friendship. If a nation shows that it knows how to act with reasonable efficiency and decency in social and political matters, if it keeps order and pays its obligations, it need fear no interference from the United States. Chronic wrongdoing, or an impotence which results in a general loosening of the ties of civilized society, may in America, as elsewhere, ultimately require intervention by some civilized nation, and in the Western Hemisphere the adherence of the United States to the Monroe Doctrine may force the United States, however reluctantly, in flagrant cases of such wrongdoing or impotence, to the exercise of an international police power. If every country washed by the Caribbean Sea would show the progress in stable and just civilization which with the aid of the Platt Amendment Cuba has shown since our troops left the island, and which so many of the republics in both Americas are constantly and brilliantly showing, all question of interference by this Nation with their affairs would be at an end. Our interests and those of our southern neighbors are in reality identical. They have great natural riches, and if within their borders the reign of law and justice obtains, prosperity is sure to come to them. While they thus obey the primary laws of civilized society they may rest assured that they will be treated by us in a spirit of cordial and helpful sympathy. We would interfere with them only in the last resort, and then only if it became evident that their inability or unwillingness to do justice at home and abroad had violated the rights of the United States or had invited foreign aggression to the detriment of the entire body of American nations. It is a mere truism to say that every nation, whether in America or anywhere else, which desires to maintain its freedom, its independence, must ultimately realize that the right of such independence can not be separated from the responsibility of making good use of it.

In asserting the Monroe Doctrine, in taking such steps as we have taken in regard to Cuba, Venezuela, and Panama, and in endeavoring to circumscribe the theater of war in the Far East, and to secure the open door in China, we have acted in our own interest as well as in the interest of humanity at large. There are, however, cases in which, while our own interests are not greatly involved, strong appeal is made to our sympathies. Ordinarily it is very much wiser and more useful for us to concern ourselves with striving for our own moral and material betterment here at home than to concern ourselves with trying to better the condition of things in other nations. We have plenty of sins of our own to war against, and under ordinary circumstances we can do more for the general uplifting of humanity by striving with heart and soul to put a stop to civic corruption, to brutal lawlessness and violent race prejudices here at home than by passing resolutions and wrongdoing elsewhere. Nevertheless there are occasional crimes committed on so vast a scale and of such peculiar horror as to make us doubt whether it is not our manifest duty to endeavor at least to show our disapproval of the deed and our sympathy with those who have suffered by it. The cases must be extreme in which such a course is justifiable. There must be no effort made to remove the mote from our brother's eye if we refuse to remove the beam from our own. But in extreme cases action may be justifiable and proper. What form the action shall take must depend upon the circumstances of the case; that is, upon the degree of the atrocity and upon our power to remedy it. The cases in which we could interfere by force of arms as we interfered to put a stop to intolerable conditions in Cuba are necessarily very few. Yet it is not to be expected that a people like ours, which in spite of certain very obvious shortcomings, nevertheless as a whole shows by its consistent practice its belief in the principles of civil and religious liberty and of orderly freedom, a people among whom even the worst crime, like the crime of lynching, is never more than sporadic, so that individuals and not classes are molested in their fundamental rights—it is inevitable that such a nation should desire eagerly to give expression to its horror on an occasion like that of the massacre of the Jews in Kishenef, or when it witnesses such systematic and long-extended cruelty and oppression as the cruelty and oppression of which the Armenians have been the victims, and which have won for them the indignant pity of the civilized world.

8. TO ROOSEVELT

The 1903 U.S. intervention in Panama and the prospect of a U.S.-controlled canal across the isthmus prompted expressions of concern and distrust by many Latin Americans. One of the most eloquent of these expressions was Nicaraguan poet and diplomat Rubén Darío's famous ode "To Roosevelt." Darío's damning critique of the culture of U.S. imperialism has proven immensely popular in Latin America ever since. The many historical and literary allusions—typical of the modernist poetry of the period—include references to American poet Walt Whitman, biblical hunter Nimrod, Russian novelist and social critic Leo Tolstoy, conqueror-tyrants Alexander the Great and Nebuchadnezzar, French novelist Victor Hugo, American president Ulysses Grant, pre-Conquest Mexican poet-king Netzahualcóyotl, Aztec emperor Moctezuma, and the martyred Aztec leader Cuauhtémoc (Cortés had his feet burned to force him to reveal the location of Aztec treasure). Darío also suggests connections between Latin America and the lost world of Atlantis mentioned in the work of Plato.

It would take a voice from the Bible or a verse of Walt Whitman, to reach you, Hunter!

———

Rubén Darío, "A Roosevelt," in *Cantos de Vida y Esperanza*, 1905. Excerpt translated by the editors.

Primitive and modern, simple and complicated,
with a dash of Washington and four of Nimrod.
You are the United States,
you are the future invader
of the ingenuous America that has indigenous blood,
that still prays to Jesus Christ and still speaks in Spanish.
You are an arrogant and forceful exemplar of your race;
you are cultured, you are skillful; you are the opposite of Tolstoy.
Taming horses or assassinating tigers,
you are an Alexander-Nebuchadnezzar.
(You are a professor of energy,
as today's lunatics say.)
You think that life is incendiary,
that progress is eruption;
that where you put the bullet
you put the future.
    No.

The United States are powerful and great.
When they shake themselves there is a deep shudder
that runs down the enormous vertebrae of the Andes.
If you clamor, it is heard as the roar of the lion.
As Hugo said to Grant: "The stars are yours."
(Barely shining the Argentine sun dawns
and the Chilean star rises . . .) You are rich.
You join together the cult of Hercules and the cult of Mammon;
and lighting the road of facile conquest,
Liberty raises her torch in New York.

But our America, that has had poets
since the old times of Netzahualcóyotl,
that has watched over the footprints of the great Bacchus,
that at one time learned the Panic alphabet;
that consulted the stars, that knew Atlantis,
whose name comes resounding down to us in Plato,
that from the remote moments of its life,
has lived on light, on fire, on perfume, on love,
the America of the great Moctezuma, of the Inca,
the fragrant America of Christopher Columbus,
the Catholic America, the Spanish America,
the America where noble Cuauhtémoc said:
"I am not on a bed of roses"; that America
trembling with hurricanes and subsisting on Love,
men of Saxon eyes and barbaric souls, lives.

And dreams. And loves, and vibrates; and it is the daughter of the Sun.
Take care. Long live Spanish America!
There are a thousand loose cubs of the Spanish Lion.
You would need, Roosevelt, to be God himself,
the terrible Rifleman and the strong Hunter,
in order to have us in your ferrous claws.

And, though you count on all; you are missing one thing: God!

9. MEXICO'S PRESIDENT LOOKS NORTH

Even Latin American leaders with close economic and political ties to the United States harbored serious concerns about their position vis-à-vis the "Colossus to the North." James Creelman's 1908 interview with Mexican president Porfirio Díaz included the following astute, measured analysis of Pan-Americanism, U.S.-Latin American relations, and even the regional implications of the U.S. annexation of the Philippines. In a less guarded moment, Díaz is reputed to have remarked, "Poor Mexico, so far from God, so close to the United States!"

"Is there a real foundation for the Pan-American movement? Is there an American idea that can bind the peoples of this hemisphere together and distinguish them from the rest of the world?"

The President listened to the question and smiled. Only a few weeks before, the American Secretary of State had been the guest of Mexico, lodged in Chapultepec Castle like a king, with its hill turned into a fairyland, and the nation, from President to peon, exerting itself to show that, in all the American republics he had visited, none could equal the land of the Montezumas in the grandeur of its welcome.

"There is an American sentiment and it is growing," said the President. "But it is useless to deny a distinct feeling of distrust, a fear of territorial absorption, which interferes with a closer union of the American republics. Just as the Guatemalans and other peoples of Central America seem to fear absorption by Mexico, so there are Mexicans who fear absorption by the United States. I do not share this fear. I have full confidence in the intentions of the American Government, yet"—with a sudden twinkling of the eyes—"popular sentiment changes and governments change and we cannot always tell what the future may bring."

James Creelman, "President Díaz, Hero of the Americas," *Pearson's Magazine* 19, no. 3 (March 1908): 247–250.

"The work done by the Bureau of the American Republics at Washington is a good one and it has a great field of usefulness. It deserves hearty support. All that is needed is that the peoples of the American nations shall know one another better. The Bureau of the American Republics is doing a great deal in that direction." ...

"It is important that the leading men of the hemisphere should visit one another's countries. The visit of Secretary Root to Mexico and the words he spoke here have already been fruitful. Ignorant Mexicans have been led to think that their enemies live on the other side of our northern frontier. But when they see a distinguished American statesman and Cabinet officer like Mr. Root entertained in Mexico, and learn the words of friendship and respect he spoke, they cannot be misled again. Let the leaders of the Americas see more of one another and the Pan-American idea will grow more rapidly, as the republics understand that they have nothing to fear and much to hope for from one another."

"And the Monroe Doctrine?"

"Limited to a particular purpose the Monroe Doctrine deserves and will receive the support of all the American republics. But as a vague general claim of power by the United States, a claim easily associated with armed intervention in Cuba [in the 1898 Spanish-American War], it is a cause of profound suspicion. There is no good reason why the Monroe Doctrine should not be made a general American doctrine, rather than a mere national policy of the United States. The American nations might bind themselves for self-defense, and each nation agree to furnish its proportion of means in case of war. They might even provide a penalty for a failure to fulfill the agreement. Such a Monroe Doctrine would make each nation feel that its national self-respect and sovereign dignity was not compromised, and would secure the American republics forever against monarchical invasion or conquest."

"How does the present tendency of national sentiment in the United States strike you at this distance, Mr. President? You have as the leader of the Mexican people studied us for more than thirty years." ...

"The people of the United States are distinguished by public spirit," he said. "They have a singular love of country. I meet thousands of Americans every year, and I find them to be, as a rule, intelligent workers and men of great energy of character. But their strongest characteristic is love of country. In my opinion, when war comes this spirit will change into military spirit."

"In taking the Philippines and other colonies you have set your flag far away from your shores. That means a great navy. I have no doubt that if President Roosevelt remains in office four years more, the American navy will equal the British navy in power."

"But, Mr. President, Cuba is to be given back to its people, and it is well understood in the United States that the people of the Philippines will receive their political and territorial independence as soon as they are fitted to govern themselves." ...

"When the United States gives independence to Cuba and the Philippines," he said slowly and with some show of feeling, "she will take her place at the head of the nations and all fear will or distrust will disappear from the American republics."

It is impossible to convey an accurate idea of the gravity and earnestness with which the President spoke.

"While you hold the Philippines you will be compelled not only to keep a great navy, but your army will increase in size."

"We are trying to make American school teachers take the place of soldiers in the Philippines," I ventured.

"I appreciate that, but I feel satisfied that in the end the people of the Philippines will gain more than the people of the United States and that the sooner you give up your Asiatic possessions the better it will be from every point of view. No matter how generous you may be, the people you govern will always consider themselves a conquered people." . . .

"And the trust question, Mr. President? How is a country like Mexico, with such vast natural resources awaiting development, to protect itself against the oppressions of such alliances of wealth and industrial combination as have grown up in your nearest neighbor, the United States?"

"We welcome and protect the capital and energy of the whole world in this country. We have a field for investors that perhaps cannot be found elsewhere. But, while we are just and generous to all, we are seeing to it that no enterprise shall be an injury to our people."

"For instance, we passed a law providing that no owner of oil-producing lands should have the right to sell them to any other person without the consent of the Government. Not that we objected to the operation of our oil fields by your American oil king, but that we were determined that our oil wells should not be suppressed in order to prevent competition and keep up the price of American oil."

"There are some things which governments do not talk about, because each case must be dealt with on its own merits, but the Mexican Republic will use its powers to preserve to its people a just share of its wealth. We have maintained free and fair conditions in Mexico thus far, and I believe we can maintain them for the future."

"Our invitation to the investors of the world is not to be found in idle promises, but in the way we treat them when they come among us."

10. NATIONAL SECURITY

During World War II, Latin American countries sided with the Allies, including the United States, in their struggle against the Axis powers (although U.S. diplomats regularly expressed concern about Argentina's alleged fascist sympathies). Conferences at

Chapultepec (Mexico 1945), Rio de Janeiro (Brazil 1947), and Bogotá (Colombia 1948) attempted to solidify this hemispheric alliance. The Bogotá conference produced the institutional framework for the Organization of American States. In addition, Resolution 32, The Preservation and Defense of Democracy in America, committed member nations to fight alongside the United States against communism in the new cold war.

In order to safeguard peace and maintain mutual respect among states, the present world situation requires that urgent measures be taken, to proscribe the tactics of totalitarian domination that are irreconcilable with the tradition of the American Nations, and to prevent serving international communism or any other totalitarian doctrine from seeking to distort the true and the free will of the peoples of this continent,

The Republics Represented at the Ninth International Conference of American States

Declare:

That, by its anti-democratic nature and its interventionist tendency, the political activity of international communism or any other totalitarian doctrine is incompatible with the concept of American freedom, which rests upon two undeniable postulates: the dignity of man as an individual and the sovereignty of the nation as a state,

Reiterate:

The faith that the peoples of the New World have placed in the ideal and in the reality of democracy, under the protection of which they shall achieve social justice, offering to all increasingly broader opportunities to enjoy the spiritual and material benefits that are the guarantee of civilization and the heritage of mankind;

Condemn:

In the name of international law, interference by any foreign power, or by any other political organization serving the interests of a foreign power, in the public life of the nations of the American continent,

And resolve:

1. To reaffirm their decision to maintain and further an effective social and economic policy for the purposes of raising the standard of living of their peoples; and their conviction that only under a system founded upon a guarantee of the essential freedoms and rights of the individual is it possible to attain this goal.
2. To condemn the methods of every system tending to suppress political and civil rights and liberties, and in particular the action of international communism or any other totalitarian doctrine.

United States Department of State, *Ninth International Conference of American States, in Bogotá, Colombia, 30 March–2 May 1948, Report of the United States of America with Related Documents*, Department of State Publication 3263.

3. To adopt, within their respective territories and in accordance with their respective constitutional provisions the measures necessary to eradicate and prevent activities directed, assisted or instigated by foreign governments, organizations or individuals tendings to overthrow their institutions by violence, to foment disorder in their domestic political life or to disturb, by means of pressure, subversive propaganda, threats or by any other means, the free and sovereign right of their peoples to govern themselves in accordance with their democratic aspirations.
4. To proceed with a full exchange of information concerning any of the aforementioned activities that are carried on within their respective jurisdictions.

11. OPERATION GUATEMALA

In the years that followed World War II, rifts began to appear in the New World alliance. Latin America's "revolution of rising expectations" and its demand for drastic social reform inevitably threatened vested interests at home and abroad, particularly in the United States. A major crisis soon arose in Guatemala. In 1944, following the overthrow of the tyrant Jorge Ubico by a revolutionary movement led by the distinguished educator Juan José Arévalo, the new government launched a sweeping land reform in a country where twenty-two families owned about 1.25 million acres of land. Native and foreign interests affected by this and other reforms, including the powerful United Fruit Company, hurled charges of communist control at the Guatemalan government, then headed by President Jacobo Arbenz. A major U.S. diplomatic campaign to isolate Guatemala, together with large-scale financial and military assistance to an invasion force of right-wing dissidents and mercenaries, brought the collapse of the Arbenz regime in 1954. Guillermo Toriello, Guatemalan ambassador to the United States at the time, describes the preparation of Operation Guatemala and his futile efforts to prevent its success.

In 1947 the United States Ambassador to Guatemala was Richard C. Patterson, a friend of President Truman, to whose election campaign he had contributed. A man of imperious, arbitrary temper, he soon identified himself with the United Fruit Company and with the domestic opposition because of his dislike for the Guatemalan Revolutionary Movement. On one occasion he actually had the nerve to say to President Arbenz: "I don't like Zotano and

Guillermo Toriello, *La batalla de Guatemala* (Santiago de Chile, 1955), pp. 45–57. Excerpt translated by Benjamin Keen.

Mangano, and I would like you to remove these officials." Another time he said to a government minister: "Fifteen million dollars could settle all our problems with you." Let me say in his behalf that he did not always show antagonism toward our government; he sometimes tried in a friendly, though crude way to gain the goodwill of high officials by bribery. In a single day he destroyed the splendid work of rapprochement, of broad and cordial understanding, achieved by his predecessor, Ambassador Edwin Kyle. In 1950 his fraternization with the domestic opposition and his interference in our internal affairs reached such a point that the Guatemalan government had to declare him persona non grata.

Under Dean Acheson, the State Department fell under the influence of the hostile propaganda directed against Guatemala by the United Fruit Company, but relations were maintained on a correct if somewhat tepid level. As early as 1949, the United States refused to permit the export of military equipment to Guatemala, the Department of State alleging that this restriction conformed to the law concerning reciprocal assistance for defense (Public Law 621), which provided that before authorizing the sale or transfer of war materiel to another country the United States government must satisfy itself that that country participates with the United States in a regional agreement on collective defense. Guatemala did not adhere to the Rio Pact of Reciprocal Assistance, nor did it have—at least until June 29, 1954—a bilateral defense agreement with the United States. However, in other respects the relations between the two countries continued cordial, and there was satisfactory cooperation in matters of common interest.

In January 1953, there was a change of administration in the United States; a new party took over the reins of government. An anticipation of catastrophe ran throughout Latin America. Our peoples feared the rise of the Republican Party, symbol of the "Bad Neighbor," whose policies of the "Big Stick" and "Dollar Diplomacy" the Latin American republics had learned at painful cost under previous Republican administrations. What new mask would the Republican wolf now assume? Could the recent honeyed proposal that we be "good neighbors" represent a new technique of the same old Republican interventionist policy?

With the Republicans in power, the official attitude toward Guatemala also changed sharply. To the State Department came John Foster Dulles, member of the law firm Sullivan and Cromwell of New York, which had represented the United Fruit Company for many years past. Dulles himself drew up the draft of the contract made by the United Fruit Company with the Guatemalan government in 1930 and 1936.

John Moore Cabot, of the Boston Cabots, became Under Secretary of Inter-American Affairs. Boston was the seat of the Banana Empire, and the Cabot family has been intimately linked to the United Fruit Company for a long time. The same can be said of the Lodge family; and a Henry Cabot Lodge was head of the permanent delegation of the United States to the

United Nations. There is a popular saying in Boston concerning these families: "The Lodges speak only to Cabots, and the Cabots speak only to God." But the Cabot Lodges present something of a puzzle. To whom do they speak? To God alone, it seems.

From the point of view of the traditional Latin American policy of the Republican Party, a policy that was aggressive, interventionist, and favorable to great monopolistic interests, the Guatemalan October Revolution represented a serious danger because of its nationalist, popular, and democratic character. Guatemala was a bad example for the other peoples of Latin America. This example must not be permitted to prevail.

The traditional Republican policy fused in a very natural way with the desires of other forces of reactionary and authoritarian tendency. One was the feudal oligarchy of Guatemala, which formerly had enjoyed a monopoly of political power. Another was the secret organization created some years back by the Franco government of Spain for the undermining of Latin American democracies. Its aim was to create in America regimes that would resemble the Spanish Falangist regime [of General Francisco Franco] and that would lend the latter some of the international support that it badly needed. This organization, with abundant means and agents, was supported by some American dictators like Trujillo. It operated actively in Guatemala, had recruited some Guatemalans into its service, and had invited some officers of the national army to join its ranks. In addition to its preeminently conspiratorial activity, this secret organization carried on some activities of a visible character: the appeal to *Hispanidad*; the malicious exploitation of the Catholic sentiments of our people; the intensive diffusion of Falangist propaganda by Catholic clergy in its service.

As for the United Fruit Company, the fiasco of more than thirty conspiracies of the traditional Latin American type had evidently convinced it that that method would no longer serve to liquidate a revolutionary government like that of Guatemala, firmly rooted in the people. Something else had to be done, on a much vaster scale.

The new complexion of the Republican Administration in the United States, particularly that of the Department of State, and the traditionally aggressive Latin American policy of the Republican Party, lent itself marvelously to a union of forces that sought to employ the old procedure, dressed in a new garb, intervention.

The fact that leading figures in the United Fruit Company held key positions in the United States government made it easy for the company to achieve such a union of forces and to transform its private fight with the Guatemalan government into a formal conflict between the two countries.

This is precisely what the President of the United Fruit Company, Kenneth Redmond, had earlier announced in a confidential interview. "Henceforth it will not be a question of the people of Guatemala against the United Fruit Company; the question will become one of communism against the right to life, property, and the security of the Western Hemisphere." The interviewer added that Mr. Redmond was convinced that there would be a change of administration in Guatemala; he could not give the exact date, but it was not very distant.

Thus was formed the portentous triangle—United Fruit Company, Department of State, CIA—which was to carry out "Operation Guatemala" with the assistance of Franco's agents and the local oligarchy. In some *sanctum sanctorum* of the great Yankee Chancellery it was decreed: "*Delenda est Guatemala* (Guatemala must be destroyed)" and the lot was thrown that decided the tragic destiny of our country. . . .

Very soon it became widely known that this coalition of forces was active and delineaments of the "Master Plan," the logical result of the subservience of the State Department to the United Fruit Company, became visible. "Operation Guatemala," a consequence of that plan, also counted on the collaboration of the CIA, whose head, conveniently enough, was Allen Dulles, brother of the Secretary of State.

The plan, combining the resources of that triangle, had the following general characteristics. Two different lines of action would be pursued simultaneously. The first would carry the case of "the red menace in Guatemala" by pseudo-correct diplomatic channels to the ministries of America and inter-American conferences; the second would clandestinely prepare armed aggression against Guatemala, but giving it the name of an "internal revolt" that seemingly involved not at all the correct, "very fair" attitude of the State Department.

To support these actions, pressure should be maintained on Guatemala in all its official diplomatic and commercial relations with the United States; the Guatemalan government would suffer boycott in its relations with other countries in the United States sphere of influence; and an enormous propaganda campaign, using the Communist scarecrow, would create throughout America a state of mind that, whether from genuine alarm, cowardice, or servility, would give the United States a free hand in Guatemala.

In sum, a gigantic project, on a scale sufficient to battle a first class enemy power, was organized with the sole aim of restoring the unjust privileges of the Banana Empire and other monopolistic enterprises, but was disguised by dressing it in the evangelical cloak of a "noble struggle against communism."

The "Master Plan" was soon put into effect. The Department of State had already presented its claims in connection with the expropriation (already indemnified) of idle lands of the United Fruit Company in the Pacific zone of Guatemala. A defamatory propaganda was intensified, using the press, radio, and television in the United States and the rest of America.

To replace Ambassador Schoenfeld, an honest and thoughtful career diplomat, Washington sent to Guatemala a rascally type by the name of John E. Peurifoy.

Contact was made with the principal elements of the Guatemalan opposition and, finally, Carlos Castillo Armas, a former soldier who had rebelled against the Guatemalan government (1950) and was currently in Honduras, was selected as an ideal instrument of the United Fruit Company–State Department–CIA plan. A lawyer in New Orleans served as the go-between who paid the monthly expenses of the conspiracy and for the purchase of war materiel. Castillo Armas in turn maintained a confidential agent at the State Department whom he paid with funds that he received from the United Fruit Company.

Through an arms dealer of Dallas, Texas, Castillo Armas was provided with the military supplies he needed: machine guns, submachine guns, rifles, 100- and 200-pound bombs for aerial bombardment, hand grenades, ammunition, explosives, radio transmission equipment, uniforms, tents. He also obtained within United States territory and at nominal prices P-47 planes and transport planes that belonged to the United States government. (Note that such equipment, being property of the United States government, cannot be exported without its express authorization; even when sold to a friendly government, such government cannot transfer or otherwise dispose of it without the previous consent of the United States.)

At the end of 1953, ten pilots and ten airplane mechanics enlisted with Castillo Armas, without loss of United States citizenship. They were to receive $500 a month until summoned to their work of destruction and murder; thereafter they would receive $1000 a month plus bonuses. Recruitment of mercenaries at $300 a month, not clandestinely but publicly, even through printed fliers, began in Honduras and Nicaragua.

All this war materiel was transported from the United States to Nicaragua and Honduras without any effort at concealment. Later the base of operations and the supplies were moved to Honduras. Castillo Armas' uniformed soldiers loaded truckloads of armaments in plain view of passersby at the United States embassy in Tegucigalpa, Honduras. Castillo Armas' mercenary troops freely circulated throughout Honduras, making conspicuous show of their abundance of United States dollars. These troops were moved to Copan, campaign headquarters near the Guatemalan frontier, in full daylight, wearing their uniforms and carrying their arms, using both their own airplanes and Honduran public services of land and air transport.

Arms, munitions, United States government planes, war materiel of every kind, North American pilots and mechanics, Castillo Armas, millions of dollars changing hands, an unheard of tolerance on the part of Honduras and Nicaragua, ships equipped for commando operations, and the like. Who could believe that all this happened without the complicity of the United States government?

As long as the conspiratorial activities of the United Fruit Company and allied interests had the character of a private struggle against the Guatemalan revolutionary movement, the State Department maintained a discreet attitude and abstained from public statements about the Guatemalan situation. This does not mean that there was an absence of attacks, echoing the defamatory propaganda of the United Fruit Company, by other official figures. In the United States Congress, especially, various senators and representatives linked to the Banana Empire or allied interests made continuous capricious attacks on the Guatemalan government.

On October 14, 1953, the State Department first spoke out publicly against Guatemala. John Moore Cabot, in a speech before the Federation of Women's Clubs in the State Department auditorium in Washington, referred extensively to Guatemala, to "gratuitous attacks against the United States and its citizens from official Guatemalan sources," concluding with the warning that "no regime that openly plays the Communist game can expect from us the positive cooperation that we normally extend to all our sister republics."

Doubtless that conclusion was geared to "Operation Guatemala," now in full movement, and did not reflect a sincere ideological stand on the part of the State Department, for in the same speech the United Fruit Stockholder, referring to Argentina, noted the good relations that were being established with that country and observed: "Frankly, its different philosophy and economy are none of our business." One standard for Guatemala, another for Argentina.

This first official statement against Guatemala was systematically followed by other, increasingly aggressive statements by Cabot and Dulles himself, in line with the Master Plan.

At the end of 1953 the Council of the Organization of American States met to prepare the agenda for the Tenth Inter-American Conference.

This presented an excellent opportunity. The Master Plan called for the State Department to operate on the Inter-American diplomatic front, generally, in order to create the proper atmosphere for the armed aggression; and, especially, in order to give the United Fruit Company's struggle against Guatemala the character of a grave inter-American problem that required the collective action of the members of the continental community.

But the State Department could not find an appropriate formula that would exonerate its actions from having a clearly interventionist character. Whatever the form employed, the common action of the other American republics in the Guatemalan case had to appear for what it really was: an intervention in the internal affairs of a member of that community, in gross violation of the principles of the inter-American system.

Fortunately for the State Department, Mr. Dulles's talent, evidenced by his numerous diplomatic triumphs in Europe and Asia, found the solution for the problem of squaring the circle. In order that some may not accuse us of intervention, let us say that foreign intervention is already in progress in an American country and that we are merely going to its aid. Let us call the hateful nationalist, democratic movement in Guatemala a "Communist intervention," and then it will become clear that, inspired by the great democratic tradition of the United States, in order to save "Christian civilization," we must liberate Guatemala from that foreign aggression.

The time for action had come. The proposed agenda of the Conference had been circulated among governments and had been returned with their observations. At the last hour the State Department requested inclusion in the agenda of the point, "Intervention of International Communism in the American Republics."

None could mistake the significance of this point. By that date the shape of the conspiratorial diplomatic plan against the [Guatemalan] October Revolution was too clear for anyone not to see that the United States proposal was an integral part of that plan. . . .

And the United States policy of boycott and encirclement of Guatemala bore its fruit at the Conference: nineteen delegates folded under Mr. Dulles's pressure and voted in favor of the United States proposal, leaving Guatemala alone in defense of a fundamental principle of the international system: nonintervention.

In January 1954, I was finishing my assignment as ambassador of Guatemala to the United States. Together with my government, I felt the most profound concern over the somber perspectives that the political aggression of the United States projected for my country. We had exhausted all the possibilities of reaching a decorous understanding; all our overtures had fruitlessly broken against the intransigence of the State Department. We knew it would give us no truce or quarter.

Given this situation, we concluded that the only hope for preventing the realization of the sinister plan being prepared against Guatemala was to take the question directly to the President of the United States and discuss it with him, amply and freely.

But in the United States it is very difficult for a Latin American ambassador to obtain an interview with the President or even with the Secretary of State, by contrast with the situation in our own countries, where any chief of mission finds an easy access to the offices of those high officials.

The persons Latin American ambassadors can easily see in Washington are officials of the sixth class (in charge of the desks of the respective countries), and, by appointment, officials of the third and fourth classes, such as the Assistant Secretary and the Vice Assistant Secretary for Inter-American Affairs.

Although I had on various occasions intimated to the State Department my desire to speak with President Eisenhower, unfortunately it always turned out, so I was told, that he was very busy, "too busy, you know." . . .

[On] January 16, the President received me. He was accompanied by John C. Moore, who this time remained during the interview. If Smith was poorly informed about the Guatemalan situation, the President was even more so. All he knew was "the Communist danger to the Continent," the "Red menace" that was Guatemala. He was greatly surprised when I described the economic subjection in which the foreign monopolies held us and the conspiratorial activities in which they engaged in order to destroy the democratic movement in Guatemala. I pointed out that one of the phases of that conspiracy was precisely the gigantic campaign of defamatory propaganda which made us appear to be Communists.

He was deeply disturbed when he learned of the extraordinary privileges those enterprises enjoyed and the connections between the United Fruit Company and the State Department. He found it difficult to believe that these companies paid no customs duties and that some of their contracts would not run out until the next century. With a terrifying naiveté, he suggested that on my arrival in Guatemala I should discuss ways of reaching a settlement with Ambassador Peurifoy. Naturally—at least that was my impression—the President knew nothing of "Operation Guatemala" in which his own State Department and his own embassy in my country were involved.

I had to express my deep skepticism concerning his suggestion, discreetly noting that Mr. Dulles was a member of the law firm of the United Fruit Company and that Mr. Cabot (who was present) and his family were stockholders in the same company. The President must have found my arguments reasonable, for then he proposed formation of an impartial mixed commission of Guatemalan and United States citizens that should discuss on the highest level the problem of the monopolistic enterprises in Guatemala and all other matters causing friction between the two countries. I indicated that I was in entire agreement with him, in principle, and that I was confident my government would receive his proposal with enthusiasm.

For a few days I had the illusory hope that through President Eisenhower's intervention and the realization of his project—the mixed commission—the progress of the State Department's sinister plans could be brought to a halt. Unfortunately, very soon I had to admit that the President's good intentions were that and nothing more. They proved totally incapable of preventing the advance of the aggression that was already under way. All had been a vain hope.

12. DISSENT WITHIN THE RANKS

Interventions by the United States in Latin America have prompted vigorous dissent, sometimes at the highest levels of government. For example, both former president John Quincy Adams and future president Abraham Lincoln spoke out in Congress against President James Polk's 1846 declaration of war against Mexico. Over a hundred years later, Senator J. William Fulbright (D-Arkansas), influential chairman of the Senate Foreign Relations Committee, delivered a two-hour speech denouncing President Lyndon Johnson's 1965 decision to send 23,000 marines to occupy Santo Domingo, capital of the Dominican Republic, allegedly to prevent communist-inspired

revolutionaries from turning the country into "another Cuba." In his speech, Ful-
bright criticizes the Johnson administration for its willingness to promote repressive
regimes like the dictatorship of Rafael Trujillo (1930–1961) in the Dominican Repub-
lic over progressive social movements like the Dominican Revolutionary Party (PDR)
of former president Juan Bosch (1963)—a situation that in Fulbright's view would
undo the important work of the Alliance for Progress program promoting democratic
government and a more equitable distribution of wealth in Latin America as an alter-
native to the radical social reforms advocated by communist revolutionaries like Fidel
Castro. At the time of the U.S. intervention, Bosch was leading a revolt against the
military government that had ousted him from power in a 1963 coup d'état.

U.S. policy in the Dominican crisis was characterized initially by over-timidity and subsequently by over-action. Throughout the whole affair it has also been characterized by a lack of candor. These are general conclusions I have reached from a painstaking review of the salient features of the extremely complex situation. These judgments are made, of course, with the benefit of hindsight and in fairness it must be conceded there were no easy choices available to the United States in the Dominican Republic. Nonetheless, it is the task of diplomacy to make wise decisions when they need to be made and U.S. diplomacy failed to do so in the Dominican crisis. . . .

I am frankly puzzled as to the current attitude of the U.S. Government toward reformist movements in Latin America. On the one hand, President [Lyndon] Johnson's deep personal commitment to the philosophy and aims of the Alliance for Progress is clear; it was convincingly expressed, for example, in his speech to the Latin American Ambassadors on the fourth anniversary of the Alliance for Progress—a statement in which the President compared the Alliance for Progress with his own enlightened program for a Great Society at home. On the other hand, one notes a general tendency on the part of our policy makers not to look beyond a Latin American politician's anti-communism. One also notes in certain Government agencies, particularly the Department of Defense, a preoccupation with counterinsurgency, which is to say, with the prospect of revolutions and means of suppressing them. . . .

It is of great importance that the uncertainty as to U.S. aims in Latin America be resolved. We cannot successfully advance the cause of popular democracy and at the same time align ourselves with corrupt and reactionary oligarchies; yet that is what we seem to be trying to do. The direction of the Alliance for Progress is toward social revolution in Latin America; the direction of our Dominican intervention is toward the suppression of revolutionary movements which are supported by Communists

J. William Fulbright, "Appraisal of United States Policy in the Dominican Crisis," *Congressional Record*, Proceedings and Debates of the 89th Congress, 1st sess., vol. 3, no. 170, daily ed., September 15, 1965, pp. 22998–23005.

or suspected of being influenced by Communists. The prospect of an election in nine months [in the Dominican Republic] which may conceivably produce a strong democratic government is certainly reassuring on this score, but the fact remains that the reaction of the United States at the time of acute crisis was to intervene forcibly and illegally against a revolution which, had we sought to influence it instead of suppressing it, might have produced a strong popular government without foreign military intervention. Since just about every revolutionary movement is likely to attract Communist support, at least in the beginning, the approach followed in the Dominican Republic, if consistently pursued, must inevitably make us the enemy of all revolutions and therefore the ally of all the unpopular and corrupt oligarchies of the hemisphere. . . .

It is not surprising that we Americans are not drawn toward the uncouth revolutionaries of the non-Communist left. We are not, as we like to claim in Fourth of July speeches, the most truly revolutionary nation on earth; we are, on the contrary, much closer to being the most un-revolutionary nation on earth. We are sober and satisfied and comfortable and rich; our institutions are stable and old and even venerable; and our Revolution of 1776, for that matter, was not much of an upheaval compared to the French and Russian revolutions and to current and impending revolutions in Latin America, Asia, and Africa. . . .

We must try to understand social revolution and the injustices that give it rise because they are the heart and core of the experience of the great majority of people now living in the world. . . .

It is the revolutionaries of the non-Communist left who have most of the popular support in Latin America. The Radical Party in Chile, for example, is full of nineteenth-century libertarians whom many North Americans would find highly congenial, but it was recently crushed in national elections by a group of rambunctious, leftist Christian Democrats. It may be argued that the Christian Democrats are anti-United States, and to a considerable extent some of them are—more so now, it may be noted, than prior to the intervention of the United States in the Dominican Republic—but they are not Communists and they have popular support. . . .

The movement of the future in Latin America is social revolution. The question is whether it is to be Communist or democratic revolution and the choice which the Latin Americans make will depend in part on how the United States uses its great influence. It should be very clear that the choice is not between social revolution and conservative oligarchy but whether, by supporting reform, we bolster the popular non-Communist left or whether, by supporting unpopular oligarchies, we drive the rising generation of educated and patriotic young Latin Americans to an embittered and hostile form of communism like that of Fidel Castro. . . .

In my Senate speech of March 25, 1964, I commented as follows on the prospect of revolution: "I am not predicting violent revolutions in Latin

America or elsewhere. Still less am I advocating them. I wish only to suggest that violent social revolutions are a possibility in countries where feudal oligarchies resist all meaningful change by peaceful means. We must not, in our preference for the democratic procedures . . . close our minds to the possibility that democratic procedures may fail in certain countries and that where democracy does fail violent social convulsions may occur."

I think that in the case of the Dominican Republic we did close our minds to the causes and to the essential legitimacy of revolution in a country in which democratic procedures had failed. That, I think, is the central fact concerning the participation of the United States in the Dominican revolution and, possibly as well, its major lesson for the future. . . .

The United States intervened in the Dominican Republic for the purpose of preventing the victory of a revolutionary force which was judged to be Communist dominated. On the basis of Ambassador [William Tapley] Bennett's messages to Washington, there is no doubt that the threat of communism rather than danger to American lives was his primary reason for recommending military intervention. . . .

The evidence does not establish that the Communists at any time actually had control of the revolution. There is little doubt that they had influence within the revolutionary movement, but the degree of that influence remains a matter of speculation.

The administration, however, assumed almost from the beginning that the revolution was Communist-dominated, or would certainly become so, and that nothing short of forcible opposition could prevent a Communist takeover. In their apprehension lest the Dominican Republic become another Cuba, some of our officials seem to have forgotten that virtually all reform movements attract some Communist support, that there is an important difference between Communist support and Communist control of a political movement, that it is quite possible to compete with the Communists for influence in a reform movement rather than abandon it to them, and, most important of all, that economic development and social justice are themselves the primary and most reliable security against Communist subversion. . . .

Intervention on the basis of Communist participation as distinguished from control of the Dominican revolution was a mistake in my opinion which also reflects a grievous misreading of the temper of contemporary Latin American politics. Communists are present in all Latin American countries, and they are going to inject themselves into almost any Latin American revolution and try to seize control of it. If any group or any movement with which the Communists associate themselves is going to be automatically condemned in the eyes of the United States, then we have indeed given up all hope of guiding or influencing even to a marginal degree the revolutionary movements and the demands for social change which are sweeping Latin America. Worse, if that is our view, then we have made ourselves the prisoners of the Latin American oligarchs who are engaged in a vain attempt to preserve the status quo-reactionaries who habitually use the term "Communist" very loosely, in part out of emotional predilection and in part in a calculated effort to scare the United States into supporting their selfish and discredited aims. . . .

In the eyes of educated, energetic and patriotic young Latin Americans—which is to say the generation that will make or break the Alliance for Progress—the United States committed a worse offense in the Dominican Republic than just intervention; it intervened against social revolution and in support, at least temporarily, of a corrupt, reactionary military oligarchy.

It is not possible at present to assess the depth and extent of disillusion with the United States on the part of democrats and reformers in Latin America. I myself think that it is deep and widespread. . . . The tragedy of Santo Domingo is that a policy that purported to defeat communism in the short run is more likely to have the effect of promoting it in the long run. Intervention in the Dominican Republic has alienated—temporarily or permanently, depending on our future policies—our real friends in Latin America. These, broadly, are the people of the democratic left. . . .

By our intervention on the side of a corrupt military oligarchy in the Dominican Republic, we have embarrassed before their own people the democratic reformers who have counseled trust and partnership with the United States. We have lent credence to the idea that the United States is the enemy of social revolution in Latin America and that the only choice Latin Americans have is between communism and reaction.

If those are the available alternatives, if there is no democratic left as a third option, then there is no doubt of the choice that honest and patriotic Latin Americans will make: they will choose communism, not because they want it but because U.S. policy will have foreclosed all other avenues of social revolution and, indeed, all other possibilities except the perpetuation of rule by military juntas and economic oligarchies. . . .

The Foreign Relations Committee's study of the Dominican crisis leads me to draw certain specific conclusions regarding American policy in the Dominican Republic and also suggests some broader considerations regarding relations between the United States and Latin America. My specific conclusions regarding the crisis in Santo Domingo are as follows:

First. The United States intervened forcibly in the Dominican Republic in the last week of April 1965 not primarily to save American lives, as was then contended, but to prevent the victory of a revolutionary movement which was judged to be Communist-dominated. The decision to land thousands of marines on April 28 was based primarily on the fear of "another Cuba" in Santo Domingo.

Second. This fear was based on fragmentary and inadequate evidence. There is no doubt that Communists participated in the Dominican revolution on the rebel side, probably to a greater extent after than before the landing of U.S. marines on April 28, but just as it cannot be proved that the Communists would not have taken over the revolution neither can it be proved that they would have. There is little basis in the evidence offered the committee for the assertion that the rebels were Communist dominated or certain to become so; on the contrary, the evidence suggests a chaotic situation in which no single faction was dominant at the outset and in which everybody, including the United States, had opportunities to influence the shape and course of the rebellion.

Third. The United States let pass its best opportunities to influence the course of events. The best opportunities were on April 25, when Juan Bosch's party, the PRD [Dominican Revolutionary Party], requested a "United States presence," and on April 27, when the rebels, believing themselves defeated, requested United States mediation for a negotiated settlement. . . .

Fourth. U.S. policy toward the Dominican Republic shifted markedly to the right between September 1963 and April 1965. In 1963, the United States strongly supported Bosch and the PRD as enlightened reformers; in 1965 the United States opposed their return to power on the unsubstantiated ground that a Bosch or PRD government would certainly, or almost certainly, become Communist dominated. Thus the United States turned its back on social revolution in Santo Domingo and associated itself with a corrupt and reactionary, military oligarchy.

Fifth. U.S. policy was marred by a lack of candor and by misinformation. The former is illustrated by official assertions that U.S. military intervention was primarily for the purpose of saving American lives; the latter is illustrated by exaggerated reports of massacres and atrocities by the rebels—reports which no one has been able to verify. It was officially asserted, for example, by the President in a press conference on June 17 that according to an official State Department bulletin "some 1,500 innocent people were murdered and shot, and their heads cut off." There is no evidence to support this statement. . . .

Sixth. Responsibility for the failure of American policy in Santo Domingo lies primarily with those who advised the president. In the critical days between April 25 and April 28, these officials sent the president exaggerated reports of the danger of a Communist takeover in Santo Domingo and, on the basis of these, recommended U.S. massive military intervention. . . .

Seventh. Underlying the bad advice and unwise actions of the United States was the fear of another Cuba. The specter of a second Communist state in the Western Hemisphere—and its probable repercussions within the United States and possible effects on the careers of those who might be held responsible—seems to have been the most important single factor in distorting the judgment of otherwise sensible and competent men.

13. COVERT OPERATIONS

The 1979 revolution that overthrew the Somoza family dictatorship (1936–1979) in Nicaragua presented U.S. officials with the prospect of a second communist-led government in Latin America. Although the Jimmy Carter administration (1977– 1981) disapproved of the Somoza regime and nominally supported the broad-based coalition that deposed him, it strongly (and unsuccessfully) opposed the participation of the radical Sandinista National Liberation Front in postrevolutionary government despite the Sandinistas' central role in the revolution. The virulently anticommunist Ronald Reagan administration (1981–1989) was even less sympathetic. Noting Sandinista ties to communist Cuba and its Marxist-Leninist agenda, the Reagan administration endorsed efforts by the Central Intelligence Agency to unite and fund the anti-Sandinista groups, which became known as the Contras. The CIA manual excerpted here instructs Contra "freedom commandos" in psychological operations which include various strategies for winning the "hearts and minds" of the civilian population as well as kidnapping and assassinating government officials. Its considerable debt to the writings of prominent guerrillas like Che Guevara and Carlos Marighella (see Chapter 16) is striking, as is its insistence that the Contras were on a "Christian and democratic crusade." The manual first came to light during the 1984 presidential campaign. Concerned about the political fallout, President Reagan ordered CIA director William Casey to investigate and discipline the responsible parties. Casey reprimanded a few lower-level employees but declined to punish the senior official(s) who probably authored the manual. The controversy over the psy-ops manual served as a prelude to the 1986 Iran-Contra scandal, involving covert operations run from the White House which used money made from selling weapons to Iran (in exchange for the release of Hezbollah hostages to Israel) to fund the Contra war despite congressional opposition.

Guerrilla warfare is essentially a political war. Therefore, its area of operations exceeds the territorial limits of conventional warfare, to penetrate the political entity itself. . . . In effect, the human being should be considered the priority objective in a political war. And conceived as the military target of guerrilla war, the human being has his most critical point in his mind. Once his mind has been reached, the "political animal" has been defeated, without necessarily receiving bullets. Guerrilla warfare is born and grows in the political environment; in the constant combat to dominate that area of political mentality that is inherent to all human beings and which collectively constitutes the "environment" in which guerrilla warfare moves, and which is where precisely its victory or failure is defined. This conception of guerrilla

---

Central Intelligence Agency, "Preface," "Implicit and Explicit Terror," and "Guerrilla Weapons Are the Strength of the People over an Illegal Government," in *Psychological Operations in Guerrilla Warfare*. The complete manual is freely available online.

warfare as political war turns Psychological Operations into the decisive factor of the results. The target, then, is the minds of the population, all the population: our troops, the enemy troops and the civilian population. This book is a manual for the training of guerrillas in psychological operations, and its application to the concrete case of the Christian and democratic crusade being waged in Nicaragua by the Freedom Commandos. . . .

A guerrilla armed force always involves implicit terror because the population, without saying it aloud, feels terror that the weapons may be used against them. However, if the terror does not become explicit, positive results can be expected. In a revolution, the individual lives under a constant threat of physical damage. If the government police cannot put an end to the guerrilla activities, the population will lose confidence in the government, which has the inherent mission of guaranteeing the safety of citizens. However, the guerrillas should be careful not to become an explicit terror, because this would result in a loss of popular support. In the words of a leader of the Huk guerrilla movement of the Philippine Islands: "The population is always impressed by weapons, not by the terror that they cause, but rather by a sensation of strength/force. We must appear before the people, giving them the message of the struggle." This is, then, in a few words, the essence of armed propaganda. An armed guerrilla force can occupy an entire town or small city that is neutral or relatively passive in the conflict. In order to conduct the armed propaganda in an effective manner, the following should be carried out simultaneously:

- Destroy the military or police installations and remove the survivors to a "public place."
- Cut all the outside lines of communications: cables, radio, messengers.
- Set up ambushes in order to delay the reinforcements in all the possible entry routes.
- Kidnap all officials or agents of the Sandinista government and replace them in "public places" with military or civilian persons of trust to our movement; in addition, carry out the following:
- Establish a public tribunal that depends on the guerrillas, and cover the town or city in order to gather the population for this event.
- Shame, ridicule and humiliate the "personal symbols" of the government of repression in the presence of the people and foster popular participation through guerrillas within the multitude, shouting slogans and jeers.
- Reduce the influence of individuals in tune with the regime, pointing out their weaknesses and taking them out of the town, without damaging them publicly.
- Mix the guerrillas within the population and show very good conduct by all members of the column, practicing the following:
- Any article taken will be paid for with cash.

- The hospitality offered by the people will be accepted and this opportunity will be exploited in order to carry out face-to-face persuasion about the struggle.
- Courtesy visits should be made to the prominent persons and those with prestige in the place, such as doctors, priests, teachers, etc.
- The guerrillas should instruct the population that with the end of the operative, and when the Sandinista repressive forces interrogate them, they may reveal EVERYTHING about the military operation carried out. For example, the type of weapons they use, how many men arrived, from what direction they came and in what direction they left, in short, EVERYTHING.
- In addition, indicate to the population that at meetings or in private discussion they can give the names of the Sandinista informants, who will be removed together with the other officials of the government of repression.
- When a meeting is held, conclude it with a speech by one of the leaders of guerrilla political cadres (the most dynamic), which includes explicit references to:
- The fact that the "enemies of the people"—the officials or Sandinista agents—must not be mistreated in spite of their criminal acts, although the guerrilla force may have suffered casualties, and that this is done due to the generosity of the Christian guerrillas.
- Give a declaration of gratitude for the "hospitality" of the population, as well as let them know that the risks that they will run when the Sandinistas return are greatly appreciated.
- The fact that the Sandinista regime, although it exploits the people with taxes, control of money, grains and all aspects of public life through associations, which they are forced to become part of, will not be able to resist the attacks of our guerrilla forces.
- Make the promise to the people that you will return to ensure that the "leeches" of the Sandinista regime of repression will not be able to hinder our guerrillas from integrating with the population.
- A statement repeated to the population to the effect that they can reveal everything about this visit of our commandos, because we are not afraid of anything or anyone, neither the Soviets nor the Cubans. Emphasize that we are Nicaraguans, that we are fighting for the freedom of Nicaragua and to establish a very Nicaraguan government.

The [use of] armed propaganda in populated areas does not give the impression that weapons are the power of the guerrillas over the people, but rather that the weapons are the strength of the people against a regime of repression. Whenever it is necessary to use armed force in an occupation or visit to a town or village, guerrillas should emphasize making sure that they:

- Explain to the population that in the first place this is being done to protect them, the people, and not themselves.
- Admit frankly and publicly that this is an "act of the democratic guerrilla movement," with appropriate explanations.
- That this action, although it is not desirable, is necessary because the final objective of the insurrection is a free and democratic society, where acts of force are not necessary.
- The force of weapons is a necessity caused by the oppressive system, and will cease to exist when the "forces of justice" of our movement assume control.

If, for example, it should be necessary for one of the advanced posts to have to fire on a citizen who was trying to leave the town or city in which the guerrillas are carrying out armed propaganda or political proselytism, the following is recommended:

- Explain that if that citizen had managed to escape, he would have alerted the enemy that is near the town or city, and they could carry out acts of reprisal such as rapes, pillage, destruction, captures, etc., it this way terrorizing the inhabitants of the place for having given attention and hospitalities to the guerrillas of the town.
- If a guerrilla fires at an individual, make the town see that he was an enemy of the people, and that they shot him because the guerrilla recognized as their first duty the protection of citizens.
- The command tried to detain the informant without firing because he, like all Christian guerrillas, espouses nonviolence. Firing at the Sandinista informant, although it is against his own will, was necessary to prevent the repression of the Sandinista government against innocent people.
- Make the population see that it was the repressive system of the regime that was the cause of this situation, what really killed the informer, and that the weapon fired was one recovered in combat against the Sandinista regime.
- Make the population see that if the Sandinista regime had ended the repression, the corruption backed by foreign powers, etc., the freedom commandos would not have had to brandish arms against brother Nicaraguans, which goes against our Christian sentiments. If the informant hadn't tried to escape he would be enjoying life together with the rest of the population, because he would not have tried to inform the enemy. This death would have been avoided if justice and freedom existed in Nicaragua, which is exactly the objective of the democratic guerrilla.

Glossary of Spanish, Portuguese, and Indian Terms

ADELANTADO. Commander of a conquering expedition; governor of a frontier or recently conquered province.

ALCABALA. Sales tax.

ALCALDE. Magistrate of a Spanish or Indian town who, in addition to administrative duties, possessed certain judicial powers as a judge of first instance.

ALCALDE MAYOR. Governor of a district or province.

ALFAQUÍ. Muslim spiritual leader and teacher of the Qur'an.

AMIN. A Jewish broth.

ANDÉN. Agricultural terrace, widely used in Incan agriculture.

ARROBA. Measure of weight (about 25 pounds).

AUDIENCIA. The highest royal court of appeals within a jurisdiction, serving at the same time as a council of state to the viceroy or captain-general.

AYLLU. Indian village community and kinship group in the Andean highlands.

CABALLERIA. Tract of land, about thirty-three and a third acres.

CABILDO. Municipal council.

CACIQUE. 1. Indian chieftain. 2. A local political boss.

CAPATAZ. Overseer or foreman.

CAPITÃO-MÔR. Commander in chief of the military forces of a province in colonial Brazil.

CARGA. A measure of six and one-half bushels.

CAUDILLO (CAUDILHO). Military or political leader or strongman.

CHAPETÓN. A disparaging name applied to European-born Spaniards in the South American colonies.

COLEGIO. School or college.

COMUNERO. A member of a popular revolt movement against Bourbon tax and fiscal policies in New Granada (Colombia) in 1781.

CONQUISTADOR. Conqueror.

CONSULADO. Colonial merchant guild and tribunal of commerce.

CORREGIDOR. Governor of a district.

CORREGIMIENTO. Territory governed by a *corregidor.*

CORTÉS. Spanish parliament or legislature.

CROWN FIFTH. The *quinto,* or royal share of the spoils of war.

CRUZADO. Ancient Portuguese gold coin.

DONATARIO. Proprietor of an original land grant in colonial Brazil.

EJIDATARIO. Member of an *ejido.*

EJIDO. An agricultural community that has received land in accordance with Mexican agrarian law.

ENCILHAMENTO. Great movement of financial speculation in the first years of the Brazilian republic.

ENCOMENDERO. Holder of an *encomienda.*

ENCOMIENDA. Grant of allotment of Indians who were to serve the holder with tribute and labor.

ESTADO. Measure of length (1.85 yards).

ESTANCIA. Ranch (Argentina and Uruguay).

561

FANEGA. A measure of grain (about 1.60 bushels).

FINCA. Farm or ranch.

FISCAL. Crown attorney.

FUERO. Privilege or exemption.

GACHÚPIN. A disparaging name for European-born Spaniards in New Spain.

GAUCHO. Cowboy of the Plata region.

GUAIPIL (HUIPIL). Square, sleeveless blouse worn by Indian women in some parts of Mexico and Central America.

GUAJIRO. A small, underprivileged farmer in Cuba, especially in Oriente province.

HACENDADO. Owner of a *hacienda*.

HACIENDA. Estate or landed property.

HIDALGO. Nobleman.

HUACA (GUACA). Incan shrine or sacred object.

INTERNADO. Boarding school (Cuba).

JEFE POLÍTICO. Governor of a district.

JUICIO DE AMPARO. Protective writ; writ of injunction (Mexico).

JUNTA. Council.

LATIFUNDIO. Large landed estate.

LATIFUNDISTA. Owner of a *latifundio*.

MAMELUCO (MAMALUCO). Mixture of white and Indian (Brazil).

MAYORDOMO. Steward of an estate.

MESTIZO. Mixture of Indian and white.

MILPA. Plot of Indian maize land (Mexico).

MITA. Periodic conscription of Indian labor in the Spanish colonies.

OBRAJE. Factory or workshop in the Spanish colonies.

OIDOR. Spanish colonial judge; member of *audiencia*.

PÁRAMO. High and cold region.

PATIO. Yard or courtyard.

PATRÓN. Master, landlord.

PATRONATO REAL. Right of the Spanish crown to dispose of all ecclesiastical benefices.

PESO. Spanish coin and monetary unit.

REGIDOR. Councilman.

REPARTIMIENTO. 1. An assignment of Indians or land to a Spanish settler during the first years of the Conquest. 2. The periodic conscription of Indians for labor useful to the Spanish community. 3. The mandatory purchase of merchandise by Indians from colonial officials.

REPARTO DE MERCANCÍAS. See *repartimiento* 3.

RESIDENCIA. Judicial review of a Spanish colonial official's conduct at the end of his term of office.

SEMIINTERNADOS. Schools where children received their meals but did not sleep overnight (Cuba).

TIERRA FIRME. The northern coast of South America.

TITHE. A tenth of all tithes collected by the king in his capacity of Master of the Order of Christ; it was paid to the donatory.

VARA. Variable unit of length, about 2.8 feet.

VISITADOR GENERAL. Official charged with the investigation or inspection of a viceroyalty or captaincy general.